Essentials of

INTERNATIONAL RELATIONS

SIXTH EDITION

Essentials of

INTERNATIONAL RELATIONS

SIXTH EDITION

KAREN A. MINGST

UNIVERSITY OF KENTUCKY

IVAN M. ARREGUÍN-TOFT

BOSTON UNIVERSITY

W. W. NORTON & COMPANY
NEW YORK · LONDON

Editor: Lisa Camner McKay
Associate Editor: Jake Schindel
Project Editor: Diane Cipollone
Associate Director of Production, College: Benjamin Reynolds
Media Editor: Toni Magyar
Associate Media Editor: Lorraine Klimowich
Editorial Assistant: Sarah Wolf
Marketing Manager, Political Science: Erin Brown
Photo Editor: Nelson Colón
Permissions Manager: Megan Jackson
Text Design: Faceout Studios
Art Director: Hope Miller Goodell
Composition: Innodata Isogen
Manufacturing: Courier—Kendallville, IN

The text of this book is composed in Garamond Pro with the display set in Trade Gothic.

Library of Congress Cataloging-in-Publication Data
Mingst, Karen A., 1947–
    Essentials of international relations / Karen A. Mingst, University of Kentucky, Ivan M. Arreguín-Toft,
    Boston University. — Sixth edition
        p. cm.
    Includes bibliographical references and index.
ISBN 978-0-393-92195-3 (pbk.)
1.   International relations.   I. Arreguín-Toft, Ivan M.   II. Title.
    JZ1305.M56 2014
    327—dc23

                                    2013020312

W. W. Norton & Company, Inc., 500 Fifth Avenue, New York, NY 10110-0017
wwnorton.com

W. W. Norton & Company Ltd., Castle House, 75/76 Wells Street, London W1T 3QT
1 2 3 4 5 6 7 8 9 0

CONTENTS

08   WAR AND STRIFE 248

09   INTERNATIONAL POLITICAL ECONOMY 304

10 HUMAN RIGHTS 350

11 TRANSNATIONAL ISSUES: THE ENVIRONMENT, WORLD HEALTH, AND CRIME 384

Figures, Tables, and Maps

FIGURES

TABLES

MAPS

PREFACE

Brief textbooks are now commonplace in International Relations. This textbook was originally written to be not only smart and brief, but also, in the words of Roby Harrington of W. W. Norton, to include "a clear sense of what's essential and what's not." We are pleased that this book's treatment of the essential concepts and information has stood the test of time.

This sixth edition of *Essentials of International Relations*, published more than a decade after the first, preserves the overall structure of earlier editions. Students need a brief history of international relations to understand why we study the subject and how current scholarship is informed by what has preceded it. This background is provided in Chapters 1 and 2. Theories provide interpretative frameworks for understanding what is happening in the world, and levels of analysis—the international system, the state, and the individual—help us further organize and conceptualize the material. In Chapters 3–7, competing theories are presented and used to illustrate how each level of analysis can be applied and how international organizations, nongovernmental organizations, and international law are viewed. Then the major issues of the twenty-first century—security, economics, human rights, and transnational issues—are presented and analyzed in Chapters 8–11.

This fully revised sixth edition is enhanced by the addition of a new chapter on human rights (Chapter 10). This addition allows Chapter 11 to take a deeper look at three of the most challenging transnational issues of our time: the environment, global health, and transnational crime. In addition, the historical overview in Chapter 2 has been refocused on major events following the Cold War, up to and including the Arab Spring.

The rich pedagogical program of previous editions has been revised based on suggestions from adopters and reviewers:

- New **You Decide** boxes each take a question of contemporary significance and present arguments that could be made to support both sides of the issue. This thoughtful feature asks students to apply what they have learned in the chapter and develop a critical engagement with the application of theoretical material to real-world problems.

- Updated **Global Perspectives** units encourage students to consider a specific issue from the vantage point of a particular state.
- End-of-chapter review materials include **discussion questions** and a list of **key terms** from the chapter to help students remember, apply, and synthesize what they have learned.
- **Theory in Brief** boxes, **In Focus** boxes, and numerous maps, figures, and tables appear throughout the text to summarize key ideas.
- A new design offers a visually appealing text with illustrative photos.

Many of these changes have been made at the suggestion of expert reviewers, primarily faculty who have taught the book in the classroom. While it is impossible to act on every suggestion (not all the critics themselves agree), we have carefully studied the various recommendations and thank the reviewers for taking time to offer critiques. We thank the following reviewers for their input on this new edition: Mervyn Bain, University of Aberdeen; Robert Bartlett, University of Vermont; Abdalla Battah, Minnesota State University, Mankato; Cynthia A. Botteron, Shippensburg University; Courtney Hillebrecht, University of Nebraska–Lincoln; Cynthia M. Horne, Western Washington University; James Kim, California State Polytechnic University, Pomona; William Lahneman, Towson University; Tobias J. Lanz, University of South Carolina; Anika Leithner, California Polytechnic State University, San Luis Obispo; Laura Neack, Miami University; Fredline M'Cormack-Hale, Seton Hall University; Andrew Ross, Ohio University; Christopher Saladino, Virginia Commonwealth University; Selwyn Samaroo, University of Tennessee at Chattanooga; Jelena Subotic, Georgia State University; Julian Westerhout, Illinois State University; Gregory White, Smith College; and Susanne Zwingel, SUNY Potsdam.

In this edition, Karen Mingst owes special thanks to her husband of forty years, Robert Stauffer. He has always provided both space and encouragement, as well as holding up more than one-half of the marriage bargain. Yet he keeps asking—another book, another edition!

Ivan Arreguín-Toft owes thanks to a number of people; including Roby Harrington, Ann Shin, Jake Schindel, and more recently Lisa Camner McKay. I thank Roby Harrington in particular for bringing me into what turned out to be both a fascinating and challenging project. I also thank Karen Mingst especially for her patience, wisdom, and guidance; and for her willingness to share creative control over a decade's intellectual and pedagogical achievement:

a comprehensive, engaging, and yet remarkably compact international relations textbook. Finally, I owe a special debt of gratitude to my wife Monica Toft, and to my children Sam and Ingrid Toft.

Ann Shin, editor of the last four editions, knows this book as well as its authors. She has always been a constant fountain of ideas and enthusiasm, and successfully managed the challenging mission of keeping her authors in line and on task; understanding that we all balance a range of both professional and personal obligations. Toward the end of the process of work on the present manuscript, Ann's wonderful management and guidance responsibilities passed to a new editor, Lisa Camner McKay. She too has offered trenchant and constructive suggestions and has rather quickly come to understand our individual and collective strengths and weaknesses. In short, many talented, professional, and delightful people contributed to the making of this edition, which we feel is the best so far. And for that, we remain always grateful.

AFRICA

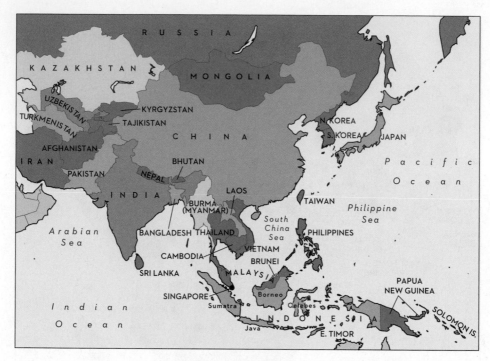

ASIA

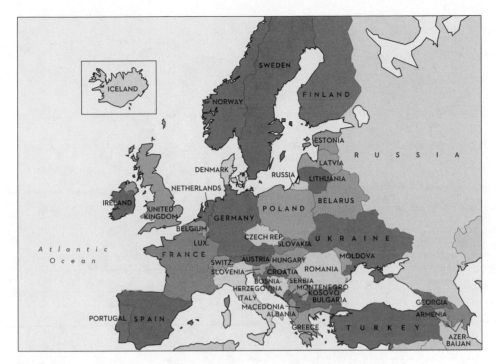

EUROPE

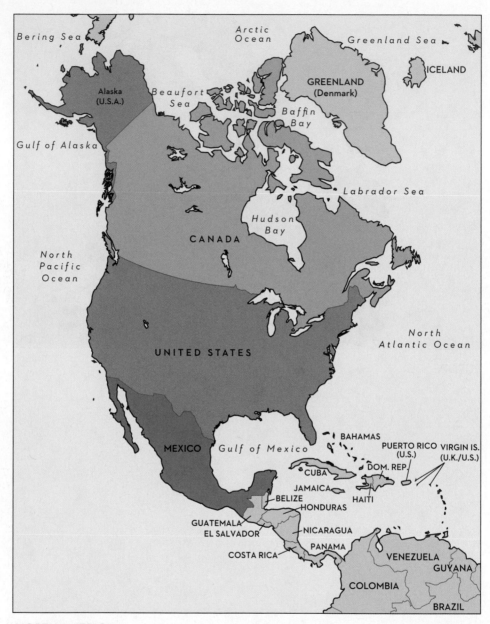

NORTH AMERICA

CENTRAL AND SOUTH AMERICA

Pacific
Ocean

Atlantic
Ocean

North
America

Europe

Central
and
South America

THE WORLD

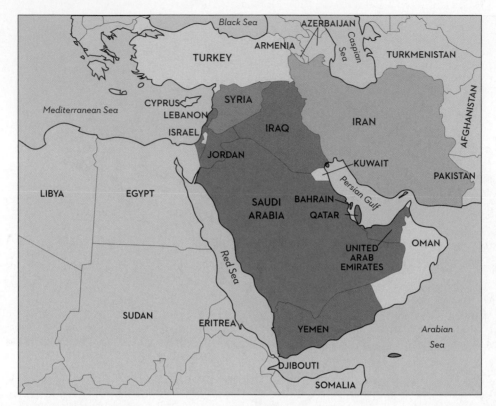

THE MIDDLE EAST

Professor of political science Fotini Christia interviewed war lords, government officials, and local residents in Balkh Province, Afghanistan, to examine the role of religion and ethnicity in war-time allegiances. This type of research is known as field work.

01

APPROACHES
TO INTERNATIONAL
RELATIONS

- *How does international relations affect you in your daily life?*

- *Why do we study international relations theory?*

- *How have history and philosophy been used to study international relations?*

- *What is the contribution of behavioralism?*

- *What alternative approaches have challenged traditional approaches? Why?*

International Relations in Daily Life

Open the door to your closet and examine your clothing labels. Workers in India, Vietnam, China, El Salvador, and Turkey sewed your clothing. Visit the produce and meat or fish counters at the supermarket. Our food is grown in Mexico and the Philippines, slaughtered in New Zealand, and fish-farmed in Thailand and China. Look at household product labels. The rug you purchased has the Rugmark signature from India, showing that child labor was not employed. Your classmates include people born in Europe, Asia, Latin America, and Africa; your fellow students have studied abroad in these same regions. People in your town or city have demonstrated in support of free elections in Iran, voiced support for Israel, and marched in silence to protest oppression in North Korea and Zimbabwe. Then visit the Web, Facebook, or Twitter and read about the wars in Syria and Mali; the negotiations on climate change and sex trafficking; and the local efforts of citizens in small South Pacific island states, Iceland, and Louisiana to prepare for the effects of coastal flooding caused by global warming. Places and events once regarded as far away now seem close at hand.

Historically, international activities were overwhelmingly the results of decisions taken by central governments and heads of state, not by ordinary citizens. Increasingly, however, these activities involve different actors, some of whom *you* directly influence. You may be a member of a nongovernmental organization (NGO)—Amnesty International, the Red Cross, or Greenpeace—with a local chapter in your community or at your college. With your fellow members around the globe, you may try to influence the local, as well as the national and international, agenda. Your city or state may be actively courting foreign private investment, competing against both neighboring municipalities and other countries to improve local employment

Changes in weather patterns have affected the environment around the globe, from the Mississippi Delta to these icebergs in Greenland. The global environment is an area of both international conflict and cooperation.

possibilities. Your campus and your town may have embarked on an energy inventory in order to develop a sustainability assessment, joining initiatives around the world to enhance environmental sustainability.

Thus the variety of actors in international relations includes not just the 194 states recognized in the world today and their leaders and government bureaucracies, but also municipalities, for-profit and not-for-profit private organizations, international organizations, and you. **International relations**, as a subfield of political science, is the study of the interactions among the various actors that participate in international politics, including states, international organizations, nongovernmental organizations, subnational entities such as bureaucracies and local governments, and individuals. It is the study of the behaviors of these actors as they participate individually and together in international political processes. International relations is also an interdisciplinary field of inquiry, using concepts and substance from history, economics, anthropology, as well as political science.

How, then, can we begin to study this multifaceted phenomenon called *international relations*? How can we begin to think theoretically about what appear to be disconnected events? How can we begin to answer the foundational questions of international relations: What are the characteristics of human nature and the state? What is the relationship between the individual and society? How is the international system organized?

Thinking Theoretically

Political scientists develop theories or frameworks both to understand the causes of events that occur in international relations every day and to answer the foundational questions in the field. Although there are many contending theories, four of the more prominent theories are developed in this book: realism and neorealism, liberalism and neoliberal institutionalism, radical perspectives whose origins lie in Marxism, and constructivism.

IN FOCUS | FOUNDATIONAL QUESTIONS OF INTERNATIONAL RELATIONS

- How can human nature be characterized?

- What is the relationship between the individual and society?

- What are the characteristics and role of the state?

- How is the international system organized?

In brief, realism posits that states exist in an anarchic international system. Each state bases its policies on an interpretation of its national interest defined in terms of power. The structure of the international system is determined by the distribution of power among states. In contrast, liberalism is historically rooted in several philosophical traditions that posit that human nature is basically good. Individuals form groups and, later, states. States generally cooperate and follow international norms and procedures that they have agreed on. Radical theory is rooted in economics. Actions of individuals are largely determined by economic class; the state is an agent of international capitalism; and the international system is highly stratified, dominated by an international capitalist system. And international relations constructivists, in contrast to both realists and liberals, argue that the key structures in the state system are not material but instead are intersubjective and social. The interests of states are not fixed but are malleable and ever changing. All four of these theories are subject to different interpretations by scholars who analyze international relations.

These different theoretical approaches help us see international relations from different viewpoints. As political scientist Stephen Walt explains, "No single approach can capture all the complexity of contemporary world politics. Therefore we are better off with a diverse array of competing ideas rather than a single theoretical orthodoxy. Competition between theories helps reveal their strengths and weaknesses and spurs subsequent refinements, while revealing flaws in conventional wisdom."[1] We will explore these competing ideas, and their strengths and weaknesses, in the remainder of this book.

Developing the Answers

How do political scientists find the answers to the questions posed? How do they find information to assess the accuracy, relevancy, and potency of their theories? The tools they use to answer the foundational questions include history, philosophy, and the scientific method.

History

Inquiry in international relations often begins with history. Without any historical background, many of today's key issues are incomprehensible. History tells us that the periodic bombings in Israel by Hamas are part of a dispute over territory between Arabs and Jews, a dispute with its origins in biblical times and with its modern roots in the establishment of the state of Israel in 1948. Sudan's twenty-year civil war between the north and south and the Darfur crisis beginning in 2003 are both products of long-standing neglect by the central government of marginalized areas. The civil war was exacerbated by religious differences (the north is Muslim; the south is Christian and animist); the Darfur crisis was magnified by natural disasters. Without that background, neither the debate over the two-state solution in Palestine nor the recent establishment of the Republic of South Sudan can be understood.

Thus, history provides a crucial background for the study of international relations. History has been so fundamental to the study of international relations that there was no separate international relations subfield until the early twentieth century. Before that time, especially in Europe and the United States, international relations was studied under the umbrella of diplomatic history in most academic institutions. Having knowledge of both diplomatic history and national histories remains critical for students of international relations.

History invites its students to acquire detailed knowledge of specific events, but it also can be used to test generalizations. Having deciphered patterns from the past, students of history can begin to explain the relationships among various events. For example, having historically documented the cases when wars occur and described the

Scholars often draw on history to help understand world politics. When the United States invaded Iraq first in the 1991 Gulf War and then in the 2003 Iraq War, some observers raised comparisons to the Vietnam War, when many Americans protested U.S. involvement. However, there were also significant differences between these events.

patterns leading up to war, the diplomatic historian can search for explanations for, or causes of, war. The ancient Greek historian Thucydides (c. 460–401 BCE), in *History of the Peloponnesian War*, used this approach. Distinguishing between the underlying and the immediate causes of wars, Thucydides found that what made that war inevitable was the growth of Athenian power. As Athens's power increased, Sparta, Athens's greatest rival, feared losing its own power. Thus, the changing distribution of power was the underlying cause of the Peloponnesian War.[2]

Many scholars following in Thucydides's footsteps use history in similar ways. But those using history must be wary, as it is not always clear what history teaches us. The "lessons" of Munich and Allied appeasement of Germany before World War II or the "lessons" of the Cuban missile crisis are not agreed on. Nor are the analogies made between the 2003 Iraq War and the U.S. war against Vietnam unambiguous. In both cases, the United States fought a lengthy war against a little understood, often unidentifiable enemy. In both, the United States adopted the strategy of supporting state building so that the central government could continue the fight, a policy labeled *Vietnamization* and *Iraqization* in the respective conflicts. The policy led to a quagmire in both places when American domestic support waned and the United States withdrew. Yet the differences are also evident. Vietnam has a long history and a strong sense of national identity, forged by wars against both the Chinese and French. Iraq, in contrast, is a relatively new state with significant ethnic and religious divisions, whose various groups seek a variety of different objectives. In Vietnam, the goal was defense of the U.S. ally South Vietnam against the communist north, backed by the Soviet Union. In Iraq, the goal was first to oust Saddam Hussein, who was suspected of building weapons of mass destruction, and second to create a democratic Iraq, which would eventually lead the region to greater stability.[3] In both, although we cannot ignore history, neither can we draw simple "lessons" from historic experiences.

Philosophy

We can also deduce answers to international relations questions from classical and modern philosophy. Much classical philosophizing focuses on the state and its leaders—the basic building blocks of international relations—as well as on methods of analysis. For example, the ancient Greek philosopher Plato (c. 427–347 BCE), in *The Republic*, concluded that in the "perfect state" the people who should govern are those who are superior in the ways of philosophy and war. Plato called these ideal rulers "philosopher-kings."[4] Though not directly discussing international relations, Plato introduced two ideas seminal to the discipline: class analysis and dialectical reasoning, both of which were bases for later Marxist analysts. Radicals, like Marxists, see economic class as the major divider in domestic and international politics; this viewpoint will be explored in depth in Chapters 3 and 9. Marxists also acknowledge the importance of dialectical reasoning—that is, reasoning from a dialogue or conversation that leads to the discovery of contradictions in the original assertions and in political reality. In contemporary Marxist terms, such an analysis reveals the contradiction between global and local policies, whereby, for example, local-level textile workers lose their jobs to foreign competition and are replaced by high-technology industries.

Just as Plato's contributions to contemporary thinking were both substantive and methodological, the contributions of his student, the philosopher Aristotle (384–322 BCE), lay both in substance (the search for an ideal domestic political system) and in method (the comparative method). Analyzing 168 constitutions, Aristotle looked at the similarities and differences among states, becoming the first writer to use the comparative method of analysis. He came to the conclusion that states rise and fall largely because of internal factors—a conclusion still debated in the twenty-first century.[5]

After the classical era, many of the philosophers of relevance to international relations focused on the foundational questions of the discipline. The English philosopher Thomas Hobbes (1588–1679), in *Leviathan*, imagined a state of nature, a world without governmental authority or civil order, where men rule by passions, living with the constant uncertainty of their own security. To Hobbes, the life of man is solitary, selfish, and even brutish. Extrapolating to the international level, in the absence of international authority, society is in a "state of nature," or **anarchy**. States in this anarchic condition act as man does in the state of nature. For Hobbes the solution to the dilemma is a unitary state—a leviathan—where power is centrally and absolutely controlled.[6]

The French philosopher Jean-Jacques Rousseau (1712–78) addressed the same set of questions but, having been influenced by the Enlightenment, saw a different solution. In "Discourse on the Origin and Foundations of Inequality among Men," Rousseau described the state of nature as an egocentric world, with man's primary concern being self-preservation—not unlike Hobbes's description of the state of nature. Rousseau posed the dilemma in terms of the story of the stag and the hare. In a hunting society, each individual must keep to his assigned task in order to find and trap the stag for food for the whole group. However, if a hare happens to pass nearby, an individual might well follow the hare, hoping to get his next meal quickly and caring little for how his actions will affect the group. Rousseau drew an analogy between these hunters and states. Do states follow short-term self-interest, like the hunter who follows the hare? Or do they recognize the benefits of a common interest?[7]

Rousseau's solution to the dilemma posed by the stag and the hare was different from Hobbes's leviathan. Rousseau's preference was for the creation of smaller communities in which the "general will" could be attained. Indeed, according to Rousseau, it is "only the general will," not a leviathan, that can "direct the forces of the state according to the purpose for which it was instituted, which is the common good."[8] In Rousseau's vision, "each of us places his person and all his power in common under the supreme direction of the general will; and as one we receive each member as an indivisible part of the whole."[9]

Still another philosophical view of the characteristics of international society was set forth by the German philosopher Immanuel Kant (1724–1804), in both *Idea for a Universal History* and *Perpetual Peace*. Kant envisioned a federation of states as a means to achieve peace, a world order in which man is able to live without fear of war. Sovereignties would remain intact, but the new federal order would be both preferable to a "super-leviathan" and more effective and realistic than Rousseau's small communities. Kant's analysis was based on a vision of human beings that was different from that of either Rousseau or Hobbes. In his view, though man is admittedly selfish, he can learn new ways of cosmopolitanism and universalism.[10]

The tradition laid down by these philosophers has contributed to the development of international relations by calling attention to fundamental relationships: those between the individual and society, between individuals *in* society, and between societies. These philosophers had varied, often competing visions of what these relationships are and what they ought to be. Some of their more important contributions are summarized in Table 1.1. The early philosophers have led contemporary international relations scholars to the examination of the characteristics of leaders, to the recognition of the importance of the internal dimensions of the state, to the analogy of the state and nature, and to descriptions of an international community.

History and philosophy permit us to delve into the foundational questions — the nature of people and the broad characteristics of the state and of international society. They allow us to speculate on the **normative** (or moral) elements in political life: What *should be* the role of the state? What *ought to be* the norms in international society? How *might* international society be structured to achieve order? When is war just? Should economic resources be redistributed? Should human rights be universalized?[11] Both history and philosophy are key tools for international relations scholars.

The Scientific Method: Behavioralism

In the 1950s, some scholars began to draw upon one understanding of the nature of humans and on history to develop a more scientific approach to the study of international relations. They built upon the philosophical assumption that man tends to act in predictable ways. If individuals act in predictable ways, might not states do the same? Are there recurrent patterns to how states behave? Are there subtle patterns to diplomatic history? Are states as power hungry as the philosophers who compare the

TABLE 1.1	CONTRIBUTIONS OF PHILOSOPHERS TO INTERNATIONAL RELATIONS THEORY
Plato (427–347 BCE)	Greek political philosopher who argued that the life force in man is intelligent. Only a few people can have insight into what is good; society should submit to the authority of these philosopher-kings. Many of these ideas are developed in *The Republic*.
Aristotle (384–322 BCE)	Greek political philosopher who addressed the problem of order in the individual Greek city-state. The first to use the comparative method of research, observing multiple points in time and suggesting explanations for the patterns found.
Thomas Hobbes (1588–1679)	English political philosopher who in *Leviathan* described life in a state of nature as solitary, selfish, and brutish. Individuals and society can escape from the state of nature through a unitary state, a leviathan.
Jean-Jacques Rousseau (1712–78)	French political philosopher whose seminal ideas were tested by the French Revolution. In "Discourse on the Origin and Foundations of Inequality among Men," described the state of nature in both national and international society. Argued that the solution to the state of nature is the social contract, whereby individuals gather in small communities where the "general will" is realized.
Immanuel Kant (1724–1804)	German political philosopher key to the idealist or utopian school of thought. In *Idea for a Universal History* and *Perpetual Peace*, advocated a world federation of republics bound by the rule of law.

anarchic international system with the state of nature would have us believe? How can we explain empirical findings? Can we use those findings to predict the future?

Behavioralism proposes that individuals, both alone and in groups, act in patterned ways. The task of the behavioral scientist is to suggest plausible hypotheses regarding those patterned actions and to systematically and empirically test those hypotheses. Using the tools of the scientific method to describe and explain human behavior, these scholars hope ultimately to predict future behavior. Many will be satisfied, however, with being able to explain patterns, because prediction in the social sciences remains an uncertain enterprise.

The Correlates of War project, research begun at the University of Michigan, permits us to see the application of behavioralism. Beginning in 1963, the political scientist J. David Singer and his historian colleague Melvin Small investigated one of the fundamental questions in international relations: Why is there war?[12] As Singer himself later acknowledged, he was motivated by the normative philosophical concern—how can peace be achieved? The two scholars chose an empirical methodological approach. Rather than focusing on one "big" war that changed the tide of history, as Thucydides did, they sought to find patterns among a number of different wars. Believing that there are generalizable patterns to be found across all wars, Singer and Small turned to statistical data to discover the patterns.

The initial task of the Correlates of War project was to collect data on international wars between 1865 and 1965 in which 1,000 or more deaths had been reported in a twelve-month period. For each of the 93 wars that fit these criteria, the researchers found data on its magnitude, severity, and intensity, as well as the frequency of war over time. This data collection process proved a much larger task than Singer and Small had anticipated, employing a bevy of researchers and graduate students.

Once the wars were codified, the second task was to generate specific, testable hypotheses that might explain the outbreak of war. Is there a relationship between the number of alliance commitments in the international system and the number of wars that are fought? Is there a relationship between the number of great powers in the international system and the number of wars? Is there a relationship between the number of wars over time and the severity of the conflicts? Which factors are *most* correlated over time with the outbreak of war? And how are these factors related to each other? What is the correlation between international system–level factors—such as the existence of international organizations—and the outbreak of war? Although answering these questions will never *prove* that a particular factor is the cause of war, the answers could suggest some high-level correlations that merit theoretical explanation. That is the goal of that research project and many others following in the behavioralist scientific tradition.

Yet methodological problems abound. The Correlates of War database looks at all international wars, irrespective of the different political, military, social, and technological contexts. Can wars of the late 1800s be explained by the same factors as the wars of the new millennium? Answering that question has led subsequent researchers to expand the data set to include militarized interstate disputes, conflicts that do not involve a full-scale war. And that data includes not only international and civil wars but also regional internal, intercommunal, and nonstate wars.[13]

Although the methods of behavioralism, as illustrated in the Correlates of War project, have never been an end in themselves, only a means to improve explanation, during the 1980s and 1990s scholars seriously questioned the behavioral approach.

Their disillusionment has taken several forms. To some, many of the foundational questions—the nature of humanity and society—are neglected by behavioralists because they are not easily testable by empirical methods. These critics suggest returning to the philosophical roots of international relations. To others, the questions behavioralists pose are the salient ones, but their attention to methods has overwhelmed the substance of their research. Few would doubt the importance of J. David Singer and Melvin Small's initial excursion into the causes of war, but even the researchers themselves admitted losing sight of the important questions in their quest to compile data and hone research methods. Some scholars, still within the behavioralist orientation, suggest simplifying esoteric methods in order to refocus on the substantive questions. Others remain firmly committed to behavioralism and the scientific method, pointing to the lack of funding and time as an explanation for their meager results.

Alternative Approaches

Some international relations scholars are dissatisfied with using history, philosophy, or behavioral tools. The postmodernists, for example, seek to deconstruct the basic concepts of the field, such as the state, the nation, rationality, and realism, by searching texts (or sources) for hidden meanings underneath the surface, in the subtext. Once those hidden meanings are revealed, the postmodernists seek to replace the once-orderly picture with disorder, to replace the dichotomies with multiple portraits.

Researchers have begun to deconstruct core concepts and replace them with multiple meanings. Cynthia Weber, for example, argues that sovereignty (the independence of a state) is neither well defined nor consistently grounded. Digging below the surface of sovereignty, going beyond evaluations of the traditional philosophers, she has discovered that conceptualizations of sovereignty are constantly shifting, depending on the exigencies of the moment and the values of different communities. The multiple meanings of sovereignty are conditioned by time, place, and historical circumstances.[14] More specifically, Karen T. Litfin shows how norms of sovereignty are shifting to address ecological destruction, although the process remains a contested one.[15] These analyses have profound implications for the theory and practice of international relations, which are rooted in state sovereignty and accepted practices that reinforce sovereignty. They challenge conventional understandings.

Postmodernists also seek to find the voices of "the others," those individuals who have been disenfranchised and marginalized in international relations. The feminist Christine Sylvester illustrates her approach with a discussion of the Greenham Common Peace Camp, a group of mostly women who in the early 1980s walked more than a hundred miles to a British air force base to protest against plans to deploy missiles at the base. Although the marchers were ignored by the media—and thus were

YOU DECIDE

How do we know what we know? How do we know *whether* we know? Historical analysis and comparison, philosophy, behavioral approaches, and discourse analysis were all introduced as methods that political scientists use to seek answers to core questions of the discipline. Think of Immanuel Kant's philosophical treatise on cooperation and peace among self-interested states, which poses the central question of international politics: Is lasting peace possible? If so, what conditions are necessary to achieve such a peace? Which method or combination of methods do you think would be most effective in answering this question?

You might argue that an examination of the historical record could answer this question. By selecting a period of time in which international relations were largely peaceful, you could read first-person accounts and detailed histories in order to identify the specific features of that period: Who were the leaders? What policies did they pursue? How did they resolve their conflicts? By exploring the rich historical record, you would come to understand what factors led to peace.

Alternately, you might take an empirical behavioral approach by first hypothesizing what conditions are necessary for peace. For instance, do changes in the volume of trade or the costs of communication explain cooperation and conflict? You could then collect data on your variables. Finally, you could evaluate statistically whether these variables are correlated with international peace. This method locates specific patterns in the data across many cases.

Or discourse analysis might provide the greatest purchase on the question. By seeking to understand how concepts like "war," "interest," and "sovereignty" have changed over time, you might show that it is what people believe these concepts to mean today that causes an observable impact on the occurrence of peace. For instance, how has our understanding of "war" changed from the seventeenth century to today? Have conceptions about the "just causes" of war evolved? How have these conceptions impacted war and peace?

Finally, you might argue that some combination of two or more approaches makes the most sense, especially given the complexity of causes and effects related to peace and war.

YOU DECIDE: What method or combination of methods do you think would be most useful in answering Kant's crucial question? What strengths and weaknesses might your preferred method(s) have?

"voiceless"—they maintained a politics of resistance, recruiting other political action groups near the camp and engaging members of the military stationed at the base. In 1988, when the Intermediate Range Nuclear Force Treaty was signed dismantling the missiles, the women moved on to another protest site, drawing public attention to the role of Britain in the nuclear era.[16] Scholars in this tradition probe how the voiceless *dalit* (or untouchables) have fought for rights, how the disabled have found a voice in international forums, and how some, like children born of rape, have not found a voice.[17]

Others, such as the constructivists, have turned to discourse analysis to answer the foundational questions of international relations. To trace how ideas shape identities, constructivists analyze culture, norms, procedures, and social practices. They probe how identities are shaped and change over time. They use texts, interviews, and archival material, and they research local practices by riding public transportation and standing in lines. By using multiple sets of data, they create thick description. The case studies found in Peter Katzenstein's edited volume *The Culture of National Security* utilize this approach. Drawing on analyses of Soviet foreign policy at the end of the Cold War, German and Japanese security policy from militarism to antimilitarism, and Arab national identity, the authors search for security interests defined by actors who are responding to changing cultural factors. These studies show how social and cultural factors shape national security policy in ways that contradict realist or liberal expectations.[18]

No important question of international relations today can be answered with exclusive reliance on any one method. History, whether in the form of an extended case study (Peloponnesian War) or a study of multiple wars (Correlates of War or militarized interstate disputes), provides useful answers. Philosophical traditions offer both cogent reasoning and the framework for the major discussions of the day. But behavioral methods still dominate. And the newer methods of deconstructionism, thick description, and discourse analysis provide an even richer base from which the international relations scholar can draw.

In Sum: Making Sense of International Relations

How can we, as students, begin to make sense of international political events in our daily lives? How have scholars of international relations helped us make sense of the world around us? In this chapter, major theories of international relations have been introduced, including the realist, liberal, radical, and constructivist approaches. These theories provide frameworks for asking and answering core foundational questions. To answer these questions, international relations scholars turn to many other disciplines, including history, philosophy, behavioral psychology, and critical studies (see Table 1.2). International relations is a pluralistic and eclectic discipline.

Where Do We Go from Here?

To understand the development of international relations theory, we need to examine general historical trends for developments in the state and the international system, particularly events in Europe during the nineteenth and twentieth centuries. This "stuff" of diplomatic history is the subject of Chapter 2. Chapter 3 is designed to help us think about the development of international relations theoretically through several frameworks—liberalism, realism, radicalism, and constructivism. Chapters 4, 5, and 6 examine the levels of analysis in international relations. Each of these chapters is organized around the theoretical frameworks. Thus, in Chapter 4 the international system is examined; in Chapter 5, the state; and in Chapter 6, the individual. In each of these chapters the focus is on comparing liberal, realist, and radical descriptions and explanations, augmented, when appropriate, with constructivism. Chapter 7 explores and analyzes the roles of international organizations, international law, and nongovernmental actors. In the last four chapters, the major issues of international relations are studied: in Chapter 8, war and strife; in Chapter 9, international political economy; in Chapter 10, human rights; and in Chapter 11, the transnational issues of the twenty-first century.

TABLE 1.2	TOOLS FOR STUDYING INTERNATIONAL RELATIONS
TOOL	**METHOD**
History	Examines individual or multiple cases
Philosophy	Develops rationales from core texts and analytical thinking
Behavioralism	Finds patterns in human behavior and state behavior using empirical methods, grounded in scientific method
Alternatives	Deconstructs major concepts and uses discourse analysis to build thick description; finds voices of "others"

Discussion Questions

1. A respected family member picked up this book and saw the word *theory* in the first chapter. She is skeptical about the value of theory. Explain to her the utility of developing a theoretical perspective.

2. Philosophy is your passion, but you find international relations moderately interesting. How can you integrate your passion with this pragmatic interest? What questions can you explore?

3. You are a history major skilled in researching the historical archives. Suggest two research projects that you might undertake to further your understanding of international relations.

4. How can the study of international relations be made more scientific? What are the problems with doing so?

Key Terms

anarchy (p. 9)

behavioralism (p. 11)

international relations (p. 5)

normative (p. 10)

Crowds celebrate the first birthday of the world's newest nation, South Sudan, on July 9, 2012. South Sudan's desire to join the international community as an independent nation-state was influenced by over 350 years of evolution of the concept of state sovereignty.

O2

THE HISTORICAL CONTEXT OF CONTEMPORARY INTERNATIONAL RELATIONS

- *Which historical periods seem to have had the most influence on the development of international relations?*

- *What are the historical origins of the state?*

- *Why do international relations scholars use the Treaties of Westphalia as a benchmark?*

- *What are the historical origins of the European balance-of-power system?*

- *How could the Cold War be both a series of confrontations between the United States and the Soviet Union and a "long peace"?*

- *What key events have shaped the post-Cold War world and the first decade of the new millennium?*

Students of international relations need to understand the events and trends of the past. Theorists recognize that core concepts in the field—concepts such as the state, the nation, sovereignty, power, and balance of power—were developed and shaped by historical circumstances. Theorists often ask the questions they do as a result of unexpected or unexplained real-world events. Policy makers search the past for patterns and precedents to guide contemporary decisions. Most importantly, and in part as a result, past events tend to shape contemporary motivations and interests. It is impossible, for example, to understand the nature of contemporary conflict in Palestine without an understanding of the Holocaust, to say nothing of the 300 years of European anti-Semitism that preceded it. Similarly, it is difficult to understand the contemporary politics of the Koreas, China, and Japan without understanding how the peoples of each present-day state remember events in World War II.

In large part, the major antecedents to the contemporary international system are found in Europe-centered Western civilization. From the ancient Greeks in particular, Western civilization inherited a view of the relation of the individual to society and to the polity, as well as root principles of legitimacy, popular sovereignty, and rule of the wise. To the Romans, we owe our contemporary understanding of the importance of the rule of law, as well as the limitations and possibilities of citizen-based militaries. Of course great civilizations thrived in other parts of the world too. India and China, among others, had extensive, vibrant civilizations long before the historical events covered here. But the European emphasis is justified because for better or worse, in both theory and practice, contemporary international relations is rooted in the European experience. In this chapter, we will begin by looking at Europe in the period immediately preceding and following the Thirty Years' War (1618–48). We then consider Europe's relationship with the rest of the world during the nineteenth century, and we conclude with an analysis of the major transitions during the twentieth and early twenty-first centuries.

The purpose of this historical overview is to trace important trends over time: the emergence of the state and the notion of sovereignty, the development of the international state *system*, the causes and continuing consequences of colonialism and two world wars, and the changes since then that appear to make states, and the state system, less relevant. These trends have a direct impact on international relations theory and foreign policy today.

The Emergence of the Westphalian System

Most international relations theorists locate the origins of the contemporary states system in Europe in 1648, the year the **Treaties of Westphalia** ended the Thirty Years' War. These treaties marked the end of rule by religious authority in Europe and the emergence of secular authorities. With secular authority came the principle that has provided the foundation for international relations ever since: the notion of the territorial integrity of states—legally equal and sovereign participants in an international system.

The formulation of **sovereignty**—a core concept in contemporary international relations—was one of the most important intellectual developments leading to the Westphalian revolution. Much of the development of the notion is found in the writings of the French philosopher Jean Bodin (1530–96). To Bodin, sovereignty was the "absolute and perpetual power vested in a commonwealth."[1] It resides not in an individual but in a state; thus it is perpetual. Sovereignty is "the distinguishing mark of the sovereign that he cannot in any way be subject to the commands of another, for it is he who makes law for the subject, abrogates law already made, and amends obsolete law."[2]

Although ideally sovereignty is absolute, in reality, according to Bodin, it is not without limits. Leaders are limited by divine law and natural law: "All the princes on earth are subject to the laws of God and of nature." They are also limited by the type of regime—"the constitutional laws of the realm"—be it a monarchy, an aristocracy, or a democracy. And last, leaders are limited by covenants, contracts with promises to the people within the commonwealth, and treaties with other states, though there is no supreme arbiter in relations among states.[3] Thus, Bodin provided the conceptual glue of sovereignty that would emerge with the Westphalian agreement.

The Thirty Years' War devastated Europe. The war, which had begun as a religious dispute between Catholics and Protestants, ended as a result of mutual exhaustion, bankruptcy, and enormous loss of life of Europe. Princes and mercenary armies ravaged the central European landscape, fought frequent battles and savage sieges, and could be supplied in the field only by plundering the civilian population. But the treaties that ended the conflict had a profound impact on the practice of international relations. First, the Treaties of Westphalia embraced the notion of sovereignty. With one stroke, virtually all the small states in central Europe attained sovereignty. The Holy Roman Empire was dead. Monarchs in the west gained the authority to decide which version of Christianity was appropriate for their people. This meant that each monarch, and not a supranational church, had religious authority over his or her population. With the pope and the emperor stripped of power, the notion of the territorial state came into focus and was increasingly accepted as normal. The treaties not only legitimized territoriality and the right of *states*—as the sovereign, territorially contiguous principalities increasingly came to be known—to choose their own religion, but the treaties also established that states could determine their own domestic policies, free from external pressure and with full jurisdiction in their own geographic space. The treaties also introduced the principle of noninterference in the affairs of other states.

Second, the leaders of Europe's most powerful countries had seen the devastation caused by mercenaries in war. Thus, after the Treaties of Westphalia, these countries sought to establish their own permanent national militaries. The growth of such forces led to increasingly centralized control, since the state had to collect taxes to pay for these militaries and leaders assumed absolute control over the troops. The state with a national army emerged, its sovereignty acknowledged and its secular base firmly established. And that state became increasingly powerful. Larger territorial units gained an advantage as armaments became more standardized and more lethal.

Third, the Treaties of Westphalia established a core group of states that dominated the world until the beginning of the nineteenth century: Austria, Russia, Prussia, England, France, and the United Provinces (the area now comprising the Netherlands and Belgium). Those in the west — England, France, and the United Provinces — underwent an economic revival under the aegis of capitalism, whereas those in the east — Prussia and Russia — reverted to feudal practices. In the west, private enterprise was encouraged. States improved their infrastructure to facilitate commerce, and great trading companies and banks emerged. In contrast, in the east, serfs remained on the land, and economic change was stifled. Yet in both regions, absolutist states dominated, with Louis XIV ruling in France (1643–1715), Peter the Great in Russia (1682–1725), and

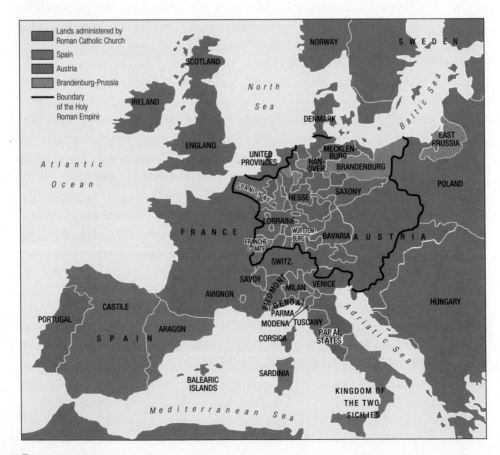

Europe, c. 1648

IN FOCUS

KEY DEVELOPMENTS AFTER WESTPHALIA

- Concept and practice of sovereignty develops.

- Capitalist economic system emerges.

- Centralized control of institutions to facilitate the creation and maintenance of military power grows.

Frederick II in Prussia (1740–86). Until the end of the eighteenth century, European politics was dominated by multiple rivalries and shifting alliances. These rivalries also played out in regions beyond Europe, where contending European states vied for power, most notably Great Britain and France in North America.

The most important social theorist of the time was the Scottish economist Adam Smith (1723–90). In *An Inquiry into the Nature and Causes of the Wealth of Nations,* Smith argued that the notion of a market should apply to all social orders. Individuals—laborers, owners, investors, consumers—should be permitted to pursue their own interests, unfettered by state regulation. According to Smith, each individual acts rationally to maximize his or her own interests. With groups of individuals pursuing their self-interests, economic efficiency is enhanced, and more goods and services are produced and consumed. At the aggregate level, the wealth of the state and that of the international system are similarly enhanced. What makes the system work is the so-called invisible hand of the market: when individuals pursue their rational self-interests, the system (the market) operates effortlessly.[4] Smith's explication of how competing units enable capitalism to ensure economic vitality has had a profound effect on states' economic policies and political choices, which we will explore in Chapter 9. But other ideas of the period would also dramatically alter governance in the nineteenth, twentieth, and twenty-first centuries.

Europe in the Nineteenth Century

Two revolutions ushered in the nineteenth century—the American Revolution (1773–1785) against British rule and the French Revolution (1789) against absolutist rule. Both revolutions were the product of Enlightenment thinking as well as social contract theory. Enlightenment thinkers saw individuals as rational, capable of understanding the laws governing them and of working to improve their condition in society.

The Aftermath of Revolution: Core Principles

Two core principles emerged in the aftermath of the American and French revolutions. The first was that absolutist rule is subject to limits imposed by man. In *Two Treatises of Government*, the English philosopher John Locke (1632–1704) attacked absolute power and the notion of the divine right of kings. Locke argued that the state is a beneficial institution created by rational men in order to protect both their natural rights (life, liberty, and property) and their self-interests. Men freely enter into this political arrangement, agreeing to establish government to ensure natural rights for all. The crux of Locke's argument is that political power ultimately rests with the people, rather than with a leader or monarch. The monarch derives **legitimacy** from the consent of the governed.[5]

John Locke's *Two Treatises of Government*, first published in 1689, continues to influence ideas about the legitimacy of the state today.

The second core principle that emerged at this time was **nationalism**, wherein a people comes to identify with a common past, language, customs, and practices. Individuals who share such characteristics are motivated to participate actively in the political process as a **nation**. For example, during the French Revolution, a patriotic appeal was made to the masses to defend the French *nation* and its new ideals. This appeal forged an emotional link between the people and the state, regardless of social class. These two principles—legitimacy and nationalism—arose out of the American and French revolutions to provide the foundation for politics in the nineteenth and twentieth centuries.

The Napoleonic Wars

The political impact of these twin principles in Europe was far from benign. The nineteenth century opened with war in Europe on an unprecedented scale. France's status as a revolutionary power made it an enticing target of other European states intent on stamping out the contagious idea of government by popular consent. Plus,

France appeared disorganized and weak, the result of years of internal conflict. As a result, following its revolution, France became embroiled in an escalating series of wars with Austria, Britain, and Prussia, which culminated in the rise of a "low-born" Corsican artillery officer named Napoleon Bonaparte to leader of the French military and, eventually, to the rank of emperor of France.

Napoleon, with help from other talented officers, set about reorganizing and regularizing the French military. Making skillful use of French national zeal, Napoleon was able to field large, well-armed, and passionately motivated armies. Modest changes in technology—in particular more efficient cultivation of the potato—made possible the advent of a *magazine* system, whereby supplies for war could be stored in prepositioned locations along likely campaign routes for retrieval by troops on the move, reducing the need to stop and forage for food. This, in combination with nationalism, made it possible for the French—who had been weakened by years of internal fighting following the French Revolution—to field larger, more mobile, and more reliable armies that could make use of innovative tactics unavailable to the smaller, professional armies of France's rivals, such as the highly regarded Prussian army. Through a series of famous battles, including those at Jena and Auerstedt (1806), in

The dramatic successes and failures of France's Napoleon Bonaparte illustrated both the power and the limits of new military technology and organization.

which Napoleon's armies shattered those of Prussia, Napoleon was able to conquer nearly the whole of Europe in a few short years.

Yet the same nationalist fervor that brought about much of Napoleon's success also led to his downfall. In Spain and Russia, Napoleon's armies met nationalists who fought a different sort of war. Rather than facing French forces in direct confrontations, Spanish *guerrillas* made use of intimate local knowledge to mount hit-and-run attacks on French occupying forces. The Spanish guerrillas also enjoyed the support of Britain, which due to its unrivaled mastery of the seas was able to lend supplies and occasional expeditionary forces. When local French forces attempted to punish the Spanish into submission by barbarism (including looting, torture, rape, and execution of prisoners and suspected insurgents without trial), resistance to French occupation escalated. The cost to France was high, draining away talented soldiers and cash and damaging French morale far beyond Spain. In Russia, which Napoleon invaded in 1812 with an army numbering a staggering 422,000, the Russians also refused to give direct battle. Instead, they retreated toward their areas of supply, destroying all available food and shelter behind them as they pursued a "scorched earth" policy. The advancing French began to suffer from severe malnutrition, the entire army slowly starving to death as it advanced to Moscow.

By the time the French reached the Russian capital, the government had already evacuated. The French army that occupied Moscow had dwindled to a mere 110,000. Napoleon waited in vain for the tsar to surrender to France. After realizing the magnitude of his vulnerability, Napoleon attempted to return in good order to France before Russia's harsh winter set in. But it was already too late.

As the French abandoned Moscow, leaving it in flames, the first snowflakes had already fallen. Now fast-moving Russian light cavalry, the Cossacks, harassed the French on their retreat to France and safety. The French sought desperately to choose a route home that offered a chance to find food and shelter, but Cossack attacks forced them to retreat along the same desolate route by which they had come. With the temperature dropping rapidly, the retreat soon became a rout. Entire French units deserted; others, decimated by exposure and starvation, simply vanished. By the time French troops crossed the original line of departure at the Nieman River, Napoleon's Grande Armeé had been reduced to a mere 10,000. The proud emperor's final defeat in 1815 by English and Prussian forces at the Battle of Waterloo (in present-day Belgium) was assured.

Peace at the Core of the European System

Following the defeat of Napoleon in 1815 and the establishment of peace by the Congress of Vienna, the five powers of Europe—Austria, Britain, France, Prussia, and Russia—ushered in a period of relative peace in the international political system, the so-called Concert of Europe. These great powers fought no major wars after the defeat of Napoleon until the Crimean War in 1854, and in that war both Austria and Prussia remained neutral. Other local wars of brief duration were fought, and in these, too, some of the five major powers remained neutral. Meeting over 30 times before World War I at a series of ad hoc conferences, the group became a club of like-minded leaders. Through these meetings they legitimized both the independence of new European states and the division of Africa among the colonial powers.

The fact that peace among great powers prevailed during this time seems surprising since major economic, technological, and political changes were radically altering the landscape.

Industrialization, a critical development during the nineteenth century, was a double-edged sword. During the second half of the nineteenth century, all attention was focused on the processes of industrialization. Great Britain was the leader, outstripping all rivals in its output of coal, iron, and steel and the export of manufactured goods. In addition, Britain became the source of finance capital, the banker for the continent and, in the twentieth century, for the world. Industrialization spread

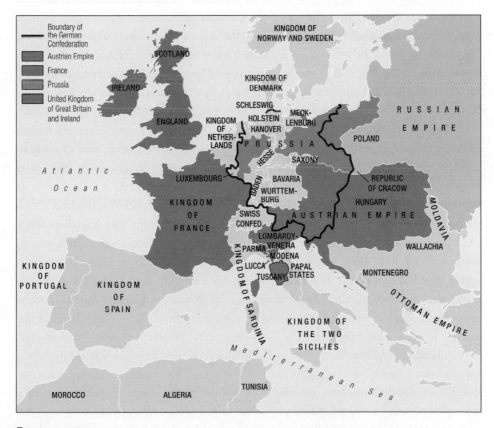

Europe, c. 1815

through virtually all areas of western Europe as the masses flocked to the cities and entrepreneurs and middlemen scrambled for economic advantage. In addition, more than any other factor, industrialization led to the capture of political power by the middle classes that were its vanguard, at the expense of the aristocratic classes. As machine power became more and more indispensable to the survival and prosperity of states, so land power—the power of land to yield surplus wealth in the form of cultivated or renewable natural resources—began to yield to machine power and to the industrious, inventive, and entrepreneurial middle classes that mastered it.

The population soared and commerce surged as transportation corridors were strengthened. Political changes were dramatic: Italy was unified in 1870; Germany was formed out of 39 different fragments in 1871; Holland was divided into the Netherlands and Belgium in the 1830s; and the Ottoman Empire gradually disintegrated, leading to independence for Greece in 1829 and for Moldavia and Wallachia (Romania) in 1856. With such dramatic changes under way, what explains the absence of major war? At least three factors were involved.

First, Europe's political elites were united in their fear of revolution among the masses. In fact, at the Congress of Vienna, the Austrian diplomat Count Klemens von Metternich (1773–1859), architect of the Concert of Europe, believed that Europe could best be managed by returning it to the age of absolutism. Elites envisioned grand alliances that would bring European leaders together to fight revolution from below. During the first half of the century, these alliances were not altogether successful. In the 1830s, Britain and France sided together against the three eastern powers (Prussia, Russia, and Austria). In 1848, all five powers were confronted by the masses with demands for reform. But during the second half of the century, European leaders acted in concert, ensuring that mass revolutions did not spread from state to state. In 1870, in the turmoil following France's defeat in the Franco-Prussian War, the leader Napoleon III was isolated quickly for fear of a revolution that never occurred. Fear of revolt from below thus united European leaders, making interstate war less likely.

Second, two of the major conflicts of interest confronting the core European states took place within rather than between culturally close territories: the unifications of Germany and Italy. Both German and Italian unification had powerful proponents and opponents among the European powers. For example, Britain supported Italian unification, making possible Italy's annexation of Naples and Sicily. Austria, on the other hand, was preoccupied with the increasing strength of Prussia and thus did not actively oppose what may well have been against its national interest—the creation of two sizable neighbors out of myriad independent units. German unification was acceptable to Russia as long as Russian interests in Poland were respected. German unification also got support from Britain's dominant middle class, which viewed a stronger Germany as a potential counterbalance to France. Thus, because the energies and resources of German and Italian peoples were concentrated on the struggle to form single contiguous territorial states, and because the precise impact of the newly unified states on the European balance of power was unknown, a wider war was averted.

The third factor in supporting peace in Europe was the complex and crucial phenomenon of imperialism/colonialism.

Imperialism and Colonialism in the European System before 1870

The discovery of the "new" world—as it was called by Europeans after 1492—led to rapidly expanding communication between the Americas and Europe. The same technology also made contact with Asia less costly and more frequent. The first to arrive were explorers seeking discovery, riches, and personal glory; merchants seeking raw materials and trade relations; and clerics seeking to convert "savages" to Christianity (Catholicism initially). But the staggering wealth that was discovered, and the relative ease with which it could be acquired, led to increasing competition among European powers for territories in far-distant lands. Most of the European powers became empires and, once established, claimed the lands sparsely occupied by indigenous peoples as sovereign territory. This is the origin of the term **imperialism**, the annexation of distant territory (most often by force) and its inhabitants to an empire. **Colonialism**, which often followed or accompanied imperialism, refers to the settling of people from the home country (say, Spain) among indigenous peoples of a distant territory (say, Mexico). The two terms are thus subtly different, because most but not all imperial powers settled their own citizens among the peoples whose territories they annexed, and some colonies were established by states that did not identify themselves as empires. Still, most scholars use the two terms interchangeably.

This process of annexation by conquest or treaty continued for 400 years. As the technology of travel and communications shifted from sail to steam, and as Europeans developed vaccines and cures for tropical diseases, the costs to European powers of imposing their will on indigenous people continued to drop. Europeans were welcomed in some places but were resisted in most. In most cases, that resistance was overcome with very little cost or risk. Spears were met with machine guns, and horses with heavy artillery. By the close of the nineteenth century, almost the whole of the globe was "ruled" by European states. Great Britain was the largest and most successful of the imperial powers, but even small states such as Portugal and the Netherlands maintained important colonies abroad.

The process also led to the establishment of a "European" identity. European states enjoyed a solidarity among themselves, based on their being European, Christian, "civilized," and white. These traits differentiated "us"—white Christian Europeans—from the "other"—the rest of the world. With the rise of mass literacy and increasing contact with the colonial world brought about by industrialization, Europeans more than ever saw their commonalities, the uniqueness of being "European." This was, in part, a return to the unity in the Roman Empire and in Roman law, a secular form of medieval Christendom, and a larger Europe as envisioned by Kant and Rousseau. The Congress of Vienna and the Concert of Europe gave more concrete form to these beliefs. The flip side of these beliefs was the ongoing exploration, conquest, and exploitation of the non-European world and the subsequent establishment of colonies.

The Industrial Revolution provided the European states with the military and economic capacity to engage in territorial expansion. Some imperial states were motivated by economic gains, seeking new external markets for manufactured goods and obtaining, in turn, raw materials to fuel their industrial growth. For others, the motivation was cultural and

In the nineteenth century, explorers often paved the way for the colonization of African, Asian, and Latin American lands by European powers. Here, a French expedition seeks to stake a claim in central Africa.

religious—to spread the Christian faith and the ways of white "civilization" to the "dark" continents and beyond. For still others, the motivation was political. Since the European balance of power prevented direct confrontation in Europe, European state rivalries were played out in Africa and Asia.

To mollify Germany's ambitions, for example, during the Congress of Berlin in 1885 the major powers divided up Africa, giving Germany a sphere of influence in east Africa (Tanganyika), west Africa (Cameroon and Togo), and southern Africa (Southwest Africa). European imperialism provided a convenient outlet for Germany's aspirations as a unified power without endangering the delicate balance of power within Europe itself. By the end of the nineteenth century, 85 percent of Africa was under the control of European states.

In Asia, only Japan and Siam (Thailand) were not under direct European or U.S. influence. China is an excellent example of the extent of external domination. Under the Qing dynasty, which began in the seventeenth century, China had slowly been losing political, economic, and military power for several hundred years. During the nineteenth century, British merchants began to trade with China for tea, silk, and porcelain, often paying for these products with smuggled opium. In 1842, the British defeated China in the Opium War, forcing China to cede various political and territorial rights to foreigners through a series of unequal treaties. European states and Japan were able to occupy large portions of Chinese territory, claiming to have exclusive trading rights in particular regions. Foreign powers exercised separate "spheres of influence" in China. By 1914, Europeans controlled four-fifths of the world.

The United States eventually became an imperial power as well. Having won the 1898 Spanish-American War, pushing the Spanish out of the Philippines, Puerto Rico, Cuba, and other small islands, the United States acquired its own colonies.

The struggle for economic power led to heedless exploitation of colonial areas, particularly in Africa and Asia. One striking aspect of the contest between the Europeans and the peoples they encountered in Africa and Asia is that European weapons and communications technology proved very difficult for indigenous peoples to resist. European states and their militaries became accustomed to winning battles against vastly more numerous adversaries, and often attributed their ability to do so to their military technology. As one famous apologist for colonialism put it: "Thank God that we have got/the Maxim gun, and they have not."[6]

But as the nineteenth century drew to a close, the assumption that vast stretches of distant territory containing large numbers of aggrieved or oppressed people could be controlled cheaply with a few colonial officers and administrators was being challenged with increasing frequency. For Great Britain, the world's most successful colonial power, the future of colonialism was clearly signaled by Britain's Pyrrhic victory in the Second Anglo-Boer War (1899–1902; also known as the South African War). In this war, which pitted British soldiers against Boer commandos (descendants of Dutch immigrants to South Africa in the 1820s), Britain was forced to fight a lengthy and bitter counterinsurgency war that claimed the lives of over 20,000 Boer women and children through the failure of the British to provide sanitary internment conditions, sufficient food, and fresh water. The war, which Britain expected to last no longer than three months and cost no more than 10 million pounds sterling, ended up costing 230 million pounds and lasting two years and eight months. It proved the most expensive war, by an order of magnitude, in British colonial history. The war was largely unpopular in Europe and led to increased tensions between Britain and Germany, because the Boers had purchased advanced infantry rifles from Germany and sought German diplomatic and military intervention during the war. However, the five European powers had still not fought major wars directly against each other.

In sum, much of the competition, rivalry, and tension traditionally marking relations among Europe's states could be acted out far beyond Europe itself. Europeans raced to acquire colonies in order to achieve increased status, wealth, and power vis-à-vis their rivals. Europeans could imagine themselves as bringing the light of civilization to the "dark" regions of the world, while at the same time acquiring the material resources (mineral wealth and "native levies") they might need in the event of a future war in Europe. Each colonial power understood it might take years to accumulate sufficient resources to gain an advantage in a major European war. Therefore each state maintained an interest in managing crises so as not to escalate a conflict of interest to all-out war. Thus the "safety valve" of colonialism both reinforced European unity and identity and prevented the buildup of tension in Europe. By the end of the nineteenth century, however, the toll of political rivalry and economic competition had become destabilizing. Germany's unification, rapid industrialization, and population growth led to an escalation of tension that could not be assuaged in time to prevent war. In 1870 France and Germany fought a war in which France was defeated. In what for France became a humiliating peace treaty, it was forced to surrender the long-contested provinces of Alsace and Lorraine, which became part of the new Germany. The war and the simmering resentments to which it gave birth were mere harbingers of conflicts to come. In addition, the legacy of colonialism, which had served to defuse tension in Europe, laid the groundwork for enduring resentment of Europeans by many Asians, Latin Americans, and Africans, resentment that continues to complicate peace, humanitarian work, and development operations in these areas of the world to this day.

Balance of Power

During the nineteenth century, colonialism, the common interests of conservative European elites, and distraction over the troubled unifications of German and Italian principalities seemed to result in a long peace in Europe. But this condition of relative peace was underpinned by another factor as well: a **balance of power**. The independent European states, each with relatively equal power, feared the emergence of any predominant state (**hegemon**) among them. As a result, they formed alliances to counteract any potentially more powerful faction, thus creating a balance of power. The idea behind a balance of power is simple. States will hesitate to start a war with an adversary whose power to fight and win wars is relatively balanced (*symmetrical*), because the risk of defeat is high. When one state or coalition of states is much more powerful than its adversaries (*asymmetrical balance*), war is relatively more likely. The treaties signed after 1815 were designed not only to quell revolution from below but also to prevent the emergence of a hegemon, such as France under Napoleon had become. Britain or Russia, at least later in the century, could have assumed a dominant leadership position—Britain because of its economic capability and naval prowess, and Russia because of its relative geographic isolation and extraordinary manpower. However, neither sought to exert hegemonic power because each one's respective capacity to effect a balance of power in Europe was declining, and because the status quo was acceptable to both states.

Britain and Russia did play different roles in the balance of power. Britain most often played the role of balancer, for example, by intervening on behalf of the Greeks in their struggle for independence from the Turks in the late 1820s, and on behalf of the Belgians during their war of independence against Holland in 1830, on behalf of Turkey against Russia in the Crimean War in 1854–56 and again in the Russo-Turkish War in 1877–78. Thus Britain ensured that other states did not interfere in these conflicts and that power in Europe remained balanced. Russia's role was as a builder of alliances. The Holy Alliance of 1815 kept Austria, Prussia, and Russia united against revolutionary France, and Russia used its claim on Poland to build a bond with Prussia. Russian interests in the Dardanelles, the strategic waterway linking the Mediterranean Sea and the Black Sea, and in Constantinople (today's Istanbul) overlapped with those of Britain. Thus, these two states, located at the margins of Europe, played key roles in making the balance-of-power system work.

During the last three decades of the nineteenth century, the Concert of Europe frayed, beginning with the Franco-Prussian War (1870) and the Russian invasion of Turkey

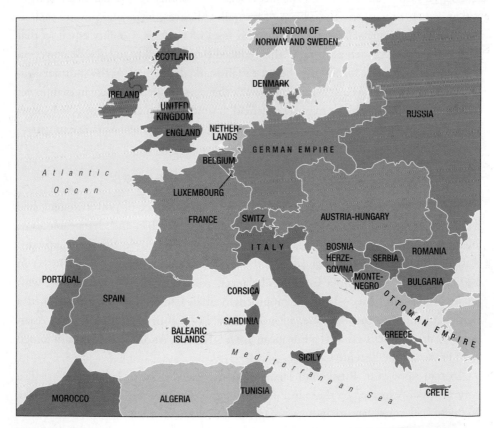

Europe, c. 1878

IN FOCUS

KEY DEVELOPMENTS IN NINETEENTH-CENTURY EUROPE

- From revolutions emerge two concepts: absolutist rule subject to limitations, and nationalism.

- A system managed by the balance of power brings relative peace to Europe. Elites are united in fear of the masses, and domestic concerns are more important than foreign policy.

- European imperialism in Asia and Africa helps to maintain the European balance of power.

- The balance of power breaks down due to imperial Germany's too-rapid growth and the increasing rigidity of alliances, resulting in World War I.

(Russo-Turkish War, 1877–78). Alliances began to solidify as the balance-of-power system began to weaken. The advent of the railroad gave continental powers such as Germany and Austria-Hungary an enhanced level of strategic mobility equal to that of maritime powers such as Britain. This reduced Britain's ability to balance power on the continent. Russia, for its part, began to fall markedly behind in the industrialization race, and its relatively few railroads meant that its massive advantage in manpower would be less and less able to reach a battlefield in time to affect an outcome. So Russia's power began to wane compared with that of France, Germany, and Austria-Hungary.

The Breakdown: Solidification of Alliances

By the waning years of the nineteenth century, the balance-of-power system had weakened. Whereas previously alliances had been fluid, flexible, and changeable, now alliances became increasingly rigid. Two camps emerged: the Triple Alliance (Germany, Austria-Hungary, and Italy) in 1882 and the Dual Alliance (France and Russia) in 1893. In 1902, Britain broke from the "balancer" role, joining in a naval alliance with Japan to prevent a Russo-Japanese rapprochement in China. This alliance marked a significant turn: for the first time, a European state (Great Britain) turned to an Asian one (Japan) in order to thwart a European power (Russia). And in 1904, Britain joined with France in the Entente Cordiale.

In that same year, Russia and Japan went to war (the Russo-Japanese War) in a contest widely expected by those in Europe to result in a Japanese defeat. After all, the Japanese had come late to industrialization, and although their naval forces looked impressive on paper, their opponents would be white Europeans. But this is where

Russia's industrial backwardness was to affect it severely. The lack of railroads made it difficult for Russia to support its forces in the Far East by rail and forced Russia to attempt to relieve its besieged Port Arthur with naval forces. These forces, in turn, had to sail all the way from Russia's Baltic ports, around Cape Hope, past India, and from there into Asian waters. Russia had been a continental power with some maritime power ambitions, but in its fight with tiny Japan, its weaknesses at sea were magnified. Port Arthur was captured while the Russian relief fleet was still on its 18,000-mile journey from its Baltic home ports. In May of 1905, the Russian and Japanese fleets met in Tsushima Bay, and the result was perhaps the greatest naval defeat in history: Russia lost 8 battleships, some 5,000 sailors were killed, and another 5,000 were captured as prisoners of war. The Japanese, under the command of Admiral Togo, lost three torpedo boats and 116 sailors. After that, Russia was forced to sue for peace, but the importance of the Japanese victory would be far greater than the mere defeat of Russia in the Far East. The war contained important insights about killing technology (modern artillery and automatic weapons in particular) that were widely ignored by European observers. More important, the defeat of a white colonial power by an Asian power seriously compromised one of the core ideological foundations of colonialism—that "whites" were inherently superior to "nonwhites." The Russian defeat spurred Japanese expansion and caused Germany to discount Russia's ability to interfere with German ambitions in Europe. Above all, Russia's defeat severely compromised the legitimacy of the tsar, setting in motion a revolution that, after 1917, was to topple the Russian empire and replace it with the Union of Soviet Socialist Republics (USSR).

The final collapse of the balance-of-power system came with World War I. The solidification of alliances at the turn of the twentieth century was accompanied by the rise in power of Germany, which made for an unstable political situation in Europe. Germany had not been satisfied with the solutions meted out at the Congress of Berlin after the Franco-Prussian War. By 1912 it had exceeded France and Britain in both heavy industrial output and population growth. Germany also feared Russian efforts to modernize its relatively sparse railroad network. Being "latecomers" to the core of European power, and having defeated France in the Franco-Prussian War (1870), many Germans felt that their nation had not received the diplomatic recognition and status it deserved. This in part explains why Germany encouraged Austria-Hungary to crush Serbia following the assassination of Archduke Franz Ferdinand (heir to the throne of the Austro-Hungarian Empire) in Sarajevo in June of 1914. Like most of Europe's leaders at the time, Germany's leaders believed war made the state and its citizens stronger, and that backing down after a humiliation would only encourage further humiliations. Besides, the outcome of a local war between Austria-Hungary and Serbia was certain to be a quick victory for Germany's most important ally.

But under the system of alliances, once the fateful shot was fired, allied states felt honor-bound to fulfill their alliance commitments. What Germany had hoped would

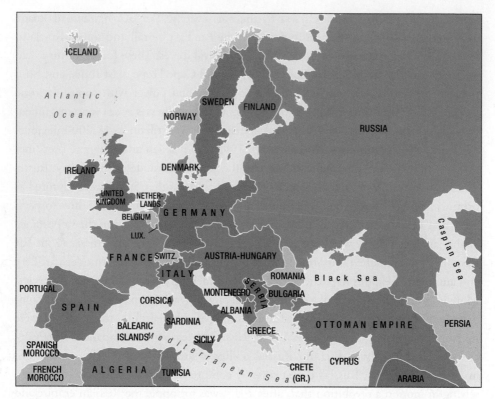

Europe, 1914

remain a local war soon escalated to a continental war once Russia's tsar ordered a pre-mobilization. And once German troops crossed into Belgium (thus violating British-guaranteed Belgian neutrality), that continental war escalated to a world war with Britain's entry on the side of France and Russia. In a twist of fate, the Ottoman Empire entered the war on the side of Germany and Austria-Hungary. Both sides anticipated a short, decisive war, but this did not happen. The initial German plan for a decisive war against both Russia and France, the famous Schlieffen Plan, failed in August 1914, leading to a ghastly stalemate. Between 1914 and 1918, soldiers from more than a dozen countries endured the persistent degradation of trench warfare and the horrors of poison gas. The "Great War," as it came to be known, saw the introduction of strategic bombing and unrestricted submarine warfare as well. Britain's naval blockade of Germany caused widespread suffering and privation for German civilians. More than 8.5 million soldiers and 1.5 million civilians lost their lives. Germany, Austria-Hungary, the Ottoman Empire, and Russia were defeated, while Britain and France—two of the three "victors"—were seriously weakened. Only the United States, a late entrant into the war, emerged relatively unscathed. The defeat and subsequent dismemberment of the Ottoman Empire by France and Britain—which created new states subject to control and manipulation by both — continues to affect interstate peace in the Middle East to this day.

The Interwar Years and World War II

The end of World War I saw critical changes in international relations. First, three European empires were strained and finally broke up during or near the end of World War I. With those empires went the conservative social order of Europe; in its place emerged a proliferation of nationalisms. Russia exited the war in 1917, as revolution raged within its territory. The tsar was overthrown and eventually replaced by not only a new leader (Vladimir Ilyich Lenin) but also a new ideology that would have profound implications for the remainder of the twentieth century. The Austro-Hungarian and Ottoman Empires also broke apart. Austria-Hungary was replaced by Austria, Hungary, Czechoslovakia, part of Yugoslavia, and part of Romania. The Ottoman Empire was also reconfigured. Having gradually lost power throughout the nineteenth century, its defeat resulted in the final overthrow of the Ottomans. Arabia rose against Turkish rule, and British forces occupied Jerusalem and Baghdad. A diminished Turkey was the successor state.

The end of the empires accelerated and intensified nationalisms. In fact, one of President Woodrow Wilson's Fourteen Points in the treaty ending World War I called for self-determination, the right of national groups to self-rule. The nationalism of these various groups (for example, Austrians, Hungarians) had been stimulated by technological innovations in the printing industry and by a mass audience, now literate. Now it was easy and cheap to publish material in the multitude of different European languages and so offer differing interpretations of history and national life. Yet in reality, many of these newly created entities had neither shared histories nor compatible political histories, nor were they economically viable.

A second critical change was that Germany emerged out of World War I an even more dissatisfied power. Germany had been defeated on the battlefield, but German forces ended the war in occupation of enemy territory, and its leaders had not been honest with the German people. Since many German newspapers had been predicting a major breakthrough and victory right up until the armistice of November 11, 1918, the myth grew that the German military had been "stabbed in the back" by "liberals" (and later "Jews") in Berlin. Even more devastating was the fact that the Treaty of Versailles, which formally ended the war, made the subsequent generation of Germans pay the economic cost of the war through reparations — $32 billion for wartime damages. As Germany printed more money to pay its reparations, Germans suffered from hyperinflation, causing widespread impoverishment of the middle classes. Finally, Germany was no longer allowed to have a standing military, and its most productive industrialized region, the Ruhr Valley, was occupied by French and British troops. Bitterness over these excessively harsh penalties provided the climate for the emergence of Adolf Hitler, who publicly dedicated himself to righting the "wrongs" that had been imposed on the German people.

Third, enforcement of the Treaty of Versailles was given to the ultimately unsuccessful **League of Nations**, the intergovernmental organization designed to prevent all future wars. But the organization itself did not have the political weight, the legal instruments, or the legitimacy to carry out the task. The political weight of the League was weakened by the fact that the United States, whose president, Woodrow Wilson, had been the principal architect of the League, itself refused to join, retreating instead to an isolationist foreign policy. Nor did Russia join, nor were any of the vanquished of the war permitted to participate. The League's legal authority was weak, and the instruments it had for enforcing the peace proved ineffective.

Fourth, the blueprint for a peaceful international order enshrined in Wilson's Fourteen Points never became reality. Wilson called for open diplomacy—"open covenants of peace, openly arrived at, after which there shall be no private international understandings of any kind but diplomacy shall proceed always frankly and in public view."[7] Point three was a reaffirmation of economic liberalism, the removal of economic barriers among all the nations consenting to the peace. This order was to be maintained by the League, a "general association of nations" that would ensure that war never occurred again. But these principles never became reality. In the words of historian E. H. Carr, "The characteristic feature of the twenty years between 1919 and 1939 was the abrupt descent from the visionary hopes of the first decade to the grim despair of the second, from a utopia which took little account of reality to a reality from which every element of utopia was rigorously excluded."[8] Liberalism and its utopian

---

IN FOCUS

KEY DEVELOPMENTS IN THE INTERWAR YEARS

- Three empires collapse: Russia by revolution, the Austro-Hungarian Empire by dismemberment, and the Ottoman Empire by external wars and internal turmoil. This leads to a resurgence of nationalisms.

- German dissatisfaction with the World War I settlement leads to facism. Germany finds allies in Italy and Japan.

- A weak League of Nations is unable to respond to Japanese, Italian, and German aggression. Nor can it respond to widespread economic depression.

and idealist elements were replaced by realism as the dominant international relations theory—a fundamentally divergent theoretical perspective. (Both realism and liberalism are developed in Chapter 3.)

The world from which these realists emerged was a turbulent one. The German economy imploded; the U.S. stock market plummeted; and the world economy collapsed. Japan marched into Manchuria in 1931 and into the rest of China in 1937; Italy overran Ethiopia in 1935; fascism, liberalism, and communism clashed. These were the symptoms of the interwar period.

World War II

In the view of most Europeans and many in the United States, World War II was started by Germany, and in particular by Adolf Hitler. But Japan and Italy also played major roles in the breakdown of interstate order in the 1930s. In 1931, Japan staged the Mukden incident as a pretext for assaulting China and annexing Manchuria. The Japanese invasion of China was marked by horrifying barbarity against the Chinese people (including the rape, murder, and torture of Chinese civilians) and by the increasing inability of Japan's civilian government to restrain its generals in China. Japan's record in Korea was equally brutal. Japan's reputation for savagery against noncombatants in China reached its peak in the Rape of Nanking, as most historians name the six-week period following the capture of the city by Japanese forces in December 1937. At that time, Nanking was the capital of China, and the Japanese were determined to capture it. In the weeks that followed, hundreds of thousands of noncombatants were murdered by Japanese forces under unspeakable conditions. Japanese historians acknowledge the killing of 100,000 to 200,000 Chinese, but dispute the charges of murder and rape. Chinese historians have estimated the death toll at 300,000, close to the 260,000 estimated by the War Crimes Tribunal following World War II. The atrocities were made known to the rest of the world as foreign business delegations and members of religious organizations witnessed the brutality firsthand and reported it. When news of the massacres and rapes reached the United States—itself already embroiled in a dispute with Japan over Japan's prior conduct in China—a diplomatic crisis ensued, the end result of which was war when Japanese forces attacked the United States at Pearl Harbor in December 1941.

In 1935, Italy invaded Ethiopia with armored vehicles, aircraft, heavy artillery, and yperite (a form of mustard gas outlawed by the Geneva Protocol of 1925, to which Italy had been a signatory). The Ethiopians fielded elite warriors but had very few rifles and no vehicles, and most fought barefoot. Although the Italians expected a rapid victory, the Ethiopians fought so bravely and tenaciously that they threatened to surround and cut off the invading Italian and allied Eritrean forces. But once the Italians resorted to spraying yperite on the Ethiopian soldiers from the air, their defeat was inevitable. In the end, it took Italy a year to conquer Ethiopia and force its emperor, Haile Selassie, to flee into exile.

But Nazi Germany proved to be the greatest challenge to the nascent interstate order that followed World War I. Rearmed under Hitler in the 1930s, buoyed by helping the Spanish fascists during the Spanish Civil War, and successful in reuniting ethnic Germans from far-flung territories, Germany was ready to right the wrongs imposed by the Treaty of Versailles. Many of these wrongs were real: Germany had been forced to accept exclusive responsibility for World War I and to pay a heavy indemnity in gold. The reparations led to hyperinflation and the impoverishment of Germany's middle class. It had lost Alsace, Lorraine, and East Prussia; its industrial heartland was occupied by French troops; and the armed forces it could have for its defense were severely restricted. The excessive harshness of the Versailles treaty, as well as the widespread hardship brought about by the Great Depression and the rise of national self-determination as a powerful new norm of interstate politics, enabled Germany's charismatic leader, Adolf Hitler, to rise to power and to persuade Britain (though not France) that his diplomatic aggression was aimed merely at uniting ethnic Germans into a single state. For these and other reasons, including the economic damage suffered by both Britain and France in World War I, Britain and France acquiesced to Germany's resurgence.

German fascism uniquely mobilized the masses in support of the state. It drew on the belief that war and conflict were noble activities from which ultimately superior civilizations would be formed. It drew strength from the belief that certain racial groups were superior and others inferior and mobilized the disenchanted and the economically weak on behalf of its cause. In 1938, Britain agreed to let Germany occupy Czechoslovakia, in the hope of averting a general war if possible, or at least delaying war until Britain's defense preparations could be sufficiently strengthened. But this was a false hope. In September 1939, after having signed a peace treaty with the Soviet Union that divided Poland between them, German forces stormed into Poland from the west while Soviet forces assaulted from the east. Hitler's real intent was to secure his eastern flank against a Soviet threat while he assaulted Norway, Denmark, Netherlands, and France (and hopefully forcing Britain into a humiliating neutrality). His grand plan then called for Germany to turn east and conquer the Soviet Union. Poland was quickly overcome, but because Britain and France had guaranteed Polish security, the invasion prompted a declaration of war, and World War II had begun.

In 1940, Hitler set his grand plan into motion and succeeded in a series of rapid conquests culminating in the defeat of France in May. In the late summer and fall, after being repeatedly rebuffed in its efforts to coerce Britain into neutrality, Germany's government, known as the Third Reich, prepared to invade and the Battle of Britain ensued. Fought almost entirely in the air, Britain eventually won the battle by a combination of extreme courage, resourcefulness, and luck; and Hitler was forced to turn east with a hostile Britain at his back. In June of 1941, the Third Reich undertook the

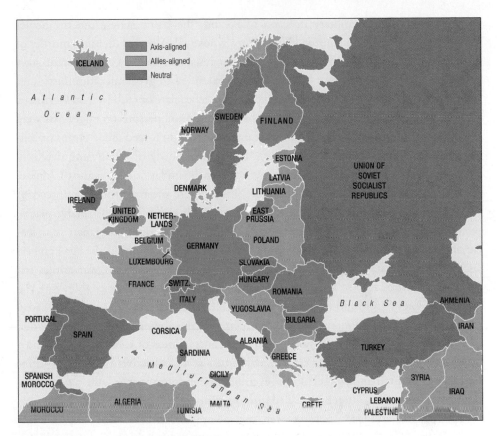

Europe, 1939

most ambitious land invasion in history in Operation Barbarossa: its long-planned yet ill-fated invasion of the Soviet Union. This surprise attack led the Soviet Union to join sides with Britain and France.

The power of fascism—in German, Italian, and Japanese versions—led to an uneasy alliance between the communist Soviet Union and the liberal United States, Great Britain, and France, among others (the Allies). That alliance was intended to check the Axis powers (Germany, Italy, and Japan), by force if necessary. Thus, during World War II, those fighting against the Axis powers acted in unison, regardless of their ideological disagreements.

At the end of the war, the Allies prevailed. Both the German Reich and imperial Japan lay in ruins. In Europe, the Soviet Union paid the highest price for Germany's aggression, and with some justification considered itself the victor in Europe, with help from the United States and Britain. In the Pacific, the United States, China, and Korea paid the highest price for Japan's aggression. With some justification, the United States considered itself the victor in the Pacific. Two other features of World War II demand attention as well.

First, the German military invasion of Poland, the Baltic states, and the Soviet Union was followed by organized killing teams whose sole aim was the mass murder of human beings, regardless of their support for or resistance to the German state. Jews in particular were singled out, but Nazi policy extended to gypsies, communists, and even ethnic Germans with genetic defects such as cleft palate or club feet. In Germany, Poland, the Baltic states, Yugoslavia, and the Soviet Union, persons on target lists were forced to abandon their homes. They were made to work in forced-labor camps or killing pits under cruel conditions, and were then either slowly or rapidly murdered by their captors. In East Asia, Japanese forces acted with similar cruelty against Chinese, Vietnamese, and Korean noncombatants. Victims were often tortured or forced to become subjects in gruesome experiments before being murdered. In many places, women were forced into army-run brothels, or "comfort stations," as Japanese rhetoric of the day described them. The nearly unprecedented brutality of the Axis powers against noncombatants in areas of occupation during the war led to war crimes tribunals and, ultimately, to a major new feature of international politics following the war: the Geneva Conventions of 1948 and 1949. These conventions—which today have the force of international law—criminalized many abuses (e.g., torture, murder, food deprivation) perpetrated against noncombatants in areas of German and Japanese occupation during World War II. The conventions are collectively known as international humanitarian law (IHL); however, because enforcement is largely voluntary, their effectiveness has often been called into question.

But German and Japanese forces were not the only forces for whom race was a factor in World War II. As documented by John Dower in his book *War without Mercy*, U.S., British, and Australian forces fighting in the Pacific tended to view the Japanese as "apes" or "monkey men." As a result, they were less likely to take prisoners and more comfortable in undertaking massive strategic air assaults on Japanese cities. In the United States, citizens of Japanese descent were summarily interned for the duration of the war. In the Pacific theater, in other words, racism affected the conduct and strategies of armed forces on *both* sides.[9]

Second, although Germany surrendered unconditionally in May 1945, the war did not end until the Japanese surrender in August of that year. By this point in the war, Japan had no hope of winning and waited only for one final effort in defense of its homeland from an expected invasion by U.S. and possibly Soviet forces. Japan had made it clear as early as January that it might be willing to surrender, so long as the emperor Hirohito was not tried or imprisoned by Allied forces. But the Allies had already agreed they would accept no less than unconditional surrender, so Japan prepared for invasion, hoping that the threat of massive Allied casualties might yet win it a chance to preserve the emperor from trial and punishment. Instead, on August 6, the United States dropped an atomic bomb on Hiroshima and three days later a second bomb on Nagasaki. The casualties were no greater than those experienced in firebombings of major Japanese cities earlier that year. But the new weapon, combined with a Soviet declaration of war on Japan the same day as the Nagasaki bombing (and Japanese calculation that the emperor might be spared), led to Japan's surrender on August 15, 1945.

All three Axis powers had suffered from overextension as well. In Germany and Japan, the widespread belief in the inherent racial superiority of Germans and Japanese (respectively) led both to a persistent underestimation of their adversaries and to a level of cruelty and genocide that backfired. In the steppes of western Russia and across the mountains of Yugoslavia and China, guerrilla armies—partisans and Mao Zedong's Red Army—proved an increasing drain on resources and on operations, setting the stage for a major shift in the pattern of conflicts that would soon follow.

The end of World War II resulted in a major redistribution of power. The victorious United States would now be pitted against the equally victorious Soviet Union. The war also changed political boundaries. The Soviet Union absorbed the Baltic states and portions of Finland, Czechoslovakia, Poland, and Romania; Germany and Korea were divided; and Japan was ousted from much of Asia. Each of these changes contributed to the new international conflict: the **Cold War**.

The Cold War

The leaders of the victors of World War II—Britain's prime minister Winston Churchill, the United States' president Franklin Roosevelt, and the Soviet Union's premier Joseph Stalin—planned during the war for a postwar order. Indeed, the Atlantic Charter of August 14, 1941, called for collaboration on economic issues and prepared for a permanent system of security. These plans were consolidated in 1943 and 1944 and came to fruition in the United Nations in 1945. Yet several other outcomes of World War II provided the foundation for the Cold War that followed.

Origins of the Cold War

The most important outcome of World War II was the emergence of two **superpowers**—the United States and the Soviet Union—as the primary actors in the international system and the attendant decline of Europe as the epicenter of international politics. The United States had been reluctant to fight, entering the war only after a direct attack on its territory at Pearl Harbor. For its part, the Soviet Union had had much more aggressive ambitions. In 1939 it fought two offensive wars—one against tiny Finland and one in alliance with Germany to dismember Poland. Hitler's assault on the Soviet Union in 1941 had come as a severe shock, first in its timing (too early), and second in its success (over 5 million Soviet soldiers were killed or captured between June and December 1941). But both the United States and the Soviet Union survived and rallied. By the end of the war, each had become a military superpower.

The second outcome of the war was the recognition of fundamental incompatibilities between these two superpowers in both national interests and ideology. Differences surfaced immediately over geopolitical national interests. Having been invaded from the west on several occasions, including during World War II, the USSR used its newfound power to solidify its sphere of influence in the buffer states of Eastern Europe — Poland, Czechoslovakia, Hungary, Bulgaria, and Romania. The Soviet leadership believed that ensuring friendly neighbors on its western borders was vital to the country's national interests. As for the United States, as early as 1947, policy makers argued that U.S. interests lay in containing the Soviet Union. The diplomat and historian George Kennan published in *Foreign Affairs* the famous "X" article, in which he argued that because the Soviet Union would always feel military insecurity, it would conduct an aggressive foreign policy. Containing the Soviets, Kennan wrote, should therefore become the cornerstone of the United States' postwar foreign policy.[10]

The United States put the notion of **containment** into action in the Truman Doctrine of 1947. Justifying material support in Greece against the communists, President Harry Truman asserted, "I believe that it must be the policy of the United States to support free peoples who are resisting attempted subjugation by armed minorities or by outside pressures. I believe that we must assist free peoples to work out their own destinies in their own way."[11] Containment as policy — essentially, the use of espionage, economic pressure, and forward-deployed military resources — emerged from a comparative asymmetry of forces in Europe. After the surrender of the Third Reich, U.S. and British forces rapidly demobilized and left, whereas the Red Army did not. In 1948, when the Soviets blocked western transportation corridors to Berlin, the German capital — which had been divided into sectors by the Potsdam Conference of 1945 — the United States realized that even as the sole state in possession of nuclear weapons, it did not possess the power to coerce the Soviet Union into retreating to its pre–World War II borders. The United States could not, in other words, roll back the Soviet advances. At best, the United States had the power to contain the Soviets in Eastern Europe, thus preserving vital U.S. interests in Western Europe, Africa, Asia, and Latin America. Thus, containment, based on U.S. geostrategic interests and a growing recognition that attempting rollback could only lead to another world war, became the fundamental doctrine of U.S. foreign policy during the Cold War.

The United States and the Soviet Union also had major ideological differences. These differences pitted two contrasting visions of society and of the international order against one another. The United States' democratic liberalism was based on a social system that accepted the worth and value of the individual; a political system that depended on the participation of individuals in the electoral process; and an economic system, **capitalism**, that provided opportunities to individuals to pursue what was economically rational with little or no government interference. At the international level, this logically translated into support for other democratic liberal regimes and support of capitalist institutions and processes, including, most critically, free trade.

Soviet communist ideology also influenced that country's conception of the international system and state practices. The Soviet state embraced Marxist ideology, which holds that under capitalism one class (the bourgeoisie) controls the ownership of the means of production and uses the institutions and authority of the state to maintain that control and exploit the workers, or proletariat. The solution to the problem of class rule, according to Marxism, is revolution, whereby the exploited proletariat takes control from the bourgeoisie by using the state to seize the means of production. Thus, capitalism is replaced by **socialism**. The leaders of the Soviet Union saw themselves in an interim period—after the demise of the capitalist state and before the victory of socialism. This ideology had critical international elements as well: capitalism will try to extend itself through imperialism in order to generate more capital, larger markets, and greater control over raw materials. Soviet leaders thus felt themselves surrounded by a hostile capitalist camp and argued that the Soviet Union "must not weaken but must in every way strengthen its state, the state organs, the organs of the intelligence service, the army, if that country does not want to be smashed by the capitalist environment."[12] Soviet leaders believed they must support other international movements, exporting the revolution in order to undermine world capitalism and promote the new socialist order in other countries.

Differences between the two superpowers were exacerbated by mutual misperceptions. Kennan cited powerful examples of such misperceptions by each superpower:

> The Marshall Plan, the preparations for the setting up of a West German government, and the first moves toward the establishment of NATO [the North Atlantic Treaty Organization] were taken in Moscow as the beginnings of a campaign to deprive the Soviet Union of the fruits of its victory over Germany. The Soviet crackdown on Czechoslovakia [1948] and the mounting of the Berlin blockade, both essentially defensive... reactions to these Western moves, were then similarly misread on the Western side. Shortly thereafter there came the crisis of the Korean War, where the Soviet attempt to employ a satellite military force in civil combat to its own advantage, by way of reaction to the American decision to establish a permanent military presence in Japan, was read in Washington as the beginning of the final Soviet push for world conquest; whereas the active American military response, provoked by this move, appeared in Moscow...as a threat to the Soviet position in both Manchuria and in eastern Siberia.[13]

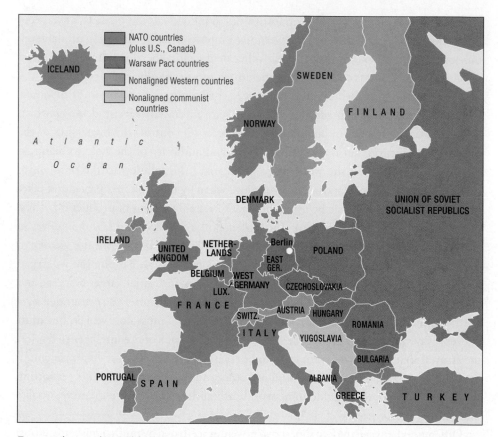

Europe during the Cold War

Although such misperceptions did not cause the Cold War, they certainly added fuel to the confrontation.

The third outcome of the end of World War II was the collapse of the colonial system, a development few foresaw. The defeat of Japan and Germany meant the immediate end of their respective imperial empires. The other colonial powers were spurred by the United Nations Charter's endorsement of the principle of national self-determination, faced with the reality of their economically and politically weakened position, and confronted with newly powerful indigenous movements for independence. These movements were equipped with leftover small arms from World War II, led by talented commanders employing indirect defense strategies such as "revolutionary" guerrilla warfare, and inspired to great self-sacrifice by the ideals of nationalism. The victorious powers granted independence to their former colonies, beginning with Britain's giving India independence in 1947. It took the military defeat of France in Indochina in the early 1950s to bring decolonization to that part of the world. African states, too, became independent between 1957 and 1963. Although the process of decolonization occurred over an extended time period, it was a relatively peaceful transition. The Europeans, together with their U.S. ally, were more interested in fighting communism than in retaining control of their colonial territories.

The fourth outcome was the realization that the differences between the two emergent superpowers would be played out indirectly, on third-party stages, rather than through direct confrontation. Both rivals came to believe the risks of a direct military confrontation were too great. The "loss" of any potential ally, no matter how poor or distant, might begin a cumulative process leading to a significant shift in the balance of power. As the number of decolonized, newly independent states proliferated in the postwar world, the superpowers wooed these new states in order to project power to areas outside their traditional spheres of influence. Thus, the Cold War resulted in the globalization of conflict to all continents. International relations became truly global.

Other parts of the world did not merely react to Cold War imperatives. They developed new ideologies or recast the dominant discourse of Europe in ways that addressed their own experience. Nowhere was this truer than in Asia. Both Ho Chi Minh of Vietnam and Zhou Enlai of China lived in Europe for a time, where they joined communist parties. Returning home, they imported communist ideology, reinterpreting it in ways compatible with their national circumstances. For example, in China, the beginning of the communist revolution predated World War II. Zhou and his colleague Mao Zedong took to the countryside to build a revolution of agrarian peasants. Although China was a semifeudal society, they focused attention on the rural peasantry, realizing that the peasantry was not the proletariat. The Chinese Communist Party

IN FOCUS

KEY DEVELOPMENTS IN THE COLD WAR

- Two superpowers emerge — the United States and the Soviet Union. They are divided by national interests, ideologies, and mutual misperceptions. These divisions are projected into different geographic areas.

- A series of crises occurs — Berlin blockade (1948-49), Korean War (1950-53), Cuban missile crisis (1962), Vietnam War (1965-73), Soviet invasion of Afghanistan (1979).

- A long peace is sustained by mutual deterrence.

became the vanguard of this group and the People's Army its instrument for guerrilla action. Mao's revolution was successful: the communists took control of mainland China in 1949 and established the People's Republic of China.

The globalization of post–World War II politics thus meant the rise of new contenders for power. Although the United States and the Soviet Union retained their dominant positions, new alternative ideologies acted as powerful magnets for populations in the independent and developing states of Africa, Asia, and Latin America. Later in the 1970s, these states advanced a new economic ideology, summarized in the program of the New International Economic Order (see Chapter 9).

The Cold War as a Series of Confrontations

The Cold War itself (1945–89) can be characterized as 45 years of overall high-level tension and competition between the superpowers but with no direct military conflict. The advent of nuclear weapons created a deterrence stalemate, in which each side acted cautiously, only once coming close to the precipice of direct war. As nuclear technology advanced, it become increasingly obvious to both sides that in a nuclear

For the United States, Vietnam became a symbol of the Cold War rivalries in Asia. The United States supported the South Vietnamese forces against the communist regime in the north. Here, a female Vietcong guerrilla prepares to fire an anti-tank rifle during the Tet Offensive of 1968.

TABLE 2.1	IMPORTANT EVENTS OF THE COLD WAR

YEAR	EVENT
1945–48	Soviet Union establishes communist regimes in Eastern Europe.
1947	Announcement of Truman Doctrine; United States proposes Marshall Plan for the rebuilding of Europe.
1948	Marshal Tito separates Yugoslavia from the Soviet bloc.
1948–49	Soviets blockade Berlin; United States and Allies carry out airlift.
1949	Soviets test atomic bomb, ending U.S. nuclear monopoly. Chinese communists under Mao win civil war, establish People's Republic of China. United States and Allies establish NATO.
1950–53	Korean War.
1953	Death of Stalin leads to internal Soviet succession crisis.
1956	Soviets invade Hungary. Gamal Abdel Nasser of Egypt nationalizes the Suez Canal, leading to confrontation with Great Britain, France, and Israel.
1957	Soviets launch the satellite *Sputnik*, symbolizing superpower scientific competition.
1960–63	Congo crisis and UN action to fill power vacuum.
1960	U.S. U-2 spy plane shot down over Soviet territory, leading to the breakup of the Paris summit meeting.
1961	Bay of Pigs invasion of Cuba, sponsored by the United States, fails. Berlin Wall constructed.
1962	United States and Soviet Union brought to the brink of nuclear war following the discovery of Soviet missiles in Cuba; eventually leads to thaw in superpower relations.
1965	United States begins large-scale intervention in Vietnam.
1967	Israel defeats Egypt, Syria, and Jordan in the Six-Day War. Glassboro summit signals détente, loosening of tensions between the superpowers.
1968	Czech government liberalization halted by Soviet invasion. Nuclear Nonproliferation Treaty (NPT) signed.

(CONTINUED)

YEAR	EVENT
1972	U.S. President Nixon visits China and Soviet Union. United States and Soviet Union sign SALT I arms limitation treaty.
1973	Yom Kippur War between Israel and Arab states leads to energy crisis.
1975	Proxy and anticolonial wars fought in Angola, Mozambique, Ethiopia, and Somalia. United States ends official military involvement in Vietnam.
1979	Shah of Iran, a U.S. ally, overthrown by Islamic revolution. United States and Soviet Union sign SALT II. Soviet Union invades Afghanistan. U.S. Senate fails to ratify SALT II.
1981–89	Reagan Doctrine provides basis for U.S. support of "anticommunist" forces in Nicaragua and Afghanistan.
1983	United States invades Grenada.
1985	Gorbachev starts economic and political reforms in Soviet Union.
1989	Peaceful revolutions in Eastern Europe replace communist governments. Berlin Wall is dismantled. Soviet Union withdraws from Afghanistan.
1990	Germany reunified.
1991	Resignation of Gorbachev. Soviet Union collapses.
1992–93	Russia and other former Soviet republics become independent states.

war each would be destroyed beyond hope of recovery. This state of affairs was called "mutual assured destruction"—aptly underlined by its acronym: MAD. Each state backed down from particular confrontations, either because its national interest was not sufficiently strong to risk a nuclear confrontation or because its ideological resolve wavered in light of military realities.

The Cold War, then, was a series of events that directly or indirectly pitted the superpowers against each other. Some of those events were confrontations just short of war, whereas others were confrontations between proxies (North Korea versus South

Korea, North Vietnam versus South Vietnam, Ethiopia versus Somalia) that, in all likelihood, neither the United States nor the Soviet Union had intended to escalate as they did. Still other confrontations were fought over words; these usually ended in treaties and agreements. Some of these confrontations involved only the United States and the Soviet Union, but more often than not, the allies of each became involved. Thus, the Cold War comprised not only superpower confrontations but also confrontations between two blocs of states: the United States, with Canada, Australia, and much of Western Europe (allied in the **North Atlantic Treaty Organization**, or **NATO**); and the Soviet Union, with its **Warsaw Pact** allies in Eastern Europe. Over the life of the Cold War, these blocs loosened, and states sometimes took positions different from that of the dominant power. But for much of this time, bloc politics was operative. Table 2.1 shows a time line of major events related to the Cold War.

One of the high-level, direct confrontations between the superpowers took place in Germany. Germany had been divided immediately after World War II into zones of occupation. The United States, France, and Great Britain administered the western portion; the Soviet Union, the eastern. Berlin, Germany's capital, was similarly divided but lay within Soviet-controlled East Germany. In 1948, the Soviet Union blocked land access to Berlin, prompting the United States and Britain to airlift supplies for 13 months. In 1949, the separate states of West and East Germany were declared. In 1961, East Germany erected the Berlin Wall around the West German portion of the city in order to stem the tide of East Germans trying to leave the troubled state. The U.S. president John F. Kennedy responded by visiting the city and declaring, "Ich bin ein Berliner" ("I am a Berliner"), committing the United States to the security of the Federal Republic of Germany at any cost. Not surprisingly, it was the dismantling of that same wall in November 1989 that symbolized the end of the Cold War.

The Cold War in Asia and Latin America

China, Indochina, and especially Korea became the symbols of the Cold War in Asia. In 1946, after years of bitter and heroic fighting against the Japanese occupation, communists throughout Asia attempted to take control of their respective states following Japan's surrender. In China, the wartime alliance between the Kuomintang (non-communist Chinese nationalists) and Mao Zedong's Red Army dissolved into renewed civil war, in which the United States attempted to support the Kuomintang with large shipments of arms and military equipment. By 1949, however, the Kuomintang had been defeated, and its leaders fled to the island of Formosa (now Taiwan).

In what was then French Indochina (an amalgamation of the contemporary states of Cambodia, Laos, and Vietnam), Ho Chi Minh raised the communist flag over Hanoi, declaring Vietnam to be an independent state. The French quickly returned to take Indochina back, but though French forces fought bravely and with skill, they proved unable to uproot the communists (known as the Viet Minh). In 1954, after having laid a trap for the Viet Minh in a fortified town called Dien Bien Phu, the French were themselves trapped: 16,000 French legionnaires were surrounded by 50,000 Viet Minh combat forces, aided by an additional 50,000 support personnel. Although in broader strategic terms, the French might have absorbed the defeat at Dien Bien Phu, in France itself the loss proved the proverbial straw that broke the camel's back. France abandoned Indochina, which was then divided by a peace treaty in Geneva of that same year into the political entities of Laos, Cambodia, and Vietnam, with the last being divided into two zones: North Vietnam and South Vietnam.

In 1950, after North Korean leader Kim Il-Sung spent years seeking support from the USSR to unify the Korean peninsula under communist rule, Joseph Stalin finally agreed to his request for tanks, heavy artillery, and combat support aircraft to facilitate North Korea's planned assault on noncommunist South Korea. On June 25 of that year, communist North Korean troops, led by heavy tanks supplied by the USSR, sliced into a weak South Korea. The North Korean offensive quickly captured Seoul, South Korea's capital, and then forced the retreat of the few surviving South Korean and American armed forces all the way to the outskirts of the port city of Pusan. In one of the most dramatic military reversals in history, U.S. forces—fighting for the first time under the auspices of the United Nations because of North Korea's "unprovoked aggression" and violations of international law—landed a surprise force at Inchon. Within days they cut off and then routed the North Korean forces. By mid-October, UN forces had captured North Korea's capital, Pyongyang, and by the end of the month, the destruction of North Korea's forces was nearly complete.

Yet the war did not end. Against the wishes of the U.S. president Harry Truman, General Douglas MacArthur ordered his victorious troops—now spread somewhat thin—to finish off the defeated North Koreans, who by this time were encamped very close to the border with communist China. The Chinese had warned they would intervene if their territory was approached too closely, and in November they did. The relatively poorly equipped but highly motivated Chinese soldiers attacked the UN forces, causing the longest retreat of U.S. armed forces in American history. The two sides became mired in a three-year stalemate. The fighting finally ended in an armistice in 1953. But as with the Berlin crisis, the armistice was followed over the years by numerous diplomatic skirmishes—over the basing of U.S. troops in South Korea, the use of the demilitarized zone between the north and the south, and North Korean attempts to become a nuclear power even after the end of the Cold War, the last still a source of conflict today.

The 1962 Cuban missile crisis was a high-profile direct confrontation between the superpowers in another area of the world. The United States viewed the Soviet Union's installation of nuclear missiles in Cuba as a direct threat to its territory: no weapons of a powerful enemy had ever been located so close to U.S. shores. The way in which the crisis was resolved suggests unequivocally that neither party sought a direct confrontation, but once the crisis became public knowledge, it became difficult for either side to back down and global thermonuclear war became a very real possibility. The United States chose to blockade Cuba—another example of containment strategy in action—in order to prevent the arrival of additional Soviet missiles. The U.S. president rejected more aggressive actions favored by the U.S. military, such as a land invasion of Cuba, or air strikes on missile sites. Through behind-the-scenes, unofficial contacts in Washington and direct communication between U.S. President Kennedy and Soviet Premier Nikita Khruschev, the Soviets agreed to remove the missiles from Cuba and the United States agreed to remove similarly capable missiles from Turkey. Thus, the crisis was defused and war was averted.

Vietnam provided a test of a different kind. The Cold War was played out there not in one dramatic crisis but in an extended civil war. Communist North Vietnam and its Chinese and Soviet allies were pitted against the "free world"—South Vietnam, allied with the United States and assorted supporters including South Korea, the Philippines, and Thailand. To most U.S. policy makers in the late 1950s and early 1960s, Vietnam was yet another test of the containment doctrine: communist influence must be stopped, they argued, before it spread like a chain of falling dominos through the rest of Southeast Asia and beyond (hence the term **domino effect**). Thus, the United States supported the South Vietnamese dictators Ngo Dinh Diem and Nguyen Van Thieu against the rival communist regime of Ho Chi Minh in the north, which was underwritten by both the People's Republic of China and the Soviet Union. But as the South Vietnamese government and military faltered on their own, the United States stepped up its military support, increasing the number of its troops on the ground and escalating the air war over the north.

In the early stages, the United States was fairly confident of victory; after all, a superpower with all its military hardware and technically skilled labor force could surely beat a poorly trained Vietcong guerrilla force. American policy makers were quickly disillusioned, however, as communist forces proved adept at avoiding the massive technical firepower of U.S. forces, and the corrupt leadership of South Vietnam siphoned away many of the crucial resources needed to win its more vital struggle for popular legitimacy. As U.S. casualties mounted, with no prospects for victory in sight, the public grew disenchanted. Should the United States use all of its conventional military capability to prevent the "fall" of South Vietnam and stave off the domino effect? Should the United States fight until victory was guaranteed for liberalism and capitalism? Or should it extricate itself from this unpopular quagmire? Should the United States capitulate to the forces of ideological communism? These questions, posed in both geostrategic and ideological terms, defined the middle years of the Cold War, from the Vietnam War's slow beginning in the late 1950s until the dramatic departure of U.S. officials from the South Vietnamese capital, Saigon, in 1975, symbolized by

YOU DECIDE

In this chapter we introduced major historical events of the last 400 years as they relate to important questions of international relations. This history includes not only wars, which affect human existence across space and time, but also societies' efforts to solve a host of problems beyond war, including economic stability, development, environmental protection, and the pressing need for mutual respect. But are history and comparative historical analysis useful guides to foreign policy decision making today, or is history too idiosyncratic?

In arguing for the usefulness of historical analysis, you might point to a formative historical event, such as the infamous "Rape of Nanking" of 1937, in which Japanese troops killed approximately 100,000–200,000 Chinese civilians and soldiers and raped thousands of women. You could argue that the contemporary politics of East Asia—including serious tensions between China and Japan across a range of policy issues—cannot be understood without at least some knowledge of each state's historical memory of the fall of Nanking. You might add that without some knowledge of these events, it would be difficult to understand how the diplomatic and economic crises that followed made Japan's attack on the United States in December 1941 more likely. The event also contributed directly to the widespread support for amendments to international law in 1949, including the prohibition of "cruel treatment and torture" in the Fourth Geneva Convention. You might add that because war—a central problem in international relations—directly engages the human body (something we all share regardless of our race, religion, or national origin), the use of history to understand war has the potential of being useful beyond its own time and place: history is not purely idiosyncratic.

In arguing against history as a basis for formulating foreign policy today, you might point out that the very questions we ask of a historical event tend to be bound by culture (or gender, for that matter), as do the answers to those questions. Moreover, history is not only literally unique, but even had we actually all been at, say, Waterloo in 1815, or at the signing of the first international arms limitation treaty at the Hague in 1899, we would all remember the events differently. Do the Chinese understand and remember the Japanese military assault on Nanking in 1937 the same way the Japanese do? If we all remember, but we all remember differently, you might argue, how can history be a useful foundation for future foreign policy?

YOU DECIDE: Does historical analysis lead to false comparisons and poor policies, or does it illuminate the causes of important features of contemporary international relations? If the latter, how useful might foreign policies based on historical knowledge and comparison be?

U.S. helicopters leaving the U.S. embassy roof while hundreds of desperate Vietnamese tried to grab on to the boarding ladders and escape with them.

The U.S. effort to avert a communist takeover in South Vietnam failed, yet contrary to expectations, the domino effect did not occur. Cold War alliances were shaken on both sides: the friendship between the Soviet Union and China had long before degenerated into a geostrategic fight and a struggle over the proper form of communism, especially in Third World countries. But the Soviet bloc was left relatively unscathed by the Vietnam War. The U.S.-led Western alliance was seriously jeopardized, as several allies (including Canada) strongly opposed U.S. policy toward Vietnam. The bipolar structure of the Cold War–era international system was coming apart. Confidence in military alternatives was shaken in the United States, undermining for over a decade the United States' ability to commit itself militarily. The power of the United States was supposed to be righteous power, but in Vietnam it was neither victorious in its outcome nor righteous in its effects.

The "Cold" in Cold War

It was not always the case that when one of the superpowers acted, the other side responded. In some cases, the other side chose not to act, or at least not to respond in kind, even though it might have escalated the conflict. Usually this was out of concern for escalating a conflict to a major war. For example, the Soviet Union invaded Hungary in 1956 and Czechoslovakia in 1968, both sovereign states and allies in the Warsaw Pact. The United States verbally condemned these aggressive actions by the Soviets. Under other circumstances it might have responded with counterforce, but the actions themselves went unchecked. In 1956, the United States, preoccupied with the Suez Canal crisis, kept quiet, aware that it was ill prepared to respond militarily. In 1968, the United States was mired in Vietnam and beset by domestic turmoil and a presidential election. The United States was also relatively complacent, although angry, when the Soviets invaded Afghanistan in 1979. The Soviets likewise kept quiet when the United States took aggressive action within the U.S. sphere of influence, invading Grenada in 1983 and Panama in 1989. Thus, during the Cold War, even blatantly aggressive actions by one of the superpowers did not always lead to a response by the other.

Many of the events of the Cold War involved the United States and the Soviet Union only indirectly; proxies often fought in their place. Nowhere was this so true as in the Middle East. For both the United States and the Soviet Union, the Middle East was a region of vital importance, because of its natural resources (including an estimated one-third of the world's oil and more than one-half of the world's oil reserves), its strategic position as a transportation hub between Asia and Europe, and its cultural significance as the cradle of three of the world's major religions. Not surprisingly, following the establishment of Israel in 1948 and its diplomatic recognition (first by the United States), the region was the scene of a superpower confrontation by proxy between the U.S.-supported Israel and the Soviet-backed Arab states Syria, Iraq, and Egypt. During the Six-Day War in 1967, Israel crushed the Soviet-equipped Arabs in six short days, seizing the strategic territories of the Golan Heights, Gaza, and the West Bank. During the Yom Kippur War of 1973, which the Egyptians had planned as a limited war, the Israeli victory was not so overwhelming, because the United States and the Soviets negotiated a cease-fire before more damage could be done. But throughout the Cold War, these "hot" wars were followed by guerrilla actions supported by all parties. As long as the basic balance of power was maintained between Israel (and the United States) on one side and the Arabs (and the Soviets) on the other, the region was left alone; when that balance was threatened, the superpowers acted through proxies to maintain the balance. Other controversies also plagued the region, as evidenced by events after the end of the Cold War.

In parts of the world that were of less strategic importance (to the two superpowers), confrontation through proxies was even more the modus operandi during the Cold War. Africa and Latin America present numerous examples of such events. When the colonialist Belgians abruptly left the Congo in 1960, a power vacuum arose. Civil war broke out, as various contending factions sought to take power and bring order out of the chaos. One of the contenders, the Congolese premier Patrice Lumumba (1925–61), appealed to the Soviets for help in fighting the Western-backed insurgents and received both diplomatic support and military supplies. However, Lumumba was dismissed by the Congolese president, Joseph Kasavubu, an ally of the United States. Still others, such as Moïse Tshombe, leader of the copper-rich Katanga province, who was also closely identified with Western interests, fought for control. The three-year civil war could have become another protracted proxy war between the United States and the Soviet Union for influence in this emerging continent. However, the United Nations averted a proxy confrontation by sending in peacekeepers, whose primary purpose was to fill the vacuum and prevent the superpowers from making the Congo yet another arena of the Cold War.

In Latin America, too, participants in civil wars were able to transform their struggles into Cold War confrontations by proxy, thereby gaining military equipment and technical expertise from one or other of the superpowers. In most cases, Latin American states were led by governments beholden to wealthy elites who maintained a virtual monopoly on the country's wealth (such as coffee in El Salvador). When popular protest against corruption and injustice escalated to violence, Communist Cuba was often asked to support these armed movements (such as the Farabundo Martí National Liberation Front, or FMLN), and in response, the United States tended to support the incumbent governments—even those whose record of human rights abuses against their own citizens had been well established. In Nicaragua, for example, after communists called Sandinistas captured the government from its dictator in 1979, the Ronald

Reagan administration supported an insurgency known as the "Contras" in an attempt to reverse what it feared would be a "communist foothold" in Latin America. Such proxy warfare served the interests of the superpowers, permitting them to project power and support geostrategic interests (e.g., oil in Angola, transportation routes around the Horn, the Monroe Doctrine in Latin America) and ideologies without directly confronting one another and risking world or thermonuclear war.

The Cold War was also fought and moderated in words, at **summits** (meetings between leaders) and in treaties. Some Cold War summits were relatively successful: the 1967 Glassboro summit (between U.S. and Soviet leaders) began the loosening of tensions known as **détente**. Others, however, did not produce results, such as the meeting between President Dwight Eisenhower and Premier Nikita Khrushchev in Vienna in 1960, which ended abruptly when the Soviets shot down a U.S. U-2 spy plane over Soviet territory. Treaties between the two parties placed self-imposed limitations on nuclear arms. For example, the first Strategic Arms Limitations Treaty (SALT I), in 1972, placed an absolute ceiling on the numbers of intercontinental ballistic missiles (ICBMs), deployed nuclear warheads, and multiple independently targetable reentry vehicles (MIRVs); and limited the number of antiballistic missile sites maintained by each superpower. So the superpowers did enjoy periods of accommodation, when they could agree on principles and policies.

The Cold War as a Long Peace

It is important to note that the term *Cold War* is itself largely an artifact of a European bias. World War III—a war widely anticipated to be as destructive in comparison to World War II as World War II had been in comparison to World War I—did not happen, or at least not in Europe. But as many as 40 million human beings lost their lives in the proxy and other wars that were fought in Asia, Africa, and Latin America from 1945 to 1991. So how "cold" the Cold War truly was is largely a matter of geopolitical perspective.

That said, if the Cold War is largely remembered as a series of crises and some direct and indirect confrontations, what explains the "cold" in Cold War or, as the diplomatic historian John Lewis Gaddis prefers, the "long peace"? The term itself was meant to dramatize the remarkable and unexpected absence of major wars among great powers during the Cold War. Just as major interstate war was averted in nineteenth-century Europe, so too has it been avoided since World War II. Why?

Gaddis attributes the long peace to five factors, no single explanation being sufficient. Probably the most widely accepted explanation revolves around the role of nuclear **deterrence**. Once both the United States and the Soviet Union had acquired nuclear weapons, neither was willing to use them, because their very deployment jeopardized both states' existence.

Another explanation attributes the long peace to the roughly equal division of power between the United States and the Soviet Union. Such a parity of power led to stability in the international system, as will be explained in Chapter 4. The argument is that a balance of power in a **multipolar** setting (less stable) was replaced by a "balance of terror" in a **bipolar** setting (very stable). However, because the advent of nuclear weapons occurred simultaneously with the emergence of the bipolar system, it is difficult to disentangle one explanation from the other.

A third explanation for the long peace is the stability imposed by the hegemonic economic power of the United States. Being in a superior economic position for much of the Cold War, the United States willingly paid the price of maintaining stability. It provided military security for Japan and much of northern Europe, and its currency was the foundation of the international monetary system. Yet although this argument explains why the United States acted to enhance postwar economic stability, it does not explain Soviet actions.

A fourth explanation gives credit for maintaining the peace not to either of the superpowers but to economic liberalism. During the Cold War, the liberal economic order solidified and became a dominant factor in international relations. Politics became more **transnational** under liberalism—based on interests and coalitions across traditional state boundaries—and thus great powers became increasingly obsolete. Cold War peace can therefore be attributed to the dominance of economic liberalism.

Finally, Gaddis explores the possibility that the long peace of the Cold War was predetermined, as simply one phase in a long historical cycle of peace and war. He argues that every 100 to 150 years, war occurs on a global scale; these cycles are driven by uneven economic growth. This explanation suggests that the Cold War is but one event in a long cycle, and specific events or conditions occurring during the Cold War have no explanatory power.[14]

Others have cited the advent of the United Nations, which many hoped would be a collective security organization that improved on the failings of the League of Nations, its predecessor. As noted in Chapter 7, the United Nations did not suffer from a lack of U.S. participation as the League of Nations had. But its contribution, if any, to the long peace remains controversial.

Whatever the "right" combination of explanations, the international relations theorist Kenneth N. Waltz has noted the irony of the long peace: both the United States and the Soviet Union, "two states, isolationist by tradition, untutored in the ways of international politics, and famed for impulsive behavior, soon showed themselves—not always and everywhere, but always in crucial cases—to be wary, alert, cautious, flexible, and forbearing."[15] The United States and the Soviet Union, wary and cautious of one another, also became predictable and familiar to one another. Common interests in economic growth and system stability overcame their long-adversarial relationship.

The Immediate Post-Cold War Era

The fall of the Berlin Wall in 1989 symbolized the end of the Cold War, but actually its end was gradual. The Soviet premier at the time, Mikhail Gorbachev, and other Soviet reformers had set in motion two domestic processes—*glasnost* (political openness) and *perestroika* (economic restructuring)—as early as the mid-1980s. *Glasnost*, combined with a new technology—the videocassette player—made it possible for the first time since the October Revolution for average Soviet citizens to compare their living standards with those of their Western counterparts. The comparison proved dramatically unfavorable. It also opened the door to criticism of the political system, culminating in the emergence of a multiparty system and the massive reorientation of the once-monopolistic Communist party. *Perestroika* undermined the foundation of the planned economy, an essential part of the communist system. At the outset, Gorbachev and his reformers sought to save the system, but once initiated, these reforms led to the dissolution of the Warsaw Pact, Gorbachev's resignation in December 1991, and the disintegration of the Soviet Union itself in 1992–93.

Gorbachev's domestic reforms also led to changes in the orientation of Soviet foreign policy. Needing to extricate the country from the political quagmire and economic drain of the war in Afghanistan while seeking to save face, Gorbachev suggested that the permanent members of the UN Security Council "could become guarantors of regional security."[16] Afghanistan was a test case, where a small group of UN observers monitored and verified the withdrawal of more than 100,000 Soviet troops in 1988 and 1989—an action that would have been impossible during the height of the Cold

---

IN FOCUS

KEY DEVELOPMENTS IN THE IMMEDIATE POST-COLD WAR ERA

- Changes are made in Soviet/Russian foreign policy, with the withdrawals from Afghanistan and Angola in the late 1980s, monitored by the United Nations.

- Iraqi invasion of Kuwait in 1990 and the multilateral response unite the former Cold War adversaries.

- *Glasnost* and *perestroika* continue in Russia, as reorganized in 1992–93.

- The former Yugoslavia disintegrates into independent states; civil war ensues in Bosnia and Kosovo, leading to UN and NATO action.

- Widespread ethnic conflict arises in central and western Africa, Central Asia, and the Indian subcontinent.

Explaining the End of the Cold War: A View from the Former Soviet Union

Many scholars of American diplomatic history attribute the end of the Cold War to policies initiated by the United States: the buildup of a formidable military capable of winning either a nuclear or a conventional war against the Soviet Union and the development of the strongest, most diversified economy the world has ever known. However, within the Soviet Union, the events leading to the end of the Cold War were perceived differently.

The predominant viewpoint in the former Soviet Union is that the explanation for the end of the Cold War can be found in a very long and complex chain of domestic developments in the Soviet Union itself. Those political, economic, and demographic factors led to what seemed to be an abrupt disintegration of the Soviet Union and hence the end of the Cold War. International relations theorists did not predict it; perhaps they were not looking at domestic factors within the Soviet state itself and did not have a sufficiently long historical perspective.

The political dominance and authority of the Communist Party, the main ideological pillar of the Soviet Union, had significantly eroded by the late 1980s. The revelation of Joseph Stalin's horrific crimes against the Soviet people, especially ethnic minorities, intensified animosity in the far-flung parts of the Soviet empire. Many of the smaller republics and subnational regions bore a grudge against the central government for forced Russification, the resettlement of certain minorities, and other atrocities such as induced famines in Russia and Ukraine in the early 1930s. Increasingly open discussion of such events undermined the ideological fervor of the common population and shook their trust in the "people's government."

During the 1960s, some Soviet leaders saw stagnation in the economic, technological, and agricultural spheres. Internal critics of the regime blamed the top-level political leadership, which had become ossified. The policy of lifelong appointments to leading posts, which remained in effect until the mid-1980s, meant that political appointees stayed in their posts for 20 or more years, regardless of their performance. There were few efforts to reform and modernize the system, and younger people had little opportunity to exercise political leadership. These failures in leadership, exemplified by the poor economy, led to widespread discontent and resentment in all layers of the society.

Moreover, the Soviet Union was a very ethnically diverse state, consisting of 15 major republics, some of which also contained "autonomous" republics and regions, inhabited by hundreds of ethnicities. Although the Soviet Union had benefitted economically from extracting resources found in the far reaches of its territories, the costs of keeping the empire together were high. Subsidies flowed to the outer regions at the expense of the Soviet state. With growing economic discontent and the erosion of the ideology promoted by the Communist Party, local nationalist movements started to fill the ideological vacuum by the late 1980s.

Before the mid-1980s, the inherent distortions and inefficiencies of the Soviet planned economy were partially offset by the profits from the energy sector based on oil and gas exports. However, the Soviet industrial and agricultural sectors lagged behind, inefficient and uncompetitive. Technological development stagnated, too. The sharp decline in world oil prices in the 1980s compounded the problems. The resulting rationing of basic food products and the poor quality of domestically manufactured products totally discredited the socialist economic model and added to the general discontent. The declining state budget could no longer bear the burden of the arms race with the United States, finance an expensive war in Afghanistan, and keep the increasingly fractured empire within its orbit.

The interplay of all these factors came to a climax when Mikhail Gorbachev took power in 1985. Acknowledging the urgent need for change, he launched ambitious domestic reforms collectively referred to as *perestroika*, literally, "restructuring" of economic relations, including stepping back from central planning and curbing government subsidies. *Glasnost* was the political component, an "opening" that relaxed censorship and encouraged democratization. In foreign policy, "New Thinking" meant improving relations with the United States and the possibility of the coexistence of the capitalist and socialist systems through shared human values. The underlying reasons for most of these domestic changes were economic. Reducing military expenditures and gaining access to Western loans became critical for the survival of the troubled state.

The rapid dissolution of the Eastern bloc led to a dramatic shift in the balance of power in the international system. Rising nationalist movements and local liberal forces gained momentum and won significant representation

Mikhail Gorbachev addresses parliament in 1991.

in the local parliaments after the first competitive elections in the former Socialist republics. Eventually, Russia became one of the first to declare independence and affirm sovereignty, with the rest of the republics following suit in the "sovereignty parade" in 1991. The de facto dissolution of the Soviet Union marked an important (final?) chapter in the history of the Cold War.

FOR CRITICAL ANALYSIS

1. How can we balance the traditional view that Western economic and military dominance caused a Soviet "defeat" with the Soviet view that internal weaknesses and contractions were primarily to blame?

2. Glasnost was supposed to make it possible for Soviet citizens to share information, but it also made it possible for them to compare their own lives with those beyond the USSR. How might this have affected the legitimacy of the Communist Party?

3. If states "learn" from their own mistakes and achievements as well as those of other states, what might a state like China have learned from the collapse of the USSR?

War. Similarly, the Soviets agreed to and supported the 1988 withdrawal of Cuban troops from Angola. The Soviet Union had retreated from international commitments near its borders, as well as others farther abroad. Most important, the Soviets agreed to cooperate in multilateral activities to preserve regional security.

These changes in Soviet policy and the eventual demise of the empire itself mark the beginning of the post–Cold War era and are the subject of much study in international relations today, not least because at the time, most Soviet and security experts completely failed to predict the outcome.

The first post–Cold War test of the so-called new world order came in response to Iraq's invasion and annexation of Kuwait in August 1990. Despite its long-standing relationship with Iraq, the Soviet Union (and later Russia), along with the four other permanent members of the UN Security Council, agreed first to implement economic sanctions against Iraq. Then they agreed in a Security Council resolution to support the means to restore the status quo — to oust Iraq from Kuwait with a multinational military force. Finally, they supported sending the UN Iraq-Kuwait Observer Mission to monitor the zone and permitted the UN to undertake humanitarian intervention and create safe havens for the Kurdish and Shiite populations of Iraq. Although forging a consensus on each of these actions (or in the case of China, convincing it to abstain) was difficult, the coalition held, a unity unthinkable during the Cold War.

The end of the Cold War denotes a major change in international relations, the end of one historical era and the beginning of another. The overwhelming military power of the United States, combined with its economic power, appeared to many to usher in an era of U.S. primacy in international affairs to a degree not matched even by the Romans or Alexander the Great. The United States seemed able to impose its will on other states even against the strong objections of its allies. Yet this moment of primacy appears doubtful today; it proved insufficient to deter or prevent ethnic conflict, civil wars, and human rights abuses from occurring. And many threats, like terrorism and the global financial crisis of 2008, have shown themselves, by their very nature, to demand *multilateral* engagement: no single state, however, powerful, can remain secure against these threats on its own.

The 1990s were marked by the struggle of former allies and enemies to find new identities and interests in a world bereft of the certainties and simplicities of the Cold War. As the threat of World War III vanished, what was the purpose of an organization such as NATO? What was the purpose or focus of state foreign policy to be if not the deterrence of aggression by other states? The United States and Israel, for example, were unparalleled in their capacity to fight and win interstate wars. But who might these other states be? What role might armed forces specialized to win interstate wars play in substate violence? Yugoslavia's violent disintegration played itself out over the entire decade despite Western attempts to resolve the conflict peacefully. At the same time, the world witnessed ethnic tension and violence in the Great Lakes region of central Africa. Genocide in Rwanda and Burundi was effectively ignored by the international community. And despite U.S. military primacy, Russia maintains enough military power and political influence to prevent U.S. intervention in ethnic hostilities in the Transcaucasus region.

These dual realities converged and diverged throughout the 1990s and continue to do so today. The disintegration of Yugoslavia culminated in an American-led war against Serbia to halt attacks on the ethnic Albanian population in Kosovo. Despite European hesitancy to engage militarily and the inability to obtain a UN resolution supporting military action, the United States drove NATO to intervene. The 78-day air war against Serbia ended with the capitulation of the Serbs and the turning over of the province of Kosovo to International administration. The war also severely challenged core principles of international law: technically, the action of NATO in Kosovo was a violation of Serbian sovereignty. Yet NATO's leaders held that Serb rapes, lootings, and murders constituted a greater harm, arguing that the harm of violating the principle of sovereignty was less than the harm of allowing Serbians to murder and torture Kosovar Albanians. The repercussions of the Kosovo precedent continue to affect interstate politics to this day.

The New Millennium: The First Decade

Perhaps the biggest change in interstate politics following the end of the Cold War was the puzzling elevation of terrorism—once a relatively minor threat—from a law-enforcement problem to a vital national security interest (and therefore a military problem). On September 11, 2001, the world witnessed deadly, psychologically disruptive, and economically devastating terrorist attacks organized and funded by Al Qaeda against New York and Washington, D.C. These attacks, directed by Osama bin Laden, set into motion a U.S.–led global "war on terrorism." Buoyed by an outpouring of support from around the world and by the first-ever invocation of Article V of the NATO Charter, which declares an attack on one NATO member to be an attack on all, the United States undertook to lead an ad hoc coalition to combat terrorist organizations with global reach. As discussed in Chapter 8, this new **war on terrorism** combines many elements into multiple campaigns with different foci in different countries. Many countries have arrested known terrorists and their supporters and frozen their monetary assets. In October of 2001, the United States launched a war in Afghanistan to oust the Taliban regime, which was providing safe haven to Osama bin Laden's Al Qaeda organization and a base from which it freely planned, organized, and trained operatives to carry out a global terror campaign against the United States and its allies.

Following an initially successful campaign in Afghanistan in 2001 and 2002 that specifically targeted terrorists and their supporters and paved the way for popular elections in that country, the United States broke from its allies. Convinced that Iraq maintained a clandestine **weapons of mass destruction (WMD)** program and posed a continued threat by backing terrorist organizations, the United States attempted to build support in the United Nations for authorization to remove Saddam Hussein forcibly from power and find the hidden WMD. When the United Nations refused to back this request, the United States built its own coalition, including key ally Great Britain. This coalition destroyed the Iraqi military and overthrew Iraq's government in 2003. No weapons of mass destruction were found, but additional justifications were offered, including promoting democracy for Iraq's three main peoples—Kurds, Sunni Arabs, and Shia Arabs—within a single state. Fighting in Iraq continues today, although Hussein himself was executed in 2006 and U.S. combat forces have withdrawn. Iraq remains riven by sectarian conflict, and its future stability and the fate of its long-suffering people remains unclear.

In an important way, Operation Enduring Freedom, the name given by the United States and its allies to the military intervention which in 2001 led to the ouster of the Taliban in Afghanistan, set a very dangerous precedent. If the United States and its allies could invade Afghanistan to punish or preempt terrorism, why couldn't it also invade any other state that hosted terrorists? After the defeat of the Taliban in 2001, much of its leadership escaped across the poorly controlled border between Afghanistan and Pakistan's Northwest Territories. But Pakistan was a formal U.S. ally, and extremely sensitive to any perceived slights to its sovereignty. This has created a dilemma that is

The collapse of the real estate sector in the United States led many people to lose their homes to foreclosure, as happened here, outside Las Vegas, Nevada. The economic repercussions of the financial crisis were quickly felt around the world.

not unique to U.S.–Pakistan relations. If the United States is to succeed in stabilizing Afghanistan, it must have the help of Pakistan to eliminate the sanctuary Pakistan currently gives to groups the U.S. and its allies consider terrorists. Yet Pakistan currently lacks both the will and the capacity either to close the border between Pakistan and Afghanistan or to stop the groups in its territory from attacking Afghan forces and the International Security Assistance Force (ISAF) within Afghanistan. If the United States attempts to use its own resources to achieve its objectives, Pakistan will vehemently resist. Because it controls many of the communications routes vital for supply of ISAF in Afghanistan, Pakistan has the capacity to cause more harm to ISAF's efforts there. Thus, the "war on terror" poses tricky dilemmas for U.S. policy makers.

In the fall of 2008, U.S. national security was severely damaged in an entirely different way. As a result of relaxed regulatory oversight and the entrepreneurial invention of complex new financial instruments, the long-steady rise in the value of domestic real estate peaked, and the financial underpinnings of housing construction and home ownership collapsed. Gigantic insurance companies and brokerage firms threatened to go bankrupt overnight. But because the fate of U.S. banks, brokerage firms, and insurance companies was intimately linked with those in Europe and Asia, the financial crisis that began in the United States quickly threatened the economies of France, Britain, and Japan, to cite but a few. Globally, investors small and large found their investments hemorrhaging value, and this led to an international economic contraction that is still being felt today. The states within the European Union, as detailed in Chapter 9, have

IN FOCUS

KEY DEVELOPMENTS IN THE FIRST DECADE OF THE NEW MILLENNIUM

- Al Qaeda terrorist network commits terrorist acts against the homeland of the United States and U.S. interests abroad; U.S. and coalition forces respond militarily in Afghanistan and Iraq.

- Terrorist attacks occur in Saudi Arabia, Spain, and Great Britain.

- A financial crisis in the United States in 2008 devastates its economy and rapidly spreads to other countries.

- In the spring of 2011, Tunisia becomes the first in a series of Arab countries in which a popular uprising topples a long-established dictator. The toppling of Tunisia's dictator was followed by the ousting of Egyptian President Hosni Mubarak and Libyan leader Muammar Qaddafi. Uprisings followed in Bahrain and Syria, but the outcomes remain indeterminate.

Protesters in Tunisia attack the office of the prime minister using a coffin draped in the Tunisian flag in January, 2011. Numerous authoritarian governments in the Middle East faced popular uprisings during the Arab Spring.

struggled to maintain the euro as its central shared currency in the face of declining productivity and ballooning government spending in Ireland, Spain, Portugal, Cyprus, and especially Greece.

Even after the economic downturn following the September 11 terrorist attacks and the financial crisis that developed in 2008, the U.S. military and economy remain the strongest in the world. Yet despite this strength, citizens of the United States do not feel secure. The global war against terrorism is far from over and appears no nearer to victory. The issue of whether U.S. power will be balanced by an emerging power (or coalition of powers) is also far from resolved. And although the U.S. military is still held in high esteem within the United States, the war in Afghanistan became widely unpopular.

Contemporary events continue to hold surprises. In December of 2010, a local protest by a single man in Tunisia sparked a massive social protest against the cruelty and corruption of Tunisia's long-standing dictator, Zine El Abidine Ben Ali. In January of 2011, Ben Ali was overthrown and fled to exile in Saudi Arabia. But protest against corrupt and brutal Arab leaders did not stop there. Soon popular protests broke out in Egypt, Libya, Yemen, Bahrain, and later Syria. Egypt's leader, Hosni Mubarak, was taken by surprise and faced a choice of mass murder and imprisonment of protestors or stepping down. With Egypt's military refusing to kill protestors, Mubarack was forced to step down. The fate of Libya's dictator, Muammar Qaddafi, was more severe: after having been forced from power by a rebellion actively supported by France and the United States, Qaddafi was captured and murdered.

The ultimate fate of what we now think of as the "Arab Spring" of 2011 remains unclear, as protest in Bahrain was brutally suppressed, and in Syria, Bashar al Assad's efforts to stay in power against widespread social protest have led to his forces killing over 70,000 of its own citizens. The Arab Spring is nevertheless remarkable for two reasons. First, it gave lie to the claims of radical and militant Islamists (such as Al Qaeda) that only through Islamic revolution, terror attacks on "the West," and the reestablishment of strict Islamic law could Arab dictators be overthrown. Second, the combined might of secret services and militaries failed to resist the power of young people armed with mobile phones, courage, and conviction.

For all states in the new millennium, there remain two major issues moving forward: (1) Will the transnational issues of the first decade—religion, organized crime, communicable disease, the environment, and terrorism—become easier to redress or harder? (2) Toward what ends should states devote their national energies, military, economic, cultural, diplomatic, and political? Will containing or rooting out terrorism become the new national aim of states? Will it be preventing global

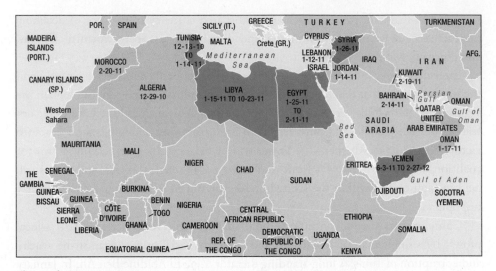

The Arab Spring, 2011

Note: Countries shaded green experienced popular protest that resulted in the collapse of an authoritarian government. Countries shaded orange experienced major protests but the government did not collapse. Countries shaded yellow experienced popular dissent but no major protests. Countries shaded red indicate an ongoing civil war.

environmental catastrophe? Will it be finding a way to overcome poverty? It remains to be seen which national and international goals will dominate the political landscape as the twenty-first century advances, and which countries—the United States, China, Brazil, Russia, South Africa, the European Union—will lead the way.

In Sum: Learning from History

Will the post–Cold War world be characterized by increasing cooperation among the great powers, or will the era be one of conflict among states and over new ideas? Does the post–Cold War era signal a return to the multipolar system of the nineteenth century? Or is the entire concept of polarity an anachronism? How can we begin to predict how the current era will best be characterized or what the future will bring? How will changing state identities affect the interests and capabilities of states moving forward?

We have taken the first step toward answering these questions by looking to the past. Our examination of the development of contemporary international relations has focused on how core concepts of international relations have emerged and evolved over time, most notably the state, sovereignty, the nation, balance of power, and the international system. These concepts, developed within a specific historical context, provide the building blocks for contemporary international relations. The state is well established, but its sovereignty may be eroding from without (Chapters 7, 9, 10) and from within (Chapter 5). The principal characteristics of the contemporary international system are in the process of changing with the end of the bipolarity of the Cold War (Chapter 4).

Moreover, we have seen that the way peoples and their leaders remember events dramatically affects their sense of the legitimacy of any given cause or action. China's remembrance of the Rape of Nanking in 1937 and its feeling that Japan has never satisfactorily acknowledged its racist brutality in China during World War II still complicate China-Japan relations today, as illustrated by the disputes over sovereignty of the islands Senkaku (to the Japanese) and Diaoyu (to the Chinese) in the South China Seas. The U.S. memory of the terrorist attacks of September 11, 2001, dramatically affect how its citizens think about terrorism, which is perceived as a grave threat and as an *Islamic*-inspired attack. Thus, understanding historical events is one way to understand the motives of leaders and those they lead.

To help us further understand the trends of the past and how those trends influence contemporary thinking, we turn to theory. Theory gives order to analysis; it provides generalized explanations for specific events. In Chapter 3 we will look at competing theories of international relations. These theories view the past from quite different perspectives.

Discussion Questions

1. The Treaties of Westphalia are often viewed as the beginning of modern international relations. Why are they a useful benchmark? What factors does this benchmark ignore?

2. Colonization by the great powers of Europe has officially ended. However, the effects of the colonial era linger. Explain with specific examples.

3. The Cold War has ended. Discuss two current events where Cold War politics persists.

4. The developments of international relations as a discipline have been closely identified with the history of Western Europe and the United States. With this civilizational bias, what might we be missing?

Key Terms

balance of power (p. 32)

bipolar (p. 58)

capitalism (p. 45)

Cold War (p. 43)

colonialism (p. 29)

containment (p. 44)

détente (p. 57)

deterrence (p. 57)

domino effect (p. 53)

hegemon (p. 32)

imperialism (p. 29)

League of Nations (p. 38)

legitimacy (p. 24)

multipolar (p. 58)

nation (p. 24)

nationalism (p. 24)

North Atlantic Treaty
Organization (NATO) (p. 51)

socialism (p. 45)

sovereignty (p. 21)

summits (p. 57)

superpowers (p. 43)

transnational (p. 58)

Treaties of Westphalia (p. 20)

war on terrorism (p. 63)

Warsaw Pact (p. 51)

weapons of mass
destruction (WMD) (p. 64)

The concept of state power is important to many international relations theories. For realists, military power is the most important source of state power. Other theorists focus on economic power and discursive power, the power of ideas.

O3

CONTENDING PERSPECTIVES:
How to Think about International Relations Theoretically

- *What is the value of studying international relations from a theoretical perspective?*

- *Why do scholars pay attention to the levels-of-analysis problem?*

- *What are the central tenents of realism and neorealism? Of liberalism and neoliberal institutionalism? Of radicalism? Of constructivism?*

- *Choose a contemporary international event and analyze it using different theoretical perspectives.*

Thinking Theoretically

How can theory help us to make sense of international relations? In this chapter, we will use the example of the 2003 Iraq War to explore major international relations theories and their explanations for political events. Why did the United States and its coalition partners invade Iraq? Why did Iraq continue to refuse to comply with the demands of the international community? We need to begin by examining the historical record. That provides the key context for understanding the actions of the United States.

The international community was concerned about Saddam Hussein's behavior, Iraq's weapons, and the possibility that Saddam was supporting international terrorist activities, especially after he expelled UN weapons inspectors from Iraq in 1998. Following the September 11, 2001, attacks on U.S. territory, that concern became urgent. In his 2002 State of the Union address, President George W. Bush included Iraq in what he described as an "axis of evil." In the fall of 2002, the administration lobbied for UN resolutions to have Iraq declared in material breach of prior UN resolutions, in particular the resolutions that resulted in a cease-fire in the previous war in 1991. Although successful in convincing the UN Security Council to declare a material breach, the United States was unable to muster support for a UN-authorized military action against Iraq. In March 2003, the United States launched a military attack against Iraq without UN authorization. Three weeks later, the Iraqi regime fell, and the United States imposed what it hoped would be temporary rule over Iraq. Table 3.1 lists the major events of the crisis and the war.

This examination of history shows that the United States was motivated by several factors: regret at not having ousted Saddam in the 1991 Gulf War; the possibility that the regime possessed weapons of mass destruction; concern that Saddam's regime was involved in both domestic and international terrorism; the need for stability in an oil-rich region; and the hope that a democratic Iraq could be the centerpiece of a new liberal democratic order in the Middle East. Similarly, to understand Iraq's refusal to comply with international demands, we must understand the roots of its strong nationalism, its history of being controlled by Western colonialists, and a Saddam Hussein who augmented his domestic power and legitimacy by standing up to the West. Of course, every event is literally unique from a historical perspective, but the motivations described here can also be seen as specific manifestations of broader historical patterns. We assess these patterns through the lenses of different *theories*. That is, we use international relations theories not only to explain a particular war, but to explain war in general, in addition to other important features of international politics. The better the theory, the greater its power is to explain or predict what might seem to be unique or isolated events.

TABLE 3.1	MAJOR EVENTS LEADING TO THE IRAQ WAR
DATE	**EVENT**
September 11, 2001	Terrorist attacks against the World Trade Center and the Pentagon are answered by an immediate commitment by the U.S. government to fight global terrorism and punish those responsible.
October 7, 2001	United States strikes targets in Afghanistan in order to oust the Taliban, whose government harbors the Al Qaeda terrorists responsible for the 9/11 attacks.
November 14, 2001	United States announces overthrow of Taliban from power in Afghanistan.
January 29, 2002	President George W. Bush labels Iraq, Iran, and North Korea members of an "axis of evil" that threaten world peace.
October 2, 2002	U.S. Congress authorizes the president to use U.S. armed forces against Iraq.
October 8, 2002	UN resolution holds Iraq in material breach of previous resolutions.
March 2003	United States stops trying to fashion a UN resolution authorizing use of military force, acknowledging failure to get approval from the five permanent members of the Security Council.
March 17, 2003	United States issues a 48-hour ultimatum for the Baathist regime and its leader, Saddam Hussein, to leave Iraq.
March 19, 2003	Decapitation attack is launched against Saddam. U.S. Special Operations forces enter Iraq, followed by the movement of coalition ground forces into Iraq.
April 9, 2003	Iraqi regime falls.
April 2003– December 2011	Efforts continue to establish security amid resistance to U.S. presence and sectarian violence.
December 2011	United States withdraws all military troops.

A **theory** is a set of propositions and concepts that combine to explain phenomena by specifying the relationships among the propositions. Theory's ultimate goal is to predict phenomena. Good theory can explain events across space (e.g., it works just as well in Argentina as in Morocco) and time (e.g., it works just as well today as in the tenth century). Good theories generate testable **hypotheses**: specific *falsifiable* statements questioning a particular relationship among two or more variables. By testing groups of interrelated hypotheses, theories are either refuted, or supported and refined (never conclusively "proven"); and new relationships are found that demand subsequent testing.

A famous example of a powerful theory from the natural sciences is Charles Darwin's theory of evolution. Darwin's theory of natural selection and his concept of survival of the fittest, for example, fit together to explain what had previously been puzzling variation in the coloration and beak shapes of identical species of birds in different environments. We say that Darwin's theory is a powerful theory because it has survived many challenges; its logic is consistent even with evidence unavailable to Darwin at the time he formulated his theory. It is therefore very general, in the sense that it can explain seemingly unique variations across space and time. Yet in neither natural nor social sciences do we ever consider theories to be "proven" or "settled" or

The destruction of a statue of Saddam Hussein in Baghdad became a symbol of his regime's defeat in 2003 by a U.S.-led coalition. Theory can help us understand why Saddam risked war with a more powerful country, and why the United States chose to invade Iraq.

"fact." Theories, whether Darwin's or Albert Einstein's or Kenneth Waltz's, can always be overturned or refuted by new evidence or better theory. Theories are therefore *not* explanations that scientists "believe in." Rather, we say they are stronger or weaker, or more or less powerful.

Moving from description to explanation to theory and from theory to testable hypotheses is not a unilinear process. Although theory depends on a logical deduction of hypotheses from assumptions and a testing of the hypotheses as more and more data are collected in the empirical world, theories often have to be revised or adjusted. This is, in part, a creative exercise, in which we must be tolerant of ambiguity, concerned about probabilities, and distrustful of absolutes.

International relations theories come in a variety of forms. In this chapter, we introduce four general theories, or theoretical perspectives, in the study of international relations: realism (and neorealism); liberalism (and its newer variant, neoliberal institutionalism); and radical theory (in this case, Marxism). We also introduce constructivism as one of the newest theoretical perspectives in international relations. Before we examine these theories more closely, we should consider one powerful strategy for understanding the bewildering complexity of the empirical world that divides it into useful and more manageable levels of analysis.

Theory and the Levels of Analysis

Why did the United States and its coalition partners invade Iraq in 2003? The list of possible explanations can be usefully organized according to three **levels of analysis** (see Figure 3.1). Dividing the analysis of international politics into levels helps orient our questions and suggests the appropriate type of evidence to explore. Paying attention to levels of analysis helps us make logical deductions and enables us to explore all categories of explanation.

In a categorization first used by Kenneth Waltz and amplified by J. David Singer, three different sources of explanations are offered. If the *individual level* is the focus, then the personality, perceptions, choices, and activities of individual decision makers (e.g., Saddam Hussein and George W. Bush) and individual participants (e.g., Defense Secretary Donald Rumsfeld and Saddam's sons) provide the explanation. If the *state level*, or domestic factors, is the focus, then the explanation is derived from characteristics of the state: the type of government (e.g., democratic or authoritarian), the type of economic system (e.g., capitalist or socialist), interest groups within the country, or even the national interest. If the *international system level* is the focus, then the explanation rests with the characteristics of that system (such as the distribution of "power") or with international and regional organizations and their relative strengths and weaknesses.[1]

Box 3.1 categorizes possible explanations of the Iraq War according to these three levels of analysis. Of course, explanations from all three levels probably contributed to the United States' decision to invade Iraq in 2003. The purpose of theory is to guide us toward an understanding of which of these various explanations are the necessary and sufficient explanations for the invasion.

Although most international relations scholars acknowledge the utility of paying attention to levels of analysis, they differ on how many levels are useful in explaining events. Most political scientists apply between three and six levels. Although adding more layers may provide more descriptive context, it makes explanation and prediction more difficult. The most important differentiation in theory must be made between the international level and the domestic level. In this book, we will use the three levels explained earlier: individual, state, and international system.

Good theory, then, should be able to explain phenomena at a particular level of analysis; better theory should also offer explanations across different levels of analysis. The general theories outlined in the rest of this chapter are all comprehensive, meaning they incorporate all three levels of analysis. Yet each of the theories is not as simple or as unified as presented. Many scholars

BOX 3.1

Possible Explanations for the United States' Invasion of Iraq in 2003 by Level of Analysis

INDIVIDUAL LEVEL

1. Saddam Hussein was an evil leader who committed atrocities against his own people and defied the West.
2. Saddam Hussein was irrational; otherwise, he would have capitulated to the superior capability of the U.S. and British coalition.
3. George W. Bush and his advisers targeted Saddam Hussein and Iraq in 2001.

STATE LEVEL

4. The United States must protect its national security, and Iraq's weapons of mass destruction threatened U.S. security.
5. Ousting the Taliban from Afghanistan was only the first step in the war on terrorism; invading Iraq, a known supporter of terrorism, was the second.
6. The United States must be assured of a stable oil supply, and Iraq has the world's second largest reserves.
7. The United States must not permit states that support terrorism or terrorist groups access to destructive weapons.
8. It is in the U.S. national interest to build a progressive Arab regime in the region.

INTERNATIONAL SYSTEM LEVEL

9. UN resolutions condemning Iraq had to be enforced in order to maintain the legitimacy of the United Nations.
10. A unipolar international system is uniquely capable of responding to perceived threats to the stability of the system, and the U.S. invasion was one manifestation of this capability.
11. There is an international moral imperative for humanitarian intervention—to oust evil leaders and install democratic regimes.

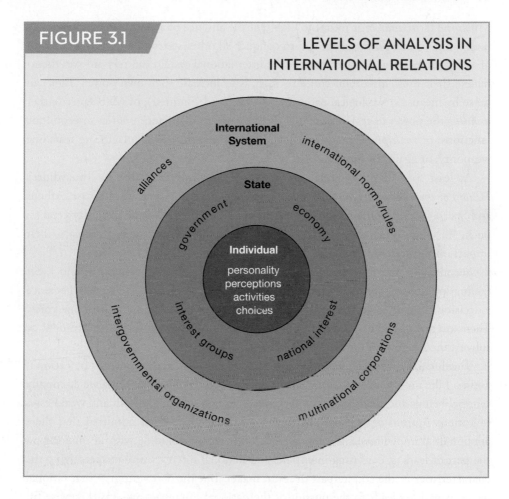

FIGURE 3.1 — LEVELS OF ANALYSIS IN INTERNATIONAL RELATIONS

have introduced variations, modifications, and problematics, and have even changed positions over time. Thus, each theoretical perspective is introduced here only in terms of its essential characteristics.

Realism (and Neorealism)

Realism is the product of a long historical and philosophical tradition, even though its direct application to international affairs is of more recent vintage. Realism is based on a view of the individual as primarily fearful, selfish, and power seeking. Individuals are organized in states, each of which acts in a unitary way in pursuit of its own **national interest**, defined in terms of power. *Power,* in turn, is primarily thought of in terms of the material resources necessary to physically harm or coerce other states: to fight and win wars. These states exist in an anarchic international system, a characterization in which the term *anarchy* is meant to highlight the absence of an authoritative hierarchy (i.e., a single state powerful enough to conquer all other states). Under this condition of anarchy, realists argue that states in the international system can rely only on themselves. Their most important concern, then, is to increase their own power. They can do so by means of two logical pathways: (1) war (and conquest); or (2) balance (either *dividing* the power of real or potential rivals by means of alliance politics or economic sanctions, or *multiplying* their own power by raising armies, manufacturing fearsome weaponry, or again, by means of alliance politics).

At least four of the essential assumptions of realism are found in Thucydides's *History of the Peloponnesian War*.[2] First, for Thucydides, the state (in this case, Athens and Sparta) is the *principal actor* in war and in politics in general, just as today's realists posit. Although other actors, such as international institutions, may participate, their impact on the system is marginal.

Second, the state is assumed to be a **unitary actor**. Although Thucydides includes fascinating debates among different officials from the same state, he argues that once a decision is made to go to war or capitulate, the state speaks and acts with one voice. There are no subnational actors trying to overturn the decision of the government or subvert the interests of the state.

Third, decision makers acting in the name of the state are assumed to be **rational actors**. Like most educated Greeks, Thucydides believed that individuals are essentially rational beings and that they make decisions by weighing the strengths and weaknesses of various options against the goal to be achieved. Thucydides admitted that there are potential impediments to rational decision making, including wishful thinking on the part of leaders, confusing intentions and national interests, and misperceiving the characteristics of the counterpart decision maker. But the core notion—that rational decision making leads to the pursuit of the national interest—remains. Likewise for modern realists, rational decisions advance the national interest—the interests of the state—however ambiguously that national interest is formulated.

Fourth, Thucydides, like contemporary realists, was concerned with security issues—the state's need to protect itself from enemies both foreign and domestic. A state augments its security by increasing its domestic capacities, building up its economic prowess, and forming alliances with other states based on similar interests. In fact, Thucydides found that before and during the Peloponnesian War, it was fear of a rival that motivated states to join alliances, a rational decision on the part of the leader. In the Melian dialogue, perhaps the most famous section of *History of the Peloponnesian War*, Thucydides posed the classic dilemma between realist and liberal thinking: "[T]he strong do what they can and the weak suffer what they must." More generally, do states have rights based on the conception of an international ethical or moral order, as liberals suggest? Or is a state's power, in the absence of an international authority, the deciding factor?

Thucydides did not identify all the tenets of what we think of as realism today. Indeed, the tenets and rationale of realism have unfolded over centuries, and not all realists agree on what they are. For example, six centuries after Thucydides lived, the Christian bishop and philosopher Saint Augustine (354–430) added a fundamental assumption of realism, arguing that humanity is flawed, egoistic, and selfish, although not predetermined to be so. Augustine blames war on these basic characteristics of humanity.[3] Although subsequent realists dispute Augustine's biblical explanation for humanity's flawed, selfish nature, few realists dispute the fact that humans are basically power seeking and self-absorbed.

The implications of humanity's flawed nature for the state are developed further in the writings of the Italian political philosopher Niccolò Machiavelli (1469–1527). In *The Prince*, Machiavelli elucidated the qualities that a leader needs to maintain the strength and security of the state. He argued that a leader needs to be ever mindful of threats to his personal security and the security of the state. In addition, Machiavelli cautioned against excessive restraint on the part of princes who might face internal or external threats; arguing that on the contrary, the responsible prince must be prepared to undertake *any* action so long as it conduced to the preservation of the state. Machiavelli is also remembered for his advocacy of the skillful use of alliances and various offensive and defensive strategies to protect the state.[4]

The central tenet accepted by virtually all realist theorists is that the chief constraint on "better" state behavior — especially enduring peace — is that states exist in an anarchic international system. This tenet was forcefully articulated by Thomas Hobbes (see Chapter 1). Hobbes, who lived and wrote during one of history's greatest periods of turmoil (the Thirty Years' War, 1618–48, and the English Civil Wars, 1641–51), maintained that just as individuals in a hypothetical "state of nature" have the responsibility and the right to preserve themselves — including a right of violence against others — so too does each state in the international system. In his most famous treatise, *Leviathan*, Hobbes argued that the only cure for perpetual war within a state was the emergence of a single powerful prince who could overawe all others: a leviathan. Applying his arguments to relations among sovereigns, Hobbes depicted a condition of anarchy where the norm for states is "having their weapons pointing, and their eyes fixed on one another."[5] In the absence of an international sovereign, few rules or norms can restrain states. War, in other words, would be perpetual.

In the aftermath of World War II, the international relations theorist Hans Morgenthau (1904–80) wrote the seminal synthesis of realism in international politics and offered what he argued was a methodological approach for testing this theory. For Morgenthau, just as for Thucydides, Augustine, and Hobbes, international politics is best characterized as a struggle for power. That struggle can be explained at the three levels of analysis: (1) the flawed individual in the state of nature struggles for self-preservation; (2) the autonomous and unitary state is constantly involved in power struggles, balancing power with power and reacting to preserve what is in the national interest; and (3) because the international system is anarchic—there is no higher power to put an end to the competition—the struggle is perpetual. Because of the imperative to ensure a state's survival, leaders are driven by a morality quite different from that of ordinary individuals. Morality, for realists, is to be judged by the political consequences of a policy.[6]

Morgenthau's international relations textbook *Politics among Nations* became the realist bible in the years following World War II. Policy implications flowed naturally from the theory: the most effective technique for managing power is balance of power. Both George Kennan (1904–2005), a writer and chair of the State Department's Policy Planning Staff in the late 1940s and later the U.S. ambassador to the Soviet Union, and Henry Kissinger (b. 1923), a scholar and foreign policy adviser and the secretary of state to presidents Richard Nixon and Gerald Ford, are known to have based their policy recommendations on realist theory.

As we saw in Chapter 2, Kennan was one of the architects of the U.S. Cold War policy of containment, an interpretation of the balance of power. The goal of containment was to prevent Soviet power from extending into regions beyond that country's immediate, existing sphere of influence (Eastern Europe). Containment was achieved by balancing U.S. power against Soviet power. Containment was an important alternative to the competing strategy of "rollback," in which a combination of nuclear and conventional military threats would be used to force the Soviet Union out of Eastern Europe and, in particular, Germany. Kennan's keen analysis of Soviet intentions and his fear of uncontrolled escalation to a third world war ultimately led to the adoption of containment as U.S. foreign policy. During the 1970s, Kissinger encouraged the classic realist balance of power by supporting weaker powers such as China and Pakistan to exert leverage over the Soviet Union and to offset India's growing power, respectively. At the time, India was an ally of the Soviets.

Whereas realism appears to offer clear policy prescriptions, not all realists agree on what an ideal realist foreign policy might look like. Defensive realists observe that few if any major wars in the last century ended up benefiting the state or states that started them. When threatened, they argue, states tend to balance against aggressors, invariably overwhelming and reversing whatever initial gains were made.

Saddam Hussein's attempt to conquer and annex neighboring Kuwait in 1990 serves as a classic example. In August of 1990, Iraq's armed forces quickly overwhelmed the paltry defenses of Kuwait, and Saddam's soldiers followed their victory with rape and looting. Before the invasion, Kuwait had been a little-known oil-rich Arab state in which a repressive hereditary elite ruled over a population composed mainly of servants hired from surrounding Arab countries (in particular, Palestinian Arabs). But though critics pointed out that Kuwait was itself a less than an ideal candidate for rescue,

Saddam's aggression provoked a powerful international reaction. In 1991, an international coalition of armed forces led by the United States invaded Kuwait and rapidly forced the retreat and later surrender of the Iraqi army. Iraq was forced to repay all the damages of its conquest, and its sovereignty was abridged by two "no-fly" zones, which protected Kurds in the north and Shia in the south from Saddam's harsh reprisals. Conquest, in other words, did not pay for Iraq.

For defensive realists, the outcome of Iraq's 1990 war forms part of a long historical pattern of effective (and inevitable) balancing. In this case, Saudi Arabia, the United States, and others supported Kuwait to balance against Iraq's regional power. As a result, defensive realists argue that states in the international system should pursue policies of restraint, whether through military, diplomatic, or economic channels. Such defensive moderate postures can be pursued without leading to dangerous levels of mistrust among states and, more importantly, without fear of unintended or uncontrolled escalation to counterproductive wars.

Offensive realists, by contrast, note that periodically demonstrating a willingness to engage in war, though perhaps costly in the short run, may pay huge dividends by way of reputation enhancement later. They argue that the credible threat of conquest can often act as a motivation to alter a target state's interests, leading states that might have opposed the threatening state to ally with it in a process international relations theorists call **bandwagoning**. The logic is that the more power you have, the more power you get. Conquest, in other words, pays. States may thus pursue expansionist politics, building up their relative power positions and intimidating potential rivals into cooperation.

Consider the stunning case of Libya's decision in December of 2003 to publicly acknowledge and then abandon its years-long efforts to acquire nuclear, chemical, and biological weapons, along with the vehicles to launch them. To an offensive realist, Libya's decision could well have been the result of the George W. Bush administration's decision to invade Iraq in March of 2003, an invasion justified to halt Saddam's production or dissemination of weapons of mass destruction. After years of opposing the United States, Libya choose instead to bandwagon in the face of this demonstration of U.S. power. By offensive realist logic, the costs of the war against Iraq were at least partly redeemed by Libya's change of policy: conquest, or the credible threat of conquest, paid.

Thus, defensive and offensive realists have significant differences of view about appropriate foreign policy.[7] In fact, realism encompasses a family of related arguments, sharing common assumptions and premises. It is not a single, unified theory. Among the various reinterpretations of realism, the most important is **neorealism** (or structural realism), as delineated in Kenneth Waltz's *Theory of International Politics.*[8] Reasoning that lack of progress in social scientific theory of international politics was due to lack of theoretical rigor (especially in comparison to steady theoretical progress in the natural sciences), Waltz undertook this reinterpretation of classical realism in order to make political realism a more rigorous theory of international politics. Neorealists therefore propose general laws to explain events: they simplify explanations of behavior in anticipation of being better able to explain and predict general trends.

Neorealists give precedence in their analyses to the structure of the international system as an explanatory factor, while traditional realists also attach importance to the characteristic of states and of human beings. According to Waltz, the most important object of study is the structure of the international system. Attempting to understand the international system by reference to states is analogous, in Waltz's view, to attempting to understand a market by reference to individual firms: unproductive at best. Neorealism thus advances two arguments. The first is that we need theory in order to understand international politics (and that prior to the publication of Waltz's book we had none); and the second is that his theory, neorealism, explains international politics since 1648, the date cited by scholars for the advent of the state system.

Critics of classical realism had noted that if the human desire for power, inscribed on states, was driving the recurrence of interstate war, how can we explain long periods of peace? How, in other words, can a constant explain a variable? Waltz responded by substituting international structure as a variable in place of the constant of human nature. He argued that the structure of a particular system is determined by its ordering principle, namely, the presence or absence of overarching authority, and the distribution of capabilities among states. While international anarchy has been a constant, the distribution of capabilities has changed over time. Those capabilities define a state's position in the system. The distribution of capabilities in an anarchic system can also be described in structural terms as having one of two values: bipolarity (two fairly equal rivals, such as Athens and Sparta at the start of the Peloponnesian Wars or the United States and Soviet Union during the height of the Cold War); or multipolarity (three or more great powers, as in Europe in 1914). According to neorealists, the structure of the system and the distribution of power within it, rather than the characteristics of individual states, determine outcomes. This is why the closer the overall distribution of power approaches the ideal of unipolarity, the greater, in the neorealist view, is the likelihood (but never the certainty) of peace.[9] Note that logically, unipolarity (the emergence of a leviathan) would suspend the condition of anarchy and overturn all the causes of war that are said to inevitably follow from that condition.

This observation leads to another key question, the answers to which lie at the root of the disagreement between liberals and realists. Why, we might ask, haven't two or more great powers ever cooperated to become a single leviathan, thus ending war? Neorealists posit two answers: first, cooperation is difficult under conditions of anarchy due to concerns over relative gains; and second, states in an anarchic system must be on constant guard against cheating. In an anarchic system, the possibilities for international cooperation are logically slim:

THEORY IN BRIEF

REALISM / NEOREALISM

KEY ACTORS	States (most powerful matter most)
VIEW OF THE INDIVIDUAL	Insecure, selfish, power-seeking
VIEW OF THE STATE	Insecure, selfish, unitary, power-seeking as evidence of rationality
VIEW OF THE INTERNATIONAL SYSTEM	Anarchic (implies perpetual threat of war); more stable as distribution of power approaches unipolarity
BELIEFS ABOUT CHANGE	Possibility of perpetual peace logically precluded; emphasis shifted to managing the frequency and intensity of war
MAJOR THEORISTS	Thucydides, Saint Augustine, Machiavelli, Hobbes, Morgenthau, Waltz, Gilpin, Mearsheimer

When faced with the possibility of cooperating for mutual gain, states that feel insecure must ask how the gain will be divided. They are compelled to ask not "Will both of us gain?" but "Who will gain more?" If an expected gain is to be divided, say, in the ratio of two to one, one state may use its disproportionate gain to implement a policy intended to damage or destroy the other. Even the prospect of large absolute gains for both parties does not elicit their cooperation so long as each fears how the other will use its increased capabilities.[10]

The importance of relative power means that states hesitate to engage in cooperation if the benefits to be gained might be distributed unevenly among participating states. Even if cooperation could produce absolute gains for any one state, these gains will be discounted by that state should cooperation produce greater gains for other states. In a neorealist's balance-of-power world, a state's survival depends on its having more power than other states. Thus all power (and gains in power) are viewed in relative terms.[11]

Neorealists are also concerned with cheating. States may be tempted to cheat on agreements in order to gain a relative advantage over other states. Fear that other states will renege on existing cooperative agreements is especially potent in the military realm, in which changes in weaponry might result in a major shift in the balance of power. Self-interest provides a powerful incentive for one state to take advantage of another. The awareness that such incentives exist, combined with states' rational desire to protect their own interests, tends to preclude long-term cooperation among states. As the popular paraphrase of Britain's Lord Palmerston (1784–1865) puts it, "Nations have no permanent friends or allies, only permanent interests."

Scholars have developed other interpretations of realism as well. Although neo-realism simplifies the classical realist theory and focuses on a few core concepts (system structure and balance of power), other reinterpretations add increased complexity to realism. In *War and Change in World Politics*, Robert Gilpin offers one such reinterpretation. Accepting the realist assumptions that states are the principal actors, decision makers are basically rational, and the international system structure plays a key role in determining power, Gilpin examines 2,400 years of history, finding that "the distribution of power among states constitutes the principal form of control in every international system."[12] What Gilpin adds is the notion of dynamism, of history as a series of cycles—cycles of the birth, expansion, and demise of dominant powers. Whereas classical realism offers no satisfactory rationale for the decline of powers, Gilpin finds the answer in economic power. Hegemons decline because of three processes: the increasingly marginal returns of controlling an empire, a state-level phenomenon; the tendency for economic hegemons to consume more over time and invest less, also a state-level phenomenon; and the diffusion of technology, a system-level phenomenon through which new powers challenge the hegemon. As Gilpin explains, "disequilibrium replaces equilibrium, and the world moves toward a new round of hegemonic conflict."[13]

In short, there is no single tradition of political realism; there are "realisms." Although each is predicated on a key group of assumptions, each attaches different importance to the various core propositions. Yet what unites proponents of realist theory—their emphasis on the unitary state in an international anarchic system, and a threat of war that can be managed but never done away with—distinguishes them clearly from both the liberals and the radicals.

Liberalism (and Neoliberal Institutionalism)

Liberalism holds that human nature is basically good and that people can improve their moral and material conditions, thus making societal progress—including lasting peace—possible. Bad or evil human behavior, such as injustice and war, is the product of inadequate or corrupt social institutions and of misunderstandings among leaders. Thus, liberals believe that injustice, war, and aggression are not inevitable but can be moderated or even eliminated through institutional reform or collective action. According to liberal thinking, the expansion of human freedom is best achieved in democracies and through well-regulated market capitalism.

The origins of liberal theory are found in eighteenth-century Enlightenment optimism, nineteenth-century political and economic liberalism, and twentieth-century Wilsonian idealism. The contribution of the Enlightenment to liberalism rests on the Greek idea that individuals are rational human beings, able to understand the universally applicable laws governing both nature and human society. Understanding such laws means that people have the capacity to improve their condition by creating a just society. If a just society is not attained, then the fault rests with inadequate institutions, the result of a corrupt environment.

The writings of the French philosopher Charles-Louis de Secondat, Baron de La Brède et de Montesquieu (1689–1755), reflect Enlightenment thinking. He argued that it is not human nature that is defective, but that problems arise as humanity enters civil society and forms separate nations. War is a product of society, not an attribute inherent in individuals. To overcome defects in society, education is imperative; it prepares one for civil life. Groups of states are united according to the law of nations, which regulates conduct even during war. Montesquieu optimistically stated that "different nations ought in time of peace to do one another all the good they can, and in time of war as little harm as possible, without prejudicing their real interests."[14]

Likewise, the writings of Immanuel Kant (1724–1804) form the core of Enlightenment beliefs. According to Kant, international anarchy can be overcome through a particular kind of collective action—a federation of republics in which sovereignties would be left intact. Like other liberal philosophers, Kant's argument held out the possibility of transcending the limitations of anarchy in the international system and the withering away of war. Unlike others, however, Kant's philosophy did not assume or require moral actors. On the contrary, Kant assumed that states would act in self-interested ways, and that the repeated interaction of self-interested states would eventually lead to an expanding zone of peace, *in spite of that self-interest*. As he famously put it, what is required for the emergence of perpetual peace is not moral angels, but "rational devils."[15]

Nineteenth-century liberalism took the rationalism of the Enlightenment and reformulated it by adding a preference for democracy over aristocracy and for free trade over national economic self-sufficiency. Sharing the Enlightenment's optimistic view of human nature, nineteenth-century liberalism saw humanity as capable of satisfying its natural needs and wants in rational ways. These needs and wants could be met most efficiently by each individual's pursuing his or her own freedom and autonomy in a democratic state, unfettered by excessive governmental restrictions. Likewise, political freedoms are most easily achieved in capitalist states, where rational and acquisitive human beings can improve their own conditions, maximizing both individual and collective economic growth and economic welfare. Free markets must be allowed to flourish, and governments must permit the free flow of trade and commerce. Liberal theorists believe that free trade and commerce create interdependencies among states, thus raising the cost of war and reducing its likelihood.

Twentieth-century idealism also contributed to liberalism, finding its greatest adherent in the U.S. president Woodrow Wilson. Wilson authored the covenant of the League of Nations—hence the term *Wilsonian idealism.* The basic proposition of Wilson's idealism is that war is preventable through the collective action of states; more than half of the League covenant's 26 provisions focused on preventing war. The covenant even included a provision legitimizing the notion of **collective security**, whereby aggression by one state would be countered by automatic and collective reaction, embodied in a "league of nations."

Thus, the League of Nations illustrated the importance that liberals place on the potential of international institutions to deal with war and the opportunity for collective problem solving in a multilateral forum. Liberals also place faith in international law and legal instruments such as mediation, arbitration, and international courts. Still other liberals think that all war can be eliminated through disarmament. Whatever the specific prescriptive solution, the basis of liberalism remains firmly embedded in the belief in the rationality of human beings, the irreducibility of the human condition to the individual (unlike realists, who model human insecurity on an isolated human being, liberals observe that humans exist everywhere in *society*), and that through learning and education, humans can develop institutions capable of ensuring and advancing human welfare.

During the interwar period, when the League of Nations proved incapable of maintaining collective security, and during World War II, when atrocities made many question the basic goodness of humanity, liberalism came under intense scrutiny. *Was* humankind inherently good? How could an institution fashioned under the best assumptions have failed so miserably? Liberalism as a theoretical perspective fell out of favor, replaced by realism and its solution to the problem of war: the balance of power.

Since the 1970s, however, liberalism has been revived under the rubric of **neoliberal institutionalism**. Neoliberal institutionalists such as the political scientists Robert Axelrod and Robert O. Keohane ask *why* states choose to cooperate most of the time, even under the anarchic conditions of the international system. One answer is found in the simple but important story of the prisoner's dilemma.[16]

The **prisoner's dilemma** is the story of two prisoners who are interrogated separately for an alleged crime. The police have enough evidence to convict both prisoners on a minor charge but need a confession in order to convict them on a major charge. An interrogator tells each prisoner that if one of them testifies against the other (defects) and the other stays silent (cooperates), the one who defects will go free, but the one who cooperates will get a one-year prison term. If both defect, both will get three-month prison terms. If neither defects (i.e., they both cooperate and stay silent), both will receive one-month prison terms for the minor charge. Let's say that both

French President François Hollande and German Chancellor Angela Merkel attend a celebration of the peaceful Franco-German relationship that has endured since the end of World War II. Liberal theorists believe France and Germany's joint membership in numerous international organizations, including the UN, NATO, and the European Union, has supported this long peace.

prisoners defect. Each will serve a longer sentence than if they had cooperated and kept silent. Why didn't each prisoner cooperate? So long as the game is played once, neither prisoner can be certain of what the other will do, so each chooses to testify against the other (defect) because each will be better off *regardless of what the other prisoner decides*. Two important points follow. First, the prisoner's dilemma is actually not a dilemma, because so long as the game is structured as it is, any rational prisoner would choose to defect: it's the only sure way of minimizing the possibility of disaster (a full year in jail). Second, the prisoner's dilemma is famous as an illustrative game because it highlights how the structure of an interaction can intervene between intention and outcome to explain unintended (or harmful) outcomes. It's an effectively realist story, which emphasizes how the structure of interactions limit the possibility of peace through cooperation. But neoliberal institutionalists added a startling question: why assume a single round of play?

If the prisoner's dilemma interaction is played over and over, the likelihood of reciprocity (known in game theory parlance as "tit for tat") makes it rational for each prisoner to cooperate rather than defect. If either prisoner testified against the other in a first round, in a second round, that prisoner could expect retaliation. As more rounds are played, rational players understand they can maximize their expected benefit by

THEORY IN BRIEF	LIBERALISM / NEOLIBERAL INSTITUTIONALISM
KEY ACTORS	States, nongovernmental groups, international organizations
VIEW OF THE INDIVIDUAL	Basically good; social; capable of cooperating
VIEW OF THE STATE	States are selfish; have relationships (enduring friends and rivals); can be good (democratic-liberal) or bad (authoritarian-autarkic)
VIEW OF THE INTERNATIONAL SYSTEM	Anarchy abridged by interdependence among actors; an international order
BELIEFS ABOUT CHANGE	Self-interest managed by structure (institutions) leads to possibility of perpetual peace
MAJOR THEORISTS	Montesquieu, Kant, Wilson, Keohane, Doyle, Ikenberry

cooperating, and over time this becomes their preferred or dominant strategy. Similarly, states in the international system are not faced with a one-time round of "play": they confront each other over and over again on a wide range of issues. Unlike classical liberals, neoliberal institutionalists do not believe that individuals naturally cooperate out of an innate characteristic of humanity. The prisoner's dilemma provides neoliberal institutionalists with a rationale for mutual cooperation in an environment where there is no international authority mandating such cooperation.

Neoliberal institutionalists arrive at the same prediction that liberals do—cooperation—but their explanation for why cooperation occurs is different. For classical liberals, cooperation emerges from humanity's establishing and reforming institutions that permit cooperative interactions and prohibit coercive actions. For neoliberal institutionalists, cooperation emerges because when actors have continuous interactions with each other, it is in the self-interest of each to cooperate. Institutions help prevent cheating in other ways: they reduce transaction costs (costs incurred in making an exchange), reduce opportunity costs (the costs of alternative possibilities), and improve the flow of information—all benefits of cooperation.

Two other additions to neoliberal institutionalist thought also explain cooperation. First, cooperation in one issue area may spill over into other areas. Thus cooperation on trade may over time lead to cooperation on security. Second, theorists such as Robert Keohane argue that institutional cooperation can deepen to the point where it may be said to have inertia: whatever the original conditions of its establishment, once established, institutional cooperation can exist and even flourish once those initial conditions have vanished. Consider NATO: it was founded after World War II to prevent Europe from being bullied or conquered by the Soviet Union, yet the Soviet Union disintegrated in 1991. Why then does NATO still exist? Neoliberal institutionalists would argue that the cooperation that originally made NATO possible and effective deepened over time to become an end in itself.

For neoliberal institutionalists, security is essential, just as it is for realists. But as theorists like G. John Ikenberry argue, realism cannot explain the duration of postwar stability following the collapse of the Soviet Union, while neoliberal institutionalists can.[17] Institutions such as NATO and the European Union's Common Foreign and Security Policy provide a guaranteed framework of interactions, and thus incorporate a powerful expectation of repeated interactions. The implication of these repeated interactions is increased cooperation not only on security issues, but across a whole range of international issues including economics and trade, human rights (a classic liberal concern), the environment, immigration, and transnational crime.[18] Thus, for neoliberals, institutions are critical: they facilitate, widen, and deepen cooperation by building on common interests, thus maximizing the gains for all parties. Institutions help shape state preferences, solidifying cooperative relationships.

With the end of the Cold War in the 1990s, liberalism as a general theoretical perspective has achieved new credibility. Two particular areas stand out. First, researchers of the so-called democratic peace (discussed in more detail in Chapter 5) have been trying to explain an empirical puzzle: although on balance, democratic states are as warlike as authoritarian states, democratic states never attack *each other*. The question is "why?" A variety of liberal explanations provide potential answers. One argument is that the democratic process inhibits aggression; leaders in democracies hear from a multiplicity of voices that tend to restrain decision makers and therefore lessen the chance of war. Another argument is that transnational and international institutions that bind democracies together through dense networks act to constrain behavior. These explanations are based on liberal theorizing. The policy implications are clear: replacing dictators with democratic governments could reduce the likelihood of interstate war, a net benefit to every state in the system of states.

Second, the scholar and former policy analyst Francis Fukuyama sees not just a revival, but a victory for international liberalism following the end of the Cold War. He admits that some groups, such as Palestinians and Israelis, and Armenians and Azeris, will continue to have grievances against one another. But the frequency of large-scale conflict has been declining over the last 20 years. For the first time, Fukuyama argues, the possibility exists for the "universalization of Western liberal democracy as the final form of human governance."[19] Indeed, the political scientist John Mueller makes the liberal argument even more strongly. Just as dueling and slavery, once acceptable practices, have become morally unacceptable, nations of the developed world increasingly see war as immoral and repugnant. The terrifying moments of World Wars I and II have led to the obsolescence of war, says Mueller (see Chapter 8).[20] And Mueller's observation that war is going out of fashion has recently been expanded by two other scholars, Steven Pinker and Joshua Goldstein. Pinker, a scholar of cognitive and evolutionary psychology, argues that not only has war gone out of fashion, but violence of all sorts is disappearing. Goldstein's analysis shows that the frequency and intensity of war between states has dropped precipitously in the past four decades: so much so that he has argued that "the war against war has been won."[21]

Liberalism, then, has provided the major counterpoint to realism. Although these two theories differ in many respects, they both assume actors are basically rational and both conceptualize power in materialist terms.

The Radical Perspective

Radicalism offers the third overarching theoretical perspective on international relations. Whereas agreement is widespread concerning the appropriate assignment of the liberal and realist labels, there is no such agreement about the label *radicalism*.

The writings of Karl Marx (1818–83) are fundamental to all radical thought, even though he did not directly address all the issues of today. Marx based his theory of the evolution of capitalism on economic change and economic class conflict: the capitalism of nineteenth-century Europe emerged out of the earlier feudal system. According to Marx, in the capitalist system, private interests control labor and market exchanges, creating bondages from which certain classes try to free themselves. Note that Marx and his partner Friedrich Engels borrowed the notion of "class" from Europe's social classes (upper classes, the aristocracy; middle classes, guildsmen; and lower classes, peasants and laborers) but reimagined them as two economic classes: a bourgeoisie—which owned all means of production—and a proletariat—exploited labor. A clash inevitably arises between the controlling, capitalist bourgeois class, and the controlled proletariat. It is from this violent clash, which the proletariat must inevitably win after a period of revolutionary struggle, that a new socialist order is born.[22]

A group of core beliefs unites those espousing a radical, largely Marxist, perspective. The first set of radical beliefs is found in historical analysis. Whereas for most realists and liberals, history provides various data points from which to glean appropriate generalizations, radicals see historical analysis as fundamental. Of special relevance is the history of the production process. During the evolution of the production process from feudalism to capitalism, new patterns of social relations were developed. Radicals are concerned most with explaining the relationships among the means of production, social relations, and power.

Basing their analyses of history on the importance of the production process, most radical theorists also assume the primacy of economics for explaining virtually all other phenomena. This clearly differentiates radicalism from either realism or liberalism. For liberals, economic interdependence is one possible explanation for international cooperation, but only one among many factors. For realists, economic factors are one of the ingredients of power, one component of the international structure. In neither theory, though, is economics the determining factor. Both realists and liberals accept that the *state* is the primary unit of analysis. In radicalism, on the other hand, economic factors (for Marxists, it is class) assume primary importance. For example, radical feminists based in the Marxist tradition suggest that the roots of oppression against women are found in an exploitative capitalist system.

A different group of radical beliefs centers on the structure of the global system. That structure, in Marxist thinking, is hierarchical and is largely the by-product of imperialism, or the expansion of certain economic forms into other areas of the world. The British economist John A. Hobson (1858–1940) theorized that expansion occurs because of three conditions in the more developed states: overproduction of goods and services, underconsumption by workers and the lower classes because of low wages, and oversavings by the upper classes and the bourgeoisie. In order to solve these three economic problems, developed states historically have expanded abroad, and radicals argue that developed countries still see expansion as a solution. Goods find new markets in underdeveloped regions, workers' wages are kept low because of foreign competition,

THEORY IN BRIEF	RADICALISM / DEPENDENCY THEORY
KEY ACTORS	Social classes, transnational elites, multinational corporations
VIEW OF THE INDIVIDUAL	Actions determined by economic class interests
VIEW OF THE STATE	An agent of the structure of international capitalism and the executing agent of the bourgeoisie
VIEW OF THE INTERNATIONAL SYSTEM	Highly stratified; dominated by international capitalist system
BELIEFS ABOUT CHANGE	Radical change inevitable
MAJOR THEORISTS	Marx, Hobson, Lenin, Prebisch

and savings are profitably invested in new markets rather than in improving the lot of the workers. Imperialism leads to rivalry among the developed countries.[23]

For radicals, imperialism produces the hierarchical international system, which offers opportunities to some states, organizations, and individuals, but imposes significant constraints on behavior for others. Developed countries can expand, enabling them to sell goods and export surplus wealth that they cannot use at home. Simultaneously, the developing countries are increasingly constrained by and dependent on the actions of the developed world. Hobson, who condemned imperialism as irrational, risky, and potentially conflictual, did not see it as necessarily inevitable. But most radicals drawing on Marx's analysis critique capitalism as inevitably leading to crises. Whereas free-market capitalists maintain that equilibrium will be found through the market, radicals predict a series of deep crises.

Radical theorists emphasize the techniques of domination and suppression that arise from the uneven economic development inherent in the capitalist system. Uneven development empowers and enables the dominant states to exploit the underdogs; the dynamics of capitalism and economic expansion make such exploitation necessary if the top dogs are to maintain their position and the capitalist structure is to survive. Whereas realists see balancing the power of other states to fight and win wars as the mechanisms for gaining and maintaining power, Marxists and radicals view the economic techniques of domination and suppression as the means of power in the world; the choices for the underdog are few and ineffective.

One latter-day school of radicalism recognizes that capitalists can apply additional, more sophisticated techniques of control to developing markets. Contemporary radicals such as **dependency theorists** attribute primary importance to the role of **multinational corporations (MNCs)** and international banks based in developed countries in exerting fundamental controls over the developing countries. These organizations are seen as key players in establishing and maintaining dependency relationships; they are agents of penetration, not benign actors, as liberals would characterize them, or marginal actors, as realists would. These organizations are able to forge transnational relationships with elites in the developing countries, so that domestic elites in both exploiter and exploited countries are tightly linked in a symbiotic relationship.

Dependency theorists, particularly those from Latin America (Raul Prebisch, Enzo Faletto, Fernando Henrique Cardoso), believe that options for states on the periphery are few. Since the basic terms of trade are unequal, these states have few external options. Nor do they have many internal options, because their internal constraints are just as real: land tenure and social and class structures.[24] Thus, like the realists, dependency theorists are rather pessimistic about the possibility of change.

Finally, virtually all radical theorists, regardless of their specific emphases, are normative in their orientation. They evaluate the hierarchical capitalist structure as "bad," its methods exploitative. They have clear normative and activist positions about what should be done to ameliorate inequalities among both individuals and states — ranging from forming radical organizations supported by Leninists to more incremental changes suggested by dependency theorists.

In some quarters, radicalism has been discredited as an international relations theory. Radicalism cannot explain why cooperation was emerging between capitalist and socialist states even before the end of the Cold War. And it cannot explain the divisiveness among noncapitalist states. For example, in 1948, communist Yugoslavia and the USSR dramatically split over the former's refusal to submit important domestic and foreign policy decisions to Stalin's approval. Neither can radicalism explain why and how some of the developing countries such as India have been able to adopt a capitalist approach and escape from economic and political dependency. Radicalism could not have predicted such developments. And radicalism, just like liberalism and realism, did not foresee or predict the demise of the Soviet Union, arguably one of the most significant changes in the twentieth century. Each theory, despite claims of comprehensiveness, has significant shortcomings.

In other circles, radicalism has survived as a theory of economic determinism and as a force advocating major change in the structure of the international system. Radicalism helps us understand the role of economic forces both within and between states and to explain the dynamics of late-twentieth-century economic globalization and the 2008 economic crisis, as discussed in Chapter 9.

Constructivism

A late-twentieth-century addition to international relations, **constructivism** has returned international relations scholars to foundational questions, including the nature of the state and the concepts of sovereignty, identity, and citizenship. In addition, constructivism has opened new substantive areas to inquiry, such as the roles of gender and ethnicity, which have been largely absent from other international relations theories. Yet like liberalism, realism, and radicalism, constructivism is not a uniform theory. Indeed, some scholars question whether it is a substantive theory at all. That said, most constructivists do share a number of ideas.

Constructivism's major theoretical proposition is that neither objects nor concepts have any necessary, fixed, or objective meaning; rather, their meanings are *constructed* through social interaction. In other words, we bring meaning to objects, not the other way around. By extension, state conduct is shaped by elite beliefs, identities, and social norms. Individuals in collectivities forge, shape, and change culture through ideas and practices. State and national interests are the result of the social identities of these actors. Thus, the objects of study are the norms and practices of individuals and the collectivity.[25] Ted Hopf offers a simple analogy:

> The scenario is a fire in a theater where all run for the exits. But absent knowledge of social practices of constitutive norms, structure, even in this seemingly overdetermined circumstance, is still indeterminate. Even in a theater with just one door, while all run for that exit, who goes first? Are they the strongest or the disabled, the women or the children, the aged or the infirm, or is it just a mad dash? Determining the outcome will require knowing more about the situation than about the distribution of mate- rial power or the structure of authority. One will need to know about the culture, norms, institutions, procedures, rules, and social practices that constitute the actors and the structure alike.[26]

Note that had realist logic been employed to predict the outcome of Hopf's fire-in-a-theater example, or, say, the demographic composition of the *Titanic*'s lifeboats in 1912, realist assumptions about the value placed on one's own survival and self-interests, and about relative power, would have forced an incorrect prediction. In real life, very often the strong yield to the weak, rather than forcing the weak to "suffer what they must." That is why the *Titanic*'s lifeboats were not filled with strong men, but with the ship's physically weakest passengers: women and children.

Constructivists thus eschew the idea that material structures have a necessary, fixed, or inherent meaning. Alexander Wendt, one of the best-known constructivists, argues that on its own, a political structure—whether one of anarchy or a particular distribution of mate- rial capabilities—cannot tell us much of interest: "It does not predict whether two states will be friends or foes, will recognize each other's sovereignty, will have dynastic ties, will have revisionist or status quo powers, and so on."[27] Many constructivists emphasize normative structures. What we need to know is identity, and identities change as a result of cooperative behavior and learning. Whether a system is anarchic depends on the distribution of identi- ties, not the distribution of military capabilities, as the realists would have us believe. If a state identifies only with itself, then the system may "be" anarchic. If a state identifies with other states, then there is no anarchy. In short, "anarchy is what states make of it."[28]

Like the realists and neoliberal institutionalists, constructivists see power as impor- tant. But whereas the former see power in primarily material terms (military, economic, political), constructivists also see power in discursive terms—the power of ideas, cul- ture, and language. Thus, to constructivists, power includes such ideas as legitimacy; states may alter their actions in order to be viewed as legitimate by other members of the international community. Power exists in every exchange among actors, and the goal of constructivists is to find the sources of that power. Their unique contribution

Constructivism offers an explanation for how ideas such as "crimes against humanity" can evolve into powerful international norms and laws. The precedent for war crimes trials established at Nuremberg after World War II has since been replicated around the world.

may well be in elucidating the sources of power in ideas and in showing how ideas shape and change identity. An example of constructivist contributions can be seen in the discussion of sovereignty. Constructivists see sovereignty not as an absolute but as a contested concept. They point out that states have never had exclusive control over territory. State sovereignty has always been challenged and is being challenged continuously by new institutional forms and new national needs.

Constructivist theory offers different explanations of change. Change can occur through diffusion of ideas or the internationalization of norms, as well as through socialization, adopting the identities of peer groups. These explanations help us understand that ideas are spread both within a national setting and cross-nationally. This is how democracy is diffused, how ideas about human rights protection have been internationalized, and how such states as the new members of the European Union become socialized into the community's norms and practices. Put another way, realism and liberalism each have a more difficult time explaining the advent, spread, and real-world *impact* of ideas and norms such as taboos against land mines or the "responsibility to

THEORY IN BRIEF

CONSTRUCTIVISM

KEY ACTORS	People, elites, cultures
VIEW OF THE INDIVIDUAL	Key component in creation of meaning; bound by education, socialization, and culture
VIEW OF THE STATE	An artifact whose significance is socially constructed through discourse
VIEW OF THE INTERNATIONAL SYSTEM	An artifact whose significance is socially constructed through discourse
BELIEFS ABOUT CHANGE	Possible by means of discourse: "[anarchy] [war] [peace] is what we make of it"
MAJOR THEORISTS	Foucault, Derrida, Kratochwil, Hopf, Wendt

protect" (see Chapter 8). Thus constructivism does *not* reduce to mere conversation and blathery, but helps provide strong explanations of shifts in our understanding of objects that have an impact on real human lives, just as realism, liberalism, and radicalism do.

But also like realism, liberalism, and radicalism, constructivism has its shortcomings. Until recently, constructivism remained mainly a powerful tool of criticism rather than a program capable of explaining outcomes in the real world. This is changing, however. Throughout this textbook, examples of constructivist scholarship will allow you to see this approach in use so that you can come to your own judgments concerning this crucial and still-relatively-new theoretical perspective.

A related but separate theory of constructivism is feminist international relations theory, which often shares constructivism's core concepts and mechanisms. For constructivists more broadly, the meaning of things is established, supported, and changed through a process of social interaction called discourse. For many feminist scholars, such as J. Ann Tickner, Cynthia Enloe, and Christine Sylvester, that discourse has been dominated by a narrowly male perspective. Paying little attention to the voices of women affects both the kinds of questions we ask and how we evaluate the answers.

According to Tickner, for example, classical realism is based on a very limited—indeed, *masculine*—notion of both human nature and power. She argues that human nature is not fixed and unalterable; it is multidimensional and contextual. Power cannot be equated exclusively with physical control and domination. Tickner thinks that all international relations theory must be reoriented toward a more inclusive notion of power, in which power is the ability to act in concert (not just in conflict) or

YOU DECIDE

Feminist scholars of international relations such as J. Ann Tickner have argued that much of what we think we know about the world—especially as filtered through classical and contemporary international relations theory—is actually about males. Tickner and other feminist theorists believe that a kind of systematic bias they call *masculinism* has led both to the too-frequent occurrence of war across history, as well as to a scholarly fixation on war as *the* central problem of international relations. Assume for the sake of argument that due to systematic exclusion from state leadership opportunities (or female self-selection out of such opportunities), Tickner is right. Would a world led by women be more peaceful?

To conclude that a world led by women would be more peaceful, you would need to first establish that in general, women and men act and think in different ways. You might assert that while women across many cultures appear to be just as conflict-prone as men, they are rarely as violent. Biology plays a role in determining behavior. Because women on average are less physically strong than men, yet face the same pressures to survive and advance, women come into adulthood with powerful incentives to innovate conflict resolution strategies that do not rely on physical coercion or defense to the extent that male-male interactions do. In this sense, a world led by women would be more peaceful.

In contrast, you might begin by arguing that observed differences between how men and women act and think are due to socialization rather than nature: men are not inherently more violent, but rather are taught by society to be so. You might also note that today both women and men are socialized differently than in the past. If true, you might expect the differences between male and female leaders to be both slight and ephemeral. Finally, in keeping with many feminist critiques, you might observe that war is not the only threat to peace, so perhaps less war might not correspond to more peace (or to a better world).

YOU DECIDE: Extend a first-level-of-analysis argument by leveraging your own anecdotal evidence in support of your position. You might recall instances in which women have been heads of state during a security crisis. Did they seem to act differently than you might have expected a male leader to act in the same situation? You might recall your own reactions to threats and those of friends and acquaintances of the opposite sex. How do your observations of male-female differences, if any, affect your arguments about whether female leadership might lead to less war?

to engage in a symbiotic relationship (instead of outright competition). In other words, power can also be a concept of connection rather than one only of autonomy.[29]

Theory in Action: Analyzing the 2003 Iraq War

The contending theoretical perspectives discussed in the preceding sections see the world and even specific events quite differently. What theorists and policy makers choose to see, what they each seek to explain, and what implications they draw—all these elements of analysis vary, even though the facts of an event seem identical. Analyzing the 2003 Iraq War by applying these different theories allows us to compare and contrast them in action.

Realist interpretations of the 2003 Iraq War would focus on state-level and international-level factors. Realists see the international system as anarchic, with no international authority and few states other than the United States able and willing to act to rid the world of the Iraq threat. Iraq posed a security threat to the United States with its supposed stockpiles of weapons of mass destruction, and the United States therefore saw a need to eliminate those weapons and at the same time to ensure a stable oil supply to the West. The only way to achieve these objectives was to oust Saddam's Baathist regime from power in Iraq. Having escalated its threats and amassed its troops on Iraq's borders to coerce the regime to give up power, the United States had no choice but to act militarily when that coercion failed.

Yet not all realists agree that the policy the United States pursued was the correct one. Realists are carrying on an interesting discussion about whether or not the U.S. operation was necessary. John Mearsheimer, an offensive realist, and Stephen Walt, a defensive realist, have jointly argued that the war was not necessary. Before the war began, they wrote that any threat posed by Saddam, even his possible attainment of nuclear weapons, could be effectively deterred by U.S. military power. They further argued that even if the war went well and had positive long-term consequences, it would be unnecessary and could engender long-term animosity toward the United States both in the Middle East and around the world. The policy of deterrence employed by the United States had worked previously and could have continued to work.[30]

But other realist theorists, as well as President George W. Bush, believed that Saddam was not being effectively deterred. Bush argued that Saddam's use of chemical weapons against the Kurds in the past meant that it was probable he would use these weapons to threaten the United States. This perceived threat influenced the Bush administration's decision to invade. In addition, some realists in the Bush administration argued that a forceful response to Saddam's flouting of his obligations to the international community (his government was in violation of agreements it signed as part of the settlement that ended the first Gulf War in 1991) would put other enemies of the United States and its allies on notice. Perhaps force would also curtail what the administration referred to as state-sponsored terrorism. Realists clearly can draw different policy prescriptions from theory.

A liberal view of the 2003 Iraq War would utilize all three levels of analysis. With respect to the individual level, Saddam was clearly an abusive leader whose atrocities against his own population were made evident in the aftermath of the war, with the discovery of mass graves. He was aggressive not only against domestic opponents of his regime but also against other peoples within the region, and even supported terrorist activities against enemies in the West. With respect to the state level, liberals would emphasize the characteristics of the Iraqi regime — mainly its authoritarian nature — and the notion that replacement by a democracy would decrease the coercive threat of the Iraqi state and would enhance stability in the Middle East. A democratic Iraq would be a beacon for other nascent democracies nearby. The fact that many liberals believed that Saddam's regime had or was very close to acquiring weapons of mass destruction (WMD) only added to the urgency of regime change. With respect to the international level, liberals would emphasize that Iraq was not conforming to its obligations under various UN Security Council resolutions. Thus, the international community had an obligation to support sanctions and continue inspections and, failing that, undertake collective action, fighting a war to punish Saddam's regime and allow an alternative government to take root.

Why did the international community not respond as some liberals would have predicted? The inability of the United States to win the endorsement of the UN Security Council for collective action can be attributed to the fact that some members of the council, including France and Russia, and some other powerful states, including Germany, believed that containment of the Iraqi regime was effective, that there was insufficient evidence of weapons of mass destruction, and that there was no need to take immediate action in light of the higher priority given to fighting Al Qaeda in Afghanistan.

A radical interpretation would tend to focus mainly on the international system structure. That system structure, for radicals, is embedded in the historical colonial system and its contemporary legacies. Radicals hold that political colonialism spawned an imperialist system in which the economic needs of the capitalist states were paramount. In the Middle East, that meant imperialist action by the West to secure oil resources. In the nineteenth-century colonial era, imperialism was state organized; today imperialism is practiced by multinational corporations. In this view, the instability of the oil supply coming from Iraq explains the U.S. invasion of Iraq in 2003. Many radicals (and many in the Arab world) believe that the United States invaded in order to gain control of Iraq's oil. They point to the fact that one of the United States' first military objectives was the seizure of the Rumaila oil field in southern Iraq. Oil fields all over the

Canadian Views of the War in Afghanistan

Policies made by states are rooted in one theoretical perspective. Skeptics or dissenters often have a different theoretical perspective. Their justifications and the evidence they provide reflect different international relations theories.

On October 7, 2001, just hours after U.S. and British planes began bombing Afghan cities, Prime Minister Jean Chrétien announced that Canada would join the U.S. war in Afghanistan. In January and February 2002, regular military troops arrived in the country. These troops soon became part of the International Security Assistance Force (ISAF). Between 2,500 and 2,800 Canadian troops were engaged in action. One key part of Canadian participation was its 330-person Kandahar Provincial Reconstruction Team (PRT), deployed to support reconstruction efforts in the region. One hundred fifty-seven Canadian troops have died in the cause, the third highest absolute number of deaths of any foreign participating state. Given the rarity of foreign war casualties in Canada's history and Canada's relatively small population, the high casualties particularly affected Canadian views of the war in Afghanistan. This contributed to Canada's decision to withdraw its combat forces completely by the end of 2011.

In 2001, the Canadian defense minister provided unequivocal support for Canadian involvement in Afghanistan as the means to address the problem of terrorism. The discovery of the 2006 plot by an Al Qaeda cell to carry out terrorism in Ottawa and Toronto reaffirmed the salience of the global terrorist threat to Canadian territory. Conservative Prime Minister Stephen Harper framed Canada's policy in realist terms: Canada's

participation in Afghanistan, he argued, amounted to a projection of Canadian power in the national interest, which was to protect itself and support the United States, its closest ally. These policies reaffirm that Canada's security, borders, and economy are interdependent with those of the United States.

Liberals in Canada initially supported Canada's involvement in Afghanistan for reasons beyond the terrorist threat. Is not the establishment of democratic institutions a worthy goal? Doesn't Canada stand for human rights for women? Clearly, economic development and respect for human rights were severely compromised under the Taliban. Liberals might point to Canadian involvement in projects that served this agenda. In 2003 under Operation Athena, for example, Canadian troops helped improve civilian infrastructure by digging wells and repairing buildings.

But liberals and conservatives alike proved disappointed by the rate of progress. Representatives from the New Democratic Party, in particular, argued that the reconstruction of Afghanistan was being undermined by the counterinsurgency operations themselves. Women's groups pointed to few improvements in the emancipation of women—girls were (and are) still being attacked and sometimes maimed for attending school. As York University's Afghanistan Canada Research Group found, few development projects of any importance have been finished by the Canadian Forces or the Canadian International Development Agency. Liberals argued that the money would have been better spent on social programs at home. This lack of progress made the casualty figures more difficult to bear.

Radical dissatisfaction with Canadian policy focused on two arguments: Canada as subservient to U.S. hegemonic ambition and Canadian arms manufacturers' vested interest in violence. Radicals argued that Canadian involvement in what they viewed as America's war proved a sad illustration of the reluctance and unwillingness of the Canadian government to distance itself from the United States. In addition, Canadian and international businesses profited from the war. Canada is the sixth-largest arms supplier in the world. And any reconstruction will need to involve expansion of Afghanistan's potentially rich mining sector. The Canadian mining industry remains the world's leader in exploration and development.

Constructivists could point to the power of Canadian identity to explain the country's policies in Afghanistan. That identity revolves around Canada's global citizenship and its support of peacekeeping, multilateralism, NGOs, and human security issues. Feminists might have the stronger argument: Canada's transition from a liberal ("girly") to a conservative ("manly") government in 2006 was marked by a shift from UN support (including humanitarian and peacekeeping missions) to a more active and aggressive search and destroy effort after 2006.

By 2009, both popular and political sentiment had shifted. The relatively high casualties and lack of progress toward well-intentioned political objectives meant that Canadians no longer supported a combat role for their troops. As of 2013, Canadian involvement in Afghanistan involves strictly non-combat support. Canada remains rightly

Canadian forces stand outside an armored sleeping container in Kandahar.

proud of its efforts to bring security and prosperity to Afghanistan, but perhaps should be even prouder of a political process that led to a bipartisan and well-reasoned decision to withdraw combat forces as gracefully as possible in 2011.

FOR CRITICAL ANALYSIS

1. To what extent does Canada's relationship with the United States influence its foreign policy strategies?

2. Canada supported U.S. policy in Afghanistan, but not American policy in Iraq. Which theory best explains the difference in the Canadian positions?

3. Domestic factors help to explain Canada's choice of foreign policy. How?

4. Which explanation of Canada's position do you find most convincing? Why?

country were protected by U.S. troops even when civil disorder and looting of precious cultural monuments went unchecked. Restarting the oil pipelines was given priority over providing for the basic needs of the Iraqi people.

Radicals, especially dependency theorists, would not be at all surprised that the core states of the capitalist system—the United States and its allies—responded with force when Iraq threatened their critical interests in oil. Nor would they expect the end of the Cold War to make any difference in the structure of the system. The major changes in international power relationships that radicals seek—and predict—have not yet come.

A constructivist view of the 2003 Iraq War would focus on several factors. These theorists would emphasize the social construction of threat; how U.S. policy makers constructed Saddam Hussein and the purported WMD as threats to the United States, even though UN inspectors claimed that the weapons program had been dismantled. The "constructed" nature of the threat becomes evident when comparing Iraq to Israel or Great Britain, both of which possess nuclear weapons but are not considered "threatening" and are in fact close allies. The rhetoric of the threat accelerated as Saddam was portrayed as an evil tyrant, having power beyond materialist considerations. Constructivists would also point to the importance of legitimacy. The United States recognized the need for legitimacy for its actions, being socialized into those norms. That explains the considerable effort the United States expended in trying to obtain UN Security Council approval for the invasion, though in the long run, those efforts failed. In constructivist thinking, international organizations such as the UN play a powerful legitimizing and socializing role in international relations.

In Sum: Seeing the World through Theoretical Lenses

How each of us sees international relations depends on our own theoretical lens. Do you see events through a realist framework? Are you inclined toward a liberal interpretation? Or do you adhere to a radical or constructivist view of the world? These theoretical perspectives differ not only in whom they identify as key actors, but also in their views about the individual, the state, and the international system—the three levels of analysis. Equally important, these perspectives support different views about the possibility and desirability of change—and in particular war and peace—in the international system.

In the next four chapters, we examine in more detail how each of these perspectives sees the international system, the state, the individual, and international organizations. We begin with the most general level of analysis—the international system.

Discussion Questions

1. Choose a current event. Describe and explain that event using the three levels of analysis.

2. Is President Barack Obama a realist, a liberal, or a radical? Provide evidence to support your position.

3. A realist and a liberal are discussing the role of domestic politics in influencing international outcomes. Re-create that conversation, highlighting the differing perspectives.

4. Constructivists assert that the power of norms and ideas is continuously shaping and reshaping state behavior. Select a political idea — equality, democracy, or human rights. How has that idea been changed over time? How has state behavior changed?

Key Terms

bandwagoning (p. 83)

collective security (p. 88)

constructivism (p. 95)

dependency theorists (p. 94)

hypotheses (p. 76)

institutions (p. 86)

levels of analysis (p. 77)

liberalism (p. 86)

multinational
corporations (MNCs) (p. 94)

national interest (p. 79)

neoliberal institutionalism (p. 88)

neorealism (p. 83)

prisoner's dilemma (p. 88)

radicalism (p. 92)

rational actors (p. 80)

realism (p. 79)

theory (p. 76)

unitary actor (p. 80)

In 1999, heads of state celebrated the 50th anniversary of the North Atlantic Treaty Organization. International relations theorists debate the role of international organizations such as NATO in the international system. While realists focus on the distribution of power among states, liberals and constructivists believe that international institutions can lead to system-level change.

O4

THE INTERNATIONAL SYSTEM

- *Why is the concept of a system a powerful descriptive and explanatory device?*

- *What concepts do realists employ to analyze the international system?*

- *How does a liberal theorist view the international system?*

- *How do radicals view the international system? Constructivists?*

- *How does each of the contending theoretical perspectives explain change in the international system?*

- *What are the problems and/or weaknesses with the notion of the international system?*

The Notion of a System

Each of the contending theoretical perspectives examined in Chapter 3 described an international system. For realists and radicals, the concept of an international system is vital to their analyses, whereas for liberals, the international system is less precise as an explanatory mechanism and less consequential. For constructivists, the concept of an international system is tied to notions of change.

To understand the international system, the notion of a system itself must be clarified. Broadly defined, a **system** is an assemblage of units, objects, or parts united by some form of regular interaction. The concept of systems is essential to the physical and biological sciences; systems are composed of different interacting units, whether at the micro (cell, plant, animal) or the macro (natural ecosystem or global climate) level. Because these units interact, a change in one unit causes changes in the others. With their interacting parts, systems tend to respond in regularized ways; their actions have patterns. Boundaries separate one system from another, but there can be exchanges across these boundaries. A system can break down when changes within it become so significant that in effect a new system emerges.

In the 1950s, the behavioral revolution in the social sciences and the growing acceptance of political realism in international relations led scholars to conceptualize international politics as a system, using the language of systems theory. Beginning with the supposition that people act in regularized ways and that their patterns of interaction with each other are largely habitual, both realists and behavioralists made the conceptual leap that international politics is a system whose major actors are individual states.[1] This notion of a system is embedded in ideas of the major theoretical schools of international relations. Of particular interest is explaining how change occurs.

The International System According to Realists

Political realists have clear notions of the international system and its essential characteristics. All realists characterize the international system as anarchic; while not chaotic, there is no overarching hierarchy. No authority exists above the state; the state is sovereign. This anarchic structure constrains the actions of decision makers and affects the distribution of capabilities among the various actors. Realists differ among themselves, however, about the degree of a state's autonomy in the international system. Traditional or classical realists acknowledge that states act and shape the international system,

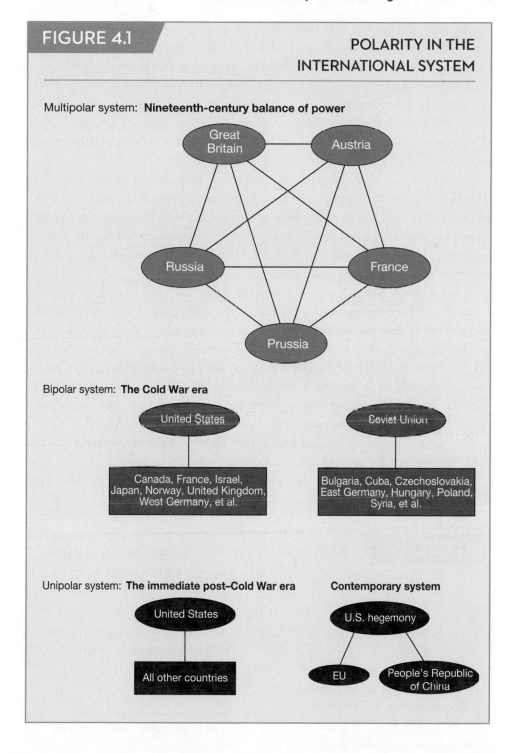

FIGURE 4.1

POLARITY IN THE
INTERNATIONAL SYSTEM

Multipolar system: **Nineteenth-century balance of power**

Great Britain · Austria · Russia · France · Prussia

Bipolar system: **The Cold War era**

United States — Canada, France, Israel, Japan, Norway, United Kingdom, West Germany, et al.

Soviet Union — Bulgaria, Cuba, Czechoslovakia, East Germany, Hungary, Poland, Syria, et al.

Unipolar system: **The immediate post–Cold War era**

United States — All other countries

Contemporary system

U.S. hegemony — EU · People's Republic of China

whereas neorealists or structural realists believe that states are constrained by the structure of the international system. Yet for both, anarchy is the basic ordering principle. Each state in the system must, therefore, look out for its own interests above all.

In order to characterize the international system, realists use the dimension of polarity. System polarity simply describes the distribution of capabilities among states in the international system by counting the number of "poles" (states or groups of states) where power is concentrated. There are at least three types of system polarity: multipolarity, bipolarity, and unipolarity (see Figure 4.1).

If there are a number of influential actors in the international system, a balance-of-power, or multipolar, system is formed. In a classical balance of power, the actors are exclusively states, and there should be at least five of them. The nineteenth-century balance of power—among Great Britain, Russia, Prussia, France, and Austria—is the real-world antecedent discussed in Chapter 2. In multipolar systems, several states—at least three or more—enjoy relative power parity.

In a balance-of-power system, the essential norms are clear to each of the state actors. The In Focus box below lists those basic norms of behavior. If an essential actor does not follow these norms, the balance-of-power system may become unstable. If the number of states declines to three, stability is threatened, because coalitions between any two are possible, which would leave the third alone and weak. In balance-of-power systems, alliances are formed for a specific purpose, have a short duration, and shift according to advantage rather than ideology. Any wars that do break out are probably limited in nature, designed to preserve the balance of power.

In bipolar systems, the essential norms are different. In the bipolar system of the Cold War, each of the blocs (the North Atlantic Treaty Organization, or NATO, and the Warsaw Pact) sought to negotiate rather than fight, to fight minor wars rather than

IN FOCUS

BASIC NORMS OF A BALANCE-OF-POWER SYSTEM

- Any actor or coalition that tries to assume dominance must be constrained.

- States want to increase their capabilities by acquiring territory, increasing their population, or developing economically.

- Negotiating is better than fighting.

- Fighting is better than failing to increase capabilities, because no one else will protect a weak state.

- Other states are viewed as potential allies.

- States seek their own national interests, defined in terms of power.

The Berlin Wall, which divided Soviet-controlled East Berlin from Allied-controlled West Berlin, was one symbol of the bipolar system that characterized the Cold War. Despite the tension between the two poles, the Cold War stayed "cold," which some realists take as evidence of the stability of a bipolar system.

major ones, and to fight major wars rather than fail to eliminate the rival bloc, although the Cold War never erupted into a "hot" war. In a bipolar system, alliances tend to be long term, based on relatively permanent, not shifting, interests. In a tight bipolar system, international organizations either do not develop or are completely ineffective, as the United Nations was during the height of the Cold War. In a looser bipolar system, international organizations may develop primarily to mediate between the two blocs, and individual states within the looser coalitions may try to use the international organizations for their own advantage. During much of the Cold War era, particularly in the 1950s and 1960s, the international system was bipolar—the United States, its allies in NATO, and Japan faced the Soviet Union and its Warsaw Pact allies. But over the course of the Cold War, the relative tightness or looseness of the bipolar system varied, as powerful states such as the People's Republic of China and France pursued independent paths.

Another possibility is that the international system is unipolar, that is, one state commands overwhelming capabilities in the international system, by virtue of size, economic and/or military capability, or organizational competence. Immediately after

the Gulf War in 1991, many states, including the United States' closest allies and virtually all developing states, grew concerned that the international system had become
unipolar. After all, the defense expenditures of the United States were greater than
those of the next 15 states combined; its economy was three times stronger than those
of the next three economies combined. With that superiority, other states were worried that there might be no effective counterweight to the power of the United States.
This concern remains in the twenty-first century. There is little debate as to whether
the United States still commands overwhelming capabilities, but there is much more
discussion over whether the United States can translate those power capabilities into
effective power. In relative terms, U.S. dominance is on the decline. China, Japan,
and the European Union are rising economically, as are Brazil and India, even though
U.S. military expenditures go unchallenged. The trend clearly suggests that although
the United States remains the unipole in absolute terms, its ability to exercise hegemony is being challenged by other states.

The type of international system in place at any given time has implications for
system management and stability. Are certain polarities more manageable and hence
more stable than others? Are wars more likely to occur in bipolar systems, multipolar
systems, or unipolar systems? These questions have dominated much of the discussion
among realists, but the studies of these relationships are inconclusive.

Bipolar systems are very difficult to regulate formally, because neither uncommitted
states nor international organizations are able to direct the behavior of either of the two
poles. Informal regulation may be easier. If either of the blocs is engaged in disruptive
behavior, the consequences are immediately evident, especially if one of the blocs gains in
strength or position as a result. Kenneth Waltz, for one, argues that because of this visibility,
the bipolar international system is the most stable structure in the long run: the two sides
are "able both to moderate the other's use of violence and to absorb possibly destabilizing
changes that emanate from uses of violence that they do not or cannot control."[2] In such a
system, there is a clear difference in the amount of power held by each pole compared with
that held by the other state actors. Because of the power disparity, each of the two sides
is able to focus its activity almost exclusively on the other. Each can anticipate the other's
actions and accurately predict its responses because of their history of repeated interactions.
Each tries to preserve this balance of power in order to preserve itself and the bipolar system. In 2012, Waltz reprised a similar argument, "Why Iran Should Get the Bomb." He
argues that Israel's nuclear capability is destabilizing the region. "If Iran goes nuclear, Israel
and Iran will deter each other, as nuclear powers always have." That would bring stability.[3]

Pointing to the stability attained in the bipolar Cold War system, John Mearsheimer
provoked controversy by suggesting that the world would miss the stability and predictability that the Cold War forged. With the end of the Cold War bipolar system,
Mearsheimer argued, more interstate conflicts would develop and hence more possibilities for war. He felt that deterrence would be more difficult and miscalculations more

⬆⬇ YOU DECIDE

Many international relations theorists believe that the likelihood of peace and war among states depends on how power is distributed in the international system: Is power shared among three or more states or coalitions (multipolar), between two states or coalitions (bipolar), or does one "hyperpower" dominate (unipolar)? As we have seen, different theorists make intriguing and even well-supported claims for their argument that certain distributions lead to peace while others increase the likelihood of war. But critics have pointed out that the concept of polarity, while sound analytically, is actually difficult to measure with precision. Thinking about today and beyond, how would you characterize the distribution of power in the international system? Is it unipolar, bipolar, or multipolar?

If you argue that the world is going to be unipolar, you must first define what you mean by "power": What are the sources of the unipole's unmatched power? You should also consider how unipolarity differs from the realist notion of leviathan (an abrogation of the condition of anarchy).

You might instead argue the world is bipolar, but perhaps the poles have yet to consolidate: the People's Republic of China appears to be gaining power rapidly, you might note, and within another decade might equal and perhaps overtake the United States as a superpower. As China rises, you might argue, many of its neighbors, including Russia and India, might feel threatened enough to ally themselves more strongly with the United States or with China, thus strengthening your argument that the world is becoming more bipolar rather than unipolar.

Finally, you might take the position that the world is actually multipolar: Europe, Africa, India, Russia, China, the United States, and Japan all seem destined to be or remain as major power poles in a re-aligned interstate system. The situation looks quite different from the bipolarity of the Cold War, you might think, as the world no longer divides neatly into two cohesive and competing camps.

YOU DECIDE: What will the world beyond today look like in terms of the distribution of power? What sort of power or powers might matter the most? Military power? Economic power? The power of ideas? Finally, what do you expect the impact of this distribution of power might be on the likelihood of peace and war? How might this affect you in your daily life?

probable. He drew a clear policy implication: "The West has an interest in maintaining peace in Europe. It therefore has an interest in maintaining the Cold War order, and hence has an interest in the continuation of the Cold War confrontation; developments that threaten to end it are dangerous. ... A complete end to the Cold War would create more problems than it would solve."[4] Most analysts do not agree with this provocative conclusion, partly because factors other than polarity can affect system stability.

Theoretically, in multipolar, or balance-of-power, systems, the regulation of system stability ought to be easier than in bipolar systems. The whole purpose of the balancer, as Great Britain was in the nineteenth century, is to act as a regulator for the system, stepping in to correct a perceived imbalance. For example, Great Britain intervened in the Crimean War of 1854–55, opposing Russia on behalf of Turkey. Under multipolarity, numerous interactions take place among all the various parties, and thus each has less opportunity to dwell on a specific relationship. Interaction by any one state actor with other states leads to crosscutting loyalties and alliances and therefore moderates hostility or friendship with any other single state actor. States are less likely to respond to the arms buildup of just one party in the system, and so war becomes less likely.

In contrast, hegemonic stability theorists claim that unipolarity, when the hegemon is willing to act, leads to the most stable international system. In *The Rise and Fall of the Great Powers,* the historian Paul Kennedy argues that it was the hegemony of Britain in the nineteenth century and that of the United States in the immediate post–World War II era that led to the greatest stability.[5] Other proponents of this theory, such as Robert O. Keohane, contend that hegemonic states are willing to pay the price of enforcing norms, unilaterally if necessary, to ensure the continuation of the system that benefits them. When the hegemon loses material capability and is no longer willing to exercise power, then system stability is jeopardized.[6]

It is clear, then, that realists do not agree among themselves as to the relationship between polarity and stability. Individual and group efforts to test this relationship have been inconclusive. The Correlates of War project (discussed in Chapter 1) did test two hypotheses flowing from the polarity-stability debate. J. David Singer and Melvin Small hypothesized that the greater the number of alliance commitments in the system, the more war the system will experience. They also hypothesized that the closer the system is to bipolarity, the more war it will experience. On the basis of the data between 1815 and 1945, however, neither argument was proven valid across the whole time span. During the nineteenth century, alliance commitments prevented war, whereas in the twentieth century, proliferating alliances seemed to predict war.[7] Other evidence from the 1970s suggests that although U.S. economic prowess declined in relative terms, the international system itself remained stable; system stability is not dependent solely on one power.[8]

Can a unipolar system endure? One group of scholars posits that if the unipole is satisfied with the status quo, the system is more likely to endure and be stable. But if the state becomes fearful and opportunistic, if it underproduces public goods and pursues more parochial interests, then the stability of the international order may be threatened.[9]

Realists and International System Change

Although realists value the continuity of systems, they recognize that international systems do change, as described earlier. Why do systems change? Realists attribute system change either to changes in the actors and hence the distribution of power or to exogenous changes, those emanating from outside the system.

Changes in either the number of major actors or the relative power relationship among those actors may result in a fundamental change in the international system. Wars are usually responsible for such fundamental changes in power relationships. For example, the end of World War II brought the relative decline of Great Britain and France, even though they were the victors. The war also signaled the end not only of Germany's and Japan's imperial aspirations but of their basic national capabilities as well. Their militaries were soundly defeated; their civil society was destroyed and their infrastructure demolished. Two other powers emerged in dominant positions—the United States, now willing to assume the international role that it had shunned after World War I, and the Soviet Union, buoyed by its victory although economically weak. The international system had fundamentally changed; the multipolar world had been replaced by a bipolar one.

Robert Gilpin, in *War and Change in World Politics,* sees another mechanism of system change. States grow at uneven rates because states respond differently to political, economic, and technological developments. It is those uneven rates that eventually lead to redistribution of power and thus change the international system. For example, the rapidly industrializing East Asian states—South Korea, Taiwan, and Hong Kong (now part of China)—have responded to technological change the fastest. By responding rapidly and with single-mindedness, these states have improved their relative positions. Thus, characteristics of the international system can be changed by the actions of a few.[10]

Exogenous changes may also lead to a shift in the international political system. Advances in technology—the instruments for oceanic navigation, the airplane for transatlantic crossings, and satellites and rockets for the exploration of space, for example—not only have expanded the boundaries of accessible geographic space, but also have brought about changes in the boundaries of the international political system. With these came an explosion of new state actors, reflecting different political interests and different cultural traditions.

No technological change has had more of an impact on the international system than the development of nuclear weapons and their use in warfare. The destructiveness of these weapons, their inability to discriminate between combatants and civilians,

THEORY IN BRIEF	THE REALIST PERSPECTIVE ON THE INTERNATIONAL SYSTEM
CHARACTERIZATION	Anarchic
ACTORS	State is primary actor
CONSTRAINTS	Polarity
POSSIBILITY OF CHANGE	Slow change when the balance of power shifts or technological change occurs

and their evident harm to future generations are all characteristics that have led policy makers to change the rules of the game. During the Cold War, this meant that the superpowers did not fight directly but preferred to spar through non-nuclear proxies using conventional military technology, as discussed in Chapter 2. Since nuclear weapons have not been used since 1945, they are no longer seen as credible in some circles. Nevertheless, they remain greatly feared, and efforts by non-nuclear states to develop such weapons, or even the threat to do so, have met sharp resistance, as occurred when North Korea and Iran announced their intentions to become nuclear. The nuclear states do not want a change in the status quo; in their view, nuclear proliferation, particularly in the hands of "rogue" states such as North Korea and Iran, leads to international system instability.

Thus, in the view of realists, international systems can change, yet the inherent bias among realist interpretations is for continuity. All realists agree that there are patterns of change in the system, although they may disagree about what time frame to look at in order to study the changes. Efforts by realists to test many of the ideas arising from their notions about the international system have proven inconclusive.

The International System According to Liberals

The international system is less consequential as an explanatory level of analysis in the view of liberals. It is therefore not surprising to find at least three different conceptions of the international system in liberal thinking.

The first conception sees the international system not as an unchanging structure but as an interdependent system, in which multiple and fluid interactions occur among different parties and where various actors learn from the interaction. Actors in this process include not only states but also international governmental organizations (such as the United Nations), nongovernmental organizations (such as Human Rights Watch), multinational corporations, and substate actors (such as parliaments and bureaucracies). Each different type of actor has interactions with all of the others. With so many different kinds of actors, a plethora of national interests defines the liberal international system. Although security interests, so dominant for realists, are also important to liberals, other interests such as economic and social issues are considered, depending on the time and circumstance. In their book *Power and Interdependence,* the political scientists Robert Keohane and Joseph Nye describe the international system as an interdependent system in which the different actors are both sensitive to (affected by) and vulnerable to (suffering costly effects from) the actions of others. Interdependent systems have multiple channels connecting states; these channels exist among governmental elites, nongovernmental elites, and transnational organizations. Multiple issues and agendas arise in the interdependent system. Military force may be useful in some situations but is not useful for all issues.[11]

Negotiating and coordinating in the liberal international system often occurs through **multilateralism**. Multilateralism is based on core principles, such as the collective security system. Briefly, collective security rests on the idea that peace is indivisible: a war against one is a war against all, meaning that the international community is obligated to respond. That idea will be examined in greater detail in Chapter 8, as it is a key liberal approach to war and strife. Thus, the possibility of coordinating behavior through multilateralism is a key component of the liberal view of the international system.

THEORY IN BRIEF   THE LIBERAL PERSPECTIVE ON THE INTERNATIONAL SYSTEM

CHARACTERIZATION	Three liberal interpretations: interdependence among actors, an international order, neoliberal institutionalism
ACTORS	States, international governmental institutions, nongovernmental organizations, multinational corporations, substate actors
CONSTRAINTS	Interdependence; institutions
POSSIBILITY OF CHANGE	Low likelihood of radical change, but may occur; constant incremental change as actors are involved in new relationships

A second liberal conception sees the international system in terms of a specific international order. Building on the tradition of Immanuel Kant and U.S. President Woodrow Wilson, as discussed in Chapter 3, this view holds that a liberal international order governs arrangements among states with basic rules and principles, similar to the principles that realists see under varying conditions of polarity. But unlike the realists principles, this order is an acknowledged order; it is not just patterned behavior or some interconnections. In this order, there is a key role for institutions. As John Ikenberrry in *After Victory* argues, the acknowledged goal of a dominant power in this international order is to establish rules that are "both durable and legitimate, but rules and arrangements that also serve the long-term interests of the leading state."[12] To do that, the dominant power limits its own autonomy and agrees to make credible commitments.

A third liberal view of the international system is held by neoliberal institutionalists. Neoliberal institutionalists see the international system as anarchic and acknowledge that each individual state acts in its own self-interest, similar to realist thinking. But neoliberal institutionists draw different conclusions about state behavior in the international system. It may be a cooperative system, wherein states choose to cooperate because they realize that they will have future interactions with the same actors, as explained in Chapter 3. Those repeated interactions provide the motivation for states to create international institutions, which in turn moderate state behavior, providing a guaranteed framework for interactions and a context for bargaining. International institutions provide focal points for coordination and serve to make state commitments more credible by specifying what is expected, thereby encouraging states to establish reputations for compliance. Thus, for neoliberals, institutions have important and independent effects on interstate interactions, both by providing information and by framing actions, but they do not necessarily affect states' underlying motivations. The international system may be anarchic but cooperation may emerge through institutions.

Liberals and International System Change

All liberals acknowledge and welcome incremental change in the international system. Liberals see change as coming from several sources. First, changes in the international system occur as the result of exogenous technological developments, that is, progress occurring independently, outside the control of actors in the system. For example, changes in communication and transportation are responsible for the increasing level of interdependence among states within the international system.

Second, change may occur because of changes in the relative importance of different issue areas. Although realists give primacy to issues of national security, liberals identify the relative importance of other issue areas. Specifically, in the last decades of the twentieth century, economic issues replaced national security issues as the leading topic of the international agenda. In the twenty-first century, transnational concerns such as human rights, the environment, and health have assumed a much more prominent role. These are fundamental changes in the international system, according to most liberal thinking.

Third, change may occur when new actors, including multinational corporations, nongovernmental organizations, or other participants in global civil society augment or replace state actors. The various new actors may enter into new kinds of relationships and may alter both the international system and state behaviors. These types of changes are compatible with liberal thinking and are discussed by liberal writers. And, like their realist counterparts, liberal thinkers also acknowledge that change *may* occur in the overall power structure among the states. In contrast, radicals *advocate* major changes.

The International System According to Radicals

Whereas realists define the international system in terms of its polarity and stability, radicals seek to describe and explain the structure in totally different terms. Hence radicals advocate for a different future.

Radicals describe the structure of the international system by stratification. **Stratification** refers to the uneven division of resources among different groups

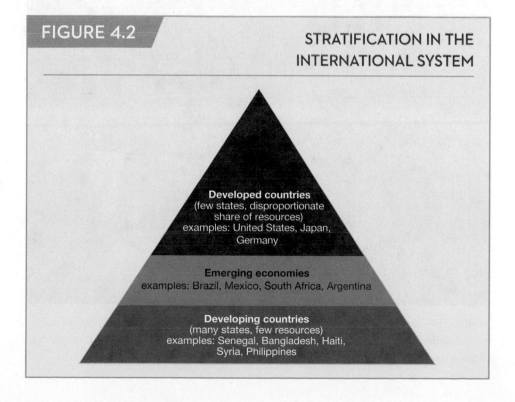

FIGURE 4.2   STRATIFICATION IN THE INTERNATIONAL SYSTEM

Developed countries
(few states, disproportionate share of resources)
examples: United States, Japan, Germany

Emerging economies
examples: Brazil, Mexico, South Africa, Argentina

Developing countries
(many states, few resources)
examples: Senegal, Bangladesh, Haiti, Syria, Philippines

of states. The international system is stratified according to which states have vital resources, such as oil or military strength or economic power. Stratification is the key to understanding the radicals' notion of the international system.

Different international systems have had varying degrees of stratification. Historically system stratification is extensive. According to one set of measures, several of the world's powers (the United States, Japan, Germany, France, Britain, Russia, and China) account for about one-half of the world's total gross domestic product (GDP). The other 180 plus states share the other half (see Figure 4.2). From the stratification of power and resources comes the division between the haves, loosely characterized as the **North**, and the have-nots, states largely located in the **South**. This distinction is vital to the discussion of international political economy found in Chapter 9.

Stratification of resources and hence influence has implications for the ability of a system to regulate itself, as well as for system stability. When the dominant powers are challenged by those states just below them in terms of access to resources, the system may become highly unstable. For example, Germany's and Japan's attempts to obtain and reclaim resources during the 1930s led to World War II. Such a group of second-tier powers has the potential to win a confrontation, but the real underdogs in a severely stratified system do not (although they can cause major disruptions). The rising

With a GDP per capita of approximately $1,500, Nigeria is one of the "have-nots" in the radical understanding of the international system. Despite its wealth of natural resources, Nigeria has been unable to successfully develop out of poverty.

THEORY IN BRIEF / THE RADICAL PERSPECTIVE ON THE INTERNATIONAL SYSTEM

CHARACTERIZATION	Highly stratified
ACTORS	Capitalist states vs. developing states
CONSTRAINTS	Capitalism; stratification
POSSIBILITY OF CHANGE	Radical change desired but limited by the capitalist structure

powers, especially those that are acquiring resources, seek first-tier status and are willing to fight wars to get it. If the challengers do not begin a war, the top powers may do so to quell the threat of a power displacement.

For Marxists, as well as most other radicals, crippling stratification in the international system is caused by capitalism. Capitalism structures the relationship between the advantaged and the disadvantaged, empowering the rich and disenfranchising the weak. Marxists assert that capitalism breeds its own instruments of domination, including international institutions whose rules are structured by capitalist states to facilitate capitalist processes, multinational corporations whose headquarters are in capitalist states but whose loci of activity are in dependent areas, and even individuals (often leaders) or classes (the national bourgeoisie) residing in weak states who are co-opted to participate in and perpetuate an economic system that places the masses in a permanently dependent position.

Radicals believe that the greatest amount of resentment will arise in systems where the stratification is most extreme. There, the poor are likely to be not only resentful but also aggressive. They want change, but the rich have very little incentive to change their behavior. The call for the **New International Economic Order (NIEO)** was voiced by radicals (and some liberal reformers) in the 1970s in most developing countries. The poorer, developing states of the South, underdogs with a dearth of resources, sought fundamental changes that would enhance their economic development and control over their own natural resources, thus increasing their power relative to the North.

In short, radicals believe that great economic disparities are built into the structure of the international system and that all actions and interactions are constrained by this structure. But some radicals recognize that transitions may occur. The hegemonic Dutch of the eighteenth century were replaced by the British in the nineteenth century and by the Americans in the twentieth. Change may occur in the semiperiphery and periphery, as states change their positions relative to each other. Capitalism goes through cycles of growth and expansion, as occurred during the age of colonialism and imperialism, followed by periods of contraction and decline. So capitalism itself is a dynamic force for change, though radicals do not view those changes in a positive light.

But can the capitalist system itself be changed? In other words, is system transformation—such as the change from the feudal to the capitalist system—possible? Here, radicals differ among themselves. Some are quite pessimistic, others more optimistic. Just as realists disagree among themselves about policy implications, radicals disagree about the likelihood that the system stratification that they all abhor can be altered.

Constructivism and Change

Constructivists argue that the whole concept of an international system is a European idea. They hold that nothing can be explained by international material structures alone. Martha Finnemore in *The Purpose of Intervention* suggests that there have been different international orders with changing purposes, different views of threat, and reliance on different ways to maintain order. She traces at least four European international orders: an eighteenth-century balance order; a nineteenth-century concert order; a sphere-of-influence system for much of the twentieth century; and after the end of the Cold War, an evolving new order whose purposes are the promotion of liberal democracy, capitalism, and human rights. Constructivists agree with other theorists that power matters in the international system, but they propose that what "power" means can change over time. As Finnemore writes, "[W]hat made 1815 a concert and 1950 a cold war was not the material distribution of capabilities but the shared meanings and interpretations participants imposed on those capabilities."[13]

Constructivists see not a material structure in the international system but rather a socially constructed process. While the prominent constructivist Alexander Wendt in *Social Theory of International Politics* agrees with the fundamental premise of realists that the system is anarchic, he contends that the whole notion of anarchy is socially constructed: anarchy is what states make of it.[14] The meaning of anarchy is not constant across geographic space or through time. Anarchy leads to no particular outcome. Neither does sovereignty or balance of power objectively exist. States debate anarchy's meaning and in turn give it meaning. Thus, constructivists reject the notion that the international system gives rise to objective rules or principles.

Constructivists believe that what does change are social norms, although not all norm changes will be transforming. Social norms can be changed both through actions of the collective and through individuals. Collectively, norms may change through coercion, but most likely through international institutions, law, and social movements. At the individual level, change occurs through persuasion and through internationalization of the new norms. So although material capabilities do matter in explaining change, just as realists and many liberals argue, "why one order emerges rather than another" can only be seen, Finnemore argues, "by examining the ideas, culture, and social purpose of the actors involved."[15]

Constructivists, then, are interested in analyzing the major changes in the normative structure: how the use of force has evolved over time, how the view of who is human has changed, and how ideas about democracy and human rights have internationalized and how states have been socialized in turn.

Advantages and Disadvantages of the International System as a Level of Analysis

For adherents of all theoretical perspectives, using the international system as a level of analysis has clear advantages. The language of systems theory allows comparison and contrasts between systems: the international system at one point in time may be compared with one at another point in time; international systems may be compared with internal state systems; political systems may be contrasted with social or even biological systems. How these various systems interact is the focus of both the social and the natural sciences.

For all the sciences, three of the most significant advantages to this level of analysis lie in the comprehensiveness of systems theory. First, important aspects of the whole are more difficult to understand by reference to their parts. If systems interest you, then trying to understand them entirely by reference to their parts will prove misleading. Second, it enables scholars to organize the seemingly disjointed parts into a whole; it allows them to hypothesize about and then to test how the various parts, actors, and rules of the system are related and to show how change in one part of the system results in changes in other parts. In this sense, the notion of a system is a significant research tool. Third, it permits theorizing about change. Even though international relations theories have not proven very accurate at predicting change, paying attention to international system changes can force scholars and students to think about the possibilities for change and hypothesize about the future.

In short, systems theory is a holistic, or top-down, approach. Although it cannot explain events at the micro level — why a particular individual acts a certain way — it does allow plausible explanations at the more general level. For realists, generalizations derived from systems theory provide the fodder for prediction, the ultimate goal of all behavioral science. For liberals and radicals, these generalizations have definite normative implications; in the former case they affirm movement toward a positive system, and in the latter case they confirm pessimistic assessments about the place of states in the economically determined international system.

The International System: A View from China

Realists posit that the international system changes as great powers gain or lose power relative to other states. As China's economic and political power has grown, many scholars have speculated whether China will catch up to the United States, leading to a new bipolarity, or surpass the United States, becoming the new hegemon in a unipolar system. Chinese government officials have stated their intentions.

Following almost a century of seeing itself as a victim of the great powers and after decades of internal revolution when it was closed to the world, China is becoming a confident great power. The country wields increasing economic and political influence using both bilateral and multilateral diplomacy. China's interests are aligned quite closely with those of other major powers, although they are not parallel. The country now operates within the rules of the contemporary international system; it has become socialized into the prevailing international norms.

The economic revolution in China, its embrace of free market capitalism, and its opening to foreign investment and enterprise have led to almost four decades of unprecedented economic growth of more than 9 percent per year. Deng Xiaoping and the Chinese Communist Party learned from the policy mistakes of the Cultural Revolution and focused on economic liberalization as a path out of poverty for China's 1.3 billion citizens. As the world's second largest economy, it is in China's interest to continue this "peaceful rise," or *zhongguo heping jueqi*, serving as a viable economic model for many states.

China's participation in world trade regimes has increased its global presence to the benefit of all parties. China's accession to the World Trade Organization (WTO) and its Free Trade Agreement with the United States has allowed it to maximize economic output while demonstrating to the world that it can adhere to WTO regulations such as nondiscrimination policies, elimination of price controls, and revision of domestic laws to comply with WTO obligations. China is continuing its efforts to enforce new intellectual property laws. China is also now actively engaged in regional trade and economic agreements, particularly with South East Asian Nations (ASEAN) states and with Asia-Pacific Economic Cooperation (APEC).

China has acted responsibly toward both the advanced capitalist states and the developing world. China finances a large portion of American debt because of its large balance of trade surplus with the United States. During the 2008 international financial crisis, China refrained from putting pressure on the U.S. dollar and on interest rates. To help rebalance the international economy, China is encouraging domestic consumption, increasing workers' pay, and allowing its currency to appreciate gradually. Even though China has geopolitical disputes with Japan, the economic ties between the two countries remain strong.

Like many other states, China needs natural resources. Thus, China has forged relationships with states congruent with China's national interest. China is building relations with African countries by investing in infrastructure, technology, and natural resources, amounting to an estimated $40 billion. With trade of more than $166 billion, China is Africa's top business partner. China continues its relationships with resource-rich countries like Nigeria, Algeria, South Africa, Sudan, and Zambia. But China has expanded its interests into non-resource sectors in places like the Congo and Ethiopia. Chinese private companies, businessmen, and tourists are finding Africa fertile territory. Whereas the West colonized these lands and often stripped them of their resource wealth, China seeks a peaceful, mutually beneficial relationship. China does not interfere in the domestic affairs of other states or impose unwanted conditions on issues that are within the state's own responsibility. This illustrates that China is acting as a responsible global power.

Like all great powers, China has increased its military expenditures, although the United States spends six times more on defense than China. China will continue to modernize its nuclear forces and strengthen its second-strike abilities. It will develop cyberwarfare capabilities. But these advances may have been exaggerated by Western observers. After all, China's military began at a much lower baseline than that of other great powers.

China has chosen not to use its military capabilities. China has not fought to expand its territory. But China will defend its national interest consistent with the One-China policy: In China's view, Tibet, Taiwan, and the islands in the South China Seas including Diaoyu are part of China. China will oppose the designs of neighboring states, including Japan, Korea, Vietnam, and even the United States, who might refute those claims.

China has not engaged in military activities far from its shores. Unlike its principal rival, it has not invaded and occupied states thousands of miles away. China has not openly exercised its financial power, unlike its principal rival. And

China financed the construction of this stadium in Ndola, Zambia.

like other powers, China is now exercising its soft power. Over 300 Confucius Institutes have been established in almost 100 countries to promote Chinese language, culture, and exchanges. Meanwhile, China has acted responsibly to try to solve major international issues like the North Korea nuclear standoff. China has benefited from the international order of the last decades and is committed to a stable order.

FOR CRITICAL ANALYSIS

1. Why does China have an interest in sustaining the contemporary international system even if it does not dominate it?

2. How would an offensive realist react to China's explanation of its role in the international system?

3. China has consistently argued in favor of sovereignty and noninterference in the domestic affairs of states. How does this position support China's international role?

4. Constructivists argue that changes in norms lead to system change. Has China learned new norms? Or is it merely acting in its own self-interest, as realists suggest?

But systems theory also has some glaring weaknesses and inadequacies. The emphasis at the international system level means that politics is often neglected. The generalizations are broad and sometimes obvious. Who disputes that most states seek to maintain their relative capability or that most states prefer to negotiate rather than fight under all but a few circumstances? Who doubts that some states occupy a preeminent economic position that determines the status of all others?

International system theorists have always been hampered by the problem of boundaries. If they use the notion of the international system, do they mean the international *political* system? What factors lie outside of the system? In fact, much realist theory systematically ignores this critical question by differentiating several different levels within the system but only one international-system-level construct. Liberals do better, differentiating factors external to the system and even incorporating those factors into their expanded notion of an interdependent international system. Yet if you cannot clearly distinguish between what is inside and what is outside of the system, do you in fact have a system? Even more important, what shapes the system? What is the reciprocal relationship between international system constraints and unit (state) behavior? By way of contrast, constructivists do not acknowledge such boundaries. They argue that there is no natural or necessary distinction between the international system and the state or between international politics and domestic politics and no distinction between endogenous and exogenous sources of change.

Furthermore, the testing of system theories is very difficult. In most cases, theorists are constrained by a lack of historical information. After all, few systems theorists besides some radical and cyclical theorists discuss systems predating 1648. In fact, most begin with the nineteenth century. Those using earlier time frames are constrained both by a poor grounding in history and by glaring lapses in the historical record. Although these weaknesses are not fatal, they restrict scholars' ability to generalize their findings.

Perhaps the most fundamental critique is the attention paid to one international system in particular. Is not the idea of one international system really a Eurocentric notion? Here, the critics have a valid point. The idea of an international system evolved out of the statecentric, post-Westphalian world. In that world, the international system consisted of sovereign European states that shared common pre-Westphalian traditions: the Roman Empire, which had imposed order and unity by force on a large geographic expanse and used a common language, and the Christian tradition, as exemplified by the Catholic Church of the medieval era with its authority and law. From those common social roots, the idea of the international system arose. Some scholars, the so-called English school, call this system an **international society**, because it is grounded in a common culture that was a foundation for common rules and institutions. According to two of the principal architects, the scholars Hedley Bull and Adam Watson, although the international system comprises a group of independent political communities, an international society is more than that. In an international society, the various actors

THEORY IN BRIEF	CONTENDING PERSPECTIVES ON THE INTERNATIONAL SYSTEM			
	REALISM / NEOREALISM	LIBERALISM / NEOLIBERAL INSTITUTIONALISM	RADICALISM / DEPENDENCY THEORY	CONSTRUCTIVISM
CHARACTERIZATION	Anarchic	Three liberal interpretations: interdependence, international order, and neoliberal institutionalism	Highly stratified	International system exists as social construct
ACTORS	State is primary actor	States, international governmental institutions, nongovernmental organizations, substate actors	Capitalist states vs. developing states	Individuals matter; no differentiation between international and domestic
CONSTRAINTS	Polarity; distribution of power	Interdependence; institutions	Capitalism; stratification	Ongoing Interactions
POSSIBILITY OF CHANGE	Slow change when the balance of power shifts	Low possibility of radical change; constant incremental change as actors are involved in new relationships	Radical change desired but limited by the capitalist structure	Emphasis on change in social norms and identities

communicate; they consent to common rules and institutions and recognize common interests. Actors in international society share a common identity, a sense of "we-ness"; without such an identity, a society cannot exist.[16]

Yet were there not international systems—or more accurately international societies—beyond the European world? Perhaps those societies were based on other sets of rules and institutions. For example, various kingdoms flourished in China for centuries before unification in 200 BCE. Imperial China endured for 2,000 years, united around a common culture that the Chinese thought was the center of the universe. The Islamic peoples, too, shared a common identity as Islam spread across the Middle East to Africa, Asia, and even Europe. That social identity can be seen in the belief in the *umma*, or community of believers. The *umma* was symbolized by the institution of the caliphate, the Islamic political authority, and was an identity that overrode tribe, race, and even the state itself. That unity broke down in the division between Sunni and Shia, a dispute over who was the rightful successor to the Prophet Muhammad. Some advocate restoration of the caliphate as a renewal of Islamic civilization's former historical greatness. International relations scholars have often paid too little attention to non-European international societies.

As the Europe-based international system emerged as the most powerful and dominant one, how did other regions become part of it? Colonialism and the spread of capitalism by the European powers brought many areas into the new system, as traced in Chapter 2.

Struggles persist among these different international societies. The political scientist Samuel Huntington identified these struggles as civilizational, positing that there was not one international system sharing common culture and traditions, but different societies, or civilizations. He believed that variety would be the basis of international conflict.[17] Thus, although the notion of one international system may reflect power realities from the nineteenth century to the early years of the twenty-first, that idea is disputed because of its Eurocentric bias, its neglect of the international systems of "others," and the empirical difficulties involved in differentiating the international system and its component parts.

In Sum: From the International System to the State

Of all the theoretical approaches, the international system level of analysis receives the most attention from realists and radicals. For realists, the defining characteristic of the international system is polarity; for radicals, it is stratification. In both perspectives, the international system constrains state behavior. Realists generally view such constraints as positive, depending on the distribution of power, whereas for radicals the constraints are negative, preventing economically depressed states from achieving equality and justice. Liberals view the international system from a more neutral perspective as an arena and process for interaction. Constructivists take an evolutionary approach, emphasizing how changes in norms and ideas shape the system, seeing little differentiation between international and domestic systems and discounting the importance that other theorists attach to international system structure.

States and foreign policy decision makers operate within the confines of the international system. In the next chapter, we examine the state, models of state decision making, and challenges to the state.

Discussion Questions

1. Is the international system like physical or biological systems? How are these systems similar? How are they different?

2. Realists, liberals, radicals, and constructivists view sovereignty differently. Explain.

3. The realist view of the international system has been criticized as oriented to the status quo. To what extent is that critique valid? Is that characteristic desirable or not?

4. Neorealists and neoliberals agree on an essential characteristic of the international system. How do they disagree? Why is that disagreement important?

5. After the collapse of the Soviet Union, some theorists argued that Marxism had been discredited and was, in fact, dead. Is that true? How can radicalism help us explain some features of the international system?

6. What kind of international system would you like to live in? Why?

Key Terms

international society (p. 126)

multilateralism (p. 117)

New International Economic Order (NIEO) (p. 121)

North (p. 120)

South (p. 120)

stratification (p. 119)

system (p. 108)

The state is an important international actor, in part because of the resources it can command. States have many sources of power, including natural resource wealth, such as this iron ore in South Africa. States can trade their resources for currency to invest in education or build a military; or they can refuse to trade in order to hurt adversaries.

05

THE STATE

- *How is the state, the major actor in international relations, defined?*

- *What are the different views of the state held by the various theoretical perspectives?*

- *How is state power measured?*

- *What methods do states use to exercise their power?*

- *Do democracies behave differently from nondemocracies?*

- *What models help us explain how states make foreign policy decisions?*

- *What are the major contemporary challenges to the state?*

In thinking about international relations, the state is central. Much of the history traced in Chapter 2 was the history of how the state emerged from the post-Westphalian framework and developed in tandem with sovereignty and the nation. Two of the theoretical perspectives — realism and liberalism — acknowledge the primacy of the state. Yet despite this emphasis on the state, it is inadequately conceptualized. As the scholar James Rosenau laments, "All too many studies posit the state as a symbol without content, as an actor whose nature, motives, and conduct are so self-evident as to obviate any need for precise conceptualizing. Often, in fact, the concept seems to be used as a residual category to explain that which is otherwise inexplicable in macro politics."[1] We need to do better. How do states behave in international relations, and why do they matter?

The State and the Nation

For an entity to be considered a state, four fundamental legal conditions must be met. First, a state must have a territorial base, with geographically defined boundaries. Second, within its borders, a stable population must reside. Third, there should be a government to which this population owes allegiance. Finally, a state has to be recognized diplomatically by other states.

These legal criteria are not absolute and are subject to various interpretations. Most states do have a territorial base, though the precise borders are often the subject of dispute. Until the Palestinian Authority was given a measure of control over the West Bank and Gaza, for instance, Palestine was not territorially based. It was, however, given special observer status in international bodies and was viewed as a quasi state. In 2012, the territory was upgraded to nonvoting observer status in the UN General Assembly. Most states have a stable population, but migrant communities and nomadic peoples cross borders, as the Masai peoples of Kenya and Tanzania do, undetected by state authorities. Most states have some type of institutional structure for governance, but whether the people are obedient to it can be unknown, because of lack of information, or it can be problematic, because the institutional legitimacy of the government is constantly questioned. A state need not have a particular form of government, but most of its people must acknowledge the legitimacy of that government. In 2010, the people of Egypt told the international community that they no longer recognized the legitimacy of the government led by Hosni Mubarak, leading to demonstrations and ultimately the downfall of his government. Finally, other states must recognize the state diplomatically; but how many states' recognition does it take for this criterion to be fulfilled? The Republic of Transkei — a tiny piece of real estate carved out of South Africa — was recognized by just one state, South Africa; that proved insufficient to give Transkei status as a state, and the territory was soon reincorporated into South Africa.

Disputes between nations over state territories are a recurrent source of international conflict. Here, Palestinians plant an olive tree on land confiscated by Israel in the West Bank, which is claimed by both Israelis and Palestinians.

Some states are currently contested. In early 2008, Kosovo, once a semiautonomous part of Yugoslavia and later a province of Serbia, declared unilateral independence from Serbia. A constitution was accepted and a ministry of foreign affairs established. By the end of 2012, 100 states recognized Kosovo's independence, but not Serbia. While the supervisory International Civilian Office was closed in 2012, security is maintained by a NATO-led peacekeeping force. Abkhazia and Nagorno-Karabakh are also "quasi-countries teetering on the brink of statehood," which are in "the international community's prenatal ward."[2] So although the legal conditions for statehood provide a yardstick, that measuring stick is not absolute.

The definition of a state differs from that of a **nation**. A nation is a group of people who share a set of characteristics. Do a people share a common history and heritage, a common language and customs, or similar lifestyles? If so, then the people make up a nation. It was this feeling of commonality, of people uniting together for a cause, that provided the foundation for the French Revolution and spread to Central and South America and to central Europe. It was nationalism—the belief that nations should form their own states—that propelled the formation of a unified Italy and Germany in the nineteenth century. At the core of the concept of a nation is the notion that people with commonalities owe their allegiance to the nation and to its

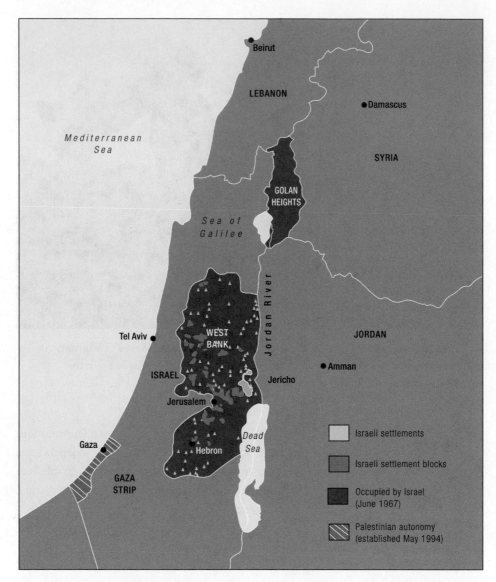

Central Middle Eastern Region, 2012

legal representative, the state. The recognition of commonalities among people (and hence of differences from other groups) spread with new technologies and education. When the printing press became widely used, the masses could read in their national languages; with improved methods of transportation, people could travel, witnessing firsthand similarities and differences among other groups. With better communications, elites could use the media to promote unity or sometimes to exploit differences.

Some nations, like the Danes and Italians, formed their own states. That coincidence between state and nation, the **nation-state**, is the foundation for national self-determination, the idea that peoples sharing nationhood have a right to determine how and under what conditions they should live. Other nations are spread among several states. For example, Germans resided and still live not only in a united Germany but in the far regions of eastern Europe; Somalis live in Kenya, Ethiopia, and Djibouti as well as in Somalia. Still other states have within their borders several different nations—India, Russia, and South Africa are prominent examples. In the United States and Canada, a number of different Native American nations are a part of the state, as are multiple immigrant communities. The state and the nation do not always coincide. Yet over time in the latter cases, a common identity and nationality have been forged, even in the absence of religious, ethnic, or cultural similarity. In the case of the United States, national values reflecting commonly held ideas are expressed in public rituals including reciting the Pledge of Allegiance, singing the national anthem, and volunteering in one's community.[3] States are both complex and constantly evolving.

Some of the hundreds of national subgroups around the world, which count some 900 million people, identify more with a particular culture or religion than with a particular state, often experiencing discrimination or persecution because of their identity. This situation is not new. The gradual disintegration of the Ottoman Empire between the 1830s and World War I reflected increasing ethnic demands for self-determination from Egypt and Greece to Albania, Montenegro, and Bulgaria.

Yet not all ethnonationalists aspire to the same goals. Some want recognition of a unique status, the right to speak and write a particular language or practice their religion, or special seats in representative bodies, as the Basques in Spain and France desire. Some seek solutions in federal arrangements, hoping to guarantee autonomy within an established state, as the Kurds have sought in Iraq. Yet the Kurds' 2009 constitution, proclaiming exclusive rights to oil and gas resources beneath their territory, suggests they may want more authority. Still other groups seek separation and the right to form their own state, as Catalonians in Spain expressed in mass demonstrations in 2012. The Republic of South Sudan, after two decades of civil war, became a separate state in 2011. And some prefer **irredentism**, joining with another state that is populated by fellow ethnonationalists.

One persistent dispute over the state and nation involves the People's Republic of China (PRC) and Taiwan, also called the Republic of China (ROC). After World War II, Mao Zedong and his communist revolutionaries took over the territory and government of mainland China, forcing the former Nationalist government to flee to Taiwan, a small island about 100 miles to the southeast. Both governments claimed to represent the Chinese nation. For ideological and geopolitical reasons, the United States originally recognized the ROC, while the Soviet Union recognized the PRC. Over time, however, the growing political and economic power of the PRC meant that the ROC was sidelined; notably, in 1972, the PRC assumed China's permanent seat in the Security Council at the United Nations. Today, the PRC is recognized by 171 states, while the ROC is recognized by only 23. The PRC has always maintained that Taiwan is an inseparable part of China, a policy it calls "the One China policy," which the United States supports. The relationship between China and Taiwan became more complicated after democracy was established in Taiwan in 1990, as one major political party supports independence for Taiwan while the other supports a continuation of the status quo. The so-called China question, the conflict over the state and nation of China, continues today.

Disputes over state territories and the desires of nations to form their own states have been major sources of instability and even conflict since the end of colonialism in Africa and the Middle East, and most recently after the breakups of the Soviet Union and Yugoslavia. Another of these intractable conflicts is that between Israeli Jews and Palestinian Arabs, who each claim the same territory. This conflict has been complicated by several factors—that Jews, Christians, Muslims, and Bahá'ís each claim certain land and monuments as sacred, the intense opposition from Arab states to the existence of the state of Israel, and Israel's gradual expansion of its territory through war and settlements. Since the founding of Israel in 1948, the Arab and Jewish peoples of Palestine have been involved in six interstate wars and three popular uprisings. Civilians on both sides have been harmed and killed, and many continue to live as refugees. This leads to a major debate: Should Israel and the Palestinian territories be divided into two separate independent states?

Contending Conceptualizations of the State

Just as the nation is more than a historic entity, the state is more than a legal entity. There are numerous competing conceptualizations of the state, many of which emphasize ideas absent from the legalistic approach.

Other concepts of the state include the following: The state is a normative order, a symbol for a particular society and the beliefs that bind the people living within its borders. It is also the entity that has a monopoly on the legitimate use of violence within a society. The state is a functional unit that takes on a number of important responsibilities, centralizing and unifying them. These perspectives of the state parallel the general international relations theories discussed in Chapters 3 and 4. For two of these theoretical perspectives, the state is paramount.

The Realist View of the State

Realists generally hold a statist, or state-centric, view. They believe that the state is an autonomous actor constrained only by the structural anarchy of the international system. The state enjoys sovereignty, that is, the authority to govern matters that are within its own borders and that affect its people, economy, security, and form of

IN FOCUS   THE REALIST VIEW OF THE STATE

The state is:

- an autonomous actor.
- constrained only by the anarchy of the international system.

- sovereign.
- guided by a national interest that is defined in terms of power.

government. As a sovereign entity, the state has a consistent set of goals—that is, a national interest—defined in terms of power. Different kinds of power can be translated into military power. Although power is of primary importance to realists, as we will see later in this chapter, ideas also matter in their estimation; ideology, for example, can determine the nature of the state, as with the North Korean state under communism. But in international relations, once the state (with power and ideas) acts, according to the realists, it does so as an autonomous, unitary actor.

The Liberal View of the State

In the liberal view, the state enjoys sovereignty but is not an autonomous actor. Just as liberals believe the international system is a process occurring among many actors, they see the state as a pluralist arena whose function is to maintain the basic rules of the game. These rules ensure that various interests (both governmental and societal) compete fairly and effectively in the game of politics. There is no single explicit or consistent national interest; there are many. These interests often compete against each other within a pluralistic framework. A state's national interests change over time, reflecting

IN FOCUS   THE LIBERAL VIEW OF THE STATE

The state is:

- a process, involving contending interests.
- a reflection of both governmental and societal interests.

- the repository of multiple and changing national interests.
- the possessor of fungible sources of power.

the interests and relative power positions of competing groups inside and sometimes also outside the state.

The Radical View of the State

Radicals offer two alternative views of the state, each emphasizing the role of capitalism and the capitalist class in the formation and functioning of the state. The *instrumental* Marxist view sees the state as the executing agent of the bourgeoisie. The bourgeoisie reacts to direct societal pressures, especially to pressures from the capitalist class. The *structural* Marxist view sees the state as operating within the structure of the capitalist system. Within that system, the state is driven to expand, not because of the direct pressure of the capitalists but because of the imperatives of the capitalist system. In neither view is there a national interest: state behavior reflects economic goals. In neither case is real sovereignty possible, because the state is continually reacting to external and internal capitalist pressures.

The Constructivist View of the State

Because constructivists see both national interests and national identities as social constructs, they conceptualize the state very differently from theorists with other perspectives. To constructivists, national interests are neither material nor given. They are ideational and ever-changing and evolving, both in response to domestic factors and in response to international norms and ideas. States share a variety of goals and values, which they are socialized into by international and nongovernmental organizations. Those norms can change state preferences, which in turn can influence state behavior. So, too, do states have multiple identities, including a shared understanding of national identity, which also changes, altering state preferences and hence state behavior. In short, the state "makes" the system and the system "makes" the state.[4]

IN FOCUS   THE RADICAL VIEW OF THE STATE

The state is:

- the executing agent of the bourgeoisie.

- influenced by pressures from the capitalist class.

- constrained by the structure of the international capitalist system.

Contrasting the Various Views of the State

The four theoretical conceptualizations of the state can be easily contrasted using the example of an important primary commodity—oil.[5]

A realist interpretation posits a uniform national interest that is articulated by the state. States recognize certain strategic commodities as vital for their national security. Thus, states desire stability in the availability and prices of these commodities. For example, the United States needs to be assured of a safe and secure supply of oil and seeks to obtain it at relatively uniform prices. When the United States negotiates in international forums with individual supplier states or with multinational companies, the national interest of the state defined in strategic terms is the bottom line of the negotiations. This is also the case with China. Oil is the engine of its rapidly expanding economy, and therefore it has forged strong bilateral ties with oil-exporting states such as Iran, Sudan, and Angola, among others.

Liberals believe that multiple national interests influence state actions: consumer groups desire oil at the lowest price possible; manufacturers, who depend on bulk supplies to run their factories, value a stable supply of oil, otherwise they risk losing their jobs; producers of oil, including domestic producers, want high prices, so that they will make profits and have incentives to reinvest in drilling. The state itself reflects no consistent viewpoint about the oil; its task is to ensure that the "playing field is level" and that the procedural rules are the same for the various players in the market. The substantive outcome of the game—which group's interests predominate—changes depending on circumstances and is of little import to the state. When negotiations occur, the state ensures that the various interests have a voice and provides a forum for the interactions. There is no single or consistent national interest: at times, it is low

IN FOCUS

THE CONSTRUCTIVIST VIEW OF THE STATE

The state is:

- a socially constructed entity.

- the repository of national interests that change over time.

- shaped by international norms that change preferences.

- influenced by changing national interests that shape and reshape identities.

- socialized by IGOs and NGOs.

consumer prices; at other times, stability of prices; and at still other times, high prices in order to stimulate domestic production.

In the radical perspective, a state's policy toward primary commodities reflects the interests of the owner capitalist class aligned with the bourgeoisie (in the instrumental Marxist view) and reflects the structure of the international capitalist system (in structural Marxist thinking). Both views would more than likely see the negotiating process as exploitative, where the weak (poor and dependent groups or states) are exploited for the advancement of strong capitalists or capitalist states. According to radical thinking, the international petroleum companies are the capitalists, aligned with hegemonic states. They are able to negotiate favorable prices, often to the detriment of weaker oil-producing states such as Mexico or Nigeria. Radicals may explain U.S. and European interests in the Middle East in terms of the need for a reliable petroleum and natural gas supply.

By way of contrast, although constructivists may pay little heed to materialist conceptions of power defined in terms of oil resources, they may try to tease out how the identities of states are forged by having such a valuable resource. Saudi Arabia and the Persian Gulf states have developed an identity based on a seemingly limitless, valuable resource. Oil permits them to merge that identity with their identity as Islamic states that export the faith to other countries.

Thus, each theory holds a different view about the state. These differences can be seen in four topic areas: the nature of state power (What is power? What are important sources of power?), the exercise of state power (the relative importance of different techniques of statecraft), how foreign policy is made (the statist versus the bureaucratic or the pluralist view of decision making), and the determinants of foreign policy (the relative importance of domestic versus international factors).

The Nature of State Power

States are critical actors because they have **power**, which is the ability not only to influence others but also to control outcomes so as to produce results that would not have occurred naturally. States have power with respect to each other and with respect to actors within the state. All theoretical perspectives acknowledge the importance of power. But each pays attention to different types of power. Realists, liberals, and radicals all conceptualize power in materialist terms, realists and radicals primarily in natural and tangible sources, while liberals also pay attention to intangible power sources. Constructivists emphasize the nonmaterialist sources found in the power of ideas, one of the intangible sources. All agree that power is multidimensional, dynamic, and situational.

Natural Sources of Power

Through the exercise of power, states have influence over others and can control the direction of policies and events. Whether power is effective at influencing outcomes depends, in part, on the **power potential** of each party. A state's power potential depends in part on its natural sources of power, which is critical to both realist and radical perspectives. The three most important natural sources of power potential are geographic size and position, natural resources, and population.

Geographic size and position were the natural sources of power recognized first by international relations theorists. A large geographic expanse gives a state automatic power potential (when we think of power, we think of large states — Russia, China, the United States, Australia, India, Canada, or Brazil, for instance). Long borders, however, may be a weakness: they must be defended, an expensive and often problematic task.

Two different views about the importance of geography in international relations emerged at the turn of the century within the realist tradition. In the late 1890s, the naval officer and historian Alfred Mahan (1840–1914) wrote of the importance of controlling the sea. He argued that the state that controls the ocean routes controls the world. To Mahan, sovereignty over land was not so critical as having access to and control over sea routes.[6] In 1904, the British geographer Sir Halford Mackinder (1861–1947) countered this view. To Mackinder, the state that had the most power was the one that controlled the Eurasian geographic "heartland": "He who rules Eastern Europe commands the Heartland of Eurasia; who rules the Heartland commands the World Island of Europe, Asia, and Africa, and who rules the World Island commands the world."[7]

Both views have empirical validity. British power in the eighteenth and nineteenth centuries was determined largely by its dominance on the seas, a power that allowed Britain to colonialize distant places, including India, much of Africa, and North and Central America. Russia's lack of easy access to the sea and its resultant inability to wield naval power has been viewed as a persistent weakness in that country's power potential. Control of key oceanic choke points — the Straits of Malacca, Gibraltar, and Hormuz; the Dardanelles; the Persian Gulf; and the Suez and Panama canals — is viewed as a positive indicator of power potential.

Yet geographic position in Mackinder's heartland of Eurasia has also proven to be a significant source of power potential. More than any other country, Germany has acted to secure its power through its control of the heartland of Eurasia, acting very clearly according to Mackinder's dictum, as interpreted by the German geographer Karl Haushofer (1869–1946). Haushofer, who had served in both the Bavarian and the German armies, was disappointed by Germany's loss in World War I. Arguing that

Germany could become a powerful state if it could capture the Eurasian heartland, he set out to make geopolitics a legitimate area for academic inquiry. He founded an institute and a journal, thrusting himself into a position as the leading supporter and proponent of Nazi expansion.

But geographic power potential is magnified or constrained by natural resources, a second source of natural power. Controlling a large geographic expanse is not a positive ingredient of power unless that expanse contains natural resources. Petroleum-exporting states such as Kuwait, Qatar, and the United Arab Emirates, which are geographically small but have a crucial natural resource, have greater power potential than their sizes would suggest. States need oil and are ready to pay dearly for it, and will even go to war when access to it is denied. States that have such valuable natural resources, regardless of their geographic size, wield power over states that do not. The United States, Russia, and South Africa exert vast power potential because of their diverse natural resources—oil, copper, bauxite, vanadium, gold, and silver. Russia has leveraged its power from its control of natural resources to influence political outcomes in other states. For instance, Russia cut off natural gas supplies to Ukraine, thereby slowing supplies to Europe, which gets one-quarter of its gas through Ukraine. The conflict, which began as a commercial dispute over pricing, has become a tool Russia can use to punish Ukraine for bringing an anti-Russian government into power during the 2005 Orange Revolution and for its rapprochement with the West. Mainland China, which supplies over 95 percent of the demand for so-called rare earth minerals essential in high-tech manufacturing, has been able to use its monopoly to deny access for political purposes and drive up prices. Yet China's monopoly may not last, as the high prices are leading to opening of new mines in Australia, the United States, India, and Vietnam. Even natural resource–based power may have its limits.

Of course, having a sought-after resource may prove a liability, making states targets for aggressive actions, as Kuwait soberly learned in 1990. Nor does the absence of natural resources mean that a state has no power potential; Japan is not rich in natural resources, but it has parlayed other elements of power so as to make itself an economic powerhouse.

Population is a third natural source of power. Sizable populations, such as those of China (1.3 billion people), India (1.2 billion), the United States (314 million), Indonesia (237 million), Brazil (192 million), and Russia (143 million), automatically give power potential, and often great power status, to a state. Although a large population produces a variety of goods and services, characteristics of that population (health status, age distribution, level of social services) may magnify or constrain state power. States with small, highly educated, skilled populations, such as Switzerland, Norway, Austria, and Singapore, can fill disproportionately large economic and political niches. States with large but relatively poor populations, such as Ethiopia (with 84 million people but a gross national product of only $390 per capita), can exercise less power. States with a declining population or a rapidly aging one may in the future suffer from

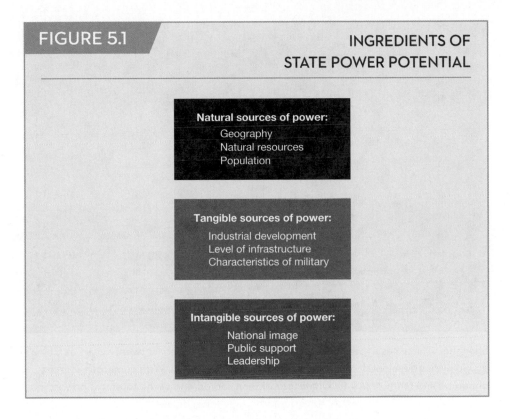

FIGURE 5.1

INGREDIENTS OF STATE POWER POTENTIAL

Natural sources of power:
Geography
Natural resources
Population

Tangible sources of power:
Industrial development
Level of infrastructure
Characteristics of military

Intangible sources of power:
National image
Public support
Leadership

a decline in this power source: China and Russia both are predicted to have a rapidly aging population needing financial support from a declining working population, thus undermining one natural source of power.

The degree to which these natural sources of power potential are translated into actual power can be affected by both tangible and intangible sources. These sources are used to enhance, modify, or constrain power potential, as shown in Figure 5.1.

Tangible Sources of Power

Among the tangible sources of power, industrial development, economic diversification, level of infrastructure, and characteristics of the military are among the most critical. With an advanced industrial capacity, the advantages and disadvantages of geography diminish. Air travel, for example, makes geographic expanse less of a barrier to commerce, yet at the same time makes even large states militarily vulnerable. With industrialization, the importance of population is modified, too. Large but poorly equipped armies are no match for small armies with advanced equipment. Industrialized states generally have higher educational levels, more advanced technology, and more efficient use of capital, all of which add to their tangible power potential.

Shanghai, China, has undergone a major transformation in the last twenty years as China's economy has developed rapidly from agricultural to industrial. With numerous sources of natural and tangible power, China today is considered one of the foremost powers in the world.

Intangible Sources of Power

Intangible power sources—national image, quality of government, public support, leadership, and morale—may be as important as the tangible ones, although not to radicals, who emphasize material sources of power. People within states have images of their own state's power potential—images that translate into an intangible power ingredient. Canadians have typically viewed themselves as internationally responsible and eager to participate in multilateral peacekeeping missions, to provide generous foreign aid packages, and to respond unselfishly to international emergencies. The state has acted on and, indeed, helped to shape that image, making Canada a more powerful actor than its small population (34 million) would otherwise dictate.

The perception by other states of public support and cohesion is another intangible source of power. China's power was magnified during the leadership of Mao Zedong (1893–1976), when there appeared to be unprecedented public support for the communist leadership and a high degree of societal cohesion. A state government's actual support among its own population can also be a powerful mediator of state power. Israel's successful campaigns in the Middle East in the 1967 and 1973 wars can be attributed in large part to strong public support, including the willingness of Israeli citizens to pay the cost and die for their country when necessary. When that public support is absent, particularly in democracies, the power potential of the state is diminished. Witness the U.S. loss in the Vietnam War, when challenges to and disagreement with the war effort undermined military effectiveness. Loss of public support may also inhibit authoritarian systems. In both the 1991 Gulf War and the 2003 Iraq War, Saddam Hussein's support from his own troops was woefully inadequate: many were not ready to die for the Iraqi regime and fled. And in Libya, Muammar Qaddafi's military, composed of mercenaries from poor neighboring countries, was not willing to fight indefinitely in 2011.

Leadership is another source of intangible power. Visionaries and charismatic leaders, such as India's Mohandas Gandhi, Germany's Otto von Bismarck, and Britain's Winston Churchill, were able to augment the power potential of their states by taking bold initiatives. Poor leaders, those who squander public resources and abuse the public's trust, such as Zimbabwe's Robert Mugabe and Iraq's Saddam Hussein, diminish the state's power capability and its capacity to exert power over the long term. Liberals, in particular, pay attention to leadership: good leaders can avoid resorting to war; bad leaders may not be able to prevent it.

More generally, intangible power characteristics can be exercised. Joseph S. Nye labeled such power **soft power**, the ability to attract others because of the legitimacy of the state's values or its policies.[8] Rather than exerting its natural and tangible power, such a state influences other states by being what it is. In the case of the United States, its soft power resources may include its model of functioning democracy and commitment to political and civil rights.

Clearly, when coupled with the tangible, intangible power sources either augment a state's capacity or diminish its power. Liberals, who have a more expansive notion of power, would more than likely place greater importance on these intangible ingredients, because several are characteristics of domestic processes. Yet different combinations of the sources of power may lead to different outcomes. The victory by the NATO alliance over Slobodan Milošević's Yugoslavian forces in 1999 and over Libya in 2011 can be explained by the alliance's overwhelming natural sources of power coupled with its strong tangible sources of power. But how can Afghanistan's victory over the Soviet Union in the early 1980s be explained, or the North Vietnamese victory over the United States in the 1970s, or the Algerian victory over France in the early 1960s? In each case, a country with limited natural and tangible sources of power was able to prevail over those with strong natural and tangible power resources. In these cases, the intangible sources of power, including the willingness of the populations to continue to fight against overwhelming odds, explains victory by the objectively weaker side.[9] Success involves using various forms of state power. Nye calls that **smart power**, the combination of the hard power of coercion and payment with the soft power of persuasion and attraction, with the appropriate combination depending on context.[10]

Constructivists, in contrast, offer a unique perspective on power. They argue that power includes not only the tangible and intangible sources. In addition, it includes the power of ideas and language—as distinguished from ideology, which fueled the unlikely victory of the objectively weaker side in the cases described earlier. It is through the power of ideas and norms that state identities and nationalism are forged and changed.

The Exercise of State Power

In all theoretical perspectives, power is not just to be possessed, it is to be used. Using state power is a difficult task.

States use a variety of techniques to translate power potential into effective power, namely, diplomacy, economic statecraft, and force. In a particular situation, a state may begin with one approach and then try a number of others to influence the intended target. In other cases, several different techniques may be utilized simultaneously. Which techniques political scientists think states emphasize varies across the theoretical perspectives. In addition, different types of states may make different choices.

The Art of Diplomacy

Traditional **diplomacy** entails states trying to influence the behavior of other actors by negotiating, by taking a specific action or refraining from such an action, or by conducting public diplomacy.

According to Harold Nicolson, a British diplomat and writer, diplomacy usually begins with negotiation, through direct or indirect communication, in an attempt to reach agreement. This negotiation may be conducted tacitly among the parties, each of which recognizes that a move in one direction leads to a response by the other that is strategic. The parties may conduct open, formal negotiations, where one side offers a formal proposal and the other responds in kind; this is generally repeated many times until a compromise is reached. In either case, reciprocity usually occurs, whereby each side responds to the other's moves in kind.

Yet for negotiations to be successful, each party needs to be credible, that is, each party needs to make believable statements, assume a likely position, and be able to back up its position by taking action. Well-intentioned and credible parties will have a higher probability of engaging in successful negotiations.

States seldom enter diplomatic bargaining or negotiations as power equals. Each state knows its own goals and power potential, of course, and has some idea of its opponent's goals and power potential, although information about the opponent may be imperfect, incomplete, or even just wrong. Thus, although the outcome of the bargaining is almost always mutually beneficial (if not, why bother?), that outcome is not likely to please the parties equally. And the satisfaction of each party may change as new information is revealed or as conditions change over time.

Bargaining and negotiations are complex processes, complicated by at least two critical factors. First, most states carry out two levels of bargaining simultaneously: international bargaining between and among states and the bargaining that must occur between the state's negotiators and its various domestic constituencies, both to arrive at a negotiating position and to ratify the agreement reached by the states. The political scientist Robert Putnam refers to this as a "two-level game."[11] International trade negotiations within the World Trade Organization are such a two-level game. The Doha Round of trade negotiations reached an impasse in 2008 between the United States and European Union on the one hand, and the emerging states of India, China, and Brazil on the other. The United States and the European Union (EU) opposed significant reductions in agricultural subsidies, while India and China sought, if not an end to subsidies, then special safeguards for their poor farming constituencies. All countries were each conducting two sets of negotiations: one with the foreign states and the other within the domestic political arena. What makes the game unusually complex is that "moves that are rational for one player at one board … may be impolitic for that same player at the other board."[12] The negotiator is the formal link between the two levels of negotiation. Realists see the two-level game as constrained primarily by the structure of the international system, whereas liberals more readily acknowledge domestic pressures and incentives.

Second, bargaining and negotiating are, in part, a culture-bound activity. Approaches to bargaining vary across cultures—a view accepted among liberals, who place importance on state differences. At least two styles of negotiations have been identified.[13] These two different styles may lead to contrasting outcomes. The more advanced industrialized states like the United States, Great Britain, and Germany favor discussion of concrete detail, eschewing grand philosophical debate, addressing concrete problems, and resolving specific issues before broader principles are crystallized. Other states, many in the developing world, argue in a deductive style—from general principles to particular applications. This approach may mask conflict over details until a later stage in the process. These differences in negotiating approaches can lead to stalemate or even negotiation failure, as it did in the discussions over the New International Economic Order (NIEO), discussed in Chapter 9.

The use of **public diplomacy** is an increasingly popular diplomatic technique in a communication-linked world. Public diplomacy involves targeting both foreign publics and elites, attempting to create an overall image that enhances a country's ability to achieve its diplomatic objectives. For instance, as secretary of state, Hillary Rodham

Clinton traveled to over 100 countries, highlighting the role of women and promoting values, democracy, and human rights. China's public diplomacy has utilized Confucius Institutes to promote Chinese language and culture worldwide. Before and during the 2003 Iraq War, public diplomacy became a particularly useful diplomatic instrument. American administration officials not only made the case for war to the American people in news interviews and newspaper op-ed pieces but also lobbied friendly and opposing states both directly in negotiations and indirectly through various media outlets, including independent Arab media such as the Qatar-funded Al Jazeera television network. The Department of State established the Middle East Radio Network, comprising both Radio Sawa and Alhurra. Radio Sawa broadcasts both Western and Middle Eastern popular music with periodic news briefs. The more controversial Alhurra begun in 2004 has attracted much of the Iraqi market, and during the Arab Spring in Egypt, an estimated 25 percent of people living in Cairo and Alexandria listened to this news source. Al Jazeera remains the number one news source for an estimated 55 percent of the Arab world. States in the communication age clearly have another diplomatic instrument at their disposal, but whether public diplomacy changes "hearts and minds" is debatable.

Celebrity diplomacy is another form of public diplomacy, but celebrity diplomacy aims at influencing not only the public but persuading decision makers as well. Celebrities like Bob Geldof, Bono, Angelina Jolie, and George Clooney are able to use their access to the media to support a particular cause, lobby for action, and speak directly to world leaders. No celebrity has been as effective as George Clooney and his work on behalf of the people of Darfur and South Sudan. Called a "21st-century statesman" and becoming an issue expert and privately funding a satellite to monitor military movements, Clooney sees his role as helping "focus news media where they have abdicated their responsibility. We can't make policy, but we can 'encourage' politicians more than ever before."[14]

But diplomacy may need to encompass more than conducting negotiations and persuading the public. Negotiators may find they need to utilize other measures of statecraft, including positive incentives such as diplomatic recognition, foreign aid in return for desired actions, and the threat of negative consequences (reduction or elimination of foreign aid, severance of diplomatic ties, use of coercive force) if the target state continues to move in a specific direction. The tools of statecraft are not only diplomatic but also economic and military.

The liberal view is that talking, via all forms of diplomacy, is better than not talking to one's adversaries. Whatever the differences, liberals assert, discussion clarifies the issues, narrows differences, and encourages bargaining. Use of more forceful actions, like both economic statecraft and use of force, may make diplomacy less effective and should be used only as a last resort. Realists are more skeptical about the value of diplomacy. While not ignoring some benefits, realists tend to see state goals as inherently conflictual. Thus, to them, negotiations and diplomacy are apt to be effective only if they are backed by force, either economic or military.

Economic Statecraft

States use more than words to exercise power. They may use economic statecraft—both positive and negative **sanctions**—to try to influence other states.[15] Positive sanctions involve offering a "carrot," enticing the target state to act in the desired way by rewarding moves made in the desired direction. The assumption is that positive incentives will lead the target state to change its behavior. Negative sanctions, however, may be imposed more often: threatening to act or actually taking actions that punish the target state for moves made in the direction not desired. The goal of using the "stick" (negative sanctions) may be to punish or reprimand the target state for actions taken or may be to try to change the future behavior of the target state. Table 5.1 provides examples of positive and negative sanctions used in economic statecraft.

Since the mid-1990s, states have increasingly imposed **smart sanctions**, including freezing assets of governments and/or individuals and imposing commodities sanctions (e.g., on oil, timber, or diamonds). Targeting has involved not just "what" but also "who," as the international community has tried to affect specific individuals and rebel groups, reduce ambiguity and loopholes, and avoid the high humanitarian costs of general sanctions. Despite these modifications, liberals are still wary of sanctions, believing instead that diplomacy is a more effective way for states to achieve international goals. Realist theorists, on the other hand, believe it is necessary in exercising power to resort to or threaten to use sanctions or force on a more regular basis.

A state's ability to use these instruments of economic statecraft depends on its power potential. States with a variety of power sources have more instruments at their disposal. Clearly, only economically well-endowed countries can grant licenses, offer investment guarantees, grant preferences to specific countries, house foreign assets, or boycott effectively. Radicals often point to this fact to illustrate the hegemony of the international capitalist system.

Although radicals disagree, liberals argue that developing states do have some leverage in economic statecraft under special circumstances. If a state or group of states controls a key resource whose production is limited, their power is strengthened. Among the primary commodities, petroleum has this potential, and it gave the Arab members of the Organization of the Petroleum Exporting Countries (OPEC) the ability to impose oil sanctions on the United States and the Netherlands when those two countries strongly supported Israel in the 1973 Arab-Israeli War.

The ability of sanctions to alter a target state's behavior appears mixed. South Africa illustrates a case of relative success in the use of economic sanctions. When positive sanctions in the form of the Reagan administration's "constructive engagement" policy failed to work, the U.S. Congress approved harsh sanctions against South Africa's apartheid regime in 1986, over a presidential veto. Under the Comprehensive Anti-Apartheid Act, the United States joined with other countries and the United Nations, which had already imposed economic sanctions. In 1992, the white-controlled South African regime announced a political opening that led to the end of apartheid and white-minority rule. Most commentators conclude that sanctions probably had an important effect on the regime's decision to change policy.

Yet economic statecraft does not always lead to the intended outcome. In 1960 the U.S. imposed an economic, commercial, and financial embargo against Cuba, designed to punish the communist regime under Fidel Castro; those restrictions were strengthened and codified in 1992, making it the longest trade embargo in history. Only in 2000 were some of the restrictions relaxed for agribusiness and medicine. Despite its cost to American business and its failure to weaken the regime, the embargo remains. The political power of the Florida-based Cuban refugee community explains the continuation of the policy even though its objective has not been achieved.

Iraq represents another case of ambiguous results for sanctioning. Between 1991 and 2003, the Iraq regime was subject to comprehensive sanctions designed to pressure the Saddam Hussein regime to dismantle its weapons of mass destruction and ultimately to bring down the government. While the sanctions may have achieved their first goal, Saddam remained firmly in power while the people suffered. Similarly, steps taken by the United States and the European Union in 2011–13 to cut off Iran from the international financial system and impose sanctions on companies in the petrochemical and oil industries have choked off revenue (an estimated $9 billion every quarter) and caused a dramatic decline in the value of its currency, weakening the Iranian economy. But the ultimate objective—convincing the leaders to renounce Iran's nuclear program—has not been achieved. These ambiguous results lead realist theorists to conclude that states must use the threat of force to achieve their objectives.

The Use of Force

Force (and the threat of force) is another critical instrument of statecraft and is central to realist thinking. Like economic statecraft, force or its threat may be used either to get a target state to do something or to undo something that state has done—compellence—or to keep an adversary from doing something—deterrence.[16] Liberal theorists are more likely to advocate compellent strategies, moving cautiously to deterrence, whereas realists promote deterrence.

With the strategy of **compellence**, a state tries, by threatening to use force, to get another state to do something or to undo an act that it has undertaken. The prelude to the 1991 Gulf War is an excellent example. The United States, the United Nations, and coalition members tried to get Saddam Hussein to change his actions with the

TABLE 5.1	TYPES OF SANCTIONS IN ECONOMIC STATECRAFT

Positive Sanctions

SANCTION	EXAMPLE
Give the target state the same trading privileges given to your best trading partner (most-favored-nation [MFN] status) as incentive for policy change.	U.S. granted MFN status to China, in spite of that country's poor human rights record.
Allow sensitive trade with target state, including militarily useful equipment.	France and Germany export equipment to Iran, even though Iran's government is hostile to the West.
Give corporations investment guarantees or tax breaks as incentives to invest in target state.	U.S. offered insurance to U.S. companies willing to invest in post-apartheid South Africa.
Allow importation of target state's products into your country at best tariff rates.	Industrialized states allow imports from developing countries at lower tariff rates.

Negative Sanctions

SANCTION	EXAMPLE
Freeze target state's assets.	U.S. froze Iranian assets during 1979 hostage crisis; UN froze Libyan assets 1993–99; UN froze Afghanistan's assets under Taliban 1999–2001.
Blacklist target state.	Arab states blacklisted companies that conducted business in Israel.
Boycott goods and services of target states.	South Africa was boycotted for apartheid policy in 1970s and 1980s; exports of dual-use technologies were prohibited to Iraq, Iran, Syria, Libya, North Korea, Sudan in the 1990s and after because of their support of terrorism.
Ban importation of one or all products of target state.	Iraq was forbidden to sell oil internationally 1991–2003 as punishment for the 1991 Gulf War; UN sanctions were imposed against Haiti 1990 and 1993–94 to try to overthrow the military government there.

compellent strategy of escalating threats. Iraq's invasion of Kuwait was initially widely condemned. Formal UN Security Council measures gave multilateral legitimacy to the condemnation. Next, Iraq's external economic assets were frozen and economic sanctions were imposed. Finally, U.S. and coalition military forces were mobilized and deployed, and specific deadlines were given for Iraq to withdraw from Kuwait. At each step of the compellent strategy of escalation, one message was communicated to Iraq: withdraw from Kuwait or more coercive actions will follow. The Western alliance followed a similar strategy to try to compel Serbia to stop abusing the human rights of Kosovar Albanians and to withdraw its military forces from the region. Compellence was also used before the 2003 Iraq War, when the United States and others threatened Saddam Hussein that if certain actions were not taken, then war would follow. Threats began when George W. Bush labeled Iraq a member of the "axis of evil"; they escalated when the United Nations found Iraq to be in material breach of a UN resolution. Then in March 2003, Great Britain, one of the coalition partners, gave Iraq ten days to comply with the UN resolution. And on March 17, the last compellent threat was issued: U.S. president George W. Bush gave Saddam's Baathist regime 48 hours to leave Iraq as its last chance to avert war. In all of these cases, it was necessary to resort to an invasion because compellence via an escalation of threats failed. Note that compellence ends once the use of force begins.

With the strategy of deterrence, states commit themselves to punishing a target state if that state takes an undesired action. Threats of actual war are used as an instrument of policy to dissuade a state from pursuing certain courses of action. If the target state does not take the undesired action, deterrence is successful and conflict is avoided. If it does choose to act despite the deterrent threat, then the first state will presumably deliver a devastating blow.

Since the advent of nuclear weapons in 1945, deterrence has taken on a special meaning. Today if a state chooses to resort to violence against a nuclear state, it is possible that nuclear weapons will be launched against it in retaliation. If this happens, the cost of the aggression will be unacceptable, especially if both states have nuclear weapons, in which case the viability of both societies will be at stake. Theoretically, therefore, states that recognize the destructive capability of nuclear weapons will be hesitant to take aggressive action. It is difficult for a state to know for absolute certain that it could annihilate its adversary's nuclear capability in one go—called **first-strike capability**—and even the possibility that the adversary can respond with its **second-strike capability** will result in restraint. Deterrence is then successful.

For either compellence or deterrence to be effective, states have to lay the groundwork. They must clearly and openly communicate their objectives and capabilities, be willing to make good on threats or to fulfill promises, and have the capacity to follow through with their commitments. In short, a state's credibility is essential for compellence and deterrence. Yet this is not a one-sided, unilateral process; it is a strategic

↑↓ **YOU DECIDE**

In a televised speech on September 11, 2001, U.S. President George W. Bush assured the people of the United States that the country and its allies stood ready to win a "war against terrorism." But war is a serious matter. Did the terrorist attacks of 9/11 justify the U.S. going to war?

In support of declaring a war on terrorism, you might argue that war was essential because it could act as a rallying point to garner both domestic and international political support. You might add that, by and large, the United States and its allies have been victors in war and collectively possess the world's most concentrated and advanced war-fighting forces. Moreover, the United States was attacked first, by a group of religiously-inspired individuals who considered themselves warriors engaging in an act of war. Finally, you might argue that a law-enforcement approach is inadequate because due process of law would be too time-consuming, and the delay in bringing those responsible for terrorism to justice might endanger the lives of U.S., British, Japanese, Russian, Chinese (and so on) citizens. By contrast, the use of force, while regulated, is a more effective way of securing states and their vulnerable populations and infrastructures from 9/11-style attacks than a law-enforcement approach. In war, enemies are (hopefully) quickly killed while potential adversaries are deterred from attack. On the other hand, during legal proceedings, our adversaries would be held in prison, which could encourage attacks by co-conspirators in hopes of obtaining their release.

In opposing a policy of war on terrorism, you might argue that as painful as terrorist attacks are, they don't actually threaten the state's survival, and therefore war is not a proportionate response. You might add that by their very nature, terrorists aren't soldiers (they don't wear uniforms and they systematically target the weak and defenseless), and targeting them with soldiers means that many civilians who are not terrorists will be unintentionally harmed or killed as well. Wars demand militaries, and militaries are too blunt an instrument with which to counter terrorism. Finally, you might point out that declaring war might blind us to the uncomfortable fact that in rare cases the terrorists have a legitimate grievance (though even a legitimate grievance cannot justify murder), and a declaration of war may make it more difficult to reach a political solution.

YOU DECIDE: Did the terrorist attacks of September 11, 2001, justify the U.S. going to war, or was war the wrong response? Strengthen your argument by citing the benefits of both a war-fighting and law enforcement approach before settling on one as the better of the two.

interaction where the behavior of each state is determined not only by one's own behavior, but by the actions and responses of the other.

Compellence and deterrence can fail, however. If they do, states may go to war, but even during war, states have choices. They choose the type of weaponry (nuclear or nonnuclear, strategic or tactical, conventional or chemical and biological), the kind of targets (military or civilian, urban or rural), and the geographic locus (city, state, region) to be targeted. They may choose to respond in kind, to escalate, or to de-escalate. In war, both implicit and explicit negotiation takes place, over both how to fight the war and how to end it. We will return to a discussion of war in Chapter 8.

Democracy and Foreign Policy

Although all states use diplomacy, economy, and force to conduct foreign policy, do policy choices vary by type of government? Specifically, do democratic states conduct foreign policy and make policy choices that are any different from the choices and policies made by authoritarian states and leaders? We might expect that in democratic states, the intangible sources of power—national image, public support, and leadership—would matter more, because the leaders are responsible to the public through elections. If that is true, then is the foreign policy behavior of democratic states any different from the behavior of nondemocratic or authoritarian states?

This question has occupied philosophers, diplomatic historians, and political scientists for centuries. In *Perpetual Peace* (1795), Immanuel Kant argued that the spread of democracy would change international politics by eliminating war. He reasoned that the public would be very cautious in supporting war because they, the public, are likely to suffer the most devastating effects. Thus, leaders will act in a restrained fashion and tend to abstain from war because of domestic constraints.[17] Since Kant's time, other explanations have been added to the democratic peace hypothesis. Liberals point to the notion of shared domestic norms and joint membership in international institutions to explain peace among democracies. And because democratic states trade more with each other, they prefer to benefit from those economic gains made during peacetime. Many of these ideas found resonance with Woodrow Wilson, a major advocate of the democratic peace. Realists, too, add to the democratic peace explanation. By belonging to the same alliances, democratic states are more effective at practicing balance of power, decreasing the probability of war.

Political scientists have developed an extensive research agenda related to the **democratic peace** theory. Are democracies more peaceful than nondemocracies? More specifically, do democracies fight each other less than nondemocracies do? Do democracies fight nondemocracies more than they fight each other? Gathering data on different kinds of warfare over several centuries, researchers have addressed these questions.

One study has confirmed the hypothesis that democracies do not go to war against each other: since 1789 no wars have been fought strictly between independent states with democratically elected governments. Another study has found that wars involving democracies have tended to be less bloody but more protracted, although between 1816 and 1965, democratic governments were not noticeably more peaceable or passive.[18] But the evidence is not that clear-cut, and explanations are partial. Why are states in the middle of transitions to democracy more susceptible to conflict? How can we explain when democratic states have not gone to war? It may, after all, have had little to do with their democratic character.

Why have some of the findings on the democratic peace been so divergent? Even within a single research program there may be serious differences in conclusions, based on the assumptions made by researchers and the methods used. Scholars who use the behavioral approach themselves point to some of the difficulties. Some researchers analyzing the democratic peace use different definitions of the key variables, democracy and war. Some researchers distinguish between liberal democracies (for example, the United States and Germany) and illiberal democracies (Yugoslavia in the late 1990s). Also, the data for war would be different if wars with fewer than 1,000 deaths were included, as they are in some studies. And other studies of the democratic peace examine different time periods. Such differences in research protocols might well lead to different research findings. Yet even with these qualifications, the basic finding from the research is that democracies do not engage in militarized disputes against each other. That finding *is* statistically significant—that is, it does not occur by random chance. Overall, democracies are not more pacific than nondemocracies; democracies simply do not fight *each other*. In fact, autocracies are just as peaceful with each other as are democracies.

Models of Foreign Policy Decision Making

How are specific foreign policy decisions actually made? Do democracies make foreign policy choices differently from nondemocracies? How do the different theories view the decision-making process? Differences depend in large part on how subnational actors—interest groups, **nongovernmental organizations (NGOs)**, and businesses—are viewed.

The Rational Model

Most policy makers, particularly during crises, and most realists begin with the rational model, which conceives of foreign policy as actions chosen by the national government

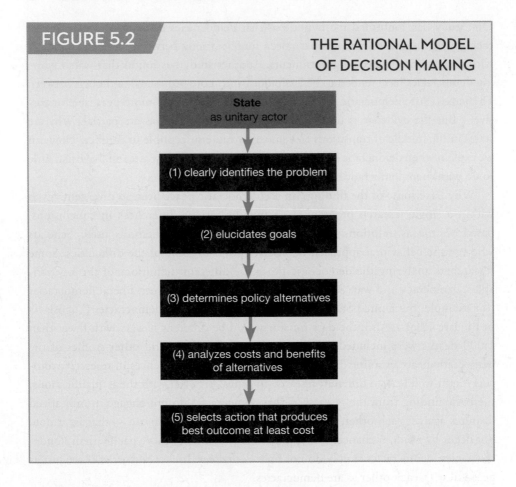

FIGURE 5.2   THE RATIONAL MODEL
                                                  OF DECISION MAKING

State
as unitary actor

(1) clearly identifies the problem

(2) elucidates goals

(3) determines policy alternatives

(4) analyzes costs and benefits
of alternatives

(5) selects action that produces
best outcome at least cost

to maximize its strategic objectives. The state is assumed to be a unitary actor with established goals, a set of options, and an algorithm for deciding which option best meets its goals. The process is relatively straightforward, as shown in Figure 5.2. Taking as our case the 1996 incident in which the People's Republic of China (PRC) tested missiles by launching them over the Republic of China (ROC; Taiwan), a rational approach would view Taiwan's decision-making process about how to respond in the following manner (the numbers correspond to the numbered steps in Figure 5.2):

1. The PRC was testing missiles over the ROC in direct threat to the latter's national security and just prior to Taiwan's first democratic election.
2. The goal of both the ROC and its major supporter, the United States, was to stop the firings immediately.
3. The ROC decision makers had several options: do nothing; wait until after the elections, in hopes that the PRC would then stop; issue diplomatic protests; bring the issue to the UN Security Council; threaten or conduct military operations

against the PRC by bombing its missile sites or mounting a land invasion; or threaten or use economic statecraft (cut trade, impose sanctions or embargoes).

4. The ROC leaders analyzed the benefits and costs of these options: the PRC would exercise its veto in the UN Security Council; economic or military actions undertaken by the ROC were unlikely to be successful against the stronger adversary, potentially leading to the destruction of Taiwan, an unacceptable side effect.

5. The ROC, with U.S. support, chose diplomatic protest as a first step, in the hope that the antagonistic missile tests would cease after the election. Doing nothing clearly would have suggested that the missile testing was acceptable, which it was not. Military action against the PRC was too extreme, with possibly disastrous consequences.

Crises such as the preceding example have a unique set of characteristics: decision makers are confronted by a surprising, threatening event; they have only a short time to make a decision about how to respond; often a limited number of decision makers are involved in top secret proceedings; and there is little time for substate actors to have much influence. In these circumstances, using the rational model as a way to assess the other side's behavior is an appropriate choice.

In a noncrisis situation in which when a state knows very little about the internal domestic processes of another state—as the United States knew little about mainland China during the era of Mao Zedong—then decision makers have little alternative but to assume that the other state will follow the rational model. Indeed, in the absence of better information, most U.S. assessments of decisions taken by the Soviet Union during the Cold War were based on a rational model: the Soviet Union had a goal, its alternatives were clearly laid out, and decisions were taken to maximize its achievement of that goal. Only after the opening of the Soviet governmental archives following the

THEORY IN BRIEF — THE REALIST PERSPECTIVE ON STATE POWER AND POLICY

NATURE OF STATE POWER	Emphasis on power as key concept in international relations; geography, natural resources, population especially important
USING STATE POWER	Emphasis on coercive techniques of power; use of force acceptable
HOW FOREIGN POLICY IS MADE	Emphasis on rational model of decision making; unitary state actor assumed once decision is made
DETERMINANTS OF FOREIGN POLICY	Largely external/international determinants

end of the Cold War did historians find that, in fact, the Soviets had no concrete plans for turning Poland, Hungary, Romania, or other East European states into communist dictatorships or socialist economies, as the United States believed. The Soviets appear to have been guided by events happening in the region, not by specific ideological goals and rational plans.[19] The United States was incorrect in imputing the rational model to Soviet decision making, but in the absence of complete information, this was the least risky approach: the anarchy of the international system means that a state assumes that its opponent engages in rational decision making.

The Bureaucratic/Organizational Model

Not all decisions occur during crises, and not all decisions are taken with so little knowledge of domestic politics in other countries. In these instances, foreign policy decisions may be products of either subnational governmental organizations or bureaucracies (departments or ministries of government). **Organizational politics** emphasizes the standard operating procedures and processes of an organization. Decisions arising from organizational processes depend heavily on precedents; major changes in policy are unlikely. Conflicts can occur when different subgroups within the organization have different goals and procedures. Often those different goals have been strongly influenced by particular interest groups or NGOs.

Bureaucratic politics, on the other hand, occurs among members of the bureaucracy representing different interests. Decisions determined by bureaucratic politics flow from the push and pull, or tug-of-war, among these departments, groups, or individuals. In either political scenario, the ultimate decision depends on the relative strength of the individual bureaucratic players or the organizations they represent (see Figure 5.3).

Both trade and environmental policy are prominent examples of the bureaucratic/organizational model of decision making at work in noncrisis situations. Bureaucracies in the ministries of agriculture, industry, and labor in the case of trade, and environment, economics, and labor in the case of the environment, fight particularly hard within their own governments for policies favorable to their constituencies. Substate groups develop strong relationships with these ministries to ensure favorable outcomes. When time is no real constraint, informal bureaucratic groups and departments are free to mobilize. They hold meetings, hammering out positions that satisfy all the contending interests. The decisions arrived at are not always the most rational ones; rather, the groups are content with **satisficing**—that is, settling for a decision that satisfies the different constituents without ostracizing any, even if it is not the best possible outcome.

Liberals especially turn to this model of decision-making behavior in their analyses because for them the state is only the playing field; the actors are the competing interests in bureaucracies and organizations. The model is most relevant in large democratic

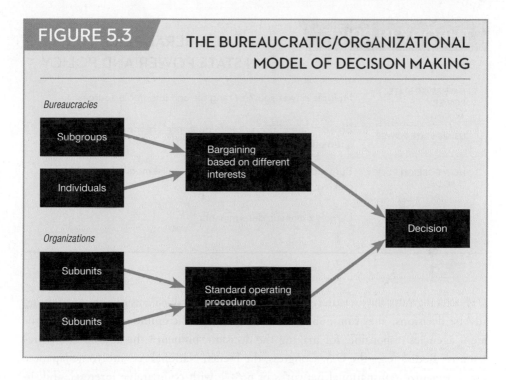

FIGURE 5.3   THE BUREAUCRATIC/ORGANIZATIONAL MODEL OF DECISION MAKING

Bureaucracies

Subgroups

Individuals

Bargaining based on different interests

Organizations

Subunits

Subunits

Standard operating procedures

Decision

countries, which usually have highly differentiated institutional structures for foreign policy decision making and where responsibility and jurisdiction are divided among a number of different units. But to use this model in policy-making circles to analyze or predict other states' behavior or to use it to analyze decisions for scholarly purposes, one must have detailed knowledge of a country's foreign policy structures and bureaucracies. In the absence of such information and in a crisis situation where policy must be determined quickly, the rational model is the best alternative.

The Pluralist Model

The pluralist model, in contrast to the other two alternatives, attributes decisions to bargaining conducted among domestic sources—the public, interest groups, mass movements, and multinational corporations (see Figure 5.4). In noncrisis situations and on particular issues, especially economic ones, societal groups may play very important roles. No one doubts the power of the rice farmer lobbies in both Japan and South Korea in preventing the importation of cheap, U.S. grown rice. No one denies the power of U.S. shoe manufacturers in supporting restrictions on the importation of Brazilian-made shoes into the United States, despite U.S. governmental initiatives to allow imports of products from developing countries.

THEORY IN BRIEF   **THE LIBERAL PERSPECTIVE**
                                  ON STATE POWER AND POLICY

NATURE OF STATE POWER	Multiple power sources; tangible and intangible sources
USING STATE POWER	Broad range of power techniques; preference for noncoercive alternatives
HOW FOREIGN POLICY IS MADE	Bureaucratic/organizational and pluralist models of decision making
DETERMINANTS OF FOREIGN POLICY	Largely domestic determinants

Societal groups have a variety of ways of forcing favorable decisions or constraining adverse decisions. They can mobilize the media and public opinion, lobby the government agencies responsible for making the decision, influence the appropriate representative bodies (e.g., the U.S. Congress, the French National Assembly, the Japanese Diet), organize transnational networks of people with comparable interests, and, in the case of high-profile heads of multinational corporations, make direct contacts with the highest governmental officials. The decision made will reflect these diverse societal interests and strategies—a result that is particularly compatible with liberal thinking. The movement to ban land mines in the 1990s is an example of a societally based pluralist foreign policy decision, a process reflecting democratic practices.

Both realists and liberals acknowledge that states have real choices in foreign policy, no matter which model explains their behavior; radicals, however, see fewer real choices. In the radical view, capitalist states' interests are determined by the structure of the international system, and their decisions are dictated by the economic imperatives of the dominant class. Internal domestic elites have been co-opted by international capitalists such as multinational corporations.

Constructivists hold that foreign policy decisions are based on the decision makers' adherence to international norms. Because elite socialization with international norms is evident to the public (in contrast to the power-driven interests that neorealists and neoliberals assume to underlie decisions), leaders are inclined to build policies through processes open to domestic and international civil society, the mass media, and international partners. Foreign policy decisions are determined by leaders' beliefs that their actions are congruent with the international norms that they have appropriated.

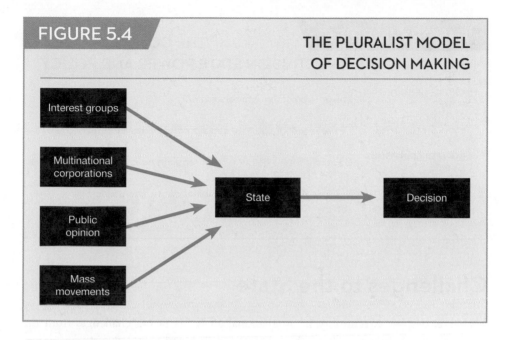

FIGURE 5.4

THE PLURALIST MODEL OF DECISION MAKING

Interest groups

Multinational corporations

Public opinion

Mass movements

State

Decision

Each alternative model offers a simplification of the foreign policy decision-making process. Each provides a window into how groups (both governmental and nongovernmental) influence the foreign policy process. But these models do not provide answers to other critical questions. They do not tell us the content of a specific decision or indicate the effectiveness with which the foreign policy was implemented.

THEORY IN BRIEF

THE RADICAL PERSPECTIVE ON STATE POWER AND POLICY

NATURE OF STATE POWER	Economic power organized around classes
USING STATE POWER	Weak states have few instruments of power
HOW FOREIGN POLICY IS MADE	States have no real choices; decisions dictated by economic capitalist elites
DETERMINANTS OF FOREIGN POLICY	Largely external determinants; co-opted internal elements

THEORY IN BRIEF

THE CONSTRUCTIVIST PERSPECTIVE ON STATE POWER AND POLICY

NATURE OF STATE POWER	Power subject to norm socialization
USING STATE POWER	Power is tool of elites for socializing societies through norms
HOW FOREIGN POLICY IS MADE	Decisions based on norms that regulate policy sector
DETERMINANTS OF FOREIGN POLICY	External determinants in combination with domestic civil society

Challenges to the State

The state, despite its centrality in international affairs, is facing challenges from the processes of globalization, religiously and ideologically based transnational movements, ethnonational movements, transnational crime, and failed states (see Table 5.2). In each of these processes, new and intrusive technologies—e-mail, Facebook, Twitter, cell phones with cameras, direct satellite broadcasting, worldwide television networks such as CNN—increasingly undermine the state's control over information and hence its control over its citizens, nongovernmental groups, and their activities. Both the Persian Gulf states and China have fought losing battles trying to "protect" their populations from either crass Western values or dangerous political ideas transmitted through modern media. These new communication technologies have facilitated the organization of transnational and ethnonational movements and transnational crime. As Jessica Mathews explains, "The most powerful engine of change in the relative decline of the state and the rise of non-state actors is the computer and telecommunications revolution, whose deep political and social consequences have been almost completely ignored. … In every sphere of activity, instantaneous access to information and the ability to put it to use multiplies the number of players who matter and reduces the number who command great authority."[20]

Globalization

Externally, the state is buffeted by globalization, the growing integration of the world in terms of politics, economics, and culture, a process that increasingly undermines traditional state sovereignty. In political terms, states, an overwhelming number of which are now democracies, are confronted by transnational issues—environmental

TABLE 5.2	CHALLENGES TO STATE POWER
FORCES	**EFFECTS ON THE STATE**
Globalization—political, economic, cultural	Undermines state sovereignty; interferes with state exercise of power; exacerbated by the rise of new media
Transnational religious and ideological movements	Seek loyalty and commitment of individuals and groups beyond the state; change state behavior on a specific problem or issue
Ethnonational movements	Seek own state; attempt to replace current government with one representing the interests of the movement
Transnational crime	Challenges state authority
Failed states	Threaten lives of persons within states and security of other states in international system

degradation, disease, crime, and intrusive technologies—that governments cannot manage alone, as discussed in Chapter 11. Increasingly, cooperative actions to address these issues require states to compromise their sovereignty. In the economic realm, states' financial markets are increasingly tied inextricably together; multinational corporations and the internationalization of production and consumption make it ever more difficult for states to regulate their own economic policies and make states more subject to international forces, as discussed in Chapter 9. Culturally, globalization has prompted both homogenization and differentiation. On the one hand, people around the world share a culture by watching the same cinema and listening to the same music. At the same time, people are also increasingly eager to differentiate themselves within this homogenizing cultural force by maintaining local languages or pressing for local political autonomy. An outgrowth of globalization has been both increasing democratization and the emerging power of transnational movements.

Transnational Religious and Ideological Movements

Transnational movements, particularly religious and ideological movements, have become political forces in their own right. Different religions have always existed, and their current numbers reveal the diversity (2.1 billion Christians; 1.5 billion Muslims; 900 million Hindus; 376 million Buddhists; 14 million Jews; 900 million atheists).

The Arab Spring: A View from Egypt

The Arab Spring, a series of popular protests against authoritarian governments in the Middle East, has captured international headlines since 2011. Initial enthusiasm has been tempered as the politics of democratization became messy, however. Egypt illustrates the promise and pitfalls of the process of democratization.

In power since 1981, Hosni Mubarak and the Egyptian military ruled over a stable but dysfunctional authoritarian government. Widespread corruption and brutal tactics by the state's security forces had broken the ties between the state and society. Mubarak failed to keep his promise to implement liberal economic reforms, and economic conditions were dire. Unemployment reached 40 percent for those under 30 years old, the majority of the population. Job growth had actually declined as the gulf between rich and poor widened. In 2010, as rumors spread that Mubarak's son Gamal would soon assume office, anger grew into action. Organizers from many political persuasions rose to protest Gamal as the next leader of Egypt.

Thus, when Mohammad Bouazizi, a Tunisian fruit seller, set himself ablaze in December 2010 to protest Tunisian government malfeasance, Egyptians listened, as did the masses in Yemen, Bahrain, Libya, Syria, and beyond. When the Tunisian autocrat Zine al-Abidine Ben Ali fled for exile less than a month later, people realized that autocratic leaders were not immune to popular protest. On January 25, 2011, which many Egyptians now call "Revolution Day," opposition forces occupied Cairo's Tahir Square. A week later, one million protesters took to the streets. Social media and an energized press played a catalytic role, facilitating mass mobilization as demonstrations spread throughout the country. Mubarak

frantically tried to hold onto power; however, under pressure from Egyptians and international actors, he resigned on February 11. Two days later, the constitution was suspended and parliament dissolved. However, military leaders and Mubarak's confidants remained in charge, leading some to argue that this was more of an intra-regime coup than a real revolution.[a] Since 1952, the Egyptian army had been a symbol of national pride and was interwoven in the country's political and economic life. That was not to change with the departure of Mubarak.

Those gathered at Tahir Square were united in their desire to be rid of the Mubarak regime, but there was little agreement beyond that. The Muslim Brotherhood, an established transnational solidarity-based social and educational organization, was one of the most organized, as the group had struggled for a political voice for over 80 years. Yet the Brotherhood joined the revolution only belatedly. After February 21, the conservative wing of the Brotherhood formed the Freedom and Justice Party, advocating for a more literal interpretation of the Koran and calling for a reassessment of Egypt's relationship with the United States. A second vision of Egypt's future was espoused by leading expatriates, including Mohammed ElBaradei. ElBaradei and others returned home with ideas about constituting Egypt as a secular democracy. A competing vision was advocated by a group espousing a strict interpretation of Islam, the Salafists, who organized as the Nour Party.

These contending voices competed over the future of Egypt. In the parliamentary elections between November 2011 and January 2012, the Freedom and Justice Party won 50 percent of the vote, the Salafists won 25 percent, and other parties split the rest. In the June 2012 election for president, the Muslim Brotherhood candidate, Mohammed Morsi, won by a narrow margin over the military's candidate, Ahmed Shafiq. By the end of the month, the parliament was dissolved by the judiciary for election irregularities, however. In the absence of a constitution or parliament, fears of a presidential dictatorship were real. Meanwhile, in the absence of economic reform, the economy has continued to decline. Hard currency reserves fell from $43 billion to $15 billion, foreign investment has dried up, and tourism is now at an all-time low.

In late 2012, a constitutional convention drafted a constitution that called for democratic government. Most contentious was the role of Sharia law. Secularists and Coptics, a Christian minority, preferred that "the principles of Sharia" be the basis for legislation. Islamists generally preferred that a stricter interpretation of "the rules of Sharia" be the foundation. Disagreement also arose over who should interpret Sharia—should it be religious scholars, or should it be the courts? In December 2012, a new constitution was approved by the electorate, with the principles of Sharia wording and with the stipulation that religious scholars must be consulted.

Another political issue involves the tension over control of the economy. The military's economic interests are extensive, perhaps 25 to 40 percent of the national economy, including resource-intensive sectors. Thus, the military demands that the final constitution give it control over the budget. But the Muslim Brotherhood also commands economic assets,

Protesters in Tahir Square, Cairo, Egypt.

with interests in consumer goods and services and the financial sector.

The struggle continues for a new Egypt. When President Morsi seized more power and called protesters "thugs," just as the Mubarak regime had done, the protests grew louder. While forced to soften his stance, the relationships among the main power brokers—the president, the courts, and the military—remain tense. In July 2013, the military removed Morsi from power, as massive protests by both Morsi's supporters and opponents led to violence in the streets. In Egypt, the Arab Spring is now in the winter of its discontent.

[a] Ewan Stein, "Revolution or Coup? Egypt's Fraught Transition," *Survival* 54:4 (Aug.–Sept. 2012): 45–66.

FOR CRITICAL ANALYSIS

1. What evidence can you provide that democracy is on the march in Egypt?

2. The new constitution does not settle many issues regarding Egypt's new political order. What issues would you expect to appear in the near future?

3. Why do Islamic states seem to have difficulty establishing democracies?

What has changed is that increasing democratization has emerged as a by-product of globalization, providing an opening for members of the same religion to organize transnationally and therefore increase their political influence. Able now to communicate with their adherents and compete for political power both within states and transnationally, some of these groups, antisecular and antimodern, pose stark challenges to state and international authorities.[21]

Political protests have become globalized, a result in part of new communication technology. Here, an Iranian living in Greece holds a poster with an image of a blood-drenched woman allegedly killed in protests in Tehran. The video became an Internet sensation, increasing pressure on the Iranian government.

Extremist Islamic fundamentalism poses such a dual threat. Although Islamic extremists come from many different countries and support different strategies for reaching their end goal, believers are united in their belief that political and social authority should be based in the Koran. This movement presents both a basic critique of what is wrong in many secular states as well as a solution that calls for radical state transformation. Islamic extremists see a long-standing discrepancy between the political and economic aspirations of states and the actual conditions of uneven economic distribution and rule by corrupt elites. Extremist groups advocate violence as the means to overthrow these corrupt rulers and install religious authority in their place.

The fight by the Afghans and their Islamic supporters against the Soviet Union in the 1980s proved to be a galvanizing event for extremist Islamic fundamentalism. It brought together religiously committed yet politically and economically disaffected young Islamists from all over the world; fighting the "godless" enemy forged group cohesion, and fighting the better-equipped Soviet military allowed them to hone their guerrilla tactics. These *mujahideen* (holy warriors) gained confidence by beating the Soviets into retreat. When they returned to their homelands in Saudi Arabia, Egypt, and other parts of the Middle East, they were imbued with a mission—to wage *jihad* (holy war) against what they view as illegitimate regimes. During the fight in Afghanistan,

Osama bin Laden, a Saudi national, emerged as a charismatic leader. When the Taliban assumed power in Afghanistan in 1996, bin Laden and what remained of the *mujahideen* formed Al Qaeda. Yet, as we will see in Chapter 8, Al Qaeda is just one of many Islamic fundamentalist groups, although its successful terrorist attacks on September 11, 2001, have made it the most widely known.

Although extremist Islamic fundamentalists are only a very small proportion of the over 1.5 billion Muslims worldwide, theirs is still a powerful transnational movement and a challenge to states from the Philippines and Indonesia, to Nigeria and Algeria, to Saudi Arabia, Iran, and Pakistan. In Nigeria, for example, the Boko Haram (meaning "Western education is sinful") formed after sectarian violence in the northeastern region in 2009. Since that time, over 1,000 people have been killed in attacks on the police, at churches, and in restaurants. Boko Haram followers view the Nigerian state as the enemy, a corrupt regime that systematically discriminates against the north, causing economic deprivation. The group advocates Sharia law in place of the existing state. While its violent actions are mainly local, the group has links with Al Qaeda in the Islamic Maghreb. More recently, the state of Mali has been under attack from both its own Toureg ethnic group and extremists from neighboring countries. They are terrorizing the local population in northern Mali, trying to impose unwelcome Sharia law, leading thousands of refugees to flee to Mauritania, and threatening the viability of the Mali state. This led to a French military intervention in 2013. Such examples have led some to believe the predictions that Samuel Huntington made 20 years ago that the next great international conflict would be a "clash of civilizations" arising from underlying differences between Western liberal democracy and Islamic fundamentalism.[22]

Members of **extremist Christian groups**, too, have posed serious problems for state authority. One such group, The Covenant, the Sword, and the Arm of the Lord, is examined in Jessica Stern's revealing book, *Terror in the Name of God.*[23] The cult began as a commune, with members living under primitive conditions and sharing Bible readings and prayer, but the group gradually cut itself off from the outside world. Members came to believe that Zionists, socialists, communists, and others had taken over the United States, as exemplified by the UN, the International Monetary Fund (IMF), and the Council on Foreign Relations—all indications of Satan's power. Joining forces with other right-wing groups, they planned—as directed by God—to poison residents in American cities and to destroy the so-called Zionist Occupied Government. Although federal authorities foiled the plot, the group has since joined with Christian Identity, an anti-government, racist group. Among its adherents were Timothy McVeigh, responsible for the Oklahoma City Federal Building bombing in 1995.

Not all transnational movements pose such direct challenges to the state. Indeed, many such movements, rather than forming around major cleavages such as religion or ideology as discussed earlier, develop around progressive goals such as the environment, human rights, and development, or around conservative goals such as opposition to abortion, family planning, or immigration. Often spurred by nongovernmental organizations that frame the issue and mobilize resources, these social movements want change, developing new approaches to problems and pushing governments to take action, but these movements do not generally undermine state sovereignty.

Ethnonational Movements

Another dramatic challenge to the state is found in **ethnonational movements**. The end of the Cold War witnessed the demise of multiethnic states such as the Soviet Union and Yugoslavia followed by the rise of democratic states in their stead. This political change, coupled with the communications revolution of fax, cell phone, and Internet, has led to increasing demands by ethnonational movements. While the demands differ in degree and kind, each poses a threat to the viability and sovereignty of established states.

One of the more complex ethnonational movements with international implications involves Kashmir—a mountainous area at the intersection of India, Pakistan, and China—and the Kashmiris, a people who are overwhelmingly Muslim but who have traditionally been ruled by Hindus. When India (dominated by Hindus) and Pakistan (dominated by Muslims) separated into two independent states in 1947, the maharaja of Kashmir, Hari Singh, opted to join India, much to the displeasure of the majority population, which wanted national affiliation with Pakistan. In 1947–48 and again in 1965, India and Pakistan fought over the territory, which has been plagued ever since by tensions and periodic skirmishes. A Line of Control (LOC) was reestablished in 1972, dividing Kashmir into India-administered Kashmir to the east and south, with 9 million people, and Pakistan-administered Kashmir to the north and west, with 3 million people. In addition to the rival claims of India and Pakistan, since 1989 a growing violent separatist movement has fought against Indian rule in Kashmir. The most prominent separatist group is the pro-Pakistani Hizbul Mujahideen, seeking union with Pakistan. The largest pro-independence group is the Jammu and Kashmir Liberation Front, but its influence has been declining. The Kashmiri ethnonational conflict has been particularly difficult because its factions are not only fighting for control of territory but are also tied into the larger conflict between India and Pakistan. In 2003, India and Pakistan signed a cease-fire along their borders in Kashmir and established diplomatic ties, reopening transportation links. But despite rounds of Indo-Pakistani peace talks, the dispute continues. In 2007, a devastating train bombing ignited violence, and in 2012 soldiers from both parties were killed in skirmishes.

Ethnonationalist movements pose a challenge even to the strongest states. China has been confronted by ethnic uprisings within the Muslim Uighur minority in the Xinjiang

Uighur Autonomous Region, its northwestern-most province, over the past several decades. Today, Xinjiang (a name the Uighurs find offensive), which makes up one-sixth of China's land area, is home to 20 million people and 13 ethnic groups. Of these, 45 percent are Uighurs and 40 percent are ethnic Han. The Uighurs migrated to the Chinese border region from the Mongolian steppe in the tenth century. They are a Turkic-speaking race that follows a branch of Sunni Islam. Their diaspora is centered in this area, but

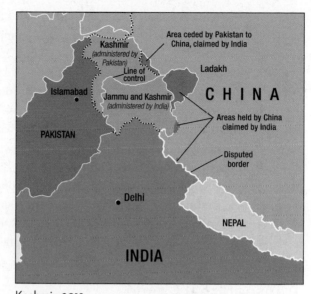

Kashmir, 2012

Note: The Line of Control separates the two sides in the Kashmir conflict.

Uighurs also live in Kazakhstan, Kyrgyzstan, and Uzbekistan, with smaller numbers in Mongolia and Afghanistan. They have a long history of fighting for independence as Uighuristan or East Turkestan.

When vast mineral and oil deposits were found in Xinjiang in the 1950s, Han Chinese began to move into the region at the urging of the government, which promised the settlers infrastructure and jobs. But to the Uighurs, the ethnic Han Chinese migrants are colonists; Uighur Islamic faith, traditional language, and economic prosperity are being repressed by the official Han policies.

Following 9/11, the Chinese government began to refer to Uighurs as terrorists, and greater repression has followed. Demonstrations broke out in the summer of 2009, when police tried to stop 1,000 Uighurs from demonstrating to protest judicial discrimination. Uighurs attacked Han Chinese, who responded in kind. More than 200 people were killed and 2,000 people wounded. The Chinese government is concerned about ethnic revolts and instability within its borders and justifies its own response as a war against terrorism. In 2012, Chinese officials charged that Uighur militants, calling themselves the East Turkestan Islamic Movement, have ties to Pakistan-based terror groups.

Chinese policy toward minorities is one of official recognition, granting limited autonomy with an extensive effort at central control. Although only 9 percent of China's population consists of ethnic minorities, those minorities are spread across resource-rich areas. They are actually the majorities in the strategically important border areas of not only Xinjiang but also Tibet, Inner Mongolia, and Yunan. These minorities also have higher birthrates than the Han Chinese, due to policies that permit the minorities more children.

The Chinese government's suppressions of Tibet in 1959 and 2008 and of Xinjiang in 2009 demonstrate Beijing's determination to exert dominance and authority across the entire country. However, with increasing economic problems and the internal struggle for succession, the state may continue to be challenged by ethnic minorities.

Some ethnonational challenges lead to civil conflict and even war, as the case of Kashmir illustrates. The political scientist Jack Snyder has identified the causal mechanism whereby ethnic nationalists challenge the state on the basis of the legitimacy of their language, culture, or religion. Particularly when countervailing state institutions are weak, elites within these ethnonational movements may be able to incite the masses to war.[24] Table 5.3 lists some of the ethnonational challengers in the world today.

Transnational Crime

Nowhere is the challenge to the state more evident than in the rise of transnational crime—illicit activities made easier by globalization. Growing in value, extending in scope, and becoming highly specialized, these activities have been facilitated by more and faster transportation routes, rapid communication, and electronic financial networks. Transnational crime has led to the accelerating movement of illegal drugs, counterfeit goods, smuggled weapons, laundered money, trade in body parts, piracy, and trafficking in poor and exploited people. (This is further explored in Chapter 11.) Organized around flexible networks and circuitous trafficking routes, and lubricated by electronic transfers of funds, transnational crime has created new businesses while distorting national and regional economies. States and governments are largely incapable of responding: rigid bureaucracies, laborious procedures, interbureaucratic fighting, and corrupt officials undermine states' efforts. In fact, some states—such as China, North Korea, and Nigeria—actively participate in these illicit activities or do nothing to stop them because key elites are making major profits.[25]

Other states such as Mexico have made concerted efforts to stop transnational crime. Since 2006, Mexico has undertaken a major effort to break up the drug cartels. That effort has escalated in violence, killing an estimated 55,000 people since 2006, mostly cartel members but also 1,000 children and almost 100 local government officials and reporters. The effort has had transnational implications. Small arms smuggled into Mexico from the United States fuel the violence; gang violence crosses the border into American cities; American tourists are staying away from Mexican resorts, with adverse effects on the economy. Many states are finding it very difficult to control and punish the transgressors, undermining their own sovereignty and that of their neighbors.

TABLE 5.3	ETHNONATIONAL CHALLENGERS, REPRESENTATIVE CASES
STATE(S)	**ETHNONATIONAL GROUPS**
Indonesia	Timorese, Papuans, Moluccans
People's Republic of China	Tibetans, Uighurs, Manchus
Nigeria	Yorubas, Ibos
Burundi, Rwanda	Hutus, Tutsis
Syria, Iraq, Iran, Turkey	Kurds
Moldova	Ukranians, Russians
Serbia, Macedonia	Albanians
Mexico, Guatemala	Maya, Zapotecs, Mixtecs
Burma, Thailand	Karens
India	Kashmiris
Afghanistan	Pashtuns, Hazaras, Tajiks, Uzbeks, Turkmens
Georgia	Abkhaz, Ossetes

Failed States

"Widespread lawlessness, ineffective government, terrorism, insurgency, crime, and well publicized pirate attacks against foreign vessels"—such is the description of a **failed state**.[26] Failed states entered the political lexicon in 1992 with the case of Somalia. In 2012, the index of failed states, based on 12 social, economic, and political indicators published by *Foreign Policy*, listed Somalia once again on top of the list, followed by the Democratic Republic of Congo, Sudan, Chad, Zimbabwe, Afghanistan, Haiti, Yemen, Iraq, and the Central African Republic. Other terms are often used in place of failed states—fragile, flailing, brittle, weak, and dysfunctional states, to name a few. But the implications are the same.

Failed states pose an internal threat to the people residing in the territory. The state is failing to perform one of its vital functions—protection of its people from violence and crime. Political, civil, as well as economic rights of its population are in continuous jeopardy. Failed states are unable to serve their citizenry, one of the requisites of sovereignty.

THEORY IN BRIEF

CONTENDING PERSPECTIVES ON STATE POWER AND POLICY

	REALISM/ NEOREALISM	LIBERALISM/ NEOLIBERAL INSTITUTIONALISM	RADICALISM/ DEPENDENCY THEORY	CONSTRUCTIVISM
Nature of State Power	Emphasis on power as key concept in international relations; geography, natural resources, population especially important	Multiple power sources; tangible and intangible sources	Economic power organized around classes	Power subject to norm socialization
Using State Power	Emphasis on coercive techniques of power; use of force acceptable	Broad range of power techniques; preference for noncoercive alternatives	Weak states have few instruments of power	Power is tool of elites for socializing societies through norms
How Foreign Policy is Made	Emphasis on rational model of decision making; unitary state actor assumed once decision is made	Organizational/ bureaucratic and pluralist models of decision making	States have no real choices; decisions dictated by economic capitalist elites	Decisions based on norms that regulate policy sector
Determinants of Foreign Policy	Largely external/ international determinants	Largely domestic determinants	Largely external determinants; co-opted internal elements	External determinants in combination with domestic civil society

Failed states also pose an international threat, serving as a hideaway for transnational terrorists, criminals, and pirates. In response, so-called failed states may develop alternative arrangements. By 2012 Somalia had been effectively split into five or six zones of influence and regional leaders have agreed to work toward a federal system. But the verdict is out whether that approach will alleviate the challenges that the "state" faces.

In Sum: The State and Challenges Beyond

The centrality of the state in international politics cannot be disputed. In this chapter, we have conceptualized the state according to the contending theoretical perspectives. We have looked inside the state to describe the various forms of state power. We have discussed the ways that states are able to use power through the diplomatic, economic, and coercive instruments of statecraft. We have explored the question of whether certain kinds of governments—democracies in particular—behave differently from nondemocracies. We have disaggregated the subnational actors within the state to identify different models of foreign policy decision making. And we have examined the ways in which globalization, transnational religious and ideological movements, ethnonationalist movements, transnational crime, and failed states pose threats to state sovereignty and to the stability of the international system. Such movements, however, depend on individuals; it is individuals who lead the challenge. Some are elites who are charismatic and powerful leaders in their own right. Some are part of a mass movement. It is these individuals to whom we now turn.

Discussion Questions

1. You are the leader of an emerging economy such as Indonesia. What tools of statecraft do you have at your disposal to influence your neighbors? What if instead you are the leader of a rising power like the People's Republic of China? What tools could you use?

2. Find two newspaper articles that suggest the use of soft power. How can you tell whether soft power "works"?

3. Ethnonationalist movements are a major source of state instability. Compare two recent cases of such conflict. How are the respective states addressing the issue? Are they addressing it at all?

4. Choose one state labeled as a failed state. What recommendations can you make to turn the state into a viable one?

Key Terms

bureaucratic politics (p. 158)

celebrity diplomacy (p. 148)

compellence (p. 150)

democratic peace (p. 154)

diplomacy (p. 146)

ethnonational movements (p. 168)

extremist Christian groups (p. 167)

extremist Islamic fundamentalism (p. 166)

failed state (p. 171)

first-strike capability (p. 152)

irredentism (p. 135)

nation (p. 133)

nation-state (p. 134)

nongovernmental organizations (NGOs) (p. 155)

organizational politics (p. 158)

power (p. 140)

power potential (p. 141)

public diplomacy (p. 147)

sanctions (p. 149)

satisficing (p. 158)

second-strike capability (p. 152)

smart power (p. 145)

smart sanctions (p. 149)

soft power (p. 145)

state (p. 132)

transnational movements (p. 163)

International political news is often dominated by the names of individuals, from U.S. President Barack Obama to democratic activist Aung San Suu Kyi, who won the Nobel Peace Prize for her efforts to bring democracy and human rights to Myanmar. As leaders, philanthropists, celebrities, soldiers, even as anonymous members of mass publics, individuals can influence world events in meaningful ways.

06

THE INDIVIDUAL

- *Which individuals matter most in international relations?*

- *What psychological factors have an impact on elite foreign policy decision making?*

- *What roles do private individuals play in international relations?*

- *What roles do mass publics play in foreign policy?*

- *According to the various theoretical perspectives, how much do individuals matter?*

International relations certainly affects the lives of individuals, as discussed in Chapter 1, but how individuals are viewed by international relations theorists varies. Does the structure of the international system make individuals merely passive agents or mere recipients of foreign policy? Are individuals really agents of the state acting in the national interest? Or can individuals, both elites and individuals acting in a large group, play a significant role that should be considered as a third level of analysis?

Recall the possible explanations given in Chapter 3 for why the United States invaded Iraq in 2003. One explanation pointed to the beliefs of President George W. Bush and his security advisers and to their response to Saddam Hussein, his personal characteristics, and his advisers. Clearly, one group of individuals that makes a difference to international relations is leaders. But individuals holding more informal roles can also have significant influence on international events, including war and peace, as well as international policies. For example, Srdja Popovic, a Serb activist and founder of CANVAS, the Centre for Applied NonViolent Action and Strategies, has trained revolutionaries in 46 countries, including Georgia, Ukraine, Moldova, and Egypt. And Wangari Maathai, the late Kenyan environmentalist, founded the Green Belt Movement, which promotes environmental management. In this chapter, we explore the various roles individuals play in international relations.

Foreign Policy Elites: Individuals Who Matter

Do individuals matter in the making of foreign policy? Liberals and constructivists recognize that leaders do make a difference. Whenever there is a leadership change in a major power such as the United States, China, or Russia, speculation always arises about possible changes in the country's foreign policy. This speculation reflects the general belief that individual leaders and their personal characteristics do make a difference in foreign policy, and hence in international relations. Ample empirical proof has been offered for this position. For instance, in March 1965 Nicolae Ceauşescu became the new leader of the Communist party of Romania. During his 22 years as Romania's head of state, the course of Romanian security policy changed significantly, reflecting the preferences and skills of Ceauşescu himself. He established diplomatic relations with West Germany before the Soviets agreed to reconciliation, he denounced the Warsaw Pact invasion of Czechoslovakia in 1968, and he strengthened ties to another maverick, Yugoslavia. A strong leader, Ceauşescu significantly changed Romania's foreign policy, moving it in a direction that deviated from the preferences of its closest ally, the Soviet Union.

The example of the Soviet leader Mikhail Gorbachev also illustrates the fact that leaders can effect real change. After coming to power in 1985, he began to frame the challenges confronting the Soviet Union differently, identifying the Soviet security problem as part of the larger problem of weakness in the Soviet economy. Through a process of trial and error, and by living through and then studying failures, Gorbachev came to the realization that the economic system had to be reformed in order to improve the country's security. He then took action to implement major reforms. Although he eventually lost power, he is responsible for initiating broad economic foreign policy change, including extricating the Soviet Union from its war in Afghanistan. Some constructivists credit the changes not only to Gorbachev, but also to a network of Western-oriented policy entrepreneurs who promoted new ideas.[1]

For realists, individuals are of little importance. This position comes from the realist assumption of a unitary actor. Thus, states are not differentiated by their government type or personalities or styles of the leaders in office but by the relative power they hold in the international system. Hans J. Morgenthau explained as follows:

> The concept of national interest defined as power imposes intellectual discipline upon the observer, infuses rational order into the subject matter of politics, and thus makes the theoretical understanding of politics possible. On the side of the actor, it provides for rational discipline in action and creates the astounding continuity in foreign policy which makes American, British, or Russian foreign policy appear as an intelligible, rational continuum, by and large consistent with itself, regardless of the different motives, preferences, and intellectual and moral qualities of successive statesmen.[2]

Yet, sometimes, individual motives and preferences seem to make a difference. *Glasnost* and *perestroika* were introduced in the Soviet Union beginning in 1986, Romania did carve a foreign policy niche independent of the Soviet Union during the 1970s, and the Chinese leader Deng Xiaoping established himself as the architect of the new China after 1978. Under his socialist market economy, the state permitted limited private competition and gradually opened itself economically to the outside world. Were these individuals in fact responsible for these major changes, or did individual leaders just happen to be the right (or wrong) people at the time? Given the same situation, would different individuals have made different decisions, thus charting different courses through international relations?

Two questions are most pertinent to determining the role of individuals in international relations: When are the actions of individuals likely to have a greater or lesser effect on the course of events? And under what circumstances do actors' different personal characteristics cause them to behave differently?

The Impact of Elites: External Conditions

An individual's actions affect the course of events when at least one of several factors is present (see Figure 6.1). When political institutions are unstable, young, in crisis, or collapsed, leaders are able to provide powerful influences. Founding fathers, be they the United States' George Washington, India's Mohandas Gandhi, Russia's Vladimir Lenin, or South Africa's Nelson Mandela, have a great impact because they lead in the early years of their nations' lives, when institutions and practices are being established. Adolf Hitler, Franklin Roosevelt, Mikhail Gorbachev, and Vladimir Putin had more influence precisely because their states were in economic crises when they were in power.

Mohandas Gandhi tirelessly led a mass non-violent movement for Indian independence from British rule. His actions helped to establish India as an independent state, with major international ramifications. Here, Gandhi visits the British prime minister's residence in London in 1931.

Individuals also affect the course of events when they have few institutional constraints. In dictatorial regimes, top leaders are relatively free from domestic constraints such as political opposition or societal inputs, and thus are able to chart courses and implement foreign policy relatively unfettered, as illustrated by the Romanian and Soviet examples. In democratic regimes, too, occasionally top decision makers are able to change policy in a dramatic fashion. For example, U.S. president Richard Nixon in 1972 was able to engineer a complete foreign policy reversal in relations with the People's Republic of China, secretly sending his top foreign policy adviser, Henry Kissinger, for several meetings with the Chinese premier Zhou Enlai and his advisers. These moves were an unexpected change, given Nixon's Republican Party affiliation and prior anticommunist record. But that may be the exception, as many democratic leaders are constrained by bureaucracies and societal groups, as illustrated by Israeli leaders' delicate balancing of interests between peace activists and hardline conservatives with respect to settlements on the West Bank.

The specifics of a situation also determine the extent to which individuals matter. Decision makers' personal characteristics have more influence on outcomes when the issue is peripheral rather than central, when the issue is not routine—that is, standard operating procedures are not available—or when the situation is ambiguous and information is unclear. Crisis situations, in particular, when information is in short supply and standard operating procedures are inapplicable, create scenarios in which a decision maker's personal characteristics count most. Such a scenario arose during the Cuban missile crisis, when President John F. Kennedy's personal openness to alternatives and attention to group dynamics played a role in the resolution.

The Impact of Elites: The Personality Factor

Even among elite leaders working amid similar external conditions, some individuals seem to have a greater impact on foreign policy than others; this leads us to examine both the personal characteristics that matter and the thought processes of individuals.

Political psychologist Margaret Hermann has found a number of personality characteristics that affect foreign policy behaviors. Because top leaders do not generally take personality tests, Hermann used a different research strategy. She systematically collected spontaneous interviews and press conferences with 80 heads of state holding office in 38 countries between 1959 and 1968. From these data, she found key personality characteristics that she felt influence a leader's orientation toward policy.[3] Those characteristics are listed in the top section of Figure 6.2.

These personality characteristics orient an individual's view of foreign affairs. Two orientations emerge from the personality traits. One group, leaders with high levels of nationalism, a strong belief in their own ability to control events, a strong need for

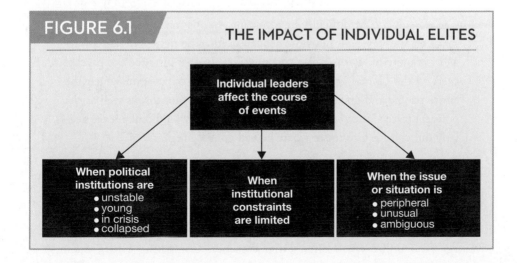

FIGURE 6.1   **THE IMPACT OF INDIVIDUAL ELITES**

Individual leaders affect the course of events

When political institutions are
- unstable
- young
- in crisis
- collapsed

When institutional constraints are limited

When the issue or situation is
- peripheral
- unusual
- ambiguous

power, low levels of conceptual complexity, and high levels of distrust of others, tend to develop an independent orientation to foreign affairs. The other group, leaders with low levels of nationalism, little belief in their ability to control events, a high need for affiliation, high levels of conceptual complexity, and low levels of distrust of others, tend toward a participatory orientation in foreign affairs. (The bottom of Figure 6.2 illustrates these orientations.) Then Hermann tested whether these personal characteristics and their respective orientations were related to the foreign policy style and the behavior of the leaders.

Both Hermann and subsequent researchers using the same schema have found that these characteristics and orientations matter. For example, one study analyzed the personality characteristics of the former British prime minister Tony Blair using Hermann's categories to organize Blair's foreign policy answers to questions posed in the House of Commons.[4] The researcher found that Blair had a strong belief in his own ability to control events and a high need for power, accompanied by a low conceptual complexity. These personality findings go a long way toward explaining British foreign policy toward the 2003 Iraq War, a policy that many in the government and the British public opposed. Thus, even in democracies, where institutional constraints are high, individual personality characteristics influence foreign policy orientation and behavior.

Political scientist Betty Glad has developed a profile of the former president Jimmy Carter that suggests how his personality characteristics played a key role in influencing the course of U.S. policy during the 1979–81 hostage crisis. The crisis began when Iranian militants kidnapped more than 60 Americans and held them for more than a year. Carter personalized the hostage taking. He was humiliated, obsessed, wanting above all to have *his* decisions vindicated. After an attempted helicopter rescue mission failed, he rationalized the failure as a "worthy effort," feeling that some action was better than nothing. Glad points to Carter's personality characteristics:

> Carter's subsequent difficulty in admitting that he made mistakes in this situation was based on his more general need to be right. He had always had difficulty in learning from his mistakes. In this instance the psychic costs to the United States of its impotence in a crisis upon which the entire people and government focused for several months, as well as the political price Carter had to pay for that fixation, would make it particularly difficult for him to see where he had gone wrong.[5]

Personality characteristics affect the leadership of dictators more than that of democratic leaders because of the absence of effective institutional checks, as Glad has also investigated. She analyzed the personalities of tyrants—those who rule without attention to law, capitalize on grandiose self-presentations and projects, look for every advantage, and utilize cruel, often extreme tactics. Comparing Hitler, Stalin, and

FIGURE 6.2 — PERSONALITY CHARACTERISTICS OF LEADERS

Personality Characteristics of Leaders

Nationalism: strong emotional ties to nation; emphasis on national honor and dignity

Perception of control: belief in ability to control events; high degree of control over situations; governments able to influence state and nation

Need for power: need to establish, maintain, and project power or influence over others

Need for affiliation: concern for establishing and maintaining friendly relationships with others

Conceptual complexity: ability to discuss with other people places, policies, ideas in a discerning way

Distrust of others: feelings of doubt, uneasiness about others; doubt about motives and actions of others

Foreign Policy Orientations

Independent leader: high in nationalism

high in perception of control

high in need for power

low in conceptual complexity

high in distrust of others

Participatory leader: low in nationalism

low in perception of control

high in need for affiliation

high in conceptual complexity

low in distrust of others

Source: Margaret G. Hermann, "Explaining Foreign Policy Behavior Using the Personal Characteristics of Political Leaders," *International Studies Quarterly* 24:1 (March 1980): 7–46.

A View from Venezuela: Hugo Chávez

Leaders are usually more complex than the simplistic labels that are attached to them: "good" or "bad," "weak" or "strong," "democrat" or "tyrant." Former President Hugo Chávez of Venezuela, who governed for 14 years until his death in 2013, was one such leader: he was a complicated individual who supported populist domestic policies and revolutionary policies abroad.

President Hugo Chávez was a charismatic, democratically elected authoritarian leader. After mounting a failed coup attempt in 1992, he decided that the way to win power was through the ballot box. He was first elected in 1998 and won re-election twice. Inspired by Simón Bolívar, Che Guevara, the Chilean socialist president Salvador Allende, and Fidel Castro, Chávez adopted a style and policies that put Venezuela on a new course.

Arguing that the model of economic development imposed on Latin American governments by the United States has failed, Chávez called his agenda a twenty-first century socialist revolution. Inspired by the teachings of Jesus, he spent large amounts of money on social programs such as housing, health care, and food subsidies. In one year alone, state spending for such programs increased by more than 30 percent and in the election year of 2012, the economy grew at 5.5 percent, in large part due to social spending. Due to the efforts of Chávez's Bolivarian Missions (named after Bolívar) to combat disease, illiteracy, and poverty, the number of poor Venezuelans fell from 49.4 percent in 1999 to 27.6 percent in 2008, according to the UN Economic Commission for Latin America. As Alberto Müller Rojas, a leader of Chávez's United Socialist Party of Venezuela, optimistically argues, "a social consciousness has been created. It's improbable that we will regress to the way it was before."[a]

Chávez also broadened popular political participation through the Bolivarian Circles, grassroots political and social groups. That participation can be seen both in poor neighborhoods around the capital and in rural areas. Bringing technology to these areas connected people and gave them a means of political participation.

Chávez's economic and political programs were funded by escalating export revenues from petroleum since 1999. The government assumed full control over Venezuela's national oil company, PDVSA, in 2004. Yet several government policies regarding oil were counterproductive. Investment in technical capacity to extract oil has declined. And policies that require PDVSA to supply cheap oil to other countries in the region, including allies in Bolivia, Ecuador, Cuba, and Nicaragua, have led to an overall decline in revenue. But Chávez continued to find support in these countries not only because of foreign aid packages but because his critique of U.S. neoliberal economic policies tapped a deep animosity toward the United States.

During his tenure, Chávez exercised his democratic authority by reducing the size of the political center and confronting his political opposition, but not banning them. He lavished his supporters with gifts and withheld resources from those who opposed him. He controlled the judiciary and the institution that supervised elections. He dominated the media. His strategy, sometimes called "Chavenomics," entailed the overwhelming presence of the state in the economy and presidential involvement in state management.

Chávez also forged relationships with other oil-producing countries, including Iran and Russia. Cooperation between Russia and Venezuela has increased in the areas of military hardware and nuclear technology acquisition and development. Chávez purchased more than $4 billion worth of Russian arms, including jet fighters and assault rifles.

With the elimination of the term limits for the presidency, which the legislature passed in 2009, Chávez ran again for office in 2012. As he stated then, "There's still much to do; I need more time."[b] Yet time is what he did not have. Venezuela's economic situation had become more difficult. Galloping inflation, food shortages, and the deteriorating quality of medical and educational services, coupled with a precipitous drop in oil revenue, has led to decline. In 2012, the inflation rate was estimated to be 20 percent and the Venezuelan currency traded for one-third of its rate on the black market. In 2011, Chávez was diagnosed with cancer and received extensive treatment in Cuba for long periods of time. Despite this, in 2012 Chávez won re-election with 55 percent of the vote. He never took the oath of office, and Chávez died in March 2013.

Both populist domestic economic measures and anti-American rhetoric continues in Venezuela. The question of whether "chavismo" will continue without Chávez looms large. His appointed vice president, Nicolás Maduro, won a contested election to become the next president. While not as charismatic or emotional as Chávez, Maduro has forged strong ties with China, Russia, and Iran, while keeping the hope alive that chavismo will continue. But internal divisions within the movement make the future uncertain. Meanwhile, the construc-

Chavez's supporters march in Caracas in 2011.

tion of a controversial 170-foot tall mausoleum designed for the remains of Bolívar (and as a monument or tomb for Chávez) continues in earnest.

[a] Quoted in Sara Miller Llana, "Where Has Chávez Taken Venezuela?" *Christian Science Monitor,* February 2, 2009, www.csmonitor.com/World/Americas/2009/0202/p01s03-woam.html (accessed 1/15/09).

[b] Llana, "Chávez."

FOR CRITICAL ANALYSIS

1. Using Hermann's personality characteristics, how would you describe Hugo Chávez?

2. Was it personality or policies that made Chávez both popular and powerful?

3. Can the policies that a charismatic leader like Chávez implement be continued when the individual is no longer the leader? Support your position.

4. Realists argue that individuals themselves are not key actors. Explain that viewpoint, using this case.

Saddam Hussein, she labels them as having malignant narcissism syndrome. Glad explains how "project over-reach and creation of new enemies leads to increasing vulnerability, a deepening of the paranoiac defense, and volatility in behavior."[6] The late North Korean leader Kim Jong-Il (the "Dear Leader") and his father, Kim Il-Sung (the "Great Leader") exhibited some of these same characteristics. Kim Il-Sung erected more than 34,000 monuments to himself during his 50-year rule, and his photo was prominently displayed in buildings and other public places. Likewise, Kim Jong-Il expressed his megalomania with gigantic pictures of himself, spending millions of dollars on spectacles with historical themes while millions of his people starved. One former CIA psychiatrist suggested that Kim Jong-Il was self-absorbed, lacked an ability to empathize, and was capable of "unconstrained aggression."[7]

Following Kim Jong-Il's death in 2011, North Korean propaganda immediately began to elevate his son, Kim Jong-Un, to deity, noting his talents and extraordinary deeds—all in an effort to legitimize the succession. How Kim Jong-Un will lead remains an engima. He has shown a "human touch" toward his own people, while threatening war against South Korea and the United States.

Personality characteristics, then, partly determine what decisions individual leaders make. But those decisions also reflect the fact that all decision makers are confronted with the task of putting divergent information into an organized form.

Individual Decision Making

The rational model of decision making that we discussed in Chapter 5 suggests that the individual possesses all the relevant information, stipulates a goal, examines the relevant choices, and makes a decision that best achieves that goal. In actuality, however, individuals are not always rational decision makers. Confronted by information that is neither perfect nor complete, and often overwhelmed by a plethora of information and conditioned by personal experience, the decision maker selects, organizes, and evaluates incoming information about the surrounding world.

Individuals use a variety of psychological techniques to process and evaluate information. In perceiving and interpreting new and often contradictory information, individuals rely on existing perceptions, usually based on prior experiences. Such perceptions are the "screens" that enable individuals to process information selectively; these perceptions have an integrating function, permitting the individual to synthesize and interpret the information. Perceptions also serve an orienting function, providing guidance about future expectations and expediting planning for future contingencies. If those perceptions form a relatively integrated set of images, then they are called a **belief system**.

International relations scholars have devised methods to test the existence of elite perceptions, although research has not been conducted on many individuals because sufficient data is usually unavailable. Ole Holsti systematically analyzed 434 of the publicly available statements of Secretary of State John Foster Dulles concerning the Soviet Union during the years 1953–54. His research showed convincingly that Dulles held a very specific and unwavering image of the Soviet Union, one focused on atheism, totalitarianism, and communism. To Dulles, the Soviet people were good, but their leaders were bad; the state was good, the Communist party bad. This image was unvarying; the character of the Soviet Union in Dulles's mind did not change. Whether this perception, gleaned from Dulles's statements, affected U.S. decisions during the period cannot be stated with certainty. He was, after all, only one among a group of top leaders. Yet a plethora of decisions made during that time are consistent with his perception.[8]

The political scientists Harvey Starr and Stephen Walker both completed similar empirical research on Henry Kissinger.[9] Elucidating Kissinger's operational code (the rules he operated by) from his scholarly writings, Walker found that the conduct of the Vietnam War, orchestrated in large part by Kissinger between 1969 and 1973, was congruent with the premises of his operational code and his conception of mutually acceptable outcomes. He wanted to negotiate a mutual withdrawal of external forces and to avoid negotiating about the internal structure of South Vietnam. He used enough force, applied in combination with generous peace terms, so that North Vietnam was faced with an attractive peace settlement versus unpalatable alternatives — stalemate or escalation.

These elite mind-set studies were possible because the particular elites left behind extensive written records from before, during, and after they held key policy-making positions. Since few leaders leave such a record, however, our ability to empirically reconstruct elite beliefs, perceptions, or operational codes is limited, as is our inability to state with certainty their influence on a specific decision.

Information-Processing Mechanisms

Our images and perceptions of the world are continually bombarded by new, sometimes overwhelming, and often discordant information. Images and belief systems, however, are not generally changed, and almost never are they radically altered. Thus, individual elites utilize, usually unconsciously, a number of psychological mechanisms to process the information they encounter in the world. These mechanisms are summarized in Table 6.1.

First, individuals strive for **cognitive consistency**, ensuring that their beliefs fit together into a coherent whole. For example, individuals like to believe that the enemy of an enemy is a friend, and the enemy of a friend is an enemy. Because of the tendency to be cognitively consistent, individuals select or amplify information that supports existing beliefs and ignore or downplay contradictory information. For example, because both Great Britain and Argentina were friends of the United States prior to their war over the Falkland/Malvinas Islands in 1982, U.S. decision makers denied the seriousness of the conflict. They did not think that its ally would go to war with Argentina over barren islands thousands of miles from Britain's shores. The United States underestimated the strength of British public support for military action and misjudged the precarious domestic position of the Argentinian generals, who were trying to bolster their power by diverting attention to a popular external conflict.

Individuals also perceive and evaluate the world according to what they have learned from past events. They look for details of a present episode that look like those of a past one, perhaps ignoring the important differences. Such similar details are often referred to as an **evoked set**. During the 1956 Suez crisis, for instance, the British prime minister Anthony Eden saw Egyptian president Gamal Abdel Nasser as another Hitler. Eden recalled prime minister Neville Chamberlain's failed effort to appease Hitler with the Munich agreement in 1938 and thus believed that Nasser, likewise, could not be appeased. Similar thinking led some American elites to describe Iraq as another Vietnam or to see the Soviet defeat in Afghanistan as that country's Vietnam, despite critical differences.

Individual perceptions are often shaped in terms of **mirror images**: whereas one considers one's own actions good, moral, and just, the enemy's actions are automatically found to be evil, immoral, and unjust. Mirror imaging often exacerbates conflicts, making it all the more difficult to resolve a contentious issue.

The psychological mechanisms that we have discussed so far affect the functioning of both individuals and small groups. But small groups themselves also have psychologically based dynamics that undermine the rational model. Psychologist Irving Janis called this dynamic **groupthink**. Groupthink, according to Janis, is "a mode of thinking that people engage in when they are deeply involved in a cohesive in-group, when members' strivings for unanimity override their motivation to realistically appraise alternative courses of action."[10] The dynamics of the group, which include the illusion of invulnerability and unanimity, excessive optimism, the belief in the group's own morality and the enemy's evil, and the pressure placed on dissenters to change their views, leads to groupthink. During the Vietnam War, for example, a top group of U.S. decision makers, unified by bonds of friendship and loyalty, met in what they called the Tuesday lunch group. In the aftermath of President Lyndon Johnson's overwhelming electoral win in 1964, the group basked in self-confidence and optimism, rejecting out of hand pessimistic information about North Vietnam's military buildup. When information mounted about increasing South Vietnamese and American casualties and external stresses intensified, the group further closed ranks, its members taking solace in the security of the group. Individuals who did not share the group's thinking were both informally and formally removed from the group, as their prognosis that the war effort was going badly fell on deaf ears.

Participants in small groups, then, are likely to employ the same psychological techniques, such as the evoked set and the mirror image, to process new incoming

TABLE 6.1   PSYCHOLOGICAL MECHANISMS USED TO PROCESS INFORMATION

TECHNIQUE	EXPLANATION	EXAMPLE
Cognitive Consistency	Tendency to accept information that is compatible with what has previously been accepted, often ignoring inconsistent information. Desire to be consistent in attitude.	Just prior to the Japanese attack on Pearl Harbor, military spotters saw unmarked planes approaching Hawaii. Not believing the evidence, they discounted the sightings.
Evoked Set	Details in a present situation that are similar to information gleaned from past situations. The tendency to look for an evoked set leads one to conclusions that are similar to those of the past.	During the Vietnam War, U.S. decision makers saw the Korean War as a precedent, although there were critical differences.
Mirror Image	Seeing in one's opponent the opposite of characteristics seen in oneself. Opponent is viewed as hostile and uncompromising, whereas one views oneself as friendly and compromising.	During the Cold War, U.S. elites and public viewed the Soviet Union in terms of their own mirror image: the United States was friendly, the Soviet Union hostile.
Groupthink	Thought process whereby small groups form consensus and resist criticism of that core position, often disregarding contradictory information.	During the U.S. planning for the Bay of Pigs operation against Cuba in 1961, opponents were ostracized from the planning group.
Satisficing	Tendency for groups to search for a "good enough" solution, rather than an optimal one.	Decision of NATO to bomb Kosovo in 1999 in an attempt to stop the ethnic cleansing against the Albanian Kosovars, rather than sending in ground troops.

information at the individual level. But additional distorting tendencies affect small groups, such as the pressure for group conformity and solidarity. Larger groups seeking accommodation look for what is possible within the bounds of their situation, searching for a "good enough" solution, rather than an optimal one. Herbert Simon has labeled this trait *satisficing,* as introduced in Chapter 5.[11]

Political scientist Robert Jervis offers suggestions on how decision makers can safeguard their thinking and minimize mistakes due to various kinds of misperceptions.[12] They need to make their assumptions and beliefs as explicit as possible, be cognizant of the pitfall of interpreting data only as consistent with one's own theory, and be willing to consider information from different angles. Yet even this awareness does not necessarily lead to a rational model of decision making. It is not just the tyrants (Uganda's Idi Amin or Cambodia's Pol Pot), but also the visionaries (Tanzania's Julius Nyerere, India's Mohandas Gandhi), and the political pragmatists (Great Britain's Margaret Thatcher or Liberia's Ellen Johnson Sirleaf) who make an impact on the basis of their perceptions and misperceptions.

After the devastating reigns of corrupt authoritarian leaders such as Saddam Hussein in Iraq, Mobutu Sese Seko in Congo (formerly Zaire), and Robert Mugabe in Zimbabwe, whose people have been unwitting hostages to their cruelty, some pundits and politicians have suggested that "bad" or "corrupt" leaders should be removed by the international community by force, even assassination, if necessary.[13] That debate brings up numerous normative and pragmatic issues for students of international relations.

Private Individuals

Although leaders holding formal positions have more opportunity not only to participate in but to shape international relations, private individuals can and do play key roles. Private individuals, independent of any official role, may by virtue of circumstances, skills, or resources carry out independent actions in international relations. Less bound by the rules of the game or by institutional norms, such individuals engage in activities in which official representatives are either unable or unwilling to participate. The donations by Microsoft's founder Bill Gates and his wife, Melinda, to global vaccinations, water sanitation, and AIDS programs is one such example.

In the area of conflict resolution, for instance, private individuals increasingly play a role in so-called **track-two diplomacy**. Track-two diplomacy utilizes individuals outside of governments to carry out the task of conflict resolution. High-level track-two diplomacy has met with some success. In the spring of 1992, for example, Eritrea signed a declaration of independence, seceding from Ethiopia after years of both low- and high-intensity conflict. The foundation for the agreement was negotiated in numerous informal meetings in Atlanta, Georgia, and elsewhere between the affected parties

⬆⬇ YOU DECIDE

This chapter focuses on the explanatory power of theories that identify the individual as a key lever of international politics. A long history of corrupt, tyrannical, and violent state leaders prompts an important question: When a leader engages in particularly cruel and aggressive behavior, causing massive death and suffering, should assassination be considered as a legitimate tool of foreign policy, or should assassination continue to be prohibited, as it is now under international law?

On the pro assassination side, you might argue that assassination would be kinder than an economic intervention that is likely to cause widespread starvation or a military intervention that might harm not only to the target state's military but also its roads, bridges, water, agriculture, and energy sectors. Moreover, a well-executed assassination might not only avert a costly war, but it could dramatically improve the lives and opportunities of that leader's people. You might add that a policy of assassination would likely deter a subsequent leader from engaging in similarly violent and cruel policies.

On the other hand, you might point out that the prohibition against assassination of foreign heads of state is based not only on the principle of sovereign immunity, but on the more ancient principle of reciprocity: any act of state justifies a reciprocal act so long as that act is proportionate in kind and degree. Thus, you could argue that once a leader is assassinated, reciprocal assassination attempts become likely. You might add that if assassination becomes successful and widespread, negotiation to halt costly wars or sanctions becomes impossible: With whom would one negotiate? All heads of state would fear to leave their homes. Finally, you might argue that assassination, even if welcomed by an oppressed people, in some important way deprives that people of the chance to determine their own fate by doing away with a tyrant on their own. Perhaps people get the leaders they deserve?

YOU DECIDE: Would assassination of an "obviously" bad leader be a good idea, sparing all sides from suffering, or should it remain off limits as a tool of interstate politics?

and former president Jimmy Carter, acting through the Carter Center's International Negotiation Network at Emory University. In the fall of 1993, the unexpected framework for reconciliation between Israel and the Palestine Liberation Organization was negotiated through track-two informal and formal processes initiated by Terje Larsen, a Norwegian sociologist, and Yossi Beilin of the opposition Labor party in Israel. A series of preparatory negotiations was conducted over a five-month period in total secrecy. Beginning unofficially, the talks gradually evolved into official negotiations, building up trust in an informal atmosphere and setting the stage for an eventual agreement.[14]

Such high-level track-two diplomatic efforts are not always well received. For example, Jimmy Carter's eleventh-hour dash in 1994 to meet with North Korea's Kim Il-Sung to discuss the latter's nuclear buildup was met by a barrage of probing questions. Was the U.S. government being preempted? For whom did

In 2009, former president Bill Clinton played an instrumental role in arranging the release of two American journalists being held by North Korea. Private individuals, including former leaders who no longer hold any government position, can sometimes shape international relations.

Carter speak? Could the understandings become the basis of a formal intergovernmental agreement? Despite the misgivings and the eventual unraveling of North Korea's promises, Carter received the Nobel Peace Prize in 2002 for this and other efforts to promote peace around the world. Similar objections were raised when former president Bill Clinton journeyed to North Korea in 2009 to negotiate the release of two jailed American journalists. Did Clinton's meeting with the North Korean leader amount to negotiations with the errant regime? Was this private citizen actually speaking on behalf of the U.S. administration? The fact that Clinton is a former president and his wife the U.S. secretary of state at the time added to the confusion.

Other types of track-two diplomacy involve the lengthier process of sustained dialogue.[15] In some cases, unofficial individuals from different international groups are brought together in small problem-solving workshops in order to develop personal relationships and understanding of the problems from the perspective of others. It is hoped that these individuals will then seek to influence public opinion in their respective states, trying to reshape, and often rehumanize, the image of the opponent. This approach has been used to address the conflict between Protestants and Catholics in Northern Ireland and the Arab-Israeli dispute. Problem-solving workshops have been conducted over two decades and cooperative activities encouraged.

Other private individuals have played linkage roles between different countries. Armand Hammer, a U.S. corporate executive, was for years a private go-between for the Soviet Union and the United States. His long-standing business interests in the Soviet Union and his carefully nurtured friendships with both Soviet economic and political leaders and U.S. officials provided a channel of communication at a time when few informal contacts existed between the two countries. In the immediate aftermath of the 1986 Chernobyl nuclear plant explosion, Hammer convinced Gorbachev to accept U.S. medical personnel and expertise.

The Cases of Mohamed Bouazizi, A. Q. Khan, and Aung San Suu Kyi

Occasionally individuals are propelled into the international arena by virtue of one spontaneous act that has significant repercussions. Mohamed Bouazizi, a Tunisian vendor, set himself on fire outside a government building after his goods were confiscated by state authorities in December 2010. The video posted on the Internet of his self-immolation was seen around the Arab world, not only leading to the overthrow of the Tunisian president, Zine al-Abidine, in the Jasmine Revolution, but also providing the spark for the broader democratic opening in the Arab world, the Arab Spring.

The actions of A. Q. (Abdul Qadeer) Khan, the scientist dubbed the father of Pakistan's atomic bomb, led to a different kind of outcome, but just as profound. He confessed to selling nuclear technology and components to Libya, Iran, and North Korea in 2004. Through his activities, Khan has enabled nuclear proliferation, which many believe has made the world a less secure place. Under pressure from the West, the Pakistani government placed Khan in house detention but then released him in 2009.

Aung San Suu Kyi became yet a different symbol: the face of the opposition movement to the repressive military government of Myanmar (formerly Burma). Her father, General Aung San, negotiated that country's independence from Great Britain in 1947. Assassinated the same year, he is viewed by many as the father of modern-day Burma. His daughter's public acts began after the 1962 military coup. Defying a ban on political gatherings, she spoke to large crowds, demanding democratic government.

After spending many years outside of the country, she returned to Burma in 1988 and became the secretary-general of the newly formed National League for Democracy. Advocating nonviolence and civil disobedience, she traveled across the country, speaking to large audiences. In 1989, the government placed her under house arrest, where she stayed for more than two decades.

Awarded the Nobel Peace Prize in 1991, Aung San Suu Kyi became an international symbol of the opposition. That opposition demanded the release of political prisoners and broader political change, similar to those demands made by UN and U.S. negotiators. Then in 2010, in a sign of government reform, Aung San Suu Kyi was released from house arrest. She immediately began to rebuild the National League for Democracy. Since then, political prisoners have been freed, trade unions have been legalized, and Aung San Suu Kyi herself won election to the Parliament. She made triumphant trips to Europe and the United States, bringing international attention to the Burmese plight, and continues to pressure the government for more change. Less clear is whether her presence led the government to change course or whether government elites made the decision independently. Either way, contrary to the realist position, this individual mattered, serving as an example of peaceful resistance.

Alternative critical and postmodernist approaches are attempting to draw mainstream theorists' attention to other less well-known and less-publicized stories, because they, too, are part of the fabric of international relations. Feminist writers in particular have sought to bring attention to the role of private individuals and especially women. In *Bananas, Beaches, and Bases*, political scientist Cynthia Enloe shows strikingly how "the personal is international" by documenting the many ways that women influence international relations. She points to women in economic roles participating in the international division of labor, as seamstresses, light-industry "girls," nannies, and fashion models. She also identifies women more directly involved in foreign policy—the women living around military bases, diplomatic wives, domestic servants, and women in international organizations.[16] Theirs are the untold stories of marginalized groups that critical theorists, postmodernists, and constructivists are increasingly bringing to light.

Mass Publics

Mass publics have the same psychological tendencies as elite individuals and small groups. They think in terms of perceptions and images, they see mirror images, and they use similar information-processing strategies. For example, following the seizure of the U.S. embassy in Iran in November 1979, public-opinion surveys showed the prevalence of mirror images. The majority of U.S. respondents attributed favorable qualities to the United States and its leader and unfavorable ones to Iran and its leader.

The United States was strong and brave; Iran, weak and cowardly. The United States was deliberate and decisive; Iran, impulsive and indecisive. President Carter was safe; the Ayatollah Khomeini, dangerous; Carter, humane; Khomeini, ruthless. In a relatively short period of time, under crisis conditions, the public's perception of Iran had crystallized. Yet whether this had an impact on top decision makers is unclear.[17] President Carter focused almost exclusively on the hostages, becoming obsessed with his mission of freeing them. But was this because of the public attention being paid to the hostages? Or did Carter's personality characteristics predispose him to focus so exclusively and so passionately on the hostages?

The influence that mass publics have on foreign policy might be explained in three ways. First, it could be argued that elites and masses hold similar beliefs and act in similar ways because they share common psychological and biological characteristics. Second, it could be that the masses have opinions and attitudes about foreign policy and international relations, both general and specific, that are different from those of the elites. If these differences are captured by public-opinion polls, will the elites listen to these opinions? Will policy made by the elites reflect the public's attitudes? The third possibility is that the masses, uncontrolled by formal institutions, may occasionally act in ways that have a profound impact on international relations, regardless of anything that the elites do.

Elites and Masses: Common Traits

Some scholars argue that there are psychological and biological traits common to every man, woman, and child and that societies reflect those characteristics. For example, individuals, like animals, are said to have an innate drive to gain, protect, and defend territory — the "territorial imperative." This, according to some, explains the preoccupation with defending territorial boundaries, such as Britain's determination in 1982 to defend its position on the Falkland Islands. Individuals and societies also share the frustration-aggression syndrome: when societies become frustrated, just like individuals, they become aggressive. Frustration, of course, can arise from a number of different sources — economic shocks such as those Germany suffered after World War I or those Russia experienced in the 1990s, or failure to possess what is felt to be rightfully one's own, for example, the Palestinian claim to territory of the Israeli state.

The problem with both the territorial imperative and the frustration-aggression notion is that even if all individuals and societies share these innate biological predispositions, not all leaders and all peoples act on these predispositions. So general predispositions of all societies or the similarities in predispositions between elites and masses cannot explain the extreme variation found in individual behavior and state behavior.

Another possibility is that elites and masses share common traits differentiated by gender. Male elites and masses possess characteristics common to each other, whereas female elites and masses share traits different from those of males. These differences can explain political behavior. Although there is considerable interest in this possibility, the research is sketchy. One much-discussed difference is that males, both elites and masses, are power seeking, whereas women are consensus builders, more collaborative, and more inclined toward compromise. One study, for example, sees the direct implications of these gender differences for peace negotiations. Because women often come to the negotiating table with experience in civic activism, nongovernmental organizations, and citizen-empowering movements, they bring with them different attitudes and skill-sets. Drawing on this research, the European Union (EU) has mandated that 40 percent of all peacekeeping, reconciliation, and peace-building posts be given to women, and the United Nations and the Organization of Security and Cooperation in Europe have both tried to include more women in peace processes, in anticipation that gender differences may lead to better outcomes.[18]

If there are differences in male and female attitudes and behavior, are these differences rooted in biology or are they learned from the culture? Most feminists, particularly the constructivists, contend that these differences are socially constructed products of culture and can thus be reconstructed over time. Yet, once again, these general predispositions, whatever their origin, cannot explain extreme variation in individual behavior.

The Impact of Public Opinion on Elites

Publics do have general foreign policy orientations and specific attitudes about issues that can be revealed by public-opinion polls. Sometimes these attitudes reflect a perceived general mood of the population that leaders can detect. President Johnson probably accurately gauged the negative mood of the U.S. people toward the Vietnam War when he chose not to run for reelection in 1968. President George H. W. Bush was able to capitalize internationally on the positive public mood in the aftermath of victory in the 1991 Gulf War, although the domestic effect was short lived; he did not win reelection. Even leaders of authoritarian regimes pay attention to dominant moods, since these leaders also depend on a degree of legitimacy.

More often than not, however, publics do not express a single, dominant mood; top leaders are usually confronted with an array of public attitudes. These opinions are registered in elections, but elections are an imperfect measure of public opinion because they merely select individuals for office — individuals who may share voters' attitudes on some issues but not on others.

Occasionally and quite extraordinarily, the masses may vote directly on an issue with foreign policy significance. For example, many issues related to the European Union have been put to public referendum, including the Maastricht Treaty, the EU Constitution, and the Lisbon Treaty, as discussed in Chapter 7. The Norwegian public chose by a referendum to remain outside of the EU. Similarly, in 2002 the Swiss people voted in a referendum to join the United Nations. These are rather rare instances of direct public input on a foreign policy decision.

In most democratic regimes, public-opinion polling, a vast and growing industry, provides information about public attitudes. The European Union, for example, conducts the Eurobarometer, a scientific survey of public attitudes on a wide range of issues in EU countries. Because the same questions are asked during different polls over time, state officials and the EU leadership can avail themselves of reliable data on public opinion. Likewise, the Latin American Public Opinion Project has conducted systematic surveys of Latin American citizens since the 1970s. But do leaders fashion policy with these attitudes in mind? Do elites change policy to reflect the preferences of the public?

Evidence from the United States suggests that elites do care about the preferences of the public, although they do not always directly incorporate those attitudes into policy decisions. Presidents care about their popularity because it affects their ability to work; a president's popularity is enhanced if he or she follows the general mood of the masses or fights for policies that are generally popular. Such popularity gives the president more leeway to set a national agenda. But mass attitudes may not always be directly translated into policy. For example, opinion polls suggest that U.S. elites, including top decision makers, are more supportive of an activist international agenda and of free trade and less supportive of economic protectionism than the mass public is. Thus, elite-made policy is not a direct reflection of public attitudes; the relationship between elite and mass public opinion is a complex one.

Mass Actions and the Role of Elites

The relationship between the masses and leaders is not always clear. At times, the masses, essentially appearing leaderless, take collective actions that have significant effects on the course of world politics. It was the individual acts of thousands fleeing East Germany that led to the construction of the Berlin Wall in 1961. Twenty-eight years later, it was the spontaneous exodus of thousands of East Germans through Hungary and Austria that led to the tearing down of the wall in 1989. The spontaneous movement of "boat people" fleeing Vietnam and the ragged ships leaving Cuba and Haiti for the U.S. coast resulted in changes in U.S. immigration policy.

At other times, a small elite may have acted behind the scenes or even organized mass protests, as illustrated by the "people's putsch" during October 2000 against the Yugoslavian leader Slobodan Milošević. After 13 years of rule, people from all walks of Serbian life joined 7,000 striking miners, crippled the economic system, blocked transportation routes, and descended on Belgrade, the capital. Aided by the new technology of the time—the cell phone—they were able to mobilize citizens from all over the country, driving tractors into the city, attacking the Parliament, and disrupting Milošević's radio and TV stations. But the opposition elite was behind the scenes, aiding in the mobilization of the masses for policy change, and as *Time* reported, "the Serbs took back their country and belatedly joined the democratic tide that swept away the rest of Eastern Europe's communist tyrants a decade ago."[19]

The people's revolution in Serbia against Milošević (the Bulldozer Revolution) proved to be a blueprint for action in other states of the post-communist world. In Georgia, in 2003, the Rose Revolution brought to power President Mikheil Saakashvili, and a political dynasty was broken. In the Ukraine in 2004, after

Google executive Wael Ghonin used Facebook and YouTube to help organize anti-government protests in Egypt, demonstrating how private individuals can harness technology to challenge elites, ultimately leading to changes in domestic governance and international relations.

17 days of demonstrations in bitter cold, the opposition leader Viktor Yushchenko won a hotly contested election in the Orange Revolution. In March 2005, the dictator of Kyrgyzstan was forced to flee to Moscow in the Tulip Revolution after holding power since the independence of that tiny republic in Central Asia. Although these events illustrate the power of the masses and of mass communications, opposition elites played a key role.

Iran is another case where mass opposition to a regime is strong. During the contested 2009 election, the rival to incumbent president Mahmoud Ahmadinejad, Mir Hussein Moussavi, became the symbol of mass demonstrations. Believing the elections were unfair, tens of thousands of demonstrators, wearing bright green, marched in Tehran, the capital, along with prominent members of the opposition. For the first time, events were communicated to the rest of the world via Twitter. When groups were prohibited from congregating, individuals were arrested, imprisoned, and reportedly raped and tortured by authorities. Three months later that "green" mass opposition demonstrated again, illustrating real internal challenges to Iranian religious and political elites.

Although a Tunisian vendor sparked the Arab Spring as described earlier, subsequent events in Egypt and elsewhere saw key participation by elites. A group of young private citizens led by Google executive Wael Ghonin organized a Facebook and YouTube campaign, calling on its 130,000 followers for the ouster of the government of President Hosni Mubarak. They connected with human rights groups, raising the public awareness of the average Egyptian about governmental abuses. Collaborating with Mohamed ElBaradei (former director-general of the International Atomic Energy Agency and leader of an opposition political party), they became the voice behind the January 25 demonstration. Ghonin wrote, "This is Revolution 2.0. No one was a hero because everyone was a hero."[20]

THEORY IN BRIEF

CONTENDING PERSPECTIVES ON THE INDIVIDUAL

	REALISM/ NEOREALISM	LIBERALISM/ NEOLIBERAL INSTITUTIONALISM	RADICALISM/ DEPENDENCY THEORY	CONSTRUCTIVISM
FOREIGN POLICY ELITES	Constrained by anarchic international system and national interests	Significant impact on international relations through choices made and personality factors	Constrained by international capitalist system	Shape popular understanding and incorporation of events and processes
PRIVATE INDIVIDUALS	Actions of private individuals have effect only in aggregate, as reflected in national interest	Secondary role, but may be involved in track-two diplomacy and may fund important initiatives	Individual capitalists may be influential	Actions of individuals less important than beliefs
MASS PUBLICS	Actions may be reflected in national interest	May affect international relations through mass actions that pressure state decision makers	Agents of potential revolutionary change	Agents of potential change through discourse

The long-term impact of these revolutions, where the masses played a role with elite support, remains in doubt. In several color-revolution states, newly instituted reforms have subsequently been curbed and the NGOs that they spawned have been severely restricted (see the Global Perspectives box in Chapter 7). So, too, has the opposition in Iran been quieted as the public copes with international sanctions. And the future for democracy is unclear in Egypt (review the Global Perspectives box in Chapter 5) and other Arab states. While new regimes have been voted into power, they face high expectations, steep challenges, and lingering societal opposition.

In Sum: How Much Do Individuals Matter?

For liberals, the actions of individuals matter. Individual elites can make a difference: they have choices in the kinds of foreign policy they pursue and therefore can affect the course of events. Thus, we need to pay attention to personality characteristics and understand how individuals make decisions, how they employ various psychological mechanisms to process information, and what impact these processes have on individual and group behavior. Mass publics matter to liberals because liberals believe they help formulate the state's interests. Private individuals also matter, although they are clearly of secondary importance even in liberal thinking. Constructivists, too, see individuals as important. Individuals form collective identities; elites can be key policy entrepreneurs who can promote change through ideas. But only in more recent post-modernist and some constructivist scholarship, especially in feminist scholarship, have private individuals' stories found salience.

Realists and radicals do not recognize individuals as important, independent actors in international relations. They see individuals primarily as constrained by the international system and by the state. To realists, individuals are constrained by an anarchic international system and by a state seeking to project power consonant with its national interest. Similarly, radicals see individuals only as members of a class often misled or deluded by elites in the international capitalist system and within a state driven by economic imperatives. In neither case are individuals believed to be sufficiently unconstrained to be considered at the same level of analysis as either the international system or the state.

Individuals and states are not only important in themselves. They also form groups and operate in both international organizations and nongovernmental organizations, within a framework of international law. We turn to these topics in the next chapter.

Discussion Questions

1. Leaders such as Iran's former president Mahmoud Ahmadinejad, Equitorial Guinea's Teodoro Obiang Nguema Mbasogo, and North Korea's Kim Jong-Un are often dismissed as "crazy" or "nuts." What do we mean by this? What other explanations can be offered for their behavior?

2. You are a top decision maker in a government bureaucracy. What strategies would you use to try to minimize the effects of misperceptions in decision making?

3. If more women held major leadership positions in international affairs, would policies be any different? What theories would explain behavior by women leaders as similar to or different from that of male leaders?

4. Mass publics are often stimulated by the media and connected by new technologies. How? Show how the Internet, cell phones, and Twitter have made a difference to international relations.

Key Terms

belief system (p. 186)

cognitive consistency (p. 187)

evoked set (p. 188)

groupthink (p. 188)

mirror images (p. 188)

track-two diplomacy (p. 190)

Election monitoring is one of the many ways that international organizations can directly touch the lives of individuals. Here, a volunteer from Canada wears the distinctive United Nations blue as he assists with elections as part of the United Nations Transitional Administration in East Timor.

07

INTERGOVERNMENTAL ORGANIZATIONS, INTERNATIONAL LAW, AND NONGOVERNMENTAL ORGANIZATIONS

- *Why do intergovernmental organizations form?*

- *What have intergovernmental organizations such as the United Nations contributed to international peace and security?*

- *How has the European Union changed over time?*

- *What is the role of international law in international relations?*

- *What roles do nongovernmental organizations play?*

- *What contending perspectives do international relations theorists bring to their analysis of intergovernmental organizations, nongovernmental organizations, and international law?*

States and individuals are not the only actors in international politics. **Intergovernmental organizations (IGOs)** also play a role in the international system. In this chapter, we trace their roles in international relations. We illustrate how international law differs from domestic law and how both states and IGOs are embedded in that law. Understanding the international legal framework is key to understanding the liberal view of international politics. We then examine nongovernmental organizations (NGOs), which are relatively new but increasingly powerful actors. Finally, we explore the realist, radical, and constructivist responses.

Intergovernmental Organizations

The Creation of IGOs

Why have states chosen to organize themselves collectively? The response is found in liberalism: within the framework of institutions and rules, cooperation is possible. International organizations are the arenas where states interact and cooperate to solve common problems. During the 1970s, neoliberal institutionalists, as described in Chapters 3 and 4, revived the study of international organizations, arguing that "even if … anarchy constrains the willingness of states to cooperate, states nevertheless can work together and can do so especially with the assistance of international institutions."[1]

Neoliberal institutionalists recognize that continuous interaction among states provides the motivation for states to create international organizations. In turn these organizations moderate state behavior, provide a framework for interactions, establish mechanisms for reducing cheating by monitoring others and punishing the uncooperative, and facilitate transparency for state actions. Organizations are the focal points for coordination and make state commitments more credible, specifying expectations and establishing reputations for compliance.

International organizations are particularly useful for solving two sets of problems. One set of problems arises out of the need to cooperate on technical, often nonpolitical, issues where states are not the appropriate units for resolving these problems. As the scholar David Mitrany writes in *A Working Peace System*, units (states, subnational actors) need to "bind together those interests which are common, where they are common, and to the extent to which they are common."[2] This functional approach advocates building on and expanding the habits of cooperation nurtured by groups of technical experts, outside of formal state channels. This explains why international cooperation began in specific, technical issue areas such as health and communications during the nineteenth century. The expectation, according to functionalist thinking, was that solving problems in these technical areas (e.g., curbing epidemics, facilitating international mail and telegraphic services) would spill over into cooperation in political and military affairs, and new international organizations would form.

IN FOCUS

FUNCTIONALISM

- War is caused by economic deprivation.

- Economic disparity cannot be solved in a system of independent states.

- New functional units should be created to solve specific economic problems.

- People and groups will develop habits of cooperation, which will spill over from economic cooperation to political cooperation.

- In the long run, economic disparities will lessen and war will be eliminated.

International organizations also form around collective goods, the second type of problem. In "The Tragedy of the Commons," biologist Garrett Hardin tells the story of a group of herders who share a common grazing area. Each herder finds it economically rational to increase the size of his own herd, allowing him to sell more in the market. Yet if all herders follow what is individually rational behavior, then the group loses: too many animals graze the land and the quality of the pasture deteriorates, which leads to decreased output for all. As each person rationally attempts to maximize his own gain, the collectivity suffers, and eventually all individuals suffer.[3]

What Hardin describes—the common grazing area—is a **collective good**. The grazing area is available to all members of the group, regardless of individual contribution. The use of collective goods involves activities and choices that are interdependent. Decisions by one state have effects for other states—that is, states can suffer unanticipated negative consequences as a result of the actions of others. For example, the decision by wealthy countries to continue the production and sale of chlorofluorocarbons affects all countries through long-term depletion of the ozone layer. With collective goods, market mechanisms break down. Alternative forms of management are needed.

Hardin proposed several possible solutions to the tragedy of the commons. First, use coercion. Force nations or peoples to control the collective goods. States, for example, could force people to limit the number of children they have in order to prevent a population explosion that harms the environment by drawing heavily on scarce natural resources. Second, restructure the preferences of states through rewards and punishments. Offer positive incentives for states to refrain from engaging in the destruction of the commons; tax or threaten to tax those who fail to cooperate, say, by making it cheaper for a polluter to treat pollutants than to discharge them untreated. Third, alter the size of the group. Smaller groups can more effectively exert pressure on their members, because violations of the commons will be more easily noticed. China's population policy of one child per couple is administered at the local level, by individuals residing on the same street or in the same apartment building, or working in the same workplace. Close monitoring by these individuals, coupled with strong social pressure, is more likely to lead to compliance with the one-child policy. These alternatives can also be achieved through international organizations. For many, they are the preferred way to address problems of the commons — the sea, space, the environment. However, not all international problems are collective goods problems.

The Roles of IGOs

Intergovernmental organizations, such as the United Nations, the World Bank, and the International Civil Aviation Organization, can play key roles at each level of analysis.[4] In the international system, IGOs contribute to habits of cooperation; through IGOs, states become socialized to regular interactions, a development that functionalists advocate. Such regular interactions occur between states in the United Nations. Some programs of IGOs, such as the International Atomic Energy Agency's nuclear monitoring program, establish regularized processes of information gathering, analysis, and surveillance that are particularly relevant to collective goods theory. Some IGOs, such as the World Trade Organization, develop procedures for making rules, settling disputes, and punishing those who fail to follow the rules. Other IGOs conduct operational activities that help to resolve major substantive international problems. Some IGOs also play key roles in international bargaining, facilitating the formation of transgovernmental and transnational networks composed of both subnational and nongovernmental actors. And IGOs may be the place where major changes in the international distribution of power are negotiated.

IGOs, along with states, often spearhead the creation and maintenance of international rules and principles based on their common concerns. They establish expectations about the behavior of other states. These rules and principles have come to be known generally as **international regimes**. Charters of IGOs incorporate the norms, rules, and decision-making processes of regimes. By bringing members of the regime together, IGOs help to reduce the incentive to cheat and enhance the value of a good reputation. The principles of the international human rights regime, for example, are articulated in a number of international treaties, including the Universal Declaration of Human Rights. Some IGOs, such as the United Nations (through its Office of the High Commissioner for Human Rights) and the European Union, institutionalize those principles into specific norms and rules. They establish processes designed to monitor states' human rights behavior and compliance with human rights principles. These same organizations provide opportunities for different members of the regime—states, other IGOs, NGOs, and individuals—to meet and evaluate their efforts.

For states, IGOs both enlarge the possibilities for foreign policy making and add to the constraints under which states conduct and, in particular, implement foreign policy. States join IGOs to use them as instruments of foreign policy. IGOs may legitimate a state's viewpoints and policies—thus, the United States sought the support of the Organization of American States during the Cuban missile crisis in 1962. IGOs increase available information about other states, thereby enhancing predictability in the policy-making process. Small states, in particular, use the UN system to gather information about the actions of others. Some IGOs, such as the UN High Commissioner for Refugees and UNICEF, may conduct specific activities. These functions are compatible with or augment state policy.

But IGOs also constrain member states by setting international and hence national agendas and forcing governments to make decisions; by encouraging states to develop specialized decision making and implementing processes to facilitate and coordinate IGO participation; and by creating principles, norms, and rules of behavior with which states must align their policies if they wish to benefit from their membership. Both large and small states are subject to such constraints. For example, members of the UN General Assembly have at times set the international agenda to the displeasure of the United States, forcing the United States to take a stand it would not have taken otherwise.

IGOs also affect individuals by providing opportunities for leadership. As individuals work with or in IGOs, they, like states, may become socialized to cooperating internationally.

Not all IGOs perform all of these functions, and the manner in and extent to which each carries out particular functions varies. Clearly, the United Nations has been given an extensive mandate to carry out many functions. The UN's stature has evolved over time, a product of a historical process that allows the UN to carry out its designated roles.

At the UN headquarters in New York City, political representatives from 193 member countries debate many critical issues, including whether to respond to civil strife in Mali and Syria and how to address enviromental and health threats.

The United Nations

BASIC PRINCIPLES AND CHANGING INTERPRETATIONS   The United Nations was founded on three fundamental principles. Yet over the life of the organization, each of these principles has been significantly challenged by changing realities.[5]

First, the United Nations is based on the notion of the sovereign equality of member states, consistent with the Westphalian tradition. Each state—the United States, Lithuania, India, or Suriname, irrespective of size or population—is legally the equivalent of every other state. This legal equality is the basis for each state's having one vote in the General Assembly. However, the actual inequality of states is recognized in the veto power given to the five permanent members of the Security Council, the special role reserved for the wealthy states in budget negotiations, and the weighted voting system used by the World Bank and the International Monetary Fund.

Second is the principle that only international problems fall within the jurisdiction of the United Nations. Indicative of the Westphalian influence, the UN Charter does not "authorize the United Nations to intervene in matters which are essentially within the domestic jurisdiction of any state" (Article 2, Section 7). Over the life of the United Nations, the once-rigid distinction between domestic and international issues has weakened, leading to an erosion of sovereignty. Global telecommunications and economic interdependencies, international human rights, election monitoring, and environmental regulation all infringe on traditional areas of domestic jurisdiction and hence on states' sovereignty. War is increasingly civil war, which is not legally under the purview of the United Nations. Yet because international human rights are being abrogated, because refugees cross national borders, and because weapons are supplied through transnational networks, such conflicts are increasingly viewed as international, and the United Nations is viewed by some as the appropriate venue for action. These changes have led to a growing body of precedent for humanitarian intervention without the consent of the host country.

The third principle is that the United Nations is designed primarily to maintain international peace and security. This has meant that member states should refrain from the threat or the use of force; settle disputes by peaceful means, as detailed at the Hague conferences; and support enforcement measures.

Although the foundations of both the League of Nations and the United Nations focused on security in the realist, classical sense—protection of national territory—the United Nations is increasingly confronted with demands for action to support a broadened view of security. UN operations to feed the starving populations of Somalia and Niger or to provide relief in the form of food, clothing, and shelter for Haitians forced out of their homes are examples of this broadened notion of security—**human security**. Expansion into these newer areas of security collides head on with the domestic authority of states, undermining the principle of state sovereignty. The United Nations' founders recognized the tension between the commitment to act collectively against a member state and the affirmation of state sovereignty. But they could not foresee the dilemmas that changing definitions of security would pose.

STRUCTURE   The structure of the United Nations was developed to serve the multiple roles assigned by its charter, but incremental changes in that structure have accommodated changes in the international system, particularly the increase in the number of states. The central UN organs comprise six major bodies, as shown in Table 7.1.

The power and prestige of these various organs has changed over time. The **Security Council** was kept small to facilitate swift decision making in response to threats to international peace and security. Its five permanent members—the United States, Great Britain, France, Russia (successor state to the Soviet Union in 1992), and the People's Republic of China (replaced the Republic of China in 1971)—are key to council decision making, each having veto power on substantive issues where unanimity is required. In the early years of the Cold War, the Security Council became deadlocked by the Soviet Union's frequent use of the veto. Since the 1970s, the United

TABLE 7.1		PRINCIPAL ORGANS OF THE UNITED NATIONS
ORGAN	**MEMBERSHIP AND VOTING**	**RESPONSIBILITIES**
Security Council	15 members: 5 permanent with veto, 10 rotating members elected by region	Peace and security: identifies aggressor; decides on enforcement measures
General Assembly	193 members; each state has one vote; work in 6 functional committees	Debates any topic within charter's purview; admits states; elects members to special bodies
Secretariat, headed by Secretary-General	Secretariat of 55,000; secretary-general elected for 5-year renewable term by General Assembly and Security Council	Secretariat: gathers information, coordinates and conducts activities; Secretary-general: chief administrative officer, spokesperson
Economic and Social Council (ECOSOC)	54 members elected for 3-year terms	Coordinates economic and social welfare programs; coordinates action of specialized agencies (FAO, WHO, UNESCO)
Trusteeship Council	Originally composed of administering and nonadministering countries; now made up of 5 great powers	Supervision has ended; proposals have been floated to change function to that of forum for indigenous peoples, NGOs, or nation building
International Court of Justice	15 judges	Noncompulsory jurisdiction on cases brought by states and international organizations

States has used its veto more times than any other permanent member. The majority of these vetoes have concerned the Arab-Israeli-Palestinian conflict.

Since the end of the Cold War, the Security Council has regained power, because the use of the veto has dropped precipitously. The number of annual official meetings has risen, the number of resolutions passed has increased with consensus voting, and informal meetings among the permanent members have been more frequent. With greater cooperation among the permanent powers — especially since 1990, beginning with the council's authorization of force against Iraq after its invasion of Kuwait — the Security Council has taken on more armed conflicts, imposed more types of sanctions in more situations, created war crimes tribunals to prosecute war criminals, authorized protectorates in Kosovo and East Timor, and after 9/11 expanded involvement in anti-terrorism activities. But although the Security Council has enormous formal power, it does not have direct control over the means to use that power. It depends on states for funding, personnel, and enforcement of sanctions and military action. A state's willingness to contribute depends on whether it perceives the council as legitimate.

The **General Assembly** is the main deliberative body of the United Nations and permits debate on any topic under its purview. All member states are represented in the General Assembly, which has grown in membership from 51 in 1946 to 193 in 2013. The bulk of the work of the General Assembly is done in six functional committees: Disarmament and Security; Economic and Financial; Social, Humanitarian, and Cultural; Political and Decolonization; Administrative and Budgetary; and Legal. Debate on resolutions emerging from the committees is organized around regionally based voting blocs, with member states using their one vote to coordinate positions and build support for them. Since the end of the Cold War, the General Assembly's work has been increasingly marginalized, as the epicenter of UN power has shifted back to the Security Council and a more active Secretariat, much to the dismay of various caucusing groups, including the **Group of 77**, the coalition of developing states; regional groups (Africa, Asia, Latin America); and some members of the **Group of 20**, a coalition of the emerging economies. Occasionally, the work of the General Assembly attracts public attention, as it did during the 2011 and 2012 debates over the status of Palestine.

The Secretariat has expanded to employ a global staff of around 55,000, with about one-quarter located at UN headquarters. The role of the secretary-general has expanded significantly. Having few formal powers, the secretary-general depends for authority on persuasive capability and an aura of neutrality. With this power, the secretary-general, especially in the post–Cold War era, can potentially forge an activist agenda, as Secretary-General Kofi Annan did until his retirement in 2006. In 1998, he negotiated a compromise between Iraq and the United States over the authority, composition, and timing of UN weapon inspections in Iraq; he mediated between Iraq and the rest of the international community; he also implemented significant administrative and budgetary reforms and worked hard to establish a better relationship with the U.S. Congress. Annan used the office to push other initiatives, including the international response to the AIDS epidemic and the promotion of better relations between the private sector and the United Nations. A highly visible secretary-general, he was awarded the Nobel Peace Prize in 2001. His successor, Ban Ki-moon of the Republic of Korea, was reelected to a second term in 2011. He has undertaken strong initiatives on climate change, empowering women, and support for countries in crisis. However, he has met criticism as a weak leader and ineffective administrator.

Throughout the United Nations, when one organ has increased in importance, others have diminished, most notably the Economic and Social Council (ECOSOC) and the Trusteeship Council, albeit for very different reasons. ECOSOC was originally established to coordinate the various economic and social activities within the UN system through a number of specialized agencies. But the expansion of those activities and the increase in the number of programs has made ECOSOC's task of coordination a problematic one. In addition to covering such broad issues as human rights, the status of women, population and development, and social development, ECOSOC is charged with coordinating the work of the family of UN specialized institutions (discussed later). In contrast, the Trusteeship Council has worked its way out of a job. Its task was to supervise decolonization and to phase out trust territories placed under UN guardianship during the transition of colonies to independent states. Thus, the very success of the Trusteeship Council has led to its demise.

KEY POLITICAL ISSUES   The United Nations has always mirrored what is happening in the world, and the world has, in turn, been shaped by the United Nations and its organs. The United Nations played a key role in the decolonization of Africa and Asia. The UN Charter endorsed the principle of self-determination for colonial peoples, and former colonies such as India, Egypt, Indonesia, and the Latin American states seized on the United Nations as a forum to push the agenda of decolonization. By 1960, a majority of the United Nations' members favored decolonization. UN resolutions condemned the continuation of colonial rule and called for annual reports on the progress toward independence of all remaining territories. The United Nations was key to the legitimation of the new international norm that colonialism and imperialism are unacceptable state policies. By the mid-1960s, most former colonies had achieved independence with little threat to international peace, and the United Nations had played a significant role in this transformation.

The emergence of the newly independent states transformed the United Nations and international politics more generally. These states formed a coalition of the South, or Group of 77 — developing states whose interests lie in economic development, a group often at loggerheads with the developed countries of the North. The split between the North and the South became the basis for the call by the Group of 77 for a New International Economic Order. The North-South conflict continues to be a central feature of world politics and of the United Nations, although the coalitions have become more fluid with the rise of the emerging economies.

PEACEKEEPING   Of the many issues the United Nations confronts, none is as vexing as peace and security. A new approach, labeled *peacekeeping*, evolved as a way to limit the scope of conflict and prevent it from escalating into a Cold War confrontation. Peacekeeping operations fall into two types, or generations. In **traditional peacekeeping**, multilateral institutions such as the United Nations seek to contain conflicts between two states through third-party military forces. Ad hoc military units, drawn from the armed forces of nonpermanent members of the UN Security Council (often small, neutral members), have been used to prevent the escalation of conflicts and

TABLE 7.2   TRADITIONAL PEACEKEEPING OPERATIONS, REPRESENTATIVE CASES

OPERATION	LOCATION(S)	DURATION	STRENGTH
UNEF I (First UN Emergency Force)	Suez Canal, Sinai Peninsula	Nov. 1956–June 1967	3,378 troops
ONUC (UN Operation in the Congo)	Congo	June 1960–June 1964	19,828 troops
UNFICYP (UN Peacekeeping Force in Cyprus)	Cyprus	March 1964–present	857 troops; 68 police; 143 civilians
UNMISS (UN Mission In the Republic of the Sudan)	South Sudan	2011–present	5,476 troops; 124 military observers; 479 police; 2,195 civilians
UNIFIL (UN Interim Force in Lebanon)	Southern Lebanon	March 1978–present	11,530 troops; 1,007 civilians

Source: United Nations.

to keep the warring parties apart until the dispute can be settled. Invited in by the disputants, the troops operate under UN auspices, supervising armistices, trying to maintain cease-fires, and physically interposing themselves in a buffer zone between warring parties. Table 7.2 lists some of these traditional UN peacekeeping operations.

In the post–Cold War era, UN peacekeeping has expanded to address different types of conflicts and to take on new responsibilities. Whereas traditional peacekeeping activities primarily address interstate conflict, **complex peacekeeping** activities respond to civil war and ethnonationalist conflicts within states that may not have requested UN assistance. To deal with these new conflicts, peacekeepers have taken on a range of both military and nonmilitary functions. On the military side, they have aided in the verification of troop withdrawal (the Soviet Union from Afghanistan) and have separated warring factions until the underlying issues could be settled (Bosnia). Sometimes resolving underlying issues has meant organizing and running national elections, as in Cambodia and Namibia; sometimes it has involved implementing human rights agreements, as in Central America. At other times UN peacekeepers have tried to maintain law and order in failing or disintegrating societies by aiding in civil administration, policing, and rehabilitating infrastructure, as in Somalia, East Timor, and Afghanistan. (This is often referred to as **peacebuilding**.) And peacekeepers have provided humanitarian aid, supplying food, medicine, and a secure environment in part of an expanded conception of human security in Africa. Table 7.3 lists some representative cases of complex peacekeeping operations.

Complex peacekeeping has had successes and failures, as illustrated by the two African cases of Namibia and Rwanda. Namibia (formerly South-West Africa), a former German colony, was administered by South Africa following the end of World War I. Over the years, pressure was exerted on South Africa to relinquish control of the territory, but as long as Soviet-backed Cuban troops occupied neighboring Angola, South Africa refused to consider a change, citing security concerns. Finally in 1988, Cuba and Angola agreed to a withdrawal of Cuban troops as part of a regional peace settlement that included Namibian independence. The UN peacekeeping operation supervised the cease-fire, monitored the withdrawal of South African forces, supervised the civilian police force, secured the repeal of discriminatory legislation, and created conditions for free and fair elections. The UN Transition Assistance Group in Namibia (UNTAG) became the model for UN complex peacekeeping and nation building in Cambodia in the early 1990s and in East Timor in the late 1990s.

But not all UN peacekeeping operations have been successful. Rwanda is an example of a situation where a limited UN peacekeeping force proved to be insufficient and where genocide subsequently escalated as the international community watched and did nothing. Rwanda and neighboring Burundi have seen periodic outbreaks of devastating ethnic violence between Hutus and Tutsis since the 1960s. In the 1990s, intermittent fighting once again broke out. A 1993 peace agreement called for a UN force

TABLE 7.3	COMPLEX PEACEKEEPING OPERATIONS, REPRESENTATIVE CASES		
OPERATION	LOCATION(S)	DURATION	MAXIMUM STRENGTH
UNTAG (UN Transition Assistance Group)	Namibia, Angola	April 1989–March 1990	4,493 troops; 15,000 police
UNPROFOR (UN Protection Force)	Former Yugoslavia (Croatia, Bosnia and Herzegovina, Macedonia)	March 1992–Dec. 1995	38,000 troops; 4,600 civilians
UNTAC (UN Transition Authority in Cambodia)	Cambodia	Feb. 1992–Sept. 1993	15,900 troops; 3,600 police; 2,400 civilians
UNOSOM I, II (UN Operation in Somalia)	Somalia	Aug. 1992–March 1995	28,000 troops; 2,800 civilians
MONUSCO (UN Organization Stabilization Mission in the Democratic Republic of Congo); Renamed	Congo	1999–present	16,700 troops; 691 military observers; 1,376 police; 3,767 civilians
UNAMID (African Union/ United Nations Hybrid Operation in Darfur)	Darfur	July 2007–present	16,934 troops; 277 military observers; 4,895 police; 4,054 civilians

Source: United Nations.

(the UN Assistance Mission in Rwanda, or UNAMIR) to monitor the cease-fire. Yet less than a year later, large-scale violence erupted following the death of the Rwandan president in a plane crash, with Hutu extremists in the Rwandan military and police slaughtering minority Tutsis, resulting in 750,000 Tutsi deaths in a ten-week period.

UNAMIR was not equipped to handle the crisis, and despite its commander's call for more troops, the UN Security Council failed to respond until it was too late. Although UNAMIR did establish a humanitarian protection zone and provided security for relief-supply depots and escorts for aid convoys, peacekeeping failed disastrously.

The UN's response to the crisis in Darfur, Sudan, has also proven problematic. When in 2003 thousands of people fled their villages to escape attacks from the government-based Arab militias (the Janjaweed), the UN system and NGOs responded with humanitarian aid, setting up refugee camps and providing emergency food and health care. The Security Council, however, issued only weak warnings to Sudan as both China and Russia opposed coercive measures, despite evidence that Darfur was witnessing a genocide, with over 300,000 killed and 2.7 million displaced. Eventually, Sudan did accept a small African Union (AU) monitoring force, and in 2007 a stronger UN-AU peacekeeping force, just as the crisis has become more complex, with the number of factions increasing. By 2012, relative peace had been achieved; the Sudan-Chad border is relatively secure; some rebel groups have made peace; and 100,000 refugees have returned to an increasingly urbanized Darfur.

Most problematic has been the UN's complex peacekeeping operating in the Democratic Republic of Congo. Since 1998, "Africa's first world war" has led to an estimated 5.4 million deaths and 1.4 million people displaced. The crisis is multidimensional: internationalized civil war with multiple belligerents; long-standing local conflicts over land, lootable resources, and political power; continuing violence; and humanitarian crises are all occurring within a weak and failing state. Despite being one of the largest UN forces ever mounted, the organization has been unable to craft an overall strategy, since the strategic interests of key member states and organizations diverge. And the logistical and operational difficulties are enormous due to the size of the country, the lack of transportation infrastructure, the inability to protect the civilian population, the lack of preparedness of UN troops, and the difficulty in managing the behavior of the UN troops who, themselves, have been accused of sex crimes and corruption. This operation has clearly tarnished the UN's reputation. This has led many to wonder whether it is better to undertake a weak operation or perhaps to refrain from any operation when there is a lack of will and resources for a more robust operation.

ENFORCEMENT AND CHAPTER VII   Since the end of the Cold War, the Security Council has intervened in situations deemed threatening to international peace and security as authorized in Chapter VII of the UN Charter. That provision enables the Security Council to take measures (economic sanctions, direct military force) to prevent or deter threats to international peace or to counter acts of aggression. Previously, such actions had been invoked only twice, as the UN preferred the more limited, traditional peacekeeping route. The disarmament provisions overseen by the U.S. Special Commission for the Disarmament of Iraq and the International Atomic Energy Agency (IAEA), one of the United Nations' specialized agencies, and the economic sanctions against Iraq during

The United Nations has undertaken more than 65 peacekeeping missions since 1946. While some have successfully established peace, others, like the ongoing mission in the Democratic Republic of the Congo, are still struggling after a decade to prevent violence and rebuild state capacity.

the 1990s were enforcement actions under Chapter VII. Indeed, the 1990s were labeled the "sanctions decade" for the numerous times targeted sanctions were imposed. But getting agreement on when to impose sanctions can be difficult, as explained in Chapter 5. In 2008, the United States and the European Union sought targeted sanctions against the Mugabe regime in Zimbabwe for its systematic human rights abuses against its citizens. But Russia and China vetoed a draft proposal in the Security Council, reiterating the principle of noninterference in the domestic affairs of states.

The 1991 Gulf War was an enforcement action under Chapter VII. The Security Council authorized members "to use all necessary means," a mandate that led to direct military action by the multinational coalition under U.S. command. In 2002, the United States went to the Security Council seeking Chapter VII enforcement against Iraq again, claiming that Iraq was in material breach of its obligations under previous UN resolutions. The Security Council was divided, with the United States and Great Britain supporting enforcement and France, Russia, and China opposing the action. When the stalemate solidified, the United States chose not to return to the Security Council to seek formal authorization for the use of force. Thus, the U.S.-led coalition in the 2003 Iraq War was not authorized by the United Nations, leading many to ponder whether the United Nations is still a relevant player in international politics.

PEACEKEEPING AND ENFORCEMENT: SUCCESS OR FAILURE?   Scholarly studies using empirical data from multiple cases find that traditional peacekeeping has
reduced the propensity of interstate belligerents to fight in the future. The Cyprus
peacekeeping mission averted overt hostilities between Greeks and Turks on the island.
For 11 years, the Arab and Israeli states were kept apart, and India-Pakistan hostilities
over Kashmir were contained to intermittent intervals, thanks in large part to traditional peacekeeping operations.

But success in traditional peacekeeping in interstate wars has not been matched
by success in the more complex operations, notably in intrastate civil wars. In those
cases, although the risk of war has been reduced by half, the risk of another war occurring within five years ranged from 23 to 43 percent.[6] When those complex operations involved verification of arms, monitoring, or election supervision, they were
more successful. But in the most difficult conflicts, with a long history of violence and
multiple belligerents, peacekeeping and peacebuilding have been less successful, as the
Democratic Republic of Congo case illustrates.

UN REFORM: SUCCESS AND STALEMATE   Faced with escalating demands and
saddled with structures that no longer reflect the power realities of the international
system, the United Nations has been confronted with persistent calls for reform.
Although many reforms have been undertaken, the challenges remain critical. Because
amending the charter is difficult — requiring ratification of two-thirds of the members,
including all five permanent members of the Security Council — most reforms have
been undertaken without actually amending the charter.

To address management problems publicized in the 2004 oil-for-food scandal,
when UN officials were accused of taking bribes and showing favoritism in awarding
contracts in Iraq, new financial accountability mechanisms have been put in place
and internal oversight has been established. To address new transnational concerns,
structures have been created or reorganized, including the High Commissioner for
Human Rights in 1997 and the Counter-Terrorism Committee in 2001 to help countries become more effective in addressing terrorism. To manage peacekeeping operations more efficiently, the Department of Peacekeeping Operations has been expanded;
a Department of Field Support has been organized to address financial, logistical, and
information issues; military staff have been added from the troop-contributing countries, and rapid deployment teams have been organized. Since 2006, the Peacebuilding
Commission addresses postconflict recovery issues, including monitoring economic
stabilization, building government capacity, and coordinating economic development
activities through meeting among the heads of UN programs and agencies, including
the World Bank, the International Monetary Fund, and the World Trade Organization.[7]

Security Council reform remains the persistent reform issue critical to the legitimacy of the Security Council's role in enforcement. The five permanent members of

the Council, the victors of World War II who possess veto power over substantive issues, are an anachronism. Europe is overrepresented; China is the only emerging economy and the only Asian member; both Germany and Japan contribute more financially to the organization than the four permanent members other than the United States do. Virtually all agree that membership should be increased. But agreement ends there. What other countries should be admitted? Germany, Japan, and/or Italy? India, Pakistan, South Africa, and/or Nigeria from the developing world? Argentina or Brazil? Should the new members have the veto? Should the differentiation between permanent and nonpermanent membership be maintained? Contending proposals continue to be discussed and debated, but no agreement has been reached. As President Obama has stated, the UN is both "flawed and indispensible."[8]

A COMPLEX NETWORK OF IGOs   The central organs of the United Nations discussed earlier are only a small part of the UN system of organizations. Today, there are 19 specialized agencies formally affiliated with the United Nations, each a reflection of functionalist thinking dedicated to specialized areas of activity that individual states cannot manage alone. Public health and disease do not respect national borders; neither do weather systems. Specialized expertise across states is needed to monitor such phenomena. Mail and telecommunications move across national borders; marine transport and airplanes fly between states; technical rules are needed to govern these areas. Given the importance of these functional activities, it is not surprising that many of the specialized UN agencies actually predate the United Nations itself. The International Telecommunications Union dates from 1865, the Universal Postal Service from 1874, and international sanitary conferences from the middle of the nineteenth century. Others, such as the International Civil Aviation Organization and the International Maritime Organization, date from immediately after World War II.

Other specialized UN agencies and UN programs perform operational activities dedicated to limited tasks, although those tasks may be much more controversial: delivering food to those in need (World Food Programme), settling refugees and internally displaced people (UN High Commissioner for Refugees), or establishing labor standards (International Labor Organization). Many of the tasks that these programs and agencies perform began under the auspices of the League of Nations following World War I. These organizations have separate charters, memberships, budgets, and secretariats. Although each reports directly or indirectly to the UN's Economic and Social Council, none can be instructed by it or by the General Assembly (see Table 7.4).

Included under the specialized agencies are the Bretton Woods institutions—the International Monetary Fund and the World Bank—examined in Chapter 9. The United Nations is not the only important IGO, of course, and there are numerous other intergovernmental organizations not affiliated with the United Nations, including the World Trade Organization and the Organization of the Petroleum Exporting

TABLE 7.4	REPRESENTATIVE INTERNATIONAL AND REGIONAL ORGANIZATIONS	

UN Specialized Agencies	Independent Organizations
World Health Organization	Organization of the Petroleum Exporting Countries
Food and Agriculture Organization	World Trade Organization
International Labor Organization	Organisation of the Islamic Conference
International Atomic Energy Agency	North Atlantic Treaty Organization
World Bank Group	International Organization for Migration
Regional Organizations	**Subregional Organizations**
European Union	European Free Trade Association
African Union	Economic Community of West African States
Organization of American States	Mercosur
Arab League	Gulf Cooperation Council

Countries (both also examined in Chapter 9), as well as a plethora of regional and subregional organizations. These IGOs perform critical functions relating to interstate economic and security cooperation.

The European Union—Organizing Regionally

Regional organizations also play an increasingly visible role in international relations. But none has been as visible, as strong, or as copied as the **European Union (EU)**. The idea of a united Europe goes back centuries. Both Immanuel Kant and Jean-Jacques Rousseau presented plans on how to unite Europe.[9] After World War I, idealists dreamed that a united Europe could have forestalled the conflagration. World War II only intensified these sentiments. Hence, after its conclusion, vigorous debate ensued over the future organization of Europe. On the one hand were the federalists: drawing on the writings of Rousseau, they believed that because sovereign states instigated wars, peace could be attained only if states gave up their sovereignty and invested in a higher federal body. If states joined together with other states, each surrendering some pieces of sovereignty to a higher unit, the root cause of war, military competition among states, could eventually be eliminated. Advocates of federalism proposed the European Defense Community, which would have placed the military under community control, thus touching the core of national sovereignty.

On the other hand were the functionalists. Their principal proponent, Jean Monnet, believed that the forces of nationalism could in the long run be undermined by the logic of economic integration. Beginning with the creation of the European Coal and Steel Community (the predecessor of the European Economic Community, or EEC), he proposed cooperative ventures in nonpolitical issue areas. It was anticipated that these ventures would spill over eventually from the economic arena to issues of national security. The federalist European Defense Community was defeated by the French Parliament in 1954, and the functionalists' logic prevailed. No one at the time could have envisioned a union that in 2013 would bring together 506.5 million citizens in 28 countries, allowing each of them to travel freely with a burgundy EU passport, enjoying an economy of over $17.7 trillion, and with many of them (17) using a common currency, the euro. It is the euro zone crisis of 2011–12, discussed in Chapter 9, that poses the most significant challenge to the future of the European Union.

HISTORICAL EVOLUTION   The impetus for the creation of the European Union grew not only from the devastation of the wartime experience but also from the security threat that remained. Urged on by the United States, an economically strong Europe (made possible by the reduction of trade barriers) knew it would be better equipped to counter the threat of the Soviet Union if it integrated. Europe also understood that if the Germans were enmeshed in such agreements, they would pose less of a threat to other states. Of course, U.S.-based multinational corporations would also benefit from an expanded market. Thus, security threats, economic incentives, and a postwar vision all played a role in the drive of political elites for European integration.[10]

The European Coal and Steel Community, placing French and (West) German coal and steel production under a common "High Authority," was the first step toward realizing this idea. Although Germany was treated as an equal, its key economic sector supporting the arms industry was brought into a community with France, Italy, and the Benelux countries (Belgium, Netherlands, Luxembourg). This functionalist experiment was so successful in boosting coal and steel production that the member states agreed to expand cooperation under the European Atomic Energy Community and the European Economic Community. Thus the Treaties of Rome, signed in 1957, committed the six states to create a common market—removing restrictions on internal trade; imposing a common external tariff; reducing barriers to the movement of people, services, and capital; and establishing a common agricultural and transport policy. In 1968, two years ahead of schedule, most of these goals had been achieved.

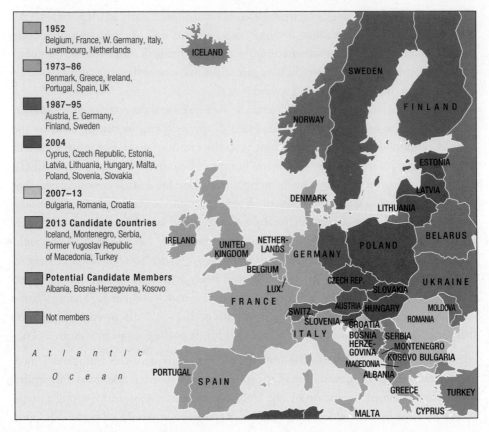

1952
Belgium, France, W. Germany, Italy,
Luxembourg, Netherlands

1973–86
Denmark, Greece, Ireland,
Portugal, Spain, UK

1987–95
Austria, E. Germany,
Finland, Sweden

2004
Cyprus, Czech Republic, Estonia,
Latvia, Lithuania, Hungary, Malta,
Poland, Slovenia, Slovakia

2007–13
Bulgaria, Romania, Croatia

2013 Candidate Countries
Iceland, Montenegro, Serbia,
Former Yugoslav Republic
of Macedonia, Turkey

Potential Candidate Members
Albania, Bosnia-Herzegovina, Kosovo

Not members

Expansion of European Union, 1952–2013

New policy areas were gradually brought under the umbrella of the community, including health, safety, and consumer standards. As success in these areas waxed and waned, and economic stagnation hindered progress, action was taken. The first initiative was expanding the size of the community in the so-called widening process. The original six members were joined by three others in 1973. Six successive enlargements followed, resulting in today's 28-state membership. These enlargements have increased the influence of the organization but complicated its decision making (see map above).

In 1986, the most important step was taken in deepening the integration process—the signing of the Single European Act (SEA), which established the goal of completing a single market by the end of 1992. This meant a complicated process of removing the remaining physical, fiscal, and technical barriers to trade; harmonizing national standards of health; varying levels of taxation; and eliminating the barriers to movement of peoples. New environmental and technological issues were also addressed. Three thousand specific measures were needed to complete the single market.

Even before that process was completed, the Maastricht Treaty was signed in 1992. The European Community became the EU. Members committed themselves not only to an economic union, but also to a political one, including the establishment of common foreign and defense policies, a single currency, and a regional central bank. Five years later, in 1997, the Amsterdam Treaty was signed, making some changes to the previous treaties, including granting more power to the European Parliament but generally putting more emphasis on the rights of individuals, citizenship, justice, and home affairs.

The increased power of the EU has not been without its opponents. As several national votes have illustrated, while the European public generally supports the idea of economic and political cooperation, it also fears a diminution of national sovereignty and is reluctant to surrender democratic rights by placing more power in the hands of bureaucrats and other nonelected elites. The debate over the proposed European Constitution brought that issue to a head. Pushed forward by elites, the European Constitution was signed by the heads of state in 2004, only to be rejected in two national referendums a year later. In its stead, in 2007, the Treaty of Lisbon replaced the Constitution. This treaty is another attempt to enhance the efficacy of the EU by creating the offices of president of the European Council and a High Representative for Foreign Affairs who leads a more united policy, and increasing the use of qualified majority voting in place of unanimity. The treaty is also aimed at improving the democratic legitimacy of the EU by increasing the authority of the European Parliament. The treaty became law on December 1, 2009 (see Table 7.5).

STRUCTURE Table 7.6 provides the basic information about the EU's decision-making bodies, membership, voting, and responsibilities. Just as power has shifted among the UN organs, so, too, has power shifted in the EU. Initially, power resided in the European Commission, which is designed to represent the interests of the community as a whole. Although each state is entitled to one member, Commission members are expected to be impartial and are not national representatives. Each is responsible for a particular policy area, known as a directorate-general, which, in turn, is divided into directorates that cover specific parts of that policy area. For much of its history, the EU Commission has played this engine role, with the Council of Ministers ratifying, modifying, or vetoing proposals, even though the Commission formally reports to the Council. Increasingly, the Council, with its weighted voting system, has assumed more power; some policy decisions in foreign and security affairs, immigration, and taxation even require unanimous support.

The increasing power of the European Parliament is another change. Since the mid-1980s, it has gained a greater legislative and supervisory role. Because members are elected by universal suffrage, this body has an element of democratic accountability not found in the other institutions. The relatively low turnout in the 2009 parliamentary elections indicates that the legitimacy of the institutions remains a problem that the provisions of the Lisbon Treaty are intended to rectify.

TABLE 7.5

SIGNIFICANT EVENTS IN THE DEVELOPMENT OF THE EUROPEAN UNION

YEAR	EVENT
1952	European Coal and Steel Community created by Belgium, France, Italy, Luxembourg, Netherlands, and West Germany.
1954	French National Assembly rejects proposal to form the European Defense Community.
1957	Treaties of Rome establish the European Economic Community (EEC) and the European Atomic Energy Community, comprising same six members.
1968	Customs union is completed; all internal customs, duties, and quotas are removed and common external tariff is established.
1975	Lomé Convention between the EEC and 46 developing countries in Africa, the Caribbean, and the Pacific signed.
1979	High-level negotiations on European Monetary System are completed; first direct elections to the European Parliament.
1986	Signing of the Single European Act designed to ensure faster decisions; more attention to environmental and technological issues; list of measures compiled that need to be taken before achieving single market in 1992.
1992	Maastricht Treaty completed, committing members to political union, including the establishment of common foreign and defense policies, a single currency, and a regional central bank; name changed to European Union (EU); controversial referendums held in several countries.
1997	Treaty of Amsterdam extends competence on Justice and Home Affairs, defines European citizenship.
1999	Common monetary policy and single currency (the euro) launched.
2002	Euro in circulation.
2004	European Constitution negotiated.
2005	French and Dutch publics reject the proposed constitution; ongoing discussions.
2007	Lisbon Treaty proposes changes in institutions and decision making.
2009	Lisbon Treaty approved.
2011–Present	Euro-zone crisis.

TABLE 7.6	PRINCIPAL INSTITUTIONS OF THE EUROPEAN UNION (2013)	
INSTITUTION	MEMBERSHIP AND VOTING	RESPONSIBILITIES
European Commission	28 members; 4-year terms; plus 38,000 support staff (Eurocrats)	Initiates proposals; guards treaties; executes policies
Council of Ministers	Ministers of member states; unanimity or qualified majority voting depending on issue; 1 minister per state	Legislates; sets political objectives; coordinates; resolves differences
European Parliament	750 members, divided among member states; elected every 5 years by citizens; organized around political parties	Legislates; approves budget; supervises executive
European Council	Heads of government; summit meetings twice yearly	Key body for EU initiatives
Economic and Social Committee	Approx. 350 members drawn from economic and social interest groups; represents employers, employees, others	Has consultative role; acts as platform for civil society; forwards opinions to other institutions
European Court of Justice	Judges (28) and advocates-general; appointed by states for 6-year terms	Adjudicates disputes over EU treaties; ensures uniform interpretation of EU laws; renders advisory opinions to states

So, too, has the power of the European Court of Justice (ECJ) expanded. The Court's wide-ranging responsibilities for interpreting and enforcing EU law include ruling on the constitutionality of all EU law; interpreting treaties; providing advisory opinions to national courts; and settling disputes among member states, EU institutions, corporations, and individuals. Member states are obligated to uphold EU law. If they fail to comply, the European Commission may undertake infringement proceedings that may include fines or imposition of sanctions. Virtually every member state has been brought before the court at some point for failing to fulfill its obligations. The 28 judges of the ECJ have heard nearly 20,000 cases and issued more than 800 opinions covering such diverse topics as disputes over customs duties, tax discrimination, elimination of nontariff barriers, agricultural subsidies, environmental law, consumer safety issues, and mobility of labor. More than its founders ever envisioned, the ECJ plays a major institutional role in European regionalism and the new legal order that is embodied in EU law.

POLICIES AND PROBLEMS   The EU has moved progressively into more policy areas, from trade and agriculture (discussed in Chapter 9) to transport, competition, social policy, monetary policy, the environment, justice, and common foreign and security policy. Among the many controversial issues has been the failed effort to develop a common European foreign and security policy. The split between those states that supported the United States' Iraq policy (Great Britain and Spain) and those that opposed it (Germany and France) is suggestive, as is the difficulty in forging a united EU foreign policy against Iran. The difficulties in security policy have had repercussions in other arenas as well. The war against terrorism has brought into question key EU policies, including open borders versus the security threats resulting from the absence of border controls, and the commitment to human rights versus the increased call for limitations on immigration and on revising the rights of aliens. Thus, disputes over deepening cooperation continue to be vexing. Should current members continue to widen the range of cooperation? Should members try to reduce the tensions that develop when states differ over foreign policy?

Equally problematic are the issues surrounding membership. Should the EU continue to expand its membership by reaching out to the newly democratic states of eastern Europe and the former Soviet Union, or to those in need, such as Iceland? How rapidly can new members come to adhere to the 80,000 pages of EU law and regulations currently in effect? How will the special concessions these countries won affect the functioning of the Union? Although new members such as Croatia, which joined in 2013, have been given extra time to phase in EU law, they also need to wait before receiving full benefits that range from agricultural subsidies to free movement of labor. Can Turkey, the first candidate state with a majority Muslim population, eventually meet the criteria for membership: stable democratic institutions, a functioning market, and a capacity to meet union obligations? Turkey has already made enormous improvements in its human rights record and minority protection, but its admission is still undecided. Will candidate member Serbia be accepted more rapidly? Will the EU governing institutions be able to change? So far, the debate over the European Constitution suggests that the answers will not be easy ones.

⬆⬇ YOU DECIDE

One of the major political developments of the past sixty years is the evolution of the European Union. The EU stands as one of the most extensive economic and political associations among sovereign states in world history. Critics argue, however, that like other IGOs such as the United Nations, the EU is insufficiently democratic: there is a lack of accountability to the population and a lack of transparency in decision making. This is ironic since EU members are themselves democratic states.

Critics refer to the fact that the European Parliament, which is the only EU body that is directly elected by citizens in member states, is also one of the weakest EU institutions. Much of the actual business of the EU is managed by eurocrats located in Brussels, appointed by and responsible to the appointed European Commission. The rejection in 2005 of the European Constitution by France and Netherlands reflected citizen dissatisfaction with EU institutions. Across the EU, people feel that unless reformed, the EU might evolve into a supra-national government with more authority than responsibility. Is a lack of accountability and transparency necessarily detrimental?

You might argue that the EU's lack of democracy has made progress on technical issues possible. Standards on food safety, labor conditions, healthcare, and the environment might have been slowed or halted by democratic participation. And if democratic processes were employed, would not that privilege the members with larger populations, putting smaller states at risk of having their interests ignored?

In contrast, you might argue that while technocratic rule was once useful, now participation by citizens is necessary. Many more states and people need to be accommodated now, with 28 member states and 506.5 million people. And the issues the EU is facing, including budget deficits and unemployment, directly affect the lives of its citizens. Without democratic participation and accountability, will voices from all sectors of society be heard in the EU halls in Brussels?

YOU DECIDE: Are democratic processes useful for the EU? Helpful? Or not? Can democracy ever be a negative for the functioning of international organizations?

Other Regional Organizations: The OAS, the AU, and the League of Arab States

For many years, the critical question was whether other regions would follow the European Union model. Clearly the circumstances surrounding the development of the European Union were unlikely to be duplicated precisely. Although most Asian leaders strongly thought the European model inappropriate for that region, some sub-regional groups, such as the Economic Community of West African States and the Caribbean Community (CARICOM), saw the EU as a model. (We will examine the North American Free Trade Agreement in Chapter 9.)

Continent-wide regional organizations, such as the Organization of American States (OAS) and the African Union (AU), have followed a different path. At its establishment in 1948, the OAS adopted wide-ranging goals: political (now promotion of democracy), economic (enhancing development, preferential treatment in trade and finance), social (promotion of human rights), and military (collective defense against aggression from outside the region and peaceful settlement of disputes within). No other regional organization includes such a North/South split between a hegemonic member such as the United States (and Canada) on the one hand and a "southern constituency" on the other. With that division, the OAS has adopted many of the foreign policy concerns of the hegemon: the defeat of communist/leftist factions during the Cold War and an emphasis on democracy promotion. In 1985, the OAS resolved to take action should an irregular interruption of democracy occur, and a member should be suspended if its government is overthrown by force. The OAS has acted against coups or countercoups nine times, including, for example, in Haiti (1991–94), Peru (1992), Paraguay (1996, 2000), and Venezuela (1992, 2002). It instituted sanctions against Haiti, and in 2009 suspended Honduras from membership after that country's coup. The overall record in achieving its political, economic, and social goals is mixed, however, constrained by a dearth of economic resources and political will. Unlike the EU, the OAS has played a limited role in economic development of the region.

The African Union replaced the Organization of African Unity in 2002. The latter had been deliberately designed as a weak intergovernmental body at its founding in 1964. The newly independent countries at the time sought to protect their new sovereignty. They were in no mood to permit interference in domestic affairs, and they preferred sovereign equality of all states. Although the illegality of apartheid in South Africa remained a rallying cry of the OAU, members were largely silent on the major economic and development issues of the day. The newly reconstituted AU is an attempt to give African states an increased ability to respond to the issues of economic globalization and democratization affecting the continent. Thus, the AU is committed to good governance and democratic principles, suspending illegitimate governments and pledging to intervene in the affairs of members should genocide and crimes against humanity occur. Such promises are predicated on the belief that better governance is key to economic development and necessary for external development funds. Yet although the AU did suspend Mauritania from membership (2008), impose sanctions on Togo (2005), and reverse a coup in the Comoros Islands (2008), additional measures were not taken, nor has the AU acted in the Zimbabwe crisis, despite its own findings of major human rights abuses in 2007 and evidence of election fraud in 2008. Following through on obligations and enforcement remains a problem not only for the OAS and the AU, but for most regional organizations, as funding is limited and commitment waxes and wanes.

An example of varying commitment over time is illustrated by the League of Arab States. Established in 1945, for many years the only action the league undertook was to oppose Israel. Member states forged little agreement on other issues. Yet following the initial shock of the Arab Spring of 2011, the Arab League seized the opportunity. With the outbreak of hostilities in Libya and Syria, the league took unprecedented steps, suspending those countries' memberships, calling for multilateral action, condemning the respective governments for their use of force, and in the case of Syria, sending in a multilateral observer mission and calling for the peaceful transfer of power. These activities represent a major change for the league, as it interferred in a member state's domestic policy, called for a democratic transition, and highlighted human rights.

In reality, IGOs, of which there are now over 240, seldom act alone. Often they carry out their activities with the cooperation of other international or regional organizations and with nonstate actors, including nongovernmental organizations. Furthermore, they are embedded in a structure of international law.

International Law

International law developed thousands of years before contemporary international organizations. Treaties between city-states and communities can be found in Mesopotamia; the Greeks and the Romans differentiated among different kinds of law, including international law; and during the Middle Ages, the authority of the Catholic Church developed canon law applying to all believers internationally. In the seventeenth and eighteenth centuries, European writers like Hugo Grotius (1583–1645), among others, wrote of international relations based on the rule of law, earning him the title of father of international law.

Despite its long history, international law has captured the American public's attention relatively recently. In the aftermath of 9/11, the U.S. military actions in Afghanistan and Iraq, and mounting humanitarian crises, international treaties have become well-known documents: the Geneva Conventions (technically the Geneva Convention for Victims of War, 1949), the Convention against Torture (the UN Convention against

Torture and Other Cruel, Inhuman or Degrading Treatment or Punishment, 1984, 1987), and the Genocide Convention (Convention on the Prevention and Punishment of Genocide, 1948). Debate has raged over the definitions of terms such as torture, genocide, terrorism, enemy combatants, enemy detainees, and rendition. NGOs such as the International Committee of the Red Cross and Human Rights Watch, once known to only a few, have attained international visibility. Thus, understanding the characteristics of international law and its limitations is all the more urgent.

International Law and Its Functions

International law consists of a body of both rules and norms regulating interactions among states, between states and IGOs, and in more limited cases among IGOs, states, and individuals. Laws serve several purposes: setting a body of expectations, providing order, protecting the status quo, and legitimating the use of force by a government to maintain order. Law provides a mechanism for settling disputes and protecting states from each other. It serves ethical and moral functions, aiming in most cases to be fair and equitable and delineating what is socially and culturally desirable. These norms demand obedience and compel behavior.

At the state level, law is hierarchical. Established structures exist for both making law (legislatures and executives) and enforcing law (executives and judiciaries). Individuals and groups within the state are bound by law. Because of a general consensus within the state on the particulars of law, compliance with the law is widespread. It is in the interest of everyone to maintain order and predictability. But if the law is violated, the state authorities can compel violators to judgment and use the instruments of state authority to punish wrongdoers.

In the international system, authoritative structures are absent. There is no international executive, no international legislature, and no judiciary with compulsory jurisdiction. So can there be international law, given the absence of a sovereign body with enforcement power and the inability to compel compliance with effective physical coercion? The late legal scholar Christopher C. Joyner argues "yes": binding legal rules are created, states recognize their obligations, and resorting to force is not necessary for the international legal system to operate. After all, "international legal rules obtain their normative force not because any superior power or world government prescribes them but because they have been generally accepted by states as rules of conduct, with the expectation that states will follow suit."[11]

The Sources of International Law

International law, like domestic law, comes from a variety of sources. Virtually all law emerges from custom. Either a hegemon or a group of states solves a problem in a particular way; these habits become ingrained as more states follow the same custom, and eventually the custom is codified into law. For example, Great Britain and later the United States were primarily responsible for developing the law of the sea. As great sea-faring powers, each state adopted practices—rights of passage through straits, methods of signaling other ships, conduct during war, and the like—that became the customary law of the sea and were eventually codified into treaties. The laws protecting diplomats and embassies likewise emerged from long-standing customs.

But customary law is limited. For one thing, it develops slowly; British naval custom evolved into the law of the sea over several hundred years. Sometimes customs become outmoded. For example, the 3-mile territorial extension from shore was established because that was the distance a cannonball could fly. Eventually, law caught up with changes in technology, and states were granted a 12-mile extension of territory into the ocean. Furthermore, not all states participate in the making of customary law, let alone give assent to the customs that have become law through European-centered practices. And the fact that customary law is initially uncodified leads to ambiguity in interpretation.

International law also arose from treaties, the dominant source of law today. Treaties, explicitly written agreements among states, number more than 25,000 since 1648 and cover myriad issues. When deciding cases, most judicial bodies look to treaty law first. Treaties are legally binding: only major changes in circumstances give states the right not to follow treaties they have ratified.

Authoritative bodies have also formulated and codified international law. Among these bodies is the UN International Law Commission, composed of prominent international jurists. That commission has codified much customary law: the Law of the Sea (1958), the Vienna Convention of the Law of Treaties (1969), and the Vienna Conventions on Diplomatic Relations (1961) and on Consular Relations (1963). The commission also drafts new conventions for which there is no customary law. For example, laws on product liability and on the succession of states and governments have been formulated in this way, then submitted to states for ratification.

Courts are also sources of international law. Although the International Court of Justice (ICJ), with its 15 judges located in The Hague, the Netherlands, has been responsible for some significant decisions, the ICJ is basically a weak institution for several reasons. First, the court actually hears very few cases; between 1946 and 2012, the ICJ has had 126 contentious cases brought before it and has issued only 26 advisory opinions, although since the end of the Cold War its caseload has increased. Ever since the small developing country of Nicaragua won a judicial victory over the United States in 1984, such countries have shown greater trust in the court. Although procedures have changed to speed up the lengthy process, the court's noncompulsory jurisdiction provision still limits its caseload. Both parties must agree to the court's jurisdiction before a case is taken. This stands in stark contrast to domestic courts, which enjoy compulsory jurisdiction. Accused of a crime, you are compelled to judgment. No state is compelled to submit to the ICJ. Second, when cases are heard, they rarely deal with the major controversies of the day, such as the war in Vietnam, the invasion of Afghanistan, or the unraveling of the Soviet Union or of Yugoslavia, although Kosovo's status was referred to the ICJ after its 2008 declaration of independence. Those controversies are generally political and outside the court's reach, although interstate boundary disputes are major issues on the court's agenda. Third, only states may initiate proceedings; individuals and nongovernmental actors such as multinational corporations cannot. Hence, with such a limited caseload concerning few fundamental issues, the court could never be a major source of law. In contrast, the European Court of Justice of the European Union is a significant source of European law. It has a heavy caseload, covering virtually every topic of European integration.

National and even local courts are also sources of international law. Such courts have broad jurisdiction; they may hear cases occurring on their territory in which international law is invoked or cases involving their own citizens who live elsewhere, and they may hear any case to which the principle of universal jurisdiction applies. Under **universal jurisdiction**, states may claim jurisdiction if the conduct of an individual is sufficiently heinous to violate the laws of all states. Several states claimed such jurisdiction as a result of the genocide in World War II and more recently for war crimes in Bosnia, Kosovo, and Rwanda. In the European Union, national and local courts are a vital source of law. A citizen of an EU country can ask a national court to invalidate any provision of domestic law found to be in conflict with provisions of the EU treaty. A citizen can also seek invalidation of a national law found to be in conflict with self-executing provisions of community directives issued by the EU's Council of Ministers. Thus, in the European system, national courts are both essential sources of European community law and enforcers of that law.

Compliance and Enforcement of International Law

Why, then, in the absence of an international executive and an international legislature, and with only a weak international court with limited authority, do states voluntarily comply with international law? The answer can be explained in terms of self-interest. Both realists and liberals agree that international law compliance relies on self-interest. States benefit from participating in making the rules through treaties, or else they would not participate or ratify; they can ensure through participation that those rules will be compatible with their interests. States benefit from knowing that territory, airspace, and property rights are generally respected, that international products and people are safe to move across national borders, and that diplomats can safely carry out their duties with international protection. And thus, states comply most of the time.

Some liberals might point to the ethical argument that compliance occurs because it is the "right thing to do." States want to do what is right and moral, and international law reflects what is right. States want to be looked on positively, according to liberal thinking. They want to be respected by world public opinion, and they fear being labeled as pariahs and losing face and prestige in the international system.

Who, then, enforces international law when there is no international police force or an international executive? The answer is that states enforce international law through self-help. Should states choose not to obey international law, other states have instruments at their disposal. Both realists and liberals point to states' reliance on self-help mechanisms, including the tools of diplomacy, economic statecraft, and use of force, as discussed in Chapter 5.

But liberals contend, rightly in many cases, that self-help mechanisms of enforcement by one state alone are apt to be ineffective. A diplomatic protest from an enemy or a weak state is likely to be ignored, although a protest from a major ally or a hegemon may carry weight. Economic boycotts and sanctions by one state will be ineffective as long as the transgressor state has multiple trading partners. And war is both too costly and unlikely to lead to the desired outcome. In most cases, then, for the enforcement mechanism to be effective, several states have to participate. For enforcement to be most effective, all states have to join together in collective action against the violator of international law and norms. In the view of liberals, states find protection and solace in collective action and in collective security. Hence multilateral action, often organized through IGOs, is essential. Yet even states and IGOs do not act alone; nonstate actors are also part of the international system, though they do not have a firm basis in traditional international law.

Nongovernmental Organizations

Nonstate actors include nongovernmental organizations (NGOs), transnational networks, foundations, and multinational corporations, though they are not sovereign and do not have the same kinds of power resources as states. In this chapter, the emphasis is on NGOs. We will examine multinational corporations in Chapter 9.

NGOs are generally private, voluntary organizations whose members are individuals or associations that come together to achieve a common purpose, often oriented to a public good. They are incredibly diverse entities, ranging from entirely local and/or grassroots organizations to those organized nationally and transnationally. Some are entirely private—that is, their funding comes only from private sources. Others rely partially on government funds or aid in kind. Some are open to mass membership; others are closed-member groups or federations. These differences have led to an alphabet soup of acronyms specifying types of NGOs. These include GONGOs (government-organized NGOs), BINGOs (business and industry NGOs), DONGOs (donor-organized NGOs), and ONGOs (operational NGOs), to name a few.

The number of NGOs has grown dramatically, as recorded in the *Yearbook of International Organizations*. While there may be as many as 10,000 nongovernmental organizations that have an international dimension in terms of either their membership or their commitment to conducting activities in several states, national and grassroots local NGOs number in the millions. Their exponential growth can be explained by the global spread of democracy, which provides an opening for NGO inputs; by the explosion of UN-sponsored global conferences in the 1990s, where NGOs took on new tasks; and by the electronic communication revolution, which enables NGOs to communicate and network both with each other and with their constituencies, providing a more forceful voice in the international policy arena.

The Growth of NGO Power and Influence

Although NGOs are not new actors in international politics, they are growing in importance.[12] In Chapter 10, we discuss one of the earliest NGO-initiated efforts at transnational organization dedicated to the abolition of slavery. While they took the first steps by defining the practice as inhumane and unjust, these NGOs were not strong enough to accomplish international abolition. NGOs organizing on behalf of peace and noncoercive methods of dispute settlement also appeared during the 1800s, as did the International Committee of the Red Cross, which advocated for humanitarian treatment for wounded soldiers, and international labor unions fighting for better working conditions. During the first half of the twentieth century, these same groups were instrumental in lobbying for a "league of nations" and the International Labor Organization, and subsequently in supporting the establishment of the United Nations and the related agencies protecting different groups of people, including refugees (UN High Commissioner for Refugees) and women and children (UNICEF), among others.

During the 1970s, as the number of NGOs grew, networks and coalitions were formed among various groups, and by the 1990s these NGOs were able to mobilize the mass public effectively and influence international relations. A number of factors explain the remarkable resurgence of NGO activity and their increased power as actors in international politics. First, the issues seized on by NGOs have been increasingly viewed as interdependent, or transnational, ones that states cannot solve alone and whose solutions require transnational and intergovernmental cooperation. Airline hijackings during the 1970s; acid rain pollution and ocean dumping during the 1970s and 1980s; and global warming, land mines, and the AIDS epidemic during the 1990s are examples of issues that require international action and that are "ripe" for NGO activity. Some have been increasingly viewed as human security issues, an argument many NGOs have promoted. Second, global conferences became a key venue for international activity beginning in the 1970s, each designed to address one of the transnational issues—the environment (1972, 1992, 2012), population (1974, 1984), women (1975, 1985, 1995), and food (1974, 1996, 2002). A pattern emerged when NGOs began to organize separate but parallel conferences on the same issues. This creates opportunities for NGO representatives not only to network with each other and form coalitions on specific issues but also to lobby governments and international bureaucrats. In some cases, those linkages between the governmental and nongovernmental conferees enhance the power of the latter. Third, the end of the Cold War and the expansion of democracy in the former communist world and developing countries have provided an unprecedented political opening for NGOs into parts of the world previously untouched by NGO activity. Finally, the communications revolution also partly explains the newly prominent role of NGOs. First the fax, then the Web, e-mail, Facebook, and Twitter have each enabled NGOs to communicate with core constituencies, build coalitions with other like-minded groups, and generate mass support. They can disseminate information rapidly, recruit new members, launch publicity campaigns, and encourage individuals to participate in ways unavailable two decades before. NGOs have benefited from these changes and have been able to capitalize on them to increase their own power.

Functions and Roles of NGOs

NGOs perform a variety of functions and roles in international relations. They advocate specific policies and offer alternative channels of political participation, as Amnesty International has done through its letter-writing campaigns on behalf of victims of human rights violations. They mobilize mass publics, as Greenpeace did in saving whales (through international laws limiting whaling) and in forcing the labeling of "green" (non-environmentally damaging) products in Europe and Canada. They distribute critical assistance in disaster relief and to refugees, as Médecins Sans Frontières (Doctors Without Borders), Catholic Relief Services, and Oxfam have done in Somalia, Yugoslavia, Rwanda, Sudan, Haiti, and Democratic Republic of Congo. They are the principal monitors of human rights norms and environmental regulations and provide warnings of violations, as Human Rights Watch has done in China, Latin America, and elsewhere.

NGOs are also the primary actors at the grassroots level in mobilizing individuals to act. For example, during the 1990 meeting to revise the 1987 Montreal Protocol on Substances that Deplete the Ozone Layer, NGOs criticized the UN Environment Program secretary-general, Mostafa Tolba, for not advocating more stringent regulations on ozone-destroying chemicals. Friends of the Earth International, Greenpeace International, and the Natural Resources Defense Council held press conferences and circulated brochures to the public, media, and officials complaining of the weak

By taking purposeful and public actions, NGOs can direct media attention to their cause, which in turn can result in pressure on politicians to change policy. Here, Greenpeace activists highlight the environmental degradation of palm oil production in Indonesia.

regulations. The precise strategy of each group varied. Friends of the Earth approached the matter analytically, whereas Greenpeace staged a drama to show the effects of environmental degradation. But the intent of each was the same—to focus citizen action on strengthening the Montreal Protocol. By publicizing inadequacies, NGOs force discussion both within states and among states in international forums.

Nowhere has the impact of NGOs been felt more strongly than at the 1992 UN Conference on the Environment and Development (UNCED) in Rio de Janeiro. NGOs played key roles in both the preparatory conferences and the Rio conference itself, adding representation and openness (or "transparency") to the process. They made statements from the floor; they drafted informational materials; they scrutinized working drafts of UN documents; they spoke up to support or oppose specific phrasing. The UNCED also provided extensive opportunities for NGO networking. Among the more than 400 accredited environmental organizations were not only traditional, large, well-financed NGOs, such as the World Wildlife Fund, but also those working on specific issues and those with grassroots origins in developing countries, many of which were poorly financed and had had few previous transnational linkages.

The persistence of the NGOs paid off. Agenda 21, the official document produced by the conference, recognized the unique capabilities of NGOs and recommended their participation at all levels, from policy formulation and decision making to implementation. What began as a parallel informal process of participation within the UN system evolved into a more formal role, which was replicated at the 1994 International Conference on Population and Development in Cairo and again at the 1995 Fourth World Conference on Women in Beijing. But since the 1990s, subsequent conferences have been less successful, as illustrated by the Rio+20 in 2012, as the conference format is increasingly viewed as ineffective and the negotiations unproductive.

NGOs also play unique roles at the national level. In a few unusual cases, NGOs take the place of states, either performing services that an inept or corrupt government is not providing or stepping in for a failed state. Bangladesh hosts the largest NGO sector in the world, a response in part to that government's failure and the failure of the private for-profit sector to provide for the poor. Thus, NGOs have assumed responsibility in education, health, agriculture, and microcredit, originally all government functions. Other NGOs work to change various countries' public institutions, as illustrated by the Muslim Brotherhood in Egypt. Dating back to 1928, the brotherhood had a long, confrontational relationship with the Egyptian government until its political party successfully contested in the 2011 parliamentary elections and assumed power.

Yet NGOs seldom work alone. The communications revolution has linked NGOs with each other, formally and informally. Increasingly, NGOs are developing regional and global networks through linkages with other NGOs. These networks and coalitions create multilevel linkages among different organizations, each of which retain its separate organizational character and membership, but through the linkages enhance each other's power. These networks have learned from each other, just as constructivists would have predicted. Environmentalists and women's groups have studied human rights campaigns for guidance in building international norms. Environmentalists seeking protection of spaces for indigenous peoples also increasingly use the language of human rights.

We usually associate NGOs with humanitarian and environmental groups working for a greater social, economic, or political good, but NGOs may also be formed for malevolent purposes—the Mafia, international drug cartels, and even Al Qaeda being prominent examples. The Mafia, traditionally based in Italy but with networks in Russia, eastern Europe, and the Americas, is engaged in numerous illegal business practices, including money laundering, tax evasion, and fraud. International drug cartels, many with origins in Colombia, function with suppliers in such far-reaching states as Peru, Venezuela, Afghanistan, and Myanmar, while maintaining links with middlemen in Nigeria, Mexico, Guinea, and the Caribbean in order to deliver illegal drugs to North America and Europe, as discussed in Chapter 11. What these NGOs share is a loose series of networks across national boundaries, moving illicit goods and services in international trade. Their leadership is dispersed and their targets everchanging, making their activities particularly difficult to contain.

Al Qaeda, too, is such an NGO—decentralized, dispersed, with individuals deeply committed to a cause, even at the price of death, and able and willing to take initiatives independent of a central authority. The organization has changed and expanded its goals over time, which has enabled it to recruit members willing to die for diverse causes. Osama bin Laden had forged broad links and alliances with various groups until his death in 2011. Like all NGOs, Al Qaeda has benefited from new communications technologies, using the Internet to collect information and train individuals and e-mail to transfer funds and communicate messages, all virtually untrackable.[13] Opponents of Al Qaeda and these other NGOs are waging a different battle, a war on organized crime, a war on drugs, and a war against terror.

The Power of NGOs

What gives NGOs the ability to play such diverse roles in the international system? What are their sources of power? NGOs rely on soft power, meaning credible information, expertise, and the moral authority that attracts the attention and admiration of governments and the public. This means that NGOs have resources such as flexibility to move staff rapidly depending on need, independent donor bases, and links with grassroots groups that enable them to operate in different areas of the world. This very flexibility enables them to create networks to increase their power potential, banding together with other like-minded NGOs and forming coalitions to promote their respective agendas. The new communication technologies have facilitated this networking and coalition-building source of NGO power.

NGOs have distinct advantages over individuals, states, and intergovernmental organizations. They are usually politically independent from any sovereign state, so that they can make and execute international policy more rapidly and directly, and with less risk to national sensitivities, than IGOs can. They can participate at all levels, from policy formation and decision making to implementation, if they choose. Yet they can also influence state behavior by initiating formal, legally binding action; pressuring authorities to impose sanctions; carrying out independent investigations; and linking issues together in ways that force some measure of compliance. Thus, NGOs are versatile and increasingly powerful actors, especially if they are able to network with other NGOs.

The International Campaign to Ban Landmines (ICBL) is an outstanding example of the power of an NGO network. Beginning in 1992, nine NGOs were eventually joined by more than 1,000 other NGOs and local groups (such as the Landmine Survivors Network, Vietnam Veterans of America Foundation, and Human Rights Watch) in more than 60 countries. They used electronic media to craft the message that land mines are a human rights issue and have devastating effects on innocent civilians. Not only was the issue framed to resonate with a large constituency, the leaders formed a network. What became known as the Ottawa Process was bolstered by the death in 1997 of Diana, Princess of Wales, one of its vocal supporters; coordinated by Jody Williams, a founder of the ICBL and winner of the 1997 Nobel Peace Prize for her efforts; and joined by Canada, whose foreign minister pushed the issue, hosted the conference, and provided financial support. The Convention to Ban Landmines was ratified in 1999. But not every attempt to forge such networks has been successful, as illustrated by the failure of the movement to curb small arm sales—NGOs have limits.

The Limits of NGOs

NGOs often lack material forms of power. Except for some of the malevolent groups, they do not have military or police forces as governments do, and thus they cannot command obedience through physical means.

Most NGOs have very limited economic resources, because they do not collect taxes as states do. Thus, the competition for funding is fierce; NGOs sharing the same concerns—for example, human rights organizations—often compete for the same donors. They have a continuous need to raise money, leading some NGOs to find new causes to widen their donor base. To expand their resources, NGOs increasingly rely on governments, an alternative that comes with its own set of limitations. If NGOs choose to accept state assistance, then their neutrality and legitimacy are potentially compromised. They may be forced to continually report "success" in order to renew their financing, even though success may be difficult to prove or even be an inaccurate description of reality. In short, NGOs are locked in a competitive scramble for resources.[14]

Do most NGOs succeed in accomplishing their goals? This is difficult to evaluate, because the NGO community is itself diverse; they have no single agenda, and NGOs often work at cross-purposes, just as states do. Groups can be found on almost any side of every issue, resulting in countervailing pressures. In a world that is increasingly viewed as democratic, are NGOs appropriate? To whom are NGOs accountable if their leaders are not elected? How do they maintain transparency when they have no publicly accountable mechanism? Do NGOs reflect only liberal values? Incomplete or unsatisfactory answers to these questions have led scholars to suggest that NGOs may be more like other actors and less altruistic than supposed—self-interested, self-aggrandizing, concerned with their own narrow agendas, hierarchical rather than democratic, more worried about financial gains than achieving progressive social purposes. This suggestion has led some critics to refer to NGOs as "wild cards" and "benign parasites."[15] Some disturbing case studies have found that NGOs' actions have led to unintended and detrimental consequences. In refugee camps in Rwanda run by NGOs such as Doctors Without Borders and the International Rescue Committee, the leaders of the genocide were actually being protected. When NGOs are active in war zones, are they becoming more like "force multipliers"?[16] The roles NGOs play and the legitimacy they may or may not have depend in part on how they answer critical questions of accountability and transparency. Whether accountable and transparent or not, NGOs increasingly work with states, IGOs, and regional organizations.

NGOs: Views from the Former Soviet States

The formation and rise of NGOs in the newly independent states of the former Soviet Union can be traced back to the early 1990s, following the disintegration of the USSR. At first, international NGOs flocked to the region, eager to advance democracy, human rights, and social programs. But NGOs are increasingly facing problems.

In the Baltic states (Lithuania, Latvia, and Estonia), civil society development generally was successful. NGOs in these countries enjoy wide-spread legitimacy and a strong financial base, due to expanded public and private resources. Those donating to NGOs are awarded tax advantages, resulting in not only more material resources but also broader public commitment to the NGOs' activities and national ownership of their goals and achievements. NGOs benefit from being operated mostly by professionals. In short, NGO strength and reach are rapidly approaching those of NGOs based in well-established Western democracies.

But as other countries in the region experienced an increasingly difficult transition from socialism to liberal economic systems and an uncertain legal environment, the NGOs that were formed were overly dependent on contributions from Western governments, overseas foundations, and international NGOs themselves. Leadership was too often provided by external donors. In some countries, certain NGOs received support from the national government, which immediately undermined their independence and neutrality. Generally cautious about affiliating with these new actors, the population chose not to participate or support their activities. Nationals became the beneficiaries of NGO services without helping to shape policies.

In the first few years of the new millennium, a number of democratic revolutions swept through several formerly socialist states within a relatively short period of time: the Rose Revolution in Georgia in 2003, the Orange Revolution in Ukraine in 2004-5, and the Tulip Revolution in Kyrgyzstan in 2005. All of these "color" revolutions followed a similar initial pattern: a pro-American profile and general support from Washington and sharply anti-Russian rhetoric. Very quickly, the suspicion that a foreign hand was behind these revolutions, which arose through civil society associations, turned into a firm belief.

Several U.S.-based groups and organizations—such as the National Democratic Institute, the International Republican Institute, Freedom House, and the Open Society Institute—became closely identified with these revolutions. By providing financial support, training, and consultative assistance to domestic opposition groups, they became known as "color revolutions exporters." In Kyrgyzstan, for example, it was believed that the photos of the former president Askar Akayev's mansion in a Kyrgyz newspaper were printed on a press financed by an American NGO or even the American government itself.

These events have led many of these governments to review their internal policies toward NGOs and impose strict governmental control over their operations. That decision affected all NGOs regardless of their sphere of activities and their level of political involvement. For example, as the result of a 2006 law,

Russia has increasingly denied entry to individuals working for NGOs, closed NGO offices, conducted long audits, and challenged the organizations' tax-exempt status. In 2012, that pressure on NGOs increased. A bill passed that requires nonprofit organizations that receive funding from outside Russia to identify themselves as "foreign agents," a term reminiscent of the Cold War era. Purportedly aimed at nonprofits advocating political change, the legislation is causing alarm in the NGO community. But as Alekrandr Sidyakin, a United Russia deputy justifies it, "The ultimate goal of funding nonprofit organizations, as a form of 'soft power,' is a colored revolution.... This is not a myth of government propaganda, it is objective political reality. The United States is trying to affect Russian politics."[a]

Uzbekistan and Tajikistan mandate state registration and reregistration of all public associations in their territory. In the process, many "undesirable" NGOs are denied registration under various pretexts. Belarus, too, imposes strict procedures: registration of all technical assistance or humanitarian projects involving foreign funds and submission of detailed reports on their implementation to relevant ministries. As a result, the government exercises control over specific projects. Severe monetary penalties and revoked registration follow in cases of alleged improper use of funds or for projects not approved by the government. Outright closure of NGO offices, confiscation of assets, frequent financial audits, increased control of NGO workers' movements, and denial of visas for NGO workers have become widespread examples of bureaucratic "red tape" in Russia, Turkmenistan, Belarus, and Uzbekistan. The governments want full control over the NGOs' sources of funding, finances, and activities.

In the former communist states, NGOs are now viewed by the governments with a good deal of suspicion and hostility. This is

Opposition protesters wave flags during the Rose Revolution, Tbilisi, Georgia.

especially true of American-financed NGOs promoting democracy or human rights. These states see such activities as encroachment on their sovereignty and contrary to the national interest of the sovereign state. With full implementation of these restrictions, each state has enhanced its capacity to control what occurs within its borders. The governments of the region will not accept interference from the agents of what they regard as an imperialistic state that tortures people abroad and occupies foreign lands.

[a] Quoted in Ellen Barry, "Russian Bill Would Limit Nonprofits' Foreign Aid," *New York Times*, July 3, 2012, p. A8.

FOR CRITICAL ANALYSIS

1. NGOs are not independent actors; they exist by consent of host states. Explain.

2. How can NGOs use soft power? What other kinds of power do they have at their disposal?

3. How might realists and radicals justify a state's opposition to foreign-financed NGOs?

4. To constructivists, NGOs may be the conduit for transmitting or socializing norms. How might they do so in the newly independent states of the former Soviet Union?

The Realist View of International Organization and Law

Realists are skeptical about intergovernmental organizations, international law, and nongovernmental organizations, though they do not completely discount their place. Recall that realists see anarchy in the international system, wherein each state is forced to act in its own self-interest and obliged to rely on self-help mechanisms. While it may be useful to utilize IGOs, states prefer not to out of distrust and skepticism. Realists doubt that collective action is effective and believe states will refuse to rely on the collectivity for the protection of their individual national interests. They can point to the failure of the council of the League of Nations to act when Japan invaded Manchuria in 1931 and its slow response to the Italian invasion of Ethiopia in 1935 as evidence. These failures confirmed the fundamental weaknesses of the League and of its collective approach to punishing aggressors. Realists likewise do not put much faith in the United Nations. They can legitimately point to the Cold War era, when the Security Council proved impotent in addressing the conflict between the United States and the Soviet Union. And the failure in 2003 of the United Nations to enforce Security Council resolutions against Iraq and the history of weak sanctions against Iran are more reminders of the organization's weakness and supposed irrelevance.

To realists, international law may create some order, but they remind us that states can opt out of following international law, and if the more powerful do so, other states can do little about it.

In the state-centric world of the realists, NGOs are generally not on the radar screen at all. After all, most NGOs exist at the pleasure of states; it is states that grant them legal authority, and it is states that can take away that authority. To realists, NGOs are not independent actors.

The Radical View of International Organization and Law

Radicals in the Marxist tradition are also very skeptical about IGOs, international law, and many NGOs, albeit for very different reasons from those of the realists. Radicals see contemporary international law and organization as the product of a specific time and historical process. Emerging from Western capitalist state experiences, international law and organization serve the interests of the dominant capitalist classes. The actions by the United Nations following the Iraqi invasion of Kuwait in 1990, including a series of resolutions condemning Iraq and imposing sanctions on that country, were designed to support the position of the West, most notably the interests of the hegemonic United States and its capitalist friends in the international petroleum industry. To radicals, the UN-imposed sanctions provide an excellent example of hegemonic interests injuring the marginalized—Iraqi men, women, and children striving to eke out meager livings. Radicals also view NATO's actions in Kosovo as another example of hegemonic power harming the poor and the unprotected.

International law is biased against the interests of socialist states, the weak, and the unrepresented. For example, international legal principles, such as the sanctity of national geographic boundaries, were developed during the colonial period to reinforce the claims of the powerful. Attempts to alter such boundaries are, according to international law, wrong, even though the boundaries themselves may be unfair or unjust. Radicals are quick to point out these injustices and support policies that overturn the traditional order.

To most radicals, the lack of representativeness and the lack of accountability of NGOs are key issues. NGOs are largely based in the North and are dominated by members of the same elite that run the state and international organizations. They see NGOs as falling under the exigencies of the capitalist economic system and as captive to those dominant interests. According to radicals, only a few NGOs have been able to break out of this mold and develop networks enabling mass participation designed to change the fundamental rules of the game. After all, radicals desire major political and economic change in favor of an international order that distributes economic resources and political power more equitably. Contemporary international law and organizations are not the agents of such change.

The Constructivist View of International Organization and Law

Constructivists place critical importance on institutions and norms.[17] Both IGOs and NGOs can be norm entrepreneurs that socialize and teach states new norms. Those norms may change state preferences, which in turn may influence state behavior. Constructivists acknowledge that new international institutions have been developing at a rapid rate and are taking on more tasks. But, Michael Barnett and Martha Finnemore argue in *Rules for the World*, international organizations may produce conflict, acting in ways that are contrary to the interests of their constituency. They may pursue particularistic goals, creating a bureaucratic culture that tolerates inefficiency and lack of accountability. International institutions may become dysfunctional, serving the interests of international bureaucrats.[18]

THEORY IN BRIEF

CONTENDING PERSPECTIVES ON IGOs, INTERNATIONAL LAW, AND NGOs

	LIBERALISM/ NEOLIBERAL INSTITUTION- ALISM	REALISM / NEOREALISM	RADICALISM/ DEPENDENCY THEORY	CONSTRUCTIVISM
INTERGOVERN- MENTAL ORGANIZATIONS	Important independent actors for collective action; neoliberals see as forums	Skeptical of their ability to engage in collective action	Serve interests of powerful states; biased against weak states and the unrep- resented	Both IGOs and NGOs can be norm entrepreneurs and socialize actors, which may change state behavior
INTERNATIONAL LAW	Key source of order in the international system; states comply because law ensures order	Acknowledges that international law creates some order, but stresses that states comply only when it is in their self- interest; states prefer self-help	Skeptical because origins of law are in Western capitalist tradition; international law only reaffirms claims of the powerful	Law reflects changing norms; shapes state expectations and behavior
NONGOVERN- MENTAL ORGANIZATIONS	Increasingly key actors that represent different interests and facilitate collective action	Not independent actors; power belongs to states; any NGO power is derived from states	Represent dominant economic interests; unlikely to effect major political or economic change	Both IGOs and NGOs may lead to dysfunctional behavior, but may also represent new ideas and norms

Law plays a key role in constructivist thinking, not because law establishes precise rules, but because it reflects changing norms. Thus, both adherents of customary international law and constructivists see the critical role such norms play in providing shared expectations about appropriate state behavior. Over time, those norms are internalized by states themselves, they change state preferences, and they shape behavior. A number of key norms are of particular interest to constructivists, for example, multilateralism, the practice of joining with others in making decisions. Occurring both outside and within formal organizations, participants learn the value of this norm. Through multilateral participation, states have also learned other norms, including the emerging prohibition against the use of nuclear weapons, the norm of humanitarian intervention, and the increasing attention to human rights norms. Yet just as these norms and ideas affect state behavior, states also participate in shaping them. All of these norms are discussed in coming chapters. Thus, with the steady expansion of international institutions and international law and influence, constructivists have an active research agenda.

In Sum: Do Intergovernmental Organizations, International Law, and Nongovernmental Organizations Make a Difference?

Liberals and constructivists are convinced that IGOs, international law, and NGOs do matter in international politics, albeit with different emphases. To liberals, these organizations and international law do not replace states as the primary actors in international politics, although in a few cases they may be moving in that direction. They do provide alternative venues, whether intergovernmental or private, for states themselves to engage in collective action and for individuals to join with other like-minded individuals in pursuit of their goals. They permit old issues to be seen in new ways, and they provide both a venue for discussing new transnational issues and an arena for action. To constructivists, the emphasis is on how changing norms and institutions shape issues. Realists and radicals remain skeptical. And in the state-centered world of security, examined in the next chapter, that skepticism is warranted.

Discussion Questions

1. Everyone agrees that reform of the UN Security Council is necessary. What proposal for reform would you support? Why?

2. Do international organizations, NGOs, and international law threaten state sovereignty, or do they not? Substantiate your position.

3. Find two recent newspaper articles that give examples of states complying with international law and two other articles about states that are failing to comply. What explains the difference between the two sets of cases?

4. What problems arise when NGOs take over the tasks of states?

Key Terms

collective good (p. 205)

complex peacekeeping (p. 214)

European Union (EU) (p. 220)

General Assembly (p. 211)

Group of 77 (p. 211)

Group of 20 (p. 211)

human security (p. 209)

intergovernmental organizations (IGOs) (p. 204)

international regimes (p. 207)

peacebuilding (p. 214)

Security Council (p. 209)

traditional peacekeeping (p. 213)

universal jurisdiction (p. 232)

War is one of the recurrent features of international relations, and its devastation has been immense: World War I, for instance, resulted in the death of close to 5 percent of the population of both France and Germany. Since 1945, the incidence of interstate war has declined significantly, but lethal violence—including civil war, genocide, and terrorism—continues within states.

08

WAR AND STRIFE

- *What makes security a preeminent value in international relations?*

- *How do the levels of analysis help us to explain the causes of wars?*

- *Is interstate war becoming obsolete? Why?*

- *What are the key characteristics of asymmetric conflict?*

- *Is the terrorism of the last decade different from earlier forms of terrorism? If so, different how?*

- *When is a war "just"? How, if at all, can we fight "justly"?*

- *How do realist and liberal approaches to managing insecurity differ?*

Among the many issues engaging the actors in international relations, war is generally viewed as the oldest, the most prevalent, and in the long term, the most important. Wars—in particular major wars between states—have been the focus of historians of international relations for centuries. Major works on war include Thucydides's *History of the Peloponnesian War* (431 BC) and Carl von Clausewitz's *On War* (1832). World War I and its aftermath (the founding of the League of Nations) led American diplomatic historians and legal scholars to create a new discipline called international relations. Since that time, prominent scholars in this field have addressed many of the critical and vexing issues surrounding war—its causes, its conduct, its consequences, its prevention, and even the possibility of its elimination. This attention to war and security is clearly warranted. Of all human values, physical security—security from violence, starvation, and the elements—comes first. All other human values that are crucially important to the quality of our lives—good government, economic development, a clean environment—presuppose a minimal level of physical security. Consider the difficulties the United States and its NATO allies have had in Afghanistan in trying to revive the economy, establish legal authority, and guarantee human rights, especially for women. In the absence of a minimum level of physical security (in this case, security from violence), these important goals have proven very difficult to achieve.

Yet history suggests that a minimum level of security has not always been attainable. Historians have recorded approximately 14,500 armed struggles over time, with about 3.5 billion people dying as either a direct or an indirect result. Since 1816, there have been between 224 and 559 international and intrastate wars, depending on how war is defined. As more and more states industrialized, interstate war became more lethal and less controllable, and it engaged ever-wider segments of belligerents' societies. This new reality of interstate war culminated in two horrific convulsions: World Wars I (1914–18) and II (1939–45).

However, following the world wars and the Korean War (1950–53), and perhaps as a consequence of their destructiveness and potential to escalate to nuclear war, both the frequency and intensity of interstate war began a slow decline. Since 1991 that decline has accelerated: both the frequency and intensity of war dropped by one-half in the years between 1991 and 2006. The number of battlefield deaths dropped by 80 percent in that span.[1] Yet, because our contemporary understanding of war remains incomplete, many international relations scholars worry that there is no reason this trend could not reverse itself. War therefore remains perhaps the most compelling issue in world politics, and international relations theorists continue to analyze why international and intrastate conflicts occur.

This analysis leads theorists to examine the possibility of *transcending* war as a means of settling conflicts of interest. Is war natural and hence inevitable? Or is it a deliberate practice that can be usefully abandoned? The four theoretical traditions answer this question differently. For realists, war is a necessary condition of interstate politics: it can be managed but never eradicated. Classical realists, ranging from Thucydides to Machiavelli to Hobbes to Hans Morgenthau, argued that human nature made transcending war unlikely. Neorealists replaced the emphasis on human nature with an emphasis on structure, arguing that war will be a permanent feature of interstate politics so long as anarchy remains. This formulation at least hints at a possibility that war might be eliminated if a single state amasses sufficient power to defeat all other states. Because this possibility is remote, neorealists effectively share the pessimism of classical realists: as a prominent feature of interstate politics, war can never be transcended. One key concept that informs realism is the prisoner's dilemma (see Chapter 3), a conflict of interest structured in such a way that rational actors choose to harm each other as a best strategy for avoiding a worse outcome. Another key concept is the **security dilemma,** in which even actors with no hostile or aggressive intentions may be led by their own insecurity into a costly and risky arms race. As the political scientist John Herz described it, "Striving to attain security from attack, [states] are driven to acquire more and more power in order to escape the power of others. This, in turn, renders the others more insecure and compels them to prepare for the worst. Since none can ever feel entirely secure in such a world of competing units, power competition ensues, and the vicious circle of security and power accumulation is on."[2] The security dilemma, then, results in a permanent condition of tension and power conflicts among states even when none actually seek conquest and war.

For liberals, in contrast, the possibility of transcending war is real, though it will likely take generations to achieve. The core logic of the liberal position acknowledges the structural constraint of anarchy and accepts the priority of state insecurity as a factor motivating interstate relations, but argues that states seeking power, including economic power, will be led by self-interest into successively deeper and broader cooperation with other states, punctuated at times by war. Over time, cooperation may be institutionalized, reducing the costs of transactions and increasing the costs and risks of cheating. Liberals also focus on the nature of a state's political system, arguing that, in contrast to the realist view, there are essentially "good" (liberal and open) and "bad" (authoritarian and closed) states. Over time, the rewards that accrue to good states will create pressures and incentives on more and more bad states to become responsible partners in an interstate system. Finally, liberal theorists argue that the democratic peace provides powerful empirical support for their arguments, because it is virtually impossible to cite an example of two democratic states going to war against one another.

Radicals, including Marxists, share liberal optimism regarding the possibility of transcending war as a permanent feature of interstate politics. For Marxists, war is expected to end when the "state" (as a form of political association) ends, as it must after the triumph of socialism worldwide. They believe that this system of exploitation and repression creates the very forces that will inevitably combine to destroy the state

a worker's revolution, leading to communism: a secular paradise in which the state has withered away (and with it war and poverty), replaced by a world of workers who share the fruits of their labors with all, obviating scarcity and any need for a state. In Marxist theory, a key question is whether humans are inherently self-interested, which might mean that a system based on collective rather than individual interest could never exist. The Marxist response is that self-interest is not natural but is socially constructed—a kind of "false consciousness" that could be corrected by reeducation.

Constructivists argue along similar lines when they note that much of the world we perceive is socially constructed: objects have no necessary or inherent meaning. Instead, human beings bring meaning to objects. This is why, when constructivists analyze the security dilemma, they point to the simple mechanism of "friend or foe" to show that the acquisition of, say, 50 new long-range missiles by Great Britain has a dramatically different implication for U.S. security than does the acquisition of missiles with the same destructive power by North Korea or Iran. If the missiles had a fixed meaning—a fixed *threat* as suggested by realist theory—then Great Britain's missiles should alarm the United States just as much as North Korea's. Yet they don't. Constructivists then ask, Where else are the implications of material objects (capabilities) assumed rather than explained and compared? For constructivists then, war is not a necessary, natural, or inevitable feature of interstate politics. Instead, actors have been socialized to understand key features of interstate politics (for example, anarchy) as threatening. If human beings, and by extension, states were socialized differently, the possibilities of either cooperation or nonviolent competition would be sufficient to reduce war to a historical footnote.

Over time, some mix of realism and liberalism has held sway as a theoretical guide to foreign policy in advanced industrial states. In general, the more a state feels threatened by physical conquest (for example, contemporary Iran, Israel, Pakistan, North Korea, Taiwan, Georgia, and Poland), the more likely it is that some variation of realism will become a guide to that state's foreign policy. Where physical threats seem less intense (for example, northern and western Europe), realism often plays a subsidiary role compared to liberalism. This chapter focuses on each theoretical tradition's explanation of the causes of war and, by extension, each tradition's understanding of the requirements of peace.

Defining War

Before exploring the question of what causes war, it makes sense to define war. International relations scholars maintain a healthy debate about what counts and what does not count as a war, but over time a number of key features have been established as agreed-upon standards. Three in particular stand out. First, a war demands organized, deliberate violence by an identifiable political authority. Riots are often lethal, but they are not considered "war" because by definition a riot is neither deliberate nor organized. Second, wars are relatively more lethal than other forms of organized violence. Pogroms, bombings, and massacres are deliberate and organized but generally not sufficiently lethal to count as war. Currently, most international relations scholars accept that in order to count as a war, organized and deliberate violence by an established political authority must result in at least 1,000 deaths in a calendar year. Third and finally, in order to count as a war, both sides must have some real capacity to harm each other, although that capacity need not be equal on both sides—one side might be stronger than the other. We don't count genocides, massacres, terrorist attacks, and pogroms as wars because in a genocide, for example, only one side has any real capacity to kill, while the other side is effectively defenseless.

In sum, **war** is an organized and deliberate political act by an established political authority, which must cause 1,000 or more deaths in a twelve-month period, and which requires at least two actors capable of harming each other.

These definitional issues are not simply academic. They have real-world consequences. An important case in point was the 1994 Rwandan genocide, in which over 750,000 men, women, and children were murdered in the space of four months. Had the international community named this violence properly as a genocide, the pressure to intervene militarily to halt it might have saved thousands of lives, although there remains a vigorous debate on whether those lives could have been saved. But the violence was initially characterized as a renewal of *civil war*, raising the legitimate question whether international intervention should occur in Rwanda's internal affairs. The actual turn of events is less controversial: what began as a genocide—the organized mass murder of defenseless civilians sharing a particular characteristic—by government-supported extremists soon *escalated* to a civil war in which a former combatant, the Rwandan Patriotic Front, remobilized, rearmed, and attacked the government, systematically destroying the forces of the extremists and ending the genocide by forcing the government and its surviving *genocidaires* to flee.

The Causes of War

In an analysis of any war—Vietnam, Angola, Cambodia, World War II, or the Franco-Prussian War, to take but a few examples—we will find more than one cause for the outbreak of violence. This multiplicity of explanations can seem overwhelming. Can we study the causes of war systematically, when the causes often seem idiosyncratic? In order to identify patterns and variables that might explain not just one war but war more generally, international relations scholars have found it useful to consider causes of war at the three levels of analysis identified by Kenneth Waltz in *Man, the State, and War*[3]—the individual, the state, and the international system.

The Individual: Realist and Liberal Interpretations

Both the characteristics of individual leaders and the general attributes of people (discussed in Chapter 6) have been blamed for war. Some individual leaders are aggressive and bellicose; they use their leadership positions to further their causes. Thus, according to some realists and liberals, war occurs because of the personal characteristics of major leaders. It is impossible, however, to prove the general veracity of this position. Would past wars have occurred had different leaders—perhaps more pacifist ones—been in power? What about wars that nearly happened but didn't, due to the intervention of a charismatic leader? As we can see, the impact of individual leaders on war is difficult to generalize. We can identify some wars in which individuals played a crucial role, but overall, we can only speculate.

If it is not the innate character flaws of individuals that cause war, is it possible that leaders, like all individuals, are subject to misperceptions that might lead to war? According to liberals, misperceptions by leaders—seeing aggressiveness where it may not be intended, attributing the actions of one person to a group—can indeed lead to the outbreak of war. Historians have typically given a key role to misperceptions. Several types of misperceptions may lead to war. One of the most common is exaggerating the hostility of the adversary, believing that it is more hostile than it may actually be or that it has greater military or economic capability than it actually has. This tendency to magnify a potential rival's hostility or capability may lead a state to build up its own arms or seek new allies, which, in turn, may be viewed as hostile acts by its actual or potential rivals. Misperceptions thus spiral, leading to costly arms races, new alliances, and potentially to war. The events leading up to World War I are often viewed as a conflict spiral, caused by misperceived intentions and actions of the principal protagonists.

Beyond the characteristics of leaders, perhaps factors particular to the masses lead to the outbreak of war. Some realist thinkers—Saint Augustine and Reinhold Niebuhr, for example—take this position. Augustine wrote that every act is an act of self-preservation on the part of individuals. For Niebuhr the link goes even deeper; the origins of war reside in the depths of the human psyche.[4] This approach is compatible with that of sociobiologists who study animal behavior. Virtually all species are equipped to use violence to ensure survival; it is biologically innate. Yet the implications of this fact remain controversial. For one thing, violence is not the same thing as aggression: a cheetah does not hate the gazelle it attacks and kills. Moreover, this view does not explain subtle differences among species: as with violence, many animals (in particular *homo sapiens*) appear equally well equipped to engage in cooperative behavior as an aid to survival. In either case, contemporary sociobiologists regard human beings as an infinitely more complex species than other animal species. If true, these presumptions lead to two possible alternative assessments, one pessimistic and the other optimistic. For pessimists, if war is the product of innate human characteristics or human nature, then there can be no reprieve. For optimists, if war or aggression is innate, the only hope of eliminating war resides in changing social institutions, socializing or educating individuals out of destructive tendencies.

Of course, war does not, in fact, happen all the time; it is an *unusual* event, not the norm. Thus, characteristics inherent in all individuals cannot be the only cause of war. Nor can the explanation be that human nature has, indeed, fundamentally changed, because wars still occur. Most experiments aimed at changing mass human behavior have failed miserably, and there is no visible proof that basic attitudes affecting insecurity, greed, aggression, and identity have been altered sufficiently to preclude war.

Thus, the individual level of analysis, though clearly implicated in some wars, is unlikely to stand as a good cause of war *in general*. Individuals, after all, do not make war. Only groups of political actors (for example, clans, tribes, nations, organizations, states, and alliances) make war.

State and Society: Liberal and Radical Explanations

A second level of analysis suggests that war occurs because of the internal structures of states. States vary in size, geography, ethnic homogeneity, and economic and government type. The question, then, is how do the characteristics of different states affect the possibility of war? Are some state characteristics more correlated with the propensity to go to war than others?

State and societal explanations for war are among the oldest. Plato, for example, posited that war is less likely where the population is cohesive and enjoys a moderate level of prosperity. Since the population would be able to thwart an attack, an enemy is likely to refrain from attacking it. Many thinkers during the Enlightenment, including Immanuel Kant, believed that war was more likely in aristocratic states.

Drawing on the Kantian position, liberals posit that republican regimes (those with representative governments and separation of powers) are least likely to wage war against each other; that is the basic position of the theory of the democratic peace introduced in Chapter 5. Democratic leaders, so the theory goes, hear from multiple voices, including the public, which tend to restrain decision makers, decrease the likelihood of misperceptions, and therefore lessen the chance of war. Ordinary citizens may be hesitant to go to war because they bear the cost of fighting, paying with their lives (in the case of soldiers), the lives of friends and family, and taxes. To thrive in a democratic state, individuals learn the art of compromise. In the process, extreme behavior such as waging war is curbed. Democratic states are thus especially unlikely to go to war with each other, because the citizens in each state can trust that the citizens in the other state are as disinclined to go to war as they are. This mitigates the threat that a democratic opponent represents, even one with greater relative power. But by this logic, the corollary is true also: citizens in democratic states tend to magnify the threat of nondemocratic states in which the government is less constrained by the will of the public, even when such states appear to have a lesser capacity to fight and win wars. More broadly, democracies engage in war only periodically and then only when the public and their chosen leaders deem it necessary to make them safe.

Other liberal tenets hold that some types of economic systems are more susceptible to war than others. Liberal states are likely to be states whose citizens enjoy relative wealth. Such societies feel no need to divert the attention of dissatisfied masses to an external conflict; the wealthy masses are largely satisfied with the status quo. And even when they are not satisfied presently, liberal economies are marked by the possibility of upward economic (and social) mobility: in a liberal state, even the poorest person may one day become one of the richest. Liberals argue that such conflicts as do arise can be limited by altering terms of trade, or by other concessions short of outright war. Furthermore, war interrupts trade, blocks profits, and causes inflation. Thus, liberal capitalist states are more likely to avoid war and to promote peace.

But not every theorist sees the liberal state as benign and peace loving. Indeed, radical theorists offer the most thorough critique of liberalism and its economic counterpart, capitalism. They argue that capitalist, liberal modes of production inevitably lead to competition for economic dominance and political leadership between the two major social classes within the state—the bourgeoisie and the proletariat. This struggle leads to war, both internal and external, because the state, dominated by the entrenched bourgeoisie, is driven to accelerate the engine of capitalism at the expense of the proletariat and for the economic preservation of the bourgeoisie.

This view attributes conflict and war to the internal dynamics of capitalist economic systems, which stagnate and slowly collapse in the absence of external stimulation. Three different explanations have been offered for what happens to capitalist states and why they must turn outward. First, the British economist John A. Hobson claimed that the internal demand for goods will slow down in capitalist countries, leading to pressures for imperialist expansion to find external markets to sustain economic growth. Second, according to Lenin and other Marxists, the problem is not underdemand but declining rates of return on capital. Capitalist states expand outward to find new markets; expanding markets increase the rates of return on capital investment. Third, Lenin and many later-twentieth-century radicals point to the need for raw materials to sustain capitalist growth; external suppliers are needed to obtain such resources. So according to the radical view, capitalist states inevitably expand, but radical theorists disagree among themselves as to precisely why expansion occurs.

Although radical interpretations help explain colonialism and imperialism, the link to war is more tenuous. One possible link is that capitalist states spend not only on consumer goods but also on the military, leading inevitably to arms races and eventually war. Another link points to leaders who resort to external conflict in order to divert public attention from domestic economic crises, corruption, or scandal. Such a conflict is called a **diversionary war** and is likely to provide internal cohesion, at least in the short run. For example, considerable evidence supports the notion that the Argentinian military used the Falkland/Malvinas conflict in 1982 to rally the population around the flag and draw attention away from the country's economic contraction. Still another link suggests that the masses may push a ruling elite toward war. This view is clearly at odds with the liberal belief that the masses are basically peace loving. Adherents of this view point to the Spanish-American War of 1898 as an example in which the U.S. public, supported or inflamed by stilted reports in the new mass print media, pushed a reluctant McKinley administration into aggressive action. And many in the United States saw a clear three-way link between the terrorist attacks of September 11, 2001, the support for the attacks from Afghanistan's ruling Taliban, and Iraq's Saddam Hussein. As a result, both the Afghanistan and Iraq wars—the first, beginning in October of 2001, named Operation Enduring Freedom; and the second, beginning in March of 2003, named Operation Iraqi Freedom—enjoyed widespread popular support early on.

Those who argue that contests over the nature of a state's government are a basic cause of war have identified another explanation for the outbreak of some wars. Many civil wars have been fought over which groups, ideologies, and leaders should control a state's government. The United States' own civil war (1861–65) between the North and the South; Russia's civil war (1917–19) between liberal and socialist forces; China's civil war (1927–49) between nationalist and communist forces; and the civil wars in Vietnam, Korea, the Sudan, and Chad—each pitting north against south—are stark illustrations. In many of these cases, the struggle among competing economic systems and among groups vying for scarce resources within a state illustrates further the proposition that internal state dynamics are responsible for the outbreak of war. The American Civil War was fought not only over slavery and which region should control policy, but also over Southerners' belief that the government inequitably and unfairly allocated economic resources. China's civil war pitted a wealthy landed elite supportive of the nationalist cause against an exploited peasantry struggling, often unsuccessfully, for survival. The intermittent Sudanese civil war pitted an economically depressed south against a northern government that poured economic resources into the region of the capital.

Yet in virtually every case cited here, neither characteristics of the state nor state structures are solely responsible for the outbreak of war. State structure is embedded in the characteristics of the international system.

The International System: Realist and Radical Interpretations

If one key issue or argument distinguishes realists from their liberal and radical critics, it is that for realists, war is a natural, and hence an inevitable and immutable, feature of interstate politics. War is as tragic and unpreventable as hurricanes and earthquakes. In advancing this argument, contemporary realists tend to focus on a single description of the international system as *anarchic*. Such an anarchic system is often compared with a "state of nature," after Hobbes's characterization. By extension, the international system is equivalent to a state of war, and Hobbes's description of that state perfectly characterizes the realist view. In his most famous book, *Leviathan*, Hobbes argued that whenever men live without a common power to keep them all in fear, they are in a condition of war: "every man against every man." War, Hobbes went on, was not the same thing as battle or constant fighting. Instead, it was any tract of time in which war was possible. Hobbes likened this situation to the relationship between climate and weather: it may not rain every day, but in some climates rain is much more common than in others. Essentially, Hobbes concluded that so long as a single strong man (or state) was not more powerful than all the others combined, human beings would be forced to live in a climate of war, never peace.[5]

According to realists then, war breaks out *because nothing in the interstate system prevents it*. So long as there is anarchy, there will be war. War, in such a system, might even appear to be the best course of action that a given state can take. After all, states must protect themselves. A state's security is ensured only by its accumulating military and economic power. But one state's accumulation makes other states less secure, according to the logic of the security dilemma.

An anarchic system may have few rules about how to decide among states' contending claims. One of the major categories of contested claims is territory. For almost all of the previous century, the Jewish-Arab dispute rested on competing territorial claims to Palestine; in the Horn of Africa, the territorial aspirations of the Somali people remain disputed; in the Andes, Ecuador and Peru have competing territorial claims; and in the South China Sea, Japan, China, and the Russian Federation are three of the many states struggling over conflicting claims to offshore islands such as the Spratly Islands. According to the international-system-level explanation, these disputes tend to escalate to violence because there are no authoritative and legitimized arbiters of claims. John Mearsheimer calls this the "911 problem—absence of central authority, to which a threatened state can turn for help."[6]

Neither is there an effective arbiter of competing claims to self-determination. Who decides whether Chechen, Bosnian, Catalonians, or Quebecois claims for self-determination are legitimate? Who decides whether Kurdish claims against Turkey and Iraq are worthy of consideration? Without an internationally legitimized arbiter, authority is relegated to the states themselves, with the most powerful ones often becoming the decisive, interested arbiters.

In addition, several realist variants attribute war to other facets of the anarchic nature of the international system. One system-level explanation for war, advanced in the work of Kenneth Organski, is power transition theory. To Organski and his intellectual heirs, it is not only asymmetric capabilities that tempt states to war, but *anticipation* of shifts in the relative balance of power. War occurs because power is expected to conduce to proportional influence, wealth, and security. Thus, a power transition can cause war in one of two patterns. In one pattern, a challenger might launch a war to solidify its position: according to some power transition theorists, the Franco-Prussian War (1870–71), the Russo-Japanese War (1904–5), and the two world wars (1914–18 and 1939–45, respectively) all share this pattern.[7] In a second pattern, the hegemon might launch a preventive war to keep the challenger down. Some have argued that current international pressure on Iran to halt its nuclear development (which has not yet escalated to war) fits this pattern. Either way, according to the theory, power transitions increase the likelihood of war.

A variant derived from power transition theory is that war is caused by the changing distribution of power among states that occurs because of uneven rates of economic development. George Modelski and William R. Thompson find regular cycles of power transition starting in 1494. They observe 100-year cycles between hegemonic wars—wars that fundamentally alter the structure of the international system. A hegemonic war creates a new hegemonic power; its power waxes and wanes, a struggle follows, and a new hegemon assumes dominance. The cycle begins again.[8]

To radicals also, the international system structure is responsible for war. Dominant capitalist states within the international system need to expand economically, waging war with developing regions over control of natural resources and labor markets, or with other capitalist states over control of developing regions. According to radicals, the dynamic of expansion inherent in the international capitalist system is the major cause of wars.

Realist and radical reliance on one level of explanation may be overly simplistic, however. Because the international system framework exists all the time, in order to explain why wars occur at some times but not others we also need to consider the other levels of analysis.[9] In actuality, most wars are caused by interactions between various factors at different levels of analysis (see Table 8.1). The case of civil war in Georgia in 2008 illustrates the multidimensional causes of war.

The Case of South Ossetia

Are the causes of interstate wars equally relevant for civil conflicts? The South Ossetia war of 2008 illustrates how explanations at the individual, state, and international levels are also useful for explaining key aspects of civil wars. This case also shows how what began as an intrastate war quickly became internationalized.

TABLE 8.1	CAUSES OF WAR BY LEVEL OF ANALYSIS	
LEVEL	**CAUSE OF WAR**	
Individual ("First Image")	Aggressive characteristics of leaders	
	Misperceptions by leaders	
	Communication failures	
State/Society ("Second Image")	Liberal capitalist states, according to radicals	
	Nonliberal/nondemocratic states, according to liberals	
	Domestic politics, scapegoating	
	Struggle between groups for economic resources	
	Ethnonational challengers	
International System ("Third Image")	Anarchy	
	Power transitions	
	Aggressiveness of the international capitalist class	

In 1991, South Ossetia was an autonomous region of Georgia. After Georgia sought to strip the region of its autonomous status, South Ossetia attempted to break away and become an independent state. Georgia resisted, and the conflict quickly escalated to a war that cost the lives of as many as 2,000 people. South Ossetia's bid for independence was openly supported by the Russian Federation, which lent regional authorities arms, transport, intelligence, and air support. Atrocities occurred on both sides, prompting large transfers of refugees (23,000 ethnic Georgians and about 100,000 South Ossetians). In a 1992 agreement, Georgia was forced to accept South Ossetia as a semi-independent state on its northern flank, with over 1,000 Russian Federation "peacekeepers" permanently stationed there.

The cease-fire held until the 2003 ouster of Georgia's President Eduard Shevardnadze by Mikheil Saakashvili in the Rose Revolution. Saakashvili's promises included restoring Georgian pride and securing Georgia against future pressure from the "bully" (the Russian Federation) by seeking full membership in NATO. With U.S. aid, Saakashvili strengthened Georgia's military. In 2004, in a violation of the 1992 agreement, Georgia sent troops into South Ossetia to reassert control. Although those forces were rebuffed, Georgia's actions convinced Russia to support South Ossetia's demand for full independence. Georgia responded by offering South Ossetia greater autonomy *within* Georgia, but the South Ossetians refused, demanding to be recognized as an independent republic.

In 2008, Russia increased its military presence in South Ossetia, where tensions with Georgia soon erupted into armed battle. Russian prime minister Vladimir Putin may have supported the assault as a way to both enhance his reputation as a strong leader and deter adjacent states from forming effective security alliances with other states.

In August 2008, the tension erupted into violence. Georgian forces began an assault on Russian and South Ossetian forces in the nominal capital, Tskhinvali. Despite some initial success, Georgian forces were routed. In a few days Russian Federation forces had not only pushed Georgian forces out of the disputed region but had advanced into undisputed territory in Georgia itself. Observers reported widespread abuses, particularly in areas occupied by Russian Federation forces, where ethnic Georgians were subjected to violent pogroms at the hands of angry South Ossetians. Strikingly, neither side's political leadership appeared to have full control of its troops on the ground. Russian and Georgian leaders would call a cease-fire, only to hear reports that fighting had either continued or intensified. After publicly stating that the war was over and agreeing to withdraw and leave the Georgian territory they had illegally occupied, Russian leaders were embarrassed by reports that in fact, Russian troops had not moved at all, but were maintaining their positions in defiance of orders.

For the first time since the collapse of the USSR, Russian armed forces handily defeated an opponent in battle. South Ossetia benefited as well, becoming another de facto independent state in the Caucasus. Georgia was the big loser, and its defeat weakened it considerably. In addition, Russia's aggressive policies in the region called into question the utility of Georgian membership in NATO and the wisdom of accepting or encouraging further U.S. military aid. Tensions between Russia and Georgia remain, and in 2012 militants from the Russian republic of Dagestan captured hostages in Georgia.

What caused this war? What insights might we draw from theories developed to explain interstate politics? At the most basic or human level of analysis, pride and election promises clearly contributed to the escalation of an ongoing conflict of interest to outright war. The accession of Saakashvili to the presidency marked a significant escalation of tensions. Without Russian assistance, South Ossetia could never have defeated Georgia's military. For its part, in 2008 Russia was led by prime minister Vladimir Putin, whose previous popularity as president had rested in large measure on his promise to use force and aggressive diplomacy to reestablish Russia's place as a preeminent great power in the international system.

Russia's constitution prohibits a president from serving more than two consecutive terms, but Putin was able to use his popularity to shift a great deal of executive power from the presidency to the office of the prime minister and then become prime minister, replacing his protégé Dmitry Medvedev, who was elected Russia's president in March of 2008. In 2012, at the end of Medvedev's first term, Putin again ran for president, and won a reputed 63 percent of the popular vote to serve another term as Russia's president, with Medvedev assuming the post of prime minister. As president in 1999, Putin's popularity in Russia had soared after his apparent defeat of separatist Chechens; it would have been uncharacteristic of his administration to hold back in South Ossetia.

At the state level, neither Georgia nor the Russian Federation are exemplary democracies where civil liberties, enforcement of property rights, punishment of corruption, and popular sovereignty are concerned. Both Saakashvili and Putin have been cited as "dictatorial" by opposition leaders in their own countries and by more neutral observers abroad. In short, as states they are more like the authoritarian regimes many think are most likely to go to war.

Most likely, regional and interstate politics played the greatest role in advancing the conflict to violence. Russia sought a confrontation to keep Georgia weak and divided, to enhance the reputations of Putin and Medvedev as strong leaders, and to put the United States—Georgia's distant ally—on notice that Russia would not tolerate a U.S. "satellite" and full NATO member on its southern flank. Georgia may have hoped for U.S. diplomatic support and anticipated that fear of more active U.S. engagement might deter Russia from a more active military role in South Ossetia. However, Russia acted as a good realist state should, using measured but decisive violence to deter the creation of a more powerful state on its border. In addition, Russia's willingness to use force in Georgia might warn other bordering states that attempting to increase their power relative to Russia's would be met with direct intervention ranging from economic and diplomatic pressure on the low end to support of opposition parties or outright invasion.

Thus, *each* of the three levels of analysis helps us understand why war broke out in the Caucasus in 2008. Kenneth Waltz was perhaps correct in his belief that the characteristics of the international system—a general state of anarchy, the lack of an accepted arbiter—provide the strongest overall general explanation, but to understand the particulars, we need to understand the interaction of all three levels of analysis.

Categorizing Wars

Once the decision has been made to go to war, decision makers are still faced with a variety of options on how to proceed. The nineteenth-century Prussian general Carl von Clausewitz describes the political nature of these decisions in his book, *On War*: "War is not merely a political act, but also a real political instrument, a continuation of political commerce, a carrying out of the same by other means."[10] The most significant decisions are about what proportion of the state's resources will be mobilized and toward what ends. Most often, decision makers attempt to keep the means proportional to the ends.

International relations scholars have developed many classification schemes to categorize wars. At the broadest level, we distinguish between wars that take place between sovereign states (**interstate war**) and wars that take place within states (**intrastate war**). Beyond this, we divide wars into total and limited (based on their aims and the proportion of resources dedicated to achieving these aims), and finally, the type of war fought, conventional or unconventional.

Interstate and Intrastate War

Since the advent of the state system in the years following the conclusion of the Thirty Years' War (1618–48), the state, as a form of political association, has proven ideal at organizing and directing the resources necessary for waging war. As one noted social scientist put it, "War made the state and the state made war."[11]

As a result, wars between states have captured the lion's share of attention from international relations theorists and from scholars of war. This is true for two reasons. First, by definition, states have recognizable leaderships and locations. They have legal weight among other states. When we say "France," we understand we are speaking about a government that controls a specific territory that others recognize as France. So states make good subjects for analysis and comparison. Second, states have formal militaries—some tiny and not much more than police forces, others vast and capable of projecting force across the surface of the globe and even into outer space. These militaries, and the state's capacity to marshal resources in support of them, make them very formidable adversaries. Thus, interstate wars are often characterized by relatively rapid loss of life and destruction of property. At the end of World War II, the world's states faced the prospect that a future interstate war might not only destroy them as such, but might, in a nuclear exchange, destroy all human life.

Yet over time, the number of interstate wars has declined. After World War II, they dropped dramatically, to be increasingly replaced by intrastate war—violence whose origins lay within states, sometimes supported by neighboring or distant states—as the most common type of war. The First Indochina War (1946–54), the Greek civil war (1944–49), the Malayan Emergency (1948–60), and the Korean War (1950–53) were all examples of the new pattern.

Intrastate wars—civil wars—have decreased over time as well, but not nearly as rapidly as interstate wars. Intrastate wars include those between factions within a state over control of territory; establishment of a government for control of a "failed state" (Somalia or Liberia); ethnonationalist movements seeking greater autonomy or secession (Chechens in Russia, Karens in Myanmar); or wars between ethnic, clan, or religious groups for control of the state (Colombia, Peru, Algeria, Rwanda). The American and Russian civil wars stand as prime examples.

More recent civil wars include those of the so-called Arab Spring of 2011, especially Libya (February–October 2011) and Syria (June 2012–present). Both qualify as wars because well over 1,000 battle deaths resulted from conflict between an incumbent government and rebels, and because each side had military capacity, though government forces had the greater capacity to harm the other. Both intrastate wars followed a similar course: peaceful protests by mostly young people were harshly repressed by government forces, which then led to an escalation of protests and international condemnation. That led to a more harsh government response and then protests becoming both more widespread and more violent. After evidence of government murders, rapes, torture, and massacres, there have been calls for international intervention. In Libya's case, both the incumbent government and its international supporters were caught by surprise, and limited military intervention by NATO on behalf of Libyan rebels accelerated the collapse of the incumbent government. In Syria, the incumbent government was better prepared, and more importantly, its allies (especially the Russian Federation) were prepared to offer military and diplomatic support. Nevertheless, in Syria the Assad regime's severe cruelty and barbarism has led to the progressive disintegration both of popular support for his rule and of diplomatic support from the Russian Federation. Turkey has given the rebels a territorial base and has made incursions into Syrian territory in response to Turkish deaths near the border. While the outcome of the Syrian civil war remains unclear, some fear a more general regional conflict.

Although some civil wars remain contained within state boundaries, civil wars are increasingly international. The repercussions of civil wars are felt across borders, as refugees from civil conflicts flow into neighboring states and funds are transferred out of the country. States, groups, and individuals from outside the warring country become involved, funding particular groups, selling weapons to various factions, and giving diplomatic support to one group over another. Thus, although the issues over which belligerents fight are often local, once started most civil wars quickly become internationalized, as with both Libya and Syria. In addition, escalating violence in Mali and Algeria in January 2013 is widely seen as a result of the massive inflow of relatively sophisticated weapons that followed from the looting of Libyan arms depots after Qaddafi was overthrown.

Total and Limited War

Total war tend to be armed conflicts involving massive loss of life and widespread destruction, usually with many participants, including multiple major powers. These wars are fought for many reasons: to conquer and occupy enemy territory or to take over the government and/or to control the economic resources of an opponent. Wars may also be fought over conflicts of ideas (communism versus capitalism; democracy versus authoritarianism) or religion (Catholic versus Protestant; Shiite versus Sunni Muslim; Hinduism versus Islam). In total war, decision makers utilize all available national resources—conscripted labor; indiscriminate weapons of warfare; economic, diplomatic, and natural resources—in order to force the unconditional surrender of their opponents. Importantly, even when opposing military forces are the primary target, in total war opposing civilian casualties are accepted or even deliberately sought in pursuit of victory. The Thirty Years' War (1618–48), the longest total war ever fought, involved numerous great powers (England, France, Habsburg Austria, the Netherlands, Spain, Sweden) and resulted in over 2 million battlefield deaths. The War of the Spanish Succession (1701–14) pitted most of the same powers against each other again and ended in over 1 million deaths. At the beginning of the nineteenth century, the Napoleonic Wars (1799–1815) resulted in over 2.5 million deaths in battle. In each war, civilian loss of life either equaled or dramatically exceeded battlefield deaths. For much of the seventeenth and eighteenth centuries, wars between and among great powers were common.

World War I and World War II were critical watersheds in the history of total war. The same great powers fought in both: Britain, France, Austria-Hungary (in World War II, Germany), Japan, Russia/the Soviet Union, and the United States. But just as industrialization revolutionized agriculture and transport, it also revolutionized the killing power of states. Industrialization demanded workers who moved from rural areas to concentrate in cities. Once restricted to the physical areas over which soldiers fought, after World War I the scope of the "battlefield" soon expanded to include armaments and munitions workers, and eventually even agricultural workers. Although total war had always imagined the mobilization of an entire society for war, industrialization—especially after World War I—made this ideal a reality. Casualties were horrific: most belligerents lost 4 to 5 percent of their pre-war population in World War I, and double this in World War II. After World War II, total war, as actually experienced by belligerents rather than imagined by war theorists and philosophers, had become far too blunt and costly an instrument to enter into deliberately.

This may in part explain why since the end of World War II, interstate wars, particularly large-scale wars between or among the great powers, have become less frequent; the number of countries participating in such wars has fallen; and the duration of such wars has shortened. These factors have led several political scientists to speculate on whether or not extremely costly total wars like World Wars I and II are events of the past.

For example, John Mueller argues that such wars have become obsolete. Among the reasons he cites are the memory of the devastation of World War II, the postwar satisfaction of the great powers with the status quo, and the recognition that any war among the great powers, nuclear or not, could escalate to a level that would become too costly.[12] More recent scholarship has argued other causes of peace. Joshua Goldstein, for example, argues that a long decline in interstate war (including total war) is due to increasingly effective UN peacekeeping operations. Robert Jervis has offered an explanation embedded in the notion of a security community that combines thinking drawn from the best insights of realism (for example, NATO) and liberalism (for example,

From the perspective of the International Security Assistance Force, the war in Afghanistan has been a limited one. From an Afghan point of view, however, the violence has been devastating, and is certain to affect the country for decades to come.

the UN, IMF, and GATT). In the security community composed of the United States, Western Europe, and Japan, Jervis argues, war is unthinkable.[13]

Realists explain the security community as arising from American economic and especially military hegemony. Since the end of World War II, the United States has had the world's largest economy, and in part because of that, U.S. military spending has on average exceeded the combined spending of the next eight countries. Militarily then, the United States had (and has) no peer. That military dominance is magnified by the effect of nuclear weapons and by the continued recognition that an all-out, general war would be unwinnable and hence irrational, just as Mueller posits. In short, there was no World War III because the United States, in combination with support from its allies, was both willing and able to use its economic and military power to prevent it.

The liberal explanation has two parts. First, liberals argue that had it not been for the short-sighted and self-destructive economic policies ("beggar thy neighbor" trade) of the 1920s, the economic depression that spread across the globe in the 1930s and created fertile ground for extreme ideas and demagogues would not have happened. War would have either been entirely prevented, or at least contained. This explains the liberal emphasis on trade openness and transparency as represented by the IMF and GATT (now the WTO). Second, liberals argue that the steady proliferation of democratic states has expanded the European zone of peace globally. Not only are democracies unlikely to go to war with each other, but that effect also becomes magnified if they are economically interdependent and if they share membership in international organizations.

Constructivists level an equally powerful set of propositions to explain the decline of interstate and total war since World War II. They posit that it is not change in the material conditions (American hegemony or economic interdependency) that matters, but change in the attitudes of individuals who are increasingly "socialized into attitudes, beliefs, and values that are conducive to peace."[14] As Jervis—a self-identified realist who has made increasing use of constructivist arguments in his own theory—explains, "The destructiveness of war, the benefits of peace, and the changes in values interact and reinforce each other."[15] This is effectively psychologist Steven Pinker's argument in *The Better Angels of Our Nature*. He argues that mutually reinforcing trends (the disciplinary power of states, the democratic peace, the empowerment of women) have led to a condition in which not just war but *all* interhuman violence has declined. Jervis and Pinker thus share the constructivist view that norms—such as the nature of security and the range of means permissible to pursue it—shift over time, creating new hazards and new opportunities.[16]

Both interstate and intrastate wars can be classified as either total or **limited war**, depending on the objective and on the degree to which a given actor's resources are mobilized to achieve that objective. The distinction generally rests on the aims or objectives sought: the more ambitious the aims, the more likely war will be total. Limited wars are therefore often initiated over less-than-critical issues (at least for one belligerent), and as such tend to involve less-than-total national resources. Thus, for Austria-Hungary, World War I began as a limited war in which Austria-Hungary sought to punish Serbia for its presumed support of the assassination of Archduke Franz Ferdinand. Yet by the end of August 1914, what had begun as a limited war had escalated into a total war, involving goals as ambitious as the complete conquest of adversaries (marked by their unconditional surrender) and using all national means available.

The Korean War (1950–53) and the Gulf War (1991) are excellent examples of limited wars. In the Korean War, U.S. and then UN forces were mobilized to prevent the outright conquest of South Korea by the North (the Democratic People's Republic of Korea, or DPRK). This made the war a limited one from the UN perspective, but because both sides tended to view material outcomes as representative of the validity of their respective ideologies; the war between the communist North and the non-communist UN contained powerful incentives for escalation.

After the stunning success of General Douglas MacArthur's Inchon landing, for example, the DPRK's military collapsed, and its remnants were forced to retreat all the way to the frontier with the newly communist People's Republic of China (PRC). MacArthur and many in the United States and in the U.S. government viewed this as an opportunity to unify Korea under noncommunist rule—a much more ambitious goal. So what began as war for limited aims on the UN side escalated into a war for conquest. Then in the winter of 1950, China intervened. The war could now only be thought of as "limited" in comparison to the real possibility it might escalate to include the Soviet Union as well. The U.S. president, Harry S. Truman, and his advisers decided to settle for a return to the status quo of 1950. Although the United States possessed nuclear weapons and could have mobilized and deployed many additional combat forces, the fear of escalation to another—perhaps nuclear—world war led to an armistice instead of an outright victory. In the 1991 Iraq case, after being routed from Kuwait by U.S. and British forces, Iraqi troops were pushed behind a line across which the victorious forces chose not to pass.

In limited wars, because the aims of war are relatively modest, not all available armaments are unleashed. In these two cases, conventional weapons of warfare were used—tanks, foot soldiers, aircraft, and missiles. But despite their availability, nuclear weapons were never deployed. There is no better illustration of limited war than the Arab-Israeli disputes from 1973 onward, described in Chapter 2. Israel has fought six interstate wars against its neighbors—Egypt, Syria, Jordan, and Lebanon—and struggled against repeated Palestinian uprisings in the West Bank and Gaza. Since the conclusion of the 1973 Yom Kippur War (limited from the Egyptian perspective, total from the Israeli), none of the opposing states have sought the complete destruction of their foes, and the conflict has blown "hot" and "cold." Both sides have employed some of the techniques described later. With the increased destructiveness of modern warfare, limited war has become the most common option for states contemplating violence against other states.

While the number of interstate wars has declined precipitously, limited wars and particularly civil wars that are total in nature have not. In the century between 1846 and 1918, approximately 50 civil wars were fought. In contrast, in the decade following the end of the Cold War (1990–2000), the total number of civil wars was about 195. Although the number of civil wars has declined modestly from 2000–2011, two-thirds of all conflicts since World War II have been civil wars.

Civil wars share several characteristics. They often last a long time, even decades, with periods of fighting punctuated by periods of relative calm. Whereas the goals may seem relatively limited by the standards of major interstate wars—secession, group autonomy—the human costs are often high because in the context of the rivalry between incumbent governments and rebels, these stakes are often perceived to be total. Both combatants and civilians are killed and maimed; food supplies are interrupted; diseases spread as health systems suffer; money is diverted from constructive economic development to purchasing armaments; and generations of people grow up knowing only war.

The African continent provides examples of these total civil wars; most such conflicts are now concentrated there. Ethiopia's war with two of its regions (Ogaden and Eritrea) lasted decades, as did the civil war between the north and south in both Sudan and Chad. Liberia and Sierra Leone, likewise, have also been sites of civil conflict where various factions, guerrilla groups, paramilitary groups, and mercenaries fought for control. The Democratic Republic of the Congo is another example of a civil war, but one that has become internationalized. In 1996 an internal rebellion broke out against the long-time dictator Mobutu Sese Seko. Very quickly, the rebellion was supported by both Uganda and Rwanda, the latter interested in eliminating Hutu militias that had fled Rwanda during the 1994 genocide. After Mobutu was ousted, a wider war erupted two years later. Powerful Congolese leaders and ethnic groups opposed the new leader, Laurent Kabila. They were supported by Rwanda and Uganda. Angola and Zimbabwe supported Kabila's government, as did Chad and Eritrea. Over five million people were killed between 1998 and 2012, despite the efforts of a large UN peacekeeping force, as explained in Chapter 7.

In virtually all these cases, the civil wars have been intensified by the availability of small arms, the recruitment of child soldiers, and financing from illicit commodity trades (narcotics, diamonds, oil). In all these cases, too, human rights abuses and humanitarian crises have captured media attention but not the political commitment or financial resources of the international community.

How Wars Are Fought

Conventional War

Throughout most of human history, wars were fought by people—almost invariably male—who were specially chosen, trained, and authorized to attack or defend against their counterparts in other political communities. In almost all societies, some groups are also considered off limits, at least where killing is concerned. The tools of war reflected this restriction. Weapons of choice have ranged from swords and shields to bows, guns, and cannons; to industrialized armies fielding infantry and riding in tanks; to navies sailing in specialized ships; and to air forces flying fixed-wing aircraft. Such weapons are utilized to defeat the enemy on a territorial battlefield. The key attribute of conventional weapons is that their destructive effects can be limited in space and time to those who are the legitimate targets of war. Conventional wars are won or lost when the warriors of one group, or their leaders, acknowledge defeat following a clash of arms.

The two world wars challenged the prevalence of conventional war in three ways. World War I saw the first large-scale use of chemical weapons on the battlefield. Near the Flemish (Belgian) town of Ypres, in 1915, German forces unleashed 168 tons of chlorine gas against French positions. French troops suffered 6,000 casualties in just a few minutes as prevailing winds carried the poisonous gas across the fields and into their trenches. But German forces were unable to exploit the four-mile-wide gap in French lines that opened as a result. Many of their own troops had been wounded or killed in handling the gas or by moving through areas still affected. This attack proved the first of many by both sides in the war, but subsequent attacks exhibited a similar pattern. After the gas caused horrific casualties, it proved difficult to exploit the temporary advantages gained. In addition, the effects of the weapons had proved difficult to restrict to combat. Chemicals leached into the soil and water table, affecting combat troops, their supporting troops, and agriculture for months afterward. After the war, winners and losers signed a Geneva Protocol outlawing the use of chemical weapons in war.

World War II added two additional challenges to the prevalence of conventional weapons. First, the advent of strategic bombing led both to the possibility of large-scale harm to noncombatants and to a reexamination of who or what a "noncombatant" actually was. Prior to the war, the simple rule had been that civilians were to be protected from intentional harm. But the belligerents possessed large fleets of ships, armored vehicles, and planes, all of which demanded a constant supply of inputs. Were the civilians who made and supplied these great engines of war to be protected, too? What about the farmers who fed the soldiers, airmen, and sailors? As the war intensified, the dividing line between those who were to be protected from deliberate harm and those who could be legitimately targeted broke down. By the war's end, both sides had taken to deliberately targeting civilians with massive air strikes. In March 1945, well before the atomic bombings of Hiroshima and Nagasaki in August, bombers from the U.S. Eighth Air Force targeted Japan's capital, Tokyo, with incendiary bombs. The ensuing flames killed over 100,000 Japanese in a single raid, most of them civilians. World War II also fast-forwarded the development of a nuclear weapon.

Weapons of Mass Destruction

The dropping of atomic bombs on Hiroshima and Nagasaki in 1945 did not have an immediate and dramatic impact on war-fighting capability. The destructiveness of the atomic bomb and its capacity to kill hundreds of thousands without discrimination had already been matched to some extent by conventional means. Many in the U.S. military, for example, considered atomic weapons to be simply more economical extensions of conventional bombs. But these first steps into the nuclear age—the first and last time nuclear weapons were deliberately used against human beings—had already hinted at a key problem related to their use: the long-lasting effects of radiation. During the Cold War, both the United States and the Soviet Union constructed larger and more lethal weapons, developing more accurate delivery systems, ballistic missiles, and cruise missiles, each capable of reaching around the world and killing the earth's population many times over. Thermonuclear weapons led to the possibility that the destruction of a nuclear exchange—now hundreds of times more powerful than what had been dropped on Hiroshima—could not be restricted to the target only, but might rapidly escalate into an exchange that could extinguish life on earth, either by radiation from fallout or by altering the climate in a "nuclear winter." This mutual assured destruction (or MAD) led the major antagonists to shelve plans to fight using nuclear weapons. Instead they fought through proxies using more conventional weapons, as discussed in Chapter 2.

The fact that nuclear weapons have never been employed in war since their use against Japan has led to two important debates about the political effects of nuclear weapons. First, did nuclear deterrence prevent a third world war and therefore justify the risk and expense the Soviet Union, the United States, Britain, China, and France sustained as a result of their development and deployment of nuclear weapons during the Cold War? Second, if nuclear deterrence causes peace—if the very destructiveness of nuclear weapons makes rational decision makers unlikely to use them or initiate a war that could escalate to their use—could the spread of nuclear weapons to other countries, called **nuclear proliferation**, cause peace? Scott Sagan and Kenneth Waltz debated these issues in the 1980s. They renewed the debate in the beginning of the twenty-first century after India and Pakistan—fierce rivals—had each acquired nuclear capability. Waltz argues that "more may be better," that under certain circumstances (namely, a rational government and a secure retaliatory capacity), the proliferation of nuclear weapons implies an expanding zone of deterrence and a lower of interstate war. Sagan strongly disagrees, arguing that the proliferation of nuclear weapons is more likely to lead to a failure in deterrence or an accidental war.[17] Sagan argues that the conditions Waltz cites for nuclear peace-causing are rare, and certainly not present in South Asia.

This debate over the threat posed by the possession of nuclear weapons gained a new salience as the technology to build nuclear weapons has proliferated. The tangled network of the Pakistani official A. Q. Khan, who provided elements of nuclear technology from Europe to Pakistan and then North Korea, has led many to reexamine the stabilizing effect of proliferation. More crucially, nuclear theorists have questioned whether a nuclear-capable Iran would make war in the region more or less likely. If Waltz is right, so long as Iran has a rational government and a number of weapons secure from a preemptive first strike, the risk of major conventional war in the Middle East would be dramatically reduced. If Sagan is right, even if Iran meets these minimal conditions (of which Sagan's argument is skeptical), the Middle East will be in increased danger of a nuclear exchange, an accidental launch or detonation, or perhaps an unauthorized launch.

Chemical and biological weapons, together with nuclear weapons, make up the more general category of **weapons of mass destruction (WMD)**. The key factor that separates WMD from conventional weapons is that *by their very nature* their destructive effects cannot be limited in space and time. This is why they are often referred to as "indiscriminate" weapons, a feature they share with antipersonnel land mines and cluster bombs. Chemical and biological weapons have existed for many more years than nuclear weapons have. Although surreptitious testing and use of such weapons have persisted, many technical difficulties in their effective delivery persist. As noted earlier, chemical weapons were actually used on a large scale in World War I, but they proved strategically useless while only increasing the suffering of war. Benito Mussolini's invasion of Ethiopia through Eritrea in 1935 must count as the only recent example of the effective use of chemical weapons in war; the aerial spraying of mustard gas on the mostly barefoot Ethiopian troops caused their rapid defeat. In that case, the Italians faced an adversary with no possibility to retaliate in kind. In addition, the oily chemical tended to float on water and remained lethal on vegetation and bare ground for weeks. As a result, Fascist Italy's use of mustard gas killed and maimed thousands of Ethiopian noncombatants. For its part, Mussolini's government went to great lengths to hide its violation of the 1923 Geneva Accords prohibiting the use of chemical weapons, in many cases actually violating other laws of war to do so, including strafing field hospitals marked with the red cross to eliminate evidence that Italy had used mustard gas. Possibly as a result of these costs, and of the likelihood of soon facing adversaries armed in kind, neither Fascist Italy nor any of the other belligerents used chemical weapons in World War II.

Biological weapons—in particular mutated strains of formerly common diseases such as plague and smallpox—have always suffered from the possibility that one's own troops and people could be victims as well as an adversary's. In addition, their use as a weapon comes with the cost of a high probability of violating the norm of noncombatant immunity, something few states want to do. Today, most observers are more concerned with the possibility that rogue states or terrorists might obtain and deploy biological or other weapons of mass destruction, and are less concerned that states with rational leaders will do so.

In 2003, the George W. Bush administration, frustrated with Saddam Hussein's repeated refusal to abide by the terms of the cease-fire that had ended the first Gulf War in 1991, decided to prepare for a possible military invasion of Iraq. Among the U.S. government's many concerns was the possibility that Saddam Hussein was developing WMD. This proved to be the administration's main justification for war. The fear that Saddam's Iraq would either use such weapons against the United States or its allies or transfer such a weapon to a terrorist group helped gain sufficient U.S. public support for the invasion. More recently, the realization that Iran is developing uranium enrichment capacity and refuses to renounce a nuclear option has led to some of the most contentious political conflicts of the new millennium. Likewise, North Korea's tests of nuclear weapons since 2006, and more recently new launch vehicles, have raised serious concerns in the international community.

Unconventional Warfare

Unconventional warfare is as old as conventional warfare and is distinguished in general by a willingness to ignore conventions of war, whether by flouting restrictions on legitimate targets of violence or by refusing to accept the traditional outcomes of battles— say, the destruction of a regular army, loss of a capital, or capture of a national leader—as an indicator of defeat.

Roman legions were plagued by terrorists, bandits, and guerrillas in many of their successful campaigns, but unconventional warfare, though noteworthy, rarely proved decisive when conventional armies clashed. Rome's most common response to homegrown resistance was notoriously brutal: entire communities would be killed, buildings razed, and a few survivors sold as slaves. News of such brutality often convinced others that it was better to live under the Roman yoke than face torture or certain death in resistance to Rome's will.

Two major changes progressively moved unconventional war from a side role to a prominent feature of war. First, the French Revolution unleashed the power of nationalism in support of large-scale military operations, enabling Napoleon Bonaparte's armies to make use of tactics that the older professional militaries of Europe could not at first counteract. Nationalism inflamed common people to resist "foreign" aggression and occupation, even in the face of the possibility of receiving bribes or under penalty of torture and death. Nationalism has proven a double-edged sword ever since. Although

Going Nuclear: A View from Iran

In recent years, no decision has been so controversial internationally as the one to cross the nuclear threshold. The debates over nuclear programs in India, Pakistan, North Korea, and Iran have centered on what this decision means, the reasons for this decision, and how it relates to international law. Iran, whose foreign policy aims at reestablishing the state as a major regional power, defends its decision to build a nuclear reactor on several grounds.

At the United Nations General Assembly in 2005, Iranian president Mahmoud Ahmadinejad stated it was his country's "inalienable right" to acquire nuclear technology. Indeed, under the terms of the Nuclear Nonproliferation Treaty (NPT), to which Iran is a party, states have the "inalienable right to develop research, production and use of nuclear energy for peaceful purposes without discrimination." According to the Iranian government, the country's significant deposits of petroleum and natural gas will one day be depleted, and it must be prepared to use alternative energy resources, including nuclear power. Thus, research on a centrifuge to speed enrichment is necessary. The Iranian government regarded attempts by the United Nations to block Iran's efforts with limited economic sanctions in 2006 as part of an Anglo-American plot to keep Iran from economic development.

Some Iranian officials point to legitimate security threats that might lead Iran to push for more than the right to develop nuclear-fuel-production capabilities. Iran is located near several traditional enemies: Israel, with a nuclear arsenal estimated to contain over 200 weapons; and Iraq, which fought a decade-long war against Iran in the 1980s. Shiite Iran also has unstable relations with many of the Persian Gulf states, which have large, sometimes unhappy Shiite minorities. On the country's western border is Turkey, a NATO member and close American ally with economic and political ties with Israel. On Iran's eastern border is Sunni Pakistan, another nuclear power and ally of the United States.

The Iranian decision to maintain the option to make the leap to nuclear weaponry is also influenced by national pride and domestic politics, which have been propelled by actions of the United States. Most Iranians believe the United States has been the country's enemy since the 1950s, when the CIA engineered the overthrow of Iran's reforming nationalist prime minister Mohammed Mossadegh in 1953. After the coup that toppled Mossadegh, the United States and Britain relied on the young shah of Iran, Mohammed Reza Pahlavi, who remained in power until 1979, as their favored ally. But the shah attempted to modernize Iran too quickly, first alienating and then violently suppressing Iran's clerics. Iranians remember his rule—buttressed by extensive use of secret police and torture—with considerable bitterness and consider U.S. support for the shah as further evidence of American disregard for the lives and freedoms of Iranians.

The fact that Iran has long been considered a potential target by American war planners causes further anxiety. Iran's move to develop a nuclear weapons program could be a major deterrent to the United States, decreasing the likelihood that the United States will forcibly promote regime change in Iran, as it did in the cases of Serbia in 1999, Afghanistan in 2001, Iraq in 2003, and Libya in 2011. None of these countries possessed nuclear weapons. North Korea, another member of the "axis," does possess such weapons. To many Iranians, the lesson seems clear: those who oppose U.S. interests *and* possess a nuclear deterrent are much less likely to be subject to military attack.

Even in the face of severe economic shortages and disruptions caused by escalating international sanctions against Iran, which increased public discontent with Iran's government in 2012, the domestic population strongly supports Iran's nuclear program. Iranians wonder why *they* have come under such scrutiny and criticism for what they argue is a legal right under NPT. They wonder why Israel, which already possesses *active nuclear weapons* and harshly represses a Palestinian minority, escapes such criticism and scrutiny. That double standard seems unjust not only to Iran, but also to many other states in the region. Crucially, Iran's supreme leader, Ayatollah Khamenei, has pronounced that nuclear *weapons* are "un-Islamic" and therefore forbidden. Many Iranians do not understand how they can be feared as religious zealots, but when their religious authority declares that nuclear weapons are forbidden, this is ignored.

In September 2012, Iran's top atomic official admitted that the country had engaged in a deliberate policy of misinformation about its nuclear capabilities as a form of self-defense. Iran used the opportunity to declare that Israeli agents had been responsible for escalated assassinations of Iranian nuclear scientists and facilities bombings in the past five years, and also repeated its assertion that the International Atomic Energy Agency,

Iranian president Mahmoud Ahmadinejad visits a nuclear enrichment facility in 2008.

which conducts inspections of nuclear sites, is compromised by spies.

For better or for worse then, Iran's current leadership appears set on building both peaceful nuclear power *and* the capability (likely without weaponizing) to manufacture nuclear weapons at the same time. Only in this way will Iran be able to drive the United States out of the region, chasten the Israelis, and secure a renewed leadership position in the world.

FOR CRITICAL ANALYSIS

1. Would Iran's acquisition of nuclear weapons make the region more or less stable?

2. Could the United States deter Iran should it acquire nuclear weapons? Could Iran deter the United States? How critical are Iran's intangible sources of power? Base your answers on the theory of deterrence.

3. How should Israel respond to Iran's nuclear development? What might be the consequences of a preemptive military attack on Iran by Israel?

4. Which international relations theory best explains Iran's position?

One of the longest running guerrilla conflicts today is the battle between the Colombian government and the Revolutionary Armed Forces of Colombia (FARC). Both sides are responsible for civilian casualties, which number in the tens of thousands. States are not always able to defeat guerrilla forces, despite states' traditional advantages in terms of territory, taxes, population, and outside alliances.

Napoleon's forces initially swept aside the old order, the source of his greatest defeats lay in nationalist-inspired resistance in Russia and Spain (Spanish resistance came to be called "small war" or, in Spanish, **guerrilla warfare**). But nationalist-inspired resistance was not by itself sufficient to make unconventional warfare effective against the power of states or incumbent governments. That took a strategic innovation that combined the ancient doctrine of guerrilla warfare with explicit use of the power of nationalism.

That strategy was first called "revolutionary guerrilla war" by its chief innovator, Mao Zedong. It was specifically designed to counter a technologically advanced and well-equipped industrial adversary by effectively reversing the conventional relationship between soldiers and civilians. In conventional war, soldiers risk their lives to protect civilians. In guerrilla warfare, civilians risk their lives to protect the guerrillas, who hide among them and who cannot easily be distinguished from ordinary civilians when not actually fighting.[18]

Using revolutionary guerrilla warfare during the Chinese Civil War (1927–37, 1945–49) and in China's resistance to Japanese occupation during World War II (1937–45), Mao's Red Army was able to survive many setbacks. Eventually, it defeated the well-armed and U.S.-supplied Nationalist armies of Jiang Jieshi (Chiang Kai-shek), whose forces fled to the island of Formosa, now Taiwan. This unexpected outcome left Mao with a vast storehouse of captured weapons and led to the spread of revolutionary guerrilla warfare as a template for other insurgents, particularly in Asia.

The second half of the twentieth century witnessed a string of unexpected defeats of the major advanced industrial powers, each of which lost wars against "weak" or "backward" adversaries. Britain was forced to grant independence to India. France was defeated in Indochina and Algeria; Portugal in Mozambique and Angola; the United States in Vietnam; the Soviet Union in Afghanistan; and Israel in Lebanon. In each case, well-equipped, industrialized militaries had sought to overcome smaller, nonindustrial adversaries and lost. Ominously, both the French experience in Algeria and the Soviet experience in Afghanistan added a new element to the mix: religion as a means of inspiring and aggregating resistance.

Today, this pattern of advanced industrial states pitted against either nonstate actors or relatively weak states has become commonplace. International relations theorists now refer to such contests as **asymmetric conflict**.

Asymmetric conflict undercuts an important proposition of both conventional warfare and nuclear war: that conventional weapons and nuclear confrontations are more likely to occur among states with rough equality of military strength that utilize similar strategies and tactics. If one party is decidedly weaker, the proposition goes, fear of defeat makes it unlikely to resort to war. Asymmetric conflicts, in contrast, are conducted between parties of unequal strength. The weaker party seeks to innovate around its opponent's strengths, including its technological superiority, by exploiting that opponent's weaknesses.[19]

One such strategy—revolutionary guerrilla warfare—has already been discussed. But like any strategy, revolutionary guerrilla warfare itself has weaknesses. In two asymmetric conflicts following World War II, the strong actors—Britain during the Malayan Emergency (1948–60) and the United States in the Philippines (1952–53)—were able to devise a counterinsurgency strategy that effectively defeated revolutionary guerrilla wars. That strategy aimed not at insurgent armed forces (terrorists and guerrillas) or even their leaders, but instead focused on the real strength of successful guerrilla warfare: the people. As Mao recognized in his early writings, there are only two ways for incumbent governments to defeat a well-led, well-organized guerrilla resistance: either change the minds of the people (via a conciliation, or "hearts and minds," strategy) or destroy them utterly (a strategy one theorist calls "barbarism").[20] In either case, the social support of a guerrilla resistance is destroyed, and that resistance will collapse. Mao was confident that his "Western" and democratic adversaries were too arrogant in their own power to attempt to change minds and too squeamish in their ethical conduct to pursue a genocidal counterinsurgency. Yet in both Malaya and in the Philippines, incumbent governments, supported by Britain and the United States, sought to redress the grievances that had led many of the country's poor or disaffected either to active support of guerrillas or to political apathy. Since World War II, "hearts and minds" strategies have proven the most effective method of counterinsurgency on the ground, but they are costly in political terms because they take a long time to work and in most cases they demand large numbers of troops.

Yet guerrilla warfare is only one of several strategies that might be used to overcome a more materially powerful incumbent and its allies. One such strategy is **nonviolent resistance**, resistance to authority that employs measures other than violence. Like revolutionary guerrilla warfare, nonviolent resistance deliberately places ordinary people at grave risk of harm in the pursuit of political objectives. Unlike guerrilla warfare or terrorism, however, nonviolent resistance avoids the use of violence as a means of protest. Prominent examples of nonviolent resistance include Mohandas Gandhi's resistance to British rule in the 1940s and the Reverend Dr. Martin Luther King Jr.'s civil rights movement of the 1960s. Another strategy for overcoming a materially more powerful adversary is terrorism.

Terrorism

Terrorism is a particular kind of asymmetric conflict that is increasingly perceived as a major international security threat. This is because the causes that motivate terrorists to murder defenseless civilians have become increasingly transnational rather than local, and because advances in WMD technology have made it theoretically possible for substate actors to cause state-level damage (say, with a nuclear bomb smuggled by a terrorist into a major metropolitan area). Though they did not involve WMD, Al Qaeda's attacks against U.S. embassies in Africa in 1998, against cities on U.S. soil in 2001, and in the London Underground and buses in 2005, were justified in the group's eyes as a religious imperative that recognized neither the state nor the international system of states.

Because a core feature of terrorism is the deliberate harm of noncombatants, "terrorists" are necessarily outlaws: outlaws neither observe nor are protected by the law by definition. Scholars of terrorism, a moribund subfield of international relations inquiry until 2001, today disagree on a universal definition of terrorism, but most definitions share three key elements:

1. It is *political* in nature or intent.
2. Perpetrators are *nonstate* actors.
3. Targets are *noncombatants*, such as political figures, bureaucrats, or innocent bystanders.

One contemporary terrorism expert, Audrey Kurth Cronin, adds a fourth element: terror attacks are unconventional and unpredictable.[21] Terrorism has often been called the strategy of the weak, but this argument begs the question of what "power" actually is. Is power only the material power to kill, or can it reside in the power of ideas? The Roman emperor Constantine, for example, did not convert to Christianity because Christians threatened to conquer the empire by force of arms, and Gandhi did not overcome the British and win India's independence by means of violent revolution. In each case, it was the power of ideas that proved decisive. Terrorists also hope to harness the power of ideas: they invariably justify their violence by reference to immortality imagery. This imagery tends to take one of three classic forms: nationalist, Marxist, or religious. In each case, the violent acts are intended to preserve the nation, or the proletariat, or the faithful, and ensure its immortality. In the Irish Republican Army's long struggles with British rule in Ireland, all three immortality images came into play, as predominately socialist, nationalist, and Catholic "terrorists" sought to coerce Britain into abandoning Ireland's Protestant minority, among other things.

Like guerrilla warfare, terrorism has a long history. During Greek and Roman times, terrorist acts were often carried out by individuals against a ruler. Interestingly, the contemporary sense of the word "terror" dates from the French Revolution, in which Robespierre's fragile government leveled extreme and at times indiscriminate violence against the French people. But neither state perpetration nor sponsorship of terror should be confused with terrorism as such, because, as observed earlier, a core element of terrorism is that it be perpetrated by nonstate actors. It is therefore difficult to say what to call the kind of mass killing perpetrated by states such as the United States against Native Americans, Hitler's Third Reich against Jews, Stalin's Soviet Union against Ukrainians, and Pol Pot's Cambodia against noncommunists. One scholar has suggested "barbarism" as a more broad term covering the use of violence against noncombatants for political purposes. This would make all terrorism barbarism, but not all barbarism terrorism.

Although terrorism involves physical harm, the essence of terrorism is psychological, not physical. Whatever the aims of the individual terrorist, killing is a by-product of terrorism as a strategy. The real aim of terrorism is to call attention to a cause, while at the same time calling into question the legitimacy of a target government by highlighting its inability to protect its citizens. For example, during the 1972 Summer Olympic games in Munich, Germany, a group of Palestinian Arab terrorists styling themselves "Black September" took 11 Israeli athletes hostage in the Olympic Village. Two of the hostages were murdered immediately. During a botched rescue attempt by the surprised and ill-prepared Germans, the remaining nine hostages were murdered. Black September was a part of the Palestinian Liberation Organization (PLO), a group founded by Yasser Arafat in 1964 to advance the cause of Palestinian Arab statehood by means of violence. But until Munich, few outside the Middle East had ever heard of the PLO. After the games, the PLO (and "terrorists" more broadly) became a widespread topic of conversation and state action. Another method of gaining attention was hijacking commercial airplanes. In December 1973, Arab terrorists killed 32 people in Rome's airport during an attack on a U.S. aircraft. Hostages were taken in support of the hijackers' demand for the release of imprisoned Palestinian Arabs. In 1976, a French plane with mostly Israeli passengers was hijacked by a Middle Eastern organization and flown to Uganda, where the hijackers threatened to kill the hostages unless Arab prisoners in Israel were released. In the aftermath of a number of such high-profile cases, the international community responded by signing a series of international agreements designed to tighten airport security, sanction states that gave refuge to hijackers, and condemn state-supported terrorism. The 1979 International Convention against the Taking of Hostages is a prominent example of such an agreement.

Much recent terrorist activity has its roots in the Middle East—in the ongoing quest of Palestinian Arabs for self-determination and their own internal conflicts over strategy, in the hostility among various Islamic groups toward Western forces and ideas (in particular the education and independence of women), and in the resurgence of extremist Islamic fundamentalism. Among terrorist groups with roots in the Middle East are Hamas, Hezbollah, and Palestine Islamic Jihad. Since September 11, 2001, Al Qaeda has been the most publicized of these groups. A shadowy network of extremist Islamic fundamentalists from many countries, including some outside the Middle East, Al Qaeda, led by the late Osama bin Laden, is motivated by the desire to install Islamic regimes in the Middle East, support Islamic insurgencies in Southeast Asia, and punish the United States for its support of Israel and for its tight linkages with corrupt regimes in the Middle East, including Saudi Arabia, which allowed the stationing of non-Muslim combat forces on its soil even after the defeat of Iraq in 1991.

But terrorism also has a long history in other parts of the world, reflecting diverse, often multiple, motivations. Some groups adhere to extreme religious positions, such as the Irish Republican Army, the protector of Northern Irish Catholics in their struggle against Protestant British rule. The Hindu-Muslim rivalry in India has led to many terrorist incidents. Other groups seek territorial separation or autonomy from a state. The Basque separatists (ETA) in Spain, the Tamil Tigers in Sri Lanka, Abu Sayyaf Group in the Philippines, and Chechen groups in Russia are all excellent examples.

Since the 1990s, terrorism has taken a new turn.[22] Terrorist acts have become more lethal, even as the groups responsible have become more dispersed. In the 1970s, about 17 percent of terrorist attacks killed someone, whereas in the 1990s, almost 25 percent of terrorist attacks resulted in deaths. Until 2000, the worst loss of life was the 1985 bombing of an Air India flight, in which 329 people were killed. That changed dramatically on September 11, 2001, when over 3,000 civilians died and $80 billion in economic losses were incurred. Increasingly, terrorists have made use of a diverse array of weapons. AK-47s, sarin gas, shoulder-fired missiles, anthrax, backpack explosives, and airplanes as guided missiles have all been used. The infrastructure that supports terrorism has also become more sophisticated. It is financed through money-laundering

In 2004, terrorists affiliated with Al Qaeda detonated bombs on commuter trains in Madrid, killing 191 and wounding hundreds. Terrorists often target civilians to draw attention to their cause and create an atmosphere of fear and insecurity in the target state.

schemes and illegal criminal activities. Training camps attract not just young, single, and uneducated potential terrorists, but also older, better-educated individuals who are willing to commit suicide to accomplish their objectives. Terrorist groups have also made use of the Internet as a recruitment tool.

The groups practicing terrorism have become wider ranging, from nationalists and neo-Nazis to religious, left-wing, and right-wing militants (see Table 8.2). State-sponsored terrorism, the support of terrorist groups by states, remains common. The United States and many of its allies (for example, Britain, Germany, and France) have repeatedly accused North Korea, Iran, Iraq, Syria, Libya, Sudan, and Cuba of having lent support to terrorist groups. Yet while there is strong evidence of state complicity in each case, the accusing states are apt to overlook their *own* sponsorship of groups others might call "terrorists." In the U.S. case, U.S. support of *contras*—groups opposing communist rule in Nicaragua in the 1980s—could easily count as state sponsored terrorism, because the *contras* did not limit their targets to Nicaraguan police and soldiers, but also attacked civilians. Terrorists are increasingly launching attacks in developing countries. Turkey, Morocco, Indonesia, India, Kenya, and Pakistan are all examples.

Preventing terrorist activity has become increasingly difficult, because most perpetrators have networks of supporters in the resident populations. Protecting populations from random acts of violence is an almost impossible task, given the availability of guns

TABLE 8.2 — SELECTED TERRORIST ORGANIZATIONS

GROUP	LOCATION	CHARACTERISTICS AND ATTACKS
Al Qaeda	Formerly in Afghanistan; now dispersed throughout Afghanistan, Pakistan, Iran, Indonesia, and Yemen	Formed by Osama bin Laden in the late 1980s among Arabs who fought the Soviets in Afghanistan; responsible for bombings in Africa (1998), Yemen (2000), United States (2001), Spain (2004), Great Britain (2005), India (2006)
Hamas (Islamic Resistance Movement)	Israel, West Bank, Gaza Strip	Its leader signed bin Laden's 1998 *fatwa* calling for attacks on U.S. interests; elected in 2006 as governing authority in Gaza
Hezbollah (Party of God)	Lebanon	Also known as Islamic Jihad; often directed by Iran and suspected in the bombing of the U.S. embassy and marine barracks in Beirut in 1983; dominates Lebanon politically; fights against Israel
Boko Haram (Western Education Is Sinful)	Nigeria's relatively impoverished northern states; some activities in neighboring states	Salafi jihadists who violently pursue the establishment of a strict version of Sharia law throughout Nigeria
Haqqani Network	Pashtunistan (eastern Afghanistan and western Pakistan)	Insurgent Islamist group; supported by U.S. CIA during Soviet occupation of Afghanistan; now allied with Taliban and tacitly supported by Pakistan; fights against ISAF in Afghanistan
Revolutionary Armed Forces of Colombia (FARC)	Colombia, with some activities in neighboring Brazil, Venezuela, Panama	Marxist; bombings, murder, kidnapping, extortion, narcotrafficking against Colombian officials

and bombs in the international marketplace. Pressure on governments is very strong because people worry disproportionately about terrorism, even though it kills a relatively small number of people, and because they are likely to believe a violent response by state security forces will help protect them. Despite advances in detection technology (for example, face recognition software), committed individuals or groups of terrorists are difficult to deter. Indeed, such individuals may be seen as heroes in their community.

The international community has taken action against terrorists first by creating a framework of international rules dealing with terrorism, including 12 conventions that address such issues as punishing hijackers and those who protect them; protecting airports, diplomats, and nuclear materials in transport; and blocking the flow of financial resources to global terrorist networks. Individual states have also taken steps to increase state security, such as the United States' controversial USA Patriot Act; to support counterintelligence activities; and to promote cooperation among national enforcement agencies in tracking and apprehending terrorists. States that have been seen as supporting terrorists, or as not taking effective enforcement measures, have been sanctioned by other states. Libya, Sudan, Afghanistan, Syria, Iran, and Iraq are prominent examples. But it is important to recall that even a state as developed as the United States has had difficulty in "taking effective enforcement measures" against terrorists. After all, the terrorists who attacked New York's World Trade Center and the Pentagon on September 11, 2001, learned to fly commercial airplanes in Florida.

The Just War Tradition

When, if ever, is it just for states to go to war? Is war always an illegal and immoral act, or are there conditions under which resorting to war is acceptable? What constitutes an appropriate justification—*jus ad bellum*—to enter into war? And what constitutes moral and ethical conduct—*jus in bello*—once the decision to go to war has been made? Normative political theorists draw our attention to the classical **just war tradition.** Although a Western and Christian doctrine dating from medieval times, just war theory draws on ancient Greek philosophy and precepts found in the Koran. As developed by Saint Augustine, Saint Thomas Aquinas, Hugo Grotius, and more recently the political philosopher Michael Walzer, just war theory asserts that several criteria can make the decision to enter a war a just one.[23] There must be a just cause (self-defense or the defense of others, or a massive violation of human rights) and a declaration of intent by a competent authority (which, since the formation of the United Nations, has been interpreted to mean the UN Security Council). The leaders need to have the correct intentions, desiring to end abuses and establish a just peace. They also need to have exhausted all other possibilities for ending the abuse, employing war as a last resort. Forces must be removed rapidly after the humanitarian objectives have been secured. Because states choose war for a variety of reasons, however, it is rarely easy to assess the justness of a particular cause or of particular intentions.

The just war tradition also addresses legitimate conduct in war. Combatants and noncombatants must be differentiated, with the latter protected from harm as much as possible. Violence must be proportionate to the ends to be achieved. Undue human suffering should be avoided at all costs. Particularly heinous weapons must not be employed. Because mustard gas caused especially cruel deaths during World War I, it was subsequently outlawed, thus providing the basis for future chemical and biological warfare conventions. Many of the extended norms of the just war tradition were codified in the four 1949 Geneva Conventions and two additional protocols concluded in 1977. These are designed to protect civilians, prisoners of war, and wounded soldiers, as well as to ban particular methods of war and certain weapons that cause unnecessary suffering.

Just war is an evolving practice. Key contemporary debates surround the question of how newer killing technologies — nuclear weapons, land mines, cluster munitions, fuel air explosives, and in particular drone strikes — affect our assessments of *jus in bello*. A key concern of just war theorists is the fact that some technological advances make the notion of **noncombatant immunity**, the protection of all civilians not using weapons and of prisoners of war, among others, very difficult. The use of nuclear weapons has been viewed as a just war concern for two reasons. First, as observed earlier, unlike with most conventional weapons, the destructive effects of nuclear weapons are impossible to restrict in time and space. Although as many as 110,000 Japanese were killed in the first few hours after the atomic bombings of Hiroshima and Nagasaki, the Japanese government estimates that total fatalities directly attributable to the bombings today exceed 250,000. Second, the destructive potential of contemporary thermonuclear weapons is simply unprecedented. No one can say for certain what the impact of even a limited exchange of such weapons might be on the global ecosystem. An all-out exchange, in which hundreds of such weapons were deliberately detonated, might end all life on the planet (save perhaps insect life), damage the atmosphere, or plunge the earth into an extended "nuclear winter." Thus the proportionality of means and ends, which stands as a second pillar of just war theory, would be violated.

Other weapons have also come under fire under the "nondiscriminatory nature" theory of unjust war. Two of particular note include antipersonnel land mines and cluster munitions. Although land mines originally were viewed as legitimate weapons, the International Campaign to Ban Landmines (ICBL), as discussed in Chapter 7, has succeeded in shifting perceptions of these weapons by emphasizing — as with other weapons of mass destruction — the indiscriminate effect of their capacity to harm. That approach and process has also been adopted by the Cluster Munitions Coalition, a coalition of 300 NGOs with the support of Norway and other countries. In 2008, the Convention

YOU DECIDE

The history of the twentieth century is often framed in terms of great wars, particularly the two world wars. These interstate wars resulted in the deaths of millions in the span of a few years. Today, the threat of interstate war—especially between powerful industrial states—seems far-fetched, while the threat of terrorism and insurgency seems both serious and widespread. From a state's perspective, which is the greater threat?

On the one hand, you might argue that interstate war remains the greatest threat because even if the probability of war is low, it remains above zero, and given the speed and magnitude of the destruction that might follow (including the possibility of nuclear war), states should rightly remain more concerned with interstate war than with nonstate actors. Second, you might argue that maintaining a costly conventional military, while expensive, is an important pillar of domestic economic health and productivity, and provides thousands of jobs along with national security. So even if it were never needed, it still provides real benefits without making war more likely. Third, it takes time to build up a capacity to fight interstate wars. So beyond the economic costs of demobilizing a conventional defense economy, the gap between the onset of hostilities and the re-acquisition of defense-relevant vehicles, weapons, and supplies creates a serious potential vulnerability. Thus paradoxically, the rational desire to redistribute the productive capacity of the state to other pressing needs may increase the likelihood of war, as states who are not demobilizing may see an opportunity to win a cheap victory in a conquest they otherwise might be deterred from attempting.

But you might counter that nonstate actors are in fact the bigger threat. Technological advances have increased the amount of harm that a small group can do to a state and its citizens, yet today's militaries are neither trained nor equipped to identify and carefully engage such small targets. Second, and as a result, engaging terrorists and insurgents often results in unintended civilian casualties, which tends to aid the insurgents (who gain more and more passionate recruits as a consequence). Moreover, nonstate actors tend to be more nimble and innovative than states, which are weighed down with procedure and bureaucracy. Finally, defending against individuals and small groups has troubling implications for civil liberties, as states come under pressure to suspend those civil liberties in order to increase their security.

YOU DECIDE: Which is the bigger threat to contemporary states, interstate war or terrorism and insurgency?

on Cluster Munitions was signed, banning the use of weapons with a high potential to harm noncombatants and providing assistance for clearance and victim assistance.

The campaigns against antipersonnel land mines and cluster munitions reflect growing pressure to restrict or eliminate the use of various weapons and practices in accord with just war principles. Constructivists can rightly cite the power of norms and socialization to alter the behavior (and identity) of both state and nonstate actors in this regard. After 2001, for example, the George W. Bush administration sought guidance on whether certain interrogation techniques—in particular one called "waterboarding," in which suspects are nearly suffocated repeatedly during questioning—were "torture." If waterboarding was torture, it would be illegal, even within the context of the "war on terrorism." After being assured that waterboarding was not torture, the Bush administration approved its use in interrogations. The ensuing controversy proved fierce. Most interrogation and legal experts consider waterboarding both an ineffective interrogation technique and torture. The subject was raised at a U.S. presidential debate in 2011 in which two candidates for the Republican nomination—Michelle Bachman and Herman Cain—argued that waterboarding was not torture and that they would authorize its use should they become president. But critics, including some prominent Republicans, responded that waterboarding was torture, and therefore inherently un-American. In 2013, the debate was renewed with the movie *Zero Dark Thirty*, which depicted the events leading to the death of bin Laden.

Another recent issue of *jus in bello* that has surfaced due to advances in U.S. surveillance technology is drone strikes. Initially, drones were used to place sophisticated eyes and ears over combat areas without risking pilots and expensive aircraft. But their use has increased radically over the past decade, from 50 a decade ago to over 7,000 in 2012. Many drones in the U.S. inventory are armed with missiles that can be aimed and launched by operators thousands of miles away. Two questions currently surround their use in a just war. First, what safeguards are there to ensure that those targeted by drone strikes are actually guilty of terrorism or of harming allied personnel? Most of those targeted do not wear uniforms, nor do they serve a state. The process by which U.S. intelligence agencies determine target lists remains classified. In October of 2011, the U.S. Central Intelligence Agency identified and killed an American-born Al Qaeda leader named Anwar al-Awlaki. The killing by executive order of al-Awlaki without due process marked a turning point in the use of armed drones in the war on terror, and it may have set a dangerous precedent, especially as other states and possibly terrorists come into possession of drone technology. Second, and related, how discriminate is the harm caused by the use of missiles fired from drones? Some reports of drone strikes in Pakistan, for example, indicate that many legitimate targets are killed in their homes and tents, which implies a high likelihood that the target's family is killed along with the target. Is this just?

The United States employs Predator drones like this one in its fight against radical terrorist groups in Afghanistan, Pakistan, and Yemen. When armed with missiles, Predator drones can attack the enemy without putting U.S. soldiers' lives at risk. But there is deep concern that drones may violate just war principles.

The Debate over Humanitarian Intervention

No issue emerging from the just war tradition has been more critical or controversial than the debate over humanitarian intervention. The just war tradition asserts that military intervention by states or the international community may be justified or even obligatory to alleviate massive violations of human rights. Yet that position directly contradicts a hallmark of the Westphalian tradition—respect for state sovereignty. Historically, military intervention on behalf of humanitarian causes was applied selectively. In the nineteenth century, Europeans used military force to protect Christians in Turkey and the Middle East, though they chose not to protect other religious groups. And European nations did not intervene militarily to stop slavery, though they prohibited their own citizens from participating in the slave trade.[24]

Since the end of World War II, the notion has emerged that all human beings deserve protection—not just particular groups—and that states have an obligation to intervene, called the **responsibility to protect (R2P)**. This belief gained even greater prominence during the 1990s after humanitarian crises in Somalia and Rwanda, and more recently after widespread murder, rape, and devastation in Darfur, Sudan (2003–2005). The idea is that in the case of massive violation of human rights, w domestic avenues for redress have been exhausted and actions by other states reasonably end the abuse, these states have a responsibility to interfere in the d affairs of the state in which the abuse is occurring. As two UN officials p "marks the coming of age of the imperative of action in the face of human rights abuses, over the citadels of state sovereignty."[25]

But questions remain: How massive do the violations of human rights have to be to justify intervention? Who decides when to respond to the abuses? Might some states use humanitarian intervention as a pretext for achieving other, less humanitarian goals? Do states have an obligation to intervene militarily in these humanitarian emergencies? How can some interventions be justified (e.g., Kosovo) while others were not undertaken (e.g., Rwanda)? As the same UN officials warn, military intervention can often be "devoid of legal sanction, selectively deployed and achieving only ambiguous ends."[26]

Given their experiences under colonial rule, many Asian and African countries are skeptical about humanitarian justifications for intervention by Western countries. Other states, such as Russia and China, have insisted that for a claim of humanitarian intervention to be legitimate, it must be authorized by the UN Security Council. In practice, humanitarian interventions are often multilateral, although they do not always receive authorization from the UN. For instance, when Western states sought military intervention in Kosovo, Russia opposed the measure, so Western powers turned to the North Atlantic Treaty Organization (NATO) instead. Russian opposition to intervention in what it considers to be the internal affairs of another state has a long history. Russia's argument regarding intervention in Kosovo was partly tradition; Serbia has long been an ally of Russia for reasons involving ethnicity and religion. And Russia's position was partly a hedge against setting a dangerous international precedent. If we allow some states to judge that other states have bad leaders and this justifies military intervention, what is to prevent any state from being judged and invaded should power shift in the future? Russia's position on intervention has in recent times complicated efforts to halt the civil war in Syria (2012–present).

States that have supported humanitarian interventions in the past do not always support future interventions. This change in policy can occur for a number of reasons, including the perception of the success or failure of previous missions as well as the nature of other interests at stake in the conflict. Having suffered a humiliating setback in Somalia in 1993, for instance, the United States (and UN) opposed increased use of the military to protect civilians in Rwanda in 1994, despite clear evidence of genocide. Similarly, only a small military contingent from the African Union was originally mobilized for the Darfur region, despite 300,000 deaths and the culpability of the Sudanese government. In the Darfur case, other national interests were deemed more vital than support for humanitarian intervention (China cared about access to Sudanese oil; Russia cared about export arms markets; the United States was preoccupied with Iraq and the war on terrorism). In May of 2012, a massacre in the village of Taldou of women, children, and even infants by the security forces of Syria's Bashar al Assad caused an international outcry. But China and Russia opposed UN-sanctioned military intervention. Both countries issued statements asserting that any foreign military intervention would only make the situation in Syria, and the region, worse.

So although support for R2P is an emergent norm, it remains the subject of debate. Because states do not intervene in all situations of humanitarian emergency, state sovereignty remains intact. But when gross violations of human rights are obvious, and when military intervention does not conflict with other national interests, humanitarian intervention is increasingly seen as a justifiable use of force.

Approaches to Managing Insecurity

Disparity in power between states, the inability to know the intentions of states and individuals, and the lack of an overarching international authority means that states are continually confronted by the need to manage their insecurity. This need is made more urgent by several related trends, including a steadily increasing reliance on computer networks to manage electrical power, finance, communications, transportation, and police work.

Four approaches to managing insecurity are well tested in international politics. Two of these approaches reflect realist thinking, requiring individual states themselves to maintain an adequate power potential. The other approaches reflect the liberal theoretical perspective and thus focus largely on multilateral responses by groups of states acting to coordinate their policies. Realists and liberals support different policy responses to arms proliferation, the resulting security dilemma, and managing insecurity more generally, as described in Table 8.3.

Realist Approaches: Balance of Power and Deterrence

Realist approaches to managing insecurity rely on balancing power, where *power* is broadly understood to mean the power to win wars. Although realism itself imagines inter- and intrastate warfare as enduring features of international politics, realists advance important arguments about how to decrease the frequency of wars and the intensity of wars once they break out. The core logic of power balancing is simple: when power is unbalanced, stronger actors will be tempted to use their advantage to secure still more power. The greater the imbalance, the greater the temptation. This is because for the stronger actor the costs and risks of war seem low in comparison to potential gains, thus making war a *rational* strategy. But when aggressive, insecure, or greedy actors face others with relatively equal power, they are likely to be deterred by the possibility that the costs of war will exceed expected benefits. Realism's logic therefore explains much of what we observe in interstate politics. It can provide an effective guide to policies aimed at preserving a status quo short of war. However, realist security-management strategies depend crucially on the notion that adversaries share definitions of relevant costs and benefits and that they assign roughly equal values to both. When they do not, a realist strategy for security management can easily go awry, making warfare more rather than less likely, and more rather than less destructive.

BALANCE OF POWER   In Chapter 4, we saw that a balance of power is a particular configuration of the international system. But theorists use the terms in other ways as well. So *balance of power* may refer to an equilibrium between any two parties, and *balancing power* may describe an approach to managing power and insecurity. The latter usage is relevant here.

Balance-of-power theorists posit that to manage insecurity, states make rational and calculated evaluations of the costs and benefits of particular policies that determine the state's role in a balance of power. All states in the system are continually making choices to maintain their position vis-à-vis their adversaries, thereby maintaining a balance of power. When that balance of power is jeopardized, as it was by the rise of German power in the early 1900s, insecurity leads states to pursue countervailing alliances or policies.[27] More recently, as a result of China's rapid economic growth in the last decade and its increasing investment in naval forces, the United States and Australia have agreed that Australia will host a U.S. Marine Corps infantry company, which will expand by 2016 to a presence of 2,500 marines. The U.S. Navy has also begun to redeploy its Pacific fleet to better protect U.S. allies and interests in Asia.

Alliances are the most important institutional tool for enhancing one's own security and balancing the perceived power potential of one's opponent. If an expanding state is threatening to achieve a dominant position, threatened states can join with others against the threat. This is external balancing. Formal and institutionalized military alliances play a key role in maintaining a balance of power, as the NATO and Warsaw Pact alliances did in the post–World War II world. States may also engage in internal balancing, increasing their own military and economic capabilities to counter potential threatening enemies.

A balance of power operates at both international and regional levels. At the international level during the Cold War, for instance, a relative balance of power was maintained between the United States and the Soviet Union. If one of the superpowers augmented its power through the expansion of its alliances or through the acquisition of deadlier, more effective armaments, the other responded in kind. Absolute gains were not so critical as relative gains; no matter how much total power one state accrued, neither state could afford to fall behind the other. Gaining allies among uncommitted states in the Third World through foreign aid or military and diplomatic intervention was one way to ensure that power was balanced. Not maintaining the power balance was too risky a strategy; national survival was at stake.

TABLE 8.3	APPROACHES TO MANAGING INSECURITY	
	REALIST	**LIBERAL**
Approach	Reliance on force or threat of force to manage power	International institutions coordinate actions to manage power
Policies	Balance of power; Deterrence	Collective security; Arms control and disarmament

Balances of power among states in specific geographic regions are also a way to manage insecurity. In South Asia, for example, a balance of power maintains a tense peace between India and Pakistan—a peace made more durable by the presence of nuclear weapons, according to realist thinking. In East Asia, Japan's alliance with the United States creates a balance of power with China. In the Middle East, the balance of power between Israel and its Arab neighbors continues. In some regions a complex set of other balances has developed: between the economically rich, oil-producing states of Saudi Arabia and the Persian Gulf and the economically poor states of the core Middle East; and between Islamic militants (Iran), moderates (Egypt, Tunisia), and conservatives (Saudi Arabia). With the breakup of the Soviet Union, the newly independent states of Central Asia are struggling for position within a newly emerging regional balance of power.

Realist theorists assert that balancing power is the most important technique for managing insecurity. It is compatible with human nature and that of the state, which is to act to protect one's self-interest by maintaining one's power position relative to those of others. If a state seeks preponderance through military acquisitions or offensive actions, then war against that state is acceptable under the balance-of-power system. If all states act similarly, the balance can be preserved without war.

One major limitation of the balance-of-power approach, however, is its requirement that states view the friendships they have established with allies as expendable. According to the theory, should power shift, alliances should also shift to maintain the balance regardless of friendship. But as liberals and constructivists observe, states exist in a kind of society and they resist giving up their "friends" even when power shifts.

This may explain why, after the collapse of the Soviet Union in 1991, long-standing U.S. allies such as Britain did not abandon their alliance with the United States, even though the bipolar balance of power had collapsed.

A second limitation stems from the inability to manage security during periods of rapid change. A balance-of-power approach supports the status quo. When change occurs, or if the status quo comes to be perceived as unjust, how should other states respond? Rapid change occurred at the end of the Cold War, for example, with the dismemberment of the Soviet Union and the dissolution of the Warsaw Pact alliance. A balance-of-power strategy would have suggested that U.S. allies re-align to fill the power vacuum left by the USSR's demise. Instead, the United States attempted, with mixed success, to lead its allies into a series of escalating confrontations with what it considered "dictatorships" and "supporters of terror." After 2005, the United States' European allies began to balance against U.S. hegemony and unilateralism, but their effort was stalled by the financial crisis of 2008 (which deprived them of the resources needed to balance) and the election of a more circumspect U.S. president, Barack Obama (which caused a shift from U.S. unilateralism to multilateralism and seemed to obviate the need for balancing).

DETERRENCE   Although the subject of deterrence has its own literature, it is best understood in relation to the balance of power as the mechanism that enables a balance of power to cause peace. At its most basic level, deterrence is the manipulation of fear to prevent an unwanted action. If I am much bigger than you, I can expect you to be deterred from attacking me for fear of being hurt or killed. The same is true of a balance of power: when power is balanced, aggressive states are expected to be deterred from attacking for fear of being defeated in war. By contrast, when a rapidly rising state threatens the balance of power, its confidence of victory may tempt it to war. Thus, deterrence is *how* balancing power works to reduce the likelihood of war.

Deterrence theory posits that violence such as war can be prevented by the credible *threat* of the use of force. In its 2002 National Security Strategy, for example, the United States made the threat very explicit for those who may pursue global terrorism. The United States writes that it will defend "the United States, the American people, our interests at home and abroad by identifying and destroying the threat before it reaches our border. ...We will not hesitate to act alone, if necessary, to exercise our right of self-defense by acting preemptively against such terrorists, to prevent them from doing harm against our people and our country."[28]

Deterrence theory as initially developed is based on a number of key assumptions.[29] First and most important is the assumption of the rationality of decision makers. The theory assumes that rational decision makers want to avoid resorting to war in those situations in which the anticipated cost of aggression is greater than the expected gain. Second, the theory assumes that nuclear weapons—one particularly intense form of harm—pose an unacceptable risk of mutual destruction, and thus that decision makers will not initiate armed aggression against a nuclear state. Third, the theory assumes that alternatives to war are available to decision makers irrespective of the issue of contention.

For deterrence to work, then, states must form alliances or build up their arsenals in order to present a credible threat. Information regarding the threat must be conveyed to the opponent. Thus, according to deterrence theorists, knowing that an aggressive action will be countered by a damaging reaction, the opponent will decide not to resort to force and thereby destroy its own society.

As logical as deterrence sounds and as effective as it seemed during the Cold War—after all, there was no nuclear war between the superpowers—the very assumptions on which deterrence is based are frequently subject to challenge. Are all top decision makers rational? Might not one individual or a group of individuals risk destruction in deciding to launch a first strike? Might some states be willing to sacrifice a large number of people, as Germany's Adolf Hitler, Iran's Ayatollah Khomeini, and Iraq's Saddam Hussein were willing to do in the past? How do states credibly convey information about their true capabilities to a potential adversary? Should they? Or would it make more sense to bluff or to lie? For states without nuclear weapons, or for nuclear-weapons states that are launching an attack against a nonnuclear state, the risks of war may seem acceptable: when one's own society is unlikely to be threatened with destruction (as in most asymmetric conflicts), deterrence is more likely to fail.

The security environment makes deterrence even more problematic in the new millennium. First, the rise of terrorism conducted by nonstate actors organized in horizontal networks appears to decrease the possibility that deterrence will work. Because nonstate actors do not hold territory, the threat to destroy such territory in a retalitory strike cannot be a potent deterrent. Flexible networks, spread over different geographic areas, rather than an organizational hierarchy located within a particular state, make eliminating those networks very difficult. The increasing willingness of some groups to use suicide terrorism to achieve their objectives has made the logic of deterrence appear particularly shaky. Deterrence depends on the calculation that rational actors will never deliberately act to invite costly reprisals, yet suicide terrorists are willing to sacrifice their own lives. Since loss of life has traditionally been thought of as the highest of all costs, suicide terrorism appears to render deterrence meaningless.[30]

Second, in the changed security environment, the United States is approaching nuclear primacy.[31] For the first time in nuclear history, it may be possible for the United States to destroy the long-range nuclear arsenals of both Russia and China with a first strike because of improvements in U.S. nuclear capacity, including the ability to track submarines and mobile missiles, the declining capability of the Russian military, and the slow pace of China's modernization. In fact, China has no long-range bombers and no advance-warning system. If true, U.S. nuclear primacy would deter other states from attacking the United States, but might tempt the United States to a preemptive nuclear strike against its enemies.

Realist approaches to managing insecurity rely mainly on fear, but as we have seen, they also imagine power in almost purely material terms. To the extent that changing norms, or a rise in the power of ideas, has changed world politics, can realist approaches to managing insecurity continue to be effective? If all realists have is bullets, it is hard to see how realist approaches to managing insecurity can succeed unaided. What is the liberal alternative?

Liberal Approaches: Collective Security and Arms Control/Disarmament

Liberal approaches to managing insecurity call on the international community or international institutions to coordinate actions in order to reduce the likelihood and destructiveness of war as well as other forms of harm, including global economic collapse.

THE COLLECTIVE SECURITY IDEAL   Collective security is captured in the old adage "one for all and all for one." Based on the proposition that aggressive and unlawful use of force by any state against another must be stopped, collective security posits that such unlawful aggression will be met by united action: all (or many) states will join together against the aggressor. Potential aggressors will know this fact ahead of time and thus will choose not to act.

Collective security makes a number of fundamental assumptions.[32] One assumption is that the collective benefit of peace outweighs the individual benefits of war, even a successful war. Another assumption is that aggressors—no matter who they are, friends or foes—must be stopped. This assumption presumes that the aggressor can be identified easily by other members of the international community. (In some conflicts, it is difficult to differentiate between the aggressor and the victim.) Collective security also assumes moral clarity: the aggressor is morally wrong because all aggressors are morally wrong, and all those who are right must act in unison to meet the aggression. Finally, collective security assumes that aggressors know that the international community will act to punish an aggressor.

Of course this is none other than deterrence, but with a twist. If all countries know that aggression will be punished by the international community, then would-be aggressors will be deterred from engaging in aggressive activity. The twist is that in liberal theory, states are more likely to calculate their interests collectively as shared interests rather than individually, as in the realist view. Both theoretical perspectives accept alliances as a fundamental aspect of interstate politics, but liberals put more faith in them than realists do. Hence, states will be more secure in the belief that would-be aggressors will be deterred by the prospect of united action by the international community. But for collective security to work, the threat to take action must be credible, and there must be cohesion among all the potential enforcers.

Collective security does not always work. In the period between the two world wars, Japan invaded Manchuria and Italy overran Ethiopia. In neither case did other states act as if it was in their collective interest to respond. Were Manchuria and Ethiopia really worth a world war? In these instances, collective security did not work because, as realists assert, the states capable of acting to halt the violence, particularly Britain and France, could not see sufficient national interest in doing so, especially when the threat of another war with Germany seemed increasingly likely. In the post–World War II era, two major alliance systems—NATO and the Warsaw Pact—arrayed states into two separate camps. States dared not engage in action against an ally or a foe, even if that state was an aggressor, for fear of causing another world war.

Collective security may also fail due to the problematic nature of a key assumption, that aggressors can be easily identified. But this is not always the case. In 1967, Israel launched an armed attack against Egypt: clearly an act of aggression. The week before, however, Egypt had blocked Israeli access to the Red Sea, kicked the UN out of Sinai, and, in combination with Syria and Jordan, moved hundreds of tanks and planes closer to Israel. Clearly these, too, were acts of aggression. Twenty years earlier, the state of Israel had been carved out of Arab real estate. That, too, was an act of aggression. Where does the aggression "begin"? The George W. Bush administration argued in 2003 that its invasion of Iraq was a preemptive war because Saddam Hussein was preparing to operationalize and possibly use a nuclear weapon (or transfer one to a terrorist group). So who is the aggressor? Furthermore, even if an aggressor can be identified, is that party always morally wrong? Due to an understandable fixation on the individual and collective costs of war (especially in the last century), collective-security theorists argue, by definition, yes. Yet trying to right a previous wrong is not necessarily wrong; trying to make just a prior injustice is not always unjust. Like the balance of power, at its best, collective security in practice supports the status quo at a specific point in time. If that status quo is unjust, then why isn't the collective security that supports it also unjust?

IN FOCUS

ASSUMPTIONS OF DETERRENCE THEORY

- Decision makers are rational.
- The threat of mutual destruction from warfare is great.
- Alternatives to war are available.

IN FOCUS

ASSUMPTIONS OF COLLECTIVE SECURITY THEORY

- Wars are caused by aggressive states.

- Aggressors must be stopped.

- Aggressors are easily identified.

- Aggressors are always wrong.

- Aggressors will be deterred from aggression by the threat of a collective response.

ARMS CONTROL AND DISARMAMENT   **Arms control** and general **disarmament** schemes have been the hope of many liberals over the years since the first Hague Convention of 1899. In the rich history of arms control and disarmament treaties since the nineteenth century—including hundreds of treaties limiting the militarization of the polar regions and space, the types of weapons that may be legitimately used (such as antipersonnel land mines, anti-ballistic-missile defenses, and cluster munitions), or even limiting the testing and development of certain weapons (such as nuclear weapons)—there have been two striking features overall: (1) most signatories to these treaties actually abide by their treaty obligations (that is, cheating is rare); and (2) many of those who have been signatories have been of an avowedly "realist" orientation. This is counterintuitive because, as observed in Chapter 3, realists tend to conflate "security" with "capacity to do physical harm." Yet even at the very first Hague Convention in 1899, realist states such as Germany, France, Britain, and Russia all found themselves agreeing to limit the quantity and quality of arms they would manufacture and employ in war. Whatever the rationale for reductions in each individual case, the logic of this approach to security is both powerful and straightforward: fewer weapons means greater security. Regulating arms proliferation (arms control) and reducing the amount of arms and the types of weapons employed (disarmament) should logically reduce the costs of the security dilemma.

During the Cold War, many arms control agreements were negotiated to reduce the threat of nuclear war. For example, in the 1972 Treaty on the Limitation of Antiballistic Missile Systems (ABM treaty), both the United States and the Soviet Union agreed not to use a ballistic missile defense as a shield against a first strike by the other. The Strategic Arms Limitations Talks in 1972 and 1979 (SALT I and SALT II, respectively) put ceilings on the growth of both Soviet and U.S. strategic weapons. However, due to the Soviet invasion of Afghanistan in 1979, the second SALT treaty was never ratified by the U.S. Senate. The Nuclear Nonproliferation Treaty (NPT) was negotiated in 1968 at the United Nations in response to the Cuban Missile Crisis.

The NPT illustrates both positive and negative effects of such treaties. In force since 1970, the NPT spells out the rules of nuclear proliferation. In the treaty, signatory countries without nuclear weapons agree not to acquire or develop them; states with nuclear weapons promise not to transfer the technology to nonnuclear states and to eventually dismantle their own. During the 1990s, three states that previously had nuclear weapons programs—South Africa, Brazil, and Argentina—dismantled their programs and became parties to the treaty, along with three other states—Belarus, Kazakhstan, and Ukraine—that gave up nuclear weapons left on their territory after the dissolution of the Soviet Union. As with many of the arms control treaties, however, a number of key nuclear states and threshold non-nuclear states (those that probably have or could quickly assemble nuclear weapons) remain outside the treaty, including Cuba, India, Israel, and Pakistan.

The International Atomic Energy Agency (IAEA), a UN-based agency established in 1957 to disseminate knowledge about nuclear energy and promote its peaceful uses, is the designated guardian of the treaty. The IAEA created a system of safeguards, including inspection teams that visit nuclear facilities and report on any movement of nuclear material, in an attempt to keep nuclear material from being diverted to nonpeaceful purposes and to ensure that states that signed the NPT are complying. Inspectors for the IAEA visited Iraqi sites after the 1991 Gulf War and North Korean sites in the mid-1990s. Their purpose in the first case was to verify that illegal materials in Iraq had been destroyed and in the second case to confirm that nuclear materials in North Korea were being used for nonmilitary purposes only. But the work of the IAEA has been constantly challenged. In 2009, Iran, which as a signatory to the NPT was obligated to report any facility actively enriching fissile material, was discovered to have an unreported facility in violation of its treaty obligations. In addition, signatories that already possess nuclear weapons are expected to reduce their stockpiles, but they have proven reluctant, in most cases, to do so very quickly.

The end of the Cold War and the dismemberment of the Soviet Union resulted in major new arms control agreements. More arms control agreements between the United States and Russia and its successor states are likely as the latter are forced by economic imperatives to reduce their military expenditures. Yet the logic of arms control agreements is not impeccable. Arms control does not eliminate the security dilemma. You can still feel insecure if your enemy has a bigger or better rock than you do. And as realists would argue, state policy toward such agreements is never assured. Verification is spotty and difficult to implement. For example, in 1994, the United States and North Korea signed the Agreed Framework: North Korea agreed to stop its nuclear weapons program in exchange for a U.S. package deal of energy supplies, light-water reactors, and security guarantees. The framework collapsed in 2002, when North Korea announced it was pulling out of the Nuclear Nonproliferation Treaty in response to U.S. decisions to halt shipments of fuel oil supporting North Korea's electric grid. On

North Korea's restarting of the Yongbyon nuclear reactor, used to process weapons-grade nuclear material, the United States and Japan halted aid shipments.

In 2003, North Korea publicly admitted that it was engaged in a nuclear-weapons program and has subsequently tested both long- and short-range missiles, causing great consternation in the region and in the United States. Is North Korea advancing a nuclear weapons program to enhance its own security? Or is North Korea simply bargaining for more aid in return for promising to halt its nuclear-weapons program? The agreement brokered in 2007 as a result of negotiations conducted among six parties—North Korea, China, Japan, the United States, South Korea, and Russia—directed that North Korea would close its main nuclear reactor in exchange for a package of fuel, food, and other aid. The agreement has proven highly unstable, however. In 2008, North Korea's leader, the late Kim Jong-Il, threatened to resume weapons development because the promised aid package was too small and had arrived too slowly. Later that year, further progress was stalled by rumors that Kim was near death. Kim reappeared in 2009, after which North Korea exploded a nuclear device underground, to widespread dismay and condemnation. Little progress has been made since that time. Threatening nuclear proliferation as a coercive measure to secure aid is an alarming new security twist.

Given how risky such a scheme would be, complete disarmament as envisioned by utopian liberal thinkers is unlikely. Unilateral disarmament would place the disarmed state in a highly insecure position, and cheaters could be rewarded. But incremental disarmament—as outlined in the Chemical Weapons Convention (CWC), which bans the development, production, and stockpiling of chemical weapons—remains a possibility. However, the increasing sophistication and miniaturization of chemical and biological weapons makes them difficult to detect, so that it is hard to guarantee compliance. Liberals place their faith in international institutions such as the IAEA to monitor adherence to such limited disarmament schemes.

The Example of NATO: Managing Insecurity in a Changing Environment

Managing insecurity is a particular challenge in times of transition in the international system. Such transitions can occur when major powers undergo a change in their actual or perceived ability to project power, protect allies, or threaten enemies. The end of the Cold War was such a moment of transition, as the Soviet Union dissolved and communist regimes were replaced with proto-democratic ones. The collapse of the Soviet Union brought an immediate end to the Warsaw Pact, leaving many countries in Eastern Europe without a major power ally. The end of the Cold War also affected NATO, the western alliance whose purpose was to balance the now-defunct Warsaw Pact. With this change, some scholars predicted the imminent demise of NATO. What happened however was not the organization's demise but its reconfiguration in terms of both the tasks it undertakes and the expansion of its membership.

With the bloody civil war in Yugoslavia and attendant refugee crises in Europe, NATO increasingly took on peacekeeping and stabilization roles in Bosnia. In 1999, NATO undertook its largest military operation since its creation in 1949: Operation Allied Force, the air war over Serbia. Without UN authorization, NATO forces conducted a 78-day air war against the Federal Republic of Yugoslavia in an attempt to halt attacks against ethnic Albanians in the Serbian province of Kosovo. The war resulted in a popular uprising and the attendant overthrow of the Serbian leadership, the extradition of the Serbian strongman Slobodan Milošević to the Hague War Crimes Tribunal, and the petition by Serbia to join NATO's Partnership for Peace program.

Since the "global war on terrorism" began in September 2001, NATO has sought to maintain its relevance in the new security environment.[33] NATO has enhanced its operational capabilities to keep up with technology, created a rapid reaction force to respond to crises, and streamlined its military command structure. It has employed forces "out of area" in Afghanistan and Libya. Its members have helped train the Iraqi military, although the organization did not join the U.S.-led coalition in Iraq.

NATO membership has also expanded as its tasks have diversified. In 1997, the first wave of new members following the end of the Cold War, including Poland, Hungary, and the Czech Republic, were admitted. These new members were to be contributors to enhanced security in the region, not just the recipients of a security umbrella. It has proven more difficult than anticipated, however, to convince these states to make necessary defense reforms, increase defense expenditures, and modernize equipment and training. Yet despite these problems, a second wave of members was admitted in 2004. They included Estonia, Latvia, Lithuania, Slovakia, Slovenia, Romania, and Bulgaria. Albania and Croatia formally joined in 2009, bringing the total NATO membership to 28, along with 22 Partnership for Peace member states and 7 Mediterranean Dialogue states. This round of admissions was a reaction to the war on terrorism: a search by the United States and others for dependable allies where bases more proximate to the Middle East could be maintained at a cheaper cost. The newer NATO members could curry favor with the United States and did not have to make reforms to be admitted to the organization.

During most of the 1990s, Russia opposed NATO enlargement, alarmed at seeing its old allies coming under NATO auspices. Russian concerns were reasonable. If NATO's reason for existence was the Soviet threat of invasion and conquest of Western Europe, and the Soviet Union no longer exists, why, asked the Russians, should NATO still exist, much less expand? This may explain why for many in Russia, the expansion of the alliance was viewed as a potential military threat. Yet after 9/11, Russian opposition softened, especially once it realized that NATO's newest members were turning it into a kind of "toothless lion." And Russia still has military bases in Ukraine, Armenia, Tajikistan, and Kyrgyzstan, among others.

To most member states, particularly the United States, NATO expansion was seen as a natural consequence of winning the Cold War, establishing a new post–Cold War security order, and more recently, trying to respond to new security threats posed by terrorism. Some realists see NATO expansion as a means of achieving relative gains over Russia and further enhancing Western security. Many liberals view expansion as a means of strengthening democracy in former communist states and bringing institutional stability to areas threatened with crises, and as a way to use a security institution to facilitate membership in a much more important set of economic and diplomatic institutions, in particular the European Union. NATO has worked closely with Russia to convince it that NATO's expansion is not an offensive threat, institutionalizing dialogue with Russia on key NATO issues that pertain to Russia's own security.

For constructivists, the issue of NATO expansion powerfully engages issues of national identity. For states formerly dominated by the Soviet Union, accession to NATO reflected their resentment over that domination. Russia opposed NATO expansion not only over security concerns, but also due to the implied insult. To a constructivist, then, the politics of NATO expansion highlight the nonmaterial bases of interstate relations between the successor states of the former Soviet Union and the former Warsaw Pact member states.

In Sum: A Changing View of International Security

Traditionally, international security has meant states' security and the defense of states' territorial integrity from external threats or attack by other states. This was because only states could master the technology of mass killing; as a result, interstate war proved the largest threat to life and property. Over time, this definition has broadened to include intrastate conflicts as well. In both situations, conflicts arise not only over control of territory but also over control of government and ideas. Although major interstate wars, such as the last century's two world wars, concentrate destruction in time, intrastate violence has resulted in just as much or even more destruction. By some estimates, more than 40 million human beings have lost their lives in so-called low-intensity conflicts in Africa, Asia, and Latin America since the end of World War II. Moreover, the advent of the container ship, extremely durable small arms, food-storage and water-purification technology, and improvements in communications technology have made it progressively less likely that the destruction caused by civil wars can be contained within their states of origin. Instead, civil conflicts are more likely than ever to involve regional and international actors than at any time in world history. Typically, responsibility for providing national security and humanitarian intervention has fallen to government officials in democracies, acting in consultation with society and the military. This has been the major focus of this chapter.

But a new trend is occurring more and more: the outsourcing of security from nationals in uniform to private security firms and robots.[34] Companies with such deliberately obscure names as Blackwater (currently known as Academi), Sandline International, BDM, COFRAS, and Southern Cross are new actors in security. These contracting private companies perform diverse tasks: servicing military airplanes and ships, providing food for armies, protecting high-profile officials, guarding and inter-rogating prisoners of war, training troops, and sometimes carrying out low-intensity military operations on behalf of a client. Their "soldier" employees—the mercenaries of the twenty-first century—come from all over the world, from the Ukraine to Fiji, Australia to Chile. Many are former government military personnel. They serve in locations from Sierra Leone to Sri Lanka, from Bosnia to the Democratic Republic of Congo, from Iraq to Afghanistan.

The use of semi-intelligent or guided robots in war, as in the case of drones previ-ously discussed, is another form of "outsourcing" that offers a similar benefit and simi-lar risks to private security contracting: casualties will not be human beings who are representing the state as nationals.

As of today, the logistical, legal, and ethical problems emerging from each type of outsourcing remain unclear. Are private contractors merely mercenaries acting out of pecuniary self-interest? Or are they pragmatically solving problems that the military could not otherwise solve? Are they cost effective? Where do their loyalties lie? To what state or what ideology do they belong? What is their relationship with the organized military? Can they be held accountable for actions they take in war? In other words, does *jus in bello* also apply to these forces? Should they be employed by the interna-tional community for UN-mandated peacekeeping? As regards robots such as drones, what safeguards exist to prevent their arbitrary or irresponsible use? As more and more states acquire the technology, how will they be regulated? Certain of its rectitude, the United States has already set dangerous precedents, reserving the right, for example, to target and kill terrorists on the sovereign territory of other states. How should the United States react if say, China used a drone to target and kill a person in Nebraska it considered a dangerous terrorist?

In the waning years of the twentieth century, another change occurred concerning who or what should be protected. Changing notions about what security is and who should be protected have been a key topic in constructivist discourse. Should only states be protected? Or should individuals be protected as well, not only from inter-state rivalries but from failures of their own government to protect life, property, and ideas? That states and the international community have the obligation, ind

Private security contractors, such as these Blackwater employees, were hired by the U.S. government after the start of the 2003 Iraq war to perform tasks such as protecting high-profile officials, transporting troops and materials, and engaging in occasional combat operations. The role of private contractors in international security continues to provoke troubling questions about accountability, lines of authority, and rule of law.

responsibility, to protect human beings, even if it means intervention in the affairs of another state, is the norm of humanitarian intervention.

But what should the individual be protected against? Should protection include more than that against the physical violence typically associated with interstate conflict, civil war, genocide, nuclear weapons, and terrorism as discussed in this chapter? Should the concept of security be broadened? In 2004, the UN High-Level Panel on Threats, Challenges, and Change identified additional threats to what it labeled *human security*, a term that has increasingly been used since the early 1990s. Should individuals be protected from infectious diseases and environmental degradation? Should they be protected from the harmful effects of economic globalization or from poverty? It is to economic issues that we now turn.

Discussion Questions

1. How can we identify an aggressor in international conflicts? Is such identification important? Why or why not?

2. Before World War II, European colonial powers had relatively little difficulty controlling their large overseas empires with few troops. After World War II, this changed dramatically. What explains the change?

3. An American decision maker charged with U.S.–Afghanistan policy requests policy memos from realists (an offensive realist and a defensive realist), a liberal, a radical, and a constructivist. How might their respective recommendations differ?

4. The norm of nonproliferation, embodied in the Nuclear Nonproliferation Treaty, has been challenged by North Korea. Is Iran's nuclear development also a challenge to the NPT? Or is it within the treaty's bounds? What are the legal issues? The political issues?

Key Terms

arms control (p. 296)

asymmetric conflict (p. 277)

disarmament (p. 296)

diversionary war (p. 257)

guerrilla warfare (p. 276)

humanitarian intervention (p. 287)

interstate war (p. 263)

intrastate war (p. 263)

just war tradition (p. 283)

limited war (p. 267)

noncombatant immunity (p. 284)

nonviolent resistance (p. 278)

nuclear proliferation (p. 271)

responsibility to protect (R2P) (p. 287)

security dilemma (p. 251)

terrorism (p. 278)

total war (p. 265)

unconventional warfare (p. 273)

war (p. 253)

weapons of mass destruction (WMD) (p. 272)

Economic globalization is a distinguishing feature of contemporary international relations. The value of international trade in goods and services is over $22 trillion a year, and economic decisions in one country can have a real impact on economic conditions elsewhere.

09

INTERNATIONAL POLITICAL ECONOMY

- *What are the theoretical underpinnings of the international political economy?*
- *What are the core concepts of economic liberalism?*
- *What roles do multinational corporations and the major international economic institutions play in the international political economy?*
- *How do the views of mercantilists/statists and radicals differ from those of economic liberals?*
- *How has the international economic system become globalized today in key areas: international finance, international trade, and international development?*
- *How have international petroleum markets changed economic globalization?*
- *What are the similarities and differences between the regionalism of the European Union and that of NAFTA?*
- *What are the challenges to economic globalization in light of the 2008–2009 global economic crisis and the 2009 eurozone crisis?*

Few people would dispute that economic **globalization** accurately describes the international political economy of 2013. As Chapter 1 reminds us, our clothes, food, and consumer products are produced around the world, often in several different countries; our financial and religious institutions as well as our coffee shops and NGOs enjoy an international market. At the individual level, we interact daily in the real world and in the "virtual" world by cell phones, the Internet, Facebook, and Twitter. As Thomas Friedman describes in *The Lexus and the Olive Tree*, globalization is the "inexorable integration of markets, nation-states and technologies to a degree never witnessed before in a way that is enabling individuals, corporations and nation-states to reach around the world further, faster, deeper and cheaper than ever before."[1] Economic liberalization and new technologies stimulate not only the increasing flows of capital and trade but also the decreasing territorialization of economic life both at the global and regional level. But the international political economy was not always as globalized as it is today. How has the international economy changed? What ideas propelled these changes? How does the globalized economy of today function? Will the trend towards integration be "inexorable," as Friedman posits?

The Evolution of the International Economy: Clashing Ideas and Practices

The era from the late Middle Ages through the end of the eighteenth century saw a number of key changes in technology, ideas, and practices. Spurred by advances in ship design and navigation systems, European explorers opened up new frontiers in the Americas, Asia, and the Middle East to trade and commerce. Although Greek, Phoenician, and Mesopotamian traders had preceded them, the British East India Company, the Hudson's Bay Company, and the Dutch East India Company facilitated trade in goods (and people as slaves) and provided capital for investments in the agricultural development of the new lands, transporting cotton, tobacco, and sugar to Europe. Settlers increasingly moved to these lands, linked to the motherland by economics, politics, and culture, a nascent transnational class pursuing individual economic interests.

Writing during this time was the eighteenth-century British economist Adam Smith. As we noted in Chapter 2, Smith began with the notion that human beings act in rational ways to maximize their self-interest. When individuals act rationally, markets develop to produce, distribute, and consume goods. These markets enable individuals to carry out the necessary transactions to improve their own welfare. When there are many buyers and sellers, market competition ensures that prices will be as low as possible. Low prices result in increased consumer welfare. Thus, in maximizing economic welfare and stimulating individual (and therefore collective) economic growth, markets epitomize economic efficiency. Those markets need to be virtually free from government interference; only through a free flow of commerce will efficient alloca-tion of resources occur. That is the rationale underpinnning the theory of economic liberalism.

Yet the policies of many European governments at the time reflected an alternative view, **mercantilism** (or **economic realism**). The goal of a mercantilist government was to build economic wealth as an instrument of state power. Drawing on the views of the Frenchman Jean-Baptiste Colbert (1619–83), an adviser to Louis XIV, the mercantilist view held that states needed to accumulate gold and silver to guarantee power. A strong central government was needed for efficient tax collection and maximization of exports, all geared toward guaranteeing military prowess. Such governments encouraged exports over imports and industrialization over agriculture, protected domestic production against competition from imports, and intervened in trade to promote employment. The United States' first secretary of the treasury, Alexander Hamilton (1757–1804), advocated policies to protect the growth of the new nation's manufactuers. In his "Report on Manufactures" to Congress in 1791, he supported protectionist policies and investment in inventions. Mercantilist policies included high tariffs and discour-aged foreign investment in the name of achieving national self-sufficiency.

From the beginning of the nineteenth century through World War I, the expansion of colonialism and the Industrial Revolution occurred as the result of major techno-logical improvements in transoceanic communications, transportation, and manufac-turing processes. The European states needed the raw materials found in the colonies, so international trade expanded, as did international investment; capital moved from Europe to the Americas in search of higher profits. Often those economic links were followed by political and cultural domination. Britain, in particular, was the center of the Industrial Revolution, the major trading state and source of international capital, as well as political and cultural hegemony, contested only by France. Britain facilitated

THEORY IN BRIEF / THE MERCANTILIST PERSPECTIVE ON THE INTERNATIONAL POLITICAL ECONOMY

VIEW OF HUMAN NATURE	Humans are aggressive; conflictual tendencies
RELATIONSHIP AMONG INDIVIDUALS, SOCIETY, STATE, MARKET	Goal is to increase state power, achieved by regulating economic life; economics is subordinate to state interests
RELATIONSHIP BETWEEN DOMESTIC AND INTERNATIONAL SOCIETY	International economy is conflictual; insecurity of anarchy breeds competition; state defends itself

trade by lowering its own tariffs and opening its markets; it policed the sea to provide safer transit; it encouraged investment abroad. It is no wonder that this period has been labeled the "Pax Britannica," when the hegemonic power of Great Britain, under the guise of economic liberalism, expanded so that "the sun never set on the British empire." Indeed, in the view of **hegemonic stability theorists**, a hegemon is needed to provide services in such an open liberalized economy, services that no other state can provide. Such collective goods (security, capital, common currency) facilitate the working of the international economic system and benefit the hegemon at the same time.[2]

The excesses of that period gave rise to another economic perspective, radicalism, drawing on the body of Marxist and neo-Marxist writings. Having seen the harsh living conditions of the working class during nineteenth-century industrialization and imperialist expansion, and cognizant of the economic chasm between the developed and the developing worlds during the twentieth century, radicals blame the capitalist system under liberalism. Although the interpretations vary, the core beliefs found in Marxist and neo-Marxist writings is that society is basically conflictual. Conflict emerges from the competition among groups of individuals—namely, the owners of wealth and the workers—for scarce resources. The state tends to support the owners of the means of production. Finally, the owners of capital are determined to expand and accumulate resources at the expense of the working class and those in the developing world. As Marx himself argued, it is the constant expansion of capitalist markets that leads to crises; dangerous speculation by those holders of capital only exacerbates these crises.

The most recent phase of the internationalization of the economy began at the end of World War II. This phase was a direct response to the interwar period, when the worldwide depression of the 1930s saw a major decline in trade and investment, made worse by "beggar thy neighbor" policies, when states seeking to protect themselves from the effects of the economic crisis hurt others. Thus, at the end of the war, the goal was to promote openness of trade and stimulate international capital flows while establishing a stable exchange rate system. Multinational corporations (MNCs) would play a major role in stimulating growth, benefiting from innovations in transportation and communication. And in later years, the communications revolution would expand the possibilities for international financial transactions, as well as, in the words of Friedman, flattening the playing field for individuals in ways never anticipated.[3] That is the underpinning of economic globalization.

How can we study these developments? Most international political economists have adopted a rational choice perspective. That perspective is based on the assumption that individuals are rational actors; participants in economic life have preferences that are fixed and known. The study of international political economy, then, is the study of how states make strategic choices that best promote their interests. It is grounded in liberal economic theory, as introduced in Chapter 3. Contesting the rational choice perspective are social constructivists, who acknowledge that policies are affected by

THEORY IN BRIEF / THE RADICAL/MARXIST PERSPECTIVE ON THE INTERNATIONAL POLITICAL ECONOMY

VIEW OF HUMAN NATURE	Naturally cooperative as individuals; conflictual in groups
RELATIONSHIP AMONG INDIVIDUALS, SOCIETY, STATE, MARKET	Competition among groups, particularly between owners of wealth and laborers; conflictual and exploitative
RELATIONSHIP BETWEEN DOMESTIC AND INTERNATIONAL SOCIETY	Conflictual relationships because of inherent expansion of capitalism; seeks radical change in international economic system

historical and societal factors. Neither individual nor state preferences are assumed. Rather, there is a contestation over beliefs and ideologies.

This chapter introduces liberal economic theory and the role that multinational corporations and international institutions play in the international economy. We then turn to an explanation of how the international economy functions in this globalized era in terms of major issues of international finance, trade, and development, and the emergence of economic regionalization. Finally, we examine the challenges to economic globalization both in the past and in light of the contemporary global economic crises.

The Basis of the Contemporary International Economy

Key Concepts in Liberal Economic Theory

Liberal economics is based on the recognition that states differ in their resource endowments of land, labor, and capital. Under these conditions, worldwide wealth is maximized if states engage in international trade. The British economist David Ricardo (1772–1823) developed a theory that states should engage in international trade according to their **comparative advantage**. That is, states should produce and export those products that they can produce most efficiently relative to other states. Because each state differs in its ability to produce specific products—because of differences in natural-resource bases, labor force characteristics, and land values—each state should produce and export that which it can produce relatively most efficiently and import goods that other states can produce more efficiently. Thus, gains from trade are maximized for states. However, individual actors can be hurt in this process, necessitating government intervention to ensure that all people gain.

Consider the production of cars and trucks in the United States and Canada. The United States can produce both cars and trucks using fewer workers than Canada, making production less expensive in the United States. Under the principle of *absolute* advantage, the United States would manufacture both cars and trucks and export both to Canada. However, under *comparative* advantage, each country should specialize; the United States should produce the car, for which it has a relative advantage in production, and Canada, the truck. By trading cars for trucks, each country gains by specialization. Each state minimizes its opportunity cost. Each gives up something to get something else. The United States gives up the production of trucks for more car production; Canada gives up the production of cars in favor of more truck production. Each gains by shifting resources to manufacturing more of the commodity it produces more efficiently and by trading for the other commodity. Both countries can consume more than if they remained in isolation, consuming only what they produced domestically. Liberal economics posits that under comparative advantage, production is oriented toward an international market. Efficiency in production is increased, and worldwide wealth is maximized.

In liberal economic thinking, national currencies, like goods and services, should be bought and sold in a free market system. In such a system of *floating exchange rates*, the market — individuals and governments buying and selling currencies — determines the actual value of one currency compared with other currencies. Just as for a tangible good, there is a supply and demand for each national currency, and the prices of each currency adjust continually in response to market supply and demand. According to liberal thinking, floating exchange rates will result in market equilibrium, in which supply equals demand.

THEORY IN BRIEF   ECONOMIC LIBERALISM

VIEW OF HUMAN NATURE	Individuals act in rational ways to maximize their self-interest
RELATIONSHIP AMONG INDIVIDUALS, SOCIETY, STATE, MARKET	When individuals act rationally, markets are created to produce, distribute, and consume goods; markets function best when free of government interference
RELATIONSHIP BETWEEN DOMESTIC AND INTERNATIONAL SOCIETY	International wealth is maximized with free exchange of goods and services; on the basis of comparative advantage, international economy gains

The Role of Multinational Corporations

Multinational corporations play a key role as engines of economic growth. To many economic liberals, MNCs are the vanguard of the liberal order. They are the "embodiment par excellence of the liberal ideal of an interdependent world economy. [They have] taken the integration of national economies beyond trade and money to the internationalization of production. For the first time in history, production, marketing, and investment are being organized on a global scale rather than in terms of isolated national economies."[4] To liberals, MNCs are a positive development: economic improvement is made through the most efficient mechanism. MNCs invest in capital stock worldwide, they move money to the most efficient markets, and they finance projects that industrialize and improve agricultural output. MNCs are the transmission belt for capital, ideas, and economic growth. In the liberal idea, MNCs prefer to act independently of states; the market itself will regulate their behavior. Any abuses of the market by MNCs can be best corrected by other market actors or at worse by government regulation.

According to the principle of comparative advantage, labor-intensive production will move to countries where labor is cheap, while capital-intensive production (such as research and development in technology or pharmaceuticals) will move to countries with abundant capital. China's large population makes it attractive to labor-intensive manufacturers like Nike, although that may be changing as Chinese wages increase.

THEORY IN BRIEF   CONTENDING PERSPECTIVES ON THE INTERNATIONAL POLITICAL ECONOMY

	MERCANTILISM/ ECONOMIC REALISM	ECONOMIC LIBERALISM	RADICALISM / MARXISM
VIEW OF HUMAN NATURE	Humans are aggressive; conflictual tendencies	Individuals act in rational ways to maximize their self-interest	Naturally cooperative as individuals; conflictual in groups
RELATIONSHIP AMONG INDIVIDUALS, SOCIETY, STATE, MARKET	Goal is to increase state power, achieved by regulating economic life; economics is subordinate to state interests	When individuals act rationally, markets are created to produce, distribute, and consume goods; markets function best when free of government interference	Competition occurs among groups, particularly between owners of wealth and laborers; group relations are conflictual and exploitative
RELATIONSHIP BETWEEN DOMESTIC AND INTERNATIONAL SOCIETY	International economy is conflictual; insecurity of anarchy breeds competition; state defends itself	International wealth is maximized with free exchange of goods and services; on the basis of comparative advantage, international economy gains	Conflictual relationships because of inherent expansion of capitalism; seeks radical change in international economic system

MNCs take many different forms and engage in many different activities:

- Importing and exporting goods and services
- Making significant investments in a foreign country
- Buying and selling licenses in foreign markets
- Engaging in contract manufacturing—permitting a local manufacturer in a foreign country to produce their products
- Opening manufacturing facilities or assembly operations in foreign countries

Whatever the specific form that their business takes, MNCs choose to participate in international markets for a variety of reasons. They seek to avoid tariff and import barriers, as many U.S. firms did in the 1960s when they established manufacturing facilities in Europe to circumvent the external barriers of the newly established European Economic Community. They may seek to reduce transportation costs by moving facilities closer to consumer markets. Some MNCs are able to obtain incentives such as tax advantages or labor concessions from host governments; these incentives can cut production costs and increase profitability. Others go abroad in order to meet the competition and the customers, capitalize on cheaper labor markets (e.g., Chinese firms moving production to Vietnam or Laos), or obtain the services of foreign technical personnel (e.g., computer firms in India). Note that these reasons are based in economics, but rationales based on the political policies of the host state may also play a role. MNCs may move abroad to circumvent tough governmental regulations at home, such as banking rules, currency restrictions, or environmental regulations. In the process, MNCs become not only economic organizations but also political ones, potentially influencing the policies of both home and host governments.

Some liberal economists go further than extolling the economic benefits of liberalism or the virtues of MNCs. They see a positive relationship between the international liberal economy and peace. We saw one aspect of this view in our discussion of the democratic peace in Chapter 5. Norman Angell, recipient of the 1933 Nobel Peace Prize, argued in favor of stimulating free trade among liberal capitalist states, in the belief that enhanced trade would be in the economic self-interest of all states. But more than that, Angell argued that national differences would vanish with the formation of an international market. Interdependence would lead to economic well-being and eventually to world peace; war would become an anachronism.[5] Although not all liberals agree with this formulation, economic liberalism does suggest specific economic policies (open markets, free trade, free flow of goods and services). Liberals also posit that government's role should be as limited as possible, merely protecting property rights and providing a functioning legal system. Under this formulation, liberals view international competition as healthy and desirable, with the potential to lead to more peaceful interactions.

The Role of International Economic Institutions

At the end of World War II, policy makers established a set of intergovernmental organizations to support economic liberalism. The so-called Bretton Woods institutions—the World Bank, the International Monetary Fund (IMF), and to a lesser extent the General Agreement on Tariffs and Trade (GATT), now the World Trade Organization (WTO)—have all played and continue to play key roles in the expansion of economic liberalism (see Figure 9.1).

The **World Bank** was designed initially to facilitate reconstruction in post–World War II Europe, hence its formal name: the International Bank for Reconstruction and Development. During the 1950s, the World Bank shifted its primary emphasis from reconstruction to development. It generates capital funds from member-state contributions and from borrowing in international financial markets. Like that of all banks, its purpose is to loan these funds, with interest, and in the case of the World Bank, to loan them to states for their economic development projects. Its lending is designed not to replace private capital but to facilitate the use of private capital. While a high proportion of the World Bank's funding has been used for infrastructure projects, including hydroelectric dams, basic transportation needs such as bridges and highways, and agribusiness ventures, the Bank funds governments and the private sector to carry out a wide array of economic development activities.

The **International Monetary Fund (IMF)** was designed to promote monetary cooperation and to provide stability in exchange rates. Originally, the fund established a system of fixed exchange rates and, with the United States, guaranteed currency convertibility. From the 1940s to the 1970s, the United States guaranteed the stability of this system by fixing the value of the dollar against gold at $35 an ounce. In 1972, however, this system collapsed when the United States announced that it would no longer guarantee a system of fixed exchange rates. This decision was revised in 1976 when the International Monetary Fund formalized the system of floating exchange rates, a policy more consistent with economic liberalism. At that time, monetary cooperation became the responsibility of the **Group of 7 (G7)**, composed of the United States, Japan, Germany, Great Britain, France, Italy, and Canada. The IMF was to provide short-term loans for member states confronted by temporary balance-of-payments difficulties. But as discussed later, the IMF has expanded its functions to include policy advice on macroeconomic issues and economic restructuring.

The third part of the liberal economic order was the **General Agreement on Tariffs and Trade (GATT)**. This treaty enshrined important liberal principles:

- Support of trade liberalization, because trade is the engine for growth and economic development
- Nondiscrimination in trade—the **most-favored-nation (MFN) principle**—whereby states agree to give the same treatment to all other GATT members as they give to their best (most-favored) trading partner
- Preferential access in developed markets to products from the South in order to stimulate economic development in the South
- Support for "national treatment" of foreign enterprises—that is, treating them as domestic firms

GATT established these trade principles as well as procedures for moving toward free trade. Multilateral negotiations among those countries sharing major interests in the issue (major producers and consumers of a product, for example) were hammered out and then expanded to all GATT participants. Individual states could claim exemptions (called *safeguards*) to accommodate any domestic or balance-of-payments difficulties that might occur because of the resulting trade agreements. A weak dispute resolution process was developed. Backed by U.S. hegemonic leadership, the Bretton Woods system led to postwar recovery and economic prosperity.

FIGURE 9.1

THE INTERNATIONAL ECONOMIC INSTITUTIONS

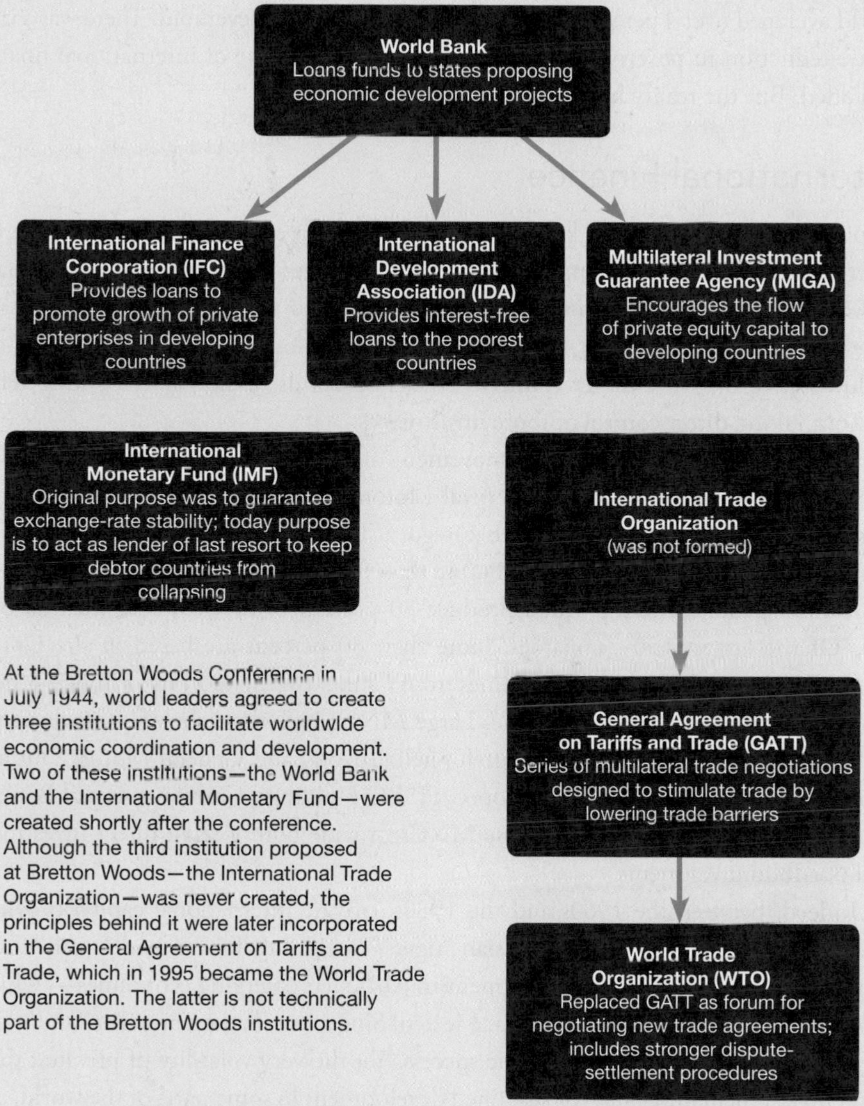

World Bank
Loans funds to states proposing economic development projects

International Finance Corporation (IFC)
Provides loans to promote growth of private enterprises in developing countries

International Development Association (IDA)
Provides interest-free loans to the poorest countries

Multilateral Investment Guarantee Agency (MIGA)
Encourages the flow of private equity capital to developing countries

International Monetary Fund (IMF)
Original purpose was to guarantee exchange-rate stability; today purpose is to act as lender of last resort to keep debtor countries from collapsing

International Trade Organization
(was not formed)

At the Bretton Woods Conference in July 1944, world leaders agreed to create three institutions to facilitate worldwide economic coordination and development. Two of these institutions—the World Bank and the International Monetary Fund—were created shortly after the conference. Although the third institution proposed at Bretton Woods—the International Trade Organization—was never created, the principles behind it were later incorporated in the General Agreement on Tariffs and Trade, which in 1995 became the World Trade Organization. The latter is not technically part of the Bretton Woods institutions.

General Agreement on Tariffs and Trade (GATT)
Series of multilateral trade negotiations designed to stimulate trade by lowering trade barriers

World Trade Organization (WTO)
Replaced GATT as forum for negotiating new trade agreements; includes stronger dispute-settlement procedures

How the Globalized Economy Works Today

For 20 years after the end of World War II, economic growth occurred much as liberal economic theory predicted. Growth rates in the developed and the developing world averaged over 4 percent. Trade volume increased over sevenfold. There was a dramatic reduction in poverty rates worldwide. And the volume of international finance exploded. But the reality has not always followed the theory.

International Finance

Capital movements played a key role in the earlier phases of the development of the international political economy, as they do today. International capital traditionally moves in two ways: **direct foreign investment** includes the building of factories and investing in the facilities for extraction of natural resources. **Portfolio investment** includes investing in another country's stocks or bonds, either short or long term, without taking direct control of those investments.

MNCs play a major role in the movement of capital. Before World War II, most MNCs were in manufacturing—General Motors, Ford, Siemens, Nestlé, and Bayer were among the many MNCs in this category. Today, there are over 80,000 MNCs (depending on one's definition), with more than 800,000 subsidiaries, employing over 90 million people. The top 1,000 produce 80 percent of the world's industrial output. Of the largest 100 companies, more than 80 percent are based in the United States, Europe, or Japan, with companies from China, Brazil, and India, among others, growing rapidly over the past decade. Large MNCs include such well-known names as Walmart, Exxon Mobil, Royal Dutch Shell, Toyota, and General Motors, but also less well-known companies, like Sinopec, HSBC Holdings, Carrefour, Royal Bank of Scotland, Gazprom, and Tesco. Those MNCs provide both foreign direct investment and portfolio investments.

Indeed, between the 1960s and the 1980s, private international capital provided essential lending to the successful Asian "tigers," including Taiwan and South Korea. In fact, the infusion of private investment in particular emerging economies—China, Brazil, Argentina, Chile, South Korea, Mexico, Singapore, Turkey, and Thailand—has played a major role in their economic success. Yet the very volatility of private capital flows makes them unreliable for sustained development in some parts of the world, and private capital alone cannot explain economic outcomes in these countries.

Some states have more difficulty attracting private investment than others. African countries typically have received the least. In 2010, total foreign direct investment to the continent topped more than $55 billion, five times more than 10 years earlier, but three-quarters of it went to just ten countries. Separate institutions within the World Bank were established to provide capital to states that were unable to attract private investment alone. The International Finance Corporation (IFC) and the International Development Association (IDA) were created in 1956 and 1960, respectively, for that purpose. The IFC provides loans to promote the growth of private enterprises in developing countries. The IDA provides capital to the poorest countries, usually in the form of interest-free loans. Repayment schedules of 50 years theoretically allow the developing countries time to reach economic takeoff and sustain growth. Funds for the IDA need to be continually replenished by major donor countries. In 1988, the Multilateral Investment Guarantee Agency (MIGA) was added to the World Bank group. This agency meets its goal—augmenting the flow of private equity capital to developing countries—by insuring investments against losses. Such losses may result from expropriation, government currency restrictions, or civil war or ethnic conflict. Even with these changes, since the mid-1980s, the flows from both multilateral institutions (the World Bank institutions, regional development banks) and official bilateral donors (the United States, Germany, Japan) have declined as a percentage of total capital flows, whereas private capital flows from MNCs and other private sources have expanded, although during the international financial crisis that began in 2008 the direction was reversed.

Beginning in the 1980s, international financial flows accelerated through several other mechanisms. Exchange rates were no longer fixed, so traders in currency exchange markets and in MNCs could capitalize on buying and selling currencies, often in very short periods of time, facilitated by increasing technological sophistication of communications. By the beginning of the new millennium, such currency transactions averaged over $3 trillion a day. Markets developed new financial instruments, such as **derivatives** (options against the future in a variety of asset classes, including loans and mortgages). These instruments were packaged and sold around the world, spreading risk and accelerating the flow of capital. New economic actors, **sovereign wealth funds**, which are state-owned investment funds composed of financial assets, including stocks, bonds, precious metal, property, or other financial instruments, formed in capital-surplus countries such as China and in the major petroleum exporters such as Kuwait, the United Arab Emirates, Norway, Russia, and Canada. Those wealth funds have been able to move capital quickly across national boundaries, taking advantage of currency differentials and buying and selling new financial instruments in order to maximize long-term economic return for what many recognize may be a declining resource. Finally, economic liberalization has led to the emergence of **offshore financial centers**, such as the Cayman Islands, Bermuda, and the British Virgin Islands. These jurisdictions have low taxation and little or no regulation. Individuals, companies, and states can move capital in and out rapidly via electronic transfers, making millions of transfers daily.

The Asian financial crisis of the 1990s illustrates the possible outcomes of the globalization of finance. Beginning in Thailand in 1997, in a relatively short period of time, 2 percent of gross domestic product fled that country. Within weeks, the crisis spread to Indonesia, Malaysia, the Philippines, and beyond. Many countries were unable to adjust to the rapid withdrawal of capital. Exchange rates plummeted to 50 percent of pre-crisis values, stock markets fell 80 percent, and real GDP dropped 4 to 8 percent. Individuals lost their jobs as companies went bankrupt or were forced to restructure. Millions of people were forced into poverty. In Southeast Asian countries such as South Korea and Taiwan, and spreading to Brazil and Russia, economies that had previously depended on external trade experienced an unparalleled sense of economic vulnerability. Fueled by instantaneous communication, global financial markets capable of moving $1.3 trillion daily, and the power of MNCs, traders, and financial entrepreneurs, economic globalization quickly displayed its pitfalls. The largely unregulated market had melted down, and states and individuals appeared helpless.

The IMF responded to the social and political upheaval with large, controversial bailout packages to three of the affected countries (Thailand, $17 billion; Indonesia, $36 billion; and South Korea, $58 billion); lengthy sets of conditions that each country was supposed to follow; and monitoring devices to ensure compliance. Extensive structural reforms would transform their economies from semimercantilist to more market-oriented ones. In South Korea, for example, the government lifted restrictions on capital movements and foreign ownership, permitted companies to lay off workers, and adopted measures to restructure the country's financial institutions. Budget cuts eliminated more social services and pushed more families below the poverty line, leading to a backlash against governments and the IMF. Solutions implemented by the international financial institutions in one country proved counterproductive in others and marginalized groups suffered. Dissatisfaction with IMF policies led many in developing countries to conclude that these institutions were captive to the interests of the developed world.

Yet following two years of economic stress and the wounded credibility of the IMF, none of the countries involved retreated from globalization or the international financial markets, and all resumed a path of strong economic growth. Critics of the IMF response focus on the so-called **moral hazard** problem: states were rescued from the consequences of their reckless behavior, providing little incentive for them to change that behavior. We will examine the international economic crises beginning in 2008 and see similar kinds of responses: the contraction of some key economies, the spillover of economic hardship around the world because of globalization, the reaction of governments and international institutions, and reminders of the moral hazard dilemma.

International Trade

Economic growth, according to economic liberal thinking, is fueled by financial flows and trade flows, ideally in an international free trade system. Yet just as happened between the world wars, while governments strive for growth through international trade, they also have other policy objectives: protection of home industries from competition to maintain domestic employment and preservation of key domestic sectors for national security reasons, among others.

The negotiating parties in GATT sought to expand international trade by lowering trade barriers. That work was carried out over the course of eight negotiating rounds, with each round progressively cutting tariffs, giving better treatment to the developing countries, and addressing new problems (subsidies and countervailing duties). For example, in the Kennedy Round between 1963 and 1967, tariff cuts averaged 35 percent on $40 billion of trade among 62 countries. In the following Tokyo Round (1973–79), 102 states negotiated tariff cuts, again amounting to more than 35 percent on $100 billion of trade. In addition, more favorable arrangements were negotiated for developing countries. Overall, between 1946 and the mid-1990s, tariffs were reduced in the major trading countries from an average of 40 percent to 5 percent on imported goods.

The final round, called the Uruguay Round, began in 1986. The Uruguay Round covered new items such as services (insurance), intellectual property rights (copyrights, patents, trademarks), and for the first time, agriculture. Previously, agriculture was seen as too contentious an issue, complicated by both U.S. agricultural subsidies and the European Union's protectionist Common Agricultural Policy (CAP). Agreement was reached to begin to phase out agricultural subsidies. In late 1994, the most comprehensive trade agreement in history was finally reached, a 400-page document covering everything from paper clips to computer chips. Tariffs on manufactured goods were cut by an average of 37 percent among members. The developing countries that participated in these tariff cuts—the liberalizers—enjoyed a full percentage point per year boost in growth compared with the nonliberalizers.[6]

In 1995, GATT became a formal institution, renaming itself the **World Trade Organization (WTO)**. The WTO incorporated the general areas of GATT's jurisdiction, as well as expanded jurisdiction in services and intellectual property. Regular ministerial meetings give the WTO a political prominence that GATT lacked. Representing states that conduct over 90 percent of the world's trade, the WTO has the task of implementing the Uruguay Round, serving as a forum for trade negotiations, and providing a venue for trade review, dispute settlement, and enforcement.

Two important procedures were initiated in the WTO. First is the Trade Policy Review Mechanism (TPRM), which conducts periodic surveillance of the trade practices of member states. Under this procedure, there is a forum where states can question each other about trade practices. Second is the Dispute Settlement Body, designed as an authoritative panel to hear and settle trade disputes. With the authority to impose sanctions against violators, this body is more powerful than earlier GATT arrangements.

Getting global participation in the WTO has proved a painstaking task. China's accession to the WTO in 2001, after 15 years of negotiations, illustrates the long process and significant concessions made. China revised its laws to permit foreign ventures in previously restricted areas, leading to a significant inflow of foreign investment in telecommunications, tourism, insurance, and banking. China continues to dismantle barriers to trade, relaxing tariffs and quotas on 7,000 products, giving it lower tariffs than either Brazil or India. WTO rules have required domestic legislation and clarification, and special courts hear WTO-related disputes. China is now proactive, initiating cases and complying when it loses. China still lags on intellectual property rights issues, long a source of contention. Vietnam, which joined the WTO in 2007, is undergoing some of the same reforms. In 2012, Russia joined as well, following 18 years of contentious negotiations largely over industrial subsidies. In each case, disentangling the government from the economy has proven to be a difficult task.

The WTO process remains contentious, as illustrated by the Doha Round launched in 2001. Seven years later, the negotiations ended in stalemate, pitting the U.S. and the EU on one hand and emerging economies, such as India, Brazil, and China, on the other. The main sticking point has been the liberalization of agricultural markets. Neither the United States nor the EU was willing to reduce farm subsidies significantly, which would have made agricultural products from developing countries more competitive in international markets. India and China, in particular, sought if not an end to farm subsidies, then special safeguard mechanisms for their own poor farmers to ensure food security. More generally, the Doha Round failed over the perception of fairness in trade. Already dissatisfied with new rules that opened competition in investment and government procurement, the developing countries sought more advantages in the politically sensitive areas of agriculture and other labor-intensive sectors. The 2009 economic slowdown made protection of domestic markets economically and politically advantageous and multilateral agreement more difficult to achieve. Will developed countries such as the United States and the members of the EU, traditionally strong supporters of the WTO, continue to support the organization? What will be the impact of Doha's failure on trade and on the development agenda? Negotiations continue; optimists claim small concessions have been made, but significant differences among the parties remain.

International Development

The Doha Round of trade negotiations had been labeled a "development round," but as one commentator noted, the round "has not filled any bellies."[7] The most developed countries, largely in the North, average $33,352 gross national income (GNI) per capita and still bask in relative wealth, with high consumption habits, high levels of education and health services, and social welfare nets. In contrast, the least developed countries, mainly in the South, still struggle to meet basic caloric needs, with poor educational and health services and no welfare nets to meet the needs of the poorest of the poor, averaging only $1,585 GNI per capita. The Human Development Index

TABLE 9.1	HUMAN DEVELOPMENT INDEX, 2011				
	LIFE EXPECTANCY AT BIRTH (YEARS)	MEAN YEARS OF SCHOOLING (YEARS)	EXPECTED YEARS OF SCHOOLING (YEARS)	GROSS NATIONAL INCOME PER CAPITA (CONSTANT 2005 PPP\$)[a]	HUMAN DEVELOPMENT INDEX VALUE[b]
Arab States	70.5	5.9	10.2	8,544	0.641
East Asia and the Pacific	72.4	7.2	11.7	6,466	0.671
Europe and Central Asia	71.3	9.7	13.4	12,004	0.751
Latin America and the Carribean	74.4	7.8	13.6	10,119	0.731
South Asia	65.9	4.6	9.8	3,435	0.548
Sub-Saharan Africa	54.4	4.5	9.2	1,966	0.463
World	69.8	7.4	11.3	10,082	0.682

[a] PPP is purchasing power parity. It is a way to compare levels of economic data cross-nationally, free of price and exchange-data distortions.

[b] The HDI combines indicators for life expectancy, educational attainment, and income into a composite value, ranging between 0 (low development) and 1 (high development).

Source: United Nations Human Development Report, 2011.

(HDI) in Table 9.1 shows these stark contrasts across several indicators. Caused by many factors—colonialism, earlier industrialization of Europe, geography, poor government policies, unaccountable governments—this is the development gap, or for the poorest, the development trap.[8] In actuality, the world has become more differentiated since the 1990s. As exemplified during the Doha Round, the G7 major economic powers are faced by both the Group of 20 collective of emerging powers and **BRICS** (Brazil, Russia, India, China, and South Africa), an informal group of emerging economic powers.

Proponents of economic liberalism point to success in closing the development gap. Beginning in the 1990s, growth in emerging markets increased, followed after 2000 with an acceleration in the developing world. Average per capita incomes in both emerging markets and developing economies in general have grown at a faster rate than in the developed economies. In particular, China's GDP has grown at an average rate of 9.5 percent a year and its GDP trebled to $11 trillion over the past decade. However, detractors of economic liberalism, including many radicals and some working within the UN development community, point to a different set of indicators. They contend that the gap between rich and poor is actually increasing. All agree that the gap between rich and poor needs to be narrowed by supporting economic growth and development.

In liberal economic theory, trade liberalization based on comparative advantage is viewed as a key engine of economic growth. Less clear is whether economic growth at the aggregate level will lead to economic improvement in the lives of individuals. Ideas about how development occurs have evolved from the work of state policy makers, officials within the UN system, and analysts within such institutions as the World Bank. In the constructivist perspective, there has been a conflict over different economic ideas and development norms.

Although the World Bank has remained largely committed to liberal economic policy, there has been some debate over the appropriate approach.[9] During the 1950s and 1960s, the Bank, like other development institutions and major donors such as the United States, adopted a strategy for development that emphasized the critical role of large infrastructure projects such as dams, electric power, and telecommunications. In the 1970s, realizing that not all groups were benefiting from such investments, the Bank began to fund projects in health, education, and housing, designed to improve the economic life of the poor. During the 1980s, the Bank shifted toward reliance on private-sector participation to meet the task of restructuring economies and reconstructing states torn apart by ethnic conflict. In the 1990s, **sustainable development**, an approach to economic development that incorporates concern for renewable resources and the environment, became part of the Bank's rhetoric, although that rhetoric did not always translate into its practices.

Of these various changes, the Bank's support of private-sector participation in reconstruction and development has been the most profound. When areas of the economy are privatized, the government's fiscal burden is reduced, and state spending in education and health can then increase. This approach to economic growth has become known as the **Washington Consensus**, a version of liberal economic ideology. Its adherents hold that only with certain economic policies—including privatization, liberalization of trade and foreign direct investment, government deregulation in favor of open competition, and broad tax reform—will development occur. The Bank and its sister institution, the International Monetary Fund, have been the leaders in advocating these policies.

Although the IMF was not originally charged with development, very quickly it realized that many countries' seemingly temporary balance-of-payments problems were actually long-term structural problems that prevented those countries from developing and which the IMF's short-term loans could not address. Thus, during the early 1980s, the IMF began to provide longer-term loans if states adopted **structural adjustment programs** consistent with the Washington Consensus. If a state adopted those policies — economic reforms (limiting money and credit growth, forcing currency devaluation, reforming the financial sector, introducing user fees, eliminating subsidies), trade liberalization reforms (removing tariffs, rehabilitating export infrastructure), government reforms (privatizing public enterprises), and private-sector policies (ending government monopolies) — then the IMF gave its stamp of approval, leading other multilateral lenders as well as bilateral and international private banks to lend as well.

DEVELOPMENT STRATEGIES IN THE TWENTY-FIRST CENTURY   During the 1990s, it became apparent that even under structural adjustment some countries could not get out from under the weight of their debt and begin to develop. That debt had been escalating; developing countries owed $2.2 trillion in 2000; 20 years earlier it had been $577 billion. There was also mounting pressure for adopting a more systematic approach to debt. Buoyed by Jubilee 2000, a social movement that promoted changes in the name of social justice and supported by radicals who thought debt doomed states to permanent underdevelopment, a major policy shift occurred, sponsored by the IMF, the World Bank, and the G7 economic powers. The Heavily Indebted Poor Countries (HIPC) Initiative was a historic one, for never before had foreign national debt been canceled or substantially rescheduled. While implementation of the plan and its attendant conditions has been slow and controversial, by 2012, 33 countries have received debt relief.

Uganda is one beneficiary, working with both local and international NGOs to develop debt-reduction strategies. A Poverty Eradication Action Plan beginning in the 1990s made major poverty issues top priorities. Resources for school construction, feeder roads, and water systems were developed by local communities during the consultative process. Debt relief proved to be part of the answer for some countries as a way to direct scarce resources for development purposes.

The demise of the Soviet Union, and with it the transition to capitalism in Russia and other former communist states, gave the IMF another role to play. The IMF gave $27 billion in assistance to help Russia and the other former communist countries make the transition to market economies. The goal was to make that adjustment an orderly one. IMF credits have helped to replenish state reserves, keeping those countries out of major debt. The results have been mixed, with the most advanced economies able to achieve success, liberalizing foreign trade and keeping inflation down.

Like the World Bank, the IMF has, too, shifted its strategies. Beginning in 2009, the IMF discontinued structural performance criteria for loans, even for loans to low-income countries, in response to both its critics and the 2008 global financial crisis.

This represents a substantial overhaul of the IMF lending framework. The amount of the loans can be greater and loans are to be tailored according to the respective state's needs, a direct response to the criticism of "cookie-cutter" approach of structural adjustment lending. Monitoring of the loans will be done more quietly to reduce the stigma attached to conditionality. Also in response to previous criticism, the IMF has urged lending to programs that encourage social safety nets for the most vulnerable within the populations. Ideas that were previously unacceptable to the IMF — that capital flows may need regulation and that states might take a proactive role in coordinating economic development — became more acceptable in response to the market failures of the global financial crisis.[10]

A broad consensus has emerged among virtually all states on the utility of market-oriented economic policies and political pluralism as the foundation for sustainable economic development. Scarce natural resources cannot be exploited as in the past; sustainability means that growth can be ensured for future generations. There must be more emphasis on human development, particularly education and health. The targets of development — the people — should have a say in how funds are allocated.

NGOs play a critical role in this new approach, organized at the grassroots level to carry out locally based projects. NGOs such as World Catholic Relief, Oxfam, and Doctors Without Borders not only deliver food and medical assistance during emergencies but also distribute seeds, drill wells, and plan local-level projects that they hope will bring economic development. NGOs can also be an alternative channel for finance to individuals and small groups, often neglected by the national or international banks. One well-publicized effort, now duplicated many times over, has been microfinance. Bangladesh's Grameen Bank in Bangladesh, created in 1983 by an academic turned banker, Muhammad Yunus (who won the Nobel Peace Prize in 2006), provides small amounts of funding for individuals and groups to invest in an economically productive enterprise. Its more than 2000 branches have made loans to more than 7.5 million borrowers, governments, and private banks. The purpose is to empower women, who are typically ignored by multilateral institutions, by providing them with income.

Microfinance institutions have grown exponentially, becoming bigger, more competitive, and more diverse. Some are not-for-profit, such as the Grameen Bank, while others are for-profit institutions; some offer just credit, while increasingly, others offer a variety of saving alternatives. But do microfinance institutions lift individuals out of poverty? Do they foster economic development and growth more generally? The Grameen Bank reports that they have moved over one-half of their borrowers above the poverty line, and enjoyed a loan recovery rate of 97 percent! In Grameen families, more children attend school, nutrition levels are higher, and child mortality is lower.[11]

Recent studies refute the anecdotal evidence, however. Two authoritative studies on microfinance find no overall impact on the borrower's household welfare after

18 months, measured by income, spending, or school attendance. However, when the borrower already owned a small business, then the new credit infusion improved income and spending. In other words, microcredit helps those who are already better off.[12]

Are the benefits of the many forms of economic globalization being distributed across the continents? Are the goals of sustainable development being met? The UN has undertaken the tasks of goal setting and monitoring. In 2001, the UN-sponsored Millennium Summit set forth eight goals known as the Millennium Development Goals (MDGs). These goals are designed to reduce poverty by 2015 and promote sustainable human development in direct response to globalization. Each substantive goal (poverty reduction, better education, improved health, environmental sustainability, and global partnerships) has specific targets, time frames, and performance indicators, along with an implementation plan. The goals have clearly raised public awareness and helped to direct aid flows to the poorer countries in targeted sectors like health and education.

Substantial progress toward achieving these goals has been made. Figure 9.2 shows selected targets of the MDGs and the progress made by region. Reporting 2010 data, the 2012 MDG Report announced that three key goals have been met. With respect to poverty trends, both the number of individuals in extreme poverty and poverty rates have fallen in every developing region including sub-Saharan Africa. The share of people living on less than $1.25 a day has dropped to less than half of the figure in 1990, the announced goal. The goal of halving the proportion of individuals without high-quality drinking water has been achieved. And the share of urban dwellers living in slums in the developing world has declined to 33 percent over the last decade. In addition, there is now parity between boys and girls in receiving primary school education.[13] But even with these goals achieved, challenges remain; by 2015, 1 billion people will still be living on less than $1.25 a day and 600 million will still not have access to clean water. And while Africa has made substantial strides, as shown in the Global Perspective feature, much more needs to be done. The critics of economic liberalism have strong arguments.

Critics of International Economic Liberalism

The triumph of economic liberalism in the twenty-first century has not been without its critics. These include both traditional critics of the theory of economic liberalism and critics of particular policies, most notably of the international financial institutions.

As they did in the seventeenth and eighteenth centuries, old-style mercantilists, with their interpretation of economic nationalism, argue that economic policy should be subservient to the state and its interests; for them, politics determines economics. This

FIGURE 9.2 — MILLENNIUM DEVELOPMENT GOALS: 2012 PROGRESS CHART (Selected Indicators)

Goals and Targets	Africa		Asia				Oceania	Latin America & Caribbean	Caucasus & Central Asia
	Northern	Sub-Saharan	Eastern	Southeastern	Southern	Western			

GOAL 1 | Eradicate extreme poverty and hunger

Goals and Targets	Northern	Sub-Saharan	Eastern	Southeastern	Southern	Western	Oceania	Latin America & Caribbean	Caucasus & Central Asia
Reduce extreme poverty by half	low poverty	very high poverty	moderate poverty	high poverty	very high poverty	low poverty	very high poverty	moderate poverty	low poverty
Productive and decent employment	large deficit in decent work	very large deficit in decent work	large deficit in decent work	large deficit in decent work	very large deficit in decent work	large deficit in decent work	very large deficit in decent work	moderate deficit in decent work	moderate deficit in decent work
Reduce hunger by half	low hunger	very high hunger	moderate hunger	moderate hunger	high hunger	moderate hunger	moderate hunger	moderate hunger	moderate hunger

GOAL 2 | Achieve universal primary education

Goals and Targets	Northern	Sub-Saharan	Eastern	Southeastern	Southern	Western	Oceania	Latin America & Caribbean	Caucasus & Central Asia
Universal primary schooling	high enrollment	moderate enrollment	high enrollment	high enrollment	high enrollment	high enrollment	–	high enrollment	high enrollment

GOAL 3 | Promote gender equality and empower women

Goals and Targets	Northern	Sub-Saharan	Eastern	Southeastern	Southern	Western	Oceania	Latin America & Caribbean	Caucasus & Central Asia
Equal girls' enrollment in primary school	close to parity	close to parity	parity	parity	parity	close to parity	close to parity	parity	parity
Women's share of paid employment	low share	medium share	high share	medium share	low share	low share	medium share	high share	high share
Women's equal representation in national parliaments	low represen-tation	moderate represen-tation	moderate represen-tation	low represen-tation	low represen-tation	low represen-tation	very low represen-tation	moderate represen-tation	low represen-tation

GOAL 4 | Reduce child mortality

Goals and Targets	Northern	Sub-Saharan	Eastern	Southeastern	Southern	Western	Oceania	Latin America & Caribbean	Caucasus & Central Asia
Reduce mortality of under-five-year-olds by two-thirds	low mortality	high mortality	low mortality	low mortality	moderate mortality	low mortality	moderate mortality	low mortality	moderate mortality

GOAL 5 | Improve maternal health

Goals and Targets	Northern	Sub-Saharan	Eastern	Southeastern	Southern	Western	Oceania	Latin America & Caribbean	Caucasus & Central Asia
Reduce maternal mortality by three-quarters	low mortality	very high mortality	low mortality	moderate mortality	high mortality	low mortality	high mortality	low mortality	low mortality
Access to reproductive health	moderate access	low access	high access	moderate access	moderate access	moderate access	low access	high access	moderate access

GOAL 6 | Combat HIV/AIDS, malaria, and other diseases

Goals and Targets	Northern	Sub-Saharan	Eastern	Southeastern	Southern	Western	Oceania	Latin America & Caribbean	Caucasus & Central Asia
Halt and begin to reverse the spread of HIV/AIDS	low incidence	high incidence	low incidence	low incidence	low incidence	low incidence	low incidence	low incidence	low incidence
Halt and reverse the spread of tuberculosis	low mortality	high mortality	low mortality	moderate mortality	moderate mortality	low mortality	high mortality	low mortality	moderate mortality

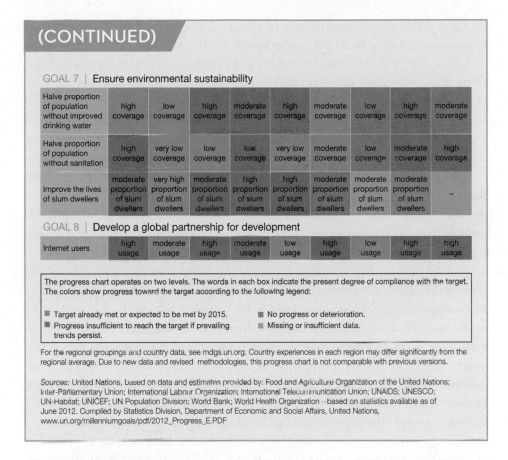

(CONTINUED)

GOAL 7 | Ensure environmental sustainability

Halve proportion of population without improved drinking water	high coverage	low coverage	high coverage	moderate coverage	high coverage	moderate coverage	low coverage	high coverage	moderate coverage
Halve proportion of population without sanitation	high coverage	very low coverage	low coverage	low coverage	very low coverage	moderate coverage	low coverage	moderate coverage	high coverage
Improve the lives of slum dwellers	moderate proportion of slum dwellers	very high proportion of slum dwellers	moderate proportion of slum dwellers	high proportion of slum dwellers	high proportion of slum dwellers	moderate proportion of slum dwellers	moderate proportion of slum dwellers	moderate proportion of slum dwellers	–

GOAL 8 | Develop a global partnership for development

Internet users	high usage	moderate usage	high usage	moderate usage	low usage	high usage	low usage	high usage	high usage

The progress chart operates on two levels. The words in each box indicate the present degree of compliance with the target. The colors show progress toward the target according to the following legend:

■ Target already met or expected to be met by 2015.
■ Progress insufficient to reach the target if prevailing trends persist.

■ No progress or deterioration.
■ Missing or insufficient data.

For the regional groupings and country data, see mdgs.un.org. Country experiences in each region may differ significantly from the regional average. Due to new data and revised methodologies, this progress chart is not comparable with previous versions.

Sources: United Nations, based on data and estimates provided by: Food and Agriculture Organization of the United Nations; Inter-Parliamentary Union; International Labour Organization; International Telecommunication Union; UNAIDS; UNESCO; UN-Habitat; UNICEF; UN Population Division; World Bank; World Health Organization —based on statistics available as of June 2012. Compiled by Statistics Division, Department of Economic and Social Affairs, United Nations, www.un.org/millenniumgoals/pdf/2012_Progress_E.PDF

mercantilist thinking dominated explanations of the economic success of Japan as well as that of the newly industrializing countries of East Asia during the 1960s and 1970s, as discussed earlier. Those states used their power to harness industrial growth. Consistent with mercantilism, they singled out certain industries for special tax advantages; they promoted exports over imports and encouraged education and technological innovations to make their respective economies more competitive internationally. Those governments could then harness MNCs in the state's interest. Setting national economic and political objectives above international economic and political objectives, statists see MNCs as economic actors to be controlled. They suggest imposing national controls on MNCs, including denying market entry to some of them, using the power of taxation to control repatriation of profits, and imposing currency controls. Mercantilists, like realists, believe that the international system is dominated by competition among states for power. States will take any action necessary to survive, protecting their self-interests.

Since 2004, a new interpretation of mercantilism has been labeled the **Beijing Consensus**, pointing to China as a potential model. Although there is no precise definition, the Beijing Consensus suggests a less dogmatic approach to development, emphasizing experimentation with policies that may be appropriate to a state's particular political structure and cultural experience. In that perspective, state capitalism is an alternative, one in which the state plays a key role not just in promoting economic growth but also in picking the winners and losers. Using capitalist tools—the stock market and professional managers—state capitalism and state enterprises have the capital for investment in their own markets and abroad. In the emerging markets of China, Russia, and Brazil, 80 percent, 62 percent, and 38 percent, respectively, of the value of the stock market is held in these institutions. As *The Economist* reports, "The invisible hand of the market is giving way to the visible, and often authoritarian, hand of state capitalism."[14] This trend is viewed more favorably since the global economic crisis.

Radical theorists have also been critical of the liberal economic path, just as they were in the nineteenth century. Development has not occurred, and for dependency theorists particularly, MNCs and their facilitators are the culprit; they exploit the resources of the poor; they perpetuate the dominance of the North and the dependency of the South. So whereas economic liberals value the interdependencies that MNCs create, radicals see them as instruments of dependency, exploitation, and even imperialism. Decisions made in the economic and financial centers of the world—Tokyo, London, New York, Seoul—create an inherently unequal and unfair international economic system. That system must be altered significantly. Because developing states cannot adequately control multinational corporations, and because many of the leaders of these states have been co-opted by those very MNCs, radicals have sought international regulations in many forums. These views undergirded much of the thinking and the agenda of the developing countries in the 1960s and 1970s. The New International Economic Order (NIEO) is one manifestation of such thinking. The Group of 77 sought changes in major areas of international economic relations: adjustment in the terms of trade by stabilizing the prices of export commodities from less-developed countries (LDCs), greater authority over natural resources and foreign investment, more favorable arrangements for technology transfer, relief for debt, and restructuring of the international financial institutions. Most of those policies were not reformed, but the debt and restructuring proposals remain prominent on the agenda for the twenty-first century, a remnant of the theoretical split between economic liberalism and radicalism over the international political economy.

Not all the critics of the current international economic system are radicals. Reformers both outside and within the international financial institutions question both governance and specific policies.[15] In terms of governance, reformers propose altering the weighted voting system used by the IMF and the World Bank in favor of greater representation for the emerging economies. In the current system, the major

The WTO's efforts to liberalize trade are controversial. WTO meetings are often accompanied by protests, like this 2009 protest in India, as farmers from developing countries and others hurt by WTO policies express their concerns about policies that seem to favor rich countries.

donors are guaranteed voting power commensurate with their contributions. The largest shareholders in each institution—the United States, the European Union states, Japan, and Canada—hold about 60 percent of the total votes. Reformists believe a more representative voting structure might lead to the promotion of different policies. Further, hiring a more diverse group of bureaucrats, instead of the current predominance of economists trained in Western developed countries, might bring new, innovative solutions to development dilemmas.

Other reformers are critical of specific policies; here the critics differ. On the one hand, some argue that both the IMF and the World Bank have strayed too far from their liberal economic foundations, taking on too many different tasks (trying to promote an environmental agenda or gender equality) and deviating from actions promoting market liberalization. In fact, some maintain that aid and loans themselves should be allocated by competition, creating a liberal market for aid funds. On the other hand, radical political economists claim the institutions promote the interests of private international capital, pointing to the economic returns to those firms that provide the services for the dams and power plants. Other bank policies that have been rigidly developed without considering local conditions and local knowledge end up disproportionately affecting the disadvantaged sectors of population: the unskilled, women, and the weak.

The World Trade Organization has also become a lightning rod for domestic groups from many countries. They feel that the WTO, a symbol of economic globalization, is usurping local decisions and degrading the welfare of individuals. NGOs are some of the major critics of WTO activities. Some of them oppose the idea that the WTO has the power to make regulations and settle disputes in high-handed ways that intrude on or jeopardize national sovereignty. Still others fear that promotion of unregulated free trade undermines the application of labor and environmental standards; they believe that the

YOU DECIDE

In the early nineteenth century, mercantilism began a slow decline and was eventually replaced by regulated free trade. Although in many ways mercantilism appeared to be an ideal economic development strategy, free trade has proved so much more successful at spurring innovation, investment, and wealth accumulation that mercantilism seemed to become extinct. But did it? In the past two decades, the People's Republic of China has pursued economic policies that to many commentators look a lot like mercantilism. Yet after decades of double-digit economic growth, in 2012 China's economy slowed significantly. Would China be better off if it changed its economic and political orientation, abandoning mercantilism in favor of economic liberalism and playing by the rules? Or are its current economic policies preferable, putting China on the path to become the world's undisputed leading economy?

On the one hand, you might argue that China's economic development has only underlined the weaknesses and risks of mercantilism as economic policy. China's growth and innovation both have been slower than they might have been had China been a fair and free trader. This would be the argument advanced by economic liberals, although it cannot be proven. In addition, the economies of China's trading partners—partners whose stability and success is needed in order for China to continue to grow—have been seriously compromised by decades of unfair trading practices. China relies on these trading partners for its own continued economic prosperity. As a result of these drawbacks, China is currently going through the painful process of reforms aimed at fully joining the global economy as a free and fair trader.

On the other hand, you might argue that China's burgeoning wealth and power stem directly from its mercantilist practices. Early on, its trading partners calculated that letting China "cheat" by protecting its domestic industries was preferable to confrontation, both because China was so far behind technologically and because the short-term gains from trade with China were very large. As a result, although China's economic growth has flattened, it remains on track to become the world's largest economy within a decade.

YOU DECIDE: Would China be better off if it gave up mercantilism to pursue liberal economic policies, or does mercantilism offer China the best possibility to become the world's largest and most successful economy?

WTO sets economic liberalization above other social values. We will examine these views in the section on the antiglobalization movement, discussed later in this chapter.

The Key Role of Petroleum Markets

No international economic issue and no single commodity is more connected to economic globalization than petroleum. Ever since World War II, the industrialized countries have relied on crude oil as their fuel for economic development and growth. For many years, the United States was both the largest producer and the largest exporter of oil. The other developed countries, including Japan and European countries, had few domestic sources, making them dependent on cheap Middle Eastern petroleum. Most developing oil-producing countries with low levels of industrialization had excess capacity and thus were eager to sell. This fundamental interdependency between producers and consumers, between developing countries and industrialized countries, has changed. World demand for oil has escalated. While petroleum supplies from existing fields are declining, new fields are being discovered in West Africa, Iran and Iraq, Brazil, China, the Arctic Ocean, Egypt, Southeast Asia, the Horn of Africa, and Australia. Moreover, unconventional oil from tar sands and shale is expanding. Prove reserves of U.S. oil and natural gas in 2010 rose by the highest amounts ever recorded since 1977. As a result of new drilling technology, new oil development has contributed to the reversal of more than two decades of generally declining U.S. proven oil reserves. The International Energy Agency predicts that the United States will be the world's leading oil producer by about 2017. This is likely to ease global oil markets from meeting U.S. demand, which stands at a quarter of the world's oil market. The export of this technology to other countries could dramatically expand global oil production.

Several other key changes have made petroleum crucial to understanding economic globalization in the twenty-first century. The Western oil giants known as the Seven Sisters — Exxon, Mobil (now Exxon-Mobil), Texaco, Shell, Standard Oil of California, British Petroleum, and Gulf — controlled the production of oil and hence the supply from the 1930s to the late 1950s. But it was the very actions of these MNCs that caused the oil-exporting countries to seize the initiative. In 1959 and 1960, the multinational oil companies acted in unison, but without consulting the oil-exporting countries, to reduce average crude prices by 5 to 7 percent to compensate for the world glut in oil. The MNCs expected the lower prices to increase demand, so they could sell their excess oil. In response to that action, the Arab producer states and Venezuela met for the first time in 1960 to restore prices to former levels and develop plans to unify policies. The Organization of the Petroleum Exporting Countries (OPEC) was born.

During the 1960s, OPEC consolidated its power. States such as Libya and Algeria won significant concessions from the oil companies and thus increased their revenue from oil exports. Iraq and Iran joined, and in 1968 the producers in the Gulf region formed their own subgroup, the Organization of Arab Petroleum Exporting Countries (OAPEC). Nigeria and Indonesia became more active participants as their oil production increased. Multinational oil companies possess the necessary technology and technical skills, but today 13 of the biggest oil firms, which together control more than three-quarters of the world's oil reserves, are state-owned or state-backed companies.

Today OPEC's 12 members combined produce between 40 and 45 percent of the world's oil, with the Middle East accounting for 65 percent of the OPEC total. Not all oil exporting countries want to be an OPEC member, however, as they can benefit from high prices without being constrained by the actions of other states. The number of oil producers outside of OPEC is expanding to include, from the largest producer to the smallest: Russia, the United States, China, Iran, Brazil, Canada, Mexico, Norway, Angola, Kazakhstan, and the United Kingdom. These non-OPEC states share about 60 percent of the world's production, giving each a key ingredient of state power, as explained in Chapter 5. Yet it is predicted that in the coming years oil production will

High demand for oil around the globe makes petroleum a valuable state resource. States with new petroleum production capacity, such as Brazil, have seized the opportunity to generate revenue, oftentimes to the detriment of the environment. Here, then-president of Brazil Lula da Silva celebrates the world's first semi-submersible petroleum platform.

increase more rapidly in the OPEC countries since their members share about 80 percent of the world's proven reserves, including Saudi Arabia (19.2 percent), Iran (10 percent), Iraq (8.4 percent), Kuwait (7.6 percent), the United Arab Emirates (7.2 percent), and Libya (3.4 percent). Another powerful contender is Venezuela, whose government announced in 2011 that they had more proven oil reserves than Saudi Arabia, increasing their estimate to almost 300 billion barrels.

The structure of the international oil market has also changed as the result of a number of shocks, each demonstrating the repercussions of economic globalization and its political ramifications. In 1974, the Arab members of OPEC began an embargo to withhold oil from states supporting Israel, causing a significant increase in oil prices (and hence revenues) and substantial economic disruption in both the United States and the Netherlands, both of which were embargoed. Inspired by OPEC's success, Southern producers of other primary commodities joined the bandwagon, forming cartels in copper, tin, cocoa, coffee, and bananas. Although these other cartels met with little success, OPEC members enjoyed the economic benefits of their political actions. This shock brought home to the American policy makers and the public the issue of natural resource interdependence and the potential vulnerability it created. Americans were forced to cut back on driving in order to conserve fuel, they faced inconvenient lines at the pump, and they had to pay much higher prices for that privilege.

Another shock occurred at the end of the 1970s following the seizure of power by extreme Islamic fundamentalists in oil-rich Iran. Although Iran's output accounted for less than 20 percent of OPEC exports, oil prices escalated dramatically in the face of the shortage and the possibility that oil could once again be a political weapon. Panic set in, as import bills for petroleum increased three- to fourfold. The outbreak of the Iran-Iraq war in 1980 only exacerbated the situation, destabilizing oil markets further, with a 10 percent drop in world production. The 1991 Gulf War resulted in a short-term doubling of oil prices, as Iraq's invasion and occupation of Kuwait cut both Iraqi and Kuwaiti production. When Iraq burned Kuwait's oil fields in its hasty retreat, production was cut even more. As in earlier crises, markets also feared that oil production in Saudi Arabia would be affected or that transportation routes would be blocked, neither of which actually occurred. The panic that spread throughout both the international petroleum and the international financial markets clearly confirms the economic interdependence characteristic of globalization.

Whereas these shocks emanated from threats to supply principally in the Middle East, the two most recent shocks emanated from demand. Since 2000, demand for oil has grown by 7 million barrels a day. China, the Middle East, and Central and South America account for most of the recent growth in demand for oil. During the high-demand period, prices of oil rose to a high of $145 a barrel in mid-2008, resulting in serious repercussions for food prices and fueling worldwide inflation. Yet just as rapidly, demand for oil fell with the onset of the global economic crisis of 2008–2009. Oil prices plunged as low as $33 a barrel in the same year. That crisis is explained at the end of this chapter. Add to the 2008–2009 crisis the recognition that global warming is caused by the burning of fossil fuels, and it becomes clear that the international petroleum markets are in the midst of a major transition. Producers and consumers are scrambling for alternative energy sources to reduce their dependence on the oil-exporting states and to slow the process of global warming.

These changes in international petroleum market dynamics have had political implications. Oil-dependent states vying for contracts have changed or modified their political allegiances to improve their chance for a reliable oil supply. For example, after 1974, Japan not only adopted a domestic policy to lessen its dependence on foreign supplies but also has tilted toward support of the Arab political position in the Middle East in hopes of securing supply routes. In the wake of the latest oil shock, China has refused to censure Sudan for its policies in Darfur for fear of losing new oil concessions. Some observers have argued that U.S. intervention in Iraq in 2003 can be partly explained by its desire to ensure steady oil supplies from that state and region.

Another implication of the global market for petroleum is the massive proceeds that oil-producing states have enjoyed. Many have formed sovereign wealth funds, investing billions of dollars in the international financial system. States with such wealth have the power to pursue domestic policies that are largely immune to international influences. For example, the so-called petrostates such as Russia, Kazakhstan, Nigeria, and even Saudi Arabia have been able to continue repressive, antidemocratic domestic practices, knowing that criticism will be muted and consuming states unlikely to initiate sanctions to force destabilizing domestic changes. Where there are fixed pipes, Russia has used oil as a strategic weapon to hold onto its share of the European market, as well as to maintain political leverage over East European neighbors. Russia has built alternative oil export pipelines bypassing some Eastern European countries, such as Belarus, who do not cooperate with it. Russia has also temporarily shut off oil to the Czech Republic when the Czech government agreed to become part of a European based anti-ballistic missile defense system designed by the U.S. government to protect Europe against an Iranian attack. And Russia initially blocked efforts by independent oil companies to build or expand pipelines from Azerbaijan and Kazakhstan to Black Sea ports for export. Similarly, Venezuela used its petrodollars to pay off Argentina's loans to the IMF to lessen that country's dependence on the U.S.-supported institution. This posture led two commentators to suggest that there is "an emerging 'axis of oil' that is acting as a counterweight to American hegemony on a widening range of issues."[16]

Even international institutions have found it more difficult to exercise their influence in getting the oil-producing states to comply with international agreements. When petroleum was discovered in Chad, the World Bank provided partial funding to build a pipeline that would deliver the product to port, with the proviso that the country use its 40 percent in government revenue to improve the life of its 9 million poor citizens. Chad was to be the new model for how oil could be used as an engine of development in Africa. But that experiment has proved short lived: the oil-empowered government elites have broken their promises.

Finally, as oil has become more valuable, it has become a target for groups (both indigenous and international) trying to disrupt established governments by blowing up pipelines and interrupting supply. Nigerian pipelines, for example, are continually compromised by the actions of people in the Delta region who feel that their development needs are not being met. Similarly, the Iraqi pipelines are the object of attacks by terrorists who hope to further undermine that country's economic recovery and general stability. Al Qaeda and its affiliates have tried to attack Saudi facilities. No wonder the new pipelines across the Caucasus Mountains are in growing need of military protection, as ethnic groups and terrorists find that these lifelines have become new areas of state vulnerability. Indeed, the entire oil-supply market chain is vulnerable, another unintended consequence of globalization.

With economic globalization, an integrated market has emerged, linking key producer and consumer states not only with multinational companies but also with international investors and financial markets. After all, although petroleum is traded as a physical commodity, it is also traded as a financial asset—not only by oil traders but also by others seeking high returns on capital, such as pension fund managers, money managers, hedge fund managers, and university endowments. Thus, the rise and fall of oil prices have a domino effect throughout the international financial system. Shifts in the distribution of power among these primary players have led to the emergence of petroleum not just as an ordinary traded commodity but also as a political weapon, with implications for the economic, political, and even strategic decisions that states, international organizations, and even subnational and transnational groups make.

Economic Globalization and Regionalism

Although economic globalization has emerged as the defining characteristic of the international political economy, regionalism has also been growing. Particularly since the 1990s, more regional economic arrangements have been negotiated, and those already operational have been strengthened. What is the relationship between globalization and regionalism? Is regionalism another step toward enhanced globalization or is regionalism really a stumbling block to globalization?

European Economic Integration

The establishment of the European Union (discussed in Chapter 7) and the accompanying economic integration have had a major impact on the international political economy and have become models for other regions. European economic integration was predicated on the notion that a larger market, along with the free movement of goods and services, would permit economies of scale and specialization to stimulate growth, competition, and innovation while enhancing opportunities for investment, all goals compatible with liberal economics. The European Union has proven successful in achieving some of these objectives, creating a single market and developing a monetary union. Yet, to achieve these objectives, the EU has relied on some protectionist measures, and in doing so, may have only diverted trade from one group to another.

The impetus for expanded European economic integration lay in part in Europe's sluggish economic growth in the 1970s and 1980s, a time when the United States and Japan were increasingly competitive. To stimulate Europe's growth and hence its international competitiveness, the Single European Act of 1987 accelerated the integration process, setting the goal of achieving a single market by 1992. That involved removing physical, fiscal, and technical barriers to trade and harmonizing national standards by adopting over 300 community directives. Some parts of the goal—the elimination of customs barriers—were quickly achieved; other areas—labor mobility—have proved more problematic. Although most countries eliminated passport controls and adopted similar visa rules, recognition of education and professional qualifications has also proven a thorny issue. Abolishing technical barriers to trade has been difficult because of differing health and safety standards, but the process is ongoing, as is the effort to break state monopolies and eliminate state aids to specific sectors.

The overall results have been positive, with the growth of all types of economic transactions across state borders, deepening integration among the national economies of the 28 member states. Exports of goods and services constitute over one-third of the GDP for the average EU member. Over 70 percent of total trade in goods is conducted with other EU members. Not only is trade integrated but so are capital flows; cross-border mergers and acquisitions have accelerated. The broad consensus is that European integration has resulted in greater trade creation and has also had a positive welfare effect on member and nonmember states.[17]

The EU is more than a regional trading area or a single market. During the discussions for the single market, the outlines of a monetary union were also negotiated. With monetary stability and a single currency, the union would grow and prosper even more. The European Monetary Union, set forth in the Maastricht Treaty in 1991, called for the establishment of a single currency, the euro; it became the unit of exchange for businesses in 1998 and for consumers in 2002. Thereafter, the individual 17 members of the eurozone would no longer be able to use exchange rates or interest rates as instruments of economic policy. Most observers agree that the euro has facilitated business transactions and eliminated the uncertainty caused by fluctuations in exchange rates. But the euro has come under unprecedented pressure since 2009, as described later in the chapter.

The European Union very early recognized, just as international trade negotiators did, that agriculture was different from other economic sectors. First, agricultural prices dramatically fluctuate with weather and disease, so there has long been a strong incentive to moderate the price fluctuations caused by supply volatility. Second, foodstuffs are viewed as vital for national security; in emergencies, no state wants its population to depend on others for food. Third, in many countries, the well-organized farm sector enjoys disproportionate political power. For all these reasons, the EU adopted the Common Agricultural Policy (CAP). The CAP has changed over time, moving gradually away from a production-oriented policy, where the EU purchases surplus crops from farmers at guaranteed prices, then either stores the surplus, anticipating higher prices in the future, or donates it to food aid programs, absorbing the losses. Since the 2003 reforms the EU has moved toward a Single Payment Scheme, where each country chooses whether the EU payment goes to the farm or the region. Farmers choose to produce any commodity, except fruit, vegetables, or potatoes. Price interventions by the EU are limited to wheat, butter, and types of milk. Large farmers are being phased out of the program.

The CAP's total budget is 42 percent of the EU budget, down from 71 percent in 1984. The CAP has proved to be one of the most controversial policies of the EU. Not only has it been a major issue for states seeking membership and wanting their share of the agricultural budget, but it is also a critical issue in multilateral negotiations, because nonmembers pay more for EU agricultural products.

Aside from the CAP, have the EU's policies contributed to economic globalization or proved an impediment? Most economists agree that the openness of the European markets has not only benefited Europeans but has also become increasingly compatible with the goals of the multilateral global system. Indeed, the EU has developed a web of preferential agreements with its neighbors in the Mediterranean area and with former colonies with shared histories in Africa, as well as with other regional trade agreements, including the North American Free Trade Agreement and Mercosur in Latin America. In general, the EU has enhanced that region's global economic power, making it more competitive with both the United States and China.

One response by other states to the economic power and success of the European Union has been to establish their own regional trading blocs or negotiate preferential trade agreements that give their members more favorable access than states outside the bloc have. There has been in fact an explosion of such preferential arrangements, numbering now almost 250 still in force.

But are conditions in Europe—similarity of economic, political, and social systems; a history of post–World War II cooperation; and the development of nascent community political institutions—also present in other parts of the world?

The North American Free Trade Agreement

The free trade area negotiated by the United States, Canada, and Mexico in 1994 differs substantially from the European Union and other regional schemes. It comprises one dominant economy and two dependent ones: Mexico's and Canada's combined economic strength is one-tenth that of the United States. The driving force behind NAFTA is not political elites but multinational corporations (MNCs) that seek larger market shares than their Japanese and European competition have. The phasing out of many restrictions on foreign investment and most tariff and nontariff barriers has allowed MNCs to shift production to low-wage labor centers in Mexico and to gain economically by creating bigger companies through mergers and acquisitions.

The social, political, and security dimensions we saw in the European Union are absent from NAFTA. Cooperation in trade and investment is not intended to lead to the free movement of labor, as championed by the European Union. The goal is quite the opposite; the United States expects that Mexican workers will *not* seek employment in the United States, because economic development in Mexico will provide ample employment opportunities. And economic cooperation does not mean political integration in NAFTA. As public questioning of the various EU treaties grows, even Europe may not be ready for this final step in regional integration. With NAFTA, economic integration is to remain just that—confined to specific economic sectors.

The North American Free Trade Agreement supports the phased elimination over ten years of tariff and nontariff barriers. In 2008, the final provisions of NAFTA were implemented, with the elimination of the last remaining trade restrictions on agricultural commodities that the United States exports to Mexico (corn, dry beans) and Mexican exports to the United States (sugar, certain horticultural products). With the completion of the free trade area and the dismantling of both trade and investment barriers, trade among the three partners was projected to increase.[18] That clearly has happened, with merchandise trade reaching almost $1 trillion in 2010, a 218 percent increase since 1993. Foreign direct investment among the three countries has increased tenfold, making NAFTA the largest free trade area in the world. Since 2005, the rate of growth in trade has slowed, however, largely because of the growth of trade with China and the latter's admission to the WTO in 2001.

Other provisions of NAFTA deal with property rights of companies making investments in the three countries and with protection of some domestic producers, notably the Mexican oil and gas industry and the U.S. shipping industry. NAFTA's sanitary and phytosanitary measures are designed to protect people and animals from health risks, although such protective measures may not be imposed for economic reasons alone. NAFTA's flexible standards permit national and local governments to impose stricter standards. Export subsidies are eventually to be eliminated, though they are permitted in the Mexican market. There are also incentives for buying within the region. Committees have been established to monitor and promote these various provisions.

Yet the economic controversies generated by NAFTA continue to be profound, illustrating that the state is not a unitary actor. Labor unions in the United States estimate that hundreds of thousands of workers have lost their jobs to Mexico. Environmental groups point to firms in the United States relocating to Mexico to take advantage of weak environmental regulations. Canadian labor contends that the country is becoming too dependent on natural resources exports while manufacturing has lagged. Mexican supporters point to major increases in labor productivity and growth of exports, while critics point to the slide in real manufacturing wages with lower-skilled jobs moving to China. To radical opponents, NAFTA is yet another example of U.S. expansionism and exploitation of the Mexican workforce.

The NAFTA case illustrates that as in all regional economic arrangements, there will be winners and losers. In NAFTA, agriculture and manufacturing in general may well be the winners. Agricultural markets are better integrated, and consumers enjoy lower prices with virtually all tariffs eliminated. Both Canada and Mexico are now large markets for U.S. agricultural exports. The share of Canadian exports absorbed by the United States has doubled, and agricultural exports from Mexico have almost trebled. Tariffs on manufactured goods have been almost entirely eliminated. While trade among the three partners has increased several times over, some manufacturers and some groups of individuals have also been losers in all countries, just as the critics argued. Both radicals and economic nationalists have ample evidence to support their analyses.

Believing that there will be more winners than losers, other regions have developed regional trading arrangements. Asia is a relative newcomer.

Asia: ASEAN Free Trade Area

Individual East Asian countries have experienced phenomenal economic growth through competitive exports; prior to the 1990s, most of the exports went to either the United States or European countries. In 1992, the Association of Southeast Asian Nations (ASEAN) established the ASEAN Free Trade Area (AFTA), now with ten member states. Its goal is twofold: to attract foreign investment to the region, taking advantage of economies of scale; and to increase members' competitive edge in the global market by eliminating tariff and nontariff barriers within ASEAN. The Common Effective Preferential Tariff is designed to do just that; for goods originating within ASEAN states, members are expected to apply a tariff rate of no more than 5 percent. Newer members (Cambodia, Laos, Myanmar, and Vietnam) have until 2015 to comply. The exception to these reductions is rice—the food staple of the region—and certain other highly sensitive products. And like the EU, AFTA has also emphasized nontariff barriers, quantitative restrictions, and harmonizing customs rules.

Compared to either the EU or NAFTA, the original AFTA agreement is relatively brief, with no binding commitments, not even a common external tariff on imported goods. Administration is by national authorities, and it has no legal authority to enforce compliance. Yet AFTA members signed agreements to form an integrated ASEAN Economic Community by 2015 (minus a common currency). The hope is that closer regional economic integration will boost growth. Whether ASEAN members can bridge their large differences in levels of development and national standards, however, remains to be seen. Thus far, it has not boosted intraregional trade, however, nor drawn more foreign direct investment to the region as hoped—except to Vietnam.

Two debates regarding regional trade agreements have emerged. First, do they improve the economic welfare of their members through trade creation or is trade actually diverted and economic welfare reduced? With regional trade agreements, some trade is created in goods produced efficiently relative to the rest of the world. Trade is also diverted from efficient nonmembers because of the preferences states grant to each other and hence state welfare is reduced.

Second, are regional trade agreements a stepping stone or a stumbling block to global trade arrangements? On the one hand, they clearly reduce the number of actors in international negotiations and enhance competitiveness of some domestic industries, making it easier to argue for liberalization. On the other hand, under regional trade agreements, larger economies can impose their will and interest groups may find it easier to lobby for their interests, inhibiting freer global trade. Economist Jagdish Bhagwati, a prominent opponent of regional trade agreements, calls this patchwork of agreements "termites in the trading system."[19] Regional agreements make states less likely to agree to global tariff cuts; freer trade may erode the narrow gains already won. Other critics point to broader challenges facing economic globalization.

Emerging Challenges to Economic Globalization

A number of practical challenges confronts economic globalization and the triumph of economic liberalism. Some of these have developed at the local level. In 1994, an army of peasant guerrillas seized towns in the southern Mexican state of Chiapas to protest against an economic and political system that they viewed as biased against them. The date of the protest coincided with the beginning of NAFTA. Feeling that economic decisions were beyond their control, the peasants protested against the structures of the international market, the state, and economic globalization. This rebellion alerted the world to the challenges of globalization. The protesters were able to tell their side of the story, ironically enough, through the Internet, one of the by-products of the globalization they opposed.

A wider antiglobalization movement has grown in response to several issues. Labor mobility is such an issue. At the outset, the EU had adopted the goal of free movement of goods, services, *and* labor. Though the last has not been achieved, the Schengen Agreement adopted in 1985 allowed the free movement of nationals from member states who no longer need passports and visas. Individuals from non-EU states have found that once they arrive in an EU country by whatever means, they can move more easily among countries. This has resulted in a flood of illegal aliens seeking better-paying jobs in EU countries as well as to a new market in human trafficking, including women and children for the sex trade. Some of those arriving may even be terrorists who seek to conduct illegal activities against a receiving country. In NAFTA, too, the porousness of the U.S.–Mexican border has fueled antiglobalist sentiments.

Another unanticipated effect of globalization is the rise of illicit markets.[20] This can include the illegal movement of commodities such as arms or even money to evade tariffs, trade restrictions, and sanctions. Or it can mean the illegal movement of banned commodities such as drugs, human organs, endangered species, or even protected intellectual property. These transnational crimes pose a threat to security of the individual, a challenge to the viability of states, as explained in Chapter 5, and are a transnational threat, as further discussed in Chapter 11.

Many in the antiglobalization movement have their own agendas—jobs, environment, better labor conditions, alternative energy strategies, control of big capital. Stimulated by unanticipated repercussions resulting from the openness of economic markets, they have forged unity in seeking more local control and more meaningful participation in economic governance. However, there has been no greater stimulus to the anti-globalization movement and to the pitfalls of economic globalization than the global economic crisis of 2008 and the eurozone crisis of 2009.

Case Studies: The Twin Crises of Economic Globalization

International crises have been a recurrent feature of the global economic system, ranging from the 1982 Mexican debt crisis, the Asian financial crisis (1997–99), the booms and busts of petroleum markets, and market panics of yesteryear. Although Marx saw such crises as a fatal weakness of the capital system, economic liberal theory predicts that the market will regain its equilibrium; it will heal. The booms and busts will self-correct; they will not bring down the global system. Indeed, reforms were undertaken after many of the historic crises to ensure that the underlying conditions would not recur. For example, after the depression of the 1930s, the banking system was reformed. When new states were formed, global financial standards in accounting, bank regulations, and ratings agencies, among others, were developed to improve information and transparency. When new and developing states encountered economic difficulties, the Bretton Woods institutions were available for temporary fixes.

THE 2008–2009 GLOBAL ECONOMIC CRISIS   A reform that was neglected, however, was ensuring transparency for the *developed* countries, mainly the United States. The 1980s and 1990s saw an explosion of unregulated (and little understood), highly leveraged financial instruments, including oil futures and derivatives markets. U.S.-based financial institutions and governmental units at all levels were participating in those markets. Excess credit against insufficient equity prevailed across a number of sectors—in the housing market, the financial sector, and consumer credit markets. That spending spree was accompanied by the importation of cheap goods from China, causing an unsustainable trade imbalance with China and with the oil-exporting countries. By 2007, it was clear the U.S. economy itself was exhibiting fundamental structural weaknesses, although few policy makers were ready to take action. First to feel the impact was the subprime mortgage market. With financial companies and international banks carrying unsustainable debt, defaults increased, and there were no assets to back up those loans. Credit became more difficult to acquire. Private investment to build factories and produce goods dried up.

What began as a financial crisis centered in the United States rapidly became a global economic crisis. The U.S.-based financial instruments that had spawned the excess lending had been sold abroad to investors ranging from local communities in Norway to banks in Europe and East Asia and investors in Japan and China. What safer place to invest in than the United States! That proved not to be the case. Financial institutions were unable to meet their obligations. Credit became almost impossible to obtain in the United States and Europe. Businesses cut expenditures and workforces. Consumer demand plummeted. States such as China, South Korea, and Japan, dependent on exports to the United States and Europe, saw their markets shrink and export earnings fall, forcing companies to curb production further. Oil prices dropped by 69 percent between July and December 2008, severely affecting such oil-exporting countries as Russia, Angola, and Venezuela. In emerging markets (especially Eastern Europe and states of the former Soviet Union) dependent on private foreign investment, investment plummeted; in 2008, it was less than one-half that of a year earlier. In late 2008, Iceland became the first state victim when its banking system collapsed and the government declared bankruptcy. European depositors in Icelandic banks lost their savings. The Baltic states, the Ukraine, and Eastern European economies virtually collapsed. As international trade declined, world shipping plummeted, with ships languishing in the ports of Singapore and Hong Kong. The crisis rippled outward to developing countries that faced the prospect of sharply reduced or negative growth and the erosion of gains from globalization-driven growth. The speed and depth of the collapse in global financial and international trade markets surprised even the experts; the self-correcting mechanisms were not working like economic liberals theorized.

Initial responses to the financial crisis were mostly unilateral. Both the United States and various EU member governments took unprecedented steps, bailing out banks and insurance companies to get credit markets functioning again and stimulate investor confidence. The United States, many EU governments, Japan, and China each responded with substantial economic stimulus packages to encourage economic growth. Some coordinated actions were taken among central bankers. The U.S. Federal Reserve, the European Central Bank, and the Bank of England engaged in currency swaps.

The IMF also responded to the crisis by making available almost $250 billion for credit lines. Iceland became the first Western country to borrow from the IMF since 1976. Substantial loans were made to Ukraine, Hungary, and Pakistan. The IMF, with an infusion of $750 billion, created the Short-Term Liquidity Facility for emerging-market countries with temporary liquidity problems. It reorganized the Exogenous Shocks Facility, designed to help low-income states by providing assistance more rapidly and streamlining conditions. But the fact was that the IMF's capacity had already been weakened by those preferring market solutions over greater regulation and those wanting to abolish the Bretton Woods system itself.

THE 2009 EUROZONE CRISIS   As growth within the states in the EU began to slow or reverse because of the global economic crisis, a crisis closer to home magnified the disequilibrium. In the early years of the new millennium, easy credit had ushered in a decade of risky borrowing and profligate spending in some EU countries. International banks were eager to oblige credit-hungry governments and individuals with low interest rates. In Greece, public sector borrowing was fueled by high public sector wages and long-term pension obligations. In Ireland and Spain, private sector borrowing accelerated, similar to the U.S. housing bubble. Then when the global economic crisis hit, households were confronted by underwater mortgages, foreclosures, and even bankruptcy. Many individuals whose net worth had dramatically declined were now confronted by the possibility of unemployment and declining wages, only deepening the debt trap. And governments dependent on borrowing in international markets were turned away, deepening their debt obligations.

But the crisis was not just a debt problem. It was also caused by an imbalance of trade. After the turn of the century, Germany's export trade grew, while that of the so-called PIGS (Portugal, Italy, Greece, Spain) had worsening balance-of-payments positions. Wages rose faster than gains in productivity, making their exports uncompetitive, while Germany's wage restraint made German exports even more competitive. Germany's trade surplus is the world's largest at $200 billion; 40 percent of that surplus comes from trade within the eurozone.

The eurozone crisis that began in 2009 precipitated an economic crisis in Greece, whose government was deeply in debt. The budget cuts implemented by the Greek government caused economic distress for many, leading to weeks of protests outside the Greek parliament.

The arrangements within the European monetary union and within the eurozone itself made addressing the twin problems of unsustainable debt and trade imbalances even more difficult. As its critics warned in the early days, how could the euro work with no fiscal union and no treasury? How could the eurozone deal with economic shocks affecting different subregions? Individual states do not have the ability to manage their monetary policy; they could not print more money; they could not devalue their currency to make their exports more competitive. Labor mobility was constrained, and there were no agreed upon procedures for transferring funds between states.[21] When the banks, including German ones, that had lent money liberally during the credit explosion became stressed, they demanded higher interest rates from the PIGS, making it more difficult for those governments to finance budget deficits and service the existing debt, a problem compounded by low growth rates.

By 2013, there had been 20 summits to address the eurozone crisis. In response, the PIGS undertook numerous reforms to reduce government debt, slashing expenditures, increasing the retirement age, promising to improve the tax collection system, and using financial transfers to avert bankruptcy. Greece, the government in the most dire straits, has received several bailouts. But these domestic reforms and economic austerity measures did not prove adequate to stem the immediate crisis, and international financial markets have reacted to the uncertainty over the prospect that other PIGS are also in an unsustainable situation. Domestic constituencies affected by the economic distress—Germans paying the bailout costs to prevent collapse, Greeks who stand in line at soup kitchens, Cypriots whose bank depositors are subject to capital controls, and Spanish youth who face an unemployment rate of 50 percent—are pressuring their democratically elected leaders for outcomes favorable to their own interests. And what is best for sectoral or national interests may not be consistent with eurozone stability or with the viability of the EU.

Commentators differ on the prognosis for the EU more generally. Economist C. Fred Bergsten acknowledges that liquidity within the PIGS must be stabilized and banking institutions supported. And fundamental reform of the eurozone arrangements are necessary, including imposing tighter constraints on government budgets and enforcing them. If those goals are accomplished, then the eurozone will survive, but integration will probably slow down. As Bergsten forecasts, "If the history of the continent's integration is any guide . . . Europe will emerge from its current turmoil not only with the euro intact but also with stronger institutions and far better economic prospects for the future."[22] Others predict that the crisis will lead to a "leveling off of European integration," where policy makers are neither widening nor deepening the EU.[23] And still another analyst points to a different future: "Without some new driving forces, without a positive mobilization among its elites and peoples, the EU, while probably surviving as an origami palace of treaties and institutions, will gradually decline in efficacy and real significance, like the Holy Roman Empire of yore."[24]

Responding to the Crises

In light of these twin crises, does the global economic system need "a scalpel or a hatchet?"[25] Scalpel-like reforms are being implemented: giving China and other BRICS a greater role in the IMF, hoping that China will channel its $2 trillion in foreign-currency savings through the IMF to stabilize markets and promote development; improving the surveillance functions of the IMF to anticipate risks and threats;[26] reinvigorating the G7 with greater participation by China; rethinking the role of the G20, including its finance ministers, central bank officials, and member state heads of state, both in terms of membership and their shifting coalitions; and reworking the rules and regulations of the private financial institutions, although the latter has proven more difficult than anticipated. Reforms in the eurozone states and in the European Central Bank are also in the proposal stage: giving the European Central Bank the role of regulator of banks in member countries and giving more authority to an IMF-like institution—namely, the European Stability Mechanism—to handle bailouts and work with the European Central Bank. Economic liberals believe that the system can be preserved merely with modest reforms, giving more transparency to market transactions. They

The Economic Crises: A View from Ghana and Kenya

Prior to the 2008–2009 global economic crises, African economies had been experiencing a resurgence. Although more than a decade ago described by The Economist as "the hopeless continent," positive changes had been occurring. Growth in real GDP averaged 4.1 percent between 1997 and 2002, and since 2003 averaged over 6 percent. Even on a per capita basis, the growth rate has climbed to over 4 percent, with the continent's GDP per capita having increased to $2,031 in 2007. Private capital investments amounted to $53 billion, a fourfold increase from 2000 to 2006, thanks in part to unprecedented Chinese and Indian economic activity. Under several multilateral debt-relief initiatives, 14 African countries with a per capita income of less than $380 a year had effectively erased their debt by 2008.

Yet when the global economic crises developed, there was legitimate worry that Africa's positive economic record would be reversed, if not irreparably harmed. After all, commodity export prices that many countries depend on would decline as demand for the products dropped. Remittances, which in many countries are a primary source of income, would fall dramatically as emigrant workers were laid off or worked fewer hours, particularly in member states of the European Union. Foreign aid would decline as donor governments cut expenditures; foreign direct investment, especially from the United States and European countries, would fall dramatically. In fact, many of these indicators did decline; foreign aid, investment, and remittances dropped. But the impact was much less than anticipated, and Africa has not followed the United States and Europe into a long recession.

Ghana and Kenya are two examples where countervailing trends have developed. Ghana is a longtime world leader in both cocoa and coffee production. When its neighbor Côte d'Ivoire became embroiled in civil war, Ghana increased cocoa production, earning $2 billion annually from international trade, a 32-year high. As a major gold producer, it benefited from higher prices as consumers moved into gold to protect themselves from declining currencies. In 2007, the country discovered a large petroleum field off its coast, with predictions that this will earn the country as much as $1 billion annually. In 2011, the first oil flowed, helping to spur its 7.7 percent annual growth rate, and optimists predict a 13 percent growth rate in the near future. Private equity, too, is now investing in projects. Cheetah Palm Oil, backed by Global Mean Capital, works with farmers to help exporters, providing microcredit and agricultural extension. The goal is to work with 50,000 small farmers. Ghanaians from the diaspora are returning, with one founding Ashesi University College to train new business leaders in Africa. A functioning multiparty democratic government has proven pivotal to economic development.

Kenya, too, has not experienced the dire effects of the economic crises. Kenya, like other East African states, is benefiting from private equity, including investment in railways that link the regional economies. Between

2000 and 2010, intraregional exports among the East African states tripled, from $700 million to almost $2 billion. Kenya has emphasized education, building more schools and proposing compulsory education so parents must send their kids to school. And more than other countries, indigenous technology companies are bringing new communication devices to education, agriculture, and services. Kenya is penetrated by increasing numbers of cell phone users, who are able not only to connect with each other but also to use them for key banking services. The technology has improved access to international markets and expedited transfers between urban workers and rural families. The mobile company M-Pesa allows users to transfer money easily through their mobile device. Finally, civil society activists are playing an increasingly vital role; in 2010, it was that sector that mobilized large numbers to vote on a referendum for a new constitution that expands democratic rights and alters electoral processes. And the democratic election in 2013 was carried out in a peaceful manner.

Both Ghana and Kenya have capitalized on infusions of funds from the emerging economies—namely, China and India. A generation ago, Brazil, Russia, India, and China accounted for 1 percent of African trade; now they account for 20 percent. In Ghana, Chinese loans and investments have gone to roads, communications systems, rural electrification, and dam building. In Kenya, about one-third of Chinese investments are in manufacturing. Construction of roads, bridges, and airports are being carried out by Chinese companies. So when investments from the United States, Europe, and MNCs declined, investments from China and other emerging economies like India were growing at an unprecedented rate.

As the World Bank optimistically reported in 2011, "Africa could be on the brink of an economic take-off, much like China was

The president of Ashesi University College, in Ghana, addresses first-year students.

30 years ago and India 20 years ago." *The Economist* has expressed regret for the "hopeless continent" label, headlining its recent analysis, "Africa's Hopeful Economies: The Sun Shines Bright."[a]

[a] See "Africa's Hopeful Economies: The Sun Shines Bright," *The Economist* Dec 3, 2011, 82–84.

FOR CRITICAL ANALYSIS

1. The African states most integrated with the global economy have the highest standards of living. How does this support a liberal economic view?

2. Not all African states enjoy the positive outlook of Ghana and Kenya. Explain the position of the poorer African states from the viewpoint of a radical theorist.

3. If you were a policy maker in Ghana or Kenya, what recommendations would you make to improve the progress toward economic development?

4. How do democratic governments contribute to achieving greater economic development?

point to the promising economic recovery after 2010 as evidence that an equilibrium can reemerge.

Those critics who argue that the crises demand the hatchet wonder, do these crises portend the end of economic globalization as now practiced? Perhaps not the end, some economic liberals admit, but certainly an end to the expectation that individuals will act rationally and that markets will always be stable and efficient. Mercantilists and economic realists might applaud the return to the state-level policies protecting their own citizens and the rise of state-controlled enterprises. Radicals recognize that delivering the hatchet to economic globalization is necessary if their goals of a more just and equitable international economic system is achieved. Social constructivists regard the contestation over ideas about the economy as an ever-evolving process.

But globalization is not only a characteristic of the international political economy. It is also reflected in the emergence of international human rights, discussed in the next chapter.

Discussion Questions

1. You are a citizen in rural Mexico. In what ways does the international political economy *directly* affect you?

2. You are an adviser to the emir of an oil-rich Gulf state. Outline to the emir the multiple ways that his state is tied to the global economy. Suggest how these ties give the emir power.

3. Liberals, mercantilists, and radicals see multinational corporations in different ways. What are those differences?

4. Does economic regionalization lead to globalization? Why or why not? Provide evidence.

5. How has your belief in the economic liberal model been modified by the global economic crises?

Key Terms

Beijing Consensus (p. 328)

BRICS (p. 321)

comparative advantage (p. 309)

derivatives (p. 317)

direct foreign investment (p. 316)

economic realism (p. 307)

General Agreement on Tariffs and Trade (GATT) (p. 314)

globalization (p. 306)

Group of 7 (G7) (p. 314)

hegemonic stability theorists (p. 308)

International Monetary Fund
(IMF) (p. 314)

mercantilism (p. 307)

moral hazard (p. 318)

most-favored-nation (MFN)
principle (p. 314)

offshore financial centers (p. 317)

portfolio investment (p. 316)

sovereign wealth funds (p. 317)

structural adjustment
programs (p. 323)

sustainable development (p. 322)

Washington Consensus (p. 322)

World Bank (p. 313)

World Trade
Organization (WTO) (p. 319)

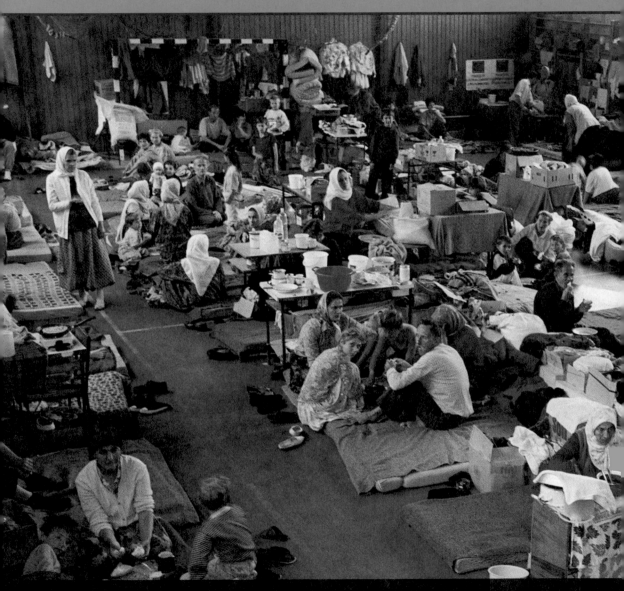

Emerging international consensus on human rights protections has not prevented egregious abuses from occurring. In the 1990s, ethnic conflict in the Balkans region resulted in massacres and displacements. Refugees received UN and NGO humanitarian aid, but the international community did not effectively halt the violence.

10

HUMAN RIGHTS

- What are the religious, philosophical, and historical foundations of human rights?

- What roles do IGOs, NGOs, and states perform in the protection of human rights?

- What human rights have been protected under international law?

- Why has the international community so often failed to respond to allegations of genocide?

- What are the advantages of using international courts to punish those guilty of human rights violations? Of using truth commissions?

- Why are women's human rights in the private sphere so difficult to address?

War and strife have always been central issues in world politics, and in the last century, so, too, has been the international political economy. Recent headlines in international relations, however, suggest new topics and narratives that demand (and have received) both academic and public attention: the international investigation of civilian deaths during the two-decade war in Sri Lanka; the call by the International Criminal Court and NGOs for the arrest of the top leader in eastern Congo for using child soldiers; the report that Syrian security forces arrested wounded hospitalized patients, tortured prisoners during interrogations, and used sarin gas; the trafficking of people and illicit goods by states and criminal organizations; the exploitation of cheap labor by multinational corporations; the widely publicized attack on a 14-year-old Pakistani girl who spoke out for education of girls. These headlines point to the emergence of international human rights as another key issue in world politics.

For several centuries after the Treaties of Westphalia, state sovereignty in this domain remained unchallenged. How states treated individuals and groups within their own jurisdiction was their own responsibility. In the twenty-first century, that is no longer true. What happens in Asian cities, African towns, European streets, and American halls of government is not only heard around the world but also watched carefully. Coercive actions by state authorities against individuals and groups are widely condemned by other states and the media, even if no others choose to act. Even what happens in the family (e.g., violence against spouses and children), is now viewed as a public issue.

While the issue has only relatively recently risen to a prominent place on the international agenda, the ethical treatment of individuals and groups of individuals—or human rights—has a long historical genesis. Over the ages, both philosophers and theologians have waxed eloquent over proper treatment of individuals and groups, while novelists and essayists have called attention to the evils of slavery, forced servitude, and the degradation of women and children. Individuals who have been prevented from freely expressing themselves or practicing their religion have emigrated, finding new homes far away from offending authorities. Civil wars have been and are still fought over acceptable treatment of individuals and groups. That people care about other people comes from religious, philosophical, and historical traditions. We briefly explore those traditions and then trace how the notion of responsibility for protection of rights of individuals and groups has become internationalized.

Religious, Philosophical, and Historical Foundations

All of the world's great religions—Hinduism, Judaism, Christianity, Buddhism, Islam, and Confucianism—assert the dignity of individuals and people's responsibilities to fellow human beings. Different religions emphasize different facets: Confucianism, the social group; Judaism, the responsibility to help those in need; Buddhism, the rejection of government policies that cause suffering.[1] But do these religions assert the inalienable rights of human beings to a standard of treatment? Or are these merely duties or responsibilities of the faithful? Who protects these rights and enforces the duties? Who acts on behalf of those whose rights are violated? Do these religions support human rights for all? The answers are not clear.

Like the world's religions, philosophers and political theorists have also conceptualized the rights of humans, each with different emphases. Liberal political theorists assert individual rights that the state can neither usurp nor undermine. John Locke, for example, wrote that individuals are equal and autonomous beings whose natural rights predate both national and international law. Public authority is designed to secure these rights. Key historic documents lay out these rights, including the English Magna Carta in 1215, the French Declaration of the Rights of Man in 1789, and the U.S. Bill of Rights in 1791. Political and civil rights, including freedom of speech, religion, and press, deserve protection. No individual should be deprived of these freedoms by authoritarian governments or by arbitrary actions. These are known as **first-generation human rights** (political and civil rights).

Theorists in the radical tradition heavily influenced by Karl Marx and other socialist writers identify social and economic rights for individuals, which the state should provide. Individuals, according to this view, enjoy material rights—rights to education, decent work, an adequate standard of living, housing—that are critical for sustaining and improving life. Without these guarantees—so-called **second generation human rights** (or socioeconomic rights)—socialist theorists believe that political and civil rights are meaningless.

What is included as a human right has continually been reconceptualized in the last two centuries, expanding into the realm of group rights. These so-called **third-generation human rights** include both group rights for marginalized peoples and collective rights for all. Group rights include protection for indigenous peoples, refugees, and more recently, the disabled and those of different sexual orientations. Collective rights include rights necessary for the collectivity to survive—namely, the right to development and the right to a clean environment. All of these rights are highly contested within states and in the international arena. This process itself has led to a debate—whether the expansion of what is included as a fundamental human right actually dilutes the very rights that others are trying to protect.

Four major debates emerge from these foundations. First, are these really human rights? That is, are they inalienable—fundamental to every person? Are they necessary to life? Are they non-negotiable—that is, are the rights so essential that they cannot be taken away? If human rights are inalienable, are they not, by definition, universal rights?

The Dharavi neighborhood is one of the biggest slums in Mumbai, India. Many of its residents lack decent work, education, housing, and health. Although human rights are often debated in lofty terms, the absence of socioeconomic rights protections has real consequences for people.

Second, if human rights are universal, are they really applicable to all peoples, in all states, religions, and cultures, without exception? Or are rights dependent on culture? Some scholars have argued for **cultural relativism**, the idea that some rights are culturally determined, and hence that different rights are relevant in different cultural settings. Particularly sensitive have been the debates on women's status, child protection, family planning, and practices such as female circumcision. Others like political scientist Jack Donnelley see both universal and contextual elements, which he calls "relative universality."[2] The Vienna Declaration adopted at the 1993 World Conference on Human Rights stated, "All human rights are universal, indivisible and interdependent and interrelated." But the same document qualified the statement, saying "the significance of national and regional particularities and various historical, cultural and religious backgrounds must be borne in mind."

Third, should some rights be prioritized over others? Just because first-generation rights have a longer historical genesis, are those rights more important than the others? Some writers from East Asia, for example, argue that advocating the rights of the individual over the welfare of the community as a whole is unsound and potentially dangerous.[3] The socialist states of the former Soviet bloc, as well as many European social welfare states, ranked economic and social rights as high or even higher than political and civil rights. Other states in the West have prioritized political-civil rights. And indeed, many of the international initiatives in articulating and enforcing rights have been on behalf of political-civil rights. Yet, to many, human rights are interdependent; the purpose of each type of human right is to treat people with respect and dignity.

Fourth, who has the responsibility and the "right" to respond to violations of human rights? And is this response an absolute obligation or merely an opportunity? Traditionally, it was the state's responsibility to protect its citizens, but if the state is the abuser, who should and can respond? How?

The first global human rights movement, the antislavery movement, illustrates the long struggle in responding to these questions.[4] In the eighteenth century, abolitionists (including religious groups, textile workers, rural housewives, and business leaders) in the United States, Great Britain, and France organized to advocate for an end to the slave trade. In 1815, when the Final Act of the Congress of Vienna was signed, it stated that the slave trade was "repugnant to the principles of humanity and universal morality." It was framed in terms of morality, not in human rights language. But the act did not declare that slavery was illegal, nor did it provide mechanisms for supporting that aspiration. At that point, to have freedom was not an inalienable right, fundamental to every person.

Nor did the right apply universally to all states and cultures. States acted individually, in response to the actions of what were generally domestic constituencies: letter writing, petition signing, and public advocacy, among other actions. Responding to these pressures, both the British and American governments banned the slave trade in their territories in 1807 (i.e., new slaves could not be imported from abroad). But it was not until a half-century later that the U.S. Civil War was fought to free the slaves. Elsewhere, Spain abolished slavery in Cuba in 1880, and Brazil ended the practice in 1888. It was not until 1926 that the International Convention on the Abolition of Slavery was ratified.

The antislavery movement suggests that political-civil rights and social-economic rights are intertwined. Since slaves were owned by another as property, they had no rights, indeed no human dignity at all. Even after political and civil rights were won, the former slaves and their descendants had and still have a long struggle to acquire full social-economic rights, rights often denied because of discrimination and racism. Since the end of institutionalized and legalized slavery, slavery has been reconceptualized in modern-day terms. In 1990, the renamed Anti-Slavery International included among its agenda the prohibition of human trafficking, child labor, and forced labor, each representing contemporary notions of slavery and often occurring because of a lack of economic opportunity. Over time, the notion of who is human expanded to include slaves and others in economically enforced servitude.

Also expanding over time is recognition of who should take responsibility to protect rights. States remain primarily responsible. But since World War II, the notion of an international community responsibility to protect human rights has developed.

Human Rights as Emerging International Responsibility

Human rights only gradually became an international issue. Just as NGOs propelled the antislavery initiatives, another nongovernmental group, the International Committee of the Red Cross, worked for protection of wounded soldiers, prisoners of war, and civilians caught in the midst of war. With states unable to guarantee protection, a third party was poised to act on behalf of those special groups. That protection was legally codified in 1864 in the first Geneva Convention for the Amelioration of the Condition of the Wounded and Sick in Armed Forces in the Field, aimed at protection of people during wartime. From that beginning of international humanitarian law in the nineteenth century came three other conventions and several protocols during the twentieth century. These are known collectively as the Geneva Conventions, rules that apply in times of conflict, including noncombatant immunity (discussed in Chapter 8).

Internationalization of human rights in other sensitive areas was slower to evolve. At the Congress of Versailles, which ended World War I, the Japanese government and its representatives, Marquis Kimmochi Saionji and Baron Nobuaki Makino, tried to convince other delegates, principally U.S. president Woodrow Wilson, to adopt a statement on human rights. As a victorious and economically advanced power, Japan felt it had a credible claim that such basic rights as racial equality and religious freedom would not be rejected. Yet the initiative was blocked, with the U.S. representatives recognizing that such a provision would doom Senate passage of the peace treaty.

The League of Nations Covenant made little explicit mention of human rights, although general procedures were articulated for protection of certain groups. For example, the Mandates Commission was authorized to protect the treatment of dependent peoples with the goal of self-determination, but they could not carry out independent inspections. Likewise, the 1919 Minorities Treaties required states to provide protection to all inhabitants regardless of nationality, language, race, or religion. Similar obligations for civil and political rights were imposed on the defeated states. The League also established the principles for assisting refugees, creating a refugee organization that would later gain protected status under the Convention Relating to the Status of Refugees.

President Franklin Roosevelt's famous "Four Freedoms" speech in 1941 called for a world based on four essential freedoms, a new moral order. But that new order would not take shape until after World War II, when the full extent of the Holocaust was shockingly revealed. With that recognition came the moral demand for international action. Thus, at the conference founding the UN, civil society groups, including churches and peace societies, successfully pushed for inclusion of human rights in the new organization. In the end, the UN Charter (Article 55c) gave a role to the organization in "promoting and encouraging respect for rights and for fundamental freedoms for all without distinction as to race, sex, language, or religion."

Drawing on that religious, philosophical, and historical foundation, the UN General Assembly approved the Universal Declaration of Human Rights in 1948, a statement of human rights aspirations. Thirty principles incorporating both political and economic rights were identified. These principles were eventually codified in two documents, the International Covenant on Economic, Social, and Cultural Rights and the International Covenant on Civil and Political Rights, approved in 1966 and ratified in 1976. Together, the three documents are known as the **International Bill of Rights**. It was the conflict between Western and socialist views that blocked conclusion of a single treaty. The fact that the United States has yet to ratify the Covenant on Economic, Social, and Cultural Rights indicates that the difference in views persists.

Subsequently, the UN and its agencies have been responsible for setting human rights standards in numerous areas, developing treaties on genocide, slavery and forced labor, refugees, racial and gender discrimination, migrant labor, and the disabled, among others (see Table 10.1). But at the same time that the Charter gave human rights a prominent place and states that ratified the conventions a standard to follow, the Charter (Article 2[7]) acknowledges the primacy of state sovereignty: "Nothing contained in the present Charter shall authorize the United Nations to intervene in matters which are essentially within the domestic jurisdiction of any state." So who protects human rights and how?

States as Protectors of Human Rights

States, as the Westphalian tradition and realists posit, are primarily responsible for protecting human rights standards within their own jurisdiction. Many liberal democratic states have based human rights practices on first-generation political and civil liberties. The constitutions of the United States and many European democracies give pride of place to freedom of speech, freedom of religion, and due process. And those same states have taken those domestic provisions and tried to internationalize them. That is, it has become part of their foreign policy agenda to support similar provisions in newly emerging states and states in transition. U.S. support for such initiatives can be seen in both Iraq and Afghanistan, where specific human rights guarantees were written into the new constitutions. And the European Union has made candidate members show significant progress toward improving political and civil liberties records before becoming a member of the EU. Consistent with the constructivist view, states can be gradually socialized to accept these new norms of international behavior.

Why do liberal democratic states support these first-generation political and civil rights in their foreign policy? One explanation is based on realist self-interest: that states sharing those values are better positioned to trade with one another and will,

TABLE 10.1 — SELECTED UN HUMAN RIGHTS CONVENTIONS

CONVENTION	OPENED FOR RATIFICATION	ENTERED INTO FORCE	RATIFICATIONS (AS OF 2012)
General Human Rights			
International Covenant on Civil and Political Rights	1966	1976	167
International Covenant on Economic, Social, and Cultural Rights	1966	1976	160
Racial Discrimination			
International Convention on the Elimination of All Forms of Racial Discrimination	1966	1969	175
International Convention on the Suppression and Punishment of the Crime of Apartheid	1973	1976	108
Rights of Women			
Convention on the Elimination of All Forms of Discrimination against Women	1979	1981	187
Human Trafficking and Other Slave-like Practices			
UN Convention for the Suppression of the Traffic in Persons and of the Exploitation of the Prostitution of Others	1949	1951	81
International Convention on the Abolition of Slavery and the Slave Trade (1926), as amended in 1953	1953	1955	99
UN Convention against Transnational Organized Crime: Protocol to Prevent, Suppress, and Punish Trafficking in Persons, Especially Women and Children	2000	2003	143

(CONTINUED)

CONVENTION	OPENED FOR RATIFICATION	ENTERED INTO FORCE	RATIFICATIONS (AS OF 2012)
Refugees and Stateless Persons			
Convention Relating to the Status of Refugees	1951	1954	144
Children			
Convention on the Rights of the Child	1989	1990	193
Physical Security			
Convention on the Prevention and Punishment of the Crime of Genocide	1948	1951	142
Convention against Torture and Other Cruel, Inhuman, or Degrading Treatment or Punishment	1984	1987	147
Convention for the Protection of All Persons from Enforced Disappearance	2006	2010	34
Other			
Convention Concerning Indigenous and Tribal Peoples in Independent Countries	1989	1991	20
International Convention on the Protection of the Rights of All Migrant Workers and Members of Their Families	1990	2003	46
Convention on the Rights of Persons with Disabilities	2007	2008	126

Sources: University of Minnesota Human Rights Library and UN High Commissioner for Human Rights.

according to the democratic peace theory discussed in Chapters 3 and 5, be less likely to go to war with one another. The second explanation is based in liberalism: that liberal democracies believe strongly in protection of individuals from unsavory governments and desire those values and beliefs to be projected abroad.

Some European socialist states have taken up the mantle of protecting economic and social rights because they see it as the role of government to play a positive role in providing those rights. In this view, governments need to do as much as possible to ensure access to education, adequate health care, and employment. But how much should the government do? What is an adequate level? Economic and social rights are achieved only gradually and over time, and thus the crux of the discussion is whether the state is acting in good faith and is doing enough to protect the economic and social welfare of its citizens.

What can states do if they believe that the human rights of individuals in another state are not being protected? A number of instruments are available. States can use their legal systems if an individual is deemed to be a particularly egregious violator. For example, Spain tried to extradite the former dictator of Chile, General Augusto Pinochet, from Britain to Spain to stand trial for abuses against Spanish citizens in Chile. Spain's attempt failed, however, even though Pinochet was ultimately returned to Chile, where he died before standing trial.

States may alternatively find that positive incentives or engagement may be used to change the human rights practices of another state. Recall Chapter 5's discussion of how states exercise power. Diplomatic engagement rests on the idea that linking multiple other interests—economic, security, and/or diplomatic—to human rights may be a way of getting a state to change the latter. For example, a state may be granted trade concessions if human rights abuses decline. Linking may work because of the notion that better economic relations and a more open economic system can create domestic pressure for more political freedom, including less offensive human rights practices. This has been an approach used with China. But although China's human rights abuses have become much more publicized, with the regime less able to hide its behavior, engagement has not brought the anticipated results.

States like the United States and European donor states can tie better human rights policies to more foreign or military aid, or reduce or take away that aid should a state's human rights records be particularly egregious. In 1976, under pressure from Congress, the U.S. Department of State began writing annual country reports on human rights. Over time, those reports have become increasingly comprehensive. Along with annual reports from NGOs like Amnesty International and Freedom House, they are used as one element in the process of deciding whether the United States should allocate foreign aid to a country. However, these reports are not the only criteria, and sometimes major human rights violators do receive aid because of other overriding strategic or political interests.

Negative sanctions, as shown in Table 5.1, are also a possibility. Following China's crackdown on dissidents and the Tiananmen Square massacre in June 1989, the United States instituted an arms embargo against China and cancelled new foreign aid; it was joined by Japan and members of the European Union. Some estimate that the coercive action may have cost China over $11 billion in bilateral aid over a four-year period. But as discussed in Chapter 5, imposing sanctions to try to pressure a state to reverse its egregious policy (or policies) often punishes the population more than the state, impinging further on their rights.

In cases of particularly severe violations like genocide or mass atrocities, states may choose to use force against offending states, although as discussed in a later section, resorting to force for human rights violations is controversial, selective, and usually carried out through multilateral actions.

States as Abusers of Human Rights

States are not just protectors, they are also violators of human rights. Both regime type and the forms of real or perceived threats to the state are explanations for state abuse. In general, authoritarian or autocratic states are more likely to abuse political and civil rights, while less developed states, even liberal democratic ones, may be unable or unwilling to meet basic obligations of social and economic rights due to scarce resources or lack of political will.

All states, including democratic ones, threatened by civil strife or terrorist activity are apt to use repression against foes, domestic or foreign. State security usually prevails over individual rights. In fact, the International Covenant on Civil and Political Rights acknowledges that heads of state may revoke some political-civil liberties when national security is threatened.

Nowhere is the potential clash between human rights and national security more focused than the issue of torture, prohibited in the Convention against Torture and Other Cruel, Inhuman, or Degrading Treatment or Punishment. May states, fearing imminent attack or grave harm, use torture or suspect acts in questioning those they believe have relevant knowledge? If states restrain themselves and avoid coercive inter-rogations, some citizens may die. Which, then, is the greater harm—violation of the rights of the detained, or the lives of innocent citizens? In 2009, former U.S. vice presi-dent Dick Cheney argued publicly that political leaders had a greater responsibility to the nation's security. Others responded by questioning whether less violent methods might not have achieved the same results. Still others, like U.S. senator John McCain, argued that Americans should not use torture because it is wrong and violates what it means to be an American. Indeed, the Convention against Torture is clear: freedom from torture is a right never to be revoked. But what acts are considered torture remains a controversial question, as the discussion on waterboarding in Chapter 8 points out.

Economic conditions also influence a country's adherence to human rights stand-ards. Poor states or states experiencing deteriorating economic conditions are apt to repress political-civil rights, in an effort by the elite to maintain authority and divert attention from economic disintegration. But economically developed states also may have difficulty meeting the demands of economic and social rights for all members of their population. And in some cases, those rights may be deliberately undermined or denied due to discrimination by race, creed, national origin, or gender.

Finally, culture and history affects a state's human rights record. Where there is a long history of communal violence, ethnic hatred, and mobilizing ideologies (like Nazism), then human rights are more apt to be abused. High degrees of factionaliza-tion along ethnic, religious, or ideological lines brings out the worst abuses.

The Role of the International Community – IGOs and NGOs

What can the international community do to protect human rights? What can the United Nations and other intergovernmental organizations do when they are them-selves composed of the very sovereign states that threaten individual and group rights?[5]

NGOs advocate for human rights by disseminating information on abuses and organizing individuals to call on political leaders for action. Though still relatively rare, sometimes NGOs can raise global awareness of a situation, as Invisible Children did with its Kony2012 video about human rights abuses in Uganda.

NGOs have been particularly vocal and sometimes very effective in the area of human rights. Of the hundreds of human rights organizations with interests that cross national borders, there is a core group that has been the most vocal and attracted the most attention, including Amnesty International (AI) and Human Rights Watch (HRW). These organizations publicize the issues, put pressure on states (both offenders and enforcers), and lobby international organizations. Furthermore, these organizations have often formed coalitions, leading to advocacy networks and social movements.[6]

With the Internet and Twitter, individuals and groups are able to voice their grievances swiftly to a worldwide audience and to solicit sympathizers to take direct actions. These technologies are particularly effective for shaping discourse surrounding an issue and generating interest among multiple constituencies. For example, during the 1970s, disability rights groups formed first in Europe and North America, generally organizing along lines of disability type. Activists were fragmented and there was no overarching approach. Over time, these various groups adopted a rights-based approach. By 1992, seven of the groups had merged into a loose network, the International Disability Alliance. As the new communication technologies were coming into the mainstream, disability activists began to elicit the support of established NGOs like HRW and AI. With the backing of HRW, AI, and funding from the Open Society Institute, a disability convention was brought to the UN General Assembly. In 2006, the Convention on the Rights of Persons with Disabilities was adopted.[7] By 2012, 126 states had become party to the treaty, which obligates signatories to prohibit all discrimination on the basis of disability. This example illustrates how concerted NGO action can result in substantive international law.

While new communication technologies have often facilitated the campaigns of NGOs, one example of a media-driven effort illustrates both the promise and problems of the approach. For over two decades, the Lord's Resistance Army and its leader, Ugandan Joseph Kony, have kidnapped children in northern Uganda and used them as child soldiers, creating fear and intimidation among the population. Invisible Children, founded in 2004, is an NGO organized to call attention to this abuse through film and organized political activity. Over the years, it has presented a simplistic but graphic message aimed at Western audiences to fight against Kony. In 2012, a half-hour video piece called *Kony2012* went viral, attracting 80 million hits. While all agree that the abuse represents an egregious violation of human rights, not everyone, including many in Uganda itself, agree with Invisible Children's solution, which supports military action. So in constructivist discourse, NGOs can aid in the spread of ideas, and in the age of new media, they often use material resources for effect. Yet NGOs also have the power to distort the message, to oversimplify a complex problem, and to offer slick solutions. And, as outlined in Chapter 7, NGOs may not be representative of all those most directly concerned. Remember, they have no independent legal standing, have few material resources compared to states, and exist at the discretion of states in which they are operating.

The human rights activities of the United Nations, other IGOs, and NGOs have been confined to several areas. First, the United Nations has been involved in setting the international human rights standards articulated in the many international treaties. NGOs have pushed for many of these new treaties, articulating emergent human rights norms. Dedicated groups often seek the involvement of some of the major NGOs like AI and HRW to legitimate the issue. In 1991, AI decided to recognize and work on lesbian and gay rights, with HRW following shortly thereafter. A decade later, AI and HRW supported the efforts of disability rights activists, as described earlier.

Second, the United Nations and the European Commission on Human Rights have worked to monitor state behavior, establishing procedures for complaints about state practices, compiling reports from interested and neutral observers about state behavior, and investigating alleged violations. Monitoring state behavior is a sensitive undertaking because it impinges directly on state sovereignty. Yet special bodies have been established to examine, advise, and publicly report on the human rights situation in a given country or on worldwide violations.

Gross violations of human rights in South Africa under apartheid, in South American countries during the 1970s, in Israel and Palestine, and in China have tended to dominate the agenda. Many criticize that focus, arguing that there is a double standard and Western bias, with inordinate attention focused on a few issues, while economic and social human rights abuses in Western countries are largely ignored.

Beginning in 2006, the UN Human Rights Council initiated a new approach, the Universal Periodic Review, wherein every member state participates in evaluating the strengths and weaknesses of its human rights record every four years. Based on that assessment, other states make recommendations, e.g., calling for the state to request assistance in a particular area; offering new approaches; suggesting that the state share its best practices with others; or even taking specific actions. For example, both Cuba and Burkina Faso have been pressured to abolish the death penalty. Recent data suggests that almost two-thirds of recommendations have been accepted; states recognize that reform "must be largely evolutionary, rather than revolutionary."[8]

NGOs have also been particularly useful in monitoring activities. Amnesty International, founded in 1961, has become perhaps the most effective human rights monitor. AI was involved in efforts to end the abuse of human rights in Uruguay and Paraguay in the 1970s. It was instrumental in bringing international attention to the Argentinian military abuses involving abductions and disappearances in the early 1980s, utilizing its research and publicity expertise. While the organization originally emphasized the protection of individual political prisoners, its agenda has now broadened to include multiple issues, including systematic abuses of economic and social rights. AI and organizations like it provide information for the UN's own monitoring activities and for the United States.[9]

Of course, monitoring is not an end in and of itself, so it is important to ask whether monitoring by either IGOs or NGOs through investigations, reports, resolutions, and naming and shaming ultimately makes a difference for rights protection. The evidence is mixed. One study found that if issues within human rights treaties are taken up by civil society groups, then the state's actual human rights practices are improved through NGO mobilization.[10] Another study of monitoring by the UN, NGOs, and the media between 1975 and 2000 found that governments identified as violators often "adopt better protections for political rights afterward, but they rarely stop or appear to lessen acts of terror.[11] Only when NGOs actively took up issues did practices improve.

Thus, IGO and NGO monitoring over time, as well as the Universal Periodic Review—which is designed to help states implement better practices—is not necessarily enough to alter practices. Achieving compliance with international human rights norms can be a long process. Moreover, when states fail to comply with existing norms, it may not be a deliberate act. Obstacles may prevent willing states from readily complying. As legal theorists Abram Chayes and Antonia Handler Chayes have argued, there is frequently ambiguity of language and intent in norms; some states may lack the capacity to implement the norms; and standards do change over time. So the goal is to reach an acceptable level of compliance.[12]

The third area in which IGOs and NGOs have operated is in taking measures to promote human rights and improve levels of state compliance. In the UN system, that responsibility rests with the coordinating office and person of the High Commissioner for Human Rights. Among the most visible of those promotional activities is ensuring fair elections. For example, since 1992, the United Nations has provided electoral assistance—election monitors, technical assistance—in over 100 countries. It has actually conducted elections in Cambodia (1992–93) and East Timor (2001–2004), and shared that responsibility with states by providing technical assistance, as in Afghanistan (2004–2005), Iraq (2005), and South Sudan (2011).

Enforcement actions by IGOs for human rights violations is also a possibility, but rare. In the case of apartheid—legalized racial discrimination against the majority black population in South Africa and a comparable policy in Southern Rhodesia (now Zimbabwe)—the international community took coercive economic measures, but as discussed in Chapter 5, the South African government did not immediately change its human rights policy, nor was the government immediately ousted from power.

In a few cases, enforcement action may involve the use of military force. In the case of the humanitarian emergency in northern Iraq after the 1991 Gulf War, as well as in reaction to the crises in Somalia in 1992 and Bosnia in the mid-1990s, the UN Security Council explicitly linked human rights violations to security threats and undertook enforcement action without the consent of the states concerned. Yet the cases where IGOs intervene are few. Many states are suspicious of strengthening international organizations' power to intervene in what they still regard as their domestic jurisdiction.

All of these activities of the international community on behalf of human rights are fraught with difficulties. A state's signature on a treaty is no guarantee of its willingness or ability to follow the treaty's provisions. Monitoring state compliance through self-reporting systems presumes a willingness to comply and to be transparent, a major caveat that cannot necessarily be taken for granted. Taking direct action by imposing economic embargoes may not achieve the announced objective—a change in human rights policy—and may actually be harmful to those very individuals whom the embargoes are trying to help. It has been reported that the international community's economic sanctions against Iraq after the first Gulf War resulted in a lower standard of living for the population and an imposition of real economic hardship on the masses, while the targeted elites remained unaffected. The sanctions did not have the intended effect of securing the elimination of Iraq's weapons of mass destruction.[13]

Despite these difficulties, the international community is moving toward the **soft law** position that international action to protect individuals is acceptable. But humanitarian intervention, or R2P, as introduced in Chapter 8, comes with its own set of problems. Can it be a legitimate response if it is used only selectively, in some cases and not in others? In 2011, why did the international community (the UN, NATO, and the League of Arab States) all voice support for military action against Libya's Colonel Muammar Qaddafi? Qaddafi's predictions of "rivers of blood" against his opponents and his threats to "cleanse Libya house by house" provided the justification for internationally sanctioned intervention.[14] But mass atrocities attributed to the Syrian regime of Bashar al Assad against the Syrian people since 2011 have not led to the same response. Might the danger be that all interventions in another state's affairs can ultimately be justified by R2P? After all, the American government, when no WMD were found in Iraq, justified the invasion by pointing to the ruthless regime of Saddam Hussein. When does use of the term become a justification for a state or group of states to act only in their national interest? Indeed, international and national actions on behalf of human rights objectives remain a very tricky business.

Explaining International and State Responses to Human Rights Abuses

What explains the lack of decisive action in responding to massive human rights atrocities? Realists respond that states have determined that it is not in their national interest to respond, since human rights abuses do not usually threaten a state's own security. If genocide committed by one state does jeopardize another state's national interest, including intruding on its core values, then it could act, in the eyes of realists, although few states are likely to act alone. As former U.S. national security adviser Henry Kissinger has warned, a wise realist policy maker would not be moved by sentiment alone or by personal welfare, but by the calculation of the national interest.[15] While national interest is generally viewed in terms of security, it may be broader than that, encompassing historical tradition or domestic values.

Liberals would be more likely to advise state intervention in response not only to genocide but also to less dramatic abuses. Liberals' emphasis on individual welfare and on the malleability of the state makes such intrusions into the actions of other states more appealing to them. Like the realists, they may prefer that nongovernmental actors or humanitarian agencies take the initiative. Hence, sending in the UN humanitarian agencies is often the first response. But liberals generally see it as a state's duty to intercede in blatant cases of human rights abuse. However, that interest may conflict with other contending interests—preserving an alliance, hamstringing an enemy, or putting resources into domestic policy initiatives.

Radicals have different reasons for not intervening. To them, the injustices in the international system stem from an unfair economic system—namely, the international capitalist system, where some groups and individuals are exploited. If intervention is justified, it must be applied without discrimination. And radicals do not believe that will occur, as the economic interests of the most powerful states will drive the interventions.

Specific Human Rights Issues

Generally, international human rights treaties address separate issues, each of which is worthy of study. In this section, we first turn to a study of genocide and mass atrocities. Protecting humans from physical violence has been a preeminent religious value over the ages. Since it was the reaction to the atrocities of World War II that led to the internationalization of human rights, focusing on these issues is appropriate. At the same time, crimes against humanity and war crimes have led to new ways of punishing violators, a subject discussed later. Then we take up the issue of protection of a specific group. The issue of women's rights is instructive, as it involves the expansion of rights across time and space and it provides parallels with other human rights issues that focus on groups of protected people, from children to indigenous people to the disabled.

The Problem of Genocide and Mass Atrocities

The twentieth century saw millions of deaths from deliberate acts of warfare, ethnic cleansing, crimes against humanity, and physical violence against individuals. Yet the word to describe one kind of physical violence—genocide—did not even exist during the first half of the century. A Polish lawyer, Raphael Lemkin, became so incensed by the destruction of Armenians in 1915 that he devoted his life to the human rights cause, penning the word *genocide* and then traveling around the world in support of an international law prohibiting it.

It took the **genocide** of Jews and other "undesirables" during World War II before the international community was ready to act. In 1948, the Convention on the Prevention and Punishment of Genocide was adopted. Genocide is defined in the convention (see Box 10.1). While the convention was signed, ratified, and recognized as an advance in international human rights, like most legal conventions it is both precise on some questions and vague on others. Such ambiguity often reflects real disagreement among the parties during the negotiating process or an inability of the negotiators to reach a compromise. From one perspective, the convention is precise in terms of defining what is a genocide. The perpetrator of the genocide has to have the intention to kill; the killing or maiming is not an unintended result of violence or a random act. The targets of the violence must be a national, ethnical, racial, or religious group. But from another view, the convention is vague. It does not specify how many people have to be killed to be considered a genocide. Nor does it specify what

---

BOX 10.1

The Genocide Convention

ARTICLE 1   The Contracting Parties confirm that genocide, whether committed in time of peace or in time of war, is a crime under international law which they undertake to prevent and punish.

ARTICLE 2   In the present convention, genocide means any of the following acts committed with intent to destroy, in whole or in part, a national, ethnical, racial or religious group, a such:

(a) Killing members of the group;
(b) Causing serious bodily or mental harm to members of the group;
(c) Deliberately inflicting on the group conditions of life calculated to bring about its physical destruction in whole or in part;
(d) Imposing measures intended to prevent births within the group;
(e) Forcibly transferring children of the group to another group.

ARTICLE 3   The following acts shall be punishable:

(a) Genocide;
(b) Conspiracy to commit genocide;
(c) Direct and public incitement to commit genocide;
(d) Attempt to commit genocide;
(e) Complicity in genocide.

---

evidence is necessary to prove intentionality. The convention provides no permanent body to monitor potential genocides or any system for early warnings. How the international community should respond is vague, but respond it should.

Despite the convention and the good intentions of "never again," the international community has failed to act decisively in cases of purported genocide. One million Bangladeshis were killed in the 1970s; India intervened, but did not stop the carnage. Two million Cambodians were killed in the same era, but Vietnam's intervention, undertaken for different reasons, was too late and the rest of the world was silent.

In the 1990s, over 750,000 Rwandans were killed while the small UN contingent on the ground sat back and watched. In the states of the former Yugoslavia, including Bosnia-Herzegovina, Croatia, Serbia, and Kosovo, people of one ethnic group were forced to move, sometimes killed or placed in concentration camps, and raped, but the reaction by the United Nations and NATO proved ineffective in stopping the carnage. In Darfur in the early 2000s, as many as 300,000 people were killed and almost 3 million people displaced. While the NGOs provided humanitarian relief, states failed to act decisively. A UN/African Union peacekeeping force was approved later, but it was too weak, having neither the mandate nor the personnel to halt the spread of violence, as discussed in Chapter 7.

In the Rwanda and Darfur cases, there was a concerted policy of major states not to use the word *genocide*, clearly aware that admitting it was genocide would necessitate an international response. Instead, at the outset these were framed as "ordinary" ethnic conflicts; in retrospect, it is clear they were anything but ordinary. Even when the NATO-backed coalition organized to stop the ethnic cleansing of Serbs in Kosovo, the word *genocide* was never used by NATO to describe what was happening.

Along with the prohibition against genocide came the codification of other crimes against humanity and crimes committed during warfare. These **crimes against humanity** are now incorporated in Article 7 of the Rome Statute of the International Criminal Court (see Box 10.2). The former Yugoslavia illustrates the dilemmas associated with the application of these conventions. During the war in the early 1990s, the term *ethnic cleansing* was coined to refer to systematic efforts by Croatia and the Bosnian Serbs to remove peoples of another group from their territory, but not necessarily to wipe out the entire group. In Bosnia, Muslim civilians were forced by Serb troops to flee towns for Muslim areas; some were deported and others placed in concentration camps.

But was this genocide or crimes against humanity? During 1992 and 1993, the UN Commission on Human Rights undertook several investigations, concluding that there were "massive and grave violations of human rights" and that Muslims were the principal victims. The Security Council Commission of Experts concluded that all sides were committing war crimes, but only the Serbs were conducting a systematic campaign of genocide. But some states and many NGOs disagreed, maintaining that all sides were guilty. Only in 2007 did the International Court of Justice rule that Serbia neither committed genocide nor conspired or was complicit in the act of genocide. The judges pointed to insufficient proof of intentionality to destroy the Bosnians.[16] In reality, Security Council members lacked the political will to stop the killing in Bosnia.

Two other cases of alleged genocide and war crimes illustrate the political sensitivity of the issues. Following the end of the Sri Lankan civil war in 2009, a UN panel was charged with investigating allegations of war crimes. Leaked in 2011, the report found that while both the government and the Tamil Tigers had committed war crimes, most civilian casualties in the final days were committed by government troops, directly contradicting the Sri Lankan government findings. Even more controversial has been the investigations of human rights violations during the Gaza war of 2008–2009 between Israel and Hamas. The UN Human Rights Council found evidence of potential war crimes and crimes against humanity by both Hamas and Israel. Like Sri Lanka, Israel investigated independently and found no deliberate targeting of civilians. The Council itself remains divided, some standing by their findings, while others concur with the Israeli findings.

As this discussion shows, international efforts to prevent or stop mass human rights abuses have been fitful. When prevention isn't possible, for practical or political reasons, the next issue is whether and how to punish the individuals responsible.

Punishing the Guilty Individuals

A key trend in the new millennium is that individuals responsible for genocide and crimes against humanity should be held accountable. This idea is not new. After World War II, the allies convened

---

BOX 10.2

Crimes Against Humanity

Article 7 of the Rome Statute of the International Criminal Court reads as follows: For the purpose of this Statute, "crime against humanity" means any of the following acts when committed as part of a widespread or systematic attack directed against any civilian population, with knowledge of the attack:

(a) Murder;

(b) Extermination;

(c) Enslavement;

(d) Deportation or forcible transfer of population;

(e) Imprisonment or other severe deprivation of physical liberty in violation of fundamental rules of international law;

(f) Torture;

(g) Rape, sexual slavery, enforced prostitution, forced pregnancy, enforced sterilization, or any other form of sexual violence of comparable gravity;

(h) Persecution against any identifiable group or collectivity on political, racial, national, ethnic, cultural, religious, gender as defined in paragraph 3, or other grounds that are universally recognized as impermissible under international law, in connection with any act referred to in this paragraph or any crime within the jurisdiction of the Court;

(i) Enforced disappearance of persons;

(j) The crime of apartheid;

(k) Other inhumane acts of a similar character intentionally causing great suffering, or serious injury to body or to mental or physical health.

---

trials in Nuremberg and Tokyo to punish German and Japanese leaders for their wartime actions. However, because these trials were the victor's punishment, they were not seen as legitimate precedents. Following the atrocities in Yugoslavia and Rwanda,

YOU DECIDE

In this chapter we've seen how the concept of human rights has evolved since World War II to become a leading discourse of the twenty-first century. Human rights today are codified to an unprecedented degree. Human rights have also become a leading justification offered by states for their economic, diplomatic, and even military intervention in the affairs of other sovereign states. Given that the principle of sovereignty was established and maintained chiefly to restrain inter-state war (particularly identity-based wars, such as nationalist or religious war), is the trend toward justifying interventions abroad as a means to support human rights a good one?

If you support humanitarian intervention on behalf of human rights abroad, you might think this trend is valuable because it pushes states to conceive of interven-tion in humanitarian terms. Sovereignty, you might argue, has no place in the debate when dictators are murdering, torturing, or imprisoning their citizens. The responsi-bility to protect makes it incumbent upon the international community to intervene in such situations. Intervention may also have the positive effect of deterring future abusers. Even lip service to such aims is valuable, you might argue, because it raises awareness of human rights and over time will result in the internalization of rights protection as an international norm.

On the other hand, you might support the idea of human rights but still think rights interventions are a bad idea. Interventions are almost always accompa-nied by their own hardships, from economic deprivation to wartime casualties. Furthermore, the most effective intervention—actual military occupation—risks turning into a colonial occupation if the intervention lasts long enough to truly establish a new, rights-respecting government. You might also be wary of the use of "human rights abuse" to justify intervention, as there are significant disagree-ments about what counts as abuse and what doesn't. For instance, in some places the punishment for stealing is having one's hand cut off in a public square. Is it fair to call this torture, or is that a western conception of rights? Permitting intervention for human rights abuse thus opens a Pandora's box to interstate conflict. Protecting sovereignty is better in the long term for avoiding war, which is good for the basic right of physical security.

YOU DECIDE: Make a case for or against human rights interventions. Take a strong position and be clear about what part of your argument is interest based, what part is morally or normatively driven, and why.

the United Nations established two ad hoc criminal tribunals, the International Criminal Tribunal for the Former Yugoslavia, in 1993, and the International Criminal Tribunal for Rwanda, in 1994. These ad hoc tribunals, approved by the UN Security Council, have developed procedures to deal with the myriad issues involved in these cases, including jurisdiction, evidence, sentencing, and imprisonment. Among the accused standing trial was former Serbian president Slobodan Milošević, until his death in 2006, and among those sentenced were a number of Rwandan officials, including former prime minister Jean Kambanda. Because of the need to establish procedures and the difficulty in finding the accused, the trials have proceeded very slowly. The Yugoslav court has indicted over 100 persons and over 50 percent of those have been sentenced; the Rwanda court has handled 40 cases. The trials are not expected to be completed until 2013 or 2014.

In light of the difficulties with the ad hoc tribunals, in 1998, states under UN auspices concluded the Rome Statute for the International Criminal Court (ICC), an innovative international court having both compulsory jurisdiction and jurisdiction over individuals.[17] Four types of crimes are covered: genocide, crimes against humanity, war crimes, and crimes of aggression. No individuals (save those under 18 years of age)

Kenyan deputy prime minister Uhuru Kenyatta, cabinet secretary Francis Muthaura, and former police chief Mohammed Hussein Ali appear before the International Criminal Court in The Hague to stand trial for murder, rape, and persecution for allegedly orchestrating postelection violence that killed 1,000 people. The ICC is the first permanent international human rights court.

are immune from jurisdiction, including heads of states and military leaders. The ICC functions as a court of last resort, hearing cases only when national courts are unwilling or unable to deal with prosecuting grave atrocities.

In 2003, the work of the ICC began. In 2012, two cases were completed. Colonel Thomas Lubanga, a Congolese rebel leader, was convicted of using child soldiers under the war crimes provision (Article 8) of the Rome Statute. A second Congolese rebel leader, Mathieu Ngudjolo Chui, was acquitted because of insufficient evidence. Most of the other cases on the ICC's docket involve crimes committed in African countries and few have been given extensive attention in the Western media. Twenty arrest warrants have been issued, including for Sudanese president Omar Hassan al-Bashir, the Lord Resistance Army (LRA)'s Joseph Kony, and General Bosco Ntaganda of the Democratic Republic of the Congo.

Yet the ICC is controversial. Widely hailed by many, including a broad-based coalition of over 1,000 NGOs, supporters see the court as essential for establishing international law and enforcing individual accountability for actions taken during conflict. Others, including the United States, China, India, and Turkey, are critical. Specifically, the United States objects to provisions of the statute that might make U.S. military personnel or the U.S. president subject to ICC jurisdiction, believing that the United States has "exceptional" international responsibilities as a hegemon that should make its military and leaders immune from the ICC's jurisdiction. The United States objects more generally on the grounds that the ICC infringes on U.S. sovereignty. The controversy continues, while the ICC proceeds despite the United States' refusal to sign the treaty (see the Global Perspectives box in this chapter).

In April 2012, the first former head of state was found guilty in an international court. Liberia's Charles Taylor was found guilty of war crimes and crimes against humanity committed in Sierra Leone between 1997 and 2003. He was sentenced to 50 years in prison. The court delivering the verdict was the Special Court of Sierra Leone, jointly organized by Sierra Leone and the United Nations. Several subsequent hybrid courts are currently in session.

Punishment of instigators, whether through international or regional courts, is controversial because of the trade-off between peace and justice. Is it more critical to try individuals for wrongdoing committed during war, or is it more critical to ensure peace? Bringing individuals to justice might jeopardize the long-term peace because those facing future prosecution may try harder to stay in power. In 2009, the ICC's indictment of Sudan's president, al-Bashir, for war crimes and his "essential role" in murder and atrocities in Darfur illustrates the dilemma. Would the war have ended sooner had his case not been referred to the ICC by the Security Council? Did the indictment complicate any potential political settlement to the Darfur conflict?

Human Rights: A View from the United States

Since the days of the Founding Fathers, the United States has viewed itself as special. As early as 1630, John Winthrop urged passengers departing for the new land to develop "a city upon a hill," a phrase drawn from Christ's Sermon on the Mount. In 1776, Thomas Paine wrote of America as a beacon of liberty. Over the centuries, that view of the United States as special or exceptional expanded: from a land of freedom for persecuted peoples, to one whose polity was one of the oldest democracies forged around liberal political and civil liberties in the Bill of Rights, to one with a unique international mission to spread abroad.

On the issue of human rights, American exceptionalism has been well entrenched. In 1941, President Franklin Roosevelt stated, "Freedom means the supremacy of human rights everywhere. Our support goes to those who struggle to gain those rights and keep them,"[a] a theme reiterated in the Atlantic Charter. At both the Tokyo and Nuremburg war crime trials of Japanese and German leaders, Americans were the prosecutors, advocating for punishing the guilty. At the UN founding conference in 1945, there was strong support for including human rights as a key area of UN responsibility. The Universal Declaration of Human Rights was attributed to the tireless effort of Eleanor Roosevelt, wife of the late U.S. president. The United States was a leader in prohibiting genocide, in supporting the Geneva Conventions on war crimes and humanitarian law, and in supporting the ad hoc tribunals for Yugoslavia and Rwanda. After all, U.S. norms and values of freedom, human rights, rule of law, and democracy are universal norms and values.

In actuality, U.S. rhetorical commitment to a human rights agenda has not always been reflected in its behavior. Racial discrimination is an area in which the United States has fared particularly poorly. Following World War I, Woodrow Wilson fought *against* an antiracial discrimination clause, not acknowledging the inconsistency of such a position. Following World War II, Mrs. Roosevelt was instructed to emphasize "safer" issues at the UN meetings, avoiding the topic of race. The U.S. record of racial discrimination, from the age of slavery, through Jim Crow laws and segregation, and continuing today with more subtle forms of discrimination, is a blemish in U.S. history.

That record became even more marred by Cold War politics, when U.S. foreign policy was dominated by fear of communism. Thus, the United States supported anti-communist regimes regardless of their record on political or civil liberties. In the name of national interest and geopolitical concerns, the United States supported right-wing dictatorships in Latin America and in Southeast Asia. Nowhere was that policy more contradictory of American exceptionalist values than in the U.S. policy toward South Africa's apartheid government. Despite that regime's blatant legal discrimination of the majority of its population, denying to blacks all the basic political, civil, and economic liberties, the United States supported the South African white regime. After all, South Africa produced key minerals necessary for U.S. economic development; it was an important way station on the oil routes around the Cape of Good Hope; and above all, it was the anticommunist bastion on the continent.

In addition, the U.S. record supporting human rights treaties has not been matched with ratification by the U.S. Senate. Thus, the United States has signed, but never ratified, many key human rights documents, including the treaties on refugees, on economic and social rights, on the child, on discrimination against women, as well as the statute on the ICC. That trend continued in 2012 when the U.S. Senate failed to ratify the UN Convention on the Rights of Persons with Disabilities.

Why has the United States not followed through with its rhetorical commitment? Although the specific reasons may vary, there are both realist and liberal institutional explanations. One justification for U.S. opposition to human rights treaties is based on the primacy of the U.S Constitution. The Constitution enshrines separation of power among the three branches of government and division of power between the federal government and the states, which can make it difficult to incorporate international law. At times, the U.S. has addressed this problem by adding an understanding to a treaty. For example, an understanding to the Convention on the Elimination of All Forms of Racial Discrimination stated that the provisions would be implemented by the federal government *to the extent it had jurisdiction*. In other cases, the treaty was never brought to the floor of the Senate.

At other times, the U.S. prefers to reinterpret or thwart treaties already in force in order to promote what is deemed to be in the national interest. In the aftermath of 9/11, the Bush administration reinterpreted international treaties, redefining torture and creating a new category of detainees called "enemy combatants" who were offered few legal protections. These actions were justified as being in the national interest.

Enemy combatants imprisoned by the United States at Guantánamo Bay, Cuba.

Several authors explain this reluctance to support and ambivalence towards international human rights treaties by referring to U.S. exceptionalism. The U.S. believes it does not have to bow to the demands of other states, nor be circumscribed by the actions of others. The U.S. is *special* and has a unique role in the world. But as constructivists argue, international human rights norms are firmly embedded and that explains why the deviant behavior of the United States has generated vigorous international debate and condemnation.

[a] Address January 6, 1941, *The Public Papers and Addresses of Franklin D. Roosevelt*, 13 vols., ed. Samuel Rosenman (New York: Random House, 1938–50), vol. 9, p. 672.

FOR CRITICAL ANALYSIS

1. Provide evidence from speeches of public officials that the United States is an exceptional power on the issue of human rights.

2. Foreign policy decisions often result in a trade-off between competing values. Explain in relation to human rights and national security.

3. What are the costs to the United States of not ratifying key international human rights treaties?

Reconciling and Rebuilding: Truth Commissions

Truth commissions are another approach that has gained popularity since their use in South Africa following the end of apartheid in that country. The idea behind such commissions is to examine in an open forum what happened during the time of crisis, to uncover the truth, and in the process move forward with the reconciliation process. This is seen as an appropriate approach in countries emerging out of civil war where violence was widespread, where blame is apportioned to all sides, and where all parties must now live side by side. Increasingly, truth commissions are used in conjunction with other legal mechanisms, such as local courts (as in Rwanda and Bosnia) or hybrid courts (as in Sierra Leone or Cambodia). The establishment of these mechanisms illustrates a movement in the direction of accepting individuals like present and former heads of state and nonstate groups as subjects of international law, where previously only states have had such a status.

Women's Rights as Human Rights: The Globalization of Women's Rights

The case of women's rights illustrates how human rights have moved from the national to the international agenda, how different generations of rights have become interconnected, and how women's human rights touch directly on cultural values and norms. Like other human rights issues, they have gradually become a globalizing issue. As a UN poster prepared for the Vienna Conference in 1993 headlined: "Women's Rights Are Human Rights." But this has not always been the case in the eyes of the world.[18]

Evolving Political and Economic Rights

Women first took up the call for political participation within national jurisdictions, demanding their political and civil rights in the form of women's suffrage. Although British and U.S. women won that right in 1918 and 1920, respectively, women in many parts of the world had to wait until World War II (France, 1944) and after (Greece, 1952; Switzerland, 1971; Jordan, 1974; Kuwait, 2006). In some Middle Eastern countries, women still do not have the right to vote or it is limited to local elections.

During the negotiations over the Universal Declaration of Human Rights (1949), Latin American representatives lobbied strongly for the inclusion of gender, even though at the time gender was not yet recognized in the context of human rights. In the immediate aftermath of the declaration, the priority of the United Nations and its Commission on the Status of Women was on getting states to grant women the right to vote, hold office, and enjoy legal rights—part of first-generation human rights. Specifically, this led to the drafting of the Conventions on the Political Rights of Women in 1952, the Nationality of Married Women in 1957, and the Consent to Marriage in 1962. These actions helped to set the standard for assessing women's political rights. More than a decade later, the 1979 Convention on the Elimination of All Forms of Discrimination against Women (CEDAW) further articulated the standard, positing that discrimination against women in political and public life is illegal.

During the 1960s and 1970s, more attention was paid to second-generation human rights—economic and social rights—for women. The development community had believed for many years that all individuals, including women, could participate and benefit equally from the economic development process. Yet as experts began to examine statistics on economic and social issues relevant to women, which were recorded beginning in the 1940s, they found that not to be the case. Esther Boserup's landmark book, *Women's Role in Economic Development*, recorded the finding that as technology improves, men benefit, while women become increasingly marginalized economically. Women would need special attention if they were to become participants in and beneficiaries of development.[19]

The result was the women in development (WID) movement—a transnational movement concerned with systematic discrimination against women and with the failure of development to make an impact on the lives of the poor. These issues developed and expanded over the life of four successive UN-sponsored world conferences on women. These conferences, with growing governmental and nongovernmental representation, mobilized women in interlocking networks, enabling them to set a critical economic agenda affecting women, including equal pay remuneration for men and women workers, minimum standards of social security, maternity protection, and nondiscrimination in the workplace. The delegates went further, however, arguing for special programs targeted to benefit women, since economic development was not assisting them. The UN system responded by establishing programs to train and mobilize women in the development process and to give financial assistance for projects run by women. Virtually all the UN specialized agencies, including the World Bank, initiated programs for women's economic enhancement. Today the WID agenda is well integrated in most international assistance programs, under the rubric of Gender and Development and Gender mainstreaming.[20]

CEDAW addresses both political-civil and a wide range of socioeconomic rights. Although 187 states have signed the treaty, these signatories have included significant reservations or understandings that illustrate differences in how the treaty is being interpreted. Many of those reservations concern the rights of women. States like Algeria and Egypt, and many others, each expressed reservations on provisions that conflict with their own domestic and family law codes, which reflect religious and cultural values.

As before, it is important to ask whether states that signed CEDAW have subsequently taken steps to implement treaty protections. One study examined the problem of violence against women in post-communist countries. The study found that four countries did establish a government office to address the issues, but except for Kosovo, where international pressures were strong, their capacity was limited. States like Croatia did make extensive legislative changes. The Czech Republic established shelters. And in many jurisdictions, including Slovenia, Russia, and Poland, strong societal pressures pushed the state to change. Thus, with CEDAW, states became more vulnerable to NGO pressure, but compliance remains an ongoing process.[21]

From Political and Economic Rights to Human Rights

By the 1990s, the discussion of women's rights was clearly viewed as one of human rights. This shift was solidified at the 1993 Vienna Conference on Human Rights. As the Vienna Declaration asserted, "The human rights of women and of the girl-child are an inalienable, integral and indivisible part of universal human rights. ... The human rights of women should form an integral part of the United Nations human rights activities, including the promotion of all human rights instruments relating to women."[22] Included was not only human rights protection in the public sphere (first- and second-generation human rights) but also protection against human rights abuses in the private sphere, notably gender-based violence against women. The latter includes violence against women in the family and domestic life; gendered division of labor in the workplace, including work in the informal sector and sexual work; and violence against women in war, particularly rape and torture. In short, violence against women and other abuses in all arenas were identified as breaches of both human rights and humanitarian norms. Their elimination was to be pursued through national and international action. The establishment of UN Women in 2011 provides an international focus for these activities, but their agenda includes many complicated issues.

Continuing Violence against Women

Three examples illustrate the widespread and often controversial problem of violence against women as a human rights abuse. First, the systematic usurpation of women's rights and accompanying violence was an issue in Taliban-run Afghanistan. When the Taliban seized power in 1996, all women's rights were revoked in both the public and private sphere. Women were not permitted to hold jobs or attend school. They were required to wear the *burqa*, a full-body veil, and to be under the authority of male family members. Violations of the rules resulted in assaults and sometimes death.

In Afghanistan under the Taliban, women risked death by meeting clandestinely to receive education. Discrimination against women in education is prohibited under the UN Declaration of Human Rights and CEDAW. Afghanistan signed CEDAW in 1980 but did not ratify the treaty until after the Taliban was overthrown.

A secret group of Afghan women, the Revolutionary Association of the Women of Afghanistan (RAWA), organized resistance to Taliban restrictions, including setting up secret schools to educate females. Internationally, the U.S.-based Feminist Majority Foundation and over 180 human rights groups organized an international media campaign that focused on the plight of Afghani women. Not until the Taliban was ousted from power were the most restrictive measures relaxed, but the struggle for Afghan women continues.

Rape is a second example of violence against women. In Chapter 2, we discussed the massacres in Nanking by Japanese soldiers in 1937. Those atrocities included the systematic rape of thousands of Chinese women. More recently, the rape of 2,000 Kuwaiti women by Iraqi soldiers during the 1991 Gulf War, of 60,000 Bosnian women in 1993 by Serb and Croat forces, of 250,000 women in Burundi's and Rwanda's ethnic conflicts in 1993–94, and of an estimated 200,000 women during the violence in the Democratic Republic of Congo highlights the extent of this unique form of violence against women. At the Nuremberg and Tokyo war trials, rape was not brought up as a war crime, even though it was systematically employed during World War II as an instrument of war by states.

During the 1990s, rape as a systematic state policy was increasingly viewed as a human rights issue, and NGOs urged the ad hoc international criminal tribunals for Yugoslavia and Rwanda to consider the crime of rape. At the ad hoc tribunal for Rwanda, Jean-Paul Akayesu was accused of gang rape and genocide. In a controversial 1998 decision, the judges issued the unprecedented ruling that rape constitutes not only a crime against humanity but also genocide. The precedent is established, and now, thanks to NGO pressure, the statute for the International Criminal Court includes rape, sexual slavery, and forced prostitution among crimes against humanity, when such actions are part of a widespread and systematic attack against a civilian population.

Rape is not just a wartime issue. In South Asia and the Middle East, the problem is particularly acute even during peacetime. In some places, rape against women may be seen as an acceptable act of revenge against a prior wrong. The raped women, being dishonored, may be subsequently killed. Or prosecution of the crime may be difficult, as in Pakistan when a woman may be convicted of adultery unless four male witnesses corroborate her rape story. The case of the gang rape of an Indian student in 2012 and her subsequent death has brought the issue into the international limelight in a country where local police and government authorities have not vigorously prosecuted the alleged suspects.

Physical assault against women is a problem in many parts of the world, as well. Beginning in the 1990s, Ciudad Juarez, Mexico experienced a wave of attacks against women, about a third of which involved sexual assault, resulting in 304 deaths in 2010 alone. Like in Pakistan and India, Mexican authorities have been criticized for their lax investigations and failure to bring perpetrators to justice. In the U.S. military, rape of female soldiers by their male counterparts attracted widespread attention in 2012–13 as the military took measures to curb this abhorrent behavior.

Increasingly, human rights NGOs like Human Rights Watch and Amnesty International bring violations of women's rights to the attention of the international community, and public pressure is brought to bear. If state authorities fail to take these cases seriously, then the state, too, becomes complicit. But given different cultural norms, private-sphere activities are much easier to hide and more resistant to change.

Trafficking in women and children is a third form of gender-specific human rights violations. While prohibited under the CEDAW convention, the practice has become more ubiquitous, facilitated by open borders, pressures to keep labor costs low, poverty that drives women and families to seek any kind of employment (including selling their children), and the high profitability of the sex trade. The number of women forced into bonded sweatshop labor and domestic servitude is unknown, ranging between 12 to 21 million persons; estimates for those trafficked for the purposes of the sex trade vary from between 600,000 to 1.75 million women and children annually. This problem is especially vexing, because unlike rape, where consent is not given, women may choose to be trafficked for economic reasons. Yet the international community, speaking through several treaties, has made the exploitation illegal (see Table 10.1).

Although international standards against trafficking in women and children exist, monitoring and enforcement remain difficult. First, despite the international agreements, disagreement remains on the local level as to what constitutes trafficking. Second, the clandestine nature of the problem complicates enforcement. Furthermore, the issue has been framed as both a human rights problem and a transnational crime issue. Various UN-related groups, including special rapporteurs responsible for monitoring and pressuring states and anti-trafficking NGOs, are involved. A variety of different strategies are employed, from providing alternative employment opportunities to women, to educating women on the dangers, to punishing the traffickers through incarceration, to stricter law enforcement across national boundaries.

Ultimately, the solution to fully address discrimination against women, be it political, economic, or social, is to elevate women from their historically subordinate status to men. Liberal feminists see that progress has been made, as women have secured privileges that were once exclusively male prerogatives. The fact that both public and private abuses are the subject of media attention, concerted NGO activity, and state action denotes progress. However, radical (socialist) feminists do not see as much progress as they point to the economic forces that continually place women in a disadvantaged position. Encouragingly, virtually all condemn the various forms of both public and private violence against women, though their remedies for relief vary.

While the legal stage has been set by the protection provided in various human rights treaties under the auspices of international organizations, the mainstay of enforcement will continue to be at the state level. It is states that, prodded by the normative requirements of international treaties and lobbied by prominent individuals and human rights networks, undertake domestic reform. And it is states that, unilaterally or multilaterally, undertake punitive action against offending states. Yet the dilemma remains that states can be not only the protectors but also the abusers.

In Sum: A Renewed Agenda?

Human rights encompass classical liberal values that hold that individuals and groups are worthy of protection. In a world where the majority of states are democracies, we would expect an improving record on human rights. But at the domestic level, abuses occur in all states: refugees are singled out for abuse, people of color are discriminated against, and ethnic minorities are unable to enjoy the fruits of economic development. And would-be protectors—states and the international community—may have priorities other than protecting individuals abroad from a foreign state. In some cases, promoting human rights abroad might run directly counter to a state's national interest. How else can we explain why on specific issues one or more of the five permanent members of the UN Security Council exercises its veto, or makes it clear that it would exercise its veto, preventing a concerted international response to egregious violations of human rights, as occurred with the United States regarding Rwanda, China regarding Darfur, and Russia regarding Syria? How else can we explain why the United States, a longtime supporter of international tribunals for war crimes, has refused to support the International Criminal Court? However, if Zbigniew Brzezinski is right when he states that increased attention to human rights issues is "the single most magnetic political idea of the contemporary time,"[23] then we can expect that over time these ideas will shape and reshape state behavior. That is clearly the constructivist argument.

Discussion Questions

1. Which rights do you think should have priority? Political-civil rights? Socio-economic rights? Collective rights of groups? Why?

2. Find two newspaper articles that provide examples of state officials abusing the rights of their citizens. Do these citizens have any recourse?

3. Genocide is sometimes difficult to prove. Choose a specific case of state-sponsored violence (e.g., Turkey against the Armenians; Sudan against the Darfurians; the Assad government in Syria against its citizens). Does the violence qualify as genocide? What evidence would you have to collect?

4. If you are a woman whose human rights are being abused, what avenues of recourse might you use to make your case?

5. What human rights have not been discussed at the international level? Why?

Key Terms

crimes against humanity (p. 369)

cultural relativism (p. 354)

first-generation human rights (p. 353)

genocide (p. 368)

International Bill of Rights (p. 357)

second-generation human rights (p. 353)

soft law (p. 366)

third-generation human rights (p. 353)

As a result of global warming, polar ice has melted in the Arctic, opening a new shipping channel and access to natural resources on the seabed below. At least seven states are now making competing claims to explore and exploit the Arctic. Because the causes and consequences of environmental change are international, the environment is a transnational issue that cannot be addressed satisfactorily at only the local or national level.

11

TRANSNATIONAL ISSUES:
THE ENVIRONMENT,
WORLD HEALTH, AND CRIME

- *What makes the environment, health, and crime transnational issues?*

- *How do the concepts of collective goods and sustainability help us think about environmental issues?*

- *How might environmental issues lead to armed conflict?*

- *What factors make communicable diseases a particularly difficult transnational issue to manage?*

- *What technologies facilitate the spread of transnational organized crime?*

- *How do international relations theories incorporate an understanding of transnational issues, and what prescriptions might these theories offer to possibly reverse harm to the global environment, threats to world health, and transnational crime?*

The Challenge of Transnational Issues

Why study the environment, world health, and organized crime in an international relations course? The answer is that although much of international relations remains focused on relations between states, new technologies and new norms have emerged that challenge states and their citizens in increasingly important ways. In this chapter, we examine the challenges posed by these issues to international relations theorists, foreign policy makers, and nonstate actors, before turning to some reflections on how to link and engage the issues.

The date April 26, 1956, is not much remembered, but it should be. On this day, Malcom McLean, a U.S. trucking entrepreneur, shipped a load of trucks from Newark, New Jersey, to Houston, Texas. What was remarkable about McLean's shipment was that his trucks would be transported aboard a tanker ship in sealed, locked, and *standardized* containers. On being unloaded at port, the containers could simply be transferred unopened to waiting freight trucks and then sent on to their final destination. McLean did not invent what we now think of as "containerization," but he was the first to use it in the way that has become standard today.[1] Over 90 percent of the world's nonbulk cargo, including wheat, ore, liquefied natural gas, and petroleum, is now transported in container ships, the largest of which can carry as many as 15,000 containers. Each container can be unloaded and then reloaded onto waiting trains or cargo-truck platforms without being opened.

The revolutionary consequences of the advent and spread of containerization, as was true of the advent of the railroad in the nineteenth century, were not immediately obvious. But within a few decades, the process of moving cargo internationally had become relatively inexpensive. By the 1980s, the advent and miniaturization of computers would reduce the costs of shipping goods worldwide still further. The implications were staggering. Before World War II, nonbulk cargo had been transported in relatively small ships in nonstandard containers. A great deal of time and expense went into transporting cargo to ports and loading ships on the outbound side, then unloading them and transferring them to train or cargo truck on the inbound side. As these costs dropped, it became cheaper for manufacturers in advanced industrial states to hire foreign labor to manufacture parts or entire products and ship them to consumer markets than to continue to pay relatively higher wages and benefits to domestic laborers to produce the same goods. By the 1980s, businesses in many advanced industrial countries began to see the huge profit potential in exporting production and assembly abroad. Costly domestic labor and environmental regulations—which depressed profits—could be sidestepped, and the destructive environmental by-products of heavy manufacturing could be effectively exported to the producing countries. The severe harm to air and water quality resulting from this ongoing process of exporting production to the developing world could not be restricted to the producing countries. However, from a business perspective this harm made good sense, because instead of individual firms having to bear the costs of compromised air and water quality, the costs of a compromised environment would be diffused worldwide. The harmful effects might also be less concentrated in consuming countries, where many of these firms have their headquarters.

Perhaps more alarming, the container's very nature—sealed and opaque—makes it an ideal vehicle for smuggling, facilitating the inexpensive transfer of everything from human beings to exotic pets, contraband animal parts or plants, narcotics, and one day even possibly a nuclear device. Human cargo is dangerous not only because some of those "shipped" by containerization may intend harm once they arrive in their ports of destination, but because humans can spread communicable diseases.

The container ship is but one of several new communications technologies that have had both positive and negative unintended consequences; the cell phone and the Internet are two more. Each technology has made the world—not actually, but functionally—smaller. As the world shrinks and its population expands, environmental, health, and crime problems (and solutions) once limited by geography and climate become increasingly shared or "transnational."

States are interconnected and interdependent to a degree never previously experienced. Economic globalization is but one illustration. Human rights, both as norms and as emerging international law, are another. In this chapter, we introduce three additional and representative transnational issues: the environment, world health, and transnational crime. For each issue, we highlight interconnectedness, the interactions among various international actors, and the impacts of these changes on core concepts and on the study of international relations. This provides a framework from which to explore the many other transnational issues that will affect all our lives.

In the twenty-first century, more types of actors than ever participate in international politics: the state, ethnonational challengers, multinational corporations, intergovernmental organizations, nongovernmental organizations, transnational movements and networks, and individuals. The transition from states being the main actors in international relations to the growing importance of nonstate actors portends a significant power shift. Nonstate actors are of course not new, but their ability to compete or interfere with the power of states on many dimensions *is* new. They participate in a great variety of issues that are substantively and geographically interlinked, from the local to the global level. The ability of state leaders to manage this activity has diminished. For instance, one aspect of the sovereignty of the state—namely, internal control over its citizens' access to information and ideas—has eroded. The 2010 "Arab Spring" is but one recent example of this.

Containerization has transformed not only transportation but politics as well. The ability to move goods cheaply around the world has enhanced gains from international trade but has also facilitated illicit activities, such as smuggling.

In short, the revolution in transportation and communications technologies represented by the container ship, the Internet, and the cell phone have not only increased the salience and transnational impact of issues such as the environment, health, and crime, but they have also shifted the balance of power from states (even nominally powerful states) toward nonstate actors. Thus, transnational issues demand further discussion. Interest at the local and state level in health, the environment, human rights, and crime has been expressed for generations. What is new is that these are now *global* interests, and often demand global responses. How can we think conceptually about transnational issues? How do these issues intersect with traditional conceptions of sovereignty, security, and economics? Who are the various actors with interests? How would a realist, a liberal, a radical, and a constructivist address these transnational issues?

The Environment — Protecting the Global Commons

The environment powerfully affects the quality of our individual and collective lives. Every person, regardless of age, national origin, culture, or level of education needs access to clean air and water, and beyond this the physical space in which to live and prosper. Wherever they live, human beings convert some portion of the natural world to energy or objects. Many of these natural resources, such as timber, are renewable, and others, such as many metals, are recyclable, but some — in particular petroleum — are non-renewable: once they're gone, they're gone. Given our universal dependence on the environment for both our very existence and as a resource for our broader welfare, how did the environment come to be so threatened and why have the efforts of individuals, states, and international organizations to protect the environment not been more successful? If states' shared interest in peace can lead to a dramatic decline in the likelihood and destructiveness of interstate war, why cannot their shared interest in a clean environment lead to a reduction in the rate of its consumption or destruction? In this chapter, we see that issues of pollution, climate change, natural resources, population change, and energy are all intertwined, such that trends in one of these issue areas affect trends in each of the others. Costly policy decisions made to address one issue can have unintended impacts on each of the others. The complexity of the global ecosystem and the difficulty of predicting the interaction of its many parts is one partial answer to the question of why more has not already been done to slow or reverse harm to the global environment.

Conceptual Perspectives

Two conceptual perspectives help us think critically about the interrelation of environmental issues. These perspectives augment each other. First is the notion of collective goods (see Chapter 7). Collective goods help us conceptualize how to achieve shared benefits that depend on overcoming conflicting individual interests. How can individual herders in the commons be convinced to abridge their own self-interest (which is for each to increase the number of sheep s/he allows to graze on the commons) in the interest of preserving the commons for the collectivity? How can individual polluters of the global air and water commons be likewise convinced to abridge their self-interest in order to preserve these commons for the collectivity? One difficulty is that our most influential economic theories had their origins at a time when the global air, sea, and natural resources commons seemed truly infinite. Published in 1776, Adam Smith's *Wealth of Nations*, for example, suggested that individual self-interest was moved "as if by an invisible hand" to a collective good in the form of ever-cheaper and more plentiful consumer goods. Yet by the close of the nineteenth century, this seemingly infinite supply of space and resources had become bounded. Since the end of World War II, we have come to understand that our planet itself is a commons, and as such we must re-assess the collective impact of our individual self-interests. Collective goods theory both helps us understand these problems and at the same time suggests solutions.

The second conceptual perspective is sustainability, or sustainable development, as introduced in Chapter 9. Sustainability is a crucial perspective because it helps us think about advancing our survival and welfare without doing lasting damage to our environment and thereby abridging the health and welfare of our descendants. As a conceptual perspective then, sustainability reminds us that it is possible, desirable, even necessary to place value on the future quality of the earth's air, water, and land. Both perspectives underline the most fundamental problem facing those committed to slowing and ultimately reversing damage to the global ecosystem: because the costs of harm to the environment are diffused across both space and time, and the benefits of polluting and unsustainable resource consumption are concentrated, each individual state or corporation or person has a strong incentive to "free ride" and hope others will bear the costs of restraint. A pernicious logic takes root: if we do not poach the elephants, someone else will. If we install pollution controls, our competitors who did not will achieve a competitive edge. Furthermore, free-riding and cheating are very difficult to detect and monitor; and worse still, the effects of cheating may last for years even after it has been detected and halted.

But as in the example of the grazing commons, today's "farmers" have been forced by real-world evidence of harm to acknowledge an interest in acting to slow or halt further damage to our shared air, water, and land resources. This is why principles and norms concerning the environment have evolved considerably in customary international law in the past few decades. One core principle is the *no significant harm principle*, meaning a state cannot initiate policies that cause significant environmental damages to another state. Another is the *good neighbor principle* of cooperation. Beyond these are soft law principles, often expressed in conferences, declarations, or resolutions, which although currently nonbinding, often informally describe acceptable norms of behavior. These include the *polluter pays principle*, the *precautionary principle* (action should be taken on the basis of scientific warning before there is irreversible harm), and the *preventive action principle* (states should take action in their own jurisdictions). New emerging principles include sustainable development and intergenerational equity, both linking economics and the environment to future generations.

The level of attention accorded to environmental issues is reflected in the international treaties and agreements that have been ratified. As one scholar put it, "the clearest evidence for the ecological trend in world politics is the astonishing array of recent treaties on a host of environmental problems."[2] These include the protection of natural resources such as endangered species of wild fauna and flora, tropical timber, natural waterways and lakes, migratory species of wild animals, and biological diversity in general, as well as protection against polluting in marine environments, on land, and in the air. Each of these treaties sets standards for state behavior, and some provide monitoring mechanisms. In so doing, they are very controversial, because they affect core political, economic, and human rights interests, and because ultimately it is individual states that must guarantee them, even in circumstances where abiding by the treaty means a short-term cost or missed opportunity.

By studying three key environmental topics—pollution and climate change, natural resources, and population—we can see the conflicting interests in economic development, promoting human rights, and protecting the environment. Although each topic may be treated separately, and often is, they are all integrally related, and each has transnational implications.

Pollution and Climate Change

As pressures on the global commons mount, the quality of geographic space diminishes. In the 1950s and 1960s, several events dramatically publicized the deteriorating quality of the commons. The oceanographer Jacques Cousteau warned of the degradation of the ocean, a warning made prescient by the 1967 Torrey Canyon oil spill off the coast of England. Rachel Carson's 1962 book *Silent Spring* warned of the impact of pesticides and chemicals on the environment.[3] Carson's book, which highlighted the paradoxical effect of pesticides such as DDT — which could dramatically reduce the spread of diseases like malaria, but at the same time devastated the reproductive cycle of wildfowl and ultimately caused cancer in humans — became a best seller. Millions of Americans, and many others worldwide, who had never thought about the links between pesticides, the ecosystem, and human health outcomes, were suddenly aware of these connections and became concerned about the damage. More people became aware that the natural world is being degraded by human activity associated with agricultural and industrial practices, and that humans do not exist separately from the natural world. Economic development in agriculture and industry has **negative externalities** — costly unintended consequences — for everyone, as well as positive consequences.

Although many negative externalities may be local, some have national and international implications. Take the case of energy. To meet a rising demand for oil, the United States and China have turned to the oil sands of Alberta, Canada. In times of high oil prices, it becomes economically profitable to convert those sands to oil for eventual refinement into gasoline. MNCs have heavily invested in the operation. Deleterious environmental externalities are, however, becoming evident. The current extractive process, for example, requires a massive withdrawal of water, disturbing fish populations, and adversely affecting water quality. The tailing ponds containing toxic extraction residues have proliferated, imperiling wildlife. And forests are cut — the same forests that provide carbon sinks to slow the escalation of global warming.

Halfway around the world, China's thirst for energy has led to increased coal usage. Coal-burning power plants emit soot, toxic chemicals, and gases, which, with weather inversions, create air pollution not only over China, neighboring Korea, and Japan but also over the west coast of the United States. These sulfur dioxide emissions carry known health risks, including respiratory and heart disease and certain kinds of cancer. China is now taking critical initiatives to replace polluting plants, with some success in improving air quality.

In addition, the rivers that facilitate the transport of ships and commerce and that provide water for industry and human consumption can carry pollution across state boundaries. On October 4, 2010, for example, the wall of a storage pond used for toxic "red sludge" near the town of Kolontar in Hungary ruptured, and a massive wall of caustic red slime flooded nearby towns — killing four people and injuring more than

100—before making its way into rivers. Once in the water, the sludge killed fish and poisoned drinking water along the way. Hungary reacted quickly in an effort to contain the damage, but in three days a much-reduced flow of sludge reached the Danube River, a major European waterway linking Hungary to Croatia, Slovenia, Romania, and Bulgaria. Thus, an industrial accident in one state became a threat to the health and well-being of at least four states downstream.

Nothing affects our globe more than the pollution issues of the twenty-first century: ozone depletion and global warming. Both issues have characteristics in common. Both concern pollution in spaces that belong to no single state. Both result from negative externalities associated with rising levels of economic development. Both pit groups of states against one another. Both have been the subjects of highly contested international negotiations.

Thrust onto the international agenda in 1975, ozone depletion illustrates a relative success story. States recognized this environmental problem, caused by the emission of chlorofluorocarbons (CFCs), before it grew to crisis proportions and reacted with increasingly strong measures. Both the developed and the developing worlds became involved, with the latter receiving financial aid from the former to finance the change in technology. Substitutes were developed, and MNCs eventually supported the prohibition of CFCs. As a result, the depletion of the ozone layer was reversed. The story is a success story, but also highlights the risks of harmful practices in that natural systems may take centuries to recover from the ill effects of human industry, even after the harm is stopped. As recently as 2011, for example, a significant ozone hole was discovered over the Arctic. Scientists believe this hole is a legacy of the years before CFC emissions were halted.

The issue of global climate change, or greenhouse warming, has proved much more complicated. There are no inexpensive substitutes for agricultural, communications, and industrial processes that emit greenhouse gases; the costs of reducing emissions are high and must be paid now, while the benefits are diffuse and may only emerge after decades. But scientific facts are indisputable. The preponderance of greenhouse gas emissions comes from the burning of fossil fuels in the industrialized countries of the North. Greenhouse gases are also found in the developing countries, most notably from deforestation of the tropics for agriculture and the timber industry, and from the rising tight use of fossil fuels in China and India (see Table 11.1). These greenhouse emissions from developed and developing countries have consequences. A 2006 report issued by the U.S. National Academy of Sciences concluded that average temperatures in the Northern Hemisphere increased by 1 degree centigrade during the last century, much of that during the last two decades. The 2007 findings of the UN's Intergovernmental Panel on Climate Change found that human activity is more than 90 percent likely to be responsible. The two greenhouse gases blamed for retaining heat in the atmosphere—carbon dioxide and methane—have experienced

TABLE 11.1

WORLD CARBON DIOXIDE EMISSIONS BY REGION (MILLION METRIC TONS CARBON DIOXIDE)

REGION/COUNTRY	2005	2008	2035*	GROWTH RATE (2008–2035)
OECD				
OECD Americas	7,079	6,926	7,772	0.4%
United States	5,996	5,838	6,311	0.3%
Canada	620	595	679	0.5%
Mexico/Chile	463	493	782	1.7%
OECD Europe	4,400	4,345	4,257	-0.1%
OECD Asia	2,172	2,201	2,294	0.2%
Japan	1,241	1,215	1,087	-0.4%
South Korea	494	522	678	1.0%
Australia/New Zealand	437	464	528	0.5%
Total OECD	13,651	13,472	14,323	0.2%
Non-OECD				
Non-OECD Europe and Eurasia	2,782	2,832	2,964	0.2%
Russia	1,645	1,663	1,747	0.2%
Other	1,137	1,169	1,217	0.2%
Non-OECD Asia	8,359	10,100	19,688	2.5%
China	5,513	6,801	13,441	2.6%
India	1,182	1,462	3,036	2.7%
Other	1,665	1,838	3,211	2.1%
Middle East	1,400	1,581	2,659	1.9%
Africa	978	1,078	1,735	1.8%
Central and South America	1,011	1,128	1,852	1.9%
Brazil	365	423	874	2.7%
Other	646	705	978	1.2%
Total Non-OECD	14,530	16,718	28,897	2.1%
Total World	**28,181**	**30,190**	**43,220**	**1.3%**

* Estimate.

Notes: The U.S. numbers include emissions from electricity generation using nonbiogenic municipal solid waste and geothermal energy.

Sources: History: U.S. Energy Information Administration (EIA), International Energy Statistics database (as of March 2011), www.eia.gov/ies. Projections: EIA, Annual Energy Outlook 2011, DOE/EIA-0383(2011), www.eia.gov/forecasts/aeo, and World Energy Protection System Plus (2011).

sharp spikes after 12,000 years of relative consistency. The scientific community has found the evidence compelling.

Although scientists increasingly agree on the problem—that contemporary industrial, agricultural, and communications processes have strongly accelerated global warming—politicians and economists have not agreed on a solution. This is not surprising, given the competing interests of various parties. Industrialized countries seek continued growth, and the South wants to become industrialized and enjoy the North's consumer lifestyle, both made possible by the conversion of oil and gas to energy. The parties disagree on whether voluntary restraints or market-based responses will be sufficient for both "worlds" to reach their economic objectives while at the same time reducing greenhouse emissions (that is, achieve *sustainable* growth). If the global response proves insufficient, might authoritative regulations be needed, and if so what authority should be invoked to monitor and enforce them—international, state level, subnational, or even local?

The international community has made several attempts to respond to climate change through negotiated state action. One of the more recent efforts was the Kyoto Protocol of 1997, which amended a weak 1992 framework. The Kyoto Protocol provided for stabilizing the concentration of greenhouse gases and delineated international goals for reducing emissions by 2010. Under the protocol, developed countries (including the United States, Europe, and Japan) were to reduce their overall greenhouse gas emissions by at least 5 percent below 1990 levels by 2010; Japan committed to 6 percent, the United States to 7 percent, and the European Union to 8 percent. In neither the Kyoto Protocol nor the earlier agreement were developing countries included in the emission limitation requirement.

The Kyoto Protocol came into force in 2005, and was ratified by 156 states—but not the United States. The George W. Bush administration argued that the economic costs of moving away from a fossil fuel–based economy would be too high, and an unacceptable number of U.S. jobs would be lost. Furthermore, the developed northern countries would be forced to comply with restrictions, whereas rapidly developing economies like India and China would have fewer restrictions, giving them an unfair economic advantage. From a balance of power perspective, the Bush administration worried particularly about China, a nondemocratic country with long-standing territorial disputes in Asia. Allowing China's already rapidly growing economy to grow faster, while U.S. economic growth slowed, would harm long-term U.S. security and economic interests in East Asia. From an ideological perspective, the Bush administration opposed international regulations on the issue. Instead, the president argued that markets would be the best way to bring about the necessary changes, with higher prices leading to decreased consumption, and possibly a system for trading emission quotas.

European states and Japan did sign the protocol, and the protocol's cap-and-trade system appears to have worked: European signatories to the Kyoto Protocol committed to reducing average emissions by 8 percent below 1990 levels by 2012; yet by 2011 they had already exceeded those targets by 3 percent (11 percent total). Despite the success of the EU signatories, however, global emissions continued to rise: in 2010, the Global Carbon Project reported that global emissions of carbon dioxide rose by 5.9 percent, the equivalent of a half-billion extra tons of carbon pumped into the air.

In 2009, the new U.S. president, Barack Obama, attended a follow-up to Kyoto in Copenhagen, Denmark. Although the president acknowledged for the first time that the United States is responsible for more carbon emissions than any other state save China, and pledged to do more to curb emissions, the Copenhagen Accord of 2009 contained little in the way of specific guarantees, and left most environmentalists (and many small developing countries) angry and unsatisfied. Yet the 2008–2009 global economic crisis made a stronger treaty impossible, because despite the success of the EU's cap-and-trade system, most publics remain skeptical and tend to accept the argument that "regulation" is a costly luxury that cannot be pursued during times of economic hardship and uncertainty. This matters because with the exception of China, most of the major emitter economies are democracies in which leaders are necessarily responsive to public demands.

Three lines of thinking have emerged from disappointment with Kyoto and Copenhagen. First, perhaps by seeking a comprehensive global treaty, the individuals, groups, states, and coalitions of states seeking to slow, halt, and reverse global warming have aimed too high. As Robert Keohane and David Victor have argued, what seems to have emerged from the failures of Kyoto and Copenhagen is a kind of middle-ground: a "regime complex" for climate change that focuses on key *parts* of the climate change problem rather than the whole.[4] A second line of thinking is that given the reality of global warming, and the likely continued failure of efforts to slow or halt it, we should perhaps shift our resources into preparing for and remediating its effects. For example, 80 percent of the world's population lives near a coastline. As sea levels continue to rise, this population will need to move to higher ground. One problem with this solution, however, is that some states — such as Vanuatu, Netherlands, and Greenland — are particularly vulnerable to rising sea levels. Their citizens may not have the option of moving, because there simply is no higher ground their citizens might move to. Third, perhaps success can be achieved by focusing on the emissions that do the most damage rather than all emissions: this is the idea of Mexican scientist and Nobel laureate Mario Molina, who has argued that we can build on the 1987 Montreal Protocol, the most successful international environmental treaty ever, by banning hydrofluorocarbons, or HFCs. These chemicals are widely used as refrigerants and have "thousands of times the global warming potential of carbon dioxide."[5]

Thus, climate change will continue to be a high-priority agenda item across a wide spectrum of state interests, including economic development and national security. Climate change is an issue that brings with it both very real threats and opportunities in the twenty-first century.

Natural Resource Issues

The belief in the infinite supply of natural resources was not unreasonable throughout much of human history, as peoples migrated to uninhabited or only sparsely inhabited lands. Trading for natural resources became a mainstay of economic activity once people recognized that natural resources were never uniformly distributed. The assumption of an infinite supply of key economic resources was challenged by radical Marxist thinkers. According to Lenin, one of the reasons for imperialism was the inevitable quest for new sources of raw materials. Capitalist states depended on overseas markets *and* resources, precisely because resources are unevenly distributed. From this assertion, Lenin also drew his explanation for why imperialism necessarily resulted in war: capitalist states would be compelled to use armed force to secure the natural resources their factories demanded.

Nowadays we are keenly aware that natural resources *are* limited and that states do compete for resources. Two examples, both linked to pollution, climate change, and population, help highlight the importance of natural resources as a transnational issue. First is the growing importance of the Arctic as a communications (including transportation) and minerals resource, and second is the problem of fresh water.

One of the most obvious effects of global warming, particularly in the last decade, has been melting polar ice both in the Arctic and in the Antarctic. In the Arctic, receding ice has introduced an issue both old and new. As the Arctic ice recedes, waters once unnavigable become navigable, and access to natural resources on the seabed below—including strategic minerals, gold, and especially petroleum—becomes economically viable. This has led, in the last decade, to a kind of "race for the Arctic," as the seven states bordering the Arctic Circle—Canada, Denmark, Finland, Greenland, Norway, Russia, and the United States—have escalated claims and competition for the rights to access, traverse, explore, and exploit these newly available Arctic mineral resources. Of the Arctic states, only the United States has not yet ratified the international treaty governing states' rights to passage and access to seabed resources, the United Nations Convention on the Law of the Sea (UNCLOS). UNCLOS governs how far out from a state's coastline it has the right to regulate the passage of other states' vessels and exclusive rights to mineral resources on the seabed.

In the Arctic, the implications go far beyond economic interests in mineral wealth, however, because both the United States and the Russian Federation possess nuclear-powered and nuclear-armed submarines—to say nothing of surface vessels capable of bearing missiles or troops—whose legitimate patrol routes could be altered in important ways by claims made under UNCLOS. This explains why competition and claims for Arctic resources have taken on so many of the trappings of the fifteenth century "discovery" of the New World. Russia has reprised the planting of the national flag by using unmanned deep-sea submersibles to plant flags on the seabed.

While competition over access to the Arctic is a alarming to observers, perhaps *the most crucial* transnational resource issue is freshwater because it is necessary for all forms of life—human, animal, and plant. Only 3 percent of the earth's water is fresh (one-third lower than in 1970), and 70 percent of the world's total supply of freshwater is leaking away from the polar ice caps. At the same time, and partly as a consequence of global warming, the demand for freshwater is increasing. As discussed in Chapter 9, 20 percent of the world's people still lack access to safe, clean water, and one-third of those live in Africa. Worldwide, agriculture accounts for about two-thirds of the use of water, industry about one-quarter, and human consumption slightly less than one-tenth. It is estimated that by 2025, two-thirds of the world's people will live in countries facing moderate or severe water-shortage problems.

Because water resources have also become increasingly valuable as an aid to natural gas and petroleum extraction (a process most commonly known as "fracking"), freshwater shortage and contamination issues are likely to remain central concerns locally, regionally, and internationally. Fracking, short for hydraulic fracturing, takes its name from the process by which high-pressure water (often but not invariably freshwater) is injected via underground wells into hydrocarbon-rich substrata. The water, mixed with various sands and chemicals, frees natural gas or petroleum resources trapped in the earth and then returns them to the surface, where they can be separated, collected, transported, and refined. But because the process is largely unregulated in some countries (such as the United States), the potential for overconsumption or contamination of existing freshwater resources is high. In addition, the process violently alters the substructure of existing layers of earth, leading to the potential to destabilize human and natural communities on the surface, although the level of risk varies. In some communities, fracking has been implicated in micro-earthquakes.

Several additional examples illustrate the international controversies and repercussions of the limited supply of freshwater. Israel's control of scarce water on the West Bank has resulted in rationing in neighboring regions. The World Bank predicts that in the twenty-first century, water could be the major political issue not only between Israel and Jordan, but also between Turkey and Syria, between Pakistan and India, and between India and Bangladesh.

The story is much the same in Central Asia, where two upstream countries with relatively poor land, Tajikistan and Kyrgyzstan, are the water source for areas downstream with good land. Under the old system in the Soviet Union, water was freely available for downstream users. Now, conflict has arisen because water systems are in decay and no new system for water allocation has been developed. Water is also scarce in China's northern cities, so the country has embarked on a massive plan to rechannel water from the Yangtze basin via three 1,000-mile channels, at an estimated cost of $58 billion. That is more than twice the cost of China's other major water project, the Three Gorges Dam, the largest construction project ever. Three Gorges is designed to create hydropower. Both projects come at an enormous financial cost, diverting money from other sources, and are accompanied by detrimental environmental side effects. Three Gorges, for example, generates an estimated 84 billion kilowatt-hours of electricity, but the weight of the water it holds has created a risk of earthquakes and landslides that remains uncertain. In addition, the lake created by the dam has become a repository for concentrated sewage and waste dumped upstream by industry and cities. A severe drought in 2011 also highlighted how challenging regulating the flow of water downstream would be, as barge traffic (navigability) and access to drinking water by downriver communities were both interrupted.

Finally, because freshwater is a survival necessity at the individual level, we can see that the prospects for violent armed conflict within states can increase dramatically when access to water declines or is suddenly restricted and at the same time water-stressed peoples gain access to small arms. In 2003, during a time of severe drought, newly armed militias ravaged Sudan's Darfur region. In 2011, following the collapse of Libya's dictatorship, a combination of severe water shortage and a flood of Libyan small arms combined to cause increased violence in the Sahel region of Mali, Algeria, Chad, and Niger.

Population Issues

Recognition of the potential world population problem occurred centuries ago. In 1798, Thomas Malthus posited a key relationship. If population grows unchecked, it will increase at a geometric rate (1, 2, 4, 8, …), whereas food resources will increase at an arithmetic rate (1, 2, 3, 4, …). Very quickly, he postulated, population increases will outstrip food production. This scenario is referred to as the **Malthusian dilemma**. Although Malthus did not think productivity would keep up with population growth rates, he did acknowledge wars, famine, or moral restraint as ways to check excessive population.[6] Three centuries later, *The Limits to Growth*, an independent report issued by the Club of Rome in 1972, systematically investigated trends in population, agricultural production, natural resource utilization, and industrial production and pollution and the intricate feedback loops that link these trends. Its conclusion was pessimistic: the earth would reach natural limits to population growth within a relatively short period of time.[7]

Neither Malthus nor the Club of Rome proved to be correct (see Figure 11.1). Malthus did not foresee the technological changes that would lead to much higher rates of food production, nor did he predict the **demographic transition**—that population growth rates would not proceed unchecked. Although improvements in economic development led at first to lower death rates and hence to a greater population increase, over time as the lives of individuals improved, women became more educated, and people moved to urban areas, birth rates dropped dramatically. The advent of safe, reliable birth-control technologies also led to a decline in birth rates. Likewise, the Club of

Rome's predictions proved too pessimistic, as technological change stretched resources beyond the limits predicted in its 1972 report.

Although Malthus and the Club of Rome missed some key trends, their prediction that the world's population would increase dramatically has proved correct. While global population growth *rates* peaked in 1970, that is not the whole story. Several key observations make population growth rates all the more cause for concern. First, the population increase is not uniformly distributed. The developing world has higher population growth rates than the developed world. Fertility rates in the developing world have averaged 3.4 children per woman, while in the developed world fertility has declined to 1.6 children per woman as a result of the demographic transition. Thus, there is a significant demographic divide between the rich North, with low population growth rates, and the poorer South, with higher population growth rates; 98 percent of the growth in the world population is occurring in the developing countries. In

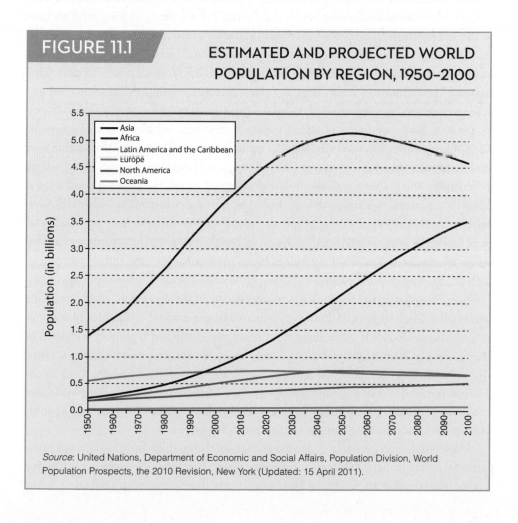

FIGURE 11.1   ESTIMATED AND PROJECTED WORLD POPULATION BY REGION, 1950–2100

Source: United Nations, Department of Economic and Social Affairs, Population Division, World Population Prospects, the 2010 Revision, New York (Updated: 15 April 2011).

addition, a long tradition of favoring male over female children in India and China has led to a gender imbalance in these two states. By 2020, men aged 15 to 34 will outnumber women in the same age bracket in these two countries by an estimated 57 million. These divides have politically sensitive consequences, as those in the South, laboring under the burden of the population explosion, attempt to meet the economic consumption standards of the North.

Realists see two threats emerging from these demographic trends that could destabilize the balance of power. First, states with burgeoning populations and insufficient food might seek to expand their territory or acquire food by means of war. Second, surplus males who might otherwise turn to domestic crime or destabilize the state from within might be channeled into state militaries and "expended" in aggressive interstate wars.[8] Both liberals and radicals see these possibilities as confirming that the South needs economic development for more than simply material needs. This is because wherever economic life improves (especially when that improvement has resulted from greater educational and workplace opportunities for women), women tend to have fewer and healthier babies (more of whom survive to adulthood). As a state's economic fortunes improve, so does better access to health care and family planning. Better education for parents and their children, in turn, opens up more economic opportunity, and the cycle reinforces itself. Thus, for these theorists, closing the development gap leads to a self-reinforcing spiral of economic improvement and demographic balance.

Second, both rapid rates of overall population growth and high levels of economic development mean increased demands for natural resources—in particular, arable land and freshwater. For countries such as China, India, and Bangladesh that already have large populations, the problem is severe. In Bangladesh and Nepal, the growing population is forced onto increasingly marginal land. In Nepal, human settlements at higher elevations have resulted in deforestation, as people cut down trees for fuel, resulting in hillside erosion, landslides, and other "natural" disasters. In Bangladesh, population pressures have led to settlements on deltas, which are vulnerable to monsoonal flooding and also strips topsoil, decreases agricultural productivity, and periodically dislocates millions of individuals.

Accelerating demand for natural resources occurs in the developed world as well. As the smaller (even slightly declining) population becomes more economically affluent, it increasingly demands more energy and resources to support its higher standards of living. People clamor for more living space, larger houses, and more highways, creating more demand for energy and resources. Wealthier people, especially those in the United States, also produce more garbage per person than in the developing world and much is not recycled, leading to a high demand for domestic landfill space and a profitable business in exporting garbage to the developing world.

High population growth rates lead to numerous ethical dilemmas for state and international policy makers. How can population growth rates be curbed without infringing on individual rights to procreate? How can cultural barriers to birth control or to the value of female children be overcome? How can the developed countries promote lower birth rates in the developing world without sounding racist or ethnocentric? Can policies be developed that both improve the standards of living for those already born and guarantee equally high standards and improvements for our descendants?

Population becomes a classic collective goods problem. It is eminently rational for a couple in the developing world to have more children: children provide valuable labor and often earn money in the wage economy, contributing to family well-being. Children are the social safety net for families in societies where no governmental programs exist. But what is economically rational for each couple is not environmentally sustainable for the collectivity. The amount of land in the commons shrinks on a per capita basis, and the overall quality of the resource declines. Over time, the finite resources of the commons have a decreasing capacity to support the population: Adam Smith's famous "invisible hand," when considered in the context of a commons, may therefore lead not to collective benefit but to collective disaster.

What actions can be taken with respect to population to alleviate or mitigate these dilemmas? The biologist Garrett Hardin's solution, using coercion to prohibit procreation, is politically untenable and pragmatically difficult, as China discovered with its one-child policy. Relying on group pressure to force individual changes in behavior is also unlikely to work in the populous states.[9] Leaving coercion aside, even if individuals may desire smaller families, family-planning methods may be unavailable to them. It is estimated that 120 million couples in the developing world want access to such methods but do not have access to them due to high costs or unavailability. Without access to family-planning methods, birth rates will continue to rise and states may feel forced to impose coercive restrictions.

But like the global environment, the connections, causes, and consequences of global population growth and decline have proven not only interlinked but complex. In the developed world, population growth has not only slowed, but in Europe, Japan, Russia, and even China, it is in decline. It is also aging. The causes of net population loss in Europe, Russia, and East Asia have similarities and differences. These regions all share in a remarkable trend of increasing women's access to education and career employment outside the home. As a result, one of the world's most powerful demographic trends — women having fewer babies and having babies later in life — can be explained by the extraordinary demands of education and career. The negative birthrate in the developed world thus becomes another kind of commons, as individual women in many of these states choose to put off motherhood in order to complete their educations and compete in the workplace. The aggregation of these individually rational decisions is a declining birthrate.

One exception to the pattern of population growth decline is the Nordic countries (in particular Norway and Sweden), where parental leave and strongly enforced antidiscrimination policies make it possible for women to avoid having to choose between becoming mothers and obtaining higher education and lifetime employment. But differences abound as well. In Russia, which the demographer Nicholas Eberstadt has characterized as a "demographic disaster," a combination of two decades of dramatic underinvestment in health care and education, widespread alcoholism, and heart disease, has led to steep declines in Russia's population, despite significant immigration into Russia from the Central Asian states. As Eberstadt puts it:

> In 2009, life expectancy at age 15 for all Russian adults was more than two years below its level in 1959; life expectancy for young men sank by almost four years over those two generations. Put another way, post-Soviet Russia has suffered a cumulative "excess mortality" of more than seven million deaths, meaning that if the country could have simply held on to its Gorbachev-era survival rates over the last two decades, seven million deaths could have been averted.[10]

In China, the population faces decline as a result of decades of its attempt to enforce a one-child policy, and in particular its surplus of males. There are simply too few women in China now, and many of China's women, like women in other growing economies, have sought higher education and the employment opportunities that follow. As a result of both trends, China's population growth rate has begun to decline.

Although the relative rate of growth of the world's population has slowed, the population has increased from 800 million in 1776, Adam Smith's era, to 7 billion in 2011. The UN estimates that by the end of the twenty-first century the global population will reach 10.1 billion. What is clear about world population growth and decline is that the problems and opportunities they create are international. Decisions affect not just states with high rates of population growth but their neighbors, as people on overcrowded land contend for scarce resources, seek a better life in other countries through migration, or turn to violence to get more desirable space, as happened in the early 2000s in Darfur, Sudan.

States are not the only actors affected by population pressures: this issue affects individuals, couples, and communities, along with their deepest-held religious and humanistic values. Population pressures also involve the nongovernmental community, including groups such as Population Connection or the Population Council that try to change public attitudes about population and procreation, as well as the Catholic Church and fundamentalist Islamic sects that oppose artificial restrictions on the size of families. It involves intergovernmental organizations such as the World Bank, charged with promoting sustainable development and yet hamstrung by the wishes of some member states to refrain from directly addressing the population issue. Perhaps most important, the population issue intersects inextricably with other environmental issues.

Populations put demands on land use for enhanced agricultural productivity; they need natural resources and energy resources. Thus, ironically, population may well be the pivotal global environmental issue, but it may also be the one that states and other international actors can do the least about.

Environmental NGOs in Action

NGOs have played a vital role in environmental issues since the 1960s. Their numbers have grown and their interests are diverse. On the issue of natural resources, for example, the Nature Conservancy and the Rainforest Action Network lobby for land protection. The Earth Island Institute and the Global Climate Coalition, the latter an industry-sponsored group opposed to limitations on greenhouse emissions, are likewise concerned with pollution issues.

NGOs perform a number of key functions in environmental affairs. First, they often act as international critics, using the media to publicize their dissatisfaction and to get environmental issues onto international and state agendas. For example, Greenpeace's condemnation of Brazil's unsustainable cutting of mahogany trees led that country to stop all mahogany exports until forestry practices could be improved. Second, NGOs may function through intergovernmental organizations, working to change the organization from within. For example, NGOs transformed the International Whaling Commission from a body that limited whaling through quotas into one that banned whale hunting altogether. Third, NGOs can aid in monitoring and enforcing environmental regulations, either by pointing out problems or by actually carrying out on-site inspections. For example, TRAFFIC, the wildlife-trade-monitoring program of the World Wildlife Fund and the International Union for the Conservation of Nature (IUCN), is authorized to conduct inspections under the Convention on International Trade in Endangered Species of Wild Fauna and Flora (CITES). Fourth, NGOs may function as part of transnational communities of experts, serving with counterparts in intergovernmental organizations and state agencies to try to change practices and procedures on an issue. One such **epistemic community** formed around the Mediterranean Action Plan of the UN Environmental Program. Experts gathered to discuss ways to improve the quality of seawater, share data, and ultimately establish monitoring programs. These same individuals also became active in domestic bargaining processes, fostering learning among government elites. Finally, and perhaps most important, NGOs can attempt to influence state environmental policy directly, providing information about policy options, sometimes initiating legal proceedings, and lobbying directly to a state's legislature or bureaucracy. For, despite the increased roles for NGOs, it is still states that have primary responsibility for taking action.

Human action has caused significant damage to our environment, but the political response has rarely proved commensurate with the harm. Many well intentioned efforts, like cleaning landfills, fail to address the larger problems of overconsumption and pollution of natural resources.

A Theoretical Take

What has made many environmental issues so politically controversial at the international level is that states have tended to divide along the developed/developing—North/South—economic axis, although some developed states have been more accommodating than others. From the perspective of some in the developed world, many environmental issues appear to stem from the population explosion, which they take to be a problem of the developing world, and furthermore one over which governments in those parts of the world have some control. In this view, the developing world's governments must enact policies that slow population growth rates, leading to a decrease in the pressure on scarce natural resources, and diminishing the negative externality of pollution locally, regionally, and internationally.

States of the developing South perceive the environmental issue differently. These states correctly point to the fact that many environmental problems—including the overutilization of natural resources and the pollution issues of ozone depletion and greenhouse gas emissions—are the result of the industrial world's excesses. By exploiting the environment in an unsustainable way, by misusing the commons, the developed countries were able to achieve high levels of—depending upon one's point of view—either economic development or consumption. Putting restrictions on developing countries by not allowing them to exploit their natural resources or by limiting their utilization of fossil fuels may impede *their* development. Thus, because the developed states have been responsible for most of the environmental excesses, it is they who should bear the burden of reduced energy consumption and environmental clean up.

The challenge in addressing transnational environmental issues is to negotiate a middle ground that reflects the fact that both sides are, in fact, correct. High population growth rates are a problem in the South—one that will not be alleviated until higher levels of economic development are achieved. Overutilization of natural resources is primarily a problem of the North. Powerful economic interests in the North are continually reminding us that changes in resource utilization may lead to a lower standard of living. Pollution is a by-product of both problems, which in the South tends to be in the form of land- and water-resource utilization because of excessive population, whereas in the North it stems from the by-products and negative externalities of industrialization. Thus, more than the other transnational issues, the environmental issue involves trade-offs with economic interests. Economic security is more likely to lead to environmental security.

Realists, liberals, radicals, and constructivists do not all have the same degree of concern for environmental issues, although each group has modified its perspectives in response to external changes. Realists' principal emphasis has been on state security, although some have identified human security concerns. Both types of security require a healthy and strong population base, near self-sufficiency in food, and a dependable supply of natural resources. Making the costs of natural resources or the costs of pollution abatement too high diminishes the ability of a state to make independent decisions. So, for example, Iceland's dependency on cod fishing as an industry made it much more vulnerable to unsustainable harvesting practices by its own fisheries and those of Britain and the United States, and to issues surrounding the rise in sea temperatures caused by global warming, which have caused cod populations to move to deeper or more northerly waters. The deeper implication is that for countries like Iceland, sovereignty is necessarily abridged, and the security of Iceland's citizens cannot be guaranteed by the state. Thus, realists fit environmental issues into the theoretical concepts of the state, power, sovereignty, and the balance of power.

Radicals are also concerned with the economic costs of the environmental problem. Radicals are apt to see the costs borne disproportionately by those in the South and by the poorer groups in the developed North. What remains striking about the most recent decade is how the most cogent part of radical—in this case, Marxist—theory has been revived by a resurgent transnational corporatism. Marxism predicts that capital must necessarily capture the state, which will then place corporate (commercial) interests above those of the state's citizens, its weakest and poorest. Thus a Marxist critique of the current period would hold that the United States—epicenter of global capitalism—gutted regulations governing health care, food safety, worker safety, and

The Environment: A View from Indonesia

Increasing economic growth and raising the standard of living can come at the expense of other values, including a commitment to environmental sustainability. Indonesia has experienced this trade-off between development and environmental quality, or between concentrated short-term gains and diffused long-term development.

Agricultural production, forestry, and mining are all key sectors in the economy of Indonesia, an archipelago nation of 6,000 islands and approximately 245 million people. The Indonesian government has limited funds for development, and as foreign-owned companies push for bigger profits, state decisions makers have found it difficult to implement and enforce laws limiting the rate of natural resource consumption. However, Indonesia has acknowledged that deforestation is now a major problem. Prized hardwood trees have been deliberately cut or burned by MNCs and local operators to speed the clearing process. Between 2000 and 2005, 1.45 million hectares a year were deforested, second only to deforestation in Brazil.

Deforestation has significant consequences for the enviroment: it erodes the soil; crops are incapable of regeneration; and animal species are lost and biodiversity is threatened. Deforestation through burning led to massive forest fires in 1987, 1994, 1997–98, 2005–2006, and yet again in 2012. The fires resulted in a cloud of haze over Indonesia as well as neighboring Malaysia, Thailand, and Singapore. Furthermore, in the long term, deforestation leads to an increase in greenhouse gas emissions and contributes to global warming: first because the carbon from burned trees rises into the atmosphere, and second because while alive, the trees are a major carbon sink, meaning they absorb more carbon than they release. Because Indonesia's islands are vulnerable to rising seas, floods, and landslides, Indonesia has an increasingly strong national interest in slowing down deforestation and thus reducing its greenhouse emissions. The country is already one of the world's biggest emitters of greenhouse gases.

But beyond the regional and local dimensions of the deforestation problem, the Indonesian government must also remain sensitive to the economic needs of its poorest population. Many people's livelihoods depend on existing old-growth forests from which they harvest nontimber forest products. Some people in the highlands use traditional swidden agriculture. They live in stationary villages, and their fields are rotated through slash-and-burn techniques, then left fallow for the forest to regenerate. Such traditional techniques are seen as a threat to the integrity of the forest both for logging and for protection of nature and biodiversity. Thus, communities that depend on the forest continually clash with national authorities over its use. Decentralization of control, urged in part to respect the wishes of forest-dependent communities and advocated by multilateral institutions such as the World Bank, has created new loci of corruption as local governments fight businesses and each other regarding how to best use forest resources.

Mining is also a significant industry in Indonesia with consequences for the environment. Gold, copper, and coal are mined throughout Indonesia and are viewed by government officials as a vital part of the country's economic development. To extract the highest profits, mining companies often disregard environmental protocols, resulting in polluted water, air, and topsoil. In 2004, Indonesia sued the Newmont Mining Corporation, a U.S.-based gold producer, for emitting toxic mercury vapors into the air. In 2006, the company paid Indonesia $30 million in a settlement to compensate for the pollution. In 2012, Bumi, a new mining conglomerate started by British financier Nat Rothschild, came under criticism for both environmental and human rights abuses. When Rothschild moved to make the company's ownership structure more transparent, he was forced from his position as Bumi's co-chairman.

In Indonesia, as in much of the developing and developed world, the very real possibility that sustainable natural resource consumption can create sustainable economic development (and jobs) is undermined by corporate venality: the wealth generated by paper, energy, and mining corporations tends to remain highly concentrated rather than distributed and reinvested.

Clearly, there are strong social and economic interests in Indonesia that contribute to and benefit from practices that pose a threat to the environment, from deforestation to mining to swidden agriculture. However, there are also countervailing pressures advocating for environmental protection. Indonesian-based umbrella NGOs publicize abuses and institute legal proceedings, frequently teaming with international NGOs such as the World Wide Fund for Nature and Greenpeace to establish more sustainable environmental initiatives. Greenpeace, for example, has turned renewed concern over Sumatran fires and global warning into an opportunity to persuade Indonesia

Logging in a tropical rainforest in Indonesia.

to pursue more sustainable forestry and mining strategies.

Indonesia may therefore lie at the forefront of a new development in global environmental threats and remediation: a convergence of individual state and collective global interests.

FOR CRITICAL ANALYSIS

1. What conflicting choices does the Indonesian government face as it considers its economic and environmental policies?

2. How are Indonesia's environmental dilemmas also transnational problems?

3. Are Indonesia's problems a tragedy of the commons? How?

4. What could international actors, such as IGOs, NGOs, and epistemic communities, do to help Indonesia achieve sustainable economic development?

environmental protection in the wake of the global economic crisis. The hammer blow of environmental harm (among others) then fell hardest on the poorest in the United States, its trading partners, and neighboring countries.

Both realists and radicals clearly recognize that controversies over natural resources and resource scarcity can lead to violence and even war. The political scientist Thomas Homer-Dixon, for example, has proposed one model that directly links the environment to conflict.[11] Figure 11.2 shows these hypothesized relationships. Although not all scholars would agree with the lines of causation, they are intellectually provocative and a source of concern for policy makers.

In contrast, liberals have typically seen environmental issues as appropriate for the international agenda in the twenty-first century. Their broadened view of security, coupled with the credence they give to the notion of an interdependent international system—perhaps even one so interconnected as to be called an international society—make environmental issues ripe for international action. Because liberal theory can accommodate a greater variety of different international actors, including

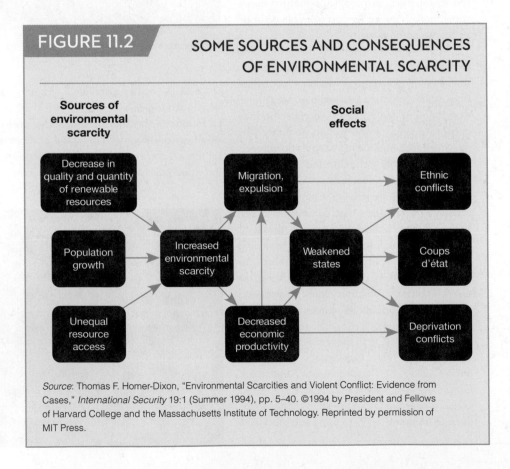

FIGURE 11.2 **SOME SOURCES AND CONSEQUENCES OF ENVIRONMENTAL SCARCITY**

Sources of environmental scarcity

Social effects

- Decrease in quality and quantity of renewable resources
- Population growth
- Unequal resource access
- Increased environmental scarcity
- Migration, expulsion
- Decreased economic productivity
- Weakened states
- Ethnic conflicts
- Coups d'état
- Deprivation conflicts

Source: Thomas F. Homer-Dixon, "Environmental Scarcities and Violent Conflict: Evidence from Cases," *International Security* 19:1 (Summer 1994), pp. 5–40. ©1994 by President and Fellows of Harvard College and the Massachusetts Institute of Technology. Reprinted by permission of MIT Press.

nongovernmental actors from global civil society, they see environmental and human rights issues as legitimate, if not key, international issues of the twenty-first century. Unlike realists and radicals, who fear dependency on other countries because it may diminish state power and therefore limit state action, liberals welcome interdependence and have faith in the technological ingenuity of individuals to be able to solve many of the natural resource dilemmas.

Constructivists, too, are comfortable with environmental issues as an arena for international action because environmental issues bring out salient discourse on environmentalism and sustainability. Constructivists are interested in how political and scientific elites define the problems and how these definitions change over time as new ideas become rooted in their belief sets. Constructivists also realize that environmental issues challenge the core concepts of sovereignty. One of the major intellectual tasks for constructivists has been to uncover the roots and practices of sovereignty.[12]

Health and Communicable Disease — Protecting Life in the Global Commons

Public health and communicable disease are ancient issues that have never respected national boundaries. But when thinking about disease as a transnational threat, we should remember that, like other threats, global health also provides opportunities for cooperation.

The threat of plagues crossing state boundaries cannot be ignored. Around 1330, for example, the bubonic plague began in China, transmitted from rodents and fleas to humans. Moving rapidly from China to Western Asia and then to Europe, by 1352 the plague had killed one-third of Europe's population, about 25 million people. The epidemic, like others before and after, followed trade routes. During the age of discovery, Europeans carried smallpox, measles, and yellow fever to the distant shores of the Americas, decimating the indigenous populations. Expanding trade and travel in the nineteenth century within Europe and between Europe and Africa accelerated the spread of deadly diseases such as cholera and malaria, leading to the first International Sanitary Conference in 1851. Between 1851 and 1903, a series of 11 International Sanitary Conferences developed procedures to prevent the spread of contagious and infectious diseases, establishing conditions of quarantine. As economic conditions improved and medical facilities expanded, the prevalence of diseases such as cholera, plague, yellow fever, and, much later, polio declined in the developed world.

Other diseases have continued to ravage the developing world. The World Health Organization (WHO), founded as one of the specialized UN agencies in 1948, tackled two of the most deadly diseases with its 1955 malaria eradication program and its 1965 smallpox campaign. Malaria eradication proved successful in the United States, the Soviet Union, Europe, and a few developing countries, using a combination of the insecticide DDT and new antimalarial drugs. Yet in most of the developing world, the program failed to curb the disease, as the number of cases of malaria soared in Burma (Myanmar), Bangladesh, Pakistan, India, and much of Africa. Efforts in malaria eradication focus today on low-cost mosquito netting to protect sleeping children, the most vulnerable victims. In contrast, the smallpox campaign was a stunning success. When the vaccination campaign began, there were an estimated 10 to 15 million smallpox cases a year, including 2 million deaths and 10 million disfigurements in the developing world. The last reported case of smallpox occurred in 1977.

Buoyed by the success of smallpox eradication, WHO tackled polio. In 1988, when the campaign began, this disease was estimated to paralyze 350,000 children a year. By working with state officials, WHO has immunized most of the world's population using an effective and inexpensive vaccine, leading to a 99 percent reduction in cases. In 2003, however, polio resurged when religious authorities in northern Nigeria halted vaccinations. Similarly, in 2010, when it was revealed that the U.S. Central Intelligence Agency had been using health workers administering inoculations to take blood samples to locate Osama bin Laden via DNA analysis, many health workers came under attack, and polio resurged in both Afghanistan and Pakistan. While polio of all strains had become virtually extinct, in 2011 Afghanistan recorded 80 new cases and Pakistan 198. Since then, the availability of more effective vaccines and new emergency inoculation initiatives have brought the number of new cases to nearly zero.

After the widely hailed eradication of certain transmissible diseases, the international community was caught unawares by the new realities spawned by globalization. Economic and social globalization has had a dramatic effect on the vulnerability of individuals and communities to disease through migration, refugees, air and truck transport, trade, and troop movements. Twenty-first-century mobility has posed major problems for containing outbreaks of newly discovered diseases such as the Ebola virus, hantavirus, SARS (severe acute respiratory syndrome), avian (bird) flu, and HIV/AIDS, as well as for preventing the transmission of older diseases such as cholera, dengue fever, and typhoid. In 2007, WHO regulations were revised to address global health emergencies in a more effective, better-coordinated manner. States committed to notifying WHO within 24 hours of an impending health threat. WHO would also be able to use nongovernmental resources, such as press reports and the Internet, to report an emergent threat.

These resources and revised reporting standards were utilized recently with the outbreak of H1N1 (swine) flu in 2009, called a flu pandemic by WHO. WHO is committed to preventing another catastrophe like the 1918 "Spanish" flu and is armed with better tools for communicating crucial information to at-risk publics than ever before in world history. But the same tools that enable WHO to develop preventive measures and quarantine standards also work against it. The costs of communications

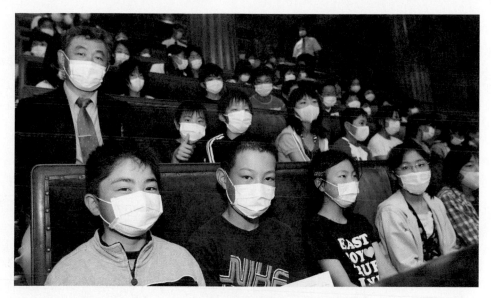

As a result of globalization, goods and services are not the only items traded around the world more quickly than ever before; communicable diseases too can spread rapidly, as humans hop airplanes to distant destinations more and more frequently. Here, Japanese students take precautions during the 2009 outbreak of the H1N1 virus, called swine flu.

of all sorts continue to drop. As they do, more and more human beings will be brought into contact with each other in ways that both benefit the world at large and place it at unprecedented risk.

HIV/AIDS as a Transnational Issue

Of all communicable diseases, the history of HIV/AIDS is the most illustrative of the challenges facing the world's peoples in the twenty-first century. HIV/AIDS is the quintessential transnational issue. Originally transmitted from animals to humans in central Africa, it then spread from person to person through the exchange of bodily fluids. Then it was carried by those infected to others around the globe as people traveled among states, all long before any symptoms appeared. HIV/AIDS rapidly became a major health and humanitarian problem, with an estimated 30 million deaths over the past several decades, and an estimated 34 million people living with the disease today. Since 2007, the number of AIDS-related deaths has declined, to 1.7 million in 2011. Two-thirds of those infected live in sub-Saharan Africa. HIV/AIDS is also an economic issue, disproportionately affecting those in their primary productive years, between 15 and 45. As teachers, workers, military personnel, and civil servants are infected, economic development is stymied, and the viability of the military as an institution is threatened. And HIV/AIDS is a social issue, as families are torn apart and children are orphaned and left to fend for themselves. These children are often then forced to turn to prostitution or crime in order to survive.

HIV/AIDS is a human rights and ethical issue, as well as a security issue. As the independent International Crisis Group has noted:

> HIV/AIDS can be so pervasive that it destroys the very fibre of what constitutes a nation: individuals, families and communities; economic and political institutions; military and police forces. It is likely then to have broader security consequences.[13]

In 2000, the UN Security Council identified HIV/AIDS as a threat to global security, the first time that a health issue has been so recognized. One of the UN's Millennium Development Goals is to halt and reverse the spread of HIV/AIDS.

Many different actors have responded to the HIV/AIDS problem, but individual states are key. Some states and leaders seized on the issue very rapidly, launching major public-relations campaigns to inform their populations of risky practices leading to transmission of the virus, distributing condoms, and now facilitating the distribution of life-extending drugs. Uganda, Botswana, and Brazil are examples of states that took initiatives very early. Each has seen the results of its national program as rates of infection have declined. Other states have been very slow to acknowledge the problem, including South Africa, India, and China. South Africa's former president Thabo Mbeki, for example, spent years denying the existence of HIV/AIDS, and as a result, South Africa's rate of infection skyrocketed. After charismatic intervention by Michel Sidibé, the new chief of UNAIDS, however, South Africa's current president, Jacob Zuma, has increased the national AIDS budget by 30 percent. Consistent with a state-centric view of international relations, states are critical actors; without their willingness to act and respond openly, programs initiated by the international community cannot penetrate national borders.

Although states are key actors in managing national health, intergovernmental organizations took the leadership role at the early stages of the HIV/AIDS epidemic. For example, WHO took steps to help states create national HIV/AIDS programs beginning in 1986. Subsequently, WHO set standards for specific levels of care and recommendations for drug treatments, adding antiretroviral drugs to its essential drug list in 2002. Following WHO's initiative, in 1996, the Joint United Nations Programme on HIV/AIDS (UNAIDS) was created, which coordinates cooperative projects among numerous UN agencies, including the WHO, the UN Development Program, and UNICEF. UNAIDS is also designed to promote joint programs with the World Bank, NGOs, corporations, and national governments. Dissatisfaction with UN leadership led to the Global Fund to Fight AIDS, Tuberculosis, and Malaria (GFATM), an independent institution that uses local expertise and local ownership of issues to advance

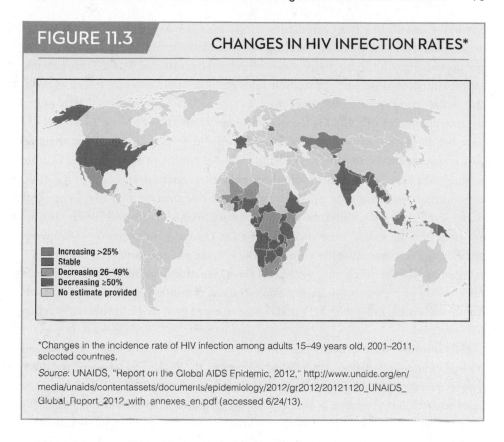

FIGURE 11.3   **CHANGES IN HIV INFECTION RATES***

- Increasing >25%
- Stable
- Decreasing 26–49%
- Decreasing ≥50%
- No estimate provided

*Changes in the incidence rate of HIV infection among adults 15–49 years old, 2001–2011, selected countries.

Source: UNAIDS, "Report on the Global AIDS Epidemic, 2012," http://www.unaids.org/en/media/unaids/contentassets/documents/epidemiology/2012/gr2012/20121120_UNAIDS_Global_Report_2012_with_annexes_en.pdf (accessed 6/24/13).

its cause. In 2010, however, GFATM reported a looming deficit, and halted all new grants pending a replenishment of funds. In 2011, the GFATM was rocked by scandal, as reports of corruption facilitated by lax accounting practices caused some donor states to withhold funds. Now a much-improved GFATM continues to support and deliver antiretroviral drugs as well as help in the fight against tuberculosis and malaria.

Many NGOs have been actively involved in the issue, including Médecins Sans Frontières (Doctors Without Borders), CARE (Cooperative for Assistance and Relief Everywhere), the International Council of AIDS Service Organizations, and the Global Network of People Living with HIV/AIDS, as well as scores of local NGOs. Some work at the grassroots level, treating victims and helping families and communities survive. Others train health-care workers in HIV/AIDS care, so that those workers can then spread out around the world to administer that care.

With the development of antiretroviral drugs to extend the lives of people living with HIV/AIDS, multinational pharmaceutical companies have become major actors, albeit controversial ones. These drugs became available for treatment in the developed countries in the mid-1990s, but in the developing world, the cost of the drugs—between $10,000 and $15,000 per person annually—made that alternative essentially unavailable. But beginning in 1998, Brazilian and Indian drug companies began manufacturing generics, reducing the cost of the treatment to less than $500 per person annually. This activity was controversial because the World Trade Organization's intellectual-property protection rules prohibit internationally traded generics that violate patent restrictions. Brazil took its case to UN human rights bodies and to the international media, arguing that patients have a human right to treatment. NGOs have led the public campaigns in both developed and developing countries, charging that pharmaceutical companies essentially withhold treatment from patients because of the prices they demand, dooming those people to certain death. Some NGOs are committed to lowering drug prices in order to provide treatment to a larger number of those infected. Others find the cost too prohibitive in any case and believe that the available funding should therefore be targeted at changing the behavior of those not yet infected. A compromise has been reached, with the pharmaceutical companies lowering prices for the developing world and the international community raising funds for a variety of prevention strategies. Successful use of antiretrovirals explains why the number of people living with HIV/AIDS has increased even as the number of fatalities has stabilized.

No organization has been more influential in global health than the Bill and Melinda Gates Foundation. Since its establishment in 2000, it has devoted considerable resources to global health initiatives, including combating HIV/AIDS. It supports basic research on prevention as well as national programs in India and Botswana. The 2006 decision by the U.S. businessman Warren Buffett to sign over his wealth to the foundation means that the organization will have assets of over $60 billion. With global health and American education as its two priorities, the foundation directs an unprecedented stream of new revenue toward supporting global health programs.

Individuals such as Bill and Melinda Gates and Bono have used their wealth, prestige, and bully pulpit in the fight against HIV/AIDS. But there are many others. President Yoweri Museveni of Uganda has played a major role in developing his country's response, as has Peter Mugyenyi, a Ugandan infectious-disease expert known for his defiant action in administering cheaper HIV/AIDS drugs. In South Africa, it is Zackie Achmat, chairperson of the Treatment Action Campaign; in China, Dr. Wan Yanhai, founder of the Beijing Aizhi (AIDS) Action Project. As in other areas of international life, individuals made a difference.

As with other technical issues in international politics, such as environmental protection, another new group of actors has become increasingly important for HIV/AIDS and other health-related issues—transnational communities of experts, or epistemic communities. Such groups are composed of experts and technical specialists from international organizations, nongovernmental organizations, and state and substate agencies. Besides sharing a set of beliefs, these communities share expertise, notions of validity, and a set of practices organized around solving a particular problem.[14]

Major research institutes, such as the U.S. Centers for Disease Control and Prevention, the U.S. National Institutes of Health, and France's Pasteur Institute, are important contributors to the global health epistemic communities. These institutions conduct research and participate in global surveillance activities. Members of epistemic communities can influence the behavior of both states and international organizations and have done so on the issue of HIV/AIDS.

Beyond HIV/AIDS

HIV/AIDS and infectious disease are not the only health issues affecting the global community. Health issues include regulations to ensure the quality of pharmaceuticals and to control what many consider to be unhealthy behaviors. Although the former is not generally controversial, the latter is. For example, in the early 1970s, health-care workers recognized that bottle-fed babies were dying at higher rates than breast-fed babies because of the use of diluted formula or impure water. Infant Feeding Action Coalition (INFACT), an NGO, organized boycotts against Nestlé, a major infant formula producer, to push the company to change its marketing strategies. Along with NGOs, WHO and UNICEF developed a controversial code of conduct regulating the marketing of infant formula. An even more politicized item is now on the WHO agenda: tobacco. After years of debate, WHO's Framework Convention on Tobacco Control came into effect in 2005, although its enforcement pits the large, profitable MNCs and states dependent on tax revenue from tobacco companies against health officials and professionals.

Increasingly, health is being recognized as a development issue. The economic development gap and the quality of individual lives cannot change without improvements in health conditions. That is why three of the Millennium Development Goals discussed in Chapter 9 are related to improving health, including reducing child mortality and improving maternal health. The fact that during the 1980s the World Bank became the largest multilateral financier of health programs in developing countries confirms the health-development connection. The Bank uses a sector approach, funding programs to increase the capacity of national and local health facilities. Even more than a development issue, health is seen in some circles as a human rights issue, just as Brazil argued with respect to access to antiretrovirals. Without a doubt, health is a transnational issue affecting politics, economics, society, and individuals.

A Theoretical Take

Health is an example of a quintessential functionalist issue (see Chapter 7). Virtually everyone agrees that prevention of disease is critical and that good health is desired by all. This consensus extends to the belief that we should rely on technical experts and highly trained medical personnel to prevent the spread of infectious disease. Given these two functionalist criteria, it is not surprising that one of the first historical areas of international cooperation was health, as states sought to harmonize quarantine practices and address the spread of communicable diseases such as the plague. This was the narrow purpose of the First International Sanitary Conference of Paris in 1851. But interstate cooperation to manage communicable disease has dramatically expanded since that time. On this issue, realists, liberals, radicals, and constructivists can all find common ground.

Differences remain, however. Because most realists focus on states and define security narrowly (as physical security), realists tend to reduce a broad array of global health issues to such goals as responding to outbreaks of communicable disease or to preparing against the possibility of the deliberate use of bioweapons by state or nonstate actors. Once conceptualized as a threat, relevant questions tend to get reduced to the capacity of the state to defend itself against the threat of infectious disease or a biological weapons attack. The result is a paradox in two respects. First, because it privileges states as independent political actors, threat rhetoric tends to attract considerable organizational and financial resources. Yet the likelihood that any single state, however powerful, can succeed in mitigating the "threat" is low. Not all transnational issues demand a multilateral response, but health care is one of them. Second, the privileging of short-term, direct threats like terrorism over longer term indirect threats like a compromised global health-care infrastructure can lead to seemingly irrational policies. Jeopardizing the polio immunization program in Pakistan and Afghanistan by using it to locate Osama bin Laden would only make sense if Al Qaeda had killed and maimed more human beings worldwide than polio, but the reverse is true.

For liberals, world health presents great opportunities along with real threats. Because liberal theory's basic unit of analysis is the state as a member of a *community* of states, concerns about acute threats of plague are no more or less important than chronic threats or preventive action. Liberals are more likely to focus on international responsibility for dealing with health issues and be willing to utilize all groups possible, including local, substate, state, international, and nongovernmental organizations when appropriate.

Perhaps no issue clarifies these disparate approaches to world health as a transnational issue more than the September 2011 announcement that a Dutch scientist in Malta had successfully modified a strain of the H5N1 virus so that it could infect humans. The team that modified the virus wanted to publish its findings. But publication was stalled by a demand from the U.S. National Science Advisory Board for Biosecurity. The Board worried that publishing the information would make it easier for a bioterrorist to create a lethal bioweapon. Virologists (an epistemic community) were appalled: publication of the information would make it much easier to stop an H5N1 pandemic in its tracks because researchers would be able to study the virus and how to treat it. Who is right?

Even among radicals there remain important differences. Marxists, for example, might argue that challenges to world health stem from capitalism's tendency to concentrate wealth. By forcing many of the earth's peoples into poverty, and compromising the health-care infrastructure of states in the developing world, the eventual emergence of a lethal pandemic that slays the owners of the means of production along with workers is yet another way that capitalists "dig their own graves."

Constructivists would focus our attention on key features of how we think we know what world health means, and how that meaning came to be established. For example, as noted earlier, the resources a state may be able to extract from its citizens in order to engage health as an issue may depend on whether in a given state, threat rhetoric is a more successful framing than cooperation and prevention rhetoric. For some feminist international relations theorists, the argument might be that women and men understand the world differently: women may think of world health in terms of long-term prevention and health-care infrastructure, and men may think of world health in terms of short-term responses to acute threats. The fact that most epistemic communities and states' bureaucracies are staffed by males means that world health issues are too often addressed as reactions to periodic health crises. More women in positions of authority or a more humanistic (as opposed to masculinist) perspective might therefore be needed before world health outcomes improve.

Transnational Crime

Over the last two decades, transnational crime has emerged alongside world health as a major issue of international relations, leading Moisés Naím to posit, "Global criminal activities are transforming the international system, upending the rules, creating new players, and reconfiguring power in international politics and economics."[15] As the frequency, intensity, and likelihood of interstate war declines, we can begin to focus on other persistent issues. And the capacity of transnational criminal organizations (TCOs) to cause harm to people (and by extension, states) has increased over time in proportion to the continual drop in the costs of communications between places. The 2011 World Development Report estimates that the annual revenue accruing to organized criminal networks may be as high as $330 billion—about half of one percent of global GDP, but a number which pales in comparison to the costs of crime, most of which cannot be reduced to an economic value. Beyond the example of human and sex trafficking (Chapter 10), two additional examples of transnational crime are narcotrafficking and cyber crime.

Narcotrafficking

Trafficking in illegal drugs—in particular highly addictive narcotics—is one form of transnational crime that garnered international attention following the end of the Cold War. **Narcotrafficking**—the transportation of large quantities of narcotics such as heroin or cocaine across state borders—has always been a problem. By the early 1970s, it had become severe enough in the United States that President Richard Nixon declared a policy of "war on drugs," reasoning that lives lost to drug abuse was akin to casualties of war; in NATO countries alone, over 10,000 people die annually from heroin overdoses. The other advantage of declaring a war on drugs was that "war" implies a shared undertaking that mobilizes all sectors of society to victory. It also implied that the best way to address the problem was to cut off the *supply* of drugs to potential customers. But the problem is that such a "war" can never be won. Even if the destruction of major tracts of land where opium poppies or coca plants are grown can bring victory closer, the costs of shipping large quantities of product long distances are so low that cultivation destroyed in one region can quickly be replaced by new sources.

Another challenge in preventing narcotrafficking is that the production, refinement, and shipment of narcotics contributes substantially to gross national product in many countries, including those that supply the raw materials for illegal narcotics (for example, Colombia, Afghanistan) and countries that are transit routes for narcotics (for example, Tajikistan). Thus, destroying poppy fields in Afghanistan or coca fields in Bolivia would be tantamount to destroying the economies of each of these states. Afghanistan, for example, produces an estimated 70 percent of the world's heroin, most of which is consumed in the Russian Federation. The economic value to Tajikistan of heroin smuggling from Afghanistan to the Russian Federation is equivalent to 30 to 50 percent of its GDP. A similar fate has befallen the West African state of Guinea-Bissau, whose offshore islands and miles of coastland have been too costly for the relatively poor country to police adequately. Narcotraffickers have established a collection and distribution base in Guinea-Bissau that may be responsible for the transit of 2,200 pounds of cocaine *per night*, with the complicity of some in the national military.

A final challenge is that because drug profits often are recycled into the purchase of arms, intelligence, and bribes for use by terrorist organizations, the harm of narcotrafficking is not restricted to destabilized countries, violent and property crime, broken families, and shattered lives. It also takes the form of organized terrorist attacks against ordinary people all around the world (see Chapter 8).

This has led to an increasing use of the term *narcoterrorism*, which highlights the links between terrorism as a political strategy and narcotrafficking as an effective method of funding terrorists. The term also serves to increase the availability of resources to counter narcotrafficking, as in much of the advanced-industrial world, framing an issue as an element of "national security" makes it more important and thus easier to compete for resources against "less-than-vital" threats.

One important shared feature of human and narcotrafficking is that the damage each does is relatively slow, and may not always result in a death. States usually pay the most attention to violence that results in a death. This may explain why TCOs are again gaining the attention of policy makers and publics: since 2010, a rapid escalation in drug cartel violence in Mexican towns and cities bordering the United States, as discussed in Chapter 5, has again pushed the salience of narcotrafficking to the forefront of public policy debates.

Cyber Crime

Cyber crime is increasingly familiar to people in the developed world. The Internet had its origins in a U.S. Department of Defense project aimed at making the U.S. nuclear command and control structure less vulnerable to a first strike. The concern was that the U.S. command and control system was too hierarchical, making command and control of a nuclear counterstrike problematic: what if that the president and his cabinet were killed in a first strike? What if they were not killed, but their ability to communicate to the military in control of a U.S. counterstrike were disrupted?

The solution offered by the Internet was that it is a network. Unlike a hierarchy, when a node in a network is destroyed, "traffic" (in this case commands) can instantly reroute around the compromised node. Networks, as a form of communication, are extremely resilient to damage. Once computing hardware technology became sufficiently inexpensive for households to own (which happened in the early 1980s), the number of nodes that could be connected in an "internet" increased dramatically. From there, the development of the Internet was exponential. As more and more personal computer users began to link to the net, the value of the net increased, providing incentives for households to buy computers and devices to access the net. Entrepreneurs began to offer "content" in the form of text, and later music and video files. The evolution of the Internet also made it possible to implement electronic commerce, or e-commerce. The rapid evolution of the Internet and e-commerce also created a lucrative potential for criminal activity. Anyone with a computer and access to the Internet can vandalize or steal. Identity and credit card fraud remain common hazards of e-commerce, as does the compromise of lucrative personal data like credit scores and social security numbers. Thus, two major categories of cyber crime or **netcrime** have become major transnational issues: (1) cyber vandalism; and (2) cyber theft.

 **YOU DECIDE**

Why do many proposed solutions to public policy problems focus on the *supply* of a harmful product or activity rather than the *demand*? In this chapter, we've seen how the international community has attempted to solve the problem of narcotrafficking by destroying or interdicting the supply of illegal narcotics. Efforts to reduce gun violence, illegal immigration, and terrorism also often fit this pattern. What explains the preference for supply-side solutions? Would a demand-side strategy be better?

On the supply side, you might start by arguing that supply-side strategies—e.g., in order to reduce death and injury due to firearms, reduce the supply of firearms—are simple to describe and logically compelling. Another argument in favor of a supply-side approach is that measuring supply is easier than measuring demand: guns, cocaine, and illegal immigrants can all be touched and counted. Thus, progress is (or at least seems to be) easier to measure. Finally, you might argue that because "supplies" tend to be physical, reduction of supply is both likely to be physical and observable. In many states, physical action that is public action (e.g., deporting illegal immigrants, seizing heroin) creates a powerful sense of something getting done, which tends to attract resources and public support.

On the demand side, you might argue that reducing demand for firearms by providing better police security and increased access to employment—though more complex to describe—can be said to address root causes of violence and narcotrafficking rather than their symptoms. You might also argue that successfully changing demand makes supply irrelevant, a crucial advantage when the costs of restricting supply (e.g., a military invasion) might be prohibitive. Border control and programs to eradicate opium, poppy, or coca fields in foreign countries are not only costly in terms of cash, but are likely to evoke a nationalistic response. Finally, you might argue that eliminating the supply of a commodity in high demand is ultimately impossible, because the costs of moving goods globally is so low that even if it were possible to, say, eliminate all opium poppy growth in Afghanistan, production would simply increase proportionally somewhere else.

YOU DECIDE: Is the focus on supply-side solutions to illegal activity the best approach? Would demand-side solutions be better, or would a combination of the two be best?

Cyber vandalism is most often associated with "hackers," who are generally young males who delight in compromising state or corporate information and communications networks or stealing private information. Cyber vandalism tends to be transnational because there is a great deal of variation in the degree to which access to the Internet is monitored and controlled. Two kinds of states do a good job of policing access to the Internet: (1) advanced-industrial states with major e-commerce stakes; and (2) authoritarian governments anxious to surveil their citizens and control public access to extra-state sources of information. Thus, many of the perpetrators of net-crime prefer to base themselves in urban areas in the developing world with weak state capacity to monitor their behavior. Cyber vandalism remains a serious problem, as the viruses hackers create often propagate well beyond initial targets, and can threaten power grids and emergency services. Every year, cyber vandals cause billions of dollars of lost revenue in the form of denial-of-service attacks and remediation costs.

Even more serious is cyber theft. In cyber theft, banking and financial networks can be attacked and large sums of money can be stolen, though this remains rare. More prevalent, and more costly, is corporate espionage. Estimates of the threat vary, largely because companies prefer not to report it for fear of stockholder lawsuits. But it is estimated that the yearly losses from Chinese cyber espionage and theft is between $800 million and $1 billion in intellectual property value. (Many states, including the United States, engage in some form of cyber espionage, but China has so far been the most expansive, sophisticated, and successful.) While experts disagree as to the magnitude of the theft, there is no dispute about where these attacks originate: China (95 percent), Russia (3 percent), and Iran (2 percent). A U.S. nonprofit monitoring group, U.S. Cyber Consequences Unit, has characterized the theft from China alone as representing "the biggest transfer of wealth in a short period of time that the world has ever seen." Entire industries are being reassembled in Southeast Asia.[16] The damage of such a theft today may not be truly felt for five, ten, or twenty years.

The ongoing and persistent threat of Chinese cyber espionage has caused U.S. corporations to go to extraordinary lengths to keep their proprietary information secure, both domestically and when traveling to China, where executives remove the batteries from their mobile phones during meetings and are not allowed to connect thumb drives or network laptops with home computers once they return.

Finally, the same capacity to steal can be turned into the capacity to disrupt communications, water, electricity, and emergency services operations in major metropolitan areas of a target state. Military networks can be compromised as well. Because each of these actions has a high potential to result in loss of life in a target community, these capabilities generally fall under the heading of cyber terror or cyber warfare (see Chapter 8).

The Impact of Transnational Issues

As an unexpected consequence of advances in communications technology, transnational issues like the environment, world health, and organized crime have advanced from tertiary and moral issues to primary and vital interests. Before World War II, developed states might have viewed more active economic, health infrastructure, and human rights interventions as morally desirable but either risky or unnecessary for reasons of state. Since the late 1970s, however, transnational issues such as organized crime, terrorism, pandemics, natural disasters, and refugees from these disasters have tended to affect the developed world much more directly. Transnational issues have *become* issues because morality-based arguments for intervention to redress damages have increasingly transitioned into interest-based arguments for undertaking the same interventions. Transnational issues have effects on four major areas of international relations theory and practice.

First, the interconnectedness of the many sub-issues within health, environment, human rights, and transnational law enforcement affects international bargaining. When states choose to go to the bargaining table, a multiplicity of issues is often at stake, and states may be willing to make trade-offs between issues to achieve a desired result. For example, in the aftermath of the 1973 oil embargo and in the face of supply shortages, the United States was willing to negotiate with Mexico on cleaning up the Colorado River. The United States built a desalination plant at the U.S.– Mexican border and helped Mexican residents reclaim land in the Mexicali Valley for agriculture. To win an ally in the supply of petroleum resources, the United States made this major concession and also accepted responsibility for past legal violations.

Other issues, however, are less accommodating to negotiation, particularly if key concerns of national security are at stake. The United States was unwilling to compromise by signing the Anti-Personnel Land Mine Ban Convention because of the security imperative to preserve the heavily mined border between North and South Korea. Supporters of the treaty framed the argument in human rights terms: innocent individuals, including vulnerable women and children, are being killed or maimed by such weapons, which must be eliminated. Yet in this case, the United States decided not to sign the treaty because of Korean security. Although some states, eager for U.S. participation, were willing to make concessions, others, afraid that the treaty would be weakened by too many exceptions, were not. Bargaining is a much more complicated process in the age of transnational issues.

Second, transnational issues themselves may be the source of conflict, just as the Marxists predicted in the nineteenth century. The need to protect the petroleum supply was a primary motivation for the West's involvement in the 1991 Gulf War. Jared Diamond's book *Collapse: How Societies Choose to Fail or Succeed* documents how the struggle for scarce resources led to the collapse of empires in the past and to state failure in Rwanda and Burundi, resulting in the abrogation of human rights. The relationship between environmental and resource issues and conflict is a complex one.[17]

Issues of resource depletion and degradation, usually worsened by population increase, are likely to result in conflicts when some groups try to capture use of the scarce resource. For example, Israeli authorities control access to scarce water on the West Bank of the Jordan River, exacerbating the conflict between the Israelis and the Palestinians. Israel permits its own settlers greater access to the resource and restricts access to the Palestinians. In the Gaza Strip, where population is growing 4.6 percent annually, resources have been depleted, intensifying the conflict with Israel.

Nonrenewable resources such as oil may lead to particularly violent conflicts, because such resources are vital for industry, economic health and welfare, and national security, and there are few viable substitutes. How else can we explain the conflict over remote and uninhabited islands in the China Seas? Only with the possibility of oil beneath the waters surrounding the islands does the conflict make sense. Changes in the distribution of these resources may lead to a shift in the balance of power, creating an instability that leads to war, just as realists fear. In contrast, issues such as ozone depletion or global warming are not particularly conducive to violent interstate conflict. In these cases, the commons and responsibility for its management are diffuse.

Third, transnational issues pose direct challenges to state sovereignty, setting off a major debate about the nature of sovereignty. In Chapter 2, we traced the roots of sovereignty in the Westphalian revolution. The notion developed that states enjoy internal autonomy and cannot be subjected to external authority. That norm — noninterference in the domestic affairs of other states — was embedded in the UN Charter.

Yet the rise of nonstate actors — multinational corporations, TCOs, nongovernmental organizations, and supranational organizations such as the European Union — and the forces of globalization, whether economic, cultural, or political, undermine Westphalian ideals of state sovereignty. Communicable diseases, the environment, human rights, and transnational crime were traditionally sovereign state concerns, and interference by outside actors was unacceptable. After World War II, those norms began to change, a process that continues today. The problems raised by transnational terrorism, for example, imply a multinational response: by transnational terrorism's very nature, single states, no matter how powerful, cannot solve the problem on their own. This is one of the main reasons that discussion has turned to a power shift, an erosion of state authority and the severe weakening of state power overall. Issues that once were the exclusive hallmark of state sovereignty are increasingly susceptible to scrutiny and intervention by global actors.

Part of the problem is that in many areas of the world, particularly since the end of the Cold War, states themselves have become weak or have failed. These so-called states then become sites for transnational crime, terrorist organizations, and disease, all of which may be exported at relatively low cost to neighboring states and even around the world. Consider the fate of Zimbabwe under Robert Mugabe's heavy hand. In 2008, Zimbabwe's collapsed health-care infrastructure was unable to prevent or control the outbreak of a cholera epidemic. The disease soon spread to affect (and infect) the citizens of neighboring states. Yet traditions of sovereignty mitigate against interventions aimed at restoring a state to full functionality. Who is to judge whether an intervention will simply restore a state or become a kind of twenty-first-century neocolonialism, as debated in Chapter 8?

How then should we reconceptualize sovereignty? How has sovereignty been transformed? Mainstream theories in the realist and liberal traditions tend to talk of an erosion of sovereignty. Constructivists go further, probing how sovereignty is and always has been a contested concept. There have always been some issues where state control and authority are secure and others where authority is shared or even undermined. After all, sovereignty is a socially constructed institution that varies across time and place. Transnational issues such as health, the environment, and human rights permit us to examine in depth long-standing but varying practices of sovereignty. These issues give rise to new forms of authority and new forms of governance, stimulating us to reorient our views of sovereignty.[18]

Fourth, transnational issues pose critical problems for international relations scholars and for the theoretical frameworks introduced at the beginning of this book. Adherents of each framework have been forced to rethink key assumptions and values, as well as the discourse of their theoretical perspective, to accommodate transnational issues.

IN FOCUS

EFFECTS OF TRANSNATIONAL ISSUES

- *On international bargaining:* More policy trade-offs; greater complexity

- *On international conflict:* May increase at international and substate levels

- *On state sovereignty:* Traditional notion challenged; need for reconceptualization

- *On study of international relations:* Core assumptions of theories jeopardized; theories modified and broadened

Transnational Issues from Different Theoretical Perspectives

The very core propositions of realist theory—the primacy of the state, the clear separation between domestic and international politics, and the emphasis on state security—are made problematic by transnational issues. Issues of health and disease, the environment, human rights, drug and human trafficking, transnational terrorism, and international crime are problems that no single state can effectively address alone. These issues have broken down the divide between the international and the domestic. They may threaten state security but may have no traditional military solution, even for a great power or superpower.

Responding to transnational issues, realists have generally adopted a nuanced argument consonant with realist precepts. Although most realists admit that other actors have gained power relative to the state, they contend that state primacy is not in jeopardy. Competitive centers of power at the local, transnational, or international level do not necessarily or automatically lead to the erosion or elimination of state power. Most important, the fundamentals of state security are no less important in this age of globalization than they were in the past. What has changed is that the decreasing salience of interstate and nuclear war as challenges to state and interstate security has forced a broadening of security discourse to encompass numerous aspects of human security. For humans to be secure, not only must state security be ensured, but economic security, environmental security, human rights security, and health and well-being must be secured as well. One form of security does not replace another; each augments the rest. Thus, although transnational issues have forced realists to add qualifications to their theory, they have preserved it and enhanced its theoretical usefulness.

Transnational issues can be more easily integrated into the liberal theoretical picture. After all, at the outset liberals asserted the importance of individuals and the possibility of both cooperative and conflictual interests. They introduced the notion that many other issues may be as important as physical security. They see power as a multidimensional concept. Later versions of liberal thinking, such as neoliberal institutionalism, recognized the need for international institutions to facilitate state interactions to ensure transparency and to add new issues to the international agenda. Though not denying the importance of state security, they quickly embraced the notion of other forms of security compatible with health, environmental, and human rights issues.

Radicals have never been comfortable with the primacy of the state or the international system that the dominant coalition of states created. For them, a shift in power away from the state and that international system is a desired transition. Marxists, for example, imagined a transnational revolution that would sweep away the state because the state's only function was the use of violence to maintain the power of capital over labor. With their pronounced emphasis on economics over security, radicals may be able to accommodate such transnational issues as communicable diseases, the environment, human rights, and transnational crime. A prominent radical interpretation of both communicable disease and the environment is that economic deprivation and perceived relative economic deprivation are the root causes of disparities in health care and environmental degradation. Human rights violations, according to radical thought, are caused by elites and privileged groups trying to maintain their edge over the less fortunate.

Constructivists have presented a different approach for analyzing transnational issues. They have alerted us to the nuances of the changing discourse embedded in discussions of health, the environment, and human rights. They have illustrated how both material factors and ideas shape debates over these issues. They have called attention to the importance of norms in influencing and changing individual and state behavior. More directly than other theorists, constructivists have begun to explore the varying impacts of these issues on the traditional concepts of the state, national identity, and sovereignty.

Feminist international relations theorists make a similar but different argument: like constructivists, they interrogate the origins and content of terms like *threat*. But feminists go on to ask whether greater participation of women in scientific, academic, and policy making processes might not lead to a more productive understanding not only of threats but also of solutions to transnational challenges. Why, for example, do "we" tend to respond to threats that are acute and direct but ignore those that are chronic and indirect, irrespective of the magnitude of potential harm? Why privilege harm that results in death as opposed to harm that abridges the quality of an affected person's life? Why speak of "threats" at all?

As transnational issues assume greater salience in the twenty-first century, all international relations theories will need modification and reformulation.

Will Transnational Issues Lead to Global Governance?

Recognition of transnational issues and their effects has led some scholars and pundits to conclude that governance processes need to be conceptualized differently than they have been in the past. The processes of interaction among the various actors in international politics are now more frequent and intense, ranging from conventional ad hoc cooperation and formal organizational collaboration to nongovernmental and network collaboration and even virtual communal interaction on the Internet. These changes imply an increasing role for the regulatory capacity of norms. **Global governance** implies that through various structures and processes, actors can coordinate interests and needs in the absence of a unifying political authority.

As noted throughout this book, the core nature of international relations has changed over time. Perhaps the most important component of that change has been variation in the *demand* for governance and, in addition, a widening variety in the forms that global governance can exhibit. Perhaps the key example of the problem and potential of global governance is the Internet. As noted earlier, the Internet had its origins in state security as a way to increase the resilience of communications after a nuclear attack. Yet by the late 1980s, it had evolved into a way for researchers to share information across national and disciplinary boundaries. As the capacity of the Internet to carry information expanded, the types of information that could be exchanged—images, and in particular video—expanded as well. Yet the Internet remained almost entirely ungoverned. For many, this was its chief virtue. But the economic and political implications of the unregulated exchange of information proved too much to remain independent of governance or the depredations of commerce. States and private corporations began to weigh in, particularly states whose governments depended for their very survival on control of public access to information (for example, China, Saudi Arabia, Russia, North Korea), and corporations whose technology had facilitated the Internet's growth and capacity. The Internet proved a double-edged sword. On the one hand, it had the potential to bring its users closer together and to dramatically facilitate international collaboration in solving tough problems. On the other hand, that same openness created vulnerabilities, which prompted states to attempt to capture and regulate that openness.

What makes the Internet so important as an example of a transnational issue is that it incorporates both a horizontal component (geographic space) and vertical components (local to global and interest heterogeneity). In a way, the complexity of the Internet stands as a perfect metaphor for the complexity, and positive potential, of global governance. The European Commission, for example, defines "Internet governance" as "the development and application by governments, the private sector and civil society, in their respective roles, of shared principles, norms, rules, decision-making procedures, and programmes that shape the evolution and use of the Internet."[19]

The implications of the Internet example for global governance are crucial. Global governance, in its idealized form, presupposes a global civil society. The political scientist Ronnie Lipschutz describes the essential component of global civil society:

> While global civil society must interact with states, the code of global civil society denies the primacy of states or their sovereign rights. This civil society is "global" not only because of those connections that cross national boundaries and operate within the "global, nonterritorial region," but also as a result of a growing element of global consciousness in the way the members of global civil society act.[20]

Some liberals would find this a desirable direction in which to be moving—a goal to be attained—whereas others fear that global governance might undermine democratic values: as the focus of governance moves further from individuals, democracy becomes more problematic.

Skeptics of global governance do not believe that anything approaching it, however defined, is possible or desirable. For realists, there can never be global governance because the more closely it is approached, the more dangerous it is perceived, and the more likely a countervailing authority or alliance is to halt or reverse the process of convergence. Outcomes are determined by relative power positions rather than by law or other regulatory devices, however decentralized and diffuse those devices might be. For Kenneth Waltz, the quintessential neorealist, the anarchic structure of the international system is the core dynamic. For other realists, such as Hans Morgenthau, there is space for both international law and international organization. His textbook includes chapters on both, but each is relatively insignificant in the face of power politics and the national interest. Few realists would talk in global governance terms. Radicals are also uncomfortable with global governance discourse. Rather than seeing global governance as a multiple-actor, multiple-process, decentralized framework, radicals fear domination by hegemons that would structure global governance processes to their own advantage. Skepticism about the possibility of global governance does not diminish the fact that there may be a need for it in the age of globalization.

In Sum: Changing You

In these eleven chapters, we have explored the historical development of international relations, from the development of the state system to notions of an international system and community and global governance. We have introduced different theories—realism, liberalism, radicalism, and constructivism—that help us organize our perspectives about the role of the international system, the state, the individual, and intergovernmental and nongovernmental organizations in international relations. From these perspectives, we have examined the major issues of the day and analyzed how these issues affect interstate bargaining, conflict, sovereignty, and even the study of international politics.

A citizenry able to articulate these arguments is better able to explain the whys and hows of events that affect our lives. A citizen who can understand these events is better able to make and support informed policy choices. In the transnational era of the twenty-first century, as economic, political, social, and environmental forces both above the state and within the state assume greater saliency, the role of individuals becomes all the more demanding—and all the more important.

Discussion Questions

1. Before World War II, crises and disasters in distant parts of the world stayed there. This is no longer the case today. What are two important implications of this new reality?

2. Global warming is a problem of the global commons, but not all environmental problems are. How should different environmental issues be approached?

3. Select two news accounts that address the trade-off between economic development and environmental sustainability. Can these two objectives be harmonized in the twenty-first century?

4. International cooperation on health has traditionally been viewed as a functionalist issue, but increasingly the issue has been politicized. What has changed? With what effect? Cite specific examples.

Key Terms

demographic transition (p. 398)

epistemic community (p. 403)

global governance (p. 426)

Malthusian dilemma (p. 398)

narcotrafficking (p. 418)

negative externalities (p. 391)

netcrime (p. 419)

NOTES

Chapter 01

1. Stephen M. Walt, "International Relations: One World, Many Theories," *Foreign Policy* 110 (Spring 1988): 30.

2. Thucydides, *History of the Peloponnesian War*, trans. Rex Warner, rev. ed. (Harmondsworth, UK: Penguin, 1972).

3. See Jeffrey Record and W. Andrew Terrill, "Iraq and Vietnam: Differences, Similarities, and Insights" (Carlisle, PA: Strategic Studies Institute, U.S. Army War College, 2004), www.strategicstudiesinstitute.army.mil/pubs/display.cfm?pubID=377 (accessed 12/15/09). For more on the use of historical analogies, see Yuen Foong Khong, *Analogies at War: Korea, Munich, Dien Bien Phu, and the Vietnam Decision of 1965* (Princeton, NJ: Princeton University Press, 1992).

4. Plato, *The Republic*, trans. Desmond Lee (Harmondsworth, UK: Penguin, 1955).

5. Aristotle, *The Politics*, ed. Trevor J. Saunders, trans. T. A. Sinclair (Harmondsworth, UK: Penguin, 1981).

6. Thomas Hobbes, *Leviathan*, ed. C. B. Macpherson (Harmondsworth, UK: Penguin, 1968).

7. Jean-Jacques Rousseau, "Discourses on the Origin and Foundations of Inequality among Men," in *Basic Political Writings of Jean-Jacques Rousseau*, ed. and trans. Donald A. Cress (Indianapolis, IN: Hackett Publishing, 1987).

8. Jean-Jacques Rousseau, "On the Social Contract," Book 2, Ch. 1, in *Basic Political Writings of Jean-Jacques Rousseau*, p. 153.

9. Rousseau, "Social Contract," Book 1, Ch. 6, p. 148.

10. See Immanuel Kant, *Idea for a Universal History from a Cosmopolitan Point of View* (1784) and *Perpetual Peace: A Philosophical Sketch* (1795), both reprinted in *Kant Selections*, ed. Lewis White Beck (New York: Macmillan Co., 1988).

11. See, for example, Michael Walzer, *Just and Unjust Wars. A Moral Argument with Historical Illustrations* (New York: Basic Books, 1977); Jack Donnelly, *Universal Human Rights in Theory and Practice*. 2nd ed. (Ithaca, NY: Cornell University Press, 2003).

12. J. David Singer and Melvin Small, *The Wages of War, 1816–1965: A Statistical Handbook* (New York: Wiley, 1972).

13. Meredith Reid Sarkees, "Defining and Categorizing Wars," in *Resort to War: A Data Guide to Inter-State, Extra-State, Intra-State, and Non-State Wars, 1816–2007*, ed. Meredith Reid Sarkees and Frank Whelon Wayman (Washington, DC: CQ Press, 2010).

14. Cynthia Weber, *Simulating Sovereignty: Intervention, the State, and Symbolic Interchange* (Cambridge, UK: Cambridge University Press, 1994).

15. Karen T. Litfin, ed., *The Greening of Sovereignty in World Politics* (Cambridge, MA: The MIT Press, 1998).

16. Christine Sylvester, "Emphatic Cooperation: A Feminist Method for IR," *Millennium: Journal of International Studies* 23:2 (1994): 315–34.

17. See articles in Clifford Bob, ed., *The International Struggle for New Human Rights* (Philadelphia: University of Pennsylvania Press, 2009).

18. Peter J. Katzenstein, ed., *The Culture of National Security: Norms and Identity in World Politics* (New York: Columbia University Press, 1996).

Chapter 02

1. Jean Bodin, *Six Books on the Commonwealth*, trans. M. J. Tooley (Oxford: Basil Blackwell, 1967), p. 25.

2. Bodin, *Commonwealth*, p. 28.

3. Bodin, *Commonwealth*, p. 28.

4. Adam Smith, *An Inquiry into the Nature and Causes of the Wealth of Nations* (New York: Modern Library, 1937).

5. John Locke, *Two Treatises on Government* (Cambridge, UK: Cambridge University Press, 1960).

6. Hilaire Belloc, as quoted in John Ellis, *A Social History of the Machine Gun* (New York: Random House, 1975), p. 18.

7. Quoted in A. C. Walworth, *Woodrow Wilson* (Baltimore, MD: Penguin, 1969), p. 148.

8. E. H. Carr, *The Twenty Years' Crisis, 1919–1939: An Introduction to the Study of International Relations* (New York: Harper Torchbooks, 1939, rep. 1964), p. 224.

9. John Dower, *War Without Mercy: Race and Power in the Pacific War* (New York: Pantheon Books, 1986).

10. George F. Kennan ["X"], "The Sources of Soviet Conduct," *Foreign Affairs* 25 (July 1947): 566–82.

11. Quoted in Charles W. Kegley Jr. and Eugene R. Wittkopf, *World Politics: Trend and Transformation*, 5th ed. (New York: St. Martin's, 1995), p. 94.

12. Joseph Stalin, "Reply to Comrades," *Pravda,* August 2, 1950.

13. George F. Kennan, "The United States and the Soviet Union, 1917–1976," *Foreign Affairs* 54 (July 1976): 683–84.

14. John Lewis Gaddis, "The Long Peace: Elements of Stability in the Postwar International System," *International Security* 10:4 (Spring 1986): 92–142.

15. Kenneth N. Waltz, *Theory of International Politics* (Reading, MA: Addison-Wesley, 1979), p. 173.

16. Mikhail Gorbachev, "Reality and Guarantees for a Secure World," as reported in Foreign Broadcast Information Service, *Daily Report, Soviet Union,* September 17, 1987, p. 25.

Chapter 03

1. Kenneth N. Waltz, *Man, the State, and War* (New York: Columbia University Press, 1954); and J. David Singer, "The Levels of Analysis Problem," in *International Politics and Foreign Policy,* ed. James N. Rosenau, rev. ed. (New York: Free Press, 1961), pp. 20–29.

2. Thucydides, *History of the Peloponnesian War,* trans. Rex Warner, rev. ed. (Harmondsworth, UK: Penguin, 1972).

3. Augustine, *Confessions* and *City of God,* in *Great Books of the Western World,* ed. Robert Maynard Hutchins, vol. 18 (Chicago: Encyclopedia Britannica, 1952, 1986).

4. Niccolò Machiavelli, *The Prince and the Discourses* (New York: Random House, 1940).

5. Thomas Hobbes, *Leviathan,* ed. C. B. Macpherson (Harmondsworth, UK: Penguin, 1968), p. 13.

6. Hans J. Morgenthau, *Politics among Nations: The Struggle for Power and Peace,* 5th ed., rev. (New York: Knopf, 1978).

7. John J. Mearsheimer, *The Tragedy of Great Power Politics* (New York: W. W. Norton, 2001), pp. 19–22.

8. Kenneth N. Waltz, *Theory of International Politics* (Reading, MA: Addison-Wesley, 1979).

9. Kenneth N. Waltz, "Realist Thought and Neorealist Theory," in *Controversies in International Relations Theory: Realism and the Neoliberal Challenge,* ed. Charles W. Kegley Jr. (New York: St. Martin's, 1995) pp. 67–82.

10. Waltz, *Theory of International Politics,* p. 105.

11. John J. Mearsheimer, "The False Promise of International Institutions," *International Security* 19:3 (Winter 1994–95): 5–49.

12. Robert Gilpin, *War and Change in World Politics* (Cambridge, UK: Cambridge University Press, 1981), p. 29.

13. Gilpin, *War and Change,* p. 210.

14. Montesquieu, *The Spirit of the Laws,* vol. 36, ed. David Wallace Carrithers (Berkeley: University of California Press, 1971), p. 23.

15. Immanuel Kant, *Perpetual Peace,* ed. Lewis White Beck (New York: Macmillan, 1957).

16. Robert Axelrod and Robert O. Keohane, "Achieving Cooperation under Anarchy: Strategies and Institutions," in *Cooperation under Anarchy,* ed. Kenneth Oye (Princeton, NJ: Princeton University Press, 1986), pp. 226–54.

17. G. John Ikenberry, *After Victory: Institutions, Strategic Restraint, and the Rebuilding of Order after Major Wars* (Princeton, NJ: Princeton University Press, 2003).

18. Robert O. Keohane and Joseph Nye, *Power and Interdependence*, 3rd ed. (New York: Longman, 2001); Robert O. Keohane and Joseph Nye, "Transnational Relations and World Politics," *International Organization* 25:3 (Summer 1971): 329–50, 721–48.

19. Francis Fukuyama, "The End of History?" *National Interest* 16 (Summer 1989): 4.

20. John Mueller, *Retreat from Doomsday: The Obsolescence of Major War* (New York: Basic Books, 1989).

21. Steven Pinker, *The Better Angels of Our Nature: Why Violence Has Declined* (New York: Viking Penguin, 2011); and Joshua S. Goldstein, *Winning the War on War: The Decline of Armed Conflict Worldwide* (New York: Dutton, 2011).

22. Karl Marx, *Capital: A Critique of Political Economy*, trans. Ben Fowkes (New York: Random House, 1977).

23. John A. Hobson, *Imperialism: A Study*, ed. Philip Siegelman (Ann Arbor: University of Michigan Press, 1965).

24. Tony Smith, "The Underdevelopment of the Development Literature: The Case of Dependency Theory," *World Politics* 31:2 (January 1979): 247–88.

25. Stephen M. Walt, "International Relations: One World, Many Theories," *Foreign Policy* 110 (Spring 1998): 29–46.

26. Ted Hopf, "The Promise of Constructivism in International Relations Theory," *International Security* 23:1 (Summer 1989): 172.

27. Alexander Wendt, "Anarchy Is What States Make of It: The Social Construction of Power Politics," *International Organization* 46:2 (Spring 1992): 396. For a more complete analysis, see Wendt, *Social Theory of International Politics* (Cambridge, UK: Cambridge University Press, 1999).

28. Wendt, "Anarchy Is What States Make of It."

29. Ann Tickner, "Hans Morgenthau's Principles of Political Realism: A Feminist Reformulation," *Millennium: Journal of International Studies* 17:3 (1988): 429–40.

30. John J. Mearsheimer and Stephen M. Walt, "An Unnecessary War," *Foreign Policy* 134 (January–February 2003): 50–59.

Chapter 04

1. See especially Morton Kaplan, *System and Process in International Politics* (New York: Krieger, 1976).

2. Kenneth N. Waltz, "International Structure, National Force, and the Balance of World Power," *Journal of International Affairs* 21:2 (1967): 229.

3. Kenneth N. Waltz, "Why Iran Should Get the Bomb," *Foreign Affairs* 91:4 (July/ August 2012): 5.

4. John J. Mearsheimer, "Back to the Future: Instability after the Cold War," *International Security* 15:1 (Summer 1990): 52.

5. Paul M. Kennedy, *The Rise and Fall of the Great Powers: Economic Change and Military Conflict from 1500 to 2000* (New York: Random House, 1987).

6. Robert O. Keohane, *After Hegemony: Cooperation and Discord in the World Political Economy* (Princeton, NJ: Princeton University Press, 1984).

7. J. David Singer and Melvin Small, "Alliance Aggregation and the Onset of War," in *Quantitative International Politics,* ed. J. David Singer (New York: Free Press, 1968), pp. 246–86.

8. Michael C. Webb and Stephen D. Krasner, "Hegemonic Stability Theory: An Empirical Assessment," *Review of International Studies* 15 (1989): 183–98.

9. G. John Ikenberry, Michael Mastanduno, and William C. Wohlforth, "Unipolarity, State Behavior, and Systemic Consequences," *World Politics* 61:1 (Jan. 2009): 1–27.

10. Robert Gilpin, *War and Change in World Politics* (Cambridge, UK: Cambridge University Press, 1981).

11. Robert O. Keohane and Joseph S. Nye, *Power and Interdependence*, 3rd ed. (New York: Longman, 2001).

12. G. John Ikenberry, *After Victory. Institutions, Strategic Restraint, and the Rebuilding of Order After Major Wars* (Princeton, NJ: Princeton University Press, 2001), p. 50.

13. Martha Finnemore, *The Purpose of Intervention: Changing Beliefs about the Use of Force* (Ithaca, NY: Cornell University Press, 2003), p. 94.

14. See Alexander Wendt, *Social Theory of International Politics* (Cambridge, UK: Cambridge University Press, 1999).

15. Finnemore, *Intervention*, p. 95.

16. Hedley Bull and Adam Watson, eds., *The Expansion of International Society* (Oxford: Oxford University Press, 1984).

17. Samuel Huntington, *The Clash of Civilizations: The Remaking of the World Order* (New York: Simon & Schuster, 1996).

Chapter 05

1. James N. Rosenau, *Turbulence in World Politics: A Theory of Change and Continuity* (Princeton, NJ: Princeton University Press, 1990), pp. 117–18.

2. Graeme Wood, "Limbo World," *Foreign Policy* (January–February 2010): 49.

3. Minxin Pei, "The Paradoxes of American Nationalism," *Foreign Policy* 134 (May–June 2003): 31–37.

4. See Martha Finnemore, *National Interests in International Society* (Ithaca, NY: Cornell University Press, 1996), chap. 1.

5. Stephen D. Krasner, *Defending the National Interest: Raw Materials Investments and U.S. Foreign Policy* (Princeton, NJ: Princeton University Press, 1978).

6. Alfred T. Mahan, *The Influence of Seapower upon History 1660–1783* (Boston: Little, Brown, 1897).

7. Halford Mackinder, "The Geographical Pivot of History," *Geographical Journal* 23 (April 1904): 434.

8. Joseph S. Nye Jr., *Soft Power: The Means to Success in World Politics* (New York: Public Affairs, 2004).

9.   Andrew Mack, "Why Big Nations Lose Small Wars: The Politics of Asymmetric Conflict," *World Politics* 27:2 (January 1975): 175–200.

10. Joseph S. Nye Jr. *The Future of Power* (New York: PublicAffairs, 2011).

11. Robert D. Putnam, "Diplomacy and Domestic Politics: The Logic of Two-Level Games," *International Organization* 42:3 (Summer 1988): 427–69.

12. Putnam, "Two-Level Games," 434.

13. Raymond Cohen, *Negotiating across Cultures: Communication Obstacles in International Diplomacy*, 2nd ed. (Washington, D.C.: U.S. Institute of Peace, 1997).

14. John Avlon, "A 21st Century Statesman," *Newsweek* (February 28, 2011), p. 16.

15. David A. Baldwin, *Economic Statecraft* (Princeton, NJ: Princeton University Press, 1985).

16. Thomas C. Schelling, *Arms and Influence* (New Haven, CT: Yale University Press, 1966).

17. Immanuel Kant, *Perpetual Peace: A Philosophical Sketch* (1795), reprinted in *Kant Selections*, ed. Lewis White Beck (New York: Macmillan, 1988).

18. See, for example, William J. Dixon, "Democracy and the Peaceful Settlement of International Conflict," *American Political Science Review* 88 (1994): 14–32; and Joe D. Hagan, "Domestic Political Systems and War Proneness," *Mershon International Studies Review* 38:2 (October 1994): 183–207.

19. Norman M. Naimark, *The Russians in Germany: A History of the Soviet Zone of Occupation, 1945–1949* (Cambridge, MA: Harvard University Press, 1995).

20. Jessica Mathews, "Power Shift," *Foreign Affairs* 76:1 (January–February 1997): 50–51.

21. See Monica Duffy Toft, Daniel Philpott, Timothy Samuel Shah, *God's Century: Resurgent Religion and Global Politics* (New York: W. W. Norton, 2011).

22. Samuel P. Huntington, *The Clash of Civilizations and the Remaking of World Order* (New York: Simon & Schuster, 1996).

23. Jessica Stern, *Terror in the Name of God: Why Religious Militants Kill* (New York: HarperCollins, 2003), pp. 9–31.

24. Jack Snyder, *From Voting to Violence: Democratization and Nationalist Conflict* (New York: W. W. Norton, 2000).

25. See Moisés Naím, *Illicit: How Smugglers, Traffickers, and Copycats Are Hijacking the Global Economy* (New York: Doubleday, 2005).

26. Defined by Fund for Peace and *Foreign Policy* Failed State Index, www.fundforpeace.org/global/?q=node/242 (accessed 1/17/13). See also www.foreignpolicy.com/failed_states_index_2012_interactive (accessed 1/17/13).

Chapter 06

1.   Robert G. Herman, "Identity, Norms, and National Security: The Soviet Foreign Policy Revolution and the End of the Cold War," in *The Culture of National Security: Norms and Identity in World Politics*, ed. P. J. Katzenstein (New York: Columbia University Press, 1996), pp. 271–316.

2. Hans J. Morgenthau, *Politics among Nations: The Struggle for Power and Peace*, brief ed., ed. Kenneth W. Thompson (New York: McGraw-Hill, 1993), p. 5.

3. Margaret G. Hermann, "Explaining Foreign Policy Behavior Using the Personal Characteristics of Political Leaders," *International Studies Quarterly* 24:1 (March 1980): 7–46.

4. Stephen Benedict Dyson, "Personality and Foreign Policy: Tony Blair's Iraq Decisions," *Foreign Policy Analysis* 2:3 (July 2006): 289.

5. Betty Glad, "Personality, Political, and Group Process Variables in Foreign Policy Decision Making: Jimmy Carter's Handling of the Iranian Hostage Crisis," *International Political Science Review* 10 (1989): 58.

6. Betty Glad, "Why Tyrants Go Too Far: Malignant Narcissism and Absolute Power," *Political Psychology* 23:1 (2002): 6.

7. Jerold Post, quoted in Peter Carlson, "The Son Also Rises," *Washington Post National Weekly Edition*, May 26–June 1, 2003, pp. 10–11.

8. Ole Holsti, "The Belief System and National Images: A Case Study," *Journal of Conflict Resolution* 6 (1962): 244–52.

9. Harvey Starr, *Henry Kissinger: Perceptions of International Politics* (Lexington: University Press of Kentucky, 1984); and Stephen Walker, "The Interface between Beliefs and Behavior: Henry Kissinger's Operational Code and the Vietnam War," *Journal of Conflict Resolution* 21:1 (March 1977): 129–68.

10. Irving L. Janis, *Victims of Groupthink: A Psychological Study of Foreign-Policy Decisions and Fiascoes* (Boston: Houghton Mifflin, 1972), p. 9.

11. Herbert Simon, "A Behavioral Model of Rational Choice," in *Models of Man: Social and Rational Mathematical Essays on Rational Human Behavior in a Social Setting* (New York: John Wiley, 1957).

12. Robert Jervis, "Hypotheses on Misperception," *World Politics* 20:3 (April 1968): 454–79.

13. Anne-Marie Slaughter, "Mercy Killings," *Foreign Policy* 134 (May–June 2003): 72–73.

14. David Makovsky, *Making Peace with the PLO: The Rabin Government's Road to the Oslo Accord* (Boulder, CO: Westview, 1996).

15. For excellent case studies of South Africa and Tajikistan dialogues, see Harold Saunders, *Politics Is about Relationships* (New York: Palgrave, 2005).

16. Cynthia H. Enloe, *Bananas, Beaches, and Bases: Making Feminist Sense of International Politics* (Berkeley: University of California Press, 1990).

17. Pamela Johnston Conover, Karen A. Mingst, and Lee Sigelman, "Mirror Images in Americans' Perceptions of Nations and Leaders during the Iranian Hostage Crisis," *Journal of Peace Research* 17:4 (1980): 325–37.

18. Swanee Hunt and Cristina Posa, "Women Waging Peace," *Foreign Policy* 124 (March–June 2001): 38–47.

19. Johanna McGeary, "The End of Milošević," *Time*, October 16, 2000, p. 60.

20. "Top Global Thinkers: Mohamed ElBaradei, Wael Ghonim," *Foreign Policy* (December 2011): 36.

Chapter 07

1. Joseph M. Grieco, "Anarchy and the Limits of Cooperation: A Realist Critique of the Newest Liberal Institutionalism," in *Neorealism and Neoliberalism: The Contemporary Debate*, ed. David A. Baldwin (New York: Columbia University Press, 1993), p. 117.

2. David Mitrany, *A Working Peace System* (London: Royal Institute of International Affairs, 1946), p. 40.

3. Garrett Hardin, "The Tragedy of the Commons," *Science* 162 (December 13, 1968): 1243–48. See also Mancur Olson Jr., *The Logic of Collective Action: Public Goods and the Theory of Groups* (New York: Schocken, 1968).

4. Margaret P. Karns and Karen A. Mingst, "The United States and Multilateral Institutions: A Framework," in *The United States and Multilateral Institutions: Patterns of Changing Instrumentality and Influence*, ed. Margaret P. Karns and Karen A. Mingst (Boston: Unwin Hyman, 1990), pp. 1–24.

5. See Karen A. Mingst and Margaret P. Karns, *The United Nations in the 21st Century,* 4th ed. (Boulder, CO: Westview, 2012).

6. See, for example, Virginia Page Fortna, "Does Peacekeeping Keep Peace? International Intervention and the Duration of Peace after Civil War," *International Studies Quarterly* 28:2 (June 2004): 269–92; Paul Collier et al., *Breaking the Conflict Trap: Civil War and Development Policy* (Washington, DC: World Bank and Oxford University Press, 2003); and Andrew Mack, "Global Patterns of Political Violence" (Working Paper, International Peace Academy, New York, March 2007).

7. United Nations, *A More Secure World: Our Shared Responsibility*, Report of the Secretary-General's High-level Panel on Threats, Challenges and Change (New York: UN, 2004), www.un.org/secureworld/ (accessed 1/28/10).

8. Quoted by Ambassador Joseph Torsella in speech delivered at Council on Foreign Relations (January 20, 2012).

9. Immanuel Kant, "Idea for a Universal History from a Cosmopolitan Point of View" (1784), reprinted in *Kant Selections*, ed. Lewis White Beck (New York: Macmillan, 1988); and Jean-Jacques Rousseau, "State of War," "Summary," and "Critique of Abbé Saint-Pierre's Project for Perpetual Peace," in *Reading Rousseau in the Nuclear Age,* trans. and ed. Grace G. Roosevelt (Philadelphia: Temple University Press, 1990), pp. 185–229.

10. This section draws on Margaret P. Karns and Karen A. Mingst, *International Organizations: The Politics and Processes of Global Governance*, 2nd ed. (Boulder, CO: Lynne Rienner, 2010), chap. 5.

11. Christopher C. Joyner, *International Law in the 21st Century: Rules for Global Governance* (Lanham, MD: Rowman & Littlefield, 2005), p. 6.

12. This section on NGOs draws on Karns and Mingst, *International Organizations*, 2nd ed., chap. 6.

13. Jessica Stern, "The Protean Enemy," *Foreign Affairs* 82:4 (July–August 2003): 27–40.

14. See Alexander Cooley and James Ron, "The NGO Scramble: Organizational Insecurity and the Political Economy of Transnational Action," *International Security* 27:1 (Summer 2002): 5–39.

15. See, for example, William DeMars, *NGOs and Transnational Networks: Wild Cards in World Politics* (London: Pluto, 2005); Volker Heins, *Nongovernmental Organizations in International Society: Struggles over Recognition* (New York: Palgrave Macmillan, 2008).

16. Fiona Terry, *Condemned to Repeat? The Paradox of Humanitarian Action* (Ithaca, NY: Cornell University Press, 2002); and Sarah Kenyon Lischer, "Military Intervention and the Humanitarian 'Force Multiplier,'" *Global Governance* 13:1 (January–March 2007): 99–118.

17. For pathbreaking theoretical and empirical work, see Martha Finnemore, *National Interests in International Society* (Ithaca, NY: Cornell University Press, 1996) and Finnemore, *The Purpose of Intervention: Changing Beliefs about the Use of Force* (Ithaca, NY: Cornell University Press, 2003); and Margaret E. Keck and Kathryn Sikkink, *Activists beyond Borders: Advocacy Networks in International Politics* (Ithaca, NY: Cornell University Press, 1998).

18. Michael Barnett and Martha Finnemore, *Rules for the World: International Organizations in Global Politics* (Ithaca, NY: Cornell University Press, 2004. Also Barnett and Finnemore, "The Politics, Power, and Pathologies of International Organizations," *International Organization* 53:4 (Autumn): 699–732.

Chapter 08

1. Data on war frequency and number of deaths can be found in several, sometimes divergent, sources. These include Quincy Wright, *A Study of War*, rev. ed., 2 vols. (Chicago: University of Chicago Press, 1942, 1965); J. David Singer and Melvin Small, *The Wages of War, 1816–1965: Statistical Handbook* (New York: Wiley, 1972); Jack S. Levy, *War in the Modern Great Power System, 1495–1975* (Lexington: University Press of Kentucky, 1983); Ruth Leger Sivard, *World Military and Social Expenditures, 1996* (Washington, DC: World Priorities, 1996); and Human Security Group, "The Human Security Report 2012," http://www.hsrgroup.org/human-security-reports/2012/overview.aspx (accessed 2/27/13).

2. John Herz, "Idealist Internationalism and the Security Dilemma," *World Politics* 2:2 (January 1950): 157–80.

3. Kenneth N. Waltz, *Man, the State, and War: A Theoretical Analysis* (New York: Columbia University Press, 1954).

4. Augustine, *Confessions* and *The City of God*, in *Great Books of the Western World*, vol. 18, ed. Robert Maynard Hutchins (Chicago: Encyclopedia Britannica, 1952, 1986); and Reinhold Niebuhr, *The Children of Light and Children of Darkness* (New York: Scribner, 1945).

5. Thomas Hobbes, *Leviathan*, rev. student ed. (New York: Cambridge University Press, 1996), pp. 88–89.

6. John J. Mearsheimer, *The Tragedy of Great Power Politics* (New York: W. W. Norton, 2001), 32.

7. F. K. Organski, *World Politics* (New York: Knopf, 1958), chap. 12; and Organski and Jacek Kugler, *The War Ledger* (Chicago: University of Chicago Press, 1980).

8. George Modelski and William R. Thompson, "Long Cycles and Global War," in *Handbook of War Studies*, ed. Manus I. Midlarsky (Boston: Unwin Hyman, 1989).

9. For a more comprehensive approach, see Jack S. Levy, "The Causes of War: A Review of Theories and Evidence," in *Behavior, Society and Nuclear War*, ed. Philip E. Tetlock et al. (New York: Oxford University Press, 1989), vol. 1, pp. 209–333.

10. Carl von Clausewitz, *On War*, ed. Anatol Rapoport (Middlesex: Penguin Books, 1968), p. 119.

11. Charles Tilly, "Reflections on the History of European State-Making," in *The Making of National States in Western Europe* (Princeton, NJ: Princeton University Press, 1975), p. 42.

12. John Mueller, "The Essential Irrelevance of Nuclear Weapons: Stability in the Postwar World," *International Security* 13:2 (Fall 1988): 55–79, and Mueller, *Retreat from Doomsday: The Obsolescence of Major War* (New York: Basic Books, 1989). See also Gregg Easterbrook, "The End of War?" *New Republic* (May 30, 2005): 18–21.

13. See Joshua S. Goldstein, *Winning the War on War: The Decline of Armed Conflict Worldwide* (New York: Dutton, 2011); and Robert Jervis, "Theories of War in an Era of Leading Power Peace," *American Political Science Review* 96:1 (March 2002), 1–14.

14. Robert Jervis, "Theories of War in an Era of Leading Power Peace," *American Political Science Review* 96:1 (March 2002): 11.

15. Jervis, "Theories of War," 9.

16. Steven Pinker, *The Better Angels of Our Nature: The Decline of Violence in History and its Causes* (New York: Viking Penguin, 2011).

17. Scott D. Sagan and Kenneth N. Waltz, *The Spread of Nuclear Weapons: A Debate Renewed* (New York: W. W. Norton, 2003).

18. Michael Walzer, *Just and Unjust Wars* (New York: Basic Books, 1992), p. 185.

19. Andrew Mack, "Why Big Nations Lose Small Wars: The Politics of Asymmetric Conflict," *World Politics* 27:2 (January 1975): 175–200.

20. Ivan Arreguín-Toft, *How the Weak Win Wars: A Theory of Asymmetric Conflict* (New York: Cambridge University Press, 2005).

21. Audrey Kurth Cronin, "Behind the Curve: Globalization and International Terrorism," *International Security* 27:3 (Winter 2002/3): 33.

22. See, for example, Dan Caldwell and Robert E. Williams Jr., *Seeking Security in an Insecure World* (Lanham, MD: Rowman & Littlefield, 2006); and Walter Enders and Todd Sandler, "Distribution of Transnational Terrorism among Countries by Income Classes and Geography after 9/11," *International Studies Quarterly* 50:2 (June 2006): 367–68.

23. For contemporary views, see Michael Walzer, *Just and Unjust Wars*, 4th ed. (New York: Basic Books, 2006).

24. Martha Finnemore, *The Purpose of Intervention: Changing Beliefs about the Use of Force* (Ithaca, NY: Cornell University Press, 2003), pp. 52–84.

25. Shashi Tharoor and Sam Daws, "Humanitarian Intervention: Getting Past the Reefs," *World Policy Journal* 18:2 (Summer 2001): 23.

26. Tharoor and Daws, 23.

27. Hans J. Morgenthau, *Politics among Nations: The Struggle for Power and Peace*, 4th ed. (New York: Knopf, 1967), pp. 161–215.

28. George W. Bush, "The National Security Strategy of the United States of America," September 17, 2002, http://georgewbush-whitehouse.archives.gov/nsc/nss/2002/index.html (accessed 2/1/10).

29. See Glenn Snyder, *Deterrence and Defense* (Princeton, NJ: Princeton University Press, 1961); and Alexander L. George and Richard Smoke, *Deterrence in American Foreign Policy: Theory and Practice* (New York: Columbia University Press, 1974).

30. For a good analysis of suicide terrorism, see Robert A. Pape, "The Strategic Logic of Suicide Terrorism," *American Political Science Review* 97:3 (August 2003): 343–61. On the discounted power of credible threats to kill as a challenge to deterrence, see Ivan Arreguín-Toft, "Unconventional Deterrence: How the Weak Deter the Strong," in *Complex Deterrence: Strategy in the Global Age*, ed. T. V. Paul, Patrick Morgan, and James Wirtz (Chicago: University of Chicago Press, 2009), pp. 204–21.

31. Keir A. Lieber and Daryl G. Press, "The Rise of U.S. Nuclear Primacy," *Foreign Affairs* 85:2 (March–April 2006): 42–54.

32. For a complete treatment, see Inis Claude, *Power and International Relations* (New York: Random House, 1962), pp. 94–204.

33. Zoltan Barany, "NATO's Post–Cold War Metamorphosis: From Sixteen to Twenty-Six and Counting," *International Studies Review* 8:1 (March 2006): 165–78.

34. Deborah Avant, *The Market for Force: The Consequences of Privatizing Security* (New York: Cambridge University Press, 2005).

Chapter 09

1. Thomas L. Friedman, *The Lexus and the Olive Tree: Understanding Globalization* (New York: Farrar, Straus, and Giroux, 1999), p. 257.

2. Charles P. Kindleberger, "International Public Goods without International Government," *American Economic Review* 76 (March 1986): 1–13.

3. Thomas L. Friedman, *The World Is Flat: A Brief History of the Twenty-first Century* (New York: Farrar, Straus, and Giroux, 2005).

4. Robert Gilpin, "Three Models of the Future," *International Organization* 29:1 (Winter 1975): 39.

5. Sir Norman Angell, *The Great Illusion* (New York: Putnam, 1933).

6. Antoni Estadadeordal and Alan Taylor, "Is the Washington Consensus Dead? Growth, Openness, and the Great Liberalization, 1970s–2000s" (Cambridge, MA: NBER Working Paper 14264, August 2008).

7. David S. J. Christy, "Round and Round We Go," *World Policy Journal* 25:2 (Summer 2008): 24.

8. Paul Collier, *The Bottom Billion: Why the Poorest Countries Are Failing and What Can Be Done about It* (New York: Oxford University Press, 2007).

9. Michelle Miller-Adams, *The World Bank: New Agendas in a Changing World* (London: Routledge, 1999); and Ngaire Woods, *The Globalizers: The IMF, the World Bank, and Their Borrowers* (Ithaca, NY: Cornell University Press, 2006).

10. Nancy Birdsall and Francis Fukuyama, "The Post-Washington Consensus: Development after the Crisis," *Foreign Affairs* 90:2 (2011): 45–53.

11. Muhammad Yunus, quoted in Judy Mann, "An Economic Bridge Out of Poverty: Grameen Bank in Bangladesh Loans Money to Poor Women Who Want to Start Business," *Washington Post*, October 14, 1994, E3. See also Muhammad Yunus, *Banker to the Poor: Micro-Lending and the Battle against World Poverty* (New York: Public Affairs, 2003).

12. David Roodman, *Due Diligence: An Impertinent Inquiry into Microfinance* (Washington, DC: Center for Global Development, 2012).

13. For progress reports broken down by goal and by region, see the United Nations Web site, www.un.org/millenniumgoals/ (accessed 1/17/13). See also United Nations, *Human Development Report 2012,* available at http://hdr.undp.org/en/reports/global/hdr2012 (accessed 1/17/13).

14. Quoted in "Special Report, State Capitalism: The Visible Hand," *The Economist* (January 21, 2012): 5.

15. William Easterly, *The White Man's Burden: Why the West's Efforts to Aid the Rest Have Done So Much Ill and So Little Good* (New York: Penguin, 2006); and Joseph E. Stiglitz, *Globalization and Its Discontents* (New York: W. W. Norton, 2002).

16. Flynt Leverett and Pierre Noel, "The New Axis of Oil," *National Interest* 84 (Summer 2006): 62.

17. Loukas Tsoukalis, "Managing Interdependence: The EU in the World Economy," in *International Relations and the European Union*, ed. Christopher Hill and Michael Smith (Oxford: Oxford University Press, 2005), pp. 232–36.

18. Robert Pastor, "The Future of North America: Replacing a Bad Neighbor Policy," *Foreign Policy* 87:4 (July–August 2008): 85.

19. Jagdish Bhagwati, *Termites in the Trading System: How Preferential Agreements Undermine Free Trade* (New York: Oxford University Press, 2008).

20. Moisés Naím, *Illicit: How Smugglers, Traffickers, and Copycats Are Hijacking the Global Economy* (New York: Doubleday, 2005).

21. C. Fred Bergsten, "Why the Euro Will Survive: Completing the Continent's Half-Built House," *Foreign Affairs* 91:5 (September/October 2012): 16–17; and Timothy Garton Ash, "The Crisis of Europe: How the Union Came Together and Why It's Falling Apart," *Foreign Affairs* 91:5 (September/October 2012): 7–8.

22. Bergsten, "Why the Euro Will Survive," 22. For a more general assessment of the viability of the EU, see Wallace J. Thies, "Is the EU Collapsing?," *International Studies Review* 14 (2012): 225–239.

23. Ash, "The Crisis of Europe," 15.

24. Andrew Moravcsik, "Europe after the Crisis: How to Sustain a Common Currency," *Foreign Affairs* 91:3 (May/June 2012): 67.

25. Roger Altman, "The Great Crash, 2008: A Geopolitical Setback for the West," *Foreign Affairs* 88:1 (January/February 2009): 13.

26. See, for example, Barry Eichengreen, "Bad Credit History," *Current History* (January 2009): 14–19; and Harry James, "The Making of a Mess: Who Broke Global Finance, and Who Should Pay for It?, *Foreign Affairs* 88:1 (January–February 2009): 162–68.

Chapter 10

1. See Paul Gordon Lauren, *The Evolution of International Human Rights. Visions Seen*, 3rd ed. (Philadelphia: University of Pennsylvania Press, 2011), chap. 1.

2. Jack Donnelly, *International Human Rights*, 4th ed. (Boulder, CO: Westview, 2013). See esp. chap. 3.

3. See, for example, Amartya Sen, "Universal Truths: Human Rights and the Westernizing Illusion," *Harvard International Review* 20:3 (Summer 1998):40–43.

4. See Paul Gordon Lauren, *Power and Prejudice: The Politics and Diplomacy of Racial Discrimination* (Boulder, CO: Westview Press, 1996).

5. See Karen A. Mingst and Margaret P. Karns, *The United Nations in the 21st Century*, 4th ed. (Boulder, CO: Westview, 2012), chap. 6

6. See Margaret E. Keck and Kathryn Sikkink, *Activists beyond Borders: Advocacy Networks in International Networks* (Ithaca, NY: Cornell University Press, 1998); and Charles Tilly, *Social Movements, 1768–2004* (Boulder, CO: Paradigm, 2004).

7. Janet E. Lord, "Disability Rights and the Human Rights Mainstream: Reluctant Gate Crashers?" in *The International Struggle for New Human Rights*, Clifford Bob, ed. (Philadelphia: University of Pennsylvania Press, 2009), pp. 83–92.

8. See Edward McMahon and Marta Ascherio, "A Step Ahead in Promoting Human Rights? The Universal Periodic Review of the UN Human Rights Council," *Global Governance* 18:2 (April–June 2012): 239.

9. On Amnesty International, see Stephen Hopgood, *Keepers of the Flame. Understanding Amnesty International* (Ithaca, NY: Cornell University Press, 2006); Ann Marie Clark, *Diplomacy of Conscience: Amnesty International and Changing Human Rights Norms* (Princeton, NJ: Princeton University Press, 2001).

10. Emilie Hafner-Burton and Kiyoteru Tsutsui, "Human Rights in a Globalized World: The Paradox of Empty Promises," *American Juornal of Sociology* 110:5 (2005): 1373–1411.

11. Emilie Hafner-Burton, "Sticks and Stones: Naming and Shaming the Human Rights Enforcement Problem," *International Organization* 62:4 (2008): 706.

12. Abram Chayes and Antonia Handler Chayes, "On Compliance," *International Organization* 47:2 (Spring 1993): 175–205.

13. David Cortright and George A. Lopez, *The Sanctions Decade: Assessing UN Strategies in the 1990s* (Boulder, CO: Lynne Rienner, 2000).

14. Jonas Claes, *Libya and the "Responsibility to Protect"* (Washington, DC: United States Institute of Peace, 2011).

15. Henry Kissinger, *Diplomacy* (New York: Simon and Schuster, 1994).

16. International Court of Justice, *Case Concerning Application of Convention on the Prevention and Punishment of the Crime of Genocide* (Bosnia and Herzegovina v. Serbia and Montenegro, 2007).

17. For an excellent study on the International Criminal Court, see Benjamin N. Schiff, *Building the International Criminal Court* (Cambridge, UK: Cambridge University Press, 2008). Also Cesare P. R. Romano, ed., *The Sword and the Scales: The United Nations and International Courts and Tribunals* (New York: Cambridge University Press, 2009).

18. V. Spike Peterson and Anne Sisson Runyan, *Global Gender Issues in the New Millennium*, 3rd ed. (Boulder, CO: Westview, 2009).

19. Esther Boserup et al., *Woman's Role in Economic Development*, with new introduction by Nazneen Kanji (London: Earthscan Publications, Ltd., 2007).

20. See Devaki Jain, *Women, Development and the UN: A Sixty-year Quest for Equality and Justice* (Bloomington: Indiana University Press, 2005).

21. Olga Avdeyeva, "When Do States Comply with International Treaties? Policies on Violence against Women in Post-Communist Countries," *International Studies Quarterly* 51 (2007): 877–900.

22. United Nations World Conference on Human Rights, Vienna Declaration and Programme of Action, July 12, 1993, Article 18, available at http://www.unhchr.ch/huridocda/huridoca.nsf/(symbol)/a.conf.157.23.en (accessed 1/17/13).

23. Zbigniew Brzezinski, *The Grand Failure: The Birth and Death of Communism in the Twentieth Century* (New York: Scribner's, 1989), p. 256.

Chapter 11

1. See Marc Levinson, *The Box: How the Shipping Container Made the World Smaller and the World Economy Bigger* (Princeton, NJ: Princeton University Press, 2006).

2. Karen T. Litfin, "Constructing Environmental Security and Ecological Interdependency," *Global Governance* 5:3 (July–September 1999): 367.

3. Rachel Carson, *Silent Spring* (Boston: Houghton Mifflin, 1962). See also Jacques Yves Cousteau with Frederick Dames, *The Silent World* (New York: Harper & Row, 1953); and Cousteau with James Dugan, *The Living Sea* (New York: Harper & Row, 1963).

4. Robert Keohane and David Victor, "The Regime Complex for Climate Change," *Perspectives on Politics* 9:1 (March 2011): 7–23.

5. John M. Broder, *The New York Times*, November 9, 2010, A1.

6. Thomas Malthus, *An Essay on the Principle of Population: Text, Sources, and Background Criticism*, ed. Philip Appleman (New York: W. W. Norton, 1976).

7. Donella H. Meadows et al., *The Limits to Growth* (New York: Signet, 1972).

8. Andrea Den Boer and Valerie M. Hudson, "A Surplus of Men, a Deficit of Peace: Security and Sex Ratios in Asia's Largest States," *International Security* 26:4 (Spring 2002): 5–38. For extended argument see Valerie M. Hudson and Andrea M. den Boer, *Bare Branches: The Security Implications of Asia's Surplus Male Population* (Cambridge, MA: The MIT Press, 2005).

9. Garrett Hardin, "The Tragedy of the Commons," *Science* 162 (December 13, 1968): 1243–48.

10. Nicholas Eberstadt, "The Dying Bear: Russia's Demographic Disaster," *Foreign Affairs* 90:6 (March 2011): 95–108.

11. Thomas F. Homer-Dixon, "Environmental Scarcities and Violent Conflict: Evidence and Cases," *International Security* 19:1 (Summer 1994): 5–40.

12. See Karen T. Litfin, *Ozone Discourses: Science and Politics in Global Environmental Cooperation* (New York: Columbia University Press, 1994).

13. International Crisis Group, "HIV/AIDS as a Security Issue," June 19, 2001, available at www.crisisgroup.org/home/index.cfm?l=1&id=1831 (accessed 2/6/10).

14. Peter M. Haas, "Introduction: Epistemic Communities and International Policy Coordination," *International Organization* 46:1 (Winter 1992): 3.

15. Moisés Naím, *Illicit: How Smugglers, Traffickers, and Copycats are Hijacking the Global Economy* (New York: Anchor Books, 2006), p. 5.

16. See Bjorn Rutten, *It's All about You: Building Capacity in Cyber Security* (New York: The Conference Board of Canada, 2011).

17. Jared Diamond, *Collapse: How Societies Choose to Fail or Succeed* (New York: Penguin, 2005).

18. See Stephen D. Krasner, *Sovereignty: Organized Hypocrisy* (Princeton, NJ: Princeton University Press, 1999); and Karen T. Litfin, ed., *The Greening of Sovereignty in World Politics* (Cambridge, MA: MIT Press, 1998).

19. See http://ec.europa.eu/information_society/policy/internet_gov/index_en.htm.

20. Ronnie Lipschutz, "Reconstructing World Politics: The Emergence of Global Civil Society," *Millennium: Journal of International Studies* 21:3 (1992): 398–99.

GLOSSARY

anarchy the absence of governmental authority

arms control restrictions on the research, manufacture, or deployment of weapons systems and certain types of troops

asymmetric conflicts war between political actors of unequal strength, in which the weaker party tries to neutralize its opponent's strength by exploiting the opponent's weaknesses

balance of power any system in which actors (e.g., states) enjoy relatively equal power, such that no single state or coalition of states is able to dominate other actors in the system

bandwagoning strategy in which weaker states join forces with stronger states

behavioralism an approach to the study of social science and international relations that posits that individuals and units like states act in regularized ways; leads to a belief that behaviors can be described, explained, and predicted

Beijing Consensus an alternative to the Washington Consensus; experimenting with economic policies in state capitalism; government plays a more active role in picking economic winners and losers

belief system the organized and integrated perceptions of individuals in a society, including foreign-policy decision makers, often based on past history, that guide them to select certain policies over others

bipolarity an international system in which there are two great powers or blocs of roughly equal strength or weight

BRICS an informal group of emerging economic powers, including Brazil, Russia, India, China, and South Africa

bureaucratic politics the model of foreign-policy decision making that posits that national decisions are the outcomes of bargaining among bureaucratic groups having competing interests; decisions reflect the relative strength of the individual bureaucratic players or of the organizations they represent

capitalism the economic system in which the ownership of the means of production is in private hands; the system operates according to market forces whereby capital and labor move freely; according to radicals, an exploitative relationship between the owners of production and the workers

celebrity diplomacy use of popular individuals to both bring attention to an issue and/ or to try to influence both the public and decision makers to pursue a course of action

cognitive consistency the tendency of individuals to accept information that is compatible with what has previously been accepted, often by ignoring inconsistent information; linked to the desire of individuals to be consistent in their attitudes

Cold War the era in international relations between the end of World War II and 1990, distinguished by ideological, economic, political, and military rivalry between the Soviet Union and the United States

collective good public goods that are available to all regardless of individual contribution — e.g., the air, the oceans, or Antarctica — but that no one owns or is individually responsible for; with collective goods, decisions by one group or state have effects on other groups or states

collective security the concept that aggression against a state should be defeated collectively because aggression against one state is aggression against all; basis of League of Nations and United Nations

colonialism the 15th–20th century practice of founding, maintaining, and expanding colonies abroad. Colonialism, now universally delegitimized, was marked by two main motivations: (1) showing indigenous peoples how best to live (a "civilizing mission"); and (2) exploiting indigenous people and their territory for labor and material resources in order to increase the power of the colonial authority

comparative advantage the ability of a country to make and export a good relatively more efficiently than other countries; the basis for the liberal economic principle that countries benefit from free trade among nations

compellence the use of threats to coerce another into taking an action it otherwise would not take

complex peacekeeping multidimensional operations using military and civilian personnel, often including traditional peacekeeping and nation-building activities; more dangerous because not all parties have consented and because force is usually used

constructivism an alternative international relations theory that hypothesizes how ideas, norms, and institutions shape state identity and interests

containment a foreign policy designed to prevent the expansion of an adversary by blocking its opportunities to expand, by supporting weaker states through foreign aid programs, and by the use of coercive force only to oppose an active attempt by an adversary to physically expand; the major U.S. policy toward the Soviet Union during the Cold War era

crimes against humanity international crimes, including murder, enslavement, ethnic cleansing, and torture, committed against civilians, as codified in the Rome Statute

cultural relativism the belief that human rights, ethics, and morality are determined by cultures and history and therefore are not universally the same

democratic peace theory supported by empirical evidence that democratic states do not fight wars against each other, but do fight wars against authoritarian states

demographic transition the situation in which increasing levels of economic development lead to falling death rates, followed by falling birth rates

dependency theorists individuals whose ideas are derived from radicalism, and explain poverty and underdevelopment in developing countries based on their historical dependence on and domination by rich countries

derivatives financial instruments often derived from an asset (mortgages, loans, foreign exchange, interest rates) which parties agree to exchange over time; a way of buying and selling risk in international financial markets

détente the easing of tense relations; in the context of this volume, détente refers to the relaxation and reappraisal of threat assessments by political rivals, for example, the United States and Soviet Union during the later years of the Cold War

deterrence the policy of maintaining a large military force and arsenal to discourage any potential aggressor from taking action; states commit themselves to punish an aggressor state

diplomacy the practice of states trying to influence the behavior of other states by bargaining, negotiating, taking specific noncoercive actions or refraining from such actions, or appealing to the foreign public for support of a position

direct foreign investment investing in another state, usually by multinational corporations, by establishing a manufacturing facility or developing an extractive industry

disarmament the policy of eliminating a state's offensive weaponry; may occur for all classes of weapons or for specified weapons only; the logic of the policy is that fewer weapons leads to greater security

discourse expanded communication dealing with a topic

diversionary war the theory that leaders start conflicts to divert attention from domestic problems

domino effect a metaphor that posits that the loss of influence over one state to an adversary will necessarily lead to a subsequent loss of control over neighboring states, just as dominos fall one after another; used by the United States as a justification to support South Vietnam, fearing that if that country became communist, neighboring countries would also fall under communist influence

economic realism modern version of mercantilism, meaning use of state power to achieve economic and social goals

epistemic communities transnational communities of experts and technical specialists who share a set of beliefs and a way to approach problems

ethnonational movements the participation in organized political activity of self-conscious communities sharing an ethnic affiliation; some movements seek autonomy within an organized state; others desire separation and the formation of a new state; still others want to join with a different state

European Union (EU) a union of twenty-eight European states, formerly the European Economic Community; designed originally during the 1950s for economic integration, but since expanded into a closer political and economic union

evoked set the tendency to look for details in a contemporary situation that are similar to information previously obtained

externalities in economics, unintended side effects that can have positive or negative consequences

extremist Christian groups groups seeking to replace secular state authority and willing to use violence in the name of God to achieve its objectives

extremist Islamic fundamentalism groups seeking to change states and societies through violent and coercive means to support imposition of Sharia law

failed state state which has ineffective or nonexistent government, widespread lawlessness, often accompanied by insurgency and crime; situation where state authorities are not protecting their own people

first-generation human rights political or civil rights of citizens that prevent governmental authority from interfering with private individuals or civil society (negative rights)

first-strike capability the ability to launch a nuclear attack capable of completely preventing a retaliatory strike

General Assembly one of the major organs of the United Nations; generally addresses issues other than those of peace and security; each member state has one vote; operates with six functional committees composed of all member states

General Agreement on Tariffs and Trade (GATT) founded by treaty in 1947 as the Bretton Woods institution responsible for negotiating a liberal international trade regime that included the principles of nondiscrimination in trade and most-favored-nation status; reformed as the World Trade Organization in 1995

genocide the systematic killing or harming of a group of people based on national, religious, ethnic, or racial characteristics, with the intention of destroying the group

global governance structures and processes that enable actors to coordinate interdependent needs and interests in the absence of a unifying political authority

globalization the process of increasing integration of the world in terms of economics, politics, communications, social relations, and culture; increasingly undermines traditional state sovereignty

Group of 7 (G7) group of the traditional economic powers (U.S., Great Britain, France, Japan, Germany, Italy, Canada) who meet annually to address economic problems; when Russia joins, the G-8 discussions turn to political issues

Group of 77 a coalition of about 125 developing countries that press for reforms in economic relations between developing and developed countries; also referred to as the South

Group of 20 group of finance ministers and heads of central banks (recently heads of state) of major economic powers, including China, Russia, Australia, Argentina, Brazil, Indonesia, Mexico, South Africa, South Korea, Turkey, as well as representatives from the G-7; meets periodically to discuss economic issues

groupthink the tendency for small groups to form a consensus and resist criticism of a core position, often disregarding contradictory information in the process; group may ostracize members holding a different position

guerrilla warfare the use of irregular armed forces to undermine the will of an incumbent government (or its foreign support) by selectively attacking the government's vulnerable points or personnel over a prolonged period of time; guerrillas hide among the people they aim to represent, and as such tend to place ordinary citizens at great risk; guerrillas require both social support (or at a minimum, social apathy) and sanctuary (either a remote base in a rugged environment or a weakly defended international border) in order to survive, and by surviving, to win

hegemon a dominant state that has a preponderance of power; often establishes and enforces the rules and norms in the international system

hegemonic stability theorists those who support the theory that a dominant state is needed to support an integrated world economy; the hegemon is willing to bear the costs of maintaining the system

humanitarian intervention actions by states, international organizations, or the international community in general, to intervene, usually with coercive force, to alleviate human suffering without necessarily obtaining consent of the state

human security a concept of security broadened to include the protection of individuals from systematic violence, environmental degradation, and health disasters; the concept gained ground after the Cold War due to the inability or unwillingness of states (see also "responsibility to protect") to adequately protect their own citizens

hypotheses tentative statements about causal relationships put forward to explore and test its logical and usually its empirical consequences

imperialism the policy and practice of extending the domination of one state over another through territorial conquest or economic domination; in radicalism, the final stage of expansion of the capitalist system

institutions processes and structures of social order around which relatively stable individual and group expectations and identities converge; for example, in most places the contemporary institution of marriage is a simultaneously social, political, and economic one

intergovernmental organizations (IGOs) international agencies or bodies established by states and controlled by member states that deal with areas of common interests

International Bill of Rights the collective name for the Universal Declaration of Human Rights, the International Covenant on Civil and Political Rights, and the International Covenant on Economic, Social, and Cultural Rights

International Monetary Fund (IMF) the Bretton Woods institution originally charged with helping states deal with temporary balance-of-payments problems; now plays a broader role in assisting debtor developing states by offering loans to those who institute specific policies, or structural adjustment programs

international regimes the rules, norms, and procedures that are developed by states and international organizations out of their common concerns and are used to organize common activities

international relations the study of the interactions among various actors (states, international organizations, nongovernmental organizations, and subnational entities like bureaucracies, local governments, and individuals) that participate in international politics

international society the states and substate actors in the international system and the institutions and norms that regulate their interaction; implies that these actors communicate, sharing common interests and a common identity; identified with British school of political theory

intrastate wars organized and deliberate violence within a state which results in at least one thousand battle-related deaths per year; civil wars are by far the most common form of intrastate war, but some terrorist attacks within states have exceeded the one-thousand deaths threshold, and might therefore be counted as wars

interstate war organized violence between internationally-recognized states which results in at least one thousand deaths from combat in a calendar year; since 1900, wars between states have been responsible for the greatest concentration of deaths in a relatively short period of time in world history—for example, World War II resulted in from fifty to seventy million casualties from 1939 to 1945

irredentism the demands of ethnonationalist groups to take political control of territory historically or ethnically related to them by separating from their parent state or taking territory from other states

just war tradition the idea that wars must be judged according to two categories of justice: (1) *jus ad bellum*, or the justness of war itself; and (2) *jus in bello*, or the justness of each actor's conduct in war

League of Nations the international organization formed at the conclusion of World War I for the purpose of preventing another war; based on collective security

legitimacy the moral and legal right to rule, which is based on law, custom, heredity, or the consent of the governed

levels of analysis analytical framework based on the ideas that events in international relations can be explained by looking at individuals, states, or the international system and that causes at each level can be separated from causes at other levels

liberalism the theoretical perspective based on the assumption of the innate goodness of the individual and the value of political institutions in promoting social progress

limited wars armed conflicts usually between states in which belligerents acknowledge limits on both the resources applied to an armed conflict, and on the political objectives sought by means of war (namely, some objective less than the total defeat of the adversary or its unconditional surrender)

Malthusian dilemma the situation that population growth rates will increase faster than agricultural productivity, leading to food shortages; named after Thomas Malthus

mercantilism economic theory that international commerce should increase a state's wealth, especially gold; state power is inhanced by a favorable balance of trade

mirror images the tendency of individuals and groups to see in one's opponent the opposite characteristics as those seen in one's self

moral hazard problem when states or individuals are not made to pay the consequences of reckless behavior; they have little incentive to change that behavior

most-favored-nation (MFN) principle principle in international trade agreements when states promise to give another state the same treatment in trade as the first state gives to its most-favored trading partner

multilateralism the conduct of international activity by three or more states in accord with shared general principles, often, but not always, through international institutions

multinational corporations (MNCs) private enterprises with production facilities, sales, or activities in several states

multipolar an international system in which there are several states or great powers of roughly equal strength or weight

narcotrafficking the transportation of large quantities of illegal narcotics like heroin or cocaine across state borders

nation a group of people sharing a common language, history, or culture

national interest the interest of the state, most basically the protection of territory and sovereignty; in realist thinking, the interest is a unitary one defined in terms of the pursuit of power; in liberal thinking, there are many national interests; in radical thinking, it is the interest of a ruling elite

nationalism devotion and allegiance to the nation and the shared characteristics of its peoples; used to motivate people to patriotic acts, sometimes leading a group to seek dominance over another group

nation-state the entity formed when people sharing the same historical, cultural, or linguistic roots form their own state with borders, a government, and international recognition; trend began with French and American Revolutions

negative externalities economies term for costly (harmful) unintended consequences of exchange, in political terms, a negative externality of a failed government might be refugees; in counterinsurgency, a negative externality for an incumbent government fighting insurgents might be increased terrorist group recruitment as a result of deliberately or inadvertently harming noncombatants in disputed areas

neoliberal institutionalism a reinterpretation of liberalism that posits that even in an anarchic international system, states will cooperate because of their continuous interactions with each other and because it is in their self-interest to do so; institutions provide the framework for cooperative interactions

neorealism a reinterpretation of realism that posits that the structure of the international system is the most important level to study; states behave the way they do because of the structure of the international system; includes the belief that general laws can be found to explain events

netcrime criminal use of the internet; may include such diverse activities as use of email or chat to bully a peer, manipulation of computer code to steal another's identity, child pornography, or theft of intellectual property

New International Economic Order (NIEO) a list of demands by the Group of 77 to reform economic relations between the North and the South, that is, between the developed countries and the developing countries

noncombatant immunity a core principle of international humanitarian law (formerly, "the laws of war") that holds that people not bearing arms in a conflict may not be deliberately targeted or systematically harmed; this category includes unarmed civilians, soldiers who have surrendered, and soldiers who are too severely injured to defend themselves

nongovernmental organizations (NGOs) private associations of individuals or groups that engage in political, economic, or social activities, usually across national borders

nonviolent resistance resistance to established authority that systematically precludes the use of violence as a tactic; common examples include strikes, sit-ins, and protest marches

normative relating to ethical rules; in foreign policy and international affairs, standards suggesting what a policy should be

North the developed countries, mostly in the Northern Hemisphere, including the countries of North America, the European countries, and Japan

North Atlantic Treaty Organization (NATO) military and political alliance between Western European states and the United States established in 1948 for the purpose of defending Europe from aggression by the Soviet Union and its allies; post–Cold War expansion to Eastern Europe

nuclear proliferation the geographic diffusion of the capacity to manage a controlled nuclear chain reaction; originally restricted to the United States and the Soviet Union, this technology—which includes peaceful nuclear power facilities as well as nuclear weapons—has spread to include the United Kingdom, France, Japan, Argentina, Germany, Switzerland, Pakistan, India, and Israel, among others

offshore financial centers states or jurisdictions with few regulations on banking and financial transactions, often with low taxation; used by individuals and international banks to transfer funds

organizational politics the foreign-policy decision making model that posits that national decisions are the products of subnational governmental organizations and units; the standard operating procedures and processes of the organizations largely determine the policy; major changes in policy are unlikely

peacebuilding post-conflict political and economic activities designed to preserve and strengthen peace settlements, includes civil administration, elections, and economic development activities

portfolio investment private investment in another state by purchasing stocks on bonds, without taking direct control of the investments

power the ability to influence others and also to control outcomes so as to produce results that would not have occurred naturally

power potential a measure of the power an entity like a state could have, derived from a consideration of both its tangible and its intangible resources; states may not always be able to transfer their power potential into actual power

prisoner's dilemma a theoretical game in which rational players (states or individuals) choose options that lead to outcomes (payoffs) such that all players are worse off than under a different set of choices

public diplomacy use of certain diplomatic methods to create a favorable image of the state or its people in the eyes of other states and their publics; methods include, for example, goodwill tours, cultural and student exchanges, and media presentations

radicalism a social theory, formulated by Karl Marx and modified by other theorists, that posits that class conflict between owners and workers will cause the eventual demise of capitalism; offers a critique of capitalism

rational actors in realist thinking, an individual or state that uses logical reasoning to select a policy; that is, it has a defined goal to achieve, considers a full range of alternative strategies, and selects the policy that best achieves the goal

realism a theory of international relations that emphasizes states' interest in accumulating power to ensure security in an anarchic world; based on the notion that individuals are power seeking and that states act in pursuit of their own national interest defined in terms of power

responsibility to protect (R2P) emerging norm that the international community should help individuals suffering at the hands of their own state or others

sanctions economic, diplomatic, and even coercive military force for enforcing an international policy or another state's policy; sanctions can be positive (offering an incentive to a state) or negative (punishing a state)

satisficing in decision making theory, the tendency of states and their leaders to settle for the minimally acceptable solution, not the best possible outcome, in order to reach a consensus and formulate a policy

second-generation human rights social and economic rights that states are obligated to provide their citizenry, including the rights to medical care, jobs, and housing (positive rights)

second-strike capability in the age of nuclear weapons, the ability of a state to respond and hurt an adversary after a first strike has been launched against that state by the adversary; ensures that both sides will suffer an unacceptable level of damage

security dilemma the situation in which one state improves its military capabilities, especially its defenses, and those improvements are seen by other states as threats; each state in an anarchic international system tries to increase its own level of protection leading to insecurity in others, often leading to an arms race

Security Council one of the major organs of the United Nations charged with the responsibility for peace and security issues; includes five permanent members with veto power and ten nonpermanent members chosen from the General Assembly

smart power using a combination of coercion (hard power) with persuasion and attraction (soft power)

smart sanctions limited sanctions targeted to hurt or support specific groups; used to avoid the humanitarian costs of general sanctions

socialism an economic and social system that relies on intensive government intervention or public ownership of the means of production in order to distribute wealth among the population more equitably; in radical theory, the stage between capitalism and communism

soft law non-binding norms of state behavior; may or may not eventually become hard or obligatory law

soft power ability to change a target's behavior based on the legitimacy of one's ideas or policies, rather than on material power (economic or military)

South the developing countries of Africa, Latin America, and southern Asia

sovereignty the authority of the state, based on recognition by other states and by nonstate actors, to govern matters within its own borders that affect its people, economy, security, and form of government

sovereign wealth funds state-controlled investment companies that manage large foreign exchange reserves; located in China or in petroleum-exporting countries (Norway, the Gulf states, Saudi Arabia)

state an organized political unit that has a geographic territory, a stable population, and a government to which the population owes allegiance and that is legally recognized by other states

stratification the uneven distribution of resources among different groups of individuals and states

structural adjustment programs IMF policies and recommendations aimed to guide states out of balance-of-payment difficulties and economic crises

summits talks and meetings among the highest-level government officials from different countries; designed to promote good relations and provide a forum to discuss issues and conclude formal negotiations

superpowers highest-power states as distinguished from other great powers; term coined during the Cold War to refer to the United States and the Soviet Union

sustainable development an approach to economic development that tries to reconcile current economic growth and environmental protection with the needs of future generations

system a group of units or parts united by some form of regular interaction, in which a change in one unit causes changes in the others; these interactions occur in regularized ways

terrorism the use of organized political violence by non-state actors against noncombatants in order to cause fear as a means to achieve a political or religious objective; a form of asymmetric warfare

theory generalized statements about political, social, or economic activities that seek to describe and explain those activities; used in many cases as a basis of prediction

third-generation human rights collective rights of groups, including the rights of ethnic or indigenous minorities and designated special groups such as women and children, and the rights to democracy and development, among others

total wars armed conflicts usually among multiple powerful states involving widespread destruction and major loss of life in which participants acknowledge no limits on the use of force to achieve their political aims, and in which those aims encompass an adversary's unconditional surrender

track-two diplomacy unofficial overtures by private individuals or groups to try and resolve an ongoing international crisis or civil war

traditional peacekeeping the use of multilateral third-party military forces to achieve several different objectives, generally to address and contain interstate conflict, including the enforcement of cease-fires and separation of forces; used during the Cold War to prevent conflict among the great powers from escalating

transnational across national or traditional state boundaries; can refer to actions of various nonstate actors, such as private individuals and nongovernmental organizations

transnational movements groups of people from different states who share religious, ideological, or policy beliefs and who work together to change the status quo

Treaties of Westphalia treaties ending the Thirty Years War in Europe in 1648; in international relations represents the beginning of state sovereignty within a territorial space

unconventional warfare wars in which either the means used (e.g., deliberately harming noncombatants) or the ends sought (e.g., genocide) violate the expectations of traditional practice

unitary actor the state as an actor that speaks with one voice and has a single national interest; realists assume states are unitary actors

universal jurisdiction a legal concept that permits states to claim legal authority beyond their national territory for the purpose of punishing a particularly heinous criminal that violates the laws of all states or protecting human rights

universal rights human rights believed to be basically the same at all times and in all cultures, a controversial notion

war organized political violence by a recognized political authority intended to coerce another polity, and which results in at least one thousand battle deaths per calendar year. All parties involved must have some real capacity to harm one another; this definition makes war distinct from terrorism, riots, massacres, genocides, and skirmishes

war on terrorism a powerful rhetorical call to exploit a given society's total available resources (both material and non-material) in order to defeat a political tactic; a key implication of declaring "war on terrorism" is that few if any limits on the use of a society's resources either should or will be observed

Warsaw Pact the military alliance formed by the states of the Soviet bloc in 1955 in response to the rearmament of West Germany and its inclusion in NATO; permitted the stationing of Soviet troops in Eastern Europe

Washington Consensus the liberal belief that only through specific liberal economic policies, especially privatization, can development result

weapons of mass destruction (WMD) chemical, biological, and radiological weapons distinguished by an inability to restrict their destructive effects to a single time and place; they therefore share a quality of irrationality in their contemplated use because attackers can never be entirely protected from the harm of any attacks they initiate with such weapons

World Bank a global lending agency focused on financing projects in developing countries; formally known as the International Bank for Reconstruction and Development, established as one of the key Bretton Woods institutions to deal with reconstruction and development after World War II

World Trade Organization (WTO) intergovernmental organization designed to support the principles of liberal free trade; includes enforcement measures and dispute settlement mechanisms; established in 1995 to replace the General Agreement on Tariffs and Trade

CREDITS

INDEX

Page numbers in *italics* refer to boxes, maps, figures, and tables.